Lecture Notes in Computer Science 11176

Commenced Publication in 1973
Founding and Former Series Editors:
Gerhard Goos, Juris Hartmanis, and Jan van Leeuwen

More information about this series at http://www.springer.com/series/7408

Manuel Mazzara · Iulian Ober
Gwen Salaün (Eds.)

Software Technologies: Applications and Foundations

STAF 2018 Collocated Workshops
Toulouse, France, June 25–29, 2018
Revised Selected Papers

 Springer

Editors
Manuel Mazzara (iD)
Innopolis University
Innopolis, Russia

Gwen Salaün
Grenoble Alpes University
Montbonnot, France

Iulian Ober
University of Toulouse
Toulouse Cedex 9, France

Workshop Editors *see next page*

ISSN 0302-9743　　　　　　ISSN 1611-3349　(electronic)
Lecture Notes in Computer Science
ISBN 978-3-030-04770-2　　　ISBN 978-3-030-04771-9　(eBook)
https://doi.org/10.1007/978-3-030-04771-9

Library of Congress Control Number: 2018962486

LNCS Sublibrary: SL2 – Programming and Software Engineering

This Springer imprint is published by the registered company Springer Nature Switzerland AG
The registered company address is: Gewerbestrasse 11, 6330 Cham, Switzerland

Workshop Editors

CoSim-CPS 2018

Cinzia Bernardeschi
University of Pisa
Italy

Peter Gorm Larsen
Aarhus University
Denmark

Paolo Masci
HASLab/INESC TEC
    and Universidade do Minho
Portugal

DataMod 2018

Antonio Cerone
Nazarbayev University
Kazakhstan

Riccardo Guidotti
KDDLab, ISTI-CNR
Pisa, Italy

Oana Andrei
University of Glasgow
UK

FMIS 2018

Yamine Aït Ameur
IRIT, Université de Toulouse
France

Philippe Palanque
IRIT, Université de Toulouse
France

FOCLASA 2018

Jean-Marie Jacquet
University of Namur
Belgium

Jacopo Soldani
University of Pisa
Italy

GCM 2018

Hans-Jörg Kreowski
Universität Bremen
Germany

MDE@DeRun 2018

Hugo Bruneliere
IMT Atlantique and LS2N
Nantes, France

Romina Eramo
University of L'Aquila
Italy

Abel Gomez
Universitat Oberta de Catalunya
Spain

MSE 2018

Antonio Bucchiarone
Fondazione Bruno Kessler
Trento, Italy

Sophie Ebersold
IRIT, Université de Toulouse
Toulouse, France

Florian Galinier
IRIT, Université de Toulouse
Toulouse, France

SecureMDE 2018

Salvador Martinez
CEA-LIST, LISE laboratory
Paris, France

Jordi Cabot
SOM Research Lab, ICREA-UOC
Barcelona, Spain

Domenico Bianculli
University of Luxembourg
Luxembourg

Preface

This volume contains the technical papers presented at the eight workshops collocated with the 2018 edition of the STAF (Software Technologies: Applications and Foundations) federation of conferences on software technologies. The workshops took place at ENSEEIHT (National Higher School of Engineering in Electrical Engineering, Hydraulics, and Digital Sciences) in Toulouse, France, during June 25–29, 2018.

The STAF 2018 conferences and workshops brought together leading researchers and practitioners from academia and industry to advance the state of the art in practical and foundational advances in software technology. They address all aspects of software technology, from object-oriented design, testing, mathematical approaches to modelling and verification, transformation, model-driven engineering, aspect-oriented techniques, and tools. The satellite workshops provided a highly interactive and collaborative environment to discuss emerging areas of software engineering, software technologies, model-driven engineering, and formal methods.

The eight workshops whose papers are included in this volume are (organizers are indicated too):

- **CoSim-CPS 2018** – Second International Workshop on Formal Co-Simulation of Cyber-Physical Systems, June 26, 2018

  - Cinzia Bernardeschi (University of Pisa, Italy)
  - Peter Gorm Larsen (Aarhus University, Denmark)
  - Paolo Masci (IIASLab/INESC TEC and Universidade do Minho, Portugal)

- **DataMod 2018** – 7th International Symposium "From Data to Models and Back," June 25–26, 2018

  - Antonio Cerone (Nazarbayev University, Kazakhstan)
  - Riccardo Guidotti (KDDLab, ISTI-CNR, Pisa, Italy)
  - Oana Andrei (University of Glasgow, UK)

- **FMIS 2018** – 7th International Workshop on Formal Methods for Interactive Systems, June 25–26, 2018

  - Yamine Aït Ameur (IRIT, Université de Toulouse, France)
  - Philippe Palanque (IRIT, Université de Toulouse, France)

- **FOCLASA 2018** – 16th International Workshop on Foundations of Coordination Languages and Self-Adaptative Systems, June 26, 2018

  - Jean-Marie Jacquet (University of Namur, Belgium)
  - Jacopo Soldani (University of Pisa, Italy)

- **GCM 2018** – 9th International Workshop on Graph Computation Models, June 27, 2018

- Hans-Jörg Kreowski (Universität Bremen, Germany)

- **MDE@DeRun 2018** – Model-Driven Engineering for Design-Runtime Interaction in Complex Systems, June 28, 2018

  - Hugo Bruneliere (IMT Atlantique and LS2N, Nantes, France)
  - Romina Eramo (University of L'Aquila, Italy)
  - Abel Gomez (Universitat Oberta de Catalunya, Spain)

- **MSE 2018** – Third International Workshop on Microservices: Science and Engineering, June 25, 2018

  - Antonio Bucchiarone (Fondazione Bruno Kessler, Trento, Italy)
  - Sophie Ebersold (IRIT, Université de Toulouse, Toulouse, France)
  - Florian Galinier (IRIT, Université de Toulouse, Toulouse, France).

- **SecureMDE 2018** – First International Workshop on Security for and by Model-Driven Engineering, June 25, 2018

  - Salvador Martinez (CEA-LIST, LISE laboratory, Paris, France)
  - Jordi Cabot (SOM Research Lab, ICREA-UOC, Barcelona, Spain)
  - Domenico Bianculli (University of Luxembourg, Luxembourg).

We would like to thank each organizer of the eight workshops at STAF 2018 for the interesting topics and resulting talks, as well as the respective Program Commitee members and external reviewers who carried out thorough and careful reviews, created the program of each workshop, and made the compilation of this high-quality volume possible. We also thank the paper contributors and attendees of all workshops. We would like to extend our thanks to all keynote speakers for their excellent presentations. We also thank the developers and maintainers of the EasyChair conference management system, which was of great help in handling the paper submission, reviewing, and discussion for all workshops, and in the preparation of this volume. Finally, we would like to thank the organizers of STAF 2018, Jean-Michel Bruel and Marc Pantel, for their help during the organization of all workshops, as well as ENSEEIHT and the IRIT laboratory that hosted the workshops.

October 2018

Manuel Mazzara
Iulian Ober
Gwen Salaün

Abstracts of Invited Talks

Testing Autonomous Robots in Virtual Worlds

Hélène Waeselynck

LAAS-CNRS, Université de Toulouse, 7 Av. du Colonel Roche,
31077 Toulouse, France
Helene.Waeselynck@laas.fr

Abstract. Autonomous robots have decisional capabilities allowing them to accomplish missions in diverse and previously unknown environments. The mission-level validation of such systems typically involves test campaigns in the field, which are costly and potentially risky in case of misbehavior. In this talk, I will discuss an alternative approach based on simulation: the robot is immersed in virtual worlds, and can be tested in a wide variety of situations without incurring damage. I will take the example of testing the autonomous navigation of outdoor robots. I will share the insights and results gained from two case studies: Mana, an academic rough-terrain robot developed at LAAS-CNRS, and Oz, an agricultural robot for autonomous weeding developed by Naïo Technologies.

Keywords: Autonomous systems · Software testing · Simulation

Data-Driven Analysis of User Interface Software in Medical Devices

Paolo Masci

INESC TEC and Universidade do Minho, Portugal
paolo.masci@inesctec.pt

User interface software in medical devices is responsible for smooth and safe use of a device. In advanced systems such as robotic-assisted surgery, user interface functions can be highly sophisticated, e.g., involve the detection and translation of doctors' hands movements into micro-movements of robotic arms, allowing doctors to perform complex surgeries that were not possible before.

Developing sophisticated software with zero defects is notoriously a hard problem. In the medical domain the problem is particularly delicate, as software defects can ultimately result in patient harm. Recent estimates on incidents with medical devices indicate an escalating trend, with software defects being constantly one of the top causes of incidents since 2016, and accounting for 22.8% of medical device recalls in the first quarter of 2018[1]. To date, several studies have been carried out providing an aggregate view of software defects in medical devices. A detailed analysis of the nature and impact of user interface software defects has not been performed yet. Such detailed analysis would bring powerful insights that can be used by developers to better understand latent software defects and identify them in advance, before incidents happen.

In this talk, I will present a study conducted in collaboration with the US Food and Drug Administration that aims to quantify and classify user interface software defects in the current generation of medical devices. The study involved a systematic and detailed analysis of nearly 8,000 medical devices recall records published by the FDA from September 2012 to August 2015. A medical device recall is a corrective action initiated by the manufacturer to fix critical defects in a device already in the market. Each recall record includes a semi-structured description of the reason for the recall and the corrective action performed by the manufacturer. I will discuss the analyzed dataset, including analysis method, challenges faced while performing the analysis, obtained results, and opportunities for improvement.

---

[1] https://www.stericycleexpertsolutions.com/wp-content/uploads/2018/08/ExpertSolutions_RecallIndex_Q22018.pdf.

Safe Composition of Software Services

Gwen Salaün

Univ. Grenoble Alpes, Inria, CNRS, Grenoble INP, LIG,
F-38000 Grenoble, France

Composition of software is a crucial topic in many different computer science areas such as Software Architectures, Component-Based Software Engineering, Web services, cloud computing, Internet of Things, etc. Composition is however a difficult task for several reasons. There is a need first for models of the services and of the way these services interact together. Several levels of expressiveness can be considered in this model (signature, behaviour, semantics, quality of service). Each facet brings different issues from a composition perspective. In this talk, we have a specific focus on behavioural models for service composition. Once a model is properly defined, one can design a composition by defining connections or bindings among the involved services. Building such a composition is error-prone and several kinds of mismatch can arise. Analysis techniques are thus required in order to validate the composition and ensure that before the composition is deployed it works correctly. Beyond models and automated verification techniques for validating service composition, we also present in this talk two different ways to develop composition of services, namely, top-down and bottom-up development processes. Last but not least, we illustrate these techniques for supporting the modelling and composition of services with a concrete approach developed in the context of the Internet of Things.

Computational Oncology: From Biomedical Data to Computational Models, and Back

Giulio Caravagna

Centre for Evolution and Cancer,
The Institute of Cancer Research, London, UK

Keynote Speaker of DataMod 2018

Cancer is a disease responsible for around 8 million deaths per year (around 13% of all deaths in 2008), and whose worldwide impact is projected to continue rising, with an estimated 13 million deaths in 2030 (as of an estimate by the World Health Organisation). Finding a cure to cancer is definitely challenging, as there are as many different types of cancer as human cells, and the progression of the disease is heterogenous across individuals. Often, histologically identical tumours have few genetic features in common, and thus reconciling heterogeneity across tumour types and patients is one of the main areas of research in the community.

In the last years, thanks to the development of new high throughput sequencing technologies that measure the genomic content of cancer cells at different resolutions, the new field of Cancer Evolution has emerged. In this field, carcinogenesis is described as an evolutionary process driven by the accumulation of genomic aberrations, and complex methodologies are used to retrieve the life history of analysed tumours. At a broad level, this opens up for the opportunity to create models that recapitulate heterogeneity, and that elucidate how genomic events orchestrate diseases initiation and progression. So doing, we can anticipate a cancer's next step, and eventually implement personalised treatment strategies that are tailored to each patient.

Computational modelling is one of the key methodologies used in Cancer Evolution. In this talk, I will give a brief introduction to the problems in the filed, from a computer science perspective. I will overview some of the major computational challenges, and the kind of data can be used to approach them. The talk will span from (very basic) cell/cancer biology, to a discussion of what types of mathematical models can be used to describe cancer growth/therapy, and what Data Science challenges we have to face to implement successful strategies for cancer data analysis.

Microservices, Microservices, Microservices?

Antonio Brogi

Department of Computer Science
University of Pisa, Pisa, Italy
brogi@di.unipi.it

Abstract. In this talk, we first tried to critically discuss some of the motivations and characteristics of microservices and some of the potentially huge advantages offered by their adoption for managing enterprise applications.

One of the main motivations for adopting microservices is the need to shorten the lead time for new features and updates, by accelerating rebuild and redeployment and by reducing chords across functional silos. Another main motivation for adopting microservices is the need to scale, quickly and effectively.

Microservices architectures define applications as sets of services, each running in its own container, communicating with lightweight mechanisms, built around business capabilities, decentralizing data management, independently deployable, horizontally scalable, and fault resilient.

In the second part of the talk, we showed how a simple formalization of the main properties of microservices can be frutifully exploited to drive the refactoring of existing applications.

After introducing a simple modelling of microservices architectures as graphs fromed by services, databases, and connectors, we discussed how some distinguishing properties of microservices can be associated with antipatterns, and how such antipatterns can be associated with refactoring patterns.

The last part of the talk was devoted to discuss how the complexity and overhead introduced by microservices can make their adoption truly effective only for a certain scale of applications and enterprises.

Contents

Foundations of Coordination Languages and Self-adaptative Systems (FOCLASA)

Graph Computation Models (GCM)

Security for and by Model-Driven Engineering (MDE)

Formal Co-Simulation of Cyber-Physical Systems (CoSim-CPS)

2nd Workshop on Formal Co-Simulation of Cyber-Physical Systems (CoSim-CPS-18)

The 2nd edition of the workshop on Formal Co-Simulation of Cyber-Physical Systems (CoSim-CPS-18)[1] was held in Toulouse, France, on June 26, 2018, as a satellite event of STAF/SEFM-18.

The workshop focuses on the integrated application of formal methods and co-simulation technologies in the development of software for Cyber-Physical Systems. Co-simulation is an advanced simulation technique that allows developers to generate a global simulation of a complex system by orchestrating and composing the concurrent simulation of individual components or aspects of the system. Formal methods link software specifications and program code to logic theories, providing developers with means to analyse program behaviours in a way that is demonstrably exhaustive. These two technologies complement each other. Using co-simulation, developers can create prototypes suitable to validate hypotheses embedded in formal models and formal properties to be analysed of the software. This is fundamental to ensure that the right system is being developed. Using formal methods, developers can extend test results obtained with co-simulation runs, and ensure that the same results apply to all program states for all possible program inputs. This enables early detection of design anomalies.

We solicited contributions were welcome on all aspects of system development, including specification, design, analysis, implementation and documentation of software for CPS. This year's edition was a one-day event with 8 technical presentation (5 peer-reviewed papers, 2 invited demonstrations, and 1 keynote talk), offering an excellent view on a variety of different approaches and tools for formal co-simulation of cyber-physical systems. Each submission was evaluated by at least three reviewers. The keynote talk "Testing autonomous robots in virtual worlds" was given by Helene Waeselynck (LAAS-CNRS).

We would like to thank all authors who submitted their work to CoSim-CPS-18, as well as our PC members for doing an excellent job in writing high-quality reviews in a timely manner. We would also like to thank the STAF/SEFM event organizers, who have accepted to host our workshop, and supported us for the publication of the workshop post-proceedings with Springer LNCS.

September 2018

Paolo Masci
Cinzia Bernardeschi
Peter Gorm Larsen

---

[1] https://sites.google.com/view/cosimcps18.

Organization

CoSim-CPS-18 – Program Committee

Giovanna Broccia	University of Pisa, Italy
Josè Creissac Campos	INESC TEC and Universidade do Minho, Portugal
Paul Curzon	Queen Mary University of London, UK
Fabio Cremona	United Technologies Research Center, Italy
Andrea Domenici	University of Pisa, Italy
Adriano Fagiolini	University of Palermo, Italy
Leo Freitas	Newcastle University, UK
Claudio Gomes	University of Antwerp, Belgium
Maurizio Palmieri	University of Pisa, Italy
Mario Porrmann	Bielefeld University, Germany
Akshay Rajhans	MathWorks, USA
Matteo Rossi	Politecnico di Milano, Italy
Neeraj Singh	INPT-ENSEEIHT/IRIT, University of Toulouse, France
Marjan Sirjani	Malardalen University, Sweden and Reykjavik University, Iceland
Frank Zeyda	University of York, UK
Yi Zhang	Center for Devices and Radiological Health, US Food and Drug Administration (CDRH/FDA), USA
Mo Zhao	MathWorks, USA

Towards the Verification of Hybrid Co-simulation Algorithms

Casper Thule[1(✉)], Cláudio Gomes[2,6], Julien Deantoni[3], Peter Gorm Larsen[1], Jörg Brauer[4], and Hans Vangheluwe[2,5,6]

[1] DIGIT, Department of Engineering, Aarhus University, Aarhus, Denmark
{casper.thule,pgl}@eng.au.dk
[2] University of Antwerp, Antwerp, Belgium
{claudio.gomes,hans.vangheluwe}@uantwerp.be
[3] Polytech Nice Sophia, Biot, France
julien.deantoni@polytech.unice.fr
[4] Verified Systems International GmbH, Bremen, Germany
brauer@verified.de
[5] McGill University, Montreal, Canada
[6] Flanders Make, Lommel, Belgium

Abstract. Engineering modern systems is becoming increasingly difficult due to the heterogeneity between different subsystems. Modelling and simulation techniques have traditionally been used to tackle complexity, but with increasing heterogeneity of the subsystems, it becomes impossible to find appropriate modelling languages and tools to specify and analyse the system as a whole.

Co-simulation is a technique to combine multiple models and their simulators in order to analyse the behaviour of the whole system over time. Past research, however, has shown that the naïve combination of simulators can easily lead to incorrect simulation results, especially when co-simulating hybrid systems.

This paper shows: (i) how co-simulation of a family of hybrid systems can fail to reproduce the order of events that should have occurred (event ordering); (ii) how to prove that a co-simulation algorithm is correct (w.r.t. event ordering), and if it is incorrect, how to obtain a counterexample; and (iii) how to correct an incorrect co-simulation algorithm. We apply the above method to two well known co-simulation algorithms used with the FMI Standard, and we show that one of them is incorrect for the family of hybrid systems under study, under the restrictions of the standard. The conclusion is that either the standard needs to be revised, or one of the algorithms should be avoided.

Keywords: Hybrid co-simulation · Hybrid systems · Model checking

This work was started in the CAMPaM 2017 Workshop, executed under the framework of the COST Action IC1404 – Multi-Paradigm Modelling for Cyber-Physical Systems (MPM4CPS), and partially supported by: Flanders Make vzw, the strategic research centre for the manufacturing industry; and PhD fellowship grants from the Agency for Innovation by Science and Technology in Flanders (IWT, dossier 151067).

M. Mazzara et al. (Eds.): STAF 2018 Workshops, LNCS 11176, pp. 5–20, 2018.
https://doi.org/10.1007/978-3-030-04771-9_1

1   Introduction

Engineered systems are becoming increasingly complex while market pressure shortens the available development time [26]. There are many causes for the increase in complexity, but to a large extent, it is caused by the number of interacting subsystems and differences between their domains [33]. Thus, there is a need for an improved development cycle with better tools, techniques, and methodologies [34]. While modelling and simulation have been successfully applied to reduce development costs, these fall short in fostering more integrated development processes [5].

A promising concept for the simulation of systems consisting of coupled components is collaborative simulation (co-simulation) [19, 21, 25], which is based on the idea that interacting subsystems are best modelled and simulated by dedicated tools and formalisms [35]. Each subsystem is then modelled by a specialised team using mature tools, tailored to the domain of the allocated subsystem. Further, each subsystem internally uses its own simulation engine, so that the most appropriate approximation techniques can be employed. The behaviour of the coupled system is computed by having the simulation tools communicate with one another by exchanging their outputs over time.

In order to run a co-simulation, all that is required is that the participating simulation tools consume the inputs and expose the outputs, of the allocated subsystem, over time. A co-simulation engine then synchronises the interface values of the different subsystems. This powerful approach eases the integration of subsystems simulated by different tools, but also poses some difficulties. In particular, subsystems are modelled and treated as black boxes, and it is difficult in some cases to understand how the coordination of the subsystems—a functionality provided by the co-simulation engine—affects the behaviour of the co-simulated system [20].

One might expect that the behaviour computed via co-simulation matches the behaviour of the coupled system. In practice, however, this expectation turns out overly optimistic, and significant deviations may become visible, which could, for example, be caused by discretization or the timing in which the inputs are set. This is not only due to the inherent limitations of approximate simulations [10], but also due to the internals of the subsystem simulations. It is therefore important to study how a faulty co-simulation can be identified. If a co-simulation preserves specific properties of a system, we then say that the properties of the system are preserved under co-simulation. To serve as a reference for correctness, we consider the properties of the implemented system, i.e. with no co-simulation effects.

This paper contributes to this line of research as follows:

- We identify a novel property called *event ordering*, which is often implicitly required to be preserved by co-simulations of systems that combine software with physical subsystems.
- We present a characterisation of the event ordering property as a model checking problem [11] based on the Functional Mock-up Interface for co-simulation

(FMI) standard [6]. Our method can be utilised to decide whether a given co-simulation satisfies this property for a restricted class of coupled systems.
– We show how, exemplified using FMI, to adapt the co-simulation master algorithm to preserve the event order, if the property is not preserved.

One of the strengths of our approach is that it yields a counterexample when the property is violated. The counter example includes a *co-simulation scenario* and an *execution trace* of the co-simulation, which provide valuable insight into how the co-simulation violates the event ordering property. The Maestro [32] master algorithm serves as a case study for our approach.

The remainder of this paper is structured as follows. First, Sect. 3 presents a primer on co-simulation and co-simulation properties. Afterwards, in Sect. 4, the event ordering property is demonstrated and described along with an encoding of the problem as a model-checking instance. Finally, the paper presents a discussion and perspective on future work in Sect. 5.

2   Background: Co-simulation

In this section, we present some background concepts in an informal manner. We adopt the definitions and nomenclature introduced in [20] and refer the reader to it for a more rigorous exposition.

A co-simulation is the behaviour trace of a coupled system, produced by the coordination of simulation units. The behaviour trace is a function mapping values to time, representing the outputs generated from each simulation unit and their timestamps. An example behaviour trace is shown in the bottom of Fig. 1.

A simulation unit is an executable software entity responsible for simulating a part of the system. To communicate with other simulation units, each simulation unit implements a predefined interface. This allows an orchestrator, described below, to communicate with it.

One such communication interface is prescribed by the Functional Mock-up Interface (FMI) standard [6]. A simulation unit implementing the FMI interface is called a Functional Mock-up Unit (FMU). The main functionality of an FMU concerns calculating outputs based on inputs and time. This is represented in FMI as three C functions: a function to set inputs, a function to perform a step with a given step size, and a function to get outputs.

In the FMI Standard, there is an important restriction [13, p. 104]:

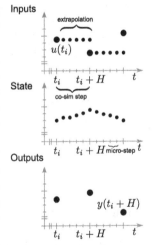

Fig. 1. Behaviour trace example.

Restriction 1. *There is the additional restriction in "slaveInitialized" state that it is not allowed to call fmi2GetXXX functions after fmi2SetXXX functions without an fmi2DoStep call in between.*

As we show later, this restriction has important consequences on the co-simulation of hybrid systems.

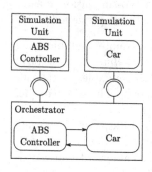

Fig. 2.   Co-simulation architecture.

An orchestrator is a software component that sets/gets inputs/outputs of each simulation unit, and asks it to estimate the state of its allocated subsystem at a future time. For example, in Fig. 1, the orchestrator sets an input to the unit at time t_i, and asks the unit to compute the state at time $t_i + H$. The unit in turn might perform multiple micro-steps and employ an input approximation scheme (this is unexposed to the orchestrator). Then, once the unit is at time $t_i + H$, the orchestrator requests an output, illustrated at the bottom of the figure.

The orchestrator follows the co-simulation scenario to know the order in which to ask the simulation unit to simulate and where to copy their outputs. A co-simulation scenario is a description of how the subsystems are interconnected and properties of the co-simulation, e.g. step size. For example, the orchestrator box contains an illustration of how the subsystems are connected, in Fig. 2.

There are three main master algorithms: Jacobi, Gauss-Seidel, and Strong-coupling [27]. We focus on the Jacobi and Gauss-Seidel, illustrated in Fig. 3a and b. The Jacobi algorithm proceeds by asking all simulators to produce outputs, then it computes and sets the inputs that all simulators need (illustrated by data transfer arrows in Fig. 3a). Afterwards, it asks all simulators to simulate their corresponding subsystem until the next communication time, after which the process repeats. This is represented by simulation step arrows in Fig. 3a, where the next communication time is $t_i + H$.

The Gauss-Seidel algorithm assigns an order to each simulator, and, in that order, computes the inputs of the simulator, then asks the same simulator to simulate to the next time point, obtains its output, and uses that output to compute the input to the next simulator. These steps are repeated until all simulators have simulated until the next time point, and then the process starts over again. See Fig. 3b.

3   Related Work: Property Preservation in Co-simulation

In this section, we introduce intuitively the notion of property preservation, and cover examples from the state of the art, where it is studied.

Given a property P that is satisfied by a coupled system, we say that the co-simulation (of the coupled system) preserves P if it also satisfies P. For example, a coupled system representing chemical kinetics always has positive concentrations. Clearly, this property (every concentration variable must be positive) should be preserved in co-simulations.

In general it is a challenge to ensure that any property of interest is preserved by co-simulations. The following paragraphs provide other examples of property preservation from the state of the art.

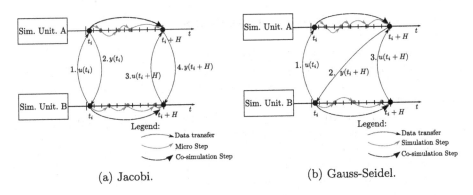

(a) Jacobi.   (b) Gauss-Seidel.

Fig. 3. Coupling algorithms.

Stability. A coupled system is stable when it eventually comes to a rest. Since many systems are engineered to be stable [3], it is important that this property is preserved under co-simulation. The works in [1, 9, 17, 24, 30] study the conditions under which the stability property is conserved for selected physical coupled systems. The same works also provide insight into how the co-simulation algorithm can preserve this property.

Energy Conservation. Systems whose models account for the flow of energy follow the principle of conservation of energy. That is, no energy is lost when flowing between subsystems. This property is not preserved in naïve co-simulation algorithms because of the input approximations, and the non-negligible communication step size. The work in [4], extended in [29], demonstrates a co-simulation algorithm that monitors the power flow between simulators and employs a correction scheme to account for the artificial energy introduced by the co-simulation. The work in [28] complements the above work by showing how the energy residual can be used as an error indicator to control the communication step size.

Event Synchrony. A co-simulation preserves event synchrony when any event happening at a specific time in the original hybrid system is also reproduced by the co-simulation at the same time. A hybrid system is a system comprising software and physical subsystems. This is one of the properties studied in [15], in the context of co-simulations involving two simulation units: one responsible for the software subsystem, and the other for a continuous subsystem. In order to enable an easier comparison of event timestamps, [12] proposes the use of integers, instead of floating point numbers, to represent time. Accurately detecting—and locating the time of—events is paramount to the preservation of the energy and stability properties in a co-simulation. As such, the work in [16] explores how the energy of a hybrid system can be increased when state events are not accurately reproduced by the co-simulation. It presents a way to find the maximum event detection delay so that the stability is preserved in the co-simulation.

4   Verification of Master Algorithms

The previous section introduced multiple properties that should be preserved in a co-simulation. In particular, it introduced the event synchrony property.

The event synchrony property states that every event happening in a hybrid system, happens at the exact same time in the corresponding co-simulation. An event is a value in the co-simulation whose timestamp should be approximated as closely as possible. For example, the time at which the output of a simulation unit crosses the zero; of the time at which a state machine based FMU changes its output because of a change in its internal discrete state.

In order to detect an event, because its exact time is often difficult to predict without actually asking the units to compute, the master algorithm only detects it after it occurs. Then, to find the exact time of the event, the orchestrator restores the co-simulation to a prior state (where the event has not yet happened) and proceeds with more caution (that is, smaller communication step size). This is repeated until the time of the event is known with sufficiently high accuracy [36]. A consequence is that this property can only be preserved up to some tolerance level, dictated by the precision required for the co-simulation experiment.

4.1   Relaxing Event Synchrony: Event Ordering

The FMI Standard partially supports master algorithms that preserve the event synchrony property. Each FMU is allowed to advance to a time prior to the one requested by the orchestrator, and supports state saving/restoring functionalities. However, making use of these capabilities in practice may be impossible due to lack of implementation (these are not mandatory), or simply due to the performance degradation entailed by saving/restoring the state multiple times.

As such, the event synchrony property might be too strong. Instead, it might be more useful to require that the sequence of events be preserved, even if the timestamps do not coincide. For example, suppose that the real/correct behaviour of a coupled system, comprised of a software and a physical component, yields 3 events: (t_1, e_1), (t_2, e_2), and (t_3, e_3), with the timestamps satisfying $t_1 < t_2 < t_3$. The co-simulation satisfies the event ordering property if it exhibits the events (t_1', e_1), (t_2', e_2), and (t_3', e_3), with the timestamps satisfying the same order, that is, $t_1' < t_2' < t_3'$, but not necessarily equal to t_1, t_2, t_3.

4.2   Problem Formulation

We focus on a restricted class of hybrid systems in order to study an essential challenge related to preserving the event synchrony property. The system under study is illustrated in Fig. 4. It consists of a software part, and a physical part. The software part is represented as a Statechart [22], and the physical part is represented by a differential equation.

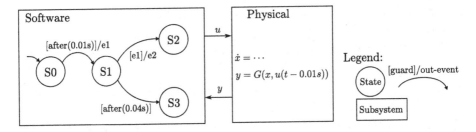

Fig. 4. Hybrid systems under study.

The software part is representative of a control system that has a timeout mechanism, triggered whenever the physical part fails to react to some stimuli (an event in this case). The details of the dynamics of the physical subsystem are not important. What is important is that its output is a delayed function of the input, so that any change in the input is reflected on the output, e.g., 0.01 s later. This is a reasonable abstraction since most physical systems have some sort of inertial reaction to inputs.

An execution of the software subsystem is plotted in Fig. 5. Immediately after time 0.01 s, the event e1 is produced. This event affects the output of the physical system (0.01 s later), which is picked up by the software unit, causing it to change to, S2 and produce event e2. If the physical plant shows no reaction within 0.04 s, then the software will change to state S3.

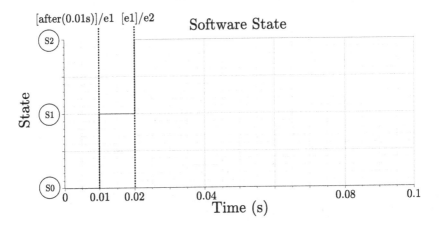

Fig. 5. Sample execution of the system in Fig. 4, with Open Modelica [14].

For the purposes of co-simulating the above system using the FMI Standard, suppose that the physical subsystem is decomposed into $N > 1$

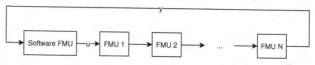

Fig. 6. Co-simulation scenario.

FMUs, connected sequentially, as shown in Fig. 6. The Software FMU implements the simulation of the software subsystem shown in Fig. 4. FMU 1 is responsible for the dynamics of the physical subsystem in the same figure, which introduces a 0.01s delay between input and output. The remaining FMUs are identity functions and will be referred to as propagate FMUs. All the FMUs here behave according to the FMI Standard 2.0, respecting Restriction 1. That is, no event is detected when a new input is set.

Using the Jacobi algorithm to co-simulate the scenario in Fig. 6, with $N = 3$ and co-simulation step size $H = 0.01$, leads to the software execution trace depicted in Fig. 7. The events produced in this trace are the same as the ones in the correct execution in Fig. 5, but their timestamps are different. Event e1 is produced at time 0.02 s instead of 0.01 s because the event should happen immediately after time 0.01 s, and not at 0.01 s. This means that it is only observed at time 0.02 s. Furthermore, the reaction of the physical subsystem is detected later at time 0.06 s, instead of 0.02 s.

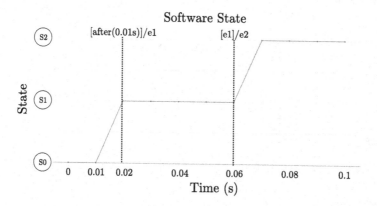

Fig. 7. Co-simulation using the Jacobi algorithm of the scenario in Fig. 6. Parameters: $N = 3, H = 0.01$. Produced with Maestro from INTO-CPS [32].

Naturally, the smaller the communication step size H, the smaller the delay introduced by the propagate FMUs.

What this example illustrates is that, due to Restriction 1, *the size of the co-simulation scenario also plays a role in the delay introduced.* By adding more propagate FMUs to the example scenario, we get a qualitatively different event sequence, as shown in Fig. 8, where the final state of the software subsystem is S3, instead of S2. The excessive delay, accidentally introduced by the Jacobi algorithm, causes the software timeout to be triggered.

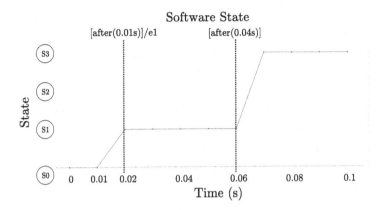

Fig. 8. Co-simulation using the Jacobi algorithm of the scenario in Fig. 6. Parameters: $N = 6, H = 0.01$. Produced with Maestro from INTO-CPS [32].

In general one would like to have co-simulations that either do not introduce artificial delays, or that, at least, introduce a delay that depend only on the communication step size, so that it is easier to satisfy the event ordering property. In the following subsections we use model checking to formally study the ordering of this property for the hybrid system shown in Fig. 4, with a variable structure co-simulation scenario illustrated in Fig. 6. In the experiments the co-simulation step size is kept the same, although it is straightforward to take its variation into account.

4.3   Model Checking the Jacobi Algorithm

We use the ProMeLa [23] notation to model the FMUs, and the master algorithm. The Promela language uses a textual syntax to describe parallel and sequential processes, communication channels, and non-determinism.

Listing 1.1. Channels

```
1  mtype:events = {e0, e1};
2  typedef channels {
3      chan in = [0] of {mtype:events};
4      chan out = [0] of {mtype:events};
5      chan step = [0] of {int};
6  }
```

The Promela model follows closely the co-simulation scenario sketched in Fig. 6. The communication between the master algorithm and the FMUs is made via three channels: one to set inputs, one to set outputs, and one to perform a co-simulation step. These channels are detailed in Listing 1.1. The in and step channels are read by the FMU, while the out channel is read by the master algorithm.

Listing 1.2. Statechart FMU

```
1   proctype stateFMU(channels chans) {
2       int t_time = 0;
3       mtype:events input;
4       do
5       :: chans.step ? t_time ->
6           if
7           /* if state is 0 and more than 1 time unit have passed, then change
                  ↪ the state to 1 and output an event. */
8           :: (state == 0) ->
9               if
10              :: (t_time > 1) ->
11                      state=1;
12                      chans.out ! e1; /* e1 is the output that we are
                                  ↪ interested in receiving again */
13              :: else -> chans.out ! e0;
14          fi;
15              /* If the state is 1 and 4 additional time units have passed, then
                  ↪ change to state 3 */
16          :: (state == 1) ->
17              if
18              :: t_time > 5 & input != e1 -> state = 3;
19              :: input == e1 -> state = 2;
20              :: else -> skip;
21              fi;
22              chans.out ! e0;
23          :: (state == 2) -> chans.out ! e1;
24          :: else -> chans.out ! e0;
25          fi;
26      :: chans.in ? input
27      :: (terminate == 1) -> break;
28      od;
29  }
```

The FMU corresponding to the software subsystem is modelled in ProMeLa by implementing the reaction to events received from the channels in and step. When an event is present in channel in, it is stored in the intermediate variable input, such that it can be accessed when an event is present in channel step. When an event is present in channel step, the FMU follows the state machine of the software subsystem, taking into account that the time is represented as an integer and the communication step size is 0.01 s. Listing 1.2 presents this model.

The other FMUs are propagate FMUs. As such, the FMU model shown in Listing 1.3 just stores and outputs whatever input it receives.

Listing 1.3. Propagate FMU

```
1   proctype propFMU(channels chans){
2       mtype:events inp;
3       int t_time = 0;
4       do
5       :: chans.in ? inp
6       :: chans.step ? t_time ->    chans.out ! inp;
7       :: (terminate == 1) -> break;
8       od;
9   }
```

The Jacobi master algorithm essentially sends events through the in channel of each FMU, asks the FMU to step via the step channel, and stores the output events at the out channels. The non-deterministic aspect of this model is encoded in the choice of the number of propagate FMUs that can be added to the scenario. The number of FMUs (maxN) is limited to 10, as it is enough to prove this property. The implementation is shown in Listing 1.4.

Listing 1.4. The Jacobi Master Algorithm in ProMeLa

```
1   proctype MAJacobi(){
2       int propagateCount;
3       select ( propagateCount : 1 .. (maxN-1) );
4       int FMUCount = propagateCount + 1;
5
6       channels fmuChannels[maxN];
7       mtype:events inputs[maxN];
8
9       smpid = run stateFMU(fmuChannels[0]);
10
11      int i;
12      for(i : 1 .. propagateCount){
13          run propFMU(fmuChannels[i]);
14      }
15
16      do
17      :: time < endTime  ->
18          /* Step the FMUs */
19          for(i : 0 .. FMUCount-1){
20              fmuChannels[i].step ! time+1;
21          }
22
23          /* Retrieve the outputs */
24          for(i : 0 .. FMUCount-1){
25              fmuChannels[i].out ? inputs[(i + 1)
26          }
27
28          /* Set inputs */
29          for(i : 0 .. FMUCount-1){
30              fmuChannels[i].in ! inputs[i]
31          }
32
33          time++;
34      :: else ->
35          terminate = 1;
36          break;
37      od;
38  }
```

The event ordering property can be encoded in this model as a reachability property: the Statechart FMU eventually reaches S2. This is shown in Listing 1.5. The state variable is global, and is set as part of the execution of the FMU.

Listing 1.5. Eventually Correct LTL formula.

```
1   ltl eventuallyCorrect { <> (state == 2)}
```

Using SPIN [23] to carry out the verification of this property, applied to Listing 1.4, quickly shows that it cannot be verified. The error trail provides a counter example execution, by showing that S3 is reached when there are four propagate FMUs. Informally, the error trail is the following: At step 2 (0.02 s), e1 is outputted from the Statechart FMU. At step 3 (0.03 s) it is outputted from the following propagate FMU. At step 4 it is outputted from the second propagate FMU, at step 5 it is outputted from the third propagate FMU. Finally, at step 6 it is outputted from the last propagate FMU but this is the same time as the Software FMU transitions to S3. Therefore, the Statechart FMU never reaches S2. This is consistent with the result in Fig. 8.

4.4   Model Checking the Gauss-Seidel Algorithm

The Gauss-seidel algorithm is introduced in Sect. 2 and illustrated in Fig. 3b. The main difference between this algorithm and the Jacobi is in the timestamp of the outputs and inputs provided to the simulation units. From the perspective of a simulation unit, the Gauss-Seidel algorithm provides future inputs to the unit, before asking it to compute a co-simulation step. This allows the unit to react to the inputs without any delay [18]. Its implementation is detailed in Listing 1.6.

Listing 1.6. The Gauss-Seidel Master Algorithm in ProMeLa

```
1   proctype MAGauss(){
2     int propagateCount;
3     select ( propagateCount : 1 .. (maxN-1) );
4     int FMUCount = propagateCount + 1;
5
6     channels fmuChannels[maxN];
7     mtype:events inputs[maxN];
8
9     run stateFMU(fmuChannels[0]);
10
11    int i;
12    for(i : 1 .. FMUCount-1){
13      run propFMU(fmuChannels[i]);
14    }
15
16    do
17    :: time < endTime  ->
18      for(i : 0 .. FMUCount-1){
19        /* Step the FMU */
20        fmuChannels[i].step ! time + 1;
21
22        /* Retrieve the output */
23        fmuChannels[i].out ? inputs[(i + 1)
24
25        /* Set the input */
26        fmuChannels[(i + 1)
27      }
28      time++;
29    :: else ->
30      terminate = 1;
31      break;
32    od;
33  }
```

Verifying Listing 1.6 with the LTL formula in Listing 1.5 shows that the Gauss-seidel algorithm correctly preserves the execution sequence of the events. This matches our intuition since the Gauss-Seidel algorithm allows each FMU to perform computation while knowing the future input. Therefore, Restriction 1 does not affect the ability to propagate events instantaneously. The next section discusses these results.

5   Discussion and Future Work

In this paper we have shown how a co-simulation using the Jacobi algorithm, and respecting the FMI Standard, can fail to preserve the event ordering property. To this end, we picked a particular class of hybrid systems that are sensitive to delays.

The correctness property we used is a weak form of event synchrony: the order of events is preserved, but their timestamps can be different than the ones happening in the correct behaviour of the coupled system. Under the restrictions of the FMI Standard, two master algorithms have been used to study the property: The Jacobi and the Gauss-Seidel. It is shown that the Jacobi algorithm does not preserve it, in general making it unsuitable for general, hybrid FMI based co-simulation.

Albeit a very simple example, the hybrid system used is meant to illustrate that, based on minimum information on the FMUs, we can prove if a co-simulation algorithm is appropriate or not for a scenario. The proof is based on an abstraction of the FMU in the form of timed automata and the definition of properties to be respected by some FMUs. To extend this preliminary work, we intend to explore how to deal with black box simulation units, so that a conservative (and provably correct) abstraction can be built for them. It is also important for an FMU to expose some of the properties that must be preserved without revealing the internal details, keeping intellectual property safe.

To illustrate, in the previous example, if we expose the shortest timed reaction of each software FMU, and the input-to-output propagation time of each FMU then we can determine which communication step size can be used in order to ensure the order of the event sequence with the Jacobi algorithm. To see how the step size H can be computed, let T denote the smallest timeout used in the software FMU, and $P(H)$ denote the largest propagation time from any output to itself, for the communication step size H. For the scenario in Fig. 6, $P(H) = H \times (N + 1)^1$. Then the communication step size must be chosen so that $P(H) < T$.

This example shows that the Jacobi algorithm is still suitable for black box co-simulations, since exposing the shortest timed reaction and the propagation time does not expose the Intellectual Property of the subsystems.

Providing abstract information from the FMU is common in research on black box co-simulation (e.g., exposing the Jacobian [31], exposing the I/O feedthrough [2], exposing the maximum allowed step size [7]). While this is usually carried out to allow the setup of a co-simulation algorithm, we propose here to expose the minimum, relevant information to have a correct co-simulation, i.e. to allow verification such as model checking of the co-simulation.

The FMI webpage[2] contains a list of tools capable of performing co-simulation, and in order to be on this list, a tool must pass some tests. These

---

[1] This formula assumes that the software FMU only outputs a timeout event **after** the timeout (as it happens in Fig. 7), and not **at** the timeout. In the latter case, the formula becomes $P(H) = H \times N$.

[2] http://fmi-standard.org/.

tests, however, are limited – for example they only concern simulation of a single FMU, and not an actual co-simulation. In the long term, this research aims at producing a set of benchmarks, for various correctness properties, that can be used by the research community in the development of co-simulation tools. This idea is inspired by the work of [8], which defined the building blocks of these benchmarks.

References

1. Arnold, M.: Stability of sequential modular time integration methods for coupled multibody system models. J. Comput. Nonlinear Dyn. **5**(3), 9 (2010)
2. Arnold, M., Clauß, C., Schierz, T.: Error analysis and error estimates for co-simulation in FMI for model exchange and co-simulation v2.0. In: Schöps, S., Bartel, A., Günther, M., ter Maten, E.J.W., Müller, P.C. (eds.) Progress in Differential-Algebraic Equations. DEF, pp. 107–125. Springer, Heidelberg (2014). https://doi.org/10.1007/978-3-662-44926-4_6
3. Aström, K.J., Wittenmark, B.: Computer-Controlled Systems: Theory and Design. Courier Corporation, Chelmsford (2011)
4. Benedikt, M., Watzenig, D., Zehetner, J., Hofer, A.: NEPCE-a nearly energy preserving coupling element for weak-coupled problems and co-simulation. In: IV International Conference on Computational Methods for Coupled Problems in Science and Engineering, Coupled Problems, pp. 1–12. Ibiza, Spain, June 2013
5. Blochwitz, T., et al.: The functional mockup interface for tool independent exchange of simulation models. In: 8th International Modelica Conference, pp. 105–114. Linköping University Electronic Press, Linköpings universitet, Dresden, Germany, June 2011
6. Blockwitz, T., et al.: Functional mockup interface 2.0: the standard for tool independent exchange of simulation models. In: 9th International Modelica Conference, pp. 173–184. Linköping University Electronic Press, Munich, Germany, November 2012
7. Broman, D., et al.: Determinate composition of FMUs for co-simulation. In: Eleventh ACM International Conference on Embedded Software, Article no. 2. IEEE Press, Piscataway, Montreal (2013)
8. Broman, D., Greenberg, L., Lee, E.A., Masin, M., Tripakis, S., Wetter, M.: Requirements for hybrid cosimulation standards. In: 18th International Conference on Hybrid Systems: Computation and Control, HSCC 2015, pp. 179–188. ACM, New York, Seattle (2015)
9. Busch, M.: Continuous approximation techniques for co-simulation methods: analysis of numerical stability and local error. ZAMM - J. Appl. Math. Mech. **96**(9), 1061–1081 (2016)
10. Cellier, F.E., Kofman, E.: Continuous System Simulation. Springer, Heidelberg (2006). https://doi.org/10.1007/0-387-30260-3
11. Clarke, E., Veith, H.: Counterexamples revisited: principles, algorithms, applications. In: Dershowitz, N. (ed.) Verification: Theory and Practice. LNCS, vol. 2772, pp. 208–224. Springer, Heidelberg (2003). https://doi.org/10.1007/978-3-540-39910-0_9
12. Cremona, F., Lohstroh, M., Broman, D., Lee, E.A., Masin, M., Tripakis, S.: Hybrid co-simulation: it's about time. Softw. Syst. Model. (2017)

13. FMI: functional mock-up interface for model exchange and co-simulation. Technical report (2014)
14. Fritzson, P., et al.: OpenModelica - a free open-source environment for system modeling, simulation, and teaching. In: 2006 IEEE Conference on Computer Aided Control System Design. 2006 IEEE International Conference on Control Applications. 2006 IEEE International Symposium on Intelligent Control, pp. 1588–1595, October 2006
15. Gheorghe, L., Bouchhima, F., Nicolescu, G., Boucheneb, H.: A formalization of global simulation models for continuous/discrete systems. In: Summer Computer Simulation Conference, SCSC 2007, pp. 559–566. Society for Computer Simulation International, San Diego, July 2007
16. Gomes, C., Karalis, P., Navarro-López, E.M., Vangheluwe, H.: Approximated stability analysis of bi-modal hybrid co-simulation scenarios. In: Cerone, A., Roveri, M. (eds.) SEFM 2017. LNCS, vol. 10729, pp. 345–360. Springer, Cham (2018). https://doi.org/10.1007/978-3-319-74781-1_24
17. Gomes, C., Legat, B., Jungers, R.M., Vangheluwe, H.: Stable adaptive co-simulation: a switched systems approach. In: IUTAM Symposium on Co-Simulation and Solver Coupling, Darmstadt, Germany (2017, to appear)
18. Gomes, C., et al.: Semantic adaptation for FMI co-simulation with hierarchical simulators. SIMULATION, 1–29 (2018)
19. Gomes, C., Thule, C., Broman, D., Larsen, P.G., Vangheluwe, H.: Co-simulation: state of the art. Technical report, February 2017. http://arxiv.org/abs/1702.00686
20. Gomes, C., Thule, C., Broman, D., Larsen, P.G., Vangheluwe, H.: Co-simulation: a survey. ACM Comput. Surv. **51**(3), Article no. 49 (2018)
21. Gomes, C., Thule, C., Larsen, P.G., Denil, J., Vangheluwe, H.: Co-simulation of continuous systems: a tutorial. arXiv:1809.08463 [cs, math], September 2018
22. Harel, D.: Statecharts: a visual formalism for complex systems. Sci. Comput. Program. **8**(3), 231–274 (1987)
23. Holzmann, G.: The model checker SPIN. IEEE Trans. Softw. Eng. **23**(5), 279–295 (1997)
24. Kalmar-Nagy, T., Stanciulescu, I.: Can complex systems really be simulated? Appl. Math. Comput. **227**, 199–211 (2014)
25. Kübler, R., Schiehlen, W.: Modular simulation in multibody system dynamics. Multibody Syst. Dyn. **4**(2–3), 107–127 (2000)
26. Lee, E.A.: Cyber physical systems: design challenges. In: 11th IEEE International Symposium on Object Oriented Real-Time Distributed Computing, ISORC, pp. 363–369 (2008)
27. Palensky, P., Van Der Meer, A.A., Lopez, C.D., Joseph, A., Pan, K.: Cosimulation of intelligent power systems: fundamentals, software architecture, numerics, and coupling. IEEE Ind. Electron. Mag. **11**(1), 34–50 (2017)
28. Sadjina, S., Kyllingstad, L.T., Skjong, S., Pedersen, E.: Energy conservation and power bonds in co-simulations: non-iterative adaptive step size control and error estimation. Eng. Comput. **33**(3), 607–620 (2017)
29. Sadjina, S., Pedersen, E.: Energy conservation and coupling error reduction in non-iterative co-simulations. Technical report, June 2016. http://arxiv.org/abs/1606.05168
30. Schweizer, B., Li, P., Lu, D.: Explicit and implicit cosimulation methods: stability and convergence analysis for different solver coupling approaches. J. Comput. Nonlinear Dyn. **10**(5), 051007 (2015)
31. Sicklinger, S., et al.: Interface Jacobian-based co-simulation. Int. J. Numer. Methods Eng. **98**(6), 418–444 (2014)

32. Thule, C., Lausdahl, K., Larsen, P.G., Meisl, G.: Maestro: the INTO-CPS co-simulation orchestration engine (2018). Submitted to Simulation Modelling Practice and Theory
33. Tomiyama, T., D'Amelio, V., Urbanic, J., ElMaraghy, W.: Complexity of multi-disciplinary design. CIRP Ann. - Manuf. Technol. **56**(1), 185–188 (2007)
34. Van der Auweraer, H., Anthonis, J., De Bruyne, S., Leuridan, J.: Virtual engineering at work: the challenges for designing mechatronic products. Eng. Comput. **29**(3), 389–408 (2013)
35. Vangheluwe, H., De Lara, J., Mosterman, P.J.: An introduction to multi-paradigm modelling and simulation. In: AI, Simulation and Planning in High Autonomy Systems, pp. 9–20. SCS (2002)
36. Zhang, F., Yeddanapudi, M., Mosterman, P.J.: Zero-crossing location and detection algorithms for hybrid system simulation. In: IFAC Proceedings Volumes, vol. 41, pp. 7967–7972. Elsevier Ltd., Seoul, July 2008

A Flexible Framework for FMI-Based Co-Simulation of Human-Centred Cyber-Physical Systems

Maurizio Palmieri[1,2] , Cinzia Bernardeschi[2] , and Paolo Masci[3(✉)]

[1] Dipartimento di Ingegneria dell'Informazione,
University of Florence, Florence, Italy
[2] Dipartimento di Ingegneria dell'Informazione, University of Pisa, Pisa, Italy
{maurizio.palmieri,cinzia.bernardeschi}@ing.unipi.it
[3] HASLab/INESC TEC and Universidade do Minho, Braga, Portugal
paolo.masci@gmail.com

Abstract. This paper presents our on-going work on developing a flexible framework for formal co-simulation of human-centred cyber-physical systems. The framework builds on and extends an existing prototyping toolkit, adding novel functionalities for automatic generation of user interface prototypes equipped with a standard FMI-2 co-simulation interface. The framework is developed in JavaScript, and uses a flexible templating mechanism for converting stand-alone device prototypes into Functional Mockup Units (FMUs) capable of exchanging commands and data with any FMI-compliant co-simulation engine. Two concrete examples are presented to demonstrate the capabilities of the framework.

1 Introduction

Human-centered Cyber-Physical Systems (CPS) are complex systems that integrate human operators, digital controllers, and the physical world. An example is a self-driving car where an advanced driver assistance system automatically adjusts the speed and navigation of the car based on inputs from sensors, and the driver can take over control of the car at any point in time, e.g., by pressing the brake or accelerator pedal.

Model-based simulation technologies applied at the early stages of system design allow developers to gain additional confidence that the system behaves as expected. To produce accurate results in model-based analysis of CPS, developers often need to use co-simulation techniques, i.e., integrated simulation of different sub-systems, each modelled and simulated with the most appropriate tool (e.g., logic-based models for digital controllers, and continuous models based on differential equations for the physical part of the system).

To date, the research community has devoted most of its effort to the development of tools for co-simulation of cyber and physical components of CPS. Relatively little attention has been dedicated to developing tool support to assess the design of the human-machine interface of CPS, even though human-CPS

© Springer Nature Switzerland AG 2018
M. Mazzara et al. (Eds.): STAF 2018 Workshops, LNCS 11176, pp. 21–33, 2018.
https://doi.org/10.1007/978-3-030-04771-9_2

interaction is often a critical aspect of the system, e.g., see the recent accidents involving self-driving cars [15,16], where the design of the car dashboard exceeded the driver's abilities and performance when the driver needed to take over control of the car because of an emergency situation.

Contribution. We present a framework designed to support modelling and co-simulation of the user interface of a CPS. The framework builds on and extends PVSio-web [12], a prototyping toolkit for model-based analysis of human-machine interfaces. We extend PVSio-web to introduce support of automatic generation of user interface prototypes equipped with a standard FMI-2 co-simulation interface. Our framework is developed in JavaScript, and uses a flexible templating mechanism to convert stand-alone device prototypes into Functional Mockup Units (FMUs) capable of exchanging commands and data with any FMI-compliant co-simulation engine. Two example co-simulations of CPS are presented to illustrate the features and utility of the framework.

Structure. Section 2 illustrates background tools and concepts used in the work. Section 3 presents the code for automatically generate an FMU implementing a device prototype previously built with PVSio-web. Section 4 shows two different example applications of our work. Section 5 presents related work on co-simulation of CPS. Finally Sect. 6 concludes the paper.

2   Background

In this section we provide details on the two main technologies used in this work, namely PVSio-web and Functional Mockup Interface (FMI). PVSio-web because is a flexible tool for simulation of graphic user interfaces of CPS based on an Higher Order Language (PVS) and FMI is an emerging standard for co-simulation of CPS.

PVSio-web. PVSio-web [12] is a toolkit for prototyping and analysis of interactive (human-centred) systems. An example prototype developed with PVSio-web is shown in the upper part of Figs. 2 and 4. Each PVSio-web prototype consists of two parts: a back-end defining the behaviour of the system; and a graphical front-end defining the visual appearance of the system. The behaviour of the system is specified as an executable formal specification in PVS [17]. The visual appearance of the system is an interactive picture of the real system. Web technologies (HTML5 & JavaScript) are used to create hotspot areas over the picture, and link input and output widgets to the PVS specification. Input widgets translate user actions over buttons into PVS expressions to be evaluated in PVSio [14], the animation component of PVS, to compute the system response. Output widgets mirror the value of state attributes of the PVS model using graphic elements reproducing the look & feel of the real system in the corresponding state. A library of widgets is provided by PVSio-web that includes common interactive elements of a system (buttons, digital displays, gauges, etc.).

Functional Mockup Interface. The Functional Mockup Interface (FMI) [3] is a tool-independent standard for co-simulation of dynamic models. Co-simulation is performed by a number of *Functional Mockup Units* (FMUs), each responsible for simulating a single model in the native formalism and execution environment of the tool used to create the model. An FMU may carry a whole simulation environment, or just information needed by an FMI-compliant host environment to simulate the model contained in the FMU. An FMI-compliant host environment provides a *master* program that communicates with other FMUs acting as *slaves*. The APIs of each FMU include: initialisation functions; a function `fmi2DoStep` that triggers one simulation step; and functions to exchange data, including getter and setter functions `fmi2Get`<*TYPE*> and `fmi2Set`<*TYPE*>, where <*TYPE*> is a concrete type name, e.g., *Integer* or *Real*.

3   Our Framework

Our framework allows developers to extend stand-alone PVSio-web prototypes with an FMI-2 compliant co-simulation interface. That is, given a prototype developed with PVSio-web, our framework generates an FMU that includes:

– The PVS model of the prototype specifying the behaviour of the prototype;
– The PVSio environment necessary for executing the PVS model;
– The XML description file used in FMI-based co-simulations to specify static information of the model (such as the list of variables);
– C code implementing the APIs of the FMU necessary for exchanging data and commands with other FMUs;
– C code implementing a web server necessary to communicate with the graphical front-end of the PVSio-web prototype;
– An external module for executing the graphical front-end of the prototype in a web browser.

The overall architecture of a co-simulation where one or more FMUs are PVSio-web prototypes is shown in Fig. 1 (additional details will be provided further below, in Subsect. 3.1).

3.1   Communication Between FMU and the Prototype Interface

FMUs encapsulating PVSio-web prototypes use a WebSocket to exchange data and commands with the graphical front-end of the prototype (see Fig. 1). That is, the graphical front-end communicates only with the FMU, and does not interact directly with the co-simulation engine. This design choice promotes a modular architecture of the FMU, and enables *hot swapping* of different look&feel of the device without restarting the co-simulation — this is useful, e.g., when using the prototypes for design exploration. In the following we briefly describe the interaction between the FMU and the user interface of the prototype.

When the user performs an action on the graphical user interface of a PVSio-web prototype, the JavaScript module sends a message to the FMU with information about the action that has been performed (e.g., button x has been clicked). Every time the co-simulation master invokes a simulation step, the FMU checks

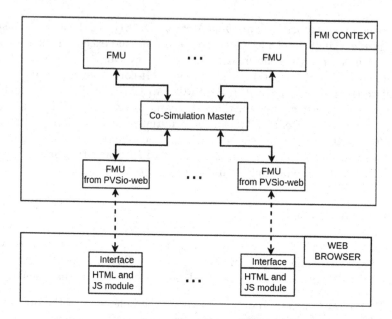

Fig. 1. FMI architecture including FMU generated from PVSio-web

if a new message has been received from the user interface (line 14 of Listing 1.4). If a message has been received, the FMU executes the user command first, and then a simulation step. After the execution of the action received from the user interface, the FMU replies to the user interface, via the same websocket connection, sending the updated state of the system.

The graphical user interface of the PVSio-web prototype is detached from the FMU. In case no user action is performed on the graphical user interface, consistency between the state of the co-simulation and feedback of the user interface is supported by an action *refresh* automatically sent by the front-end at each co-simulation step.

3.2   The APIs of Our Framework

The APIs provided by our framework include functionalities for generating the XML description file and the C code implementing the standard FMI functions necessary to extend a PVSio-web prototype with an FMI interface. The APIs are implemented in JavaScript, and the principal API function is create_FMU. An example use of the create_FMU function is as follows:

```
1  fmi_module.create_FMU("line_following_robot", {
2    fmi: [ { name : "gear", type :"string", variability: "discrete",
3            scope:"local", value:"0" },
4            ... ],
5    init: "init_LFR",
6    tick: "tick"
7  });
```

The first argument (line_following_robot) is the name of the FMU. The second argument is an object with three attributes:

```
1  <?xml version="1.0" encoding="ISO-8859-1"?>
2  <fmiModelDescription fmiVersion="2.0" modelName="{{modelName}}" ...>
3      <CoSimulation modelIdentifier="{{modelName}}"
4                    canHandleVariableCommunicationStepSize="false" ...>
5      </CoSimulation>
6      <LogCategories><Category name="logAll" /> ... </LogCategories>
7      <ModelVariables>{{#each variables}}{{#if fmi}}
8        <ScalarVariable name="{{name}}"
9                        valueReference="{{fmi.valueReference}}"
10                        causality="{{fmi.causality}}"
11                        variability="{{fmi.variability}}" >
12          <{{fmi.descriptor}} {{#if input}}start="{{value}}"{{/if}}
13                       {{#if parameter}}start="{{value}}"{{/if}} />
14        </ScalarVariable>{{/if}}{{/each}}
15      </ModelVariables>
16      <ModelStructure> ... </ModelStructure>
17  </fmiModelDescription>
```

Listing 1.1. Handlebars template for generating the XML description file.

- `fmi`: an array specifying the characteristics (name, type, variability, etc.) of the co-simulation variables;
- `init`: the name of the function in the PVS model for initializing the PVSio-web prototype;
- `tick`: the name of the function in the PVS model for advancing time.

The Handlebars[1] engine is used for generating the source code of **create_FMU** and other functions. The engine supports semantic templates with *parameters* and *helper functions*. Template parameters are instantiated at run time, using information contained in JSON objects. Helper function enable conditional compilation and iteration over arrays. The advantage of using semantic templates is that the structure of the source code can be inspected in the template, e.g., to check the correctness of syntax and semantics of the code to be generated. This makes it easier for developers to update the template when necessary, e.g., to adapt code generation to future versions of the FMI standard or to different platforms. We used the same approach in [13] for generating MISRA-C code from diagrams based on the state-charts notation. Details of the Handlebars templates developed for XML and C code generation are in the following subsections.

3.3   Generation of the XML Description File

Relevant fragments of the Handlebars template for generating the XML description file of an FMU are shown in Listing 1.1. Template parameters are characterised by unique identifiers and are adorned with curly braces. An example parameter in Listing 1.1 is {{modelName}}, which represents the name of the model described by the XML file. This and other template parameters are instantiated by invoking the Handlebars compilation engine with a JSON object whose attributes specify the actual values of those parameters. Helper functions {{if}} and {{each}} are used in the Handlebars template to perform conditional compilation (e.g., see lines 12–13 in Listing 1.1) and iteration over arrays (e.g., see lines 7–14 in Listing 1.1).

---

[1] https://handlebarsjs.com.

```
1  <?xml version="1.0" encoding="ISO-8859-1"?>
2  <fmiModelDescription fmiVersion="2.0" modelName="line_follower_robot"...>
3     <CoSimulation
4        modelIdentifier="line_follower_robot"
5        canHandleVariableCommunicationStepSize="false"
6        ...>
7     </CoSimulation>
8     <LogCategories><Category name="logAll" /> ... </LogCategories>
9     <ModelVariables>
10       <ScalarVariable name="gear" valueReference="1"
11                        causality="local" variability="discrete">
12                        <String /></ScalarVariable>
13                        ...
14       <ScalarVariable name="lightSensors_right" valueReference="10"
15                        causality="input" variability="continuous">
16                        <Real start="0" /></ScalarVariable>
17       <ScalarVariable name="motorSpeed_left" valueReference="11"
18                        causality="output" variability="discrete">
19                        <Real /></ScalarVariable>
20                        ...
21     </ModelVariables>
22     <ModelStructure> ... </ModelStructure>
23  </fmiModelDescription>
```

Listing 1.2. Example XML description file generated with our template.

An example XML file generated using the template is shown in Listing 1.2. The first part of the file provides general information about the FMU (e.g., model name, author, etc.) and information about co-simulation options supported by the FMU (e.g., step-size). The main body of the file contains information about variables used in the co-simulation, specified according to the format required by the FMI standard:

- valueReference is the buffer index where the value of the variable is stored;
- causality defines if the variable is input (i.e., received from another FMU), output (i.e., sent to another FMU), local (i.e., the variable is only used within the FMU), or if it is a parameter of the FMU;
- variability defines how the variable changes over time (i.e., discrete time or continuous time), or if the variable has a constant value.

3.4   Generation of the C Code Implementing the APIs of the FMU

The Handlebars template for generating the FMU of a PVSio-web prototype includes the definition of the standard FMI functions for exchanging data between FMUs (fmi2DoStep, fmi2Instantiate, etc.), and additional interface functions necessary to enable communication between front-end and back-end of the PVSio-web prototype. The graphical front-end is implemented in HTML5 & JavaScript, and executed in a web browser. The back-end is embedded in the FMU and executed within a web server encapsulating the PVSio animation environment. As an example, a snippet of the Handlebars template for generating function fmi2DoStep is shown in Listing 1.3. The function is used by a co-simulation master to trigger the execution of a simulation step in the FMU. It includes four arguments:

```
1  fmi2Status fmi2DoStep(fmi2Component c,
2                        fmi2Real currentCommunicationPoint,
3                        fmi2Real communicationStepSize,
4                        fmi2Boolean noSetFMUStatePriorToCurrentPoint) {
5      doStep();
6      return fmi2OK;
7  }
```

Listing 1.3. Snippet of Handlebars template for `fmi2DoStep`.

```
1  void doStep() {
2      // read input variables
3      {{#each variables}}{{#if fmi}}{{#if input}}
4      {{#if real}}
5      index_state = findVariable("{{name}}", state);
6      if (index_state != -1) {   // -1 means variable not found
7          readInputVariableDouble(index_state,{{fmi.valueReference}});
8      } {{/if}}
9      // ... code for updating other variable types omitted for brevity
10     {{/if}}{{/if}}
11     {{/each}}
12
13     // handle user action
14     handleUserAction();
15
16     // execute a simulation step
17     sendToPVSio("{{tick}}");
18     receiveFromPVSio();
19
20     // update output variables
21     {{#each variables}}{{#if fmi}}{{#if output}}
22     {{#if real}}
23     index_state = findVariable("{{name}}", state);
24     if (index_state != -1){ // -1 means variable not found
25         writeOutputVariableDouble(index_state, {{fmi.valueReference}});
26     } {{/if}}
27     // ... code for updating other variable types omitted for brevity
28     {{/if}}{{/if}}
29     {{/each}}
30 }
```

Listing 1.4. Snippet of the Handlebars template for function `doStep`.

- `fmi2Component` is the FMU;
- `currentCommunicationPoint` is the current simulation time;
- `communicationStepSize` is the simulation step;
- `noSetFMUStatePriorToCurrentPoint` is a boolean that specifies if the master can revert the state of the FMU back to a prior simulationn time.

The return of the function is of type `fmi2Status`, which is the standard return type of FMI 2.0 functions invoked by the master – possible return values are `fmi2OK` (the function has been executed correctly) and `fmi2Error` (the function produced an error). The body of the function invokes function `doStep`, which is invoked by the master to trigger the execution of a simulation step, and then returns a constant `fmi2OK` indicating that the step has been executed.

The template for function `doStep` is shown in Listing 1.4. It specifies the four main operations performed by the function: reads input variables of the FMU (lines 3–11); handles user input provided by the graphical front-end by

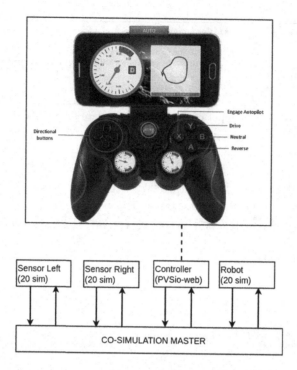

Fig. 2. Co-simulation of line follower robot case study.

executing the corresponding action in the PVS model and updating the state of the simulation (line 14); executes a step in the PVS model (lines 17–18); receives the new state of the PVS model and updates the output variables of the FMU (lines 20–29). The utility functions used in doStep are also specified as Handlebars templates.

4   Demonstrative Examples

4.1   Co-Simulation of Discrete and Continuous Components

Our first case study is based on the Line Follower Robot example provided by the INTO-CPS [10] project. In the original example, an autonomous robot has the goal of following a line painted on the ground. The controller of the robot receives the readings from two light sensors placed on the front of the robot (one slightly moved to the left and one slightly moved to the right), and sends commands to the left and right motors which are in charge of the rotation of the left and right wheels, respectively. The INTO-CPS project provides the FMU of the kinematics of the robot (created with the 20-sim [4] tool), the FMU of the sensors (created with 20-sim or OpenModelica [7]), and the FMU of the controller (created with the Overture [9] tool).

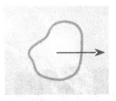

(a) U-turn due to high speed.   (b) Missed turn.

Fig. 3. Unexpected behaviours of the line follower robot.

In our previous work [20], we replaced the original controller of the robot with a more advanced controller developed with PVSio-web. The new controller allows a driver to override the automatic line following control of the robot, and operate the robot manually, using controls on a dashboard. The sensors and the mechanics of the robot are unaltered with respect to the original INTO-CPS example.

The PVSio-web prototype (shown in Fig. 2) provides a navigation display with the trajectory of the robot, two speedometer gauges to monitor the velocities of the wheels, a speedometer gauge to monitor the velocity of the robot, and various control buttons to allow a driver to accelerate (*up arrow*) or brake (*down arrow*), change direction of the robot (*left and right arrows*), and change gear (buttons *A, Y and B*). There is also a control (button *X*) to switch control mode from manual back to automatic.

In our previous work the PVSio-web prototype was created by manually developing the XML and C code necessary for the FMI interface. In this work we re-created the same prototype automatically, using the APIs of our framework. The new prototype was successfully used in co-simulation scenarios executed using the INTO-CPS Co-simulation Orchestration Engine.

The FMU connected with the PVSio-web navigation display has been used to analyse the robot behaviour when switching control mode from manual to automatic and to expose possible faults of the robot. For example, many experiments pointed out the need to perform a U-turn to get back on track when switching from manual to automatic control and the robot was moving at high speed (see Fig. 3a), and some experiments ended up with the robot going far away from the line due to the fact that it reaches perpendicularly the line, decides not to turn and moves on (see Fig. 3b).

4.2   Co-Simulation of Multiple Devices

Our second case study is based on an Integrated Clinical Environment (ICE). In this case, the co-simulation integrates the concurrent execution of three models, each representing a different device (see Fig. 4).

ICE is a prototype medical system for intensive care patients. The system includes three devices: a pump infusing morphine; a monitor checking vital signs of the patient; and a supervisor device implementing a safety interlock app that

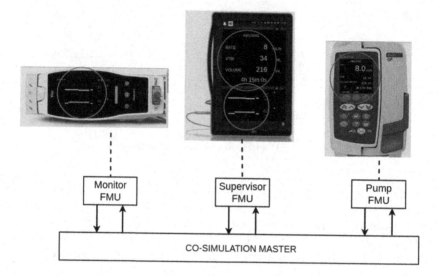

Fig. 4. Co-Simulation of ICE case study.

automatically stops the infusion when the patient monitor detects the onset of respiratory depression.

The patient monitor records two vital signs: oxygen saturation level (SpO_2), and Respiration Rate (RRa). The current value of a vital sign is reported using a numeric display. Additionally, a scan-bar trace display shows the temporal evolution of the sign. Each monitored parameter has safe range limits. An alarm is triggered if these limits are exceeded.

The front panel of the pump is used to enter the volume to be infused ($VTBI$) and the rate of the infusion of morphine, as well as to start/stop the infusion. During the infusion, the display of the pump shows the rate, the remaining volume of morphine that needs to be infused, and the time to complete the infusion.

The supervisor device has a user interface that can be used for remote monitoring of the pump state and patient monitor state. It is a portable device with a display divided into two sections. The upper section replicates the pump display, and the lower section replicates the patient monitor display.

Starting from the PVSio-web models of these devices, which were already available in the PVSio-web distribution, we used our framework to generate three FMUs, one for each device prototype. These three FMUs were integrated using the INTO-CPS Co-simulation Orchestration Engine, according to the structure shown in Fig. 4.

A similar co-simulation example for the ICE system was previously developed in [11] using a (non-standard) co-simulation engine integrated in PVSio-web, which builds on the SAPERE [23] middleware. The migration to the FMI framework did not require any substantial update to the PVSio-web prototypes, as our framework allowed us to re-route and adapt the communication channels used in the SAPERE-based co-simulation to the new FMI interface. The main advantage of the FMI-based co-simulation with respect to that based on SAPERE is that the co-simulation is not limited anymore to PVSio-web prototypes, as other interactive prototypes and system elements developed with tools other than PVSio-web can be integrated in the co-simulation. This is useful, e.g., to introduce patient models in the co-simulation, as tools other than PVS are better suited to specify these models.

5   Related Work

Significant work has been done over the last few years to develop tool support for co-simulation of CPSs. Some works use only one specification formalism for both continuous and discrete systems, like HybridSim [22]. Others support heterogeneous co-simulation [8] with customised solutions, like ForSyDe [21] that supports set of processes that may belong to a distinct Model of Computation, or *OpenICE* [1], that allows the simulation of medical devices for an Integrated Clinical Environment architectures, using a publish-subscribe middleware for communications. In our previous work [2], we developed a CPS co-simulation framework that integrates the Prototype Verification System (PVS) and Simulink.

Recent works use the Functional Mockup Interface (FMI) standard for subsystems synchronisation [19,20]. In [18] FMI co-simulation is used for modelling and analysing intelligent power systems. Another example is [6], which models the discrete aspects of the system in VDM-RT, the physical part in Modelica and the communication aspects between components in Promela. None of these framework, however, targets modelling and analysis of user interfaces of CPS.

Work on formalising models and proofs for FMI-based co-simulations has been carried out in [24] using Isabelle/UTP and an industrial case study from the railways sector. In [5], a proof-of-concept co-simulation is performed between Ptolemy II and Rodin, using Event-B for formal verification in the aeronautic field. None of these works, however, targets modelling and analysis of user interfaces of CPS.

6   Conclusion and Future Work

In this paper we present the process for transforming PVSio-web prototypes into FMUs equipped with a standard FMI-2 co-simulation interface. This activity is part of our ongoing work on the development of a framework for formal modelling, simulation and verification of human-centred CPS. In particular, the generation of the FMU, extends our framework making it possible to co-simulate our prototypes with any FMI-compliant co-simulation engine.

Our prototypes can be co-simulated with other prototypes modelled with other tools. For example, in the ICE case, the pump could have been modelled using a different formalism or a model of the patient could be included in the co-simulation. Another advantages of the FMU generation process is that the original PVSio-web prototypes are unchanged, and properties already verified for a prototype are still satisfied by the generated FMU.

Future work will focus on providing a more refined management of the simulated time and a more efficient mechanism for updating the graphical front-end of the prototype. For example, the current implementation has constraints on when time is advanced in the PVSio-web prototype. Specifically, time in the PVS model is advanced only in action *tick* by a discrete step equal to the co-simulation step-size. User actions do not advance time, and they are executed in lockstep with the simulation. The consequence is that only one user action can be handled at each simulation step. Experience shows that co-simulation steps lower than 250 ms allow for realistic simulations. We plan to remove this constraint by introducing an event-based mechanism for handling user actions continuously over time.

Acknowledgments. Paolo Masci is funded by the ERDF (European Regional Development Fund) through Operational Programme for Competitiveness and Internationalisation COMPETE 2020 Programme, within project POCI-01-0145-FEDER-006961, and by National Funds through the Portuguese funding agency FCT (Fundação para a Ciência e a Tecnologia) as part of project UID/EEA/50014/2013.

References

1. Arney, D., et al.: Simulation of medical device network performance and requirements for an integrated clinical environment. Biomed. Instrum. Technol. **46**(4), 308–315 (2012)
2. Bernardeschi, C., Domenici, A., Masci, P.: A PVS-simulink integrated environment for model-based analysis of cyber-physical systems. IEEE Trans. Softw. Eng. **44**(6), 512–533 (2018)
3. Blochwitz, T., et al.: Functional mockup interface 2.0: the standard for tool independent exchange of simulation models. In: Proceedings of the 9th International Modelica Conference, pp. 173–184. The Modelica Association (2012)
4. Broenink, J.F.: 20-SIM software for hierarchical bond-graph/block-diagram models. Simul. Pract. Theory **7**(5–6), 481–492 (1999)
5. Chaudemar, J.-C., Savicks, V., Butler, M., Colley, J.: Co-simulation of Event-B and Ptolemy II models via FMI. In: ERTS 2014, Embedded real time software and systems, Toulouse, FR (2014)
6. Couto, L.D., Basagiannis, S., Ridouane, E.H., Mady, A.E.-D., Hasanagic, M., Larsen, P.G.: Injecting formal verification in FMI-based co-simulations of cyber-physical systems. In: Cerone, A., Roveri, M. (eds.) SEFM 2017. LNCS, vol. 10729, pp. 284–299. Springer, Cham (2018). https://doi.org/10.1007/978-3-319-74781-1_20
7. Fritzson, P., et al.: The openmodelica modeling, simulation, and development environment. In: 46th Conference on Simulation and Modelling of the Scandinavian Simulation Society (SIMS2005) (2005)
8. Gomes, C., Thule, C., Broman, D., Larsen, P.G., Vangheluwe, H.: Co-simulation: state of the art. CoRR, abs/1702.00686 (2017)
9. Larsen, P.G., Battle, N., Ferreira, M., Fitzgerald, J., Lausdahl, K., Verhoef, M.: The overture initiative integrating tools for VDM. ACM SIGSOFT Softw. Eng. Notes **35**(1), 1–6 (2010)

10. Larsen, P.G., et al.: Integrated tool chain for model-based design of cyber-physical systems: the INTO-CPS project. In: 2016 2nd International Workshop on Modelling, Analysis, and Control of Complex CPS (CPS Data), pp. 1–6. IEEE (2016)
11. Masci, P., Mallozzi, P., DeAngelis, F.L., Serugendo, G.D.M., Curzon, P.: Using PVSio-web and SAPERE for rapid prototyping of user interfaces in Integrated Clinical Environments. In: Proceedings of the Workshop on Verification and Assurance (Verisure2015), Co-located with CAV2015 (2015)
12. Masci, P., Oladimeji, P., Zhang, Y., Jones, P., Curzon, P., Thimbleby, H.: PVSio-web 2.0: joining PVS to HCI. In: Kroening, D., Păsăreanu, C.S. (eds.) CAV 2015. LNCS, vol. 9206, pp. 470–478. Springer, Cham (2015). https://doi.org/10.1007/978-3-319-21690-4_30
13. Mauro, G., Thimbleby, H., Domenici, A., Bernardeschi, C.: Extending a user interface prototyping tool with automatic MISRA C code generation. arXiv preprint arXiv:1701.08468 (2017)
14. Muñoz, C.: Rapid prototyping in PVS. Technical report NIA 2003–03, NASA/CR-2003-212418, National Institute of Aerospace, Hampton, VA, USA (2003)
15. CNN News: Tesla in autopilot mode crashes into fire truck (2018). http://money.cnn.com/2018/01/23/technology/tesla-fire-truck-crash/index.html
16. CNN News: Uber self-driving car kills pedestrian in first fatal autonomous crash (2018). http://money.cnn.com/2018/03/19/technology/uber-autonomous-car-fatal-crash/index.html
17. Owre, S., Rajan, S., Rushby, J.M., Shankar, N., Srivas, M.: PVS: combining specification, proof checking, and model checking. In: Alur, R., Henzinger, T.A. (eds.) CAV 1996. LNCS, vol. 1102, pp. 411–414. Springer, Heidelberg (1996). https://doi.org/10.1007/3-540-61474-5_91
18. Palensky, P., Van Der Meer, A.A., Lopez, C.D., Joseph, A., Pan, K.: Cosimulation of intelligent power systems: fundamentals, software architecture, numerics, and coupling. IEEE Ind. Electron. Mag. 11(1), 34–50 (2017)
19. Palensky, P., van der Meer, A., Lopez, C., Joseph, A., Pan, K.: Applied cosimulation of intelligent power systems: implementing hybrid simulators for complex power systems. IEEE Ind. Electron. Mag. 11(2), 6–21 (2017)
20. Palmieri, M., Bernardeschi, C., Masci, P.: Co-simulation of semi-autonomous systems: the line follower robot case study. In: Cerone, A., Roveri, M. (eds.) SEFM 2017. LNCS, vol. 10729, pp. 423–437. Springer, Cham (2018). https://doi.org/10.1007/978-3-319-74781-1_29
21. Sander, I., Jantsch, A.: System modeling and transformational design refinement in forsyde [formal system design]. IEEE Trans. Comput.-Aided Des. Integr. Circuits Syst. 23(1), 17–32 (2004)
22. Wang, B., Baras, J. S.: HybridSim: a modeling and co-simulation toolchain for cyber-physical systems. In: 2013 IEEE/ACM 17th International Symposium on Distributed Simulation and Real Time Applications, pp. 33–40, October 2013
23. Zambonelli, F., et al.: Developing pervasive multi-agent systems with nature-inspired coordination. Pervasive Mob. Comput. 17, 236–252 (2015)
24. Zeyda, F., Ouy, J., Foster, S., Cavalcanti, A.: Formalising cosimulation models. In: Cerone, A., Roveri, M. (eds.) SEFM 2017. LNCS, vol. 10729, pp. 453–468. Springer, Cham (2018). https://doi.org/10.1007/978-3-319-74781-1_31

Towards Stochastic FMI Co-Simulations: Implementation of an FMU for a Stochastic Activity Networks Simulator

Cinzia Bernardeschi[2], Andrea Domenici[2(✉)], and Maurizio Palmieri[1,2]

[1] DINFO, University of Florence, Florence, Italy
[2] Department of Information Engineering, University of Pisa, Pisa, Italy
{cinzia.bernardeschi,andrea.domenici,maurizio.palmieri}@ing.unipi.it

Abstract. The advantage of co-simulation with respect to traditional single-paradigm simulation lies mainly in the modeling flexibility it affords in composing large models out of submodels, each expressed in the most appropriate formalism. One aspect of this flexibility is the modularity of the co-simulation framework, which allows developers to replace each sub-model with a new version, possibly based on a different formalism or a different simulator, without changing the rest of the co-simulation. This paper reports on the replacement of a sub-model in a co-simulation built on the INTO-CPS framework. Namely, an existing co-simulation of a water tank, available in the INTO-CPS distribution, has been modified by replacing the tank sub-model with a sub-model built as a Stochastic Activity Network simulated on Möbius, a tool used to perform statistical analyses of systems with stochastic behavior. This work discusses aspects of this redesign, including the necessary modifications to the Möbius sub-model. In this still preliminary work, the Stochastic Activity Network features related to stochastic models have not been used, but a simple deterministic model has proved useful in indicating an approach to the integration of Stochastic Activity Networks into a co-simulation framework.

1   Introduction

Co-simulation is gaining interest and acceptance as an approach to modeling and simulation of cyber-physical systems (CPS) [1,30], as it is based on the concept of modeling each part of a large, heterogeneous system with the most appropriate formalism, and simulating each part with a tool fit for the formalism. This requires coordinating the execution of two or more simulators, which usually have been designed as standalone tools, therefore the need arises of standards for the exchange of data and control among different modeling and simulation tools. One such standard is the *Functional Mockup Interface* (FMI), defining the common interface and protocol that must be honored by the simulators involved in a co-simulation.

The simulation of a set of heterogeneous models, called a *multi-model*, is coordinated by a *master* algorithm. Implementing a master algorithm from scratch

© Springer Nature Switzerland AG 2018
M. Mazzara et al. (Eds.): STAF 2018 Workshops, LNCS 11176, pp. 34–44, 2018.
https://doi.org/10.1007/978-3-030-04771-9_3

would be costly and inefficient, but co-simulation usually relies on a framework providing the algorithm together with a user interface to configure and control the co-simulation. An important feature of co-simulation frameworks is modularity: Developers should be able to add simulators and also to replace any simulator with another one, which simulates the same subsystem but with a different modeling technique, with a minimum effort and leaving the other simulators unchanged.

This paper is focused on (i) the development of an FMU for a modeling and simulation tool not yet used in FMI-based co-simulations, and (ii) modifying a previous multi-model by replacing one of its submodels with a new one, expressed in a completely different formalism. These two points exemplify the flexibility and modularity of the co-simulation approach. A further, longer-term goal is investigating the integration of statistical simulation techniques and co-simulation.

The simulation tool considered in this paper is Möbius, an environment for the analysis and simulation of *Stochastic Activity Networks* (SAN). SANs are a wide-ranging extension to Petri nets, oriented to the evaluation of performance and dependability. The Möbius tool has been integrated in a co-simulation built on the INTO-CPS framework. This co-simulation is a case study available in the INTO-CPS distribution, concerning the control of a water tank. The tank controller activates the tank's exhaust valve depending on the water level and is modeled in VDM, and the tank's dynamics are modeled in Modelica. This latter model has been replaced by a SAN and simulated with the Möbius tool.

2   Related Work

The co-simulation of a human heart modeled in Simulink and an implantable pacemaker modeled in PVS [21] has been presented in [5], where the PVSio-web [20] prototyping toolkit provided the communication infrastructure. A PVS model of a controller was also used in the simulation of a semi-autonomous vehicle [22] whose mechanical part was modeled with 20-SIM and OpenModelica, in the INTO-CPS framework.

The Möbius [7,9,10] tool can be seen as oriented to co-simulation, as it has been designed to build complex models by integrating submodels in different formalisms [24–26], but it requires the submodels to be developed with tools built-in in the Möbius framework. Another multi-formalism framework is SIMTHESys [14].

SAN models have been used in a large number of application fields, including biology and medicine [28,29], integrated circuits [2,3], and railway systems [19].

From the literature on the integration of deterministic and non-deterministic simulation, we may cite [16–18].

3   Background

This section introduces basic information on the tools and standards referred to in the paper, with an emphasis on Stochastic Activity Networks and the Möbius tool.

3.1   Stochastic Activity Networks

Stochastic Activity Networks [27] are an extension of Petri Nets (PN). SANs are directed graphs with four disjoint sets of nodes: *places*, *input gates*, *output gates*, and *activities*. The latter are an extension of PN *transitions*. The allowed arcs are from places to input gates, from input gates to activities, from activities to output gates, and from output gates to places.

Each SAN activity may be either *instantaneous* or *timed*. Timed activities represent actions with a duration affecting the performance of the modeled system, e.g., message transmission time. The duration of each timed activity is expressed via a *time distribution* function. An activity *completes* when its (possibly instantaneous) execution terminates.

Any instantaneous or timed activity may have mutually exclusive outcomes, called *cases*, chosen probabilistically according to the *case distribution* of the activity. Cases can be used to model probabilistic behaviors.

The state of a SAN is defined by its *marking*, i.e., a function that, at each step of the net's evolution, maps the places to non-negative integers. SANs enable the user to specify any desired enabling condition and firing rule for each activity. This is accomplished by associating an *enabling* (or *input*) *predicate* and an *input function* to each input gate, and an *output function* to each output gate. The enabling predicate is a Boolean function of the marking of the gate's input places. The input and output functions compute the next marking of the input and output places, respectively, given their current marking. If these predicates and functions are not specified for some activity, the standard PN rules are assumed.

The evolution of a SAN, starting from a given marking μ, may be described as follows: (i) The instantaneous activities enabled in μ complete in some unspecified order; (ii) if no instantaneous activities are enabled in μ, the enabled (timed) activities become *active*; (iii) the completion times of each active (timed) activity are computed stochastically, according to the respective time distributions; the activity with the earliest completion time is selected for completion; (iv) when an activity (timed or not) completes, one of its cases is selected according to the case distribution, and the next marking μ' is computed by evaluating the input functions of the input gates and the output functions of the gates connected to the selected case; (v) if an activity that was active in μ is no longer enabled in μ', it is removed from the set of active activities.

Graphically, places are drawn as circles, input (output) gates as left-pointing (right-pointing) triangles, instantaneous activities as narrow vertical bars, and timed activities as thick vertical bars. Cases are drawn as small circles on the right side of activities. Gates with default (standard PN) enabling predicates and firing rules are not shown.

3.2   The Möbius Tool

Möbius [9,10] is a software tool that provides a comprehensive framework for model-based evaluation of system dependability and performance. The main features of the tool include support for multiple high-level modeling formalisms beyond SANs, such as, among others, PEPA fault trees [13] and the ADVISE security model formalism [12], and statistical characterization of system behavior.

The Möbius tool introduces two extensions to the SAN formalism: *extended places* and *global variables*. Extended places are places whose marking is a numerical value other than non-negative integers, or a complex data structure. Global variables are (possibly complex) data structures that can be accessed by enabling predicates and input and output functions, and can be shared among different SANs.

Enabling predicates and input and output functions of the gates are specified as C++ code.

A *study model* is a set of *experiments*, i.e., assignments to the global variables. Study models enable developers to run simulations for different values of system parameters. Variable assignments can be specified manually or generated by the tool as sequences of values according to various patterns.

The tool generates a *simulation solver*, an executable file that can be run from the Möbius user interface or launched from the command line.

3.3   The FMI Standard

The FMI standard [6] defines a set of C functions to support interaction among heterogeneous simulators coordinated by a master algorithm. The interface includes operations to initialize and configure the simulators, to exchange data with setter and getter operations, and to orchestrate the co-simulation by issuing *doStep* commands to the individual simulators.

A Functional Mockup Unit is a software artifact packaging all components necessary to simulate a single model, including, if needed, a whole simulator application. Some modeling tools can produce an FMU from their user interface, or provide scripts to create it from the command line. Otherwise, a developer can adapt those scripts to modeling tools that do not yet support the FMI standard.

3.4   The INTO-CPS Framework

INTO-CPS [15] is an integrated tool-chain to support model-based development of CPSs using co-simulation according to the FMI standard. The top-level component of the tool-chain is the INTO-CPS *application*, a graphical user interface for the management of co-simulation projects. Developers create FMUs for their models using the respective tools, place them in the INTO-CPS project directory, and define their interconnections with the user interface. Simulations are executed under control of the *Co-Simulation Orchestration Engine* (COE), the core component of the tool-chain. The user interface also provides a graphical output to plot selected quantities.

The reader is addressed to the literature [11] for other important features of the tool-chain, such as design space exploration [8].

4 The SAN Water Tank Co-simulation

As anticipated in Sect. 1, the main motivations for the present work are the development of an FMU for a new modeling tool and the replacement of a sub-model into an existing multi-model, as described in this section.

4.1 The INTO-CPS Water Tank Example

The INTO-CPS application comes with a set of case studies [23] including a water tank whose level is controlled by an exit valve with two states, fully open or fully closed. The tank is fed at a constant flow and drained (when the valve is open) at a flow rate depending on the instantaneous water level. The valve tank controller reads the water level, then it opens the valve when the maximum allowed level is exceeded and closes it when the water goes below the minimum allowed level. Two models for the tank are available, one in Modelica and one in 20-SIM, while the controller model is in VDM-RT.

4.2 The SAN Model

The tank sub-model has been replaced with a SAN developed on the Möbius tool. In addition to the different modeling language, a different physical model has been chosen, adapted from the one studied in [4], and the main differences from the INTO-CPS case study are the following: (i) the intake flow is variable; (ii) the valve is opened and closed gradually, so that its area varies linearly with time; and (iii) the drain flow depends on the valve area, and not on the water level. The valve actuator, however, accepts the same control inputs as in the original model.

More precisely, the control signal takes the values 0 (*close*) or 1 (*open*) when the lower or upper level limits, respectively, are reached. Otherwise, it maintains the current value, as defined in the original INTO-CPS model. The area of the valve increases when the control signal equals 1 and decreases when the control signal is 0, unless one of the limit positions has been reached. In this case, the valve remains open or closed until a reversing control signal is received. The outgoing flow is proportional to the valve area, and the tank level is the integral of the net flow.

Figure 1 shows the SAN model, where the lighter (orange) circles are extended places, used to store quantities of interest. Let us ignore, for the moment, the *step*

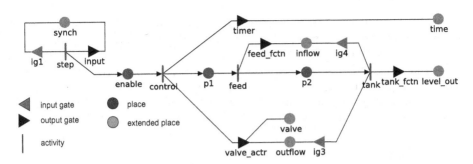

Fig. 1. SAN model of the tank (Color figure online)

Table 1. Gate functions

Gate	Predicate	Function
ig1	$synch = 1$	
input		Wait for input, then set *valve_control* and reset *synch*.
timer		Increase *time*; terminate if max time reached.
valve_actr		Set valve position; compute outflow.
feed_fctn		Compute inflow.
ig4	true	
ig3	true	
tank_fctn		Compute net flow and level; set *synch*.

activity, whose purpose is to synchronize the tank and the controller models. The input gate predicates and output gate functions are summarized in Table 1. Note that an explicit input gate is required between an extended place and an activity, hence the always enabled gates *ig3* and *ig4*. The *control* activity performs the following actions:

1. it increments the simulation time in gate *timer*;
2. it computes the valve area and the drain flow in gate *valve_actr*; and
3. it enables the next activity, *feed*, by marking place p_1.

Gate *timer* increments the marking of place *time* by a fixed amount *dt*. This is a global variable set by the user in the study model.

The valve area and the drain flow are computed by the output function of *valve_actr*, modeling the valve actuator. This function reads a global variable containing the last command from the controller, it increases or decreases the valve area accordingly, and computes the flow. The computed values are stored as the markings of the extended places *valve* and *outflow*.

The *feed* activity models the water source and enables activity *tank*. Gate *feed_fctn* computes the intake flow as a function of time and stores its value in place *inflow*. In this simulation, a sinusoidal function has been used.

Finally, the output gate *tank_fctn* of *tank* computes the net flow and the updated level. The output function executes a simple integration step increasing the current level by the product of the net flow and the time interval.

We may note that all computations are C++ fragments entered through the user interface and inserted by the tool into the functions of the output gates. However, such fragments may also call external user-defined code, for example to implement a more accurate integration method.

4.3   The FMU

Replacing a sub-model in a co-simulation multi-model involves addressing three main concerns: ensuring semantic coherence, complying with the multi-model synchronization mechanism, and translating between different syntactic representations. The third concern is not very important for the case at hand, since the submodels only exchange control and synchronization signals, the only quantitative information being the water level. In fact, the multi-model is composed only of a plant subsystem (the tank, water source, and valve) and a control subsystem. The latter receives the water level from a sensor and returns a binary signal.

The controller's signal concerns the issue of semantic coherence. In the original multi-model, its effect is to cause the valve to fully open or close, whereas in the new model the valve opens or closes gradually. Further, there are other differences between the physical behavior of the two models. However, the meaning of the controller's output remains the same, as in both cases it signals that the water level is not within the allowed limits. Therefore the new multi-model makes sense even if it simulates a system with different properties.

The synchronization mechanism is controlled by the master algorithm, which periodically invokes a *doStep* operation on each FMU to trigger one execution step. This requires the simulators to agree on a common time base and be able to pause between each simulation step.

In the INTO-CPS multi-model, the simulation step is configurable from the user interface, so the common time base is achieved by setting variable *dt* equal to the simulation step.

Pausing the SAN simulator requires adding a simple synchronization mechanism to the model. The output function of gate *input* (Fig. 1) reads the control signal from standard input, stores its value in a global variable, disables activity *step* by zeroing the marking of place *synch*, and enables the *control* activity to start a simulation step. The step terminates when the output function of *tank_fctn* prints the water level to standard output and sets the marking of place *synch* to re-enable activity *step* for the next step.

The final task is providing an FMI-compliant interface to the SAN executable. This is done by a software component that implements the FMI interface, and in particular the operations *fmi2Instantiate* and *fmi2DoStep*. The former spawns the Möbius-generated executable and connects with it through Unix pipes on which the executable's standard input and output are redirected. The module is compiled into a dynamic library that is then packed in the FMU component.

The FMU described above was installed in the INTO-CPS multi-model without changing the FMU for the controller, and simulated. Figure 2 is an example of the output for one the simulations, where the darker (blue) line is the water level and the lighter (brown) one is the controller output. This plot is consistent with the one shown in the INTO-CPS case study [23], except for the different waveform of the water level, due to the different incoming flow.

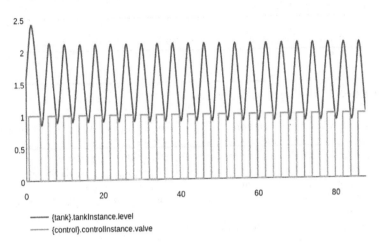

Fig. 2. Results of co-simulation

5   Conclusions

The present work shows, by means of a practical example, the "plug and play" capability of the FMI standard of the co-simulation framework adopted. A preexisting and independently developed multi-model has been modified by replacing a substantial part with a new version, differing from the original one in the modeling formalism, in the simulation engine, and even in its physical behavior. The replacement has been performed without any change to the rest of the multi-model, and has required only the inclusion of an explicit synchronization mechanism in the SAN model and the development of an FMI-compliant wrapper process to interface the model.

This simple procedure has been possible in spite of the fact that the new model is expressed in a formalism quite different from such languages as Modelica or Bond-Graphs. Making diverse modeling paradigms available gives developers the possibility to explore more aspects of the systems being developed. Stochastic Activity Networks, for example, make it easy to study probabilistic behaviors, although this capability has not been exploited in the present work. In spite of this limitation, this experience has proved useful in finding interesting aspects of the integration of SAN models that will continue to be investigated in further research. In particular, the synchronization with the master algorithm needs more study. In the present work, the straightforward solution of inserting an *ad hoc* sub-network into the SAN model has been adopted, but more modular, less invasive methods should be developed. A more fundamental issue for further work is how to synchronize the co-simulation in presence of stochastic durations of simulation steps. Finally, even if plugging the new model in the simulation "by hand" was rather easy, it should be made easier by providing generic tools that can produce FMUs for new simulator from a purely declarative description of the required interface.

Acknowledgments. The authors wish to thank the anonymous referees for their helpful suggestions.

References

1. Van der Auweraer, H., Anthonis, J., De Bruyne, S., Leuridan, J.: Virtual engineering at work: the challenges for designing mechatronic products. Eng. Comput. **29**(3), 389–408 (2013). https://doi.org/10.1007/s00366-012-0286-6
2. Bernardeschi, C., Cassano, L., Domenici, A., Sterpone, L.: ASSESS: a simulator of soft errors in the configuration memory of SRAM-based FPGAs. IEEE Trans. Comput.-Aided Des. Integr. Circuits Syst. **33**(9), 1342–1355 (2014). https://doi.org/10.1109/TCAD.2014.2329419
3. Bernardeschi, C., Cassano, L., Domenici, A.: Failure probability and fault observability of SRAM-FPGA systems. In: International Conference on Field Programmable Logic and Applications (FPL2011), pp. 385–388. IEEE, Sep 2011. https://doi.org/10.1109/FPL.2011.75
4. Bernardeschi, C., Domenici, A.: Verifying safety properties of a nonlinear control by interactive theorem proving with the Prototype Verification System. Inform. Process. Lett. **116**(6), 409–415 (2016). https://doi.org/10.1016/j.ipl.2016.02.001
5. Bernardeschi, C., Domenici, A., Masci, P.: A PVS-simulink integrated environment for model-based analysis of cyber-physical systems. IEEE Trans. Softw. Eng. **44**(6), 512–533 (2018). https://doi.org/10.1109/TSE.2017.2694423
6. Blochwitz, T., et al.: Functional mockup interface 2.0: the standard for tool independent exchange of simulation models. In: Proceedings of the 9th International MODELICA Conference, 3–5 September 2012, Munich, Germany, pp. 173–184. No. 76 in Linköping Electronic Conference Proceedings. Linköping University Electronic Press (2012). https://doi.org/10.3384/ecp12076173
7. Buchanan, C., Keefe, K.: Simulation debugging and visualization in the Möbius modeling framework. In: Norman, G., Sanders, W. (eds.) Quantitative Evaluation of Systems, pp. 226–240. Springer, Cham (2014). https://doi.org/10.1007/978-3-319-10696-0_18
8. Christiansen, M., Larsen, P., Nyholm Jørgensen, R.: Robotic design choice overview using co-simulation and design space exploration. Robotics **4**, 398–421 (2015). https://doi.org/10.3390/robotics4040398
9. Clark, G., et al.: The Möbius modeling tool. In: 9th International Workshop on Petri Nets and Performance Models, pp. 241–250. IEEE Computer Society Press, Aachen, September 2001. https://doi.org/10.1109/PNPM.2001.953373
10. Deavours, D.D., et al.: The Möbius framework and its implementation. IEEE Trans. Softw. Eng. **28**(10), 956–969 (2002). https://doi.org/10.1109/TSE.2002.1041052

11. Fitzgerald, J., Gamble, C., Larsen, P., Pierce, K., Woodcock, J.: Cyber-physical systems design: formal foundations, methods and integrated tool chains. In: Proceedings of the 2015 IEEE/ACM 3rd FME Workshop on Formal Methods in Software Engineering (FormaliSE), pp. 40–46. IEEE (2015). https://doi.org/10.1109/FormaliSE.2015.14
12. Ford, M.D., Keefe, K., LeMay, E., Sanders, W.H., Muehrcke, C.: Implementing the ADVISE security modeling formalism in Möbius. In: 2013 43rd Annual IEEE/IFIP International Conference on Dependable Systems and Networks (DSN), pp. 1–8, June 2013. https://doi.org/10.1109/DSN.2013.6575362
13. Gulati, R., Dugan, J.B.: A modular approach for analyzing static and dynamic fault trees. In: Annual Reliability and Maintainability Symposium, pp. 57–63. IEEE Computer Society Press (1997). https://doi.org/10.1109/RAMS.1997.571665
14. Iacono, M., Gribaudo, M.: Element based semantics in multi formalism performance models. In: 2010 IEEE International Symposium on Modeling, Analysis and Simulation of Computer and Telecommunication Systems, pp. 413–416, August 2010. https://doi.org/10.1109/MASCOTS.2010.54
15. Larsen, P.G., et al.: Integrated tool chain for model-based design of cyber-physical systems: the INTO-CPS project. In: 2016 2nd International Workshop on Modelling, Analysis, and Control of Complex CPS (CPS Data), pp. 1–6, April 2016. https://doi.org/10.1109/CPSData.2016.7496424
16. Lawrence, D.P.Y., Gomes, C., Denil, J., Vangheluwe, H., Buchs, D.: Coupling Petri nets with deterministic formalisms using co-simulation. In: Proceedings of the Symposium on Theory of Modeling & Simulation, TMS-DEVS 2016, pp. 6:1–6:8. Society for Computer Simulation International, San Diego (2016). https://doi.org/10.23919/TMS.2016.7918812
17. Liu, J., Jiang, K., Wang, X., Cheng, B., Du, D.: Improved co-simulation with event detection for stochastic behaviors of CPSs. In: 2016 IEEE 40th Annual Computer Software and Applications Conference (COMPSAC). vol. 1, pp. 209–214 , June 2016. https://doi.org/10.1109/COMPSAC.2016.133
18. Mancini, T., Mari, F., Massini, A., Melatti, I., Merli, F., Tronci, E.: System level formal verification via model checking driven simulation. In: Sharygina, N., Veith, H. (eds.) CAV 2013. LNCS, vol. 8044, pp. 296–312. Springer, Heidelberg (2013). https://doi.org/10.1007/978-3-642-39799-8_21
19. Nelli, M., Bondavalli, A., Simoncini, L.: Dependability modeling and analysis of complex control systems: An application to railway interlocking. In: Hlawiczka, A., Silva, J.G., Simoncini, L. (eds.) EDCC 1996. LNCS, vol. 1150, pp. 91–110. Springer, Heidelberg (1996). https://doi.org/10.1007/3-540-61772-8_32
20. Oladimeji, P., Masci, P., Curzon, P., Thimbleby, H.: PVSio-web: a tool for rapid prototyping device user interfaces in PVS. In: FMIS2013, 5th International Workshop on Formal Methods for Interactive Systems, London, UK, 24 June 2013 (2013). https://doi.org/10.14279/tuj.eceasst.69.963.944
21. Owre, S., Rajan, S., Rushby, J.M., Shankar, N., Srivas, M.: PVS: Combining specification, proof checking, and model checking. In: Alur, R., Henzinger, T.A. (eds.) CAV 1996. LNCS, vol. 1102. Springer, Berlin (1996). https://doi.org/10.1007/3-540-61474-5_91
22. Palmieri, M., Bernardeschi, C., Masci, P.: Co-simulation of semi-autonomous systems: the line follower robot case study. In: Cerone, A., Roveri, M. (eds.) SEFM 2017. LNCS, vol. 10729, pp. 423–437. Springer, Cham (2018). https://doi.org/10.1007/978-3-319-74781-1_29
23. Payne, R., et al.: Examples Compendium 2. Tech. report D3.5, INTO-CPS Deliverable, December 2008

24. Peccoud, J., Courtney, T., Sanders, W.H.: Möbius: an integrated discrete-event modeling environment. Bioinformatics **23**(24), 3412–3414 (2007). https://doi.org/10.1093/bioinformatics/btm517
25. Sanders, W.H.: Integrated frameworks for multi-level and multi-formalism modeling. In: Proceedings 8th International Workshop on Petri Nets and Performance Models (Cat. No.PR00331), pp. 2–9 (1999). https://doi.org/10.1109/PNPM.1999.796527
26. Sanders, W., Courtney, T., Deavours, D., Daly, D., Derisavi, S., Lam, V.: Multiformalism and multi-solution-method modeling frameworks: The Möbius approach. In: Proceedings of Symposium on Performance Evaluation - Stories and Perspectives, Vienna, Austria, December 2003, pp. 241–256 (2003)
27. Sanders, W.H., Meyer, J.F.: Stochastic activity networks: formal definitions and concepts. In: Brinksma, E., Hermanns, H., Katoen, J.P. (eds.) EEF School 2000. LNCS, vol. 2090. Springer, Berlin (2001). https://doi.org/10.1007/3-540-44667-2_9
28. Srivastava, R., Peterson, M.S., Bentley, W.E.: Stochastic kinetic analysis of the Escherichia coli stress circuit using σ^{32}-targeted antisense. Biotechnol. Bioeng. **75**(1), 120–129 (2001). https://doi.org/10.1002/bit.1171
29. Tsavachidou, D., Liebman, M.N.: Modeling and simulation of pathways in menopause. J. Am. Med. Inform. Assoc. **9**(5), 461–471 (2002). https://doi.org/10.1197/jamia.M1103
30. Vangheluwe, H.: Foundations of modelling and simulation of complex systems. Electronic Communications of the EASST **10** (2008). https://doi.org/10.14279/tuj.eceasst.10.162.148

Demo: Stabilization Technique in INTO-CPS

Cláudio Gomes[2,4]($\boxtimes$), Casper Thule[1], Kenneth Lausdahl[5],
Peter Gorm Larsen[1], and Hans Vangheluwe[2,3,4]

[1] DIGIT, Department of Engineering, Aarhus University, Aarhus, Denmark
{casper.thule,pgl}@eng.au.dk
[2] University of Antwerp, Antwerp, Belgium
{claudio.gomes,hans.vangheluwe}@uantwerp.be
[3] McGill University, Montreal, Canada
[4] Flanders Make, Lommel, Belgium
[5] Mjølner Informatics A/S, Aarhus, Denmark
Kenneth@lausdahl.com

Abstract. Despite the large number of applications and growing interest in the challenges that co-simulation poses, the field is fragmented into multiple application domains, with limited sharing of knowledge.

This demo promotes a deeper understanding of a well known stabilization feature in co-simulation, which is used in the INTO-CPS tool chain.

We develop the techniques that explain the empirical results of instability of the double mass-spring-damper system, and how to the stabilization feature improves the results. Moreover, we show how the restrictions of the Functional Mock-up Interface Standard impacts stability.

Keywords: Stability · Simulation · Co-simulation

1 Introduction

INTO-CPS provides an entire tool chain [8] that enables combining different tools and formalisms using co-simulation [6]. This demo provides the theoretical rationale for the stabilization feature of the Co-simulation Orchestration Engine from INTO-CPS called Maestro [12]. The feature will be illustrated with a small case study that is documented online [10].

This demo assumes that the reader is familiar with the main concepts in co-simulation (see, e.g., [7]).

This work was executed under the framework of the COST Action IC1404 – Multi-Paradigm Modelling for Cyber-Physical Systems (MPM4CPS), and partially supported by: Flanders Make vzw, the strategic research centre for the manufacturing industry; and PhD fellowship grants from the Agency for Innovation by Science and Technology in Flanders (IWT, dossier 151067).

© Springer Nature Switzerland AG 2018
M. Mazzara et al. (Eds.): STAF 2018 Workshops, LNCS 11176, pp. 45–51, 2018.
https://doi.org/10.1007/978-3-030-04771-9_4

In the next section, we describe the principles of stability analysis for linear Ordinary Differential Equations (ODEs), and linear discrete time systems. Then, in Sect. 3, we apply these principles to analyse the numerical stability of the commonly used Jacobi algorithm within the FMI context, and the stabilization method used in INTO-CPS. While the master algorithms are applicable outside the Functional Mockup Interface (FMI) context, the FMI version 2.0 has constraints that makes the stability analysis not applicable to other contexts.

2   Stability of Linear Systems

This section is based on [7].

Notation. We denote vectors with bold face, and we use capital letters for matrices and vector valued functions. Given a vector x, we denote its transpose as x^T. Furthermore, we denote the i-th element of vector x by x_i, so that $x = \begin{bmatrix} x_1\ x_2 \cdots x_n \end{bmatrix}^T$. Similarly, $F_i(x)$ denotes the i-th element of the vector returned by $F(x)$.

A linear ODE has the following form:

$$\dot{x} = Ax, \tag{1}$$

where $x(t)$ is a vector function, and A is a constant matrix. When an initial condition in the form $x(0) = x_0$ is specified, we denote Eq. (1) as an Initial Value Problem (IVP).

Example 1. The mass-spring-damper system, illustrated in Fig. 1a, is modelled by the following second order ordinary differential equation:

$$\ddot{x} = \frac{1}{m}(-cx - d\dot{x} + f_e(t)),$$

where x denotes the position of the mass, $c > 0$ is the stiffness coefficient of the spring, $d > 0$ is the damping constant of the damper, t is time, and $f_e(t)$ denotes an external force exerted on the mass.

The above equation can be put into the form of Eq. (1) by introducing a new variable for velocity, $v = \dot{x}$, and letting the vector $x = \begin{bmatrix} x\ v \end{bmatrix}^T$. Given an initial position x_0 and velocity v_0, we obtain the following:

$$\dot{x} = \begin{bmatrix} \dot{x} \\ \dot{v} \end{bmatrix} = F(\begin{bmatrix} x \\ v \end{bmatrix}, f_e(t)) = \begin{bmatrix} v \\ (1/m)(-cx - dv + f_e(t)) \end{bmatrix}, \text{ with } x(0) = \begin{bmatrix} x_0 \\ v_0 \end{bmatrix}.$$

Figure 1b shows the solution of the position component of the mass-spring-damper IVP, introduced in Example 1, and will be explained below. The solution to the velocity component is omitted.

We say that the system in Eq. (1) is *asymptotically stable* when all its solutions tend to zero as time passes, regardless of the initial value specified. Formally,

$$\lim_{t \to \infty} \|x(t)\| = 0, \text{ for all } x(t) \text{ satisfying Eq. (1).} \tag{2}$$

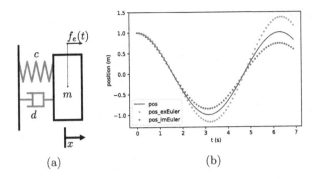

(a)   (b)

Fig. 1. Position (and its approximations) over time of the mass-spring-damper system. Parameters are: $h = 0.1, m = c = 1, d = 10^{-4}, f_e(t) = 0, x_0 = \begin{bmatrix} 1 & 0 \end{bmatrix}^T$.

An ODE in the form of Eq. (1) is asymptotically stable, i.e. it satisfies Eq. (2), if the real part of all eigenvalues of A is strictly negative. Formally,

$$\forall \lambda \in \text{Eig}(A),\ \text{Re}\{\lambda\} < 0. \tag{3}$$

This condition can be computed easily in most programming languages.

To approximate the solution to the IVP in Example 1, one can use the forward Euler method:

$$x(t + h) \approx x(t) + Ax(t)h = (I + Ah)x(t), \text{ with } x(0) = x_0, \tag{4}$$

where I is the identify matrix with the appropriate dimensions, and $h > 0$ is the given simulation step size.

In general, for a given matrix $\tilde{A}$, a system on the form

$$x(t + h) = \tilde{A}x(t), \tag{5}$$

is stable if $\rho(\tilde{A}) < 1$, where $\rho(\tilde{A})$ is the spectral radius [9] of $\tilde{A}$.

3   Stability Analysis of FMI Orchestration Algorithms

Our aim is to encode the co-simulation as a system in the form of Eq. (5). We perform this for a two-simulator system using two orchestration algorithms: the traditional Jacobi method, and the stabilization method used by INTO-CPS. A two simulator system introduced in [10] is illustrated in Fig. 2. More details about this example are given in [6, Sect. 4]. For more examples of stability analysis in co-simulation, refer to [2–5].

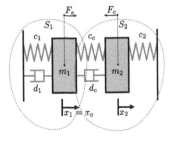

Fig. 2. Double mass-spring-damper with two subsystems: S_1 and S_2.

3.1   Co-simulation Unit Modelling

In the context of co-simulation, time is discretized into a countable set $T = \{t_0, t_1, t_2, \ldots\} \subset \mathbb{R}$, where $t_{i+1} = t_i + H_i$ is the time at step i and H_i is the communication step size at step i, with $i = 0, 1, \ldots$

Simulators exchange outputs only at times $t \in T$.

In the interval $t \in [t_i, t_{i+1}]$, each simulator S_j approximates the solution to a linear ODE,

$$\begin{aligned}
\dot{\boldsymbol{x}}_j &= A_j \boldsymbol{x}_j + B_j \boldsymbol{u}_j \\
\boldsymbol{y}_j &= C_j \boldsymbol{x}_j + D_j \boldsymbol{u}_j
\end{aligned} \tag{6}$$

where $\boldsymbol{x}_j$ is the state vector, $\boldsymbol{y}_j$ is the output vector, A_j, B_j, C_j, D_j are matrices, the initial state $\boldsymbol{x}_j(t_i)$ is computed in the most recent co-simulation step, and $j = 1, 2$.

Since the simulators only exchange outputs at times $t_i, t_{i+1} \in T$, the input $\boldsymbol{u}_j$ has to be extrapolated in the interval $[t_i, t_{i+1})$. In the simplest co-simulation strategy[1], this extrapolation is often implemented as a zero-order hold: $\tilde{\boldsymbol{u}}_j(t) = \boldsymbol{u}_j(t_i)$, for $t \in [t_i, t_{i+1})$. Then, Eq. (6) can be re-written to represent the unforced system being integrated by each simulator:

$$\begin{bmatrix} \dot{\boldsymbol{x}}_j \\ \dot{\tilde{\boldsymbol{u}}}_j \end{bmatrix} = \begin{bmatrix} A_j & B_j \\ \mathbf{0} & \mathbf{0} \end{bmatrix} \begin{bmatrix} \boldsymbol{x}_j \\ \tilde{\boldsymbol{u}}_j \end{bmatrix} \tag{7}$$

We can represent the multiple internal integration steps of Eq. (7), performed by the simulator S_j in the interval $t \in [t_i, t_{i+1}]$, as

$$\begin{bmatrix} \tilde{\boldsymbol{x}}_j(t_{i+1}) \\ \tilde{\boldsymbol{u}}_j(t_{i+1}) \end{bmatrix} = \tilde{A}_j^{k_j} \begin{bmatrix} \tilde{\boldsymbol{x}}_j(t_i) \\ \tilde{\boldsymbol{u}}_j \end{bmatrix} \tag{8}$$

where, e.g., $\tilde{A}_j = \mathbf{I} + h_j \begin{bmatrix} A_j & B_j \\ \mathbf{0} & \mathbf{0} \end{bmatrix}$ for the Forward Euler method, $k_j = (t_{i+1} - t_i)/h_j$ is the number of internal steps, and $0 < h_j \leq H_i$ is the internal fixed step size that divides H_i.

Therefore, each co-simulation unit can be modelled as a discrete time system:

$$\begin{bmatrix} \tilde{\boldsymbol{x}}_j(t_i + H) \\ \tilde{\boldsymbol{u}}_j(t_i + H) \end{bmatrix} = \begin{bmatrix} M_{1,x_j} & M_{1,u_j} \\ M_{2,x_j} & M_{2,u_j} \end{bmatrix} \begin{bmatrix} \tilde{\boldsymbol{x}}_j(t_i) \\ \boldsymbol{u}_j(t_i) \end{bmatrix} \tag{9}$$

with

$$\tilde{A}_j^{k_j} = \begin{bmatrix} M_{1,x_j} & M_{1,u_j} \\ M_{2,x_j} & M_{2,u_j} \end{bmatrix}.$$

---

[1] The derivation presented can be applied to more sophisticated input extrapolation techniques, see [1, Eq. (9)].

3.2 FMI Jacobi Algorithm

We assume without loss of generality that the two simulators are coupled in a feedback loop, that is,

$$u_1 = y_2 \text{ and } u_2 = y_1. \tag{10}$$

And, to avoid algebraic loops and keep the exposition short, we assume that either D_1 or D_2 (recall Eq. (6)) is the zero matrix. Let $D_2 = \mathbf{0}$.

The ideal Jacobi coupling would be described by:

$$\begin{aligned}
u_1(t) &= y_2(t) = C_2\tilde{x}_2(t) \\
u_2(t) &= y_1(t) = C_1\tilde{x}_1(t) + D_1u_1(t)
\end{aligned} \tag{11}$$

However, due the FMI restrictions [11, Restriction 1], the actual coupling is:

$$\begin{aligned}
u_1(t_i) &= C_2\tilde{x}_2(t_i) \\
u_2(t_i) &= C_1\tilde{x}_1(t_i) + D_1\tilde{u}_1(t_i).
\end{aligned} \tag{12}$$

Applying Eq. (12) to t_{i+1} and using Eq. (9), yields:

$$\begin{aligned}
\tilde{x}_1(t_{i+1}) &= M_{1,x_1}\tilde{x}_1(t_i) + M_{1,u_1}C_2\tilde{x}_2(t_i) \\
\tilde{u}_1(t_{i+1}) &= M_{2,x_1}\tilde{x}_1(t_i) + M_{2,u_1}C_2\tilde{x}_2(t_i) \\
\tilde{x}_2(t_{i+1}) &= M_{1,u_2}C_1\tilde{x}_1(t_i) + M_{1,u_2}D_1\tilde{u}_1(t) + M_{1,x_2}\tilde{x}_2(t_i) \\
\tilde{u}_2(t_{i+1}) &= M_{2,u_2}C_1\tilde{x}_1(t_i) + M_{2,u_2}D_1\tilde{u}_1(t) + M_{2,x_2}\tilde{x}_2(t_i)
\end{aligned} \tag{13}$$

which can be arranged to the form of Eq. (5):

$$\begin{bmatrix} \tilde{x}_1(t_{i+1}) \\ \tilde{u}_1(t_{i+1}) \\ \tilde{x}_2(t_{i+1}) \\ \tilde{u}_2(t_{i+1}) \end{bmatrix} = \begin{bmatrix} M_{1,x_1} & 0 & M_{1,u_1}C_2 & 0 \\ M_{2,x_1} & 0 & M_{2,u_1}C_2 & 0 \\ M_{1,u_2}C_1 & M_{1,u_2}D_1 & M_{1,x_2} & 0 \\ M_{2,u_2}C_1 & M_{2,u_2}D_1 & M_{2,x_2} & 0 \end{bmatrix} \begin{bmatrix} \tilde{x}_1(t_i) \\ \tilde{u}_1(t_i) \\ \tilde{x}_2(t_i) \\ \tilde{u}_2(t_i) \end{bmatrix} \tag{14}$$

3.3 INTO-CPS Method

The method used in INTO-CPS is a sucessive substitution fixed point iteration, described by:

$$\begin{aligned}
u_1(t_{i+1}) &= C_2\tilde{x}_2(t_{i+1}) \\
u_2(t_{i+1}) &= C_1\tilde{x}_1(t_{i+1}) + D_1u_1(t_{i+1})
\end{aligned} \tag{15}$$

The above equation can be expanded and simplified to:

$$\begin{aligned}
\tilde{x}_1(t_{i+1}) &= M_{1,x_1}\tilde{x}_1(t_i) + M_{1,u_1}C_2\tilde{x}_2(t_{i+1}) \\
u_1(t_{i+1}) &= M_{2,x_1}\tilde{x}_1(t_i) + M_{2,u_1}C_2\tilde{x}_2(t_{i+1}) \\
\tilde{x}_2(t_{i+1}) &= M_{1,x_2}\tilde{x}_2(t_i) + M_{1,u_2}C_1\tilde{x}_1(t_{i+1}) + M_{1,u_2}D_1u_1(t_{i+1}) \\
u_2(t_{i+1}) &= M_{2,x_2}\tilde{x}_2(t_i) + M_{2,u_2}C_1\tilde{x}_1(t_{i+1}) + M_{2,u_2}D_1u_1(t_{i+1})
\end{aligned} \tag{16}$$

which can be put in matrix form:

$$
\begin{bmatrix} \tilde{\boldsymbol{x}}_1(t_{i+1}) \\ \boldsymbol{u}_1(t_{i+1}) \\ \tilde{\boldsymbol{x}}_2(t_{i+1}) \\ \boldsymbol{u}_2(t_{i+1}) \end{bmatrix} = \begin{bmatrix} M_{1,x_1} & 0 & 0 & 0 \\ M_{2,x_1} & 0 & 0 & 0 \\ 0 & 0 & M_{1,x_2} & 0 \\ 0 & 0 & M_{2,x_2} & 0 \end{bmatrix} \begin{bmatrix} \tilde{\boldsymbol{x}}_1(t_i) \\ \boldsymbol{u}_1(t_i) \\ \tilde{\boldsymbol{x}}_2(t_i) \\ \boldsymbol{u}_2(t_i) \end{bmatrix} +
$$
$$
\begin{bmatrix} 0 & 0 & M_{1,u_1}C_2 & 0 \\ 0 & 0 & M_{2,u_1}C_2 & 0 \\ M_{1,u_2}C_1 & M_{1,u_2}D_1 & 0 & 0 \\ M_{2,u_2}C_1 & M_{2,u_2}D_1 & 0 & 0 \end{bmatrix} \begin{bmatrix} \tilde{\boldsymbol{x}}_1(t_{i+1}) \\ \boldsymbol{u}_1(t_{i+1}) \\ \tilde{\boldsymbol{x}}_2(t_{i+1}) \\ \boldsymbol{u}_2(t_{i+1}) \end{bmatrix} \tag{17}
$$

Renaming the above equation to $\bar{\boldsymbol{x}}_{i+1} = \bar{M}_i \bar{\boldsymbol{x}}_i + \bar{M}_{i+1}\bar{\boldsymbol{x}}_{i+1}$, we get an equation in the form of Eq. (5):

$$
\bar{\boldsymbol{x}}_{i+1} = (I - \bar{M}_{i+1})^{-1}\bar{M}_i\bar{\boldsymbol{x}}_i \tag{18}
$$

In most cases in practice, $\rho((I - \bar{M}_{i+1})^{-1}\bar{M}_i)$ is smaller than the spectral radius of the matrix in Eq. (14). The practical results of this analysis are shown in the case study described in [10].

This can be generalized. However, in practice, one must be aware of the internal details of each co-simulation unit, which is usually difficult. As such, this analysis can be used to determine the best orchestration algorithm, without providing guarantees.

References

1. Busch, M.: Continuous approximation techniques for co-simulation methods: analysis of numerical stability and local error. J. Appl. Math. Mech. **96**(9), 1061–1081 (2016)
2. Gomes, C., Jungers, R., Legat, B., Vangheluwe, H.: Minimally constrained stable switched systems and application to co-simulation. Technical report. arXiv:1809.02648 (2018), http://arxiv.org/abs/1809.02648
3. Gomes, C., Legat, B., Jungers, R., Vangheluwe, H.: Minimally constrained stable switched systems and application to co-simulation. In: IEEE Conference on Decision and Control, Miami Beach, FL, USA (2018). To be published
4. Gomes, C., Legat, B., Jungers, R.M., Vangheluwe, H.: Stable adaptive co-simulation: a switched systems approach. In: IUTAM Symposium on Co-Simulation and Solver Coupling, Darmstadt, Germany (2017). To appear
5. Gomes, C., Thule, C., Broman, D., Larsen, P.G., Vangheluwe, H.: Co-simulation: state of the art. Technical report, February 2017. http://arxiv.org/abs/1702.00686
6. Gomes, C., Thule, C., Broman, D., Larsen, P.G., Vangheluwe, H.: Co-simulation: a survey. ACM Comput. Surv. **51**(3) (2018). Article 49
7. Gomes, C., Thule, C., Larsen, P.G., Denil, J., Vangheluwe, H.: Co-simulation of continuous systems: a tutorial. arXiv:1809.08463 [cs, math], September 2018. http://arxiv.org/abs/1809.08463
8. Larsen, P.G., Fitzgerald, J., Woodcock, J., Gamble, C., Payne, R., Pierce, K.: Features of integrated model-based co-modelling and co-simulation technology. In: Cerone, A., Roveri, M. (eds.) SEFM 2017. LNCS, vol. 10729, pp. 377–390. Springer, Cham (2018). https://doi.org/10.1007/978-3-319-74781-1_26

9. Strang, G.: Introduction to Linear Algebra, vol. vol, p. 3. Wellesley-Cambridge Press, Wellesley (1993)
10. Thule, C.: Mass-spring-damper Case Study (2018). https://github.com/INTO-CPS-Association/example-mass_spring_damper
11. Thule, C., Gomes, C., Deantoni, J., Larsen, P.G., Brauer, J., Vangheluwe, H.: Towards verification of hybrid co-simulation algorithms. In: 2nd Workshop on Formal Co-Simulation of Cyber-Physical Systems, Toulouse, France. Springer, Cham (2018). To be published
12. Thule, C., Lausdahl, K., Larsen, P.G., Meisl, G.: Maestro: The INTO-CPSCo-simulation orchestration engine (2018). Submitted to Simulation Modelling Practice and Theory

Demo: Co-simulation of UAVs with INTO-CPS and PVSio-web

Maurizio Palmieri[1,2]([✉]), Cinzia Bernardeschi[2], Andrea Domenici[2], and Adriano Fagiolini[3]

[1] Dipartimento di Ingegneria dell'Informazione,
University of Florence, Florence, Italy
[2] Dipartimento di Ingegneria dell'Informazione, University of Pisa, Pisa, Italy
maurizio.palmieri@ing.unipi.it
[3] Dipartimento di Energia, Ingegneria dell'Informazione e Modelli Matematici
(DEIM), University of Palermo, Palermo, Italy

Abstract. This demo shows our ongoing work on the co-simulation of co-operative Unmanned Aerial Vehicles (UAVs). The work is based on the INTO-CPS co-simulation engine, which adopts the widely accepted Functional Mockup Interface (FMI) standard for co-simulation, and the PVSioweb prototyping tool, that extends a system simulator based on the PVS logic language with a web-based graphical interface. Simple scenarios of Quadcopters with assigned different tasks, such as rendez-vous and space coverage, are shown. We assumed a linearized dynamic model for Quadcopters formalized in OpenModelica, and a linearized set of equations for the flight control module written in C language. The co-ordination algorithm is modeled in PVS, while PVSio-web is used for graphical rendering of the co-simulation.

1 Introduction

Nowadays, the deployment of multi-UAVs systems is rapidly increasing in many different applications, ranging from precision farming to surveillance, search and rescue, etc. (e.g. [1,4]). Given the recent introduction of a new co-simulation standard, the Functional Mock-up Interface [2], and tool-kits to exploit such a standard, such as INTO-CPS [5], we combined these technologies with tools for formal modeling, such as PVS [8]. The result is a modular and flexible framework that can be used to co-simulate UAV coordination algorithms dealing with the heterogeneous nature of different UAV models. In this work, we will show an example where the base elements of the FMI co-simulation, the FMUs (Functional Mock-up Unit), are built using different tools (OpenModelica [3], PVSioweb [6], and C code).

In the rest of this section, we provide basic background knowledge of quadcopter representation and consensus algorithm used in the subsequent sections.

© Springer Nature Switzerland AG 2018
M. Mazzara et al. (Eds.): STAF 2018 Workshops, LNCS 11176, pp. 52–57, 2018.
https://doi.org/10.1007/978-3-030-04771-9_5

1.1 Background on Quadcopters

A quadrotor aircraft, or quadcopter, schematically consists in a cross-shaped chassis supporting one rotor at the end of each arm. The quadcopter's movements are determined by the resultant thrusts and torques of the rotors, which in turn depend on their angular speeds $\omega_1, \omega_2, \omega_3, \omega_4$. The state of the quadcopter is composed of 12 variables: (i) actual position (x, y, z); (ii) linear speeds $(\dot{x}, \dot{y}, \dot{z})$; (iii) attitude, given by the 3 angles pitch, roll, and yaw (ϕ, θ, ψ respectively); (iv) attitude angular speeds $(\dot{\phi}, \dot{\theta}, \dot{\psi})$. The values of $\omega_1, \omega_2, \omega_3, \omega_4$ are computed by the flight control module, which takes as input the desired target (x_d, y_d, z_d) and the actual state of the drone (actual position, linear speeds, attitude and attitude angular speeds) and produces the angular speeds of the four rotors required to reach the target. A simple black box schema of a quadcopter is shown in Fig. 1.

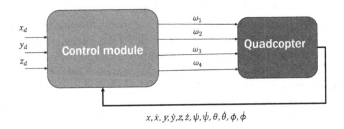

Fig. 1. Black box schema of a quadcopter

1.2 Background on the Consensus Algorithm

We have studied a well-known algorithm proposed in [7] for accomplishing the task of rendez-vous, gathering the drones in a position given by the average of their initial ones. The consensus algorithm can be expressed with the following equation:

$$x_d^{k+1}(i) = x_d^k(i) + \epsilon \sum_{j \in N_i} (x_d^k(j) - x_d^k(i)) \tag{1}$$

where $x_d^k(i)$ is the target position of the drone i at step k, $\epsilon \in (0,1)$ is a parameter of the algorithm, and N_i is the set of neighbors of drone i.

We will consider the case in which N_i is only composed of the preceding and following drones, reducing (1) to

$$x_d^{k+1}(i) = x_d^k(i) + \epsilon(x_d^k(i-1) - x_d^k(i)) + \epsilon(x_d^k(i+1) - x_d^k(i)). \tag{2}$$

2 Co-simulation Environment

In this section, we will provide details on the implementation of the FMI co-simulation used to validate the co-ordination algorithm. We have modeled a system composed of many quadcopters, each represented by 3 different sub-systems: (i) the physical part of the quadcopter; (ii) the flight control module; (iii) the coordination algorithm.

The physical part of the quadcopter has been represented with a system of linear differential equations for computing the acceleration, the speed, the position and the attitude of the quadcopter based on the angular speed of the four rotors. The system of equations has been written with OpenModelica, which allows us the automatic generation of the FMU.

The flight control module implements a system of linear equations that compute the angular speed of the rotors needed to move the quadcopter toward a target point. The system of equations has been written in C language and embedded in an FMU.

The coordination algorithm has been modeled in the PVS formal language. The PVSio-web toolkit provides the simulation environment for the coordination algorithm and the graphical animation of the interface. The PVS model, along with the whole PVS package has been automatically embedded in an FMU using the approach proposed in [9]. The communications between quadcopters are completely abstracted by connecting the output of the coordination algorithm FMU not only with the flight control FMU of the same drone but also with the coordination algorithm FMU of the other drones.

We have created a scenario to test our system with 5 drones and a fixed co-simulation step-size of 0.05 s. The parameters of the scenario are shown in Table 1 (Rendez-vous). More precisely, Fig. 2a and b, show the beginning and the end of the simulation where the drones start from different locations and converge to the same x-coordinate, reaching a vertical arrangement over the final target position on the ground. We may note that the consensus algorithm only controls the movement on the horizontal plane, independently of movements in the vertical directions.

Table 1. Parameters of the scenarios

Scenario	Parameters	Values
Rendez-vous	Duration	40 s
	ϵ	$\frac{1}{4}$
	Initial position	$\{0,1,2,5,10\}$
Space coverage 1	Duration	20 s
	ϵ	$\frac{1}{4}$
	Initial position	$\{0,1,2,3,10\}$
Space coverage 2	Duration	20 s
	ϵ	$\frac{3}{4}$
	Initial position	$\{0,1,2,3,10\}$

(a) Initial position of drones

(b) Final position of drones

Fig. 2. Rendez-vous

The co-simulation environment is flexible and other co-ordination protocols can be easily analyzed. As an example we have applied the framework to a slight variant of the consensus algorithm above, obtaining an algorithm that performs the task of space coverage along a line segment. We introduced the assumption that the leftmost drone and the rightmost drone do not change their position and they are placed at the endpoints of the line segment. In the following formula, N is the number of drones, min and max are the endpoints of the line segment, $x_d^k(i)$ is the desired position of drone i at step k, and $\epsilon > 0$ is the same parameter of the original algorithm:

$$\begin{cases} x_d^k(1) &= \min, \forall\, k \\ x_d^k(N) &= \max, \forall\, k \\ x_d^{k+1}(i) &= x_d^k(i) + \epsilon(x_d^k(i-1) - x_d^k(i)) + \epsilon(x_d^k(i+1) - x_d^k(i)), \quad i \in [2, N-1] \end{cases}$$

In the following, we show the results of the co-simulation in two scenarios whose parameters are shown in Table 1 (Space coverage). Figure 3a and b show the beginning and termination of the co-simulation for the first scenario where the three middle drones started close to each other and end up equally spaced on the x-axis.

(a) Initial position of drones.

(b) Final position of drones.

Fig. 3. Space coverage 1

Fig. 4. Space coverage 2: final position of drones

Figure 4 show the termination of the co-simulation for the second scenario where two drones collided and fell to the ground.

The two scenarios show how the value of the parameter ϵ affects the behavior of the drones, which otherwise have the same initial position and are controlled by the same algorithm in the two scenarios. From the simulation, we can see that a large value of ϵ causes the drone coordination to fail. Conditions on the admissible values of ϵ can be determined with the PVS theorem prover, which is the object of further work.

Acknowledgments. The authors would like to thank Paolo Masci for the stimulating discussion on visual interfacing for co-simulation.

References

1. Acevedo, J.J., Arrue, B.C., Maza, I., Ollero, A.: Distributed approach for coverage and patrolling missions with a team of heterogeneous aerial robots under communication constraints. Int. J. Adv. Robot. Syst. **10**(1), 28 (2013)
2. Blochwitz, T., et al.: Functional mockup interface 2.0: the standard for tool independent exchange of simulation models. In: Proceedings of the 9th International MODELICA Conference, 3–5 September 2012, Munich, Germany, no. 076, pp. 173–184. Linköping University Electronic Press (2012)
3. Fritzson, P.: Modelica - a cyber-physical modeling language and the OpenModelica environment, pp. 1648–1653. IEEE (2011)
4. Kuriki, Y., Namerikawa, T.: Consensus-based cooperative formation control with collision avoidance for a multi-UAV system. In: 2014 American Control Conference, pp. 2077–2082, June 2014
5. Larsen, P.G., et al.: Integrated tool chain for model-based design of cyber-physical systems: the INTO-CPS project. In: 2016 2nd International Workshop on Modelling, Analysis, and Control of Complex CPS (CPS Data), pp. 1–6. IEEE (2016)
6. Oladimeji, P., Masci, P., Curzon, P., Thimbleby, H.: PVSio-web: a tool for rapid prototyping device user interfaces in PVS. In: FMIS 2013 5th International Workshop on Formal Methods for Interactive Systems, London, UK, 24 June 2013
7. Olfati-Saber, R., Fax, J.A., Murray, R.M.: Consensus and cooperation in networked multi-agent systems. Proc. IEEE **95**(1), 215–233 (2007)
8. Owre, S., Shankar, N., Rushby, J.M., Stringer-Calvert, D.W.J.: PVS language reference, version 2.4. Technical report, SRI International Computer Science Laboratory, 333 Ravenswood Avenue, Menlo Park CA 94025, USA (2001)
9. Palmieri, M., Bernardeschi, C., Masci, P.: Co-simulation of semi-autonomous systems: the line follower robot case study. In: Cerone, A., Roveri, M. (eds.) SEFM 2017. LNCS, vol. 10729, pp. 423–437. Springer, Cham (2018). https://doi.org/10.1007/978-3-319-74781-1_29

Towards a Co-simulation Based Model Assessment Process for System Architecture

Benjamin Bossa[1,5], Benjamin Boulbene[1,3], Sébastien Dubé[1,4],
and Marc Pantel[1,2(✉)]

[1] Institute of Research and Technology (IRT) Saint-Exupéry, Toulouse, France
[2] University of Toulouse, INPT-ENSEEIHT/IRIT, Toulouse, France
Marc.Pantel@enseeiht.fr
[3] Chiastek, Toulouse, France
Benjamin.Boulbene@chiastek.com
[4] ESI Group, Toulouse, France
Sebastien.Dube@esi-group.com
[5] Sogeti High Tech, Toulouse, France
Benjamin.Bossa@sogeti.com

Abstract. Model Based System Engineering and early Validation &
Verification are now key enablers for the development of complex systems. However, the current state of the art is not sufficient to achieve a
seamless use in an Extended Enterprise (EE) context. Indeed, the various
stakeholders must protect their Intellectual Property (IP) while conduct-
ing system wide design exploration that relies on each part of the system.
Co-simulation standards such as Functional Mock-up Interface provide
technological assets to deal with IP management issues for an EE organization. However, this standard is not meant to provide reference processes to support such organizations. We target the development of such
a common process based on both the system of interest design models
and the EE architecture. The purpose is to build a Simulation Reference
Model as a requirement model for the whole co-simulation, the derived
IP-protected co-simulation components and the co-simulation platform
architecture as well as the method for the validation of system models. We propose to extend the work done for the Model Identity Card
and rely on detailed domain specific engineering ontologies and quantitative quality properties for models to express the requirements for
the co-simulation components and to reduce the simulation quality loss
induced by the co-simulation technologies.

Keywords: MBSE · Extended Enterprise · (co-)simulation · Quality

1 Introduction

The increasing complexity of current products and their development in
Extended Enterprise (EE) requires advanced and efficient Systems Engineering

M. Mazzara et al. (Eds.): STAF 2018 Workshops, LNCS 11176, pp. 58–68, 2018.
https://doi.org/10.1007/978-3-030-04771-9_6

(SE) activities to satisfy time to market and cost reduction constraints. Models (Model-Based Systems Engineering (MBSE)) and early Validation & Verification (V&V) activities relying on simulation were shown to be key enablers in such processes as they provide quick feedback loops to system architects using simulations of the global system. Such global simulations are built using simulation components provided by the various product stakeholders from the EE. Many constraints must be managed such as the protection of each stakeholder Intellectual Property (IP), the distribution of simulation components and computational resources among stakeholders, the heterogeneity of models and a potentially large amount of simulation components. As defined in [6], co-simulation techniques allow to mitigate such constraints where simulation platforms have to deal with EE constraints meaning distributed over companies and networks.

The Functional Mock-up Interface (FMI) Standard [2] for co-simulation offers such capabilities and can connect heterogeneous models as black boxes to prevent IP diffusion as illustrated in [4]. However, building an efficient co-simulation platform with appropriate simulation components and architecture is currently a difficult task as processes and methods are lacking to guide the involved stakeholders on the use of the existing standards and tools. This contribution does not target new tools for the co-simulation, but intends to fill the gap between SE languages and tools and co-simulation frameworks to enable a seamless transition. Moreover, we intend to provide appropriate concepts to assess the compliance of the co-simulation results (considering the potential simulation quality alteration by the introduction of co-simulation time steps between Functional Mock-up Units (FMUs)) with respect to system architecture requirements.

Our proposal is currently being defined for the validation phase of a System Architecture modelled with the Capella [10] language using the Arcadia method [16] with our proposed extensions (with simulation quality elements) thanks to co-simulation techniques. In fact, the Arcadia methodology focuses on the identification of system architecture elements (system functions, system modes & states, operational scenarios, ...). Our proposal develops additional concepts for simulation architecture and simulation components quality requirements to ensure consistency of simulation according to system expectations. In that purpose, it first integrates existing concepts from the following literature.

Sargent presents in [14] the modelling process starting from a *Problem Entity* (Real System) analysis, followed by a *Conceptual Model* design and a *Computerized Model* implementation. In Sargent's paper, the author introduces validation needs and techniques which can be used to perform model V&V. Sirin *et al.* [15] have developed the Model Identity Card (MIC) ontology to make explicit most of the available data regarding a given model. MIC is filled by all involved model stakeholders to document important characteristics and properties of the model including interface and general intentional properties (physical phenomena, maturity, etc). However, to our knowledge and understanding, first MIC proposed ontologies are very coarse and do not allow to provide precise elements about the expected models of the physical phenomena; and second MIC currently only targets relative qualitative requirements (e.g. model quality is stated to be very low, low, medium, high or very high). These kind of requirements are very difficult both to select and assess. We intend to extend MIC on these two identified weaknesses relying on existing work like Sachidananda *et al.* [13] that considers quality of simulation in order to understand the nature of the gap between real world experiments and simulations.

We will give an overview of the proposed methodology with some key definitions and then conclude with perspectives for our work.

2   Methodology Overview

Within a MBSE approach, models are exchanged between actors during the whole life-cycle of a system. Here is proposed a basic scenario with three key actors working in an EE context. In the following, the term *actor* refers to a person who has an active role with the definition or with the V&V of a system. We define three main actors:

- The System Architect (SyA) is in charge of defining, designing and providing an architecture of a system of interest. The SyA designs a system as a model in a MBSE tool such as Capella, where different views of a common model are used to describe the system in terms of functional architecture, temporal behavior, modes and physical elements (such as helixes, motors, rigid body, electronic unit, ... for a drone physical system) making explicit its interface with its operational environment. They also express V&V objectives to the Simulation Architect (SiA).
- The SiA is in charge of building a co-simulation platform for the system design provided by the SyA. He designs a co-simulation application with a Simulation Reference Model (SRM) within a MBSE tool.
- The Simulation Model Developer (SMD) is in charge of developing executable models also called Simulation Components (SCs) in this contribution.

EE means here a set of companies and individuals associated for the implementation of one or several common projects.

A Reference Model (RM) represents an executable model defined without a pragmatism [5], *i.e.* a model expressed without a tool and a methodology. In our case, a SRM is a model of an idealized system simulation with decomposition of a functional system into simulation components with abstraction of software and hardware constraints. Functional exchanges are specified as simulation data exchanges and simulation artifacts are added (such as logging mechanism, filesystem ...). The SiA defines also how system functions are allocated to simulation models and how they are grouped into different SC units (ex: FMU). Several options are available:

- All functions are included into one SC.
- Each system function has its own associated SC.
- Each macro function is represented by a SC.
- System elements are regrouped into a SC with respect to their future physical allocation (assuming the physical architecture is already known).

- Some of the system blocks are already implemented in a SC (ex: FMU) and can be re-used. This model can be an internal reuse from a previous design, a Components Off The Shelf (COTS) model or provided by a supplier.
- SC can also regroup functions by physical phenomena (all electrical functions, mechanical functions, etc) or by simulation technology or tool.

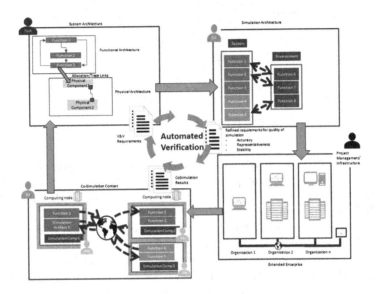

Fig. 1. Methodology overview

The roles of SiA and SyA in the methodology are illustrated in Fig. 1 making explicit the added value of the SiA in this process and the role of potential tools to support automated evaluation of architecture. The SyA designs the system as a Capella-like model containing different viewpoints. This model becomes the entry point for the SiA to create and manage the co-simulation platform. In this process, the SiA has a key role to derive from the System Architecture Requirements (SARs) the expected Architecture Requirements (SARs) the expected for the overall simulation and each individual SCs.

In order to validate some architectural choice, the SyA will provide quality requirements to a proper specification of SC. These requirements are defined by the SyA according to simulation goals and system definition maturity (Fig. 2).

Model Quality Requirements represent a qualification of SC which characterize an aspect of the model. This contribution provides three first qualifications:

- *Accuracy* that represents, in experimental sciences, the closeness of a measurement to the real value. In our case, it expresses the closeness of simulation results to the model theoretical value. Errors are usually introduced by the

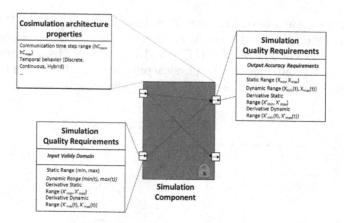

Fig. 2. SC quality requirements example

discretization of continuous behavior, the approximate solving of differential equations, the use of floating point computations, timing discrepancies due to co-simulation time-step, etc. Our work currently relies on classical accuracy models from experimental sciences.

– *Representativeness* express the gap between the real system and the mathematical models of the involved physical phenomena. It defines the degree of simplification (or abstraction) introduced by the model. As initially proposed by the MIC, we rely on ontologies for the various physical domain involved in the system to express the kind of behavior that should be modeled. These ontologies should describe precisely the various physical phenomena that should be considered, the various mathematical models that exists for these phenomena and their respective representativeness. The expected representativeness for each model is a requirements for the SC.
– *Stability* represents the ability for a model to give nearby precise solutions when inputs have a small perturbation. It is usually modeled in the frequency domain but we prefer to rely on the state based Lyapunov theory [8].

The SiA creates a model of the co-simulation platform where functional components are indicated but also how they are distributed into different clusters or FMU. This model contains specific non-existing elements used only in the context of a simulation (e.g. read/write from the file system, failures injection ...).

Other constraints are specific to the co-simulation domain: such as dependency graph related delays, numerical artifacts propagation and amplification, or strong coupling boundaries. These elements must be anticipated and monitored throughout the process. For this purpose, the methodology contains a specific simulation model to co-simulation model transition.

Then, this model can be used to generate configuration files used by a simulation engine such as simulation model library distribution or co-simulation master to prepare the simulation platform.

Once quality criteria and the co-simulation platform definition are provided, the Simulation Architect can express requirements for a simulation component development or choose a COTS component or a supplier component.

3   Use Case

3.1   Context

The V&V of a system using a co-simulation platform model prerequisites have been experimented via the IRT Saint Exupéry's case study: Aircraft Inspection by Drone Assistant (AIDA, [11]). Before take off, an operator conducts a visual pre-flight inspection to detect potential external anomalies. AIDA relies on a drone both to have a better view on the upper parts of the aircraft and to conduct a faster inspection.

As a Remotely Piloted Aircraft System (RPAS), the quadcopter drone can be piloted in automated or manual mode. In the manual mode, the pilot guides the inspection of the aircraft by the drone. In the automated mode, the drone follows a flight plan and records the video of the inspected zone. The scope of this example will be limited to the automated flight case. This RPAS shows its relevancy for such a study because enabling a division of numerous functions involving different physics with a limited impact on the physical conservation laws, making it relevant to use a loosely coupled scheme over a co-simulation bus.

A system model of the drone has already been designed in Capella. This model is the starting point for the definition of a co-simulation platform model. Model quality will also be explored in order to create a co-simulation meta-model with a definition of quality requirements. For this experiment, we intend to develop heterogeneous simulation components from drone system functions based on the Modelica language [1] to generate FMUs. The CosiMate middleware will be used as distributed co-simulation infrastructure [9] to execute distributed simulation components.

In this part will be demonstrated the key steps for the proposed methodology before setting up the whole automated toolchain:

- Definition of the drone architecture from a Systems Architecture perspective
- Definition of a Simulation Architecture perspective
- Generation of the required files for a co-simulation configuration derived from a Simulation Architecture
- An analysis of the results quality regarding a SRM depending on the chosen Simulation Architecture, setting the focus on the number of SCs.

This first approach already shows the consequences of a collaborative process, offering less accuracy when the number of stakeholders increases. Addressing the models integration at the earliest becomes a need in an EE context.

3.2 Application and Constraints

The prerequisites and limitations for this use case were:

– A System Architecture model (Fig. 3)

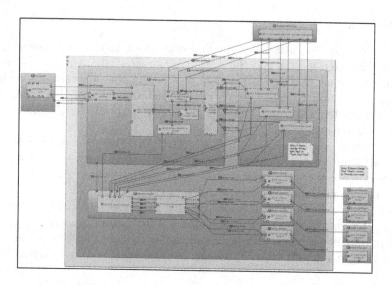

Fig. 3. Logical architecture of the AIDA main processor

The figure above presents the Co-Simulation Architecture directly derived from the Logical Architecture of the drone.

– A derived SRM Both were based on a reference work [12]
– And a mission: the AIDA drone will perform its inspection along a predetermined trajectory
– Only local co-simulations were performed
– Quality requirements are based only on a numerical analysis from the curves with no physical behavior criticism, since there is no available prototype.

The quality and relevancy of the architectural choices will be assessed regarding the accuracy of a dedicated architecture regarding an ideal trajectory setpoint. A visualization of this setpoint can be shown on Fig. 4.

To consolidate in an automatic fashion the link between the Simulation Architecture and the Co-Simulation Architecture, a generator for master files has been created.

In the first steps of this study, it had been foreseen to evaluate the relevancy of the transient co-simulation results regarding different configurations regarding the different co-simulation masters available (CosiMate [3], SimulationX [7]), different time-steps configurations and SC compositions. However, in this case,

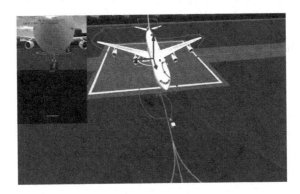

Fig. 4. Sample setpoint for an automatic drone inspection

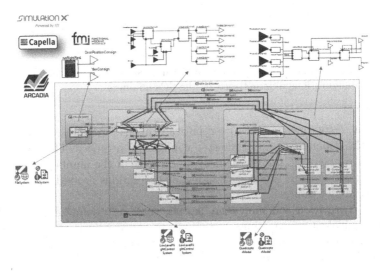

Fig. 5. Co-simulation architecture with highlighted dependencies

only the latter approach has given a sufficient discrepancy to require an analysis of the obtained curves for converging configurations. The graphs below shows an example of those results with the vertical trajectory tracking for the above-mentioned sample setpoint. Three configurations are compared:

- A Reference Simulation Model
- A 3 SCs Co-Simulation platform
- A 14 SCs Co-Simulation platform Both those co-simulation configurations have been deducted from the logical architecture of the drone implemented earlier in the modeling life cycle. All the configurations are based on an integration and exchange time-step set at the same sample time of 1 ms (Fig. 5).

3.3   Results

The results of those experiments are shown below (Fig. 6):

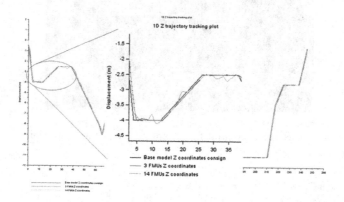

Fig. 6. Results comparison between a Reference Simulation model and two co-simulation configurations differentiated by the SCs numbers

From this experiment, it has been noticed that the results were quite similar as for the dependency and time-step configuration ranges. The main consequences of "coarsening" the problem by an increase of the number of models or the exchange time-steps are larger amplitude oscillations around the Reference Simulation Model values.

A cross-correlation and time delay has shown an approximate delay of 1 ms, which is equivalent to the time-step. However, no conclusion about the link between this time-step and the dependency graph can be given since the closed-loop behavior will be competing with the dependency graph induced latency.

Since the order of magnitude of the oscillations compared to the consign signal can appear as negligible in this case, one step further will be to enhance the complexity of the model to be able to define a validity range for the co-simulation without divergence.

4   Perspectives

This paper presents key concepts and an application to achieve earlier V&V from a System Architecture definition, using simulation, from a defined tool set (Capella/Arcadia and FMI). Beyond this proposal and basic application, the next steps achieve a complete method implementation are:

– the simulation model enrichment through
  • model complexity: the current AIDA model has shown its limitations in terms of discrepancy regarding the different co-simulation parameters (master, time-steps, SCs) to create automatic setup rules

- model representativeness: the AIDA model will require a more accurate contextual representation to achieve a validation regarding the purpose of the system of interest. Such models as 3D environment models, including cameras and localization devices, e.g. via GPS, will be added to the current configuration. This will enable to assess a real-life scenario including the visual and physical weather model (wind, light . . .), or the unintended presence of an obstacle or operator to explore the safety dimension of the design.
- The complete automation of the toolchain including consistency checking for connections, units and the relevance of the multiphysical coupling stiffnesses (conservation laws)
- Support the study case in a EE networked context
- Apply the method and tools to a real-life case.

References

1. Modelica Association, et al.: Modelica and the modelica association (2013)
2. Blochwitz, T., et al.: Functional Mockup Interface 2.0: the standard for tool independent exchange of simulation models. In: Proceedings of the 9th International Modelica Conference, pp. 173–184. The Modelica Association (2012). https://doi.org/10.3384/ecp12076173
3. Chiastek: CosiMate software (2018). https://site.cosimate.com/
4. Durling, E., Palmkvist, E., Henningsson, M.: FMI and IP protection of models: a survey of use cases and support in the standard. In: Proceedings of the 12th International Modelica Conference, Prague, Czech Republic, 15–17 May 2017, pp. 329–335, no. 132. Linköping University Electronic Press, Linköpings universitet (2017)
5. Fuhrmann, H., von Hanxleden, R.: On the pragmatics of model-based design. In: Choppy, C., Sokolsky, O. (eds.) Monterey Workshop 2008. LNCS, vol. 6028, pp. 116–140. Springer, Heidelberg (2010). https://doi.org/10.1007/978-3-642-12566-9_7
6. Gomes, C., Thule, C., Broman, D., Larsen, P.G., Vangheluwe, H.: Co-simulation: state of the art. CoRR abs/1702.00686 (2017). http://arxiv.org/abs/1702.00686
7. ITI: Simulationx software (2018). https://www.simulationx.com/simulation-software.html
8. Lyapunov, A.: The general problem of the stability of motion. Ph.D. thesis, Univ. Kharkov (1892). (in Russian). (1) Stability of Motion. Academic Press, New-York and London (1966) (2) The General Problem of the Stability of Motion, (A. T. Fuller trans.). Taylor & Francis, London (1992). Included is a biography by Smirnov and an extensive bibliography of Lyapunov's work
9. Mitts, K.J., Lang, K., Roudier, T., Kiskis, D.L.: Using a co-simulation framework to enable software-in-the-loop powertrain system development. Technical report, SAE Technical Paper (2009)
10. PolarSys: Capella (2018). http://www.polarsys.org/capella/
11. Prosvirnova, T., Saez, E., Seguin, C., Virelizier, P.: Handling consistency between safety and system models. In: Bozzano, M., Papadopoulos, Y. (eds.) IMBSA 2017. LNCS, vol. 10437, pp. 19–34. Springer, Cham (2017). https://doi.org/10.1007/978-3-319-64119-5_2

12. Quan, Q.: Introduction to Multicopter Design and Control. Springer, Singapore (2017). https://doi.org/10.1007/978-981-10-3382-7
13. Sachidananda, V., et al.: Simulation and evaluation of mixed-mode environments: towards higher quality of simulations. In: Ando, N., Balakirsky, S., Hemker, T., Reggiani, M., von Stryk, O. (eds.) SIMPAR 2010. LNCS, vol. 6472, pp. 133–143. Springer, Heidelberg (2010). https://doi.org/10.1007/978-3-642-17319-6_15
14. Sargent, R.G.: Verification and validation of simulation models. In: Proceedings of the 2011 Winter Simulation Conference, WSC, pp. 183–198, December 2011
15. Sirin, G., Paredis, C.J.J., Yannou, B., Coatanéa, E., Landel, E.: A model identity card to support simulation model development process in a collaborative multidisciplinary design environment. IEEE Syst. J. 9(4), 1151–1162 (2015). https://doi.org/10.1109/JSYST.2014.2371541
16. Voirin, J.L.: Model-based System and Architecture Engineering with the Arcadia Method, 1st edn. Elsevier, Amsterdam (2018)

Co-simulation of Physical Model and Self-Adaptive Predictive Controller Using Hybrid Automata

Imane Lamrani$^{(\boxtimes)}$, Ayan Banerjee$^{(\boxtimes)}$, and Sandeep K. S. Gupta$^{(\boxtimes)}$

iMPACT lab CIDSE, Arizona State University, Tempe, AZ 85281, USA
{ilamrani,abanerj3,sandeep.gupta}@asu.edu

Abstract. Self-adaptive predictive control (SAP) systems adjust their behavior in response to the changing physical system in order to achieve improved control. As such, models of self-adaptive control systems result in time variance of parameters. This significantly increases the complexity of model checking verification and reachability analysis techniques. In this paper, we explore recent studies on co-simulation of SAP controllers and propose a novel co-simulation platform that can be used to analyze the effectiveness of verification and reachability analysis techniques developed for SAP controllers.

Keywords: Co-simulation · Safety verification · Hybrid automata
Reachability analysis

1 Introduction

Self-adaptive predictive (SAP) control is a promising approach to regulate Cyber-Physical Systems (CPS) with changing conditions by adjusting the control parameters. In the medical domain, self-adaptive control theory has gained increasing interest where emerging innovative medical devices adopt it to deliver more accurate, personalized treatment to patients [2,4,6]. For example, recent artificial pancreas (AP) control systems adjust insulin administration based on prediction over patients' blood glucose levels, where self-adaptation mechanisms optimize control parameters based on feedback from patients to account for the ever-changing characteristics of their glycemic regulatory system [7]. Simulation-based modeling tools, such as Matlab/Simulink are often used to model and evaluate the design of medical devices with self-adaptive predictive control.

In SAP, the controller responds not only to the dynamics of the physical system but also to the subtle changes in the dynamics over time. This introduces time variance in the models used for analysis and design of SAP controllers.

This work has been partly funded by NIH grant EB019202. Thanks to Yi Zhang from CDRH, FDA for introducing the authors to the artificial pancreas model and regulatory issues.

M. Mazzara et al. (Eds.): STAF 2018 Workshops, LNCS 11176, pp. 69–76, 2018.
https://doi.org/10.1007/978-3-030-04771-9_7

Typically models deal with time variance of the parameters describing the physical system and a common method to model is through a system of differential equations involving the parameters. Formal safety verification of SAP controllers lies in verifying whether a certain unsafe set can be reached from a set of initial states. This verification is typically performed through a hybrid analysis of the co-variation of the inputs and outputs of the controller following a discrete control strategy and the time variation of the physical system parameters. As such if the physical model is time invariant, the verification problem is often intractable [18,19]. Techniques such as reachability analysis for the time invariant case cannot provide exact solutions and instead approximations are used [11]. *The time variance of the physical system models in SAP is an added complexity which further exacerbates the problem.* There has been very limited work on verification of SAP controllers assuming time variance of the physical models. Even the simpler problem of co-simulation of SAP controllers and physical systems has not been studied in extensive detail.

In this paper, we first focus on a survey of co-simulation techniques for SAP controllers and then propose a co-simulation architecture that can be used for future verification. This is the first step towards developing a complete verification methodology for SAP controllers. *In this paper, we define co-simulation as the time synchronized simulation of the SAP controller discrete decision making module, physical model update method, and physical system evolution.* The paper is organized as follows: Sect. 2 discusses different types of adaptive control system, Sect. 3 presents related works towards solving the discussed problem, Sect. 4 provides our proposed co-simulation framework for SAP systems, and finally Sect. 5 concludes the paper.

2   Types of Adaptive Control

There are different types of adaptive control systems. Open-loop adaptive control, direct adaptive control or model reference adaptive systems, and self-tuning regulators [9,20]. For self-tuning regulators, the controller automatically tunes its parameters to obtain some desired properties of the closed loop system. If the estimates of the process parameters change, then the controller parameters are updated from the solution of the controller design problem using these estimates. Plant parameters are estimated at every sampling time while controller parameters are updated every n samples, where $1/n$ is update freq.

Example of Self-Adaptive Predictive Control Systems: Artificial Pancreas (AP) systems are safety critical cyber-physical systems and are used for automated control of blood glucose level for Type 1 diabetic patients. The aim is to maintain the prescribed level of blood glucose, and avoid hypoglycemic and hyperglycemic events. These potentially dangerous events happen as a result of an inaccurate infusion rate of insulin I_t, e.g. if the glucose concentration G goes above 180 mg/dl, it can lead to hyperglycemia while low glucose level i.e. below 50 mg/dl can cause hypoglycemia. Self-adaptive predictive AP, shown in Fig. 1, consists of a sensor that measures patient's glucose concentration and predictive

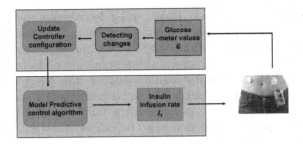

Fig. 1. Artificial pancreas: self adaptive predictive control system [6].

control algorithm which estimates the value of the patient's blood glucose concentration and computes the insulin infusion rate to maintain until the next time step. Different conditions including meal consumption and physical activity can cause tremendous change in the parameters of the predictive model describing blood glucose and insulin interaction. This model is non-linear in nature and is used by the controller to predict the value of blood glucose 30 min ahead in time and outputs the right amount of insulin infusion rate I_t for the infusion pump to maintain until the next time step. Therefore, adjusting controller parameters in response to disturbances or systemic changes is a promising approach to regulate AP and to achieve improved control [6].

3   Related Work

Model checking is one of the techniques used to ensure the correctness of the system by exploring all the possible environment states and ensuring that the system behaves as required in every state. However, the system model employed is not an accurate representation for time-invariant systems [1,21]. On the other hand, reachability analysis over hybrid automata provides a higher level of safety verification and has been extensively studied in the literature for time-invariant systems [3]. However, exact computation of reachable sets is still considered a difficult task and becomes even more complicated for time-varying systems [15]. Therefore, union of short-term simulations on a set of initial conditions has been proposed as an approach to compute overapproximation of reachable sets for time-varying systems [15].

Iftikhar and Weyns have proposed an approach to validate behavioral properties of decentralized self-adaptive systems [8]. This approach focuses on checking that the implementation of the system behaves complying with the model. The self-adaptive system is modeled with timed-automata and required properties are specified using timed-computation tree logic. The model is then verified using Uppaal [14]. Another formal verification approach of adaptive real-time systems to verify tasks schedulability has been proposed by Hatvani [10]. Hatvani uses adaptive tasks automata to model adaptive real-time systems and introduces schedulability predicates as part of the adaptive task automata to define the schedulibility of a task. Tasks can be described in the model as long as their behavior can be modeled using task automata. The main contribution of the authors lies in defining decidability to prevent missed task deadlines when adjustments to the altered environmental conditions are performed.

The following are the main assumptions of the previously discussed approaches: 1 - adaptation scenarios have to be predefined, 2 - an environment model should be available since it specifies the failure events that have to be tested, and 3 - proper test selection must be defined since exhaustive testing of systems is not feasible. None of the discussed approaches can be utilized to model and analyze SAP control systems since adaptation scenarios cannot be predefined for SAP systems where configuration functions are linear combination between the parameters of the predictive model and the changing conditions of the environment. In addition, an environmental model with changing characteristics is not available for SAP control systems. Similarly, Tan has presented a model-based framework for developping self-adaptive systems [12]. Tan introduced a configuration language to specify reconfiguration requirements and events triggering the reconfiguration are specified in temporal logic while the system behavior is depicted in the hybrid automata model of the system. However, the reconfiguration mechanism is limited to a constant function which can not be applied to predictive self-adaptive control system, where the configuration function is a linear combination between the parameters of the predictive model and the changing conditions of the environment.

In this paper, we propose a co-simulation framework for designing and formally verifying self-adaptive predictive (SAP) control systems using co-simulation and reachability analysis. This co-simulation framework represents the first step towards developing a complete verification methodology for SAP controllers. It represents a time synchronized simulation of the SAP controller discrete decision making, physical model update method, and physical system evolution.

4   Approach to Solve the Problem: Co-simulation Framework

The proposed approach depicted in Fig. 2 is an alternative modeling technique for devices with self-adaptive predictive control. For ease of understanding, we present the SAP co-simulation framework for the artificial pancreas self-adaptive predictive system presented in Sect. 2. The following represent the main steps of the co-simulation framework depicted in Fig. 2:

– A patient predictive model is used to estimate the value of blood glucose 30 min ahead in time and computes the insulin infusion rate to maintain until the next time step. This model is represented by nonlinear Eqs. 1, 2 and 3, where $\dot{X}$ represents the rate of the variation in the interstitial insulin concentration, $\dot{G}$ is the rate of change of blood glucose concentration for

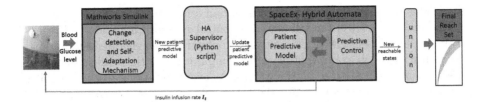

Fig. 2. SAP co-simulation framework. Mathworks and SpaceEx are executing simultaneously.

the infused insulin concentration X, and $\dot{I}$ is the variation in plasma insulin concentration [16].

$$\dot{X} = -k_2 X(t) + k_3(I(t) - I_b), \tag{1}$$

$$\dot{G} = -X(t)G(t) + k_1(G_b - G(t)), \tag{2}$$

$$\dot{I} = -k_4 I(t) + k_5(G(t) - k_6)t. \tag{3}$$

This model contains parameters $k_1, ..., k_6$ that are likely to change and need to be adapted for accuracy purposes. Some conditions including meal consumption, exercise, and emotional changes can be the cause of these changes [2]. We first derive an approximate linear system that matches closely with the real AP system [17].

- The change detection and self-adaptation mechanism detects changes in the behavior of the human body using recent blood glucose measurements. These changes physically correpond to significant change in glucose levels [7]. The change detection method compares the expected value of the model parameters and the vector of unbiased parameter estimates computed. It then adapts the predictive model accordingly by re-estimating the changing parameters of the model using the more recent data only [17].
- **The HA supervisor** is in the form of a Python script and performs the following steps:
  1. Generates initial model file in SpaceEx's XML format with initial patient predictive model settings $(k_1, k_2, ..., k_n)$ [13].
  2. Calls SpaceEx executable file to run the command line program that takes a model file in XML format and a configuration file that specifies the initial states, sampling time, and other options. The sampling time can be adaptively computed by the reachability analysis support functions or manually selected taking into consideration that a discrete transition should not occur between two consecutive sampling times [5]. SpaceEx analyzes the system and produces an output file $O_1.txt$ containing the reachable states computed.
  3. Once a change is detected, it generates a new patient predictive model XML file with new parameter settings $(k'_1, k'_2, ..., k'_n)$.
  4. Calls SpaceEx executable file to run the command line program with the new generated model file. SpaceEx analyzes the system and produces an output file $O_2.txt$ containing the reachable states.

5. This process continues until termination criterion is satisfied.
- The final reach set of the self-adaptive control system is a union of all reachable states obtained with all controller configurations generated at runtime. Figure 3 shows an example of reach set computation for the artificial pancreas self-adaptive predictive control system. At every iteration, a new controller configuration is generated and the reach set is computed accordingly. The final reach set is obtained by combining all the regions of the state space that the system has visited, as shown in Fig. 3.

The proposed approach strives to:

- Support modeling of predictive control systems using hybrid automata, and runtime self-adaption of hybrid automata based on new configurations from other modeling tools such as Simulink.
- Provide an alternative modeling technique for devices with self-adaptive predictive control.
- Verify the safety of self-adaptive predictive control devices by checking whether the sets of reachable states of the system intersects with the unsafe set.

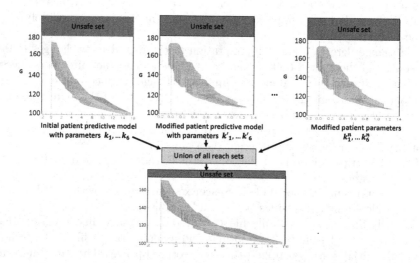

Fig. 3. Reach set of the artificial pancreas self-adaptive predictive control system.

5   Conclusions and Future Work

In this paper, we have investigated the problem of safety verification of self-adaptive control systems. We proposed a novel approach to model and verify the safety of self-adaptive predictive control systems via reachability analysis and co-simulation. Reachability analysis is performed taking into consideration the ever-changing characteristics of the system by updating the hybrid automata model of the system every time a new controller configuration is needed. Since we deal with systems where controller configurations are not predefined, the proposed method is considered a run-time verification of the self-adaptive systems using reachability analysis. Thus, one of the issues of the proposed approach is the selection of an accurate termination criteria for the safety analysis. As a future work, we plan to investigate the correctness of the computed reach set for predictive self-adaptive systems.

References

1. Jacklin, S., et al.: Verification, validation, and certification challenges for adaptive fight-critical control system software. In: AIAA Guidance, Navigation, and Control Conference and Exhibit (2004)
2. Turksoy, K., Cinar, A.: Adaptive control of artificial pancreas systems-a review. J. Healthc. Eng. **5**, 1–22 (2014)
3. Frehse, G.: Reachability of hybrid systems in space-time. In: ACM SIGBED EMSOFT (2015)
4. Sadeghi, K., et al.: Permanency analysis on human electroencephalogram signals for pervasive brain-computer interface systems. In: 39th Annual International Conference of the IEEE EMBC (2017)
5. Frehse, G.: Scalable verification of hybrid systems. Diss. Univ, Grenoble Alpes (2016)
6. Hovorka, R., et al.: Nonlinear model predictive control of glucose concentration in subjects with type 1 diabetes. Physiol. Measure. **25**(4), 905 (2004)
7. Eren-Oruklu, M., et al.: Self-tuning controller for regulation of glucose levels in patients with type 1 diabetes. In: American Control Conference, pp. 819–824. IEEE (2008)
8. Iftikhar, M.U., Weyns, D.: A case study on formal verification of self-adaptive behaviors in a decentralized system. arXiv preprint arXiv:1208.4635 (2012)
9. Landau, I.D., et al.: Adaptive Control, vol. 51. Springer, New York (1998). https://doi.org/10.1007/978-0-85729-664-1
10. Hatvani, L.: Formal verification of adaptive real-time systems by extending task automata. Diss. Mälardalen University (2014)
11. Chutinan, A., Krogh, B.H.: Computational techniques for hybrid system verification. IEEE Trans. Autom. Control **48**(1), 64–75 (2003)
12. Tan, L.: Model-based self-adaptive embedded programs with temporal logic specifications, pp. 151–158. Software IEEE (2006)
13. Frehse, G., et al.: SpaceEx: scalable verification of hybrid systems. In: Gopalakrishnan, G., Qadeer, S. (eds.) CAV 2011. LNCS, vol. 6806, pp. 379–395. Springer, Heidelberg (2011). https://doi.org/10.1007/978-3-642-22110-1_30
14. Larsen, K.G., Pettersson, P., Yi, W.: UPPAAL in a nutshell. Int. J. Softw. Tools Technol. Transf. **1**(1–2), 134–152 (1997)
15. Althoff, M., Le Guernic, C., Krogh, B.H.: Reachable set computation for uncertain time-varying linear systems. In: 14th International Conference on Hybrid Systems: Computation and Control, pp. 93–102. ACM (2011)
16. Andersen, K.E., Højbjerre, M.: A Bayesian approach to Bergman's minimal model. In: Bishop, C.M., Frey, B.J. (eds.) Ninth International Workshop on Artificial Intelligence (2003)

17. Lamrani, I., et al.: HyMn: mining linear hybrid automata from input output traces of cyber-physical systems. IEEE International Conference on Industrial Cyber-Physical Systems (2018)
18. Moon, I.-H., et al.: Approximate reachability don't cares for CTL model checking. In: In: IEEE/ACM CAD, pp. 351–358 (1998)
19. Ravi, K., Somenzi, F.: High-density reachability analysis. In: IEEE/ACM CAD, pp. 154–158 (1995)
20. Sadeghi, K., et al.: Optimization of brain mobile interface applications using IoT. In: 23rd International Conference on HiPC. IEEE (2016)
21. Sadeghi, K., et al.: SafeDrive: an autonomous driver safety application in aware cities. In: International Conference on PerCom Workshops. IEEE (2016)

From Data to Models and Back
(DataMod)

DataMod 2018 Organizers' Message

The 7th International Symposium From Data to Models and Back (DataMod 2018) was held in Toulouse, France, during 25–26 June 2018. The symposium aims at bringing together practitioners and researchers from academia, industry, government and non-government organizations to present research results and exchange experiences, ideas, and solutions for modeling and analyzing complex systems and using knowledge management strategies, technology, and systems in various domain areas such as ecology, biology, medicine, climate, governance, education, and social software engineering. After a careful review process, the Program Committee accepted eight regular papers for presentation at the symposium and inclusion in the post-proceedings, and four short presentation reports. The program of DataMod 2018 was also enriched by the keynote speeches of Paolo Masci titled "Data-driven analysis of user interface software in medical devices", Gwen Salaün titled "Safe Composition of Software Services", and Giulio Caravagna titled "Computational oncology: from biomedical data to models and back".

Several people contributed to the success of DataMod 2018. We are grateful to the DataMod Steering Committee and to the organizers of STAF 2018, in particular the workshops chairs, Manuel Mazzara, Iulian Ober, and Gwen Salaün. We would also like to thank the Program Committee and the additional reviewers for their work in reviewing the papers and their participation in the online discussion. The process of reviewing and selecting papers was significantly simplified through using EasyChair. We thank all attendees of the symposium and hope that this event enabled a good exchange of ideas and generated new collaborations among attendees. The organization of DataMod 2018 was supported by the research project "Metodologie informatiche avanzate per l'analisi di dati biomedici (Advanced computational methodologies for the analysis of biomedical data)" funded by the University of Pisa (PRA_2017_44).

September 2018

Oana Andrei
Antonio Cerone
Vashti Galpin
Riccardo Guidotti
Paolo Milazzo

Organization

DataMod 2018 - Steering Commmittee

Antonio Cerone	Nazarbayev University, Kazakhstan
Jane Hillston	University of Edinburgh, UK
Marijn Janssen	Delft University of Technology, The Netherlands
Stan Matwin	University of Ottawa, Canada
Paolo Milazzo	University of Pisa, Italy
Anna Monreale	University of Pisa, Italy

DataMod 2018 - Program Co-chairs

Oana Andrei	University of Glasgow, UK
Antonio Cerone	Nazarbayev University, Kazakhstan
Riccardo Guidotti	University of Pisa & ISTI-CNR, Italy

DataMod 2018 - Organizing Committee

Vashti Galpin	University of Edinburgh, UK
Paolo Milazzo	University of Pisa, Italy

DataMod 2018 - Program Committee

Oana Andrei (Co-chair)	University of Glasgow, UK
Luís Barbosa	United Nations University, UNU-EGOV, Portugal
Bettina Berendt	Katholieke Universiteit Leuven, Belgium
Armelle Brun	LORIA - Universite Nancy 2, France
Juliana Küster Filipe Bowles	University of St. Andrews, UK
Antonio Cerone (Co-chair)	Nazarbayev University, Kazakhstan
François Fages	Inria & Universite Paris-Saclay, France
Lei Fang	University of St. Andrews, UK
Cheng Feng	Siemens Corporate Technology, China
Giuditta Franco	University of Verona, Italy
Vashti Galpin	University of Edinburgh, UK
Yiwei Gong	Wuhan University, China
Rocio Gonzalez-Diaz	University of Seville, Spain
Riccardo Guidotti (Co-chair)	University of Pisa & ISTI-CNR, Italy
Tias Guns	Vrije Universiteit Brussel, Belgium
Joris Hulstijn	Tilburg University, The Netherlands
Mouna Kacimi	Free University of Bozen-Bolzano, Italy
Paddy Krishnan	Oracle Labs, Australia

Sotirios Liaskos	York University, Canada
Martin Lukac	Nazarbayev University, Kazakhstan
Letizia Milli	University of Pisa, Italy
Charles Morisset	Newcastle University, UK
Patrick Mukala	Eindhoven University of Technology, The Netherlands
Mirco Musolesi	University College London, UK
Laura Nenzi	TU Wien, Austria
Siegfried Nijssen	Katholieke Universiteit Leuven, Belgium
Nicola Paoletti	Stony Brook University, USA
Gwen Salaün	University of Grenoble Alpes, France
Mark Sterling	Nazarbayev University, Kazakhstan
Luca Tesei	University of Camerino, Italy

DataMod 2018 - Additional Reviewers

Dung Phan	Stony Brook University, USA
Simone Silvetti	University of Udine, Italy

Formalizing a Notion of Concentration Robustness for Biochemical Networks

Lucia Nasti[✉], Roberta Gori, and Paolo Milazzo

Dipartimento di Informatica, Università di Pisa,
Largo Bruno Pontecorvo 3, 56127 Pisa, Italy
{lucia.nasti,gori,milazzo}@di.unipi.it

Abstract. The main goal of systems biology is to understand the dynamical properties of biological systems by investigating the interactions among the components of a biological system. In this work, we focus on the robustness property, a behaviour observed in several biological systems that allows them to preserve their functions despite external and internal perturbations. We first propose a new formal definition of robustness using the formalism of continuous Petri nets. In particular, we focus on robustness against perturbations to the initial concentrations of species. Then, we demonstrate the validity of our definition by applying it to the models of three different robust biochemical networks.

Keywords: Robustness · Biochemical networks · Petri nets

1 Introduction

From the discovery of DNA structure, in 1953, there has been an increasing interest in the morphological and functional organization of living cells. A cell is a complex system. It consists of a huge number of components that interact with each other through chemical reaction networks. The cell's global behaviour, both internal and with the environment, emerges from such an interaction.

Chemical reaction networks, also called *pathways* are often based on long series of chemical reactions, also known as *signalling cascades*, activated by an initial stimulus (a chemical in the environment or entering the cell), that is perceived by a *transductor* (e.g. a receptor protein in the cell surface). The transductor causes the cascade of reactions to start, leading to the amplification and the filtering of the stimulus (or input signal), in order to suitably regulate and reconfigure cell activities as a response. Signalling pathways play a crucial role for the cell functioning. Many severe diseases, such as cancer and diabetes, are caused by the malfunctioning or the corruption of a crucial signalling pathway.

In this context, the main challenge is to explore how the components of the cells interact with each other as a *system* in order to predict how perturbations can influence the cell functioning. This is the aim of *systems biology* [1,21].

In this perspective, we focus on the definition of the *robustness* property, a fundamental feature of complex evolving systems, for which the functionality

M. Mazzara et al. (Eds.): STAF 2018 Workshops, LNCS 11176, pp. 81–97, 2018.
https://doi.org/10.1007/978-3-030-04771-9_8

of the system remains essentially intact despite the presence of internal and external perturbations.

In nature, there are different mechanisms ensuring robustness, such as system control, redundancy, modularity and structural stability [22]. *System control* is based on negative and positive feedback which, together, amplify the pathway input signals filtering out noise (other chemicals that may interfere). In this context, the most popular example is the chemotaxis of *E. Coli* [1] because it shows an evident robust adaptation to environmental changes. *Redundancy* plays a key role in robustness: pathways often have different ways to produce the same molecules, allowing them to tolerate problems such as the absence of a specific reactant. *Modularity* ensures that, if there is a damage in one of the parts of the system, this does not affect also the other parts. In this way, it is possible to avoid a total collapse, due to a local error. *Structural stability* is the quality according to which a system is able to adapt to changes even in presence of different external perturbations. Some examples of this can be found in gene regulatory circuits, that are stable for a broad range of stimuli and genetic polymorphisms [21].

The robustness of a pathway can be tested by performing wet-lab (in vitro) experiments, or through mathematical or computational (in silico) approaches on a pathway model. Model-based approaches are usually based either on mathematical analysis methods, or on numerical and simulation methods. Unfortunately, the applicability of these approaches is often hampered by the complexity of the models to be analyzed (usually expressed as ODEs or Markov chains).

To avoid analyzing complex models, Shinar and Feinberg in [34, 35] proposed a *sufficient condition* that, in some particular cases, allows robustness to be derived directly from a syntactical property of the pathway, without the need of studying or simulating its dynamics. The sufficient condition states that a mass action system can be considered robust if it admits a positive steady state, the underlying reaction network has a *deficiency* (that is a measure of *linear independence* among its reactions) equal to one and there are distinct non-terminal complexes that differ only in a single species (see [16] for the details).

This approach has the great advantage to prove robustness without executing the system. Indeed, verifying robustness would require, in general, to consider all possible initial states of the system. In particular, regarding the signalling pathways, it would be necessary to test the system behaviour by examining all the possible combinations of initial concentrations of chemical species and, in practice, this would require a huge number of simulations. On the other hand, the sufficient condition proposed in [34, 35] is not general: its syntactic constraint makes it applicable only to a particular class of pathways.

A further step towards the formal study of robustness was made in [8], where the concept of *adaptability* of a system is introducted. This consists in the capacity of the system to adapt its behaviour to different initial concentrations of some chemical species with, possibly, different degrees of robustness.

Both robustness and adaptability can be formally studied by applying the methodology proposed by Rizk et al. in [32, 33]. Such a methodology is based on the definition of robustness given by Kitano in [22] as *the ability of a system to maintain specific functionalities against perturbations*. The robustness of a system is measured as the *distance* of the system behaviour under perturbations from its reference behaviour expressed as a temporal logic formula. The distance is computed by using a notion of *violation degree* measuring how much the temporal logic formula should be changed in order to match traces of perturbed behaviours obtained, for instance, through simulations.

The approach proposed by Rizk et al. is very general, both in the description of the reference behaviour and as regards perturbations. In this paper, instead, we focus on *concentration robustness*, namely on the influence of the initial concentrations of species on what will be the steady state of the system. What we propose is a notion of α-robustness, based on continuous Petri nets [17] and interval markings, which extends the notion of *absolute concentration robustness* considered in [34,35] with the notion of *adaptability* proposed in [8].

Our definition of robustness is simpler and much less general than the one considered by Rizk et al. However, it is conceived with the aim of enabling further studies on sufficient conditions that could allow robustness to be assesses by avoiding (or significantly reducing) the number of simulations to be perfomed. This could be obtained, for instance, by adapting conditions already considered in the context of monotonicity analysis [3].

We validate our definition by modelling and simulating three different systems, two related to the Escherichia coli organism (the *EnvZ/OmpR* and bacterial chemotaxis) and the last one dealing with enzyme activity at saturation. By simulations, we verify the robustness of the system and, by varying the initial parameters, we test the degree of the robustness.

We proceed by first introducing the continuous Petri nets formalism in Sect. 2.1, which is the base of our new formal definition of robustness presented in Sect. 2.2. In Sect. 3 we validate our definition using the three biochemical examples. Finally, Sect. 4 contains some conclusions and future work.

2   Formal Definition of the Robustness Property

Many formalisms have been used to describe biological systems at different abstraction levels, as for example Petri nets [19,31], P systems [28,29], reaction systems [13], BioPepa [11] and Hybrid Automata [2,20,24,27]. These notations allow systems to be modeled unambiguously and enable the application of formal analysis techniques such as model checking [10,23], abstract interpretation [12,15,18] and, in general, logic and symbolic reasoning approaches [4–7,14].

In this work, we formalize the robustness property, using the formalism of continuous Petri nets [17]. Petri nets have many applications in different areas, since they are able to model static and dynamic behavioural aspects. They are a valid tool to study concurrent and parallel programs, communication protocols, business processes as well as biological systems.

2.1 Continuous Petri Nets

A *continuous Petri net* N can be defined as a quintuple $\langle P, T, F, W, m_0 \rangle$ where:

- P is the set of continuous *places*, conceptually one for each considered kind of system resource;
- T is the set of continuous *transitions* that consume and produce resources;
- $F \subseteq (P \times T) \bigcup (T \times P) \rightarrow \mathbb{R}_{\geq 0}$ represents the set of arcs in terms of a function giving the weight of the arc as result: a weight equal to 0 means that the arc is not present;
- $W : F \rightarrow \mathbb{R}_{\geq 0}$ is a function, which associates each transition with a *rate*;
- m_0 is the *initial marking*, that is the initial distribution of *tokens* (representing resource instances) among places. A marking is defined formally as $m : P \rightarrow \mathbb{R}_{\geq 0}$.

Tokens are movable objects, assigned to places, that are consumed by transitions in the input places and produced in the output places. Graphically, a Petri net is drawn as a graph with nodes representing places and transitions. Circles are used for places and rectangles for transitions. Tokens are drawn as black dots inside places. Graph edges represent arcs and are labeled with their weights. For simplicity, the labels of arcs with weight 1 is omitted. To faithfully model biochemical networks, the marking of a place is not an integer (the number of tokens) but a positive real number (called *token value* representing the concentration of a chemical species. Each transition is associated with a kinetic constant, that determines the rate of (continuous) flow of tokens from the input to the output places of the transition.

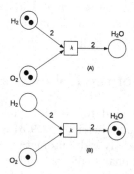

Fig. 1. Example of Petri net. In this case, it shown how represent the chemical reaction: $2\,H_2 + O_2 \xrightarrow{k} 2\,H_2O$. (A) and (B) represent two different markings for the same Petri net. The marking in (B) is obtained from the one in (A) as the result of firing transition with the rate k.

Figure 1 shows a simple example of continuous Petri net modeling the chemical reaction $2\,H_2 + O_2 \xrightarrow{k} 2\,H_2O$. In sub-figure (A), each place, H and O, has two tokens: the transition is enabled since it requires two tokens from H_2 and only one from O_2. Sub-figure (B) shows the situation after the transition has been fired: the tokens are moved (in a continuous way) to the output places. Note that in (B) the transition is no longer enabled.

The dynamics of a Continuous Petri net can be expressed in terms of ODEs (in agreement with the standard mass action kinetics of chemical reactions). Each place corresponds to a continuous variable whose value corresponds the place's marking. The dynamics of the variable is expressed by a differential equation consisting of a summation of terms corresponding to the transitions connected to the place. Each term has a positive sign if the transition is connected to the place by an outgoing arc. The sign is negative otherwise. Moreover, the term is the product of the weight of the arc with the values of the variables corresponding to all the places providing resources to the transition (i.e., having and outgoing arc connecting them to the transition). Those variables have as exponent the weight of the arc connecting them to the transition.

For example, considering the continuous Petri net in Fig. 1. The ODEs describing the dynamics of the net are as follows:

$$\frac{dH_2}{d_t} = -2kH_2^2O_2 \qquad \frac{dO_2}{d_t} = -kH_2^2O_2 \qquad \frac{dH_2O}{d_t} = +2kH_2^2O_2$$

An alternative (stochastic) dynamics can be given by using the terms of the ODEs computed for each transition as rates of a Continuous Time Markov Chain (CTMC). Both ODEs and CTMCs offer standard analytic ways to compute the steady state of the system.

Hereinafter, we refer to continuous Petri nets simply as Petri nets and we assume their dynamics to be expressed in terms of ODEs.

2.2 Formal Definition of Robustness

Given a biochemical network, the idea is to verify whether by varying the initial concentrations of some *input* species, the *output* of the network (the concentration of a species of interest) remains either constant or bounded within a given interval. We will assume the initial concentration of the input species to vary within given intervals, and the initial concentrations of all the other molecules to be fixed. Under these assumptions, we define the property of robustness of the system and we formalize it by using Petri nets.

We introduce some auxiliaries definitions. First, we extend the concept of marking. Recall that in Sect. 2.1 we defined the initial marking as an assignment of a fixed value to each place p. Now, we generalize the idea of initial marking by considering a marking as an assignment of a *interval of values* to each place p of the Petri net.

We first define the domain of intervals.

Definition 1 (Intervals). *We define the interval domain as*

$$\mathcal{I} = \{[n, m] \mid n, m \in \mathbb{R}_{\geq 0} \cup \{+\infty\} \text{ and } n \leq m\}.$$

An interval $[n, m] \in \mathcal{I}$ *is* trivial *iff* $n = m$. *Moreover, we say that* $x \in [n, m]$ *iff* $n \leq x \leq m$.

We now define interval markings.

Definition 2 (Interval marking). *Given a set of places* P, *an* interval mark-ing *is a function* $m_{[\,]} : P \to \mathcal{I}$. *We call* $M_{[\,]}$ *the domain of all interval markings.*

An interval marking in which at least one interval is non-trivial represents an infi-nite set of markings, one for each possible combination of values of the non-trivial intervals. Therefore, given an interval marking, we relate it with the markings as in the original Petri nets formalism in the following way:

$$\text{Given } m \in M \text{ and } m_{[\,]} \in M_{[\,]}, \ m \in m_{[\,]} \text{ iff } \forall p \in P, m(p) \in m_{[\,]}(p).$$

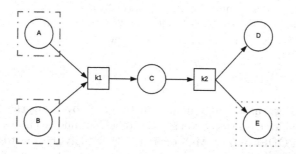

Fig. 2. Example of Petri nets, in which A and B are marked as input of the system (red dot-line) and E is marked as output (green dots). (Color figure online)

In a Petri net we assume that there exists *at least one* input place and *exactly one* output place representing input and output species of the modeled biochem-ical network, respectively. See Fig. 2 for an example. Under this assumption, we can give our formal definition of robustness.

Definition 3. (α-Robustness). *A Petri net* N *with output place* O *is* α-robust *with respect to a given interval marking* $m_{[\,]}$ *iff* $\exists k \in \mathbb{R}$ *such that* $\forall m \in m_{[\,]}$, *the marking* m' *corresponding to the steady state reachable from* m, *is such that*

$$m'(O) \in [k - \frac{\alpha}{2}, k + \frac{\alpha}{2}] \ .$$

Note that the definition of α-robustness does not explicitly mention the input places of the net. Actually, input places will be those having a non-trivial initial in $m_{[\,]}$. In other words, input places are those whose initial marking is not fixed.

Given the previous definition, it can be observed that:

– the wider are the intervals of the initial interval marking, the more robust is the network, because it means that the system gives similar outputs regardless the initial inputs;

– the smaller is the value of α, the more robust is the network.

Here, we have given a general definition that can be modified in different ways. For example, rather than considering the marking at the steady states, it could be possible to consider the marking reached at a given time T, or when the system terminates its execution (no transition is enabled).

It is worth noting that our definition is general enough to capture several notions of robustness available in literature. For example, by considering the initial intervals $[1, \infty]$ for the initial concentration of the input species and $\alpha = 0$ we obtain a formal definition for the robustness notions considered in [8,34].

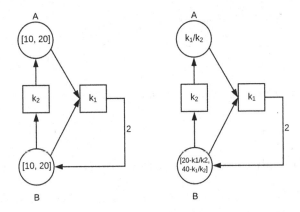

Fig. 3. Example of robust biochemical network, considering the species A as output of the system.

A simple example of robust biochemical network is given by the following two reactions:

$$A + B \xrightarrow{k_1} 2B \qquad B \xrightarrow{k_2} A$$

The Petri net representation of the network is shown in Fig. 3 (on the left with the initial marking, on the right with the steady state marking). In this case, the steady state is such that

$$A = \frac{k_2}{k_1} \qquad B = \theta - \frac{k_2}{k_1}$$

where θ is the sum of initial concentrations of A and B. If A is the output of the system, then its concentration in the steady state does not depend from the initial quantity of the (input) chemical species A and B (0-robustness with $k = \frac{k_2}{k_1}$). If we consider $[10, 20]$ as the initial interval for both A and B, we obtain that θ will be in $[20, 40]$. So, for B as the output we obtain:

$$B \in [20 - \frac{k_2}{k_1}, 40 - \frac{k_2}{k_1}]$$

Thus, for output B we have α-robustness with $\alpha = 20$, suggesting that B is not independent from the initial concentrations of A and B.

Moreover, in Fig. 4 we can see a network that is never robust neither considering A as output, nor B. Their chemical reactions are: $A \xrightarrow{k_1} B$, $B \xrightarrow{k_2} A$. In this case, the concentrations of A and B at the steady state are both always influenced by the input values. The reason of this behaviour is related to the fact that in this case the chemical species are transformed, but not consumed.

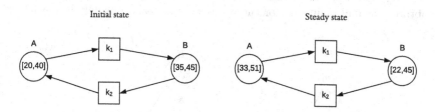

Fig. 4. Example of non robust network. In this case we chose $k_1 = 2$ and $k_2 = 3$.

3 Validating the Definition of Robustness

To validate our definition of robustness, we consider three examples of biological networks: the two component $EnvZ/OmpR$ osmoregulatory signalling system and the bacterial chemotaxis, which are related to E. coli, and a model of the behaviour of the enzyme kinetics at saturation. The first example shows absolute concentration robustness, corresponding to 0-robustness in our setting. The other two examples show a concentration robustness that it is not absolute (α-robustness with α greater than 0).

3.1 EnvZ/OmpR Osmoregulatory Signalling System in E. Coli

The $EnvZ/OmpR$ system regulates the expression of two porins, $OmpF$ and $OmpC$, which are proteins having many roles in the cell, as for example nutrients transportation, elimination of toxins and many others [9, 35].

The regulatory system consists of two components. The first one is the *histine kinase EnvZ*, a particular kind of protein having the role of adding and removing a phosphate to an aspartame acid usually on the other component of the signalling pathway, the *response regulator OmpR*, which mediates a response of the cell to changes in its environment. The role of $EnvZ$ is bifunctional because it phosphorylates and dephosphorylates $OmpR$: the model predicts that the steady state level of $OmpR_P$ (the phosporylated form of $OmpR$) is insensitive to variations in the concentration of $EnvZ$ and $OmpR$.

Table 1. The initial concentrations, the rates and the chemical reactions of *EnvZ/OmpR* system. The concentration of X and Y, marked by the symbol $\diamond$, can vary to prove the robustness in Y_P.

Initial concentrations	Rates	Chemical reactions
$X = 25 \diamond$	$k_1, k_2, k_3, k_4 = 0.5$	$XD \underset{k_2}{\overset{k_1}{\rightleftharpoons}} X$
$Y = 150 \diamond$	$k_5, k_{11} = 0.1$	$XT \underset{k_4}{\overset{k_3}{\rightleftharpoons}} X$
$XT = 0$	$k_6, k_9 = 0.02$	$XT \xrightarrow{k_5} X_P$
$X_P = 0$	$k_7, k_8, k_{10} = 0.5$	$X_P + Y \underset{k_7}{\overset{k_6}{\rightleftharpoons}} X_P Y$
$X_P Y = 0$		$X_P Y \xrightarrow{k_8} X + Y_P$
$Y_P = 10$		$XD + Y_P \xrightarrow{k_9} XDY_P$
$XDY_P = 0$		$XDY_P \xrightarrow{k_{10}} XD + Y_P$
$XD = 50$		$XDY_P \xrightarrow{k_{11}} XD + Y$

Modeling and Simulation of the EnvZ/OmpR System in E.coli. The main components of this chemical network are *EnvZ* and *OmpR*, denoted in Table 1 respectively as X and Y. *EnvZ* phosporylates *OmpR* (Y_P) and itself (X_P), by binding and breaking down *ATP*. In this sequence of chemical reactions, in fact, *ATP* and *ADP* act as cofactors (denoted as T and D).

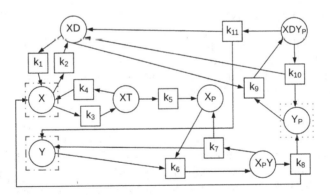

Fig. 5. The Petri nets model for the reaction network of the *EnvZ/OmpR* system. The input of the network are X and Y (red dot-lines), the output is Y_P (green dots). (Color figure online)

In order to check whether the system satisfies our definition of robustness we build the Petri nets model shown in Fig. 5, where X and Y are the input and Y_P is the output. To study the equilibrium configuration, we compute the steady state by setting the time-derivatives to zero and solving the obtained equations.

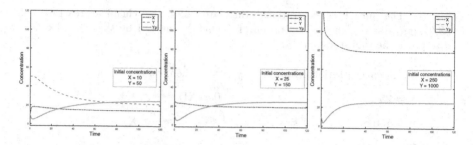

Fig. 6. Graphical results of the simulation of the *EnvZ/OmpR* system. We vary the concentrations of X and Y to show robustness in Y_P. Note that in the third case the curve of Y is out of the graph.

At the steady state, the concentration of Y_P does not depend from the input chemical species, thus, the system satisfies 0-robustness (absolute concentration robustness) for the widest intervals ($[1, \infty]$) of initial concentrations.

To illustrate the robustness of this system we show some simulation results obtained by using Dizzy [30]. Simulation results are in Fig. 6, where it is shown that the concentration of Y_P is constant even varying the initial concentrations of the input species X and Y.

Moreover, note that in this case, we can also apply the theorem in [34]: the *deficiency* of the network is 1 and the sufficient conditions required by the theorem to assure absolute concentration robustness in Y_P can be verified.

3.2   Bacterial Chemotaxis

In nature, one of the most important examples of robustness is in bacterial chemotaxis. It is the process through which bacteria sense and move along concentration gradients of specific chemicals like sugars or amino acids (as serine and aspartame) [1]. Despite their physical limitations, bacteria can detect concentration gradients to guide their motion, which consists in runs in which they alternate keeping a constant direction with *tumbles* in which they randomly change direction. The bacterium continuously compares the current attractant concentration with its concentration in the past. If it detects an increment, it reduces the tumbling frequency. After a while, if the concentration of the attractant remains constant, the bacterium increases the tumbling frequency back to the original level. This phenomenon is an example of *exact adaptation*, because the concentration of attractant does not influence the bacterium response to the ambient change (it is the gradient that matters).

Modeling and Simulation of Chemotaxis of E. coli. A detailed description of bacterial chemotaxis can be found in [1,8]. The E. coli senses the concentration of an attractant L through receptors on its external membrane. Each receptor is bound to a protein kinase, constituting a group denoted X. Rapidly, this group

Table 2. The initial concentrations, the rates and the chemical reactions of chemotaxis phenomenon of the E. coli. The concentration of the attractant L, marked by the symbol $\diamond$, can vary to prove the robustness in $CheY_P$.

Initial concentration	Rates	Chemical reaction
$X = 10$	$k_1, k_{13} = 1.15$	$X \xrightleftharpoons[k_2]{k_1} X^*$
$X^* = 10$	$k_2, k_{12} = 0.25$	$X^* + CheY \xrightarrow{k_3} CheYp + X$
$L = 0 \diamond$	$k_3 = 0.1$	$CheYp + Z \xrightarrow{k_4} CheY + Z$
$CheY = 10$	$k_4 = 10$	$CheYp \xrightarrow{k_5} CheY$
$Z = 1$	$k_5 = 0.002$	$L + X^* \xrightarrow{k_6} L + XY$
$CheYp = 1$	$k_6, k_7, k_{11} = 1$	$CheBp \xrightarrow{k_7} CheB$
$XL = 0$	$k_8 = 80$	$XY \xrightarrow{k_8} XL$
$X^*m = 1$	$k_9 = 0.01$	$CheR + XL \xrightarrow{k_9} X^*m + CheR$
$CheR = 1000$	$k_{10} = 0.2$	$X^*m + CheB \xrightarrow{k_{10}} Bp + X^*m$
$XY = 0$	$k_{14} = 0.18$	$X^*m + CheBp \xrightarrow{k_{11}} X^* + Bp$
$CheB = 2$		$X^*m \xrightleftharpoons[k_{13}]{k_{12}} Xm$
$CheBp = 0$		$X^*m + CheY \xrightarrow{k_{14}} CheYp + Xm$
$Xm = 0$		

passes from inactive state X to an active state X^*, and starts modifying the state of a regulator protein, $CheY$, by adding a phosphate group to it (which becomes $CheYp$). The complex $CheY_P$ is the main responsible of tumbles: in fact, the higher is its concentration, the higher is the tumbling frequency.

During this process, the binding of X with attractants reduces its probability to reach the active state that, consequently, reduces also the probability to attach a phospate group to $CheY$. As a consequence, the tumbling frequency is lowered.

Since the attractant (L) reduces the activity of X, there is the *methylation* mechanism to switch on again the chemical group. An enzyme $CheR$ adds at constant rate a methyl group to the XL complex, which becomes X_m and restarts behaving as X. The methyl group is removed by the enzyme $CheB$, which is influenced by X that, adding a phosphoryl group to $CheB$, makes it more active, constituting a *negative feedback loop*: the higher is the activity of X, the higher is that of $CheB$, which, in turn, reduces the activity of X. Exact adaptation is achieved because of the feedback circuit: the increased methylation of X precisely balances the reduction in activity caused by the attractant.

In Table 2 we summarize the chemical reactions of the chemotaxis network, together with rates and initial concentrations. The Petri net of the reaction network is in Fig. 7. By computing the steady state for $CheY_P$ we find that it

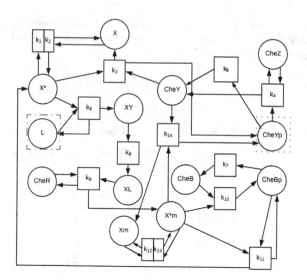

Fig. 7. The Petri nets model for the reaction network of the bacterial chemotaxis network. The input of the network are L (red dot-line), the output is the concentration of $CheYp$ (green dots). (Color figure online)

does not depend on L. Thus, according to our definition, this system is 0-robust on $CheY_P$ with respect to the variation of input L.

We simulated the chemical reactions network using again Dizzy [30]. Some simulation results are shown in Fig. 8. The first sub-figure shows that the bacterium sense the initial concentration of L and reacts by reducing the concentration of $CheY_P$ (and hence the frequency of tumbles). Since the concentration of L does not change over time, the concentration of $CheY_P$ is brought back to its original value. The second sub-figure shows that, as an effect of 0-robustness with respect to the input L, the dynamics of $CheY_P$ is the same even with a different concentration of L. The third sub-figure, instead, shows that by varying the concentration of the enzyme $CheR$, the concentration of $CheY_P$ does not

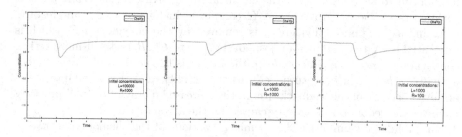

Fig. 8. Graphical results of the simulation of the bacterial chemotaxis. To show how robustness is preserved, we change the concentration of the attractant L, to study how this influences $CheY_P$.

return exactly to the initial value, hence the system is α-robust with $\alpha = 0.3$ when the species considered as input is $CheR$.

Note that the *deficiency* of this network is 3, hence the sufficient condition of [34] cannot be applied.

3.3   Enzyme Activity at Saturation

The well-known Lotka-Volterra reactions [25,26] can be interpreted as abstract chemical reactions and, in fact, they have been proposed to investigate the oscillatory dynamics of autocatalytic enzymes. Similarly, the logistic equation [36] is a model of population growth that is commonly used also in the context of biochemical reaction kinetics. It describes the growth of a population by taking the amount of available environmental resources into account (the *carrying capacity* of the environment) and it is used also to model enzyme dynamics at saturation. In this section we consider an abstract model of enzyme activity inspired by the Lotka-Volterra reactions and the logistic equation (Table 3).

Modeling and Simulation of Enzyme Activity at Saturation. We consider an abstract chemical reaction network in which an enzyme R produces a molecule X. To ensure mass conservation, we add to this idealized example the species Z, which has the role to preserve the concentration of R (i.e. R is never consumed nor produced, but transformed into Z and back).

Table 3. The initial concentrations, the rates and the chemical reactions of enzyme activity at saturation model. The concentration of P, marked by the symbol $\diamond$, can vary to prove the robustness in X.

Initial concentrations	Rates	Chemical reactions
$R = 1000$	$k_1 = 100$	$R + X \xrightarrow{k_1} X + X + Z$
$X = 30$	$k_2 = 10$	$X \xrightarrow{k_2} W$
$Z = 0$	$k_3 = 0.5$	$Z \xrightarrow{k_3} R$
$P = 1 \diamond$	$k_4 = 0.01$	$X + P \xrightarrow{k_4} P + P$
$C = 0$	$k_5 = 0.5$	$P \xrightarrow{k_5} C$
$W = 10$		

As in Lotka-Volterra, the production of X is autocatalytic (the more X are present, the higher is the production rate), but the concentration of enzymes R is limited. Hence, the enzyme activity can easily reach saturation. This reaction system is of the kind typically modeled by the logistic equation. It is expected to reach a dynamic equilibrium in which the concentration of X does not depend on its initial concentration, but only on the concentration of R. We add to this system a molecular species P acting as a "predator" for X (again, as in Lotka-Volterra). Species X can be consumed and transformed into P, by another autocatalytic reaction. In this model it can be interesting to investigate how the initial concentration of P influences the steady state concentration of X.

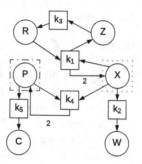

Fig. 9. The Petri nets model for enzyme activity at saturation system. The input of the network is P (red dot line), the output is X (green dots). (Color figure online)

The Petri nets model of the reactions network is shown in Fig. 9, with P as the input and X as the output species. At the steady state, the concentration of X is always constant and its value only loosely depends on the initial concentration of P. We chose $[1, 20000]$ as initial interval marking for P and we found, by the means of simulations, that the concentration reached by X is in the range $[50, 47]$, (see Fig. 10). Therefore, the system is α-robust with $\alpha = 3$ with respect to input P and the considered initial interval marking.

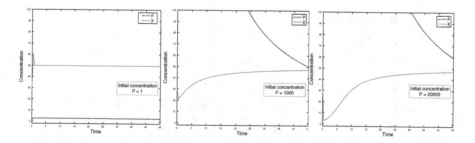

Fig. 10. Graphical results of the enzyme activity at saturation model. We change the concentration of the P to test robustness in X.

4   Conclusions

We proposed the notion of α-robustness with extends the notion of absolute concentration robustness considered in [34,35] with the notion of adaptability [8] in a way that could capture a large class of pathways exhibiting robust behaviours. We illustrated α-robustness with three examples of robust pathways.

As future work, we plan to formulate and study α-robustness by applying the more general methodology proposed by Rizk et al. in [32,33]. Moreover, we will investigate new ways to verify our α-robustness property. For example, we would like to find sufficient conditions under which the property could be verified efficiently, without computing the steady state of the system and without performing simulations in an exhaustive way. This could be obtained, for instance, by adapting conditions already considered in the context of monotonicity analysis of chemical reaction networks [3].

Acknowledgements. This work has been supported by the project "Metodologie informatiche avanzate per l'analisi di dati biomedici" funded by the University of Pisa (PRA_2017_44).

References

1. Uri, A.: An Introduction to Systems Biology: Design Principles of Biological Circuits. CRC Press, Boca Raton (2006)
2. Alur, R., Courcoubetis, C., Henzinger, T.A., Ho, P.-H.: Hybrid automata: an algorithmic approach to the specification and verification of hybrid systems. In: Grossman, R.L., Nerode, A., Ravn, A.P., Rischel, H. (eds.) HS 1991-1992. LNCS, vol. 736, pp. 209–229. Springer, Heidelberg (1993). https://doi.org/10.1007/3-540-57318-6_30
3. Angeli, D., De Leenheer, P., Sontag, E.D.: On the structural monotonicity of chemical reaction networks, pp. 7–12. IEEE (2006)
4. Antoniotti, M., Mishra, B., Piazza, C., Policriti, A., Simeoni, M.: Modeling cellular behavior with hybrid automata: bisimulation and collapsing. In: Priami, C. (ed.) CMSB 2003. LNCS, vol. 2602, pp. 57–74. Springer, Heidelberg (2003). https://doi.org/10.1007/3-540-36481-1_6
5. Barbuti, R., Gori, R., Levi, F., Milazzo, P.: Specialized predictor for reaction systems with context properties. In: International Workshop on Concurrency, Specification and Programming, CS&P 2015, pp. 31–43 (2015)
6. Barbuti, R., Gori, R., Levi, F., Milazzo, P.: Investigating dynamic causalities in reaction systems. Theoret. Comput. Sci. **623**, 114–145 (2016)
7. Barbuti, R., Gori, R., Levi, F., Milazzo, P.: Specialized predictor for reaction systems with context properties. Fundamenta Informaticae **147**(2–3), 173–191 (2016)
8. Barkai, N., Leibler, S.: Robustness in simple biochemical networks. Nature **387**(6636), 913 (1997)
9. Batchelor, E., Goulian, M.: Robustness and the cycle of phosphorylation and dephosphorylation in a two-component regulatory system. Proc. Nat. Acad. Sci. U.S.A. **100**(2), 691–696 (2003)
10. Chabrier, N., Fages, F.: Symbolic model checking of biochemical networks. In: Priami, C. (ed.) CMSB 2003. LNCS, vol. 2602, pp. 149–162. Springer, Heidelberg (2003). https://doi.org/10.1007/3-540-36481-1_13
11. Ciocchetta, F., Hillston, J.: Bio-PEPA: a framework for the modelling and analysis of biological systems. Theoret. Comput. Sci. **410**(33–34), 3065–3084 (2009)

12. Danos, V., Feret, J., Fontana, W., Krivine, J.: Abstract interpretation of cellular signalling networks. In: Logozzo, F., Peled, D.A., Zuck, L.D. (eds.) VMCAI 2008. LNCS, vol. 4905, pp. 83–97. Springer, Heidelberg (2008). https://doi.org/10.1007/978-3-540-78163-9_11

13. Ehrenfeucht, A., Rozenberg, G.: Reaction systems. Fundamenta Informaticae **75**(1–4), 263–280 (2007)

14. Eker, S., Knapp, M., Laderoute, K., Lincoln, P., Meseguer, J., Sonmez, K.: Pathway logic: symbolic analysis of biological signaling. In: Biocomputing 2002, pp. 400–412. World Scientific (2001)

15. Fages, F., Soliman, S.: Abstract interpretation and types for systems biology. Theoret. Comput. Sci. **403**(1), 52–70 (2008)

16. Feinberg, M.: Chemical reaction network structure and the stability of complex isothermal reactors-I. the deficiency zero and deficiency one theorems. Chem. Eng. Sci. **42**(10), 2229–2268 (1987)

17. Gilbert, D., Heiner, M.: From petri nets to differential equations – an integrative approach for biochemical network analysis. In: Donatelli, S., Thiagarajan, P.S. (eds.) ICATPN 2006. LNCS, vol. 4024, pp. 181–200. Springer, Heidelberg (2006). https://doi.org/10.1007/11767589_11

18. Gori, R., Levi, F.: Abstract interpretation based verification of temporal properties for bioambients. Inf. Comput. **208**(8), 869–921 (2010)

19. Goss, P.J.E., Peccoud, J.: Quantitative modeling of stochastic systems in molecular biology by using stochastic petri nets. Proc. Nat. Acad. Sci. U.S.A. **95**(12), 6750–6755 (1998)

20. Henzinger, T.A.: The theory of hybrid automata. In: Inan, M.K., Kurshan, R.P. (eds.) Verification of Digital and Hybrid Systems, pp. 265–292. Springer, Heidelberg (2000). https://doi.org/10.1007/978-3-642-59615-5_13

21. Kitano, H.: Systems biology: towards systems-level understanding of biological systems. In: Kitano, H. (ed.) Foundations of Systems Biology (2002)

22. Kitano, H.: Biological robustness. Nat. Rev. Genet. **5**(11), 826–837 (2004)

23. Kwiatkowska, M., Norman, G., Parker, D.: Using probabilistic model checking in systems biology. ACM SIGMETRICS Perform. Eval. Rev. **35**(4), 14–21 (2008)

24. Li, X., Omotere, O., Qian, L., Dougherty, E.R.: Review of stochastic hybrid systems with applications in biological systems modeling and analysis. EURASIP J. Bioinf. Syst. Biol. **2017**(1), 8 (2017)

25. Linz, P.: Analytical and Numerical Methods for Volterra Equations. SIAM (1985)

26. Lotka, A.J.: Contribution to the theory of periodic reactions. J. Phys. Chem. **14**(3), 271–274 (1910)

27. Nasti, L., Milazzo, P.: A computational model of internet addiction phenomena in social networks. In: Cerone, A., Roveri, M. (eds.) SEFM 2017. LNCS, vol. 10729, pp. 86–100. Springer, Cham (2018). https://doi.org/10.1007/978-3-319-74781-1_7

28. Paun, G.: Introduction to Membrane Computing. Springer, Heidelberg (2006). https://doi.org/10.1007/978-3-642-56196-2

29. Pérez-Jiménez, M.J., Romero-Campero, F.J.: A study of the robustness of the EGFR signalling cascade using continuous membrane systems. In: Mira, J., Álvarez, J.R. (eds.) IWINAC 2005. LNCS, vol. 3561, pp. 268–278. Springer, Heidelberg (2005). https://doi.org/10.1007/11499220_28

30. Ramsey, S., Orrell, D., Bolouri, H.: Dizzy: stochastic simulation of large-scale genetic regulatory networks. J. Bioinf. Comput. Biol. **3**(02), 415–436 (2005)

31. Reddy, V.N., Mavrovouniotis, M.L., Liebman, M.N., et al.: Petri net representations in metabolic pathways. In: ISMB, pp. 328–336 (1993)

32. Rizk, A., Batt, G., Fages, F., Soliman, S.: A general computational method for robustness analysis with applications to synthetic gene networks. Bioinformatics **25**(12), i169–i178 (2009)
33. Rizk, A., Batt, G., Fages, F., Soliman, S.: Continuous valuations of temporal logic specifications with applications to parameter optimization and robustness measures. Theoret. Comput. Sci. **412**(26), 2827–2839 (2011)
34. Shinar, G., Feinberg, M.: Structural sources of robustness in biochemical reaction networks. Science **327**(5971), 1389–1391 (2010)
35. Shinar, G., Feinberg, M.: Design principles for robust biochemical reaction networks: what works, what cannot work, and what might almost work. Mathe. Biosci. **231**(1), 39–48 (2011)
36. Weisstein, E.W.: Logistic equation. From MathWorld-A Wolfram Web Resource. http://mathworld.wolfram.com/LogisticEquation.html

Explaining Successful Docker Images
Using Pattern Mining Analysis

Riccardo Guidotti[1,2(✉)], Jacopo Soldani[1], Davide Neri[1], and Antonio Brogi[1]

[1] University of Pisa, Largo B. Pontecorvo, 3, Pisa, Italy
{riccardo.guidotti,jacopo.soldani,davide.neri,antonio.brogi}@di.unipi.it
[2] KDDLab, ISTI-CNR, Via G. Moruzzi, 1, Pisa, Italy
guidotti@isti.cnr.it

Abstract. Docker is on the rise in today's enterprise IT. It permits shipping applications inside portable containers, which run from so-called Docker images. Docker images are distributed in public registries, which also monitor their popularity. The popularity of an image directly impacts on its usage, and hence on the potential revenues of its developers. In this paper, we present a frequent pattern mining-based approach for understanding how to improve an image to increase its popularity. The results in this work can provide valuable insights to Docker image providers, helping them to design more competitive software products.

1 Introduction

Docker images are the de-facto standard for container-based virtualization in enterprise IT [16]. The aim of container-based virtualization is to provide a simple yet powerful solution for running software applications in isolated virtual environments called *containers* [23]. Containers have faster start-up time and less overhead than other existing visualization approaches, like virtual machines [12]. Docker permits building, shipping, and running applications inside portable containers. Docker containers run from Docker images, which are the read-only templates used to create them. A Docker image packages a software together with all the dependencies needed to run it (e.g., binaries, libraries).

Docker also provides the ability to distribute and search images through so-called *Docker registries*. Through Docker registries any developer can create and distribute its own created images, so that other users have at their disposal plentiful repositories of heterogeneous, ready-to-use images. In this scenario, public registries as the official Docker Hub are playing a central role in the distribution of Docker images.

DOCKERFINDER [4] enhances the support for searching Docker images. DOCKERFINDER allows to search for images based on multiple attributes. These attributes include (but are not limited to) the name and size of an image, its popularity within the Docker community (measured in terms of so-called *pulls* and *stars*), the operating system distribution they are based on, and the software distributions they support (e.g., java 1.8 or python 2.7). DOCKERFINDER

M. Mazzara et al. (Eds.): STAF 2018 Workshops, LNCS 11176, pp. 98–113, 2018.
https://doi.org/10.1007/978-3-030-04771-9_9

automatically crawls all such information from the Docker Hub and by directly inspecting the Docker containers that run from images. In this way, DOCKER-FINDER builds its own dataset of Docker images.

The popularity of an image directly impacts on its usage [15]. Understanding the reputation and usage of an image is important as for every other kind of open-source software. The higher is the usage and the endorsement of an open-source software, the higher are the chances of revenue from related products/services, the self-marketing and the peer recognition for its developers [10].

The main objective of this paper is to understand which are the *rules* characterizing the patterns leading to popular images both in terms of registered pulls and explicit endorsement from the users. With pattern we refer to the typical image composition in terms of operating system distribution, installed softwares, number of layers, size of the image, etc. In order to perform pattern analysis we develop an accurate data-to-model transformation, which considers the possible data types and distributions of variables. Finally, we extract itemsets and rules using the well known FP-Growth algorithm [8].

The analysis of such rules and itemsets highlights that most of the Docker images follow rules which are very common but that do not lead to a consistent level of popularity, while some rules only used by a small portion of the images are very stable and predictive of high level of popularity both in terms of pulls and stars. Moreover, most of the rules leading to the highest success are satisfied only by images officially supporting commercialized software distributions, and as we proof in the experiments this does not happen by chance.

The rest of the paper is organized as follows. Section 2 provides background on Docker. Section 3 formalizes the data type, the data transformation and the popularity rules used to study Docker images. Section 4 presents a dataset of Docker images and the analysis illustrating the main patterns hidden in the data. Sections 5 and 6 discuss related work and draw some concluding remarks.

2   Background

Docker is a platform for running applications in isolated user-space instances, called *containers*. Each Docker *container* packages the applications to run, along with all the software support they need (e.g., libraries, binaries, etc.).

Containers are built by instantiating so-called Docker *images*, which can be seen as read-only templates providing all instructions needed for creating and configuring a container (e.g., software distributions to be installed, folders/files to be created). A Docker image is made up of multiple file systems layered over each other. A new Docker image can be created by loading an existing image (called *parent* image), by performing updates to that image, and by committing the updates. The commit will create a new image, made up of all the layers of its parent image plus one, which stores the committed updates.

Existing Docker images are distributed through Docker *registries*, with the Docker Hub (hub.docker.com) being the main registry for all Docker users. Inside a registry, images are stored in *repositories*, and each repository can contain multiple Docker images. A repository is usually associated to a given software (e.g., *Java*), and the Docker images contained in such repository are different versions of such software (e.g., *jre7, jdk7, open-jdk8*, etc.). Repositories are divided in two main classes, namely *official* repositories (devoted to curated sets of images, packaging trusted software releases—e.g., *Java, NodeJS, Redis*) and *non-official* repositories, which contain software developed by Docker users.

The success and popularity of a repository in the Docker Hub can be measured twofold. The number of *pulls* associated to a repository provides information on its actual usage. This is because whenever an image is downloaded from the Docker Hub, the number of pulls of the corresponding repository is increased by one. The number of *stars* associated to a repository instead provides significant information on how much the community likes it. Each user can indeed "star" a repository, in the very same way as eBay buyers can "star" eBay sellers.

DOCKERFINDER is a tool for searching for Docker images based on a larger set of information with respect to the Docker Hub. DOCKERFINDER automatically builds the description of Docker images by retrieving the information available in the Docker Hub, and by extracting additional information by inspecting the Docker containers. The Docker image descriptions built by DOCKERFINDER are stored in a JSON format[1], and can be retrieved through its GUI or HTTP API.

Among all information retrieved by DOCKERFINDER, in this work we shall consider the size of images, the operating system and software distributions they support, the number of layers composing an image, and the number of pulls and stars associated to images. A formalization of the data structures considered is provided in the next section. Moreover, in the experimental section we will also observe different results for official and non-official images.

3   Proposed Analytical Model

We hereafter provide a formal representation of Docker images, and we then illustrate how to model docker patterns and popularity/endorsement rules.

A *Docker image* can be represented as a tuple indicating the operating system it supports, the number of layers forming the image, its compressed and actual size, and the set of software distributions it supports. For the sake of readability, we shall denote with $\mathbb{U}_{os}$ the finite universe of existing operating system distributions (e.g., "Alpine Linux v3.4", "Ubuntu 16.04.1 LTS"), and with $\mathbb{U}_{sw}$ the finite universe of existing software distributions (e.g., "java", "python").

Definition 1 (Image). *Let $\mathbb{U}_{os}$ be the finite universe of operating system distributions and $\mathbb{U}_{sw}$ be the finite universe of software distributions. We define a Docker image I as a tuple $I = \langle os, layers, size_d, size_a, \mathcal{S} \rangle$ where*

- *$os \in \mathbb{U}_{os}$ is the operating system distribution supported by the image I,*
- *$layers \in \mathbb{N}$ is the number of layers stacked to build the image I,*

---

[1] An example of raw Docker image data is available at https://goo.gl/hibue1.

- $size_d \in \mathbb{R}$ is the download size[2] of I,
- $size_a \in \mathbb{R}$ is the actual size[3] of I, and
- $\mathcal{S} \subseteq \mathbb{U}_{sw}$ is the set of software distributions supported by the image I.

A concrete example of a Docker image I is the following

$I = \langle$Ubuntu 16.04 LTS, 6, 0.78, 1.23, {python,perl,curl,wget,tar}$\rangle$

A *repository* contains multiple Docker images, and it stores the amount of pulls and stars associated to the images it contains. The pulls highlights the popularity of a repository, while the stars its endorsement. The main difference between pulls and stars is that stars are a *direct* appreciation of the users, while pulls are an *indirect* appreciation because a repository can be downloaded but not appreciated.

Definition 2 (Repository). *Let $\mathbb{U}_I$ be the universe of available Docker images. We define a* repository *of images as a triple $R = \langle p, s, \mathcal{I} \rangle$ where*

- $p \in \mathbb{R}$ *is the number (in millions) of pulls from the repository R,*
- $s \in \mathbb{N}$ *is the number of stars assigned to the repository R, and*
- $\mathcal{I} \subseteq \mathbb{U}_I$ *is the set of images contained in the repository R.*

For each repository, the number of pulls and stars is not directly associated with a specific image, but it refers to the overall repository. We hence define the notion of *imager*, viz., an image that can be used as a "representative image" for a repository. An imager essentially links the pulls and stars of a repository with the characteristic of an image contained in such repository.

Definition 3 (Imager). *Let $R = \langle p, s, \mathcal{I} \rangle$ be a repository, and let $I = \langle os, layers, size_d, size_a, \mathcal{S} \rangle \in \mathcal{I}$ be one of the images contained in R. We define an* imager I_R *as a tuple directly associating the pulls and stars of R with I, viz.,*

$$I_R = \langle p, s, I \rangle = \langle p, s, \langle os, layers, size_d, size_a, \mathcal{S} \rangle \rangle.$$

A concrete example of imager I_R is the following: $I_R = \langle$1.3, 1678, $\langle$Ubuntu 16.04 LTS, 6, 0.7, 1.2, {python,perl,curl,wget}$\rangle\rangle$. It is worth highlighting that an imager can be formed by picking any image I contained in R, provided that I can be considered a "medoid" [24] representing the set of images contained in R.

In order to perform frequent pattern mining analysis on imagers, we must "flatten" their representation and turn them into itemsets [1,24]. We hence provide a translation from the tuple representing an imager into a set of items, taken from discrete domains. The latter also means that the numerical domains of pulls, stars, layers and sizes have to be discretized into intervals, which will be considered instead of the concrete numeric values. The notion of *imagerset* is defined precisely to accomplish to this purpose.

---

[2] As images are downloaded as compressed archives, their download size correspond to their compressed size (in GBs).

[3] The actual size of an image corresponds to its decompressed size (in GBs).

Definition 4 (Imagerset). *Let* $I_R = \langle p, s, I \rangle = \langle p, s, \langle os, layers, size_d, size_a, S \rangle \rangle$ *be an imager. Let also* $\mathbb{P}$, $\mathbb{S}$, $\mathbb{L}$, $\mathbb{S}_b$, $\mathbb{S}_a$ *be the discretizations of the numeric domains of pulls, stars, layers, download sizes and compressed sizes, respectively. The* imagerset I_R *corresponding to* I_R *is defined as follows:* $I_R = \{\overline{p}\} \cup \{\overline{s}\} \cup \{\overline{os}\} \cup \{\overline{layers}\} \cup \{\overline{size_d}\} \cup \{\overline{size_a}\} \cup S$ *where* $\overline{x}$ *denotes the interval corresponding to the value* x *in its discretized domain (e.g.,* $\overline{p}$ *denotes the class* p *in* $\mathbb{P}$).

According to this definition, and assuming a given discretization, the previous imager I_R taken as example becomes the following imagerset I_R:

$$I_R = \{1.0 \leq p < 3.0, 1200 \leq s < 1800, \texttt{Ubuntu 16.04 LTS}, \\ 5 \leq layers < 10, 0.4 \leq size_d < 0.8, 1.0 \leq size_a < 1.5, \\ \texttt{python}, \texttt{perl}, \texttt{curl}, \texttt{wget}\}.$$

Imagersets can then be exploited to determine popularity patterns, expressed as rules determining the popularity of an imager based on its technical contents. Following [1,24], each rule is of type $X \rightarrow y$, where X is an itemset containing an operating system distribution, a class of layers, a compressed size, a download size and/or a set of supported software distribution. y is instead the popularity of an imager, expressed in terms of either pulls or stars.

Definition 5 (Popularity Rule). *Let* $\mathbb{P}$, $\mathbb{S}$, $\mathbb{L}$, $\mathbb{S}_b$, $\mathbb{S}_a$ *be the discretizations of the numeric domains of pulls, stars, layers, download sizes and compressed sizes, respectively. A* pulls popularity rule *is a pattern* $X \rightarrow y$ *where*

- $X \subseteq \mathbb{U}_{os} \cup \mathbb{L} \cup \mathbb{S}_b \cup \mathbb{S}_a \cup \mathbb{U}_{sw}$ *is an itemset, and*
- $y \in \mathbb{P}$ *is the popularity level expressed as pulls.*

A stars popularity rule *is defined analogously (with* $y \in \mathbb{S}$).

We will now exploit our modelling to analyse concrete data.

3.1 Implementing Models Transformation

In order to transform the continuous attributes $size_d, size_a, p, s$ into corresponding, discretized intervals, it is important to consider their distributions. Indeed, these attributes have a long tailed distribution with few imagers having a small set of high values, while most of the imagers are characterized by a large and various set of low values. A traditional *natural binning* [24] would result in a discretization placing most of different low values in the long tail in a single bin. This would annihilate any difference, hence resulting in a biased data model.

In order to overcome this issue we exploit the "knee method" [24] that first sorts a variable x, then considers the curve described by the sorted x, and after that it selects a threshold point pt on such curve. The latter is the point having the maximum distance from the closest point on the straight line passing through the minimum and the maximum values of x on the considered curve (examples in Fig. 2). We can then apply the natural binning only on the values lower than the threshold pt, as on these values the long tail distribution effect is less present or not present at all. Finally, the set of obtained bins is extended by including an additional bin containing all the values higher than the threshold pt.

3.2   Implementing Pattern Extraction

The transformation described in the previous section allows us to turn a given set of imagers $I_R^{\{\}} = \{I_{R1}, ..., I_{Rn}\}$ into a set of imagersets $\mathsf{I}_R^{\{\}} = \{\mathsf{I}_{R1}, ..., \mathsf{I}_{Rn}\}$. This transformation enables the usage of common algorithms for frequent pattern mining like Apriori, Eclat and FP-Growth [1,8,24]. All these approaches extract the rules form the retrieved frequent itemsets. Since we are interested in analyzing also the frequent itemsets besides the popularity rules we do not considers algorithms able to directly extract rules that have a strong relationship with a target attribute (i.e., the popularity in our case) such as algorithms for subgroup discovery [11] and contrast sets detection [2].

Given as input a set of sets of items (viz., $\mathsf{I}_R^{\{\}}$), such algorithms can be exploited to determine *(i)* the set of *itemsets* whose *support* σ is higher or equal than a user defined threshold *min_sup*, and *(ii)* the set of *rules* whose *confidence* c is higher or equal than a user defined threshold *min_conf*.

Given an itemset X, its support $\sigma(\mathsf{X})$ with respect to a set of imagersets $\mathsf{I}_R^{\{\}}$ is defined as the proportion of imagers that contain the itemset X [24], namely $\sigma(\mathsf{X}) = \frac{|\{\mathsf{I}_R \in \mathsf{I}_R^{\{\}} \mid \mathsf{X} \subseteq \mathsf{I}_R\}|}{|\mathsf{I}_R^{\{\}}|}$. The confidence of a rule instead indicates how often such rule is true. Given a rule $\mathsf{X} \to y$, its confidence $c(\mathsf{X} \to y)$ with respect to a set of imagersets $\mathsf{I}_R^{\{\}}$ is defined as the proportion of the imagers that contains X which also contains y. We recall that, in this paper, we shall consider popularity rules, i.e., $y \in \mathbb{P} \cup \mathbb{S}$. $c(\mathsf{X} \to y) = \frac{\sigma(\mathsf{X} \cup \{y\})}{\sigma(\mathsf{X})}$. We also recall two indicators that can be observed from the output of the above mentioned algorithms, viz., *coverage* and *lift*. The rule *coverage* is the proportion of records that satisfy the antecedent X of a rule: $coverage(\mathsf{X} \to y) = \sigma(\mathsf{X})$. The *lift* is the ratio of the support to that expected if X and y were independent: $lift(\mathsf{X} \to y) - \frac{\sigma(\mathsf{X} \cup \{y\})}{\sigma(\mathsf{X}) \cdot \sigma(y)}$. A lift equals to 1 implies that the probability of occurrence of the antecedent and that of the consequent are independent of each other. A lift strictly higher than 1 indicates the degree to which those two occurrences are dependent on one another, and makes the rule potentially useful for predicting the popularity.

It is finally worth recalling the definition of two particular types of itemsets, as they will be used in the following section. An itemset X is *maximal* if none of its supersets has a support greater or equal than *min_sup*, while it is *closed* if all its supersets have a lower support than $\sigma(\mathsf{X})$. We will not consider normal frequent itemsets, because maximal and closed itemsets generalize and capture variegate compositions while maintaining a better/higher level of support.

4   Experiments

4.1   Dataset and Experimental Setting

DOCKERFINDER autonomously collects information on all the images available in the Docker Hub that are contained in official repositories or in repositories that have been starred by at least three different users. The datasets collected by DOCKERFINDER[4] ranges from January 2017 to March 2018 at irregular intervals. If not differently specified in this work we refer to the most recent backup where 132,724 images are available. Since performing frequent pattern mining with the aim of understanding the rules leading to successful imagers requires a notion of popularity, i.e., pulls or stars, from the available images we select 1,067 imagers considering for each repository the "latest" image. We leave as future work the investigation of the effect of considering other extraction of imagers. Some examples can be the smallest image, the one with more softwares, or a medoid or centroid of each repository.

Table 1. Statistics of imagers: median $\tilde{x}$, mean μ and standard deviation σ.

	$size_d$	$size_a$	$layers$	$|\mathcal{S}|$	$pulls$	$stars$
$\tilde{x}$	0.16	0.41	10.00	8.00	0.06	26.0
μ	0.27	0.64	12.67	7.82	6.70	134.46
σ	0.48	1.11	9.62	2.26	46.14	564.21

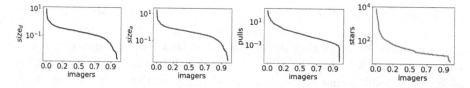

Fig. 1. Semilog distribution of $size_d$, $size_a$, pulls and stars.

Statistical details of the imagers extracted from the principal dataset analyzed can be found in Table 1. As anticipated in the previous section, $size_d$, $size_a$, p and s follow a long tailed distribution highlighted by the large difference between the median $\tilde{x}$ and the mean μ in Table 1. The power-law effect is stronger for *pulls* and *stars* (see Fig. 1). There is a robust Pearson correlation between pulls and stars of 0.76 (p-value 1.5e−165). However, saying that a high number of pulls implies a high number of stars (or vice versa) could be a tall statement. For this reason we report experiments for both popularity measures. There are no other relevant correlations. We highlight that there are 50 different *os* and the most common ones are Debian GNU/Linux 8 (jessie), Ubuntu 14.04.5 LTS and Alpine Linux v3.4. The six most common software distributions among the 28 available (without considering the version) are erl, tar, bash, perl, wget, curl, and they appear in more than 55% of the imagers. In order to avoid considering the obvious itemsets always containing such software distributions, we remove them for the imagers.

Figure 2 highlights the long tail of the aforementioned variables and which is the portion of data used for the bin containing the highest values (left of the

---

[4] Publicly available at https://goo.gl/ggvKN3.

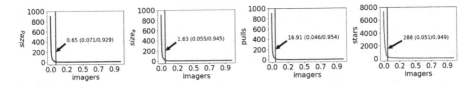

Fig. 2. Knee method effect. Numbers in parentheses indicate data used for the bin of the highest values (left) and all the rest using equal width binning (right).

parentheses) and all the rest using equal width binning (right of the parentheses). This operation removes the bias before the discretization that can be applied with natural binning on more than 94% of the variables. On the other hand, the number of *layers* and the number of softwares $|\mathcal{S}|$ do not suffer of this problem and thus can be directly discretized (see Fig. 3).

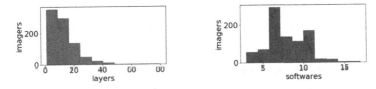

Fig. 3. Distributions of the number of layers (left) and of that of softwares (right).

The imagers to imagerset transformation and the cleaning steps return an imagerset $I_R^{\{\}}$ with an average imagerset size $|I_R|$ of $19.05 + 6.32$. We underline that the high variability of the imagersets is given by the softwares components $\mathcal{S}$ as all the other characteristics are fixed. These imagersets $I_R^{\{\}}$ are given in input to a frequent pattern mining algorithm.

Since we do not focus on particular types of itemsets or rules, a "classic" pattern mining algorithm is suitable for assessing this task. Even though performance is not an issue in this application, among the existing frequent pattern mining algorithms we selected *FP-Growth* as from the state-of-the-art it shown to have the best performances [8]. Thus, it would be the best choice in presence of larger datasets. Other pattern mining algorithms would have returned very similar results. We leave the study of the impact of the selected frequent pattern mining algorithm for future works. In particular, we used the FP-Growth Python implementation of the pyfim library[5]. As threshold parameters we fixed $min\_sup = 0.05$ and $min\_conf = 0.1$. We exploited such low values because we are interested not only in unveiling the most common patterns and rules, but especially those leading to the highest target values in terms of pulls and stars.

---

[5] http://www.borgelt.net/pyfim.html.

4.2   Pattern Mining Analysis

We hereby report on some of the most interesting results of the frequent pattern mining analysis performed specifically for itemsets and popularity rules[6].

Itemsets. FP-Growth with $min\_sup = 0.05$ retrieved 21 maximal itemsets and 45 closed itemsets having at least three components (i.e., $|X| \geq 3$).

```
{0.0037 ≤ size_a < 0.0993, 0.0019 ≤ size_d < 0.0419, httpd, ash, unzip} (0.1047)
{ping, git, python} (0.0956)
{pip, git, python} (0.0853)
{ping, unzip, python} (0.0751)
{npm, node, git, python} (0.0728)
{9 ≤ softwares < 10, Debian GNU/Linux 8 (jessie), git, python} (0.0660)
{java, Debian GNU/Linux 8 (jessie), unzip} (0.0648)
{Alpine Linux v3.4, httpd, ash, unzip} (0.0637)
{java, git, unzip, python} (0.0626)
{3 ≤ layers < 5, ash, unzip} (0.0569)
```

Fig. 4. Maximal itemsets top ten sorted by support.

```
{httpd, ash, unzip} (0.1695)
{0.0019 ≤ size_d < 0.0419, ash, unzip} (0.1286)
{0.0037 ≤ size_a < 0.0993, ash, unzip} (0.1251)
{0.0037 ≤ size_a < 0.0993, 0.0019 ≤ size_d < 0.0419, ash, unzip} (0.1229)
{git, unzip, python} (0.1229)
{Debian GNU/Linux 8 (jessie), git, python} (0.1149)
{0.0019 ≤ size_d < 0.0419, httpd, ash, unzip} (0.1104)
{0.0037 ≤ size_a < 0.0993, httpd, ash, unzip} (0.1069)
{0.0037 ≤ size_a < 0.0993, 0.0019 <= size < 0.0419, httpd, ash, unzip} (0.1047)
{9 ≤ |S| < 10, git, python} (0.1035)
```

Fig. 5. Closed itemsets top ten sorted by support.

Figures 4 and 5 report the top ten of the extracted patterns sorted by decreasing support σ (in parentheses, on the right). We underline that in these itemsets we do not consider pulls and stars as they are accurately analyzed in the popularity rules. We can notice that the closed itemset {httpd, ash, unzip} has a high support and it is contained in the maximal itemsets. Thus, it is a very typical and common pattern. Something similar happens for the pair {git, python}.

Some itemsets are also augmented with $9 \leq |S| < 10$, signaling that very commonly there are nine softwares and among them, besides the very common six filtered out, there are also git and python. Other common softwares combinations can be read in Fig. 4. By looking at sizes, we find $0.0037 \leq size_a < 0.0993$, $0.0019 \leq size_d < 0.0419$. This highlights that many Docker images are "light images" with an average compression ratio of 0.4. Finally, we underline that the maximal itemsets are more related to the software composition, while the closed

---

[6] The python code and the list of all the itemsets and popularity rules extracted can be found at https://github.com/di-unipi-socc/DockerImageMiner.

itemsets to the Docker images size. Furthermore, `java`, one of the most common programming language and tool is present only in two of reported and most supported itemsets. The reason could be that a key feature of Docker images is lightness that is generally not a prerogative of `java`.

Popularity Rules. Using FP-Growth with $min\_sup = 0.05$ and $min\_conf = 0.1$ and considering only rules having the antecedent part containing at least three components (i.e., $|X| \geq 3$), we extracted $9,325$ popularity rules where the target is the number of pulls $y \in \mathbb{P}$, and $12,900$ where the target is the number of stars $y \in \mathbb{S}$. In the following we analyze these rules with respect to the indicators previously presented (confidence and lift) and also by focusing only the rules predicting the highest values of popularity in terms of both pulls and stars. Confidence and lift are reported in the parentheses following this order.

```
{0.00 ≤ p < 0.07} ←  {8 ≤ |S| < 9, ping, unzip, python} (1.00, 1.94)
{0.00 ≤ p < 0.07} ←  {10 ≤ |S| < 11, pip, git, unzip, python} (1.00, 1.94)
{0.00 ≤ p < 0.07} ←  {Ubuntu 16.04.2 LTS, git, python} (1.00, 1.94)
{0.00 ≤ p < 0.07} ←  {size_d > 0.6419, java, git, unzip} (0.94, 1.83)
{0.00 ≤ p < 0.07} ←  {size_d > 0.6419, java, git, unzip, python} (0.93, 1.82)
```

Fig. 6. Pulls popularity rules top five sorted by confidence (first value in parentheses).

```
{13 ≤ s < 19} ←  {0.2019 ≤ size_d < 0.2419, ping, unzip} (0.77, 2.39)
{13 ≤ s < 19} ←  {0.5774 ≤ size_a < 0.6730, 10 ≤ layers < 12} (0.72, 2.23)
{13 ≤ s < 19} ←  {0.0819 ≤ size_d < 0.1219, 5 ≤ |S| < 6, python} (0.71, 2.19)
{13 ≤ s < 19} ←  {10 ≤ |S| < 11, size_d > 0.6419, unzip} (0.70, 2.15)
{13 ≤ s < 19} ←  {0.9599 ≤ size_a < 1.0555, ping} (0.70, 2.15)
```

Fig. 7. Stars popularity rules top five sorted by confidence (first value in parentheses).

Figures 6 and 7 illustrate the five most interesting rules among the ten popularity rules with the highest confidence sorted by decreasing confidence[7]. We recall that pulls are expressed in millions. The first thing we notice is that these rules with high confidence predict low popularity levels. Thus, the most common Docker image building patterns among Docker images developers perhaps do not lead to good results in terms of popularity. This confirms the idea that many users design Docker images for private usage and they are not interested in obtaining a public recognition. A second interesting aspect is that the pull popularity rules have a higher confidence than the stars popularity rules and in general (not only looking at these top fives), stars popularity rules involves the image sizes ($size_a, size_d$). Hence, pulls popularity rules are more common than stars popularity rules and they are generated by different patterns of image development. This observation is confirmed by the data because the intersection of the imagersets covered by the stars popularity rules which are covered also by the pull popularity rules is only 0.09. Moreover, since stars are given as a direct endorsement it means that image size is a very relevant aspect for Docker users.

---

[7] We discarded very similar rules in order to have a broader overview.

Even though confidence highlights common rules, it does not provide an indication of how much these rules are reliable. Indeed, all the rules reported in Figs. 6 and 7 have a high confidence but a low positive lift. This indicates that the imagerset composition suggested by the itemset X is not very predictive of the outcome y. To overcome this limitation we analyze in Figs. 8 and 9 the five most interesting rules among the ten popularity rules with the highest confidence sorted by decreasing lift. This time we can observe rules with a markedly high lift and a low confidence. By analyzing the target we notice that these rules predict high values (not the maximum value) of both pulls and stars. Hence, the rules, and consequently the patterns, which are predictors of a certain degree of success, cover less imagerset but are strongly more stable than those covering many imagerset with low popularity. The content of the itemsets of the reported rules, both for pulls and stars, is mainly related to the software composition and it is very common among the two sets of rules. The indication of these rules, which are markedly different from the previous ones, is that assembling a Docker image with these characteristics, i.e., Ubuntu 14.04.5 LTS, nginx, ping, unzip, python, ruby and an actual size of about 500MB may provide a good level of success in the community of Docker users.

$\{8.47 \le p < 8.55\} \leftarrow$ {nginx, ping, unzip, python} (0.11, 97.66)
$\{8.47 \le p < 8.55\} \leftarrow$ {Ubuntu 14.04.5 LTS, ping, git, unzip, python} (0.11, 97.66)
$\{8.47 \le p < 8.55\} \leftarrow \{0.5774 \le size_a < 0.6730,$ ping, git} (0.11, 97.66)
$\{8.47 \le p < 8.55\} \leftarrow$ {ruby, ping, git, unzip, python} (0.11, 97.66)
$\{1.69 \le p < 1.77\} \leftarrow \{0.3862 \le size_a < 0.4818,\ 5 \le layers < 7\}$ (0.11, 97.66)

Fig. 8. Pulls popularity rules top five sorted by lift (second value in parentheses).

$\{256 \le s < 263\} \leftarrow$ {nginx, ping, unzip, python} (0.11, 97.66)
$\{256 \le s < 263\} \leftarrow$ {Ubuntu 14.04.5 LTS, ping, git, unzip, python} (0.11, 97.66)
$\{256 \le s < 263\} \leftarrow \{0.5774 \le size_a < 0.6730,$ ping, git} (0.11, 97.66)
$\{256 \le s < 263\} \leftarrow$ {ruby, ping, unzip, python} (0.11, 97.66)
$\{256 \le s < 263\} \leftarrow$ {ruby, ping, unzip} (0.11, 97.66)

Fig. 9. Stars popularity rules top five sorted by lift (second value in parentheses).

Up to this point we filtered the popularity rules with respect to confidence and lift, letting emerge the most common patterns. We now wish to understand which are the itemsets leading to the highest values of pulls and stars. We report in Figs. 10 and 11 the five rules with the highest lift returning the highest values of pulls and stars, i.e., $p > 16.72$ and $s > 283$ respectively. Note that these values are those retrieved by the knee method in the imageset to imagerset transformation. First of all, we highlight that for the first time we have a high presence of the number of layers and the number of softwares of component of the itemsets. Therefore, these elements are becoming particularly interesting in defining very popular and successful images. Secondly, we notice that these rules have a confidence a bit higher than the previous set of rules observed, but also a lift coefficient markedly lower. Thus, the predictive power of these rules leading to the maximum success is not as strong as the one of the rules with the highest lift. This is because the consequence of such a success is not entirely related to the image composition but rather depends on other external and not observed factors. Something we can observe for the data we have is the fact that an imagerset is generated from an image of an official or not official repository. Examples of official images are `alpine`, `ubuntu`, `mongo`, `postgres`, `openjdk`, etc.

We underline that respecting the reported popularity rules does not automatically imply a certain degree of popularity. In other words, it is not sufficient to assemble a Docker image as described by the rules extracted to ensure successful images, as there are some external factors that can undoubtedly affect the popularity, e.g., whether a repository is official or not, or whether it uses novel, upgraded software distributions.

```
{p > 16.72} ← {3 ≤ |S| < 4, 0.12 ≤ size_d < 0.16} (0.4444, 9.3016)
{p > 16.72} ← {0.1949 ≤ size_a < 0.2906, 0.0819 ≤ size_d < 0.1219, ash, unzip} (0.33, 6.97)
{p > 16.72} ← {3 ≤ |S| < 4, 3 ≤ layers < 5} (0.33, 6.97)
{p > 16.72} ← {Debian GNU/Linux 9 (stretch), java, unzip} (0.33, 6.97)
{p > 16.72} ← {0.2906 ≤ size_a < 0.3862, 0.1219 ≤ size_d < 0.1619, 7 ≤ layers < 10} (0.25, 5.23)
```

Fig. 10. Pulls popularity rules predicting the highest value of pulls.

```
{s > 283} ← {Debian GNU/Linux 9 (stretch), java, unzip} (0.44, 8.31)
{s > 283} ← {0.1949 ≤ size_a < 0.2906, 3 ≤ layers < 5} (0.33, 6.23)
{s > 283} ← {0.2419 ≤ size_d < 0.2819, 8 ≤ |S| < 9, git, python} (0.33, 6.23)
{s > 283} ← {3 ≤ |S| < 4, 0.1219 ≤ size_d < 0.1619} (0.33, 6.23)
{s > 283} ← {Alpine Linux v3.7, 0.0037 ≤ size_a < 0.0993, 0.0019 ≤ size_d < 0.0419,
              ash, unzip} (0.27, 5.10)
```

Fig. 11. Stars popularity rules predicting the highest value of stars.

In order to quantitatively assess this point we perform an experiment using a null random model. We randomly select 1000 times 10 rules among all those extracted, both for pulls and stars. Then we calculate the average coverage of the selected rules among all the imagerset and among the imagerset referring only to official repositories. Finally, we compare these numbers with the average coverage of the ten rules with the highest lift returning the highest values of pulls and stars. Results are reported in Table 2. Both for pulls and stars a random selection of rules has a coverage considerably lower than the selection of the rules leading to maximum popularity values for official repositories. On the other hand, this phenomenon is not registered when all the repositories are considered. In conclusion, we can state that official repositories follow the rules reported in Figs. 10 and 11 not by chance and that in general they are less followed than a random selection of rules. Hence, despite the low values of confidence and rules, the rules reported in Figs. 10 and 11 are part of the reasons why official repositories are more successful besides hidden and unobserved factors.

Table 2. Comparison of average coverage (± standard deviation) between random selection of rules and rule predicting the maximum popularity values for all the repositories and for official repositories for pulls and stars.

	Pulls		Stars	
	All repositories	Officials	All repositories	Officials
Random	0.18 ± 0.45	0.14 ± 0.38	0.17 ± 0.44	0.14 ± 0.37
Max popularity	0.11 ± 0.39	0.59 ± 0.79	0.12 ± 0.44	0.83 ± 1.15

5   Related Work

The estimation and analysis of popularity of Docker images resembles the analysis of success performed in various other domains.

A well-known domain is related to quantifying the changes in impact and productivity throughout a research career in science. [26] defines a model for the citation dynamics of scientific papers. The results uncover the basic mechanisms that govern scientific impact, and they also offer reliable measures of influence that may have potential policy implications. [20] points out that, besides dependent variables, also contextual information (e.g., prestige of institutions, supervisors, teaching and mentoring activities) should be considered. The latter holds also in our context, where we can observe that official images behave differently with respect to non-official images. Sinatra et al. [22] recently designed a stochastic model that assigns an individual parameter to each scientist that accurately predicts the evolution of her impact, from her h-index to cumulative citations, and independent recognitions (e.g., prizes). The above mentioned approaches analyze the success phenomena by assuming the existence of a mathematical formulation that try to fit on the data. In our proposal, we are not looking for just an indicator but for an explainable complex model that not only permits analyzing a population, but also to reveal suggestions for improvements.

Another domain of research where the analysis of success is relevant is sport. In [3] the level of competitive balance of the roles within the four major North American professional sport leagues is investigated. The evidence in [3] suggests that the significance of star power is uncovered only by multiplicative models (rather than by the commonly employed linear ones). As shown by our experiments, this holds also in our context, where we explain with multi typical items the co-occurrences and interdependencies that lead to a certain level of popularity or endorsement. In [5], Franck et al. provide further evidence on contextual factors, by showing that the emergence of superstars in German soccer depends not only on their investments in physical talent, but also on the cultivation of their popularity. An analysis of impact of technical features on performances of soccer teams is provided in [17]. The authors find that draws are difficult to predict, but they obtain good results in simulating (and consequently quantifying) the overall championships. Instead, the authors of [18] try to understand which are the features driving human evaluation with respect to performance in soccer.

Another field of research where the study of success and popularity is quite useful is that one of online social networks, like Facebook, Instagram, Twitter, Youtube, etc. The authors of [14] propose a method to predict the popularity of new hashtags on Twitter using standard classification models trained on content features extracted from the hashtag and on context features extracted from the social graph. The difference with our approach is that we try to extract patterns to explain the reasons of a certain degree of popularity. For understanding the ingredients of success of fashion models, the authors of [19] train machine learning methods on Instagram images to predict new popular models. Instead, in [25] a regression method to estimate the popularity of an online video (from YouTube or Facebook) measured in terms of its number of views is presented. Results show that, despite the visual content can be useful for popularity prediction before content publication, the social context represents a much stronger signal for predicting the popularity of a video.

Closer to our context, some forms of analytics have been recently applied to GitHub repositories. The authors of [27] study GitHub software version evolution by developers' activities. They define four metrics to measure commit activity and code evolution and then they adopt visualization techniques to analyze the commit logs. The authors of [28] instead study popularity of GitHub developers on a sociological basis. The study is based on follow-networks built according to the follow behavior among developers in GitHub, which allows to the authors of [28] to identify and present a set of typical patterns determining a growth of developers' popularity in social coding networks. The contextual dimension given by the social network is considered in [28] find an explosive growth of the users in GitHub and construct follow-networks according to the follow behaviors among developers in GitHub. Using this network delineates four typical social behavior patterns. Further domains where the analysis and prediction of success is a challenging task are music [6,7,21], movies [13] and school performances [9]. However, to the best of our knowledge, our approach is the first that is based on complex descriptions such as those of Docker images, and which tries to understand the reasons of popularity and endorsement.

6 Conclusion

In this paper we have proposed a methodology based on frequent pattern mining to retrieve the hidden patterns leading to the popularity of Docker images. In particular, we developed an approach to use common frequent pattern mining algorithms (such as FP-Growth), which discretizes continuous variables by taking into account their distributions. The main findings highlight that most of the images follow rules which are very common but that do not lead the Docker image to a relevant level of popularity. On the other hand, we have found some rules satisfied only by a small portion of the images, which are however very stable and predictive of a consistent level of popularity in terms of pulls and stars. Finally, we have observed that the most successful rules are followed only by so-called official Docker images.

As future work, besides testing the proposed frequent pattern mining analytical framework on other domains, we would like to strengthen the experimental section by means of a real validation which involve the usage of the rules we observed in this paper. The idea is to release on DockerHub a set of images following the aforementioned rules, and to observe the level of popularity they will be obtaining in a real case study, and how long it takes to reach the estimated values. Time is indeed another crucial component that was not considered because the current version of DockerFinder is not updating the status of a repository at constant time intervals. Another extension of this study involves to also consider the temporal dimension and the evolution of the patterns. Moreover, while in this paper we propose a reasonable analysis of Docker images using basic existing approaches, as future work we would like to consider advanced *multi-instance learning* techniques [29]. These methods allow to overtake the problem of having multiple Docker images for a single repository as they takes as input a set of labeled *bags*, each containing many instances. Finally, a natural extension of this work is to build a predictor/regressor either from scratch or on top of the popularity rules extracted and observe to which extent is possible to infer the popularity of a Docker image.

Acknowledgments. Work partly supported by the EU H2020 Program under the funding scheme "INFRAIA-1-2014-2015: Research Infrastructures" grant agreement 654024 *"SoBigData"* http://www.sobigdata.eu.

References

1. Agrawal, R., Srikant, R., et al.: Fast algorithms for mining association rules. In: Proceedings of 20th International Conference Very Large Data Bases, VLDB, vol. 1215, pp. 487–499 (1994)
2. Bay, S.D., Pazzani, M.J.: Detecting group differences: mining contrast sets. Data Min. Knowl. Discov. **5**(3), 213–246 (2001)
3. Berri, D.J., Schmidt, M.B., Brook, S.L.: Stars at the gate: the impact of star power on nba gate revenues. J. Sports Econ. **5**(1), 33–50 (2004)
4. Brogi, A., Neri, D., Soldani, J.: DockerFinder: multi-attribute search of docker images. In: IC2E, pp. 273–278. IEEE (2017)
5. Franck, E., Nüesch, S.: Mechanisms of superstar formation in german soccer: empirical evidence. Eur. Sport Manag. Q. **8**(2), 145–164 (2008)
6. Guidotti, R., Monreale, A., Rinzivillo, S., Pedreschi, D., Giannotti, F.: Retrieving points of interest from human systematic movements. In: Canal, C., Idani, A. (eds.) SEFM 2014. LNCS, vol. 8938, pp. 294–308. Springer, Cham (2015). https://doi.org/10.1007/978-3-319-15201-1_19
7. Guidotti, R., Rossetti, G., Pedreschi, D.: AUDIO ERGO SUM. In: Milazzo, P., Varró, D., Wimmer, M. (eds.) STAF 2016. LNCS, vol. 9946, pp. 51–66. Springer, Cham (2016). https://doi.org/10.1007/978-3-319-50230-4_5
8. Han, J., Pei, J., Yin, Y.: Mining frequent patterns without candidate generation. In: ACM SIGMOD Record, vol. 29, pp. 1 12. ACM (2000)
9. Harackiewicz, J.M., et al.: Predicting success in college: a longitudinal study of achievement goals and ability measures as predictors of interest and performance from freshman year through graduation. JEP **94**(3), 562 (2002)

10. Hars, A., Ou, S.: Working for free? - motivations of participating in open source projects. IJEC **6**(3), 25–39 (2002)
11. Herrera, F., Carmona, C.J., González, P., Del Jesus, M.J.: An overview on subgroup discovery: foundations and applications. KAIS **29**(3), 495–525 (2011)
12. Joy, A.: Performance comparison between Linux containers and virtual machines. In: ICACEA, pp. 342–346, March 2015
13. Litman, B.R.: Predicting success of theatrical movies: an empirical study. J. Popular Cult. **16**(4), 159–175 (1983)
14. Ma, Z., Sun, A., Cong, G.: On predicting the popularity of newly emerging hashtags in twitter. JASIST **64**(7), 1399–1410 (2013)
15. Miell, I., Sayers, A.H.: Docker in Practice. Manning Publications Co., Shelter Island (2016)
16. Pahl, C., Brogi, A., Soldani, J., Jamshidi, P.: Cloud container technologies: a state-of-the-art review. IEEE Trans. Cloud Comput. (2017, in press)
17. Pappalardo, L., Cintia, P.: Quantifying the relation between performance and success in soccer. In: Advances in Complex Systems, p. 1750014 (2017)
18. Pappalardo, L., Cintia, P., Pedreschi, D., Giannotti, F., Barabasi, A.-L.: Human perception of performance. arXiv preprint arXiv:1712.02224 (2017)
19. Park, J., et al.: Style in the age of instagram: predicting success within the fashion industry using social media. In: CSCW, pp. 64–73. ACM (2016)
20. Penner, O., Pan, R.K., Petersen, A.M., Kaski, K., Fortunato, S.: On the predictability of future impact in science. Sci. Rep. **3**, 3052 (2013)
21. Pollacci, L., Guidotti, R., Rossetti, G., Giannotti, F., Pedreschi, D.: The fractal dimension of music: geography, popularity and sentiment analysis. In: Guidi, B., Ricci, L., Calafate, C., Gaggi, O., Marquez-Barja, J. (eds.) GOODTECHS 2017. LNICST, vol. 233, pp. 183–194. Springer, Cham (2018). https://doi.org/10.1007/978-3-319-76111-4_19
22. Sinatra, R., Wang, D., Deville, P., Song, C., Barabási, A.-L.: Quantifying the evolution of individual scientific impact. Science **354**(6312), aaf5239 (2016)
23. Soltesz, S., et al.: Container-based operating system virtualization: a scalable, high-performance alternative to hypervisors. In: SIGOPS, vol. 41, pp. 275–287 (2007)
24. Tan, P.-N., et al.: Introduction to Data Mining. Pearson Education India (2006)
25. Trzciński, T., Rokita, P.: Predicting popularity of online videos using support vector regression. IEEE Trans. Multimedia **19**(11), 2561–2570 (2017)
26. Wang, D., Song, C., Barabási, A.-L.: Quantifying long-term scientific impact. Science **342**(6154), 127–132 (2013)
27. Weicheng, Y., Beijun, S., Ben, X.: Mining GitHub: why commit stops–exploring the relationship between developer's commit pattern and le version evolution. In: APSEC, vol. 2, pp. 165–169. IEEE (2013)
28. Yu, Y., Yin, G., Wang, H., Wang, T.: Exploring the patterns of social behavior in GitHub. In: CrowdSoft, pp. 31–36. ACM (2014)
29. Zhou, Z.-H., Zhang, M.-L.: Multi-instance multi-label learning with application to scene classification. In: NIPS, pp. 1609–1616 (2007)

Analyzing Privacy Risk in Human Mobility Data

Roberto Pellungrini[1], Luca Pappalardo[2], Francesca Pratesi[1,2], and Anna Monreale[1(✉)]

[1] Department of Computer Science, University of Pisa, Pisa, Italy
anna.monreale@unipi.it
[2] ISTI-CNR, Pisa, Italy

Abstract. Mobility data are of fundamental importance for understanding the patterns of human movements, developing analytical services and modeling human dynamics. Unfortunately, mobility data also contain individual sensitive information, making it necessary an accurate privacy risk assessment for the individuals involved. In this paper, we propose a methodology for assessing privacy risk in human mobility data. Given a set of individual and collective mobility features, we define the minimum data format necessary for the computation of each feature and we define a set of possible attacks on these data formats. We perform experiments computing the empirical risk in a real-world mobility dataset, and show how the distributions of the considered mobility features are affected by the removal of individuals with different levels of privacy risk.

1 Introduction

In the last years, human mobility analysis has attracted a growing interest due to its importance in a wide range of applications, from urban management and public health [13], to the discovery of quantitative patterns [12] and the prediction of human future whereabouts [8]. The worrying side of this story is that human mobility data are sensitive, because they may allow the re-identification of individuals and lead to severe privacy issues if analyzed with malicious intent [18]. In order to prevent these problems, researchers have developed methodologies, frameworks and algorithms to reduce the individual privacy risk associated to the analysis of human mobility data [1]. Tools like the one presented in [15] try to balance both the individuals' privacy protection and the effectiveness of the analytical results.[1] Starting from [15], we study the empirical trade-off between individual privacy risk and data quality w.r.t. a set of state-of-the-art individual and collective mobility measures. We first introduce a set of mobility data structures, each with a different level of detail on an individual's mobility history, and then present a set of re-identification attacks based on these structures. In a scenario where a data owner wants to share human mobility data with an external

---

[1] In compliance with the new EU General Data Protection Regulation.

© Springer Nature Switzerland AG 2018
M. Mazzara et al. (Eds.): STAF 2018 Workshops, LNCS 11176, pp. 114–129, 2018.
https://doi.org/10.1007/978-3-030-04771-9_10

entity (e.g., a data analyst), it can simulate the re-identification attacks to assess the privacy risk of every individual in the dataset. Having this information, the data owner can simply delete the individuals beyond a certain threshold of privacy risk or select the most suitable privacy-preserving technique (e.g., based on k-anonymity, differential privacy) to mitigate individual privacy risk. We use a real-world human mobility dataset to compute the distribution of privacy risk for every re-identification attack. We then compare the distributions of the considered mobility features computed on the original data and on data obtained removing high risk individuals. We show how these distributions vary much less when computed on more aggregated structures.

2   Individual Mobility Features

The approach we present in this paper is tailored for human mobility data, i.e., data describing the movements of a set of individuals during a period of observation. The mobility dynamics of an individual can be described by a set of measures widely used in literature. Some measures describe specific aspects of an individual's mobility; other measures describe an individual's mobility in relation to collective mobility. The Maximum Distance is defined as the length of the longest trip of an individual during the period of observation [24]. The Sum Of Distances is the sum of all the trip lengths traveled by the individual during the period of observation [24]. The Radius of Gyration is the characteristic distance traveled by an individual during the period of observation, formally defined in [12]; this measure represents one of the major components useful for describing human mobility. The Mobility Entropy is a measure of the predictability of an individual's trajectory; formally, it is defined as the Shannon entropy of an individual's movements [7]. We can also define some measures related to locations instead of individuals, like the Location Entropy, i.e., the predictability of who visits the location. We also use Location Density, a measure of how many individuals have that location as their most visited location, and the Flow of a location defined as the number of trips that have that location as origin or destination.

3   Data Definitions

Human mobility data is generally collected in an automatic way through electronic devices (e.g., mobile phones, GPS devices) in form of raw trajectory data. A raw trajectory of an individual is a sequence of records identifying the movements of that individual during the period of observation [26]. Every record has the following fields: the identifier of the individual, a geographic location expressed in coordinates (generally latitude and longitude), a timestamp indicating when the individual stopped in or went through that location. Depending on the specific application, a raw trajectory can be aggregated into different mobility data structures introduced in the following.

Definition 1 (Trajectory). *The trajectory T_u of an individual u is a temporally ordered sequence of tuples $T_u = \langle(l_1,t_1),(l_2,t_2),\ldots,(l_n,t_n)\rangle$, where $l_i = (x_i, y_i)$ is a location, x_i and y_i are the coordinates of the geographic location, and t_i is the corresponding timestamp, $t_i < t_j$ if $i < j$.*

Definition 2 Frequency vector). *The frequency vector W_u of an individual u is a sequence of tuples $W_u = \langle(l_1,w_1),(l_2,w_2),\ldots,(l_n,w_n)\rangle$ where $l_i = (x_i, y_i)$ is a location, w_i is the frequency of the location, i.e., how many times location l_i appears in the individual's trajectory T_u, and $w_i > w_j$ if $i < j$. A frequency vector W_u is hence an aggregation of a trajectory T_u.*

Definition 3 (Probability vector). *The probability vector P_u of an individual u is a sequence of tuples $P_u = \langle(l_1,p_1),(l_2,p_2),\ldots,(l_n,p_n)\rangle$, where $l_i = (x_i, y_i)$ is a location, p_i is the probability that location l_i appears in W_u, i.e., $p_i = \frac{w_i}{\sum_{l_i \in W_u} w_i}$, and $p_i > p_j$ if $i < j$. A probability vector P_u is hence an aggregation of a frequency vector W_u.*

In the following, with the terms *visit* we refer indifferently to a tuple in a trajectory or in a frequency or probability vector. In other words, a visit indicates a pair consisting of a location and a supplementary information, e.g., the timestamp or the frequency. We denote with D a mobility dataset, i.e., a set of a one of the above data types (trajectory, frequency or probability vectors). Each data structure allows the computation of some of the mobility features presented in Sect. 2: with the trajectory, the most detailed of the three structures, we can compute all the mobility features presented. With the vector structures we can compute only Radius of Gyration, User Entropy, Location Entropy and Location Density. Lowering the detail of the structure we can compute less features but we expose less information about the individuals represented.

4   Privacy Risk Assessment Model

Several methodologies have been proposed in literature for privacy risk assessment. In this paper we start from the framework proposed in [15], which allows for the assessment of the privacy risk inherent to human mobility data. At the core of this framework, there is the identification of the minimum data structure, the definition of a set of possible attacks that a malicious adversary might conduct in order to re-identify her target and the simulation of the attacks. The privacy risk of an individual is related to her probability of re-identification in a mobility dataset w.r.t. a set of re-identification attacks. A re-identification attack assumes that an adversary gains access to a mobility dataset, then, on the basis of some background knowledge about an individual, i.e., the knowledge of a subset of her mobility data, the adversary tries to re-identify all the records in the dataset regarding the individual under attack. In this paper we use the definition of privacy risk (or re-identification risk) introduced in [19].

There can be many background knowledge categories, every category may have several background knowledge configurations, every configurations has many instances. A background knowledge category is a kind of information known by the adversary about a specific set of dimensions of an individual's mobility data. Typical dimensions in mobility data are space, time, frequency of visiting a location and probability of visiting a location. Examples of background knowledge categories are a subset of the locations visited by an individual and specific times an individual visited those locations. The number k of the elements of a category known by the adversary is called background knowledge configuration: an example is the knowledge by the adversary of $k = 3$ locations of an individual. Finally, an instance of background knowledge is the specific knowledge of the adversary, such as a visit in a specific location. We formalize these concepts as follows.

Definition 4 Background knowledge configuration. *Given a background knowledge category* $\mathcal{B}$, *we denote with* $B_k \in \mathcal{B} = \{B_1, B_2, \ldots, B_n\}$ *a specific background knowledge configuration, where* k *represents the number of elements in* $\mathcal{B}$ *known by the adversary. We define an element* $b \in B_k$ *as an* instance *of background knowledge configuration.*

Let $\mathcal{D}$ be a database, D a mobility dataset extracted from $\mathcal{D}$ (e.g., a data structure as defined in Sect. 3), and D_u the set of records representing individual u in D, we define the probability of re-identification as follows.

Definition 5 Probability of re-identification. *The probability of re-identification* $PR_D(d = u|b)$ *of an individual* u *in a mobility dataset* D *is the probability to associate a record* $d \in \mathcal{D}$ *to an individual* u, *given an instance of background knowledge configuration* $b \in B_k$.

Note that $PR_D(d=u|b) = 0$ if the individual u is not represented in D. Since each instance $b \in B_k$ has its own probability of re-identification, we define the risk of re-identification of an individual as the maximum probability of re-identification over the set of instances of a background knowledge configuration.

Definition 6 Risk of re-identification or Privacy risk. *The risk of re-identification (or privacy risk) of an individual* u *given a background knowledge configuration* B_k *is her maximum probability of re-identification* $Risk(u, D) = \max PR_D(d=u|b)$ *for* $b \in B_k$. *The risk of re-identification has the lower bound* $\frac{|D_u|}{|D|}$ *(a random choice in* D*), and* $Risk(u, D) = 0$ *if* $u \notin D$.

4.1 Privacy Attacks on Mobility Data

In this section we describe the attacks we use in this paper.

Location. In a Location attack the adversary knows a certain number of locations visited by the individual but she does not know the temporal order of the visits. This is similar to considering the locations as items of transactions [22] with the difference that a transaction is a set of items and not a multiset (an individual might visit the same location multiple times). Given an individual s, we denote by $L(T_s)$ the multiset of locations $l_i \in T_s$ visited by s. The background knowledge category of a Location attack is defined as follows.

Definition 7 Location background knowledge. *Let k be the number of locations l_i of an individual s known by the adversary. The Location background knowledge is a set of configurations based on k locations, defined as $B_k = L(T_s)^{[k]}$. Here $L(T_s)^{[k]}$ denotes the set of all the possible k-combinations of the elements in set $L(T_s)$.*

Given $b \in B_k$, we can give the definition for the set of users matching the Location background knowledge, and consequently, the probability of re-identification.

Definition 8 Location attack. *Let $b \in B_k$ be the adversary Location background knowledge. We define by $R = \{u \in U | b \subseteq L(T_u)\}$ the candidate set of users whose trajectory contains the instance b. The probability of re-identification of the user u is $\frac{1}{|R|}$.*

Location Sequence. In a Location Sequence attack [9] the adversary knows a subset of the locations and the temporal ordering of the visits. Given an individual s, we denote by $L(T_s)$ the sequence of locations $l_i \in T_s$ visited by s. The background knowledge category of a Location Sequence attack is the following.

Definition 9 Location Sequence background knowledge. *Let k be the number of locations l_i of a individual s known by the adversary. The Location Sequence background knowledge is a set of configurations based on k locations, defined as $B_k = L(T_s)^{[k]}$, where $L(T_s)^{[k]}$ denotes the set of all the possible k-subsequences of the elements in set $L(T_s)$.*

The set of users matching this background knowledge is defined in the following where we denote by $a \preceq b$ that a is a subsequence of b.

Definition 10 Location Sequence attack. *Let $b \in B_k$ be the Location Sequence background knowledge. We define by $R = \{u \in U | b \preceq L(T_u)\}$ the candidate set of users whose trajectory contains the combination b. The probability of re-identification of the user u is $\frac{1}{|R|}$.*

Visit. In a Visit attack [25] an adversary knows a subset of the locations visited by the individual and the time the individual visited these locations.

Definition 11 Visit background knowledge. *Let k be the number of visits v of a individual s known by the adversary. The Visit background knowledge is a set of configurations based on k visits, defined as $B_k = T_s^{[k]}$ where $T_s^{[k]}$ denotes the set of all the possible k-subsequences of the elements in trajectory T_s.*

We recall that in the case of trajectories we denote by visit $v \in T$ the pair (l_i, t_i) composed by the location l_i and its timestamp t_i. Formally, the set of all trajectories supporting b from both a spatial and a temporal point of view is:

Definition 12 Visit attack. *Let $b \in B_k$ be the Visit background knowledge. We define by $R = \{u \in U \mid \forall (l_i, t_i) \in b, \exists (l_i^u, t_i^u) \in T_u . l_i = l_i^u \wedge t_i \leq t_i^u\}$ the candidate set of users whose trajectories contain b. The probability of re-identification of the user u is $\frac{1}{|R|}$.*

Frequent Location, Frequent Location Sequence. We also introduce two attacks based on the knowledge of the location applied to vectors. The Frequent Location attack is similar to the Location attack but here a location can appear only once, so it follows the same principle of [22]. In the Frequent Location Sequence attack the adversary knows a subset of the locations visited by an individual and the relative ordering w.r.t. the frequencies (from most frequent to least frequent). This attack is similar to the Location Sequence attack, with two differences: a location can appear only once and locations are ordered by descending frequency. We omit the definitions of the background knowledge and attacks because they are similar to the ones defined on trajectories.

Frequency. We introduce an attack where an adversary knows the locations visited by the individual, their reciprocal ordering of frequency, and the minimum number of visits of the individual in the locations. This means that, when searching for specific subsequences, the adversary must consider also subsequences containing the known locations with a greater frequency. We recall that in the case of frequency vectors we denote by visit $v \in W$ the pair (l_i, w_i) composed by the frequent location l_i and its frequency w_i. The background knowledge category of a Frequency attack is defined as follows.

Definition 13 Frequency background knowledge. *Let k be the number of visits v of the frequency vector of individual s known by the adversary. The Frequency background knowledge is a set of configurations based on k visits, defined as $B_k = W_s^{[k]}$ where $W_s^{[k]}$ denotes the set of all possible k-combinations of frequency vector W_s.*

The set of users matching a single $b \in B_k$ is defined as follows.

Definition 14 Frequency attack. *Let $b \in B_k$ be the Frequency background knowledge. We define by $R = \{u \in U \mid \forall (l_i, w_i) \in b, \exists (l_i^u, w_i^u) \in W_u . l_i = l_i^u \wedge w_i \leq w_i^u\}$ the candidate set of users whose frequency vectors contain the instance b. The probability of re-identification of the user u is $\frac{1}{|R|}$.*

Home & Work. In the Home & Work attack [27], the adversary knows the two most frequent locations of an individual and their frequencies. This is the only attack where the background knowledge configuration is just a single 2-combination. Mechanically, this attack is identical to the Frequency attack.

Probability. In a Probability attack an adversary knows the locations visited by an individual and the probability for that individual to visit each location. This attack is similar to the one introduced by [28], but we cannot rely on matching algorithms on bipartite graph because the length of the probability vectors is not the same among the individuals and is greater than the length of the background knowledge configuration instances. We recall that in the case of probability vectors we denote by visit $v \in P$ the pair (l_i, p_i) composed by the frequent location l_i and its probability p_i. The background knowledge category for this attack is defined as follows.

Definition 15 Probability background knowledge. *Let k be the number of visits v of the probability vector of individual s known by the adversary. The Probability background knowledge is a set of configurations based on k visits, defined as $B_k = P_s^{[k]}$ where $P_s^{[k]}$ denotes the set of all possible k-combinations of probability vector P_s.*

Again, the set of users matching a single $b \in B_k$ can be defined as follows.

Definition 16 Probability attack. *Let $b \in B_k$ be the Probability background knowledge. We define by $R = \{u \in U \mid \forall \ (l_i, p_i) \ \in b, \ \exists \ (l_i^u, p_i^u) \ \in P_u \ . \ l_i = l_i^u \ \wedge \ p_i \in [p_i^u - \delta, p_i^u + \delta]\}$ the candidate set of users who in their frequency vectors contain the instance b tolerating for the probability match a tolerance δ. The probability of re-identification of the user u is $\frac{1}{|R|}$.*

Proportion. We introduce an attack assuming that an adversary knows a subset of locations and the relative proportion between the number of visits to these locations, i.e., between the frequency of the most frequent known location and the frequency of the other known locations. Given a set of visits $X \subset W$ we denote by $l1$ the most frequent location of X and with w_1 its frequency. We also denote by pr_i the proportion between w_i and w_1 for each $v_i \neq v_1 \in X$, and denote by LR a set of frequent locations l_i with their respective pr_i. The background knowledge category for this attack is defined as follows.

Definition 17 Proportion background knowledge. *Let k be the number of locations l_i of an individual s known by the adversary. The Proportion background knowledge is a set of configurations based on k locations, defined as $B_k = LR_s^{[k]}$ where $LR_s^{[k]}$ denotes the set of all possible k-combinations of the frequent locations l_i with associated pr_i.*

The set of users matching a single $b \in B_k$ is defined as follows.

Definition 18 Proportion attack. *Let $b \in B_k$ be the Proportion background knowledge. We define by $R = \{u \in U \mid \forall \ (l_i, pr_i) \ \in b, \ \exists \ (l_i^u, pr_i^u) \in LR^u \ . \ l_i = l_i^u \ \wedge \ pr_i \in [pr_i^u - \delta, pr_i^u + \delta]\}$ the candidate set of users who in their frequency vectors compatible with b. Note that δ is a tolerance factor for the matching of proportions. The probability of re-identification of the user u is $\frac{1}{|R|}$.*

Note that each attack is associated with a specific data structure: Location, Location Sequence and Visit require the trajectory data structure; Frequent Location, Frequent Location Sequence and Frequency require the frequency vector; Home & Work, Proportion and Probability require the probability vector.

5   Experiments

For all the attacks defined except the Home & Work attack we consider four sets of background knowledge configuration B_k with $k = 2, 3, 4, 5$, while for the Home & Work attack we have just one possible background knowledge configuration, where the adversary knows the two most frequent locations of an individual. Note that for the Visit attack we considered only the day as time frame for the granularity of the attack. We use a dataset provided by Octo Telematics[2] storing the GPS tracks of 9,715 private vehicles traveling in Florence from 1st May to 31st May 2011, corresponding to 179,318 trajectories. We assign each origin and destination point of trajectories to the corresponding census cells [12] provided by the Italian National Statistics Bureau. This allows us to describe the mobility of every vehicle in terms of a trajectory as defined in Sect. 3. We performed a simulation of the attacks computing the privacy risk values for all individuals in the dataset and for all B_k.[3] We then show the distribution of the mobility features presented in Sect. 2 at varying levels of risk: we compare the distribution of the features computed on the original dataset, i.e., the dataset with the complete set of trajectories, with the distributions obtained using only trajectories belonging to individuals below certain thresholds of privacy risk.

5.1 Privacy Risk Simulations

We simulated attacks using $k = 2, 3, 4, 5$: the cumulative distribution functions for the trajectory attacks are depicted in Fig. 1, where we can see that the privacy risk increase not only with increasing the amount of knowledge (from Fig. 1(a) to (c)), but also with increasing k. This is more evident for the Location attack and the Location Sequence attack (Fig. 1(a) and (b) respectively). It is interesting to note that the greater gap is present, especially for the Location attack, varying k from 2 to 3, i.e., the greatest increasing of risk of re-identification occurs when the quantity of information known is lower. This implies that adding the same absolute amount of information, i.e., one single location, has less influence if the attacker already has a quite big knowledge. For the Visit attack (Fig. 1(c)), since here the background knowledge is already enough detailed, we can see that the increasing of k does not change so much the levels of privacy risk. The number of individuals with maximum risk of re-identification, i.e., equals to 1, ranges from 60% for the Location attack to more that 80% for the Visit attack, while we do have an increase in the number of individuals with risk of re-identification of 50% (or less) across the board.

Observing Fig. 2, regarding attacks on vectors, the levels of risk decrease slightly from the attacks on trajectories. Moreover, it is clear how the the cumulative distribution function of the risk of re-identification is quite stable varying k or changing the category of knowledge. This can probably be due to the fact that, with vectors, we are dealing with distinct locations for each individual, thus, since many individuals have few distinct locations, the risk remains very similar when increasing k. With Home & Work attack (2(f)) we have significantly lower risk. Indeed, we can observe much lower levels of risk in general, even if 50% of users still have maximum risk of re-identification.

---

[2] https://www.octotelematics.com/.
[3] The Python code for attacks simulation is available here: https://github.com/pellungrobe/privacy-mobility-lib.

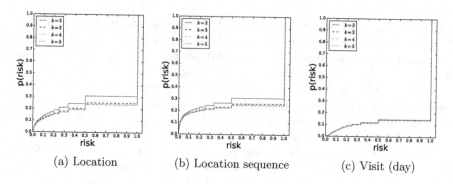

Fig. 1. Cumulative distributions for trajectory attacks.

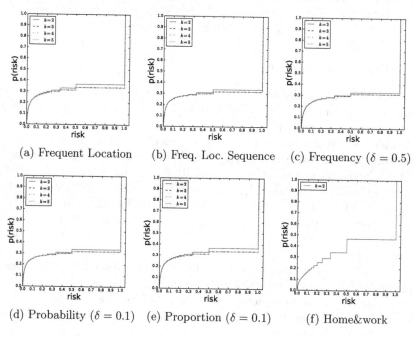

Fig. 2. Cumulative distributions for frequency vector attacks.

5.2   Correlations Between Measures and Privacy Risk

In this section we want to show the correlation between the mobility measures introduced in Sect. 2 and the levels of risk calculated for each attack. The Pearson Correlation Coefficient is a measure of the linear dependence between two variables, in this case a mobility measure and the risk assessed for each attack. It ranges from −1 to +1 where −1 indicates total negative linear correlation, 0 indicates no linear correlation and +1 indicates total positive linear correlation. Since in Sect. 5.1 we saw that, varying k, privacy risk does not change too severely, we show the correlation only for a middle value, i.e. $k = 3$. We used

Table 1. Correlation of measures and privacy risk

	RadiusGyration	UserEntropy	MaxDistance	SumDistances
Location	0.408326	0.654331	0.503459	0.352364
Location sequence	0.333477	0.668218	0.463041	0.367661
Visit (day)	0.219840	0.493934	0.320390	0.256473
Frequent location	0.359895	0.749976	0.501241	0.426581
Freq.Loc. sequence	0.352399	0.746065	0.490765	0.414132
Frequency	0.340739	0.733594	0.482271	0.410859
Probability	0.352399	0.746065	0.490765	0.414132
Proportion	0.359895	0.749976	0.501241	0.426581

only the features related to individuals and not the ones related to locations, because the privacy risk level is computed for each individual and does not have an association with locations. We show the results of correlation study in Table 1. Analyzing the attacks on trajectories, there is really no strong correlation. An interesting fact, which is compliant with the results showed in Sect. 5.1, is that the correlation tends to decrease as the levels of risk increase, thus, for the Visit attack, we observe a drop in the correlation coefficient. Another interesting result is that, especially for the attacks related to frequency and probability vectors the correlation between User Entropy and risk of re-identification is higher while no other strong correlation can be found among the various measures. So overall it seems that high levels of entropy correlate to high levels of risk.

5.3   Measure Distributions by Risk Levels

In this section we present an analysis on the distributions of mobility measures on the datasets used in the experiment, w.r.t. the changing levels of risk. We compare the distributions of the various measures and see how they vary with the levels of risk. We removed from the dataset individuals above a certain level of risk and then recomputed the measures. Thus, we obtained a set of distributions for each measure, one for each level of risk and attack. However, due to space limitations, we present the results only for two of them: the Visit and Frequency attacks. These are the two most representative of the differences between the attacks performed on different data structures, since they are two of the most powerful. For both attacks we show how each measure behaves with different levels of risk, comparing their distributions. For both datasets and for all possible attacks we selected four thresholds of risk. Then, we systematically eliminated from the original dataset users with a risk beyond the thresholds, obtaining four different derived datasets: the original dataset D_1 and $D_{0.5}$, $D_{0.33}$, $D_{0.25}$ obtained removing individuals with risk greater than 0.5, 0.33 and 0.25 respectively. Regarding the background knowledge configuration, we selected the risk calculated with $k = 2$. This for several reasons: it is a reasonable number of locations that an attacker might know, it is the level of risk that shows the most appreciable changes from one threshold of risk to the other in terms of users excluded/included, and it is also the k value that yields the lower levels of risk. In the following, we show the probability density functions (pdf) of the mobility features for the different datasets.

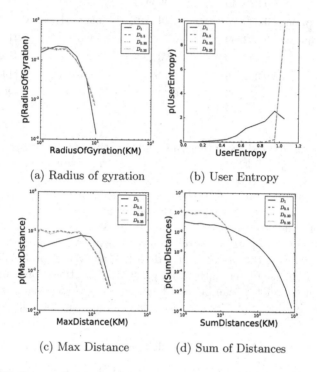

(a) Radius of gyration   (b) User Entropy

(c) Max Distance   (d) Sum of Distances

Fig. 3. Pdf of user related measures changing levels of risk (Visit attack (day))

For the Visit attack with day precision for the time frame, Fig. 3 reports results on users related measures. We observe some interesting results: User Entropy (Fig. 3(b)) becomes 1 for almost all remaining users in $D_{0.5}$, $D_{0.33}$ and $D_{0.25}$. Observing the Radius of gyration (Fig. 3(a)) we note that the shape of the distribution remains fairly similar but we find more individuals with high Radius of gyration proportionally to the total number of remaining individuals. For the Sum of Distances (Fig. 3(d)), we tend to lose the individuals who traveled the longest distances total. For Max Distance (Fig. 3(c)) the distribution remain substantially similar. Figure 4 shows that the distributions of location related measures for both datasets suffer heavy modifications. For Location Entropy (Fig. 4-left) we observe a loss of the middle values: we have a significantly higher probability of locations with very low entropy (<0.2) and a slight peak of locations with very high entropy, with no relevant values in between. This is also more evident the more we cut the data, i.e. for $D_{0.25}$. For Location Density and

Flow (Fig. 4-center and 4-right) we observe a loss of the higher values but the overall shape of the distributions remains similar.

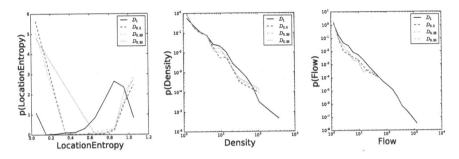

Fig. 4. Pdf of location related measures changing levels of risk (Visit attack (day))

Changing data structure from trajectory to frequency vector, we already observed in Sect. 5.1 generally lower levels of risk, thus we can maintain more individuals in the dataset cutting at the same thresholds. For this reason, we expect more similar distributions w.r.t. the original dataset. However, since we lose the information about the specific movements given by the trajectory structure, we cannot compute all the measures introduced in Sect. 2. The measures that we cannot compute are: Max Distance, Sum of Distances and Flow. For the frequency attack we show the results for individuals and locations related measures in Figs. 5 and 6 respectively. While User Entropy distribution (Fig. 5-right) still exhibits some changes w.r.t. the original distribution at changing levels of risk, we observe less dramatic differences in comparison to the distributions presented in Fig. 4-center regarding the Visit attack. For Location Entropy distribution (Fig. 6-left) we still observe a peak of locations with very low entropy but the overall shape of the distributions is closer to the original one, maintaining similar peaks around higher values. Location Density (Fig. 6-right) and Radius of gyration (Fig. 5-left) distributions appear to remain almost identical for all thresholds of risk ($D_{0.5}$, $D_{0.33}$ and $D_{0.25}$). Summarizing, the distributions presented above give an empirical demonstration to the intuition that less detailed data structures, exposing less data about an individual, lead to generally lower levels of re-identification risk. Thus, for the considered features, choosing the minimum required data structure is fundamental to improve the quality of the distributions of the mobility features we want to study when computing them from sanitized datasets.

6   Related Work

To overcome privacy leaks, many techniques have been proposed in literature. A widely used privacy-preserving model is k-anonymity [19], which requires that an individual should not be identifiable from a group of size smaller than k based

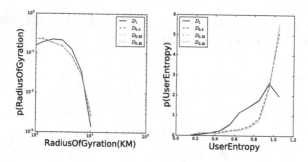

Fig. 5. Pdf of user related measures changing levels of risk (Frequency attack)

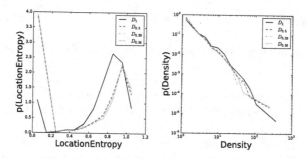

Fig. 6. Pdf of location related measures changing levels of risk (Frequency attack)

on their quasi-identifiers (QIDs), i.e., a set of attributes that can be used to uniquely identify individuals. Assuming that adversaries own disjoint parts of a trajectory, [22] reduces privacy risk by relying on the suppression of the dangerous observations from each individual's trajectory. In [25], authors propose the attack-graphs method to defend against attacks, based on k-anonymity. Other works are based on the differential privacy model [6]. [10] and [14] considers the problem of privacy on aggregations of movement data. [4] proposes to publish a contingency table of trajectory data, where each cell contains the number of individuals commuting from a source to a destination. One of the most important work about privacy risk assessment is the LINDDUN methodology [5], a privacy-aware framework, useful for modeling privacy threats in software-based systems. In the last years, different techniques for risk management have been proposed, such as NIST's Special Publication 800-30 [21] and SEI's OCTAVE [2]. Unfortunately, many of these works simply include privacy considerations when assessing the impact of threats. In [23], authors elaborate an entropy-based method to evaluate the disclosure risk of personal data, trying to manage quantitatively privacy risks. [11] studies the effect of co-location information on location privacy, considering an adversary such as a social network operator accessing to such information. The *unicity* measure proposed in [20] evaluates the privacy risk as the number of records which are uniquely identified. [3] proposes a risk-aware framework for information disclosure in tabular data supporting runtime risk assessment, using adaptive anonymization as risk-mitigation method. Lastly, in [15] authors introduced a privacy risk assessment framework specific for mobility data. Although this framework suffers from a high computational complexity, it is effective in many mobility scenarios. Other papers addressing the problem of measuring privacy risk in mobility data are [16,17].

7 Conclusion

Human mobility data contain highly sensitive information that might lead to serious violations of individual privacy. In this paper we explored a repertoire of re-identification attacks that can be conducted on mobility data, analyzing the empirical privacy risk of thousands of individuals in a real-world mobility dataset. The considered attacks were designed for three common mobility data formats: trajectories, frequency vectors and probability vectors. Through experimentation on the real-world dataset, we observed on average high level of risk across the different types of re-identification attack. We then characterize how the distributions of state-of-the-art human mobility measures changes as individuals with high level of risk are deleted from the dataset, finding two main results: (1) higher privacy risk is related to a higher distortion of the distributions of mobility measures; (2) selecting the minimum required data structure can lead to significant improvements in the overall levels of privacy risk, while guaranteeing distributions of mobility features closer to the distributions derived from the original data. We observe that the methodology experimented in this paper may be applied, without changing the attacks definitions to any dataset of mobility and sequence data; clearly, in this last case instead of locations we would have events. As future work, we plan to investigate how distributions of mobility features can be further improved using privacy transformations more sophisticated than the simple suppression of individuals with high privacy risk.

Acknowledgment. Funded by the European project SoBigData (Grant Agreement 654024).

References

1. Abul, O., Bonchi, F., Nanni, M.: Never walk alone: uncertainty for anonymity in moving objects databases. In ICDE 2008, pp. 376–385 (2008)
2. Alberts, C., Behrens, S., Pethia, R., Wilson, W.: Operationally critical threat, asset, and vulnerability evaluation (OCTAVE) framework, version 1.0. CMU/SEI-99-TR-017. Software Engineering Institute, Carnegie Mellon University (1999). http://resources.sei.cmu.edu/library/asset-view.cfm?AssetID=13473
3. Armando, A., Bezzi, M., Metoui, N., Sabetta, A.: Risk-based privacy-aware information disclosure. Int. J. Secur. Softw. Eng. 6(2), 70–89 (2015)
4. Cormode, G., Procopiuc, C.M., Srivastava, D., Tran, T.T.L.: Differentially private summaries for sparse data. In: ICDT 2012, pp. 299–311 (2012)
5. Deng, M., Wuyts, K., Scandariato, R., Preneel, B., Joosen, W.: A privacy threat analysis framework: supporting the elicitation and fulfillment of privacy requirements. Requir. Eng. 16(1), 3–32 (2011)

6. Dwork, C., McSherry, F., Nissim, K., Smith, A.: Calibrating noise to sensitivity in private data analysis. In: Halevi, S., Rabin, T. (eds.) TCC 2006. LNCS, vol. 3876, pp. 265–284. Springer, Heidelberg (2006). https://doi.org/10.1007/11681878_14
7. Eagle, N., Pentland, A.S.: Eigenbehaviors: identifying structure in routine. Behav. Ecol. Sociobiol. **63**(7), 1057–1066 (2009)
8. Gambs, S., Killijian, M.O., del Prado Cortez, M.N.: Next place prediction using mobility Markov chains. In: MPM, Article no. 4 (2012)
9. Mohammed, N., Fung, B.C.M., Debbabi, M.: Walking in the crowd: anonymizing trajectory data for pattern analysis. In: CIKM 2009, pp. 1441–1444 (2009)
10. Monreale, A., et al.: Privacy-preserving distributed movement data aggregation. In: Vandenbroucke, D., Bucher, B., Crompvoets, J. (eds.) Geographic Information Science at the Heart of Europe, pp. 225–245. Springer, Heidelberg (2013). https://doi.org/10.1007/978-3-319-00615-4_13
11. Olteanu, A.M., Huguenin, K., Shokri, R., Humbert, M., Hubaux, J.P.: Quantifying interdependent privacy risks with location data. IEEE Trans. Mob. Comput. **16**(3), 829–842 (2017)
12. Pappalardo, L., Simini, F., Rinzivillo, S., Pedreschi, D., Giannotti, F., Barabasi, A.-L.: Returners and explorers dichotomy in human mobility. Nat. Commun. **6**, 8166 (2015)
13. Pappalardo, L., Vanhoof, M., Gabrielli, L., Smoreda, Z., Pedreschi, D., Giannotti, F.: An analytical framework to nowcast well-being using mobile phone data. Int. J. Data Sci. Anal. **2**(1), 75–92 (2016)
14. Pyrgelis, A., De Cristofaro, E., Ross, G.J.: Privacy-friendly mobility analytics using aggregate location data. In: SIGSPATIAL International Conference on Advances in Geographic Information Systems, p. 34 (2016)
15. Pratesi, F., Monreale, A., Trasarti, R., Giannotti, F., Pedreschi, D., Yanagihara, T.: PRUDEnce: a system for assessing privacy risk vs utility in data sharing ecosystems. Trans. Data Priv. J., to appear
16. Rossi, L., Musolesi, M.: It's the way you check-in: identifying users in location-based social networks. In: ACM Conference on Online Social Networks, pp. 215–226
17. Rossi, L., Walker, J., Musolesi, M.: Spatio-temporal techniques for user identification by means of GPS mobility data. EPJ Data Sci. **4**(1), 11 (2015)
18. Rubinstein, I.S.: Big data: the end of privacy or a new beginning? International Data Privacy Law (2013)
19. Samarati, P., Sweeney, L.: Generalizing data to provide anonymity when disclosing information (Abstract). In: PODS, vol. 188 (1998a)
20. Song, Y., Dahlmeier, D., Bressan, S.: Not so unique in the crowd: a simple and effective algorithm for anonymizing location data. In PIR@SIGIR 2014, pp. 19–24 (2014)
21. Stoneburner, G., Goguen, A., Feringa, A.: Risk Management Guide for Information Technology Systems: Recommendations of the National Institute of Standards and Technology, vol. 800. NIST special publication (2002)
22. Terrovitis, M., Mamoulis, N.: Privacy preservation in the publication of trajectories. In: MDM, pp. 65–72 (2008)
23. Trabelsi, S., Salzgeber, V., Bezzi, M., Montagnon, G.: Data disclosure risk evaluation. In: CRiSIS 2009, pp. 35–72 (2009)
24. Williams, N.E., Thomas, T.A., Dunbar, M., Eagle, N., Dobra, A.: Measures of human mobility using mobile phone records enhanced with GIS data. PLoS One **10**(7), 1–16 (2015)

25. Yarovoy, R., Bonchi, F., Lakshmanan, L.V.S., Wang, W.H.: Anonymizing moving objects: how to hide a MOB in a crowd? In: EDBT, vol. 72, no. 83 (2009)
26. Zheng, Y.: Trajectory data mining: an overview. ACM TIST **6**, 3 (2015)
27. Zang, H., Bolot, J.: Anonymization of location data does not work: a large-scale measurement study. In: MobiCom, pp. 145–156 (2011)
28. Unnikrishnan, J., Naini, F.M.: De-anonymizing private data by matching statistics. In: Allerton, pp. 1616–1623 (2013)

Generating Synthetic Data for Real World Detection of DoS Attacks in the IoT

Luca Arnaboldi$^{(\boxtimes)}$ and Charles Morisset

School of Computing, Newcastle University, Newcastle upon Tyne, UK
{l.arnaboldi,charles.morisset}@ncl.ac.uk

Abstract. Denial of service attacks are especially pertinent to the internet of things as devices have less computing power, memory and security mechanisms to defend against them. The task of mitigating these attacks must therefore be redirected from the device onto a network monitor. Network intrusion detection systems can be used as an effective and efficient technique in internet of things systems to offload computation from the devices and detect denial of service attacks before they can cause harm. However the solution of implementing a network intrusion detection system for internet of things networks is not without challenges due to the variability of these systems and specifically the difficulty in collecting data. We propose a model-hybrid approach to model the scale of the internet of things system and effectively train network intrusion detection systems. Through bespoke datasets generated by the model, the IDS is able to predict a wide spectrum of real-world attacks, and as demonstrated by an experiment construct more predictive datasets at a fraction of the time of other more standard techniques.

1 Introduction

A Denial of Service (DoS) attack targets the availability of a device or network [16], with the intent of disrupting system usability. The most common method is referred to as Flooding DoS [16], and may be used as an attempt to deplete the devices' resources including memory, bandwidth and/or battery. A DoS attack against an Internet of Things (IoT) network has the potential to be significantly more detrimental than one against a standard network, this increased vulnerability is due in part to the low computational power and battery power characteristic of IoT devices [22].

The extant literature has delineated several potential approaches that may be effective in the mitigation of a DoS attack [23]. They widely speaking fall into two categories, host based (e.g. Client Puzzles) which puts the computational effort on the device and network based (e.g. firewall) which offloads the computational effort to a remote server or more powerful device within the system. However many of these approaches may not scale well in the IoT as computational power, heterogeneity and the large scale of these systems are all limiting

© Springer Nature Switzerland AG 2018
M. Mazzara et al. (Eds.): STAF 2018 Workshops, LNCS 11176, pp. 130–145, 2018.
https://doi.org/10.1007/978-3-030-04771-9_11

factors that deplete the available choices. One approach that sidesteps many of these standard detriments is a Intrusion Detection System (IDS) bespoke to the IoT system to protect. An IDS is a monitor placed on the network that analyses incoming messages to detect attacks and/or unwanted traffic. They are trained using system behaviour data and use these patterns to make the detection.

Organizations and researchers alike have widely recognised the advantages of adapting IDSs as the norm to monitor against DoS attacks on their systems [17]. Standard approaches used to train IDSs include using a database of known attacks (*misuse detection*) and testing systems to create a "benchmark" behaviour and flag any anomaly as a potential attack (*anomaly detection*) [15]. Implementing an IDS within an IoT network however faces multiple challenges: Firstly, it is usually challenging to establish a benchmark behaviour in dynamic IoT systems as devices may constantly shift, new devices might join and behaviours might change [10], which might prevent using anomaly detection; Secondly, protocols can vary from one network to another, which necessitates data collection to be bespoke to an individual system [11]; And thirdly, a misuse detection can be time consuming to enforce, since collecting data unique to a system and for each attack is time consuming [15] and some system changes can require data (or part of the data) to be collected from scratch (e.g. interactive smart homes where devices can change frequently).

To address the second and third challenges, we present a novel modelling approach. In brief, our model is a Markov Decision Process (MDP), representing the IoT network, the attackers, and some processes monitoring the security metrics under consideration. A trace of the model (corresponding to a sequence of actions of the MDP) should match a trace of the actual system, and vice versa, such that it becomes possible to train a IDS for the actual system on the traces of the model. The main strengths of our approach is the ability to easily represent various configurations for the IoT network as well as multiple types of attackers. MDPs have some key advantages: they have substantial tool support such as PRISM Model Checker [13], they rely on probabilities and non-determinism to recreate systems and they provide the ability to find the optimum paths through the system using the reward function. Through the reward function we create traces of behaviour that mimic attacks on systems by assigning rewards to successful (damaging) behaviour. Our results highlighted that through this methodology we were able to consistently produce datasets that resulted in accurate IDSs (detecting attacks on real world systems) and that could be trained in a fraction of the time. The core contributions of this paper are (1) A model of an IoT system that enables the generation of synthetic data sets of network behaviour (2) Modelling of attack behaviour against a system to train a real world IDS (3) A quantitative analysis and validation of this model against a real world implementation of the same system to validate our methodology.

The paper is split into the following sections; In Sect. 2 we discuss the related work; In Sect. 3 the problem overview is discussed; In Sect. 4 we introduce our IoT system model and attacks model that generates the network behaviour; In Sect. 5 we highlight our assessment methodology; In Sect. 6 we discuss the setup for the experiment; Sect. 7 provides an analysis of our results and Sect. 8 concludes and discusses future work.

2   Related Work

2.1   DoS Attacks on IoT Systems

DoS attacks have long been one of the most common and dangerous threats in any internet system. These attacks become even more dangerous as the IoT spreads across a vast amount of spectra and parts of life including safety critical and potentially life endangering ones such as IoT Healthcare and Intelligent Transportation Systems.

The extant literature highlights several new DoS attacks against IoT system taking advantage of unique qualities and IoT infrastructures [8,14,19]. One such attack, battery drain attack focuses on exhausting the devices battery power as replacing it might be costly, difficult and lead to extensive periods of downtime. These kinds of attack are very subtle as the behaviour of the attacker might not necessarily mimic more common attacks such as pure flooding, they attempt to find battery intensive operations (not necessarily malicious) and repeat them until the device is out of power. This is only one specific example of the literature cited above, however, what all of the above have in common is that they are specialised in their intent of disrupting IoT devices and many of the current detection systems do not account for them [19]. The literature highlights that there is a constant evolution of attacks, as can be seen using resources such as ExploitDB [21]. When filtering for IoT attacks we can observe that there is a huge increase in the spectrum of attacks targeting these systems.

These upwards trends in combination with the expansion of the IoT across various field makes a good argument for a simple way to observe the impact of these attacks. A formalised model would allow for intuitive means to observe and quantify these attacks as well as better defend these systems by generating network behaviour bespoke to them.

2.2   Intrusion Detection Systems

The growing use of internet services in the past few years have facilitated an increase in DoS attacks. Despite the best preventative measures, DoS attacks have been successfully carried out against various companies and organizations enforcing the need for better prevention/detection mechanisms. This is partially due to the vast new avenues of attack (often unique to IoT) that signature based schemes such as SNORT [18] struggle to detect. Further work attempts a more scalable approach that models behaviour of a network (stationary or non-stationary) and labels abnormal packets as a potential anomaly [6]. Limitations of this approach are a large number of false positives as well as lack of information regarding the attack (e.g. the specific vulnerability the attack relies on) as opposed to a signature based IDS that is able to tell you exactly what rule is broken.

The approach suggested in this paper allows for a mixture of these approaches tackling the limitations of both works. By modelling behaviour of a system, one can detect any anomaly similar to the second approach and by modelling various attacks it can also provide accurate data of the system behaviour whilst being targeted, allowing for less false positives. To predict "unknown" attacks, the modelling approach uses a stochastic attacker that attempts different behaviours allowed by the system policy. Using this data it can create a wide range of attack signatures and simulate an attacker probing the system.

2.3   Modelling IoT Systems

Several papers address modelling IoT, adopting various different approaches. Fruth [9] examines various properties of a wireless network protocol namely connectivity and energy power through PRISM, including quantifying the battery drainage of certain randomized protocols. In previous work [4] we model basic flooding DoS attacks through PRISM and look at the effectiveness of different attack strains and mitigation techniques in defending systems of interconnected IoT devices.

Our proposed method combines these approaches to recreate an accurate representation of system behaviour and represent a wide range of DoS attacks. PRISM has been widely used as a excellent method to evaluate and verify models of IoT systems and protocols, combining these two models by adapting both the system models and the attack models we successfully model the behaviour and general properties of a bespoke IoT system. We then use the inbuilt verification capabilities to ensure correctness relative to mimicking system behaviour by establishing benchmarks and tests. PRISM and its inbuilt simulation capabilities allows to simulate attacks against the verified model.

3   Formulation of Problem

An IDS is in essence an evaluator that can establish whether a set of network packets entering the system is malicious or not, by using what it has "learned" from previous data. In order to successfully train an IDS for a bespoke system, a security professional needs to therefore collect large quantities of data. The problem with this is that to gather this data there are several options each with several drawbacks [15]: (1) make use of known attack datasets to train the IDS (2) make use of existing IDS (e.g. Snort - Lightweight Intrusion Detection for Networks [18]) or (3) make use of an exploit database and simulate attacks on your own system as a pen testing approach. This latter approach is by far the most precise [7,15] as it allows to search for bespoke attacks to the IoT network and construct a dataset which is unique and effective for the specific system.

Whilst this approach produces the best suiting dataset it has some major drawbacks. Firstly, one must find and implement the attacks, which is a difficult process that might take a very long time [15]. Secondly, one would need to cause major disruptions to one's own network by running the attacks which might obstruct work and productivity. One of the many difficulties in detecting attacks on systems through the use of IDS is that one cannot (easily) predict potential attacker behaviour, or rather it is very difficult to classify an attack if its behavior differs from known attacks.

We formulate the problem as the following: Firstly, is it possible to overcome some of these difficulties and train an IDS for a specific IoT system making use of a model? The model would need to be able to produce similar results of the third approach, but would have the advantage that it could run parallel to the real system without causing downtime (Fig. 1). Secondly, by making use of non-determinism and probabilistic behavior could the modelling approach recreate behavior that mimics that of an attacker probing and finding weaknesses in the system?

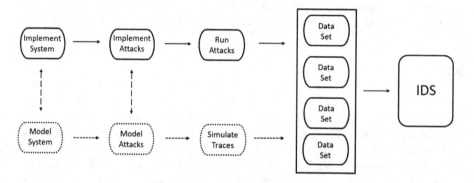

Fig. 1. Running model along-side real system to generate further datasets

4   IoT System Model

The intent of the modelled system is in essence to produce traces of behavior that correspond to the behaviour of real devices. A trace of a model under attack should be a subset of the full (finite) model trace. The traces are however limited by the drain of battery either by standard behavior or by attacker behavior, as devices out of battery stop performing actions. This means that going from a set of traces one can reconstruct a data file of what has taken place in the system. The traces can be used by the IDS to observe patterns of behavior and set out rules to use against real-world attackers.

We model the system as a synchronization of three core components: a set of devices, a set of monitors (each assigned to a device) and an attacker. The other aspect was measuring the impact of the actions on the system, specifically their effect on the devices battery and ability to operate successfully. Whilst several process calculi are available to represent traces of processes we customize the trace semantics of standard process calculus, as there are several further features we need to capture in order to be able to produce descriptive datasets. Several process calculi achieve the notion of communication however this achieves the effect of two processes performing an action simultaneously, we wish to capture the effect of a device *sending* an action and the other device *receiving* it. Looking at common process algebras such as CSP by Hoare [12], the semantics of the traces are a set of action of the processes. These kinds of traces allow for a human reader to understand the way the system operates. However an IDS can draw very little information from these traces and they fail to capture the concept of *messages* through the network. Specifically we need to be able to capture the intercommunication between devices at each transition within the trace (as per a log in a real system). This meant that output needed to hold further information rather than just the action taking place, the rules and the way the system was constructed was built around making a descriptive dataset.

The system as a whole is a tuple $\Phi = (D, M, T)$ where $D = \{D_1, .., D_n\}$ is a set of devices, $M = \{M_1, ..., M_n\}$ is a set of monitors calculating properties of their corresponding device and $T = \{t_i, ..., t_n\}$ is a set of times to calculate the changes over time of the system as a consequence of actions being triggered. We also introduce means to model an attacker as a malicious device.

4.1   Device Model

Given a global set of actions γ, a device D is a pair (A, P), where $A \subseteq \gamma \times [0, 1]$ is the set of *active* actions, where $(a, p) \in A$ means the process chooses action a with probability p, and such that $\sum \{p \mid (a, p) \in A\} = 1$; and $P \subseteq \gamma$ is the set of *passive* actions.

In order to recreate the full spectrum of potential system behaviours we model the set of actions of the device as the full capabilities of the real world device. This allows to capture the full set of abilities of its behavior and increases the accuracy of the benchmarking. This also eases the addition of further devices as they are simply modelled with the full send and receive action spectrum without the need to alter the rest of the system. The behavior of a device is in the form of a guarded communication, which in our model means that the communication is reliant on a set of conditions being true in order to be triggered. An action a in the device can only be triggered to begin a communication if it doesn't violate the capabilities of the system, such as remaining battery and time per message. This allows for realistic device behaviour, mimicking the patterns and constrictions of a real system.

4.2   Monitor Model

A monitor is the part of the system that enables its correct functioning as well as monitoring dangerous behavior. It calculates the shifts in battery of the various actions and synchronises with the devices to ensure correctness. A monitor M controls value λ, where λ is the remaining battery of the device. Given a global set of battery drains Ω the λ is measured as a quantity that is linearly drained by a ω_a where $\omega_a \in \Omega$ is a constant battery drain of an action, the monitor will update its λ value to λ' after each corresponding device action. The drain of each action is a fixed value calculated from the real world device, as such each action is associated to a single device only.

Rule 1. Given two devices $D_1 = (A_1, P_1)$ and $D_2 = (A_2, P_2)$, a communication initiated by device D_1 on an active action a, triggering corresponding receive action $\bar{a}$ in D_2, with an associated probability p takes the form:

$$\frac{(a,p) \in A_1 \quad \bar{a} \in P_2 \quad p > 0}{(A_1, P_1)||(A_2, P_2) \xrightarrow{(a,p)} (A_1, P_1)||(A_2, P_2)}$$

Rule 2. Given monitors M_1 and M_2 holding battery values λ_1 and λ_2, devices D_1 and D_2 are controlled by their respective monitors. The monitors calculate the drain in battery caused by action a and $\bar{a}$ from constant drain values ω_a and $\omega_{\bar{a}}$ in the form:

$$\frac{D_1||D_2 \xrightarrow{(a,p)} D_1||D_2 \quad \lambda_1 > \omega_a \quad \lambda_2 > \omega_{\bar{a}}}{\lambda_1 \rhd D_1||\lambda_2 \rhd D_2 \xrightarrow{(a,p)} (\lambda_1 - \omega_a) \rhd D_1||(\lambda_2 - \omega_{\bar{a}}) \rhd D_2}$$

These measurements can further aid the IDS in making informed decisions regarding the impact of the various actions in the system and were used to quantify the effectiveness of the attacker. Through this synthetic data the IDS will get a wide range of attacker behaviour that will lead to system failure, including potentially unknown attacker behaviour. Doing a similar approach without the model would require attacking one's own system and implementing an attack to collect data as per a penetration test (these approaches were compared in the experiments in Sect. 5).

4.3 Traces of the System

We differentiate each transition as a network packet running through the system, checked by the monitor of the device. Therefore they must be unique and fit all the possible behaviours of the device. As each action belongs to a single device it enables the corresponding devices to be uniquely identified.

Rule 3. Given two devices controlled by their monitors in the form: $M_1 \rhd D_1$ as CD_1 and $M_2 \rhd D_2$ as CD_2, and taking the total set of devices X, then the transition between CD1, CD2, taking system time t and being performed with probability p takes the form:

$$\frac{CD_1||CD_2 \xrightarrow{(a,p)} CD_1'||CD_2'}{(t, CD_1||CD_2||X) \xrightarrow{(a,p,t)} (t + (t_a + t_{\bar{a}}), CD_1'||CD_2'||X)}$$

In the computational view we compose a trace of the system inductively as a set of transitions in between states, where *prefix* is the prior transitions and the diagram describes a single transition in the form:

prefix	state	transition	state'	
$\overbrace{\{\}}$	$\overbrace{\bullet}$	$\overbrace{[a,p,t']}$	$\overbrace{\bullet}$	
$\downarrow$	$\downarrow$	$\updownarrow$	$\downarrow$	
$M_1\ D_1\ T_1$		$\exists\ D_i \ni b_i > \omega_a$	$M_1'\ T_1'$	$\forall\ k\ if\ k \in \{D_i,D_j\}$
$\vdots\quad\vdots\quad\vdots$		$\wedge\ \exists\ D_j \ni b_j > \omega_{\bar{a}}$	$\vdots\quad\vdots$	$\lambda_k' -= (\omega_a + \omega_{\bar{a}})$
$M_n\ D_n\ T_n$		$\wedge\ (a,p) \in D_i \wedge \bar{a} \in D_j$	$M_n'\ T_n'$	$\wedge\ t' += (t_a + t_{\bar{a}})$
				$if\ k \notin \{D_i,D_j\}\ M_k' = M_k$

The output of the system is a set of transitions following the semantics described. By generating the outputs of the system as the full behavior spectrum, the model can describe everything that can take place in the system. By updating the probabilities we can cater to the specifics of the underlying system behavior and make use of this to find unusual or potentially malicious behavior. The rules can expand to include a wide array of behaviours and specifics to regulate devices actions and when they can be activated. These can include complex policies on whether actions can be activated at a specific time or whether some actions have higher priority allowing for very specific behaviour to be modelled.

Running Example: We show an example composed of: devices D_x,D_y and D_z, corresponding monitors M_x,M_y and M_z, and global time t. Each device has different actions that are synchronized with some other devices. The monitors have battery values for the devices and each device has a set $\Omega_i \in \Omega$ of action drains. Transitions follow the described rules to construct the traces. Note that they do not represent the full possible set of traces but rather two simulations of the system until devices are drained.

Table 1. Example system model and its outputs

Devices:	$\boldsymbol{D_x} = (A_x, P_x)$ where
	$A_x = \{(read_{xy}, 0.3),(write_{xy}, 0.5),(read_{xz}, 0.2)\}$ and $P_x = \{\overline{read_{zx}}\}$
	$\boldsymbol{D_y} = (A_y, P_y)$ where
	$A_y = \{(write_{yz}, 0.8),(read_{yz}, 0.2)\}$ and $P_y = \{\overline{read_{xy}}, \overline{write_{xy}}, \overline{read_{zy}}\}$
	$\boldsymbol{D_z} = (A_z, P_z)$ where
	$A_z = \{(read_{zx}, 0.1),(read_{zy}, 0.9)\}$ and $P_z = \{\overline{read_{xz}}, \overline{write_{yz}}, \overline{read_{yz}}\}$
Monitors & drains:	$\boldsymbol{M_x} \ni \lambda_x = 5$ and $\boldsymbol{Drains_x} \ni \Omega_{A_x} = (1,3,1) \wedge \Omega_{P_x} = (1)$
	$\boldsymbol{M_y} \ni \lambda_y = 8$ and $\boldsymbol{Drains_y} \ni \Omega_{A_y} = (2,4) \wedge \Omega_{P_y} = (1,2,1)$
	$\boldsymbol{M_z} \ni \lambda_z = 2$ and $\boldsymbol{Drains_z} \ni \Omega_{A_z} = (1,1) \wedge \Omega_{P_z} = (1,2,1)$
Trace 1:	$[write_{yz}, .8, 30]\ [write_{xy}, .5, 50]\ [read_{xy}, .3, 65]$
Trace 2:	$[read_{xz}, .2, 8]\ [read_{xz}, .2, 16]\ [read_{xy}, .3, 31]\ [read_{xy}, .3, 46]\ [read_{xy}, .3, 61]$

4.4 Attacker Model

An attacker synchronizes with a subset of actions of the device. When an attacker synchronizes on the device the monitor will synchronize on that action and calculate the respective drainage. The monitor keeps track of all these measurements for its respective device. Implementing the model in a tool like PRISM allows us to make use of Probabilistic Computation Tree Logic (PCTL) [5] to calculate various conditions of pertinence to the system, to compute the optimal attack path, and to simulate traces of the model.

An attacker's intent is to behave in a manner that shortens the traces of the system by draining the value of battery in the monitor in the most efficient way possible. To model the attacker we made use of non-deterministic behavior in order to allow for anything to take place at any point. The advantage of non-determinism is that it allows for a system to arrive to an outcome using various routes. This can be manipulated to find optimal routes through the system and simulate varied behaviour. Unlike devices that are restricted by time and batteries of the devices they model, we allow for the attacker to have different levels of power to simulate various attacker strengths. An attacker, like the devices, has a set of unique actions A_A a, however unlike other devices does not have a set of passive actions as it sits outside the connectivity of devices and cannot receive messages. An Attacker may synchronise with any device in the system, and the set of actions $a_{A_i} \in A_A$ each correspond to different types of attacks in the real system. To expand further on the actions of the attacker, these should be very flexible and we make allowance for any action that can take place in the system (only restricted by the setup and protocols).

Each action label will correspond to an attack message from the real attacker and can be converted for the log file. For our specific example, each action in the attacker corresponds to the attacker in our experiment sending different packets/targeting different parts of the system as per the *attacker experiment* in Sect. 5. Beyond actions it is important for us to be able to monitor the behaviour of attackers looking at how many actions an attacking device can perform at a time T (whether by assuming a real attacker device or by simulating different powers of attack). This is highlighted by measurements of the system we implemented that were then modelled in the monitor of each device. The other information to keep track of is: the choices the attacker makes to take down the devices, as these are important behavioural patterns for the IDS to use and can give us insight on potential vulnerabilities as well as unknown attacker behaviours.

Unlike with the devices (whose intention is to cover the full spectrum of possible behaviours with the attacker), we are particularly interested in targeted behaviour. The attack actions therefore encompasses behaviours which are particularly damaging to the system (e.g. causes large drain of battery to the devices). As opposed to probabilistic behaviour we use non-determinism to find paths of behaviour that are particularly rewarding in terms of time taken to take down the system and in terms on lowering system usability (e.g. message throughput). To model non-determinism we remove the probabilities from the attacker action. This differs from probabilistic behavior because the non-deterministic choice between process A and D_x is resolved at the moment the first action takes place. Conversely in the case of a probabilistic choice is done before the actions takes place [3], so if there is a conflict in the system where both probabilistic actions and non-deterministic actions exist the probabilistic action is resolved first. By not associating a probability to an action we allow for the strategy of the attacker device to vary depending on what we are looking for in the system. Given a *policy* regulating the behaviour (corresponding to the available attack types) we allow for any action to take place at any point. This can be combined with a set of rules to find the trace of behaviour that allows to follow all the rules and yet still drain the battery as quickly as possible within these restrictions. Instead of a probability each action has an associated reward, and one can use this to find the path of most reward (or the best strategy to take down the system).

The non-determinism in combination with the reward structure *time* is used to find the optimum *attacker* strategy, or the most *rewarding* trace through the system. In PCTL it is written as $R\{$*"time"*$\}min =?[$ F *power* $= 0$ $]$ or the minimum time for the variable power (referring to battery levels) to reach 0. The value "time" is a variable calculated by the time for a single message to be sent by the attacker and cumulated for each message sent before the power reaches zero calculated in microseconds and the power drain is calculated by the formulas in Sect. 5. These reward structures allow for simulated attack strategies that an hypothetical attacker might make to take down the modelled IoT system. Not all attacks rely on speed and intensity to take down the system, as highlighted by the running example in Sect. 4.3 where the longer trace (Trace 2) is faster, so we model different rewards and observe different attacker behaviours. We can find generate traces of less detectable attack by associating an predictability score to an action and therefore keeping the behavior varied and realistic whilst still optimizing time. This can scale to several scenarios. We use these "optimized" traces to create a large dataset that mimics different kinds of attackers.

5   Experiment Methodology

To evaluate the effectiveness of the models we tested and compared the modelled system in Sect. 4.1 with the more standard approach described previously. Both the approaches output was used to train an IDS. The IDSs were then used to predict attack behavior. The verification was on the following basis: (1) Accuracy on unknown attack detection; (2) Ability to mimic devices behavior and *smart* attackers. The setup of the experiment was the following:

Experiment - Device Setup: We set up a small IoT network in the lab and then modelled it to compare the results and to test out the effectiveness of our model in creating synthetic dataset. For the sake of testing we kept the setup simple to display the tool as the thing that needs to scale and not the system. Once the simple model is created it is trivial to add more (similar) devices, whilst implementing a new system in the real world can be very time consuming. We implemented a sensor network consisting of two devices. Each device had the following *actions*; they took sensor readings and then could *send* it to the other device at any time; they could also *request* the sensor data from the other device at any point. The devices used simple HTTP protocol for communication, and the behaviour was stored in Apache log format. To accurately represent the devices and to create *smart* attackers, several measures needed to be obtained. Both devices were equipped with a Mh3500 battery. We made a basic assumption that the devices are on constantly. We argue this is a correct assumption as due to our attack the device is constantly in log mode and therefore never in sleep mode. Beyond this assumption we calculated time to send a message/log a message, baseline battery usage, percentage increase in battery usage under different DoS' strains (taken this value and dividing it by messages processed for second) and battery drain per message.

Experiment - Attacker: To validate the model we implemented a common DoS attack both in the real world and in the model. Our attack of choice was HULK, a DoS attacking tool which relies on several obfuscation techniques. In order to not be spotted whilst still outputting intense strain enough to take down systems very quickly [2]. The attack specifies it has the following properties: (1) obfuscation of source client - this is achieved by using a list of known user agents, and for every request that is constructed, the user agent is a random value out of the known list, (2) reference forgery - the referrer that points at the request is obfuscated and points into either the host itself or some major pre-listed websites, (3) stickiness - using some standard Http command to try and ask the server to maintain open connections by using Keep-Alive with variable time window and (4) unique transformation of URL - to eliminate caching and other optimization tools, they crafted custom parameter names and values and they are randomized and attached to each request. The tool was able to take down a web server within minutes from just a single host. Seeing as IoT devices will have less capabilities than any web server we hypothesized that this would be a good attack to use as its properties make for a good dataset that is not straightforward to detect. These properties and obfuscations led to different combinations of message structure that we used in the non-deterministic attacker.

To measure the time it takes per message we measure how many messages can be sent within a time period. This helps evaluate the accuracy in respect to the real world of our test attacker. In order to measure voltage usage across the different IoT devices, we attached an extra component in between the battery supply and the device to take the readings required. To measure battery drainage we utilized IoT battery lifespan estimator tool by Farnell [1]. This was used in combination with a variance we introduced on top of the calculator, to represent attack intensity and change to current. Through this we were able to estimate the different drains of the devices as an outcome of the actions they performed. We created datasets utilising three approaches and compared each dataset in two different experiments.

The first dataset (RWD) was constructed from data from the real system. We implemented the system of devices and the real-world attack and monitored the behavior of the system. The data was logged across a period of twelve hours and used to train the first IDS. The second approach was a naive approach, we constructed a synthetic dataset (ND) without attacking the system but rather attempting random behavior. This gave a comparison of the model with a different synthetic dataset this will help evaluate the effectiveness of the IDS predictions as they effectively should be random guesses. And finally, we followed our proposed approach (MD) following Sect. 4.

5.1   Experiment 1

As our dataset relies on stochastic events and actions, we created three datasets from the approach and evaluated each one to benchmark its effectiveness, a mean score was taken. Whilst our model is able to recreate very large datasets quickly we choose to keep the dataset size uniform across the initial experiment to get a fair comparison against the other two datasets. The comparison was based on accuracy of prediction against unknown attacks given IDSs trained with each of the datasets. The unknown dataset consisted of real world data of the systems behavior whilst being targeted by attacks that we had not modelled nor contained in the RWD. To measure accuracy we made use of the F score. The F score is a measure of a predictors accuracy, it is a measure of its precision over recall (a measure which takes in consideration both false positives and false negatives).

5.2   Experiment 2

The second experiment we ran was to test the effectiveness of the model in creating large quantities of behavior and the ability to readjust in case of network reconfiguration. We used deep learning classifiers catered to large datasets and created a much more efficient IDS purely through synthetic data. One of the core strengths of our approach is that once the model is setup the datasets are very easy to generate and we wanted to test whether this, in combination with our *smart* attackers, will lead to the ability to train better performing IDS.

6   Experiment Setup

To perform experiments described in Sect. 5 we implement a Python framework that runs through the various steps required to test the IDSs: data generation, data processing, standardization and setting up of the IDS's classifiers. This automatic framework prepares the datasets and trains the IDSs so that we may perform Experiment 1 and 2. It is implemented using the scikit-learn machine learning libraries.

6.1   Data Generation

Achieving a rich descriptive dataset was paramount in training an effective IDS. Through the outputted model traces we were able to generate a dataset of different transitions through the modelled system. These traces were descriptive enough for a machine learning algorithms to construct rules about negative behavior through supervised learning. The traces of the model correspond to the real system behavior and each transition was labelled as either normal or abnormal behavior, therefore they can be used to make informed decisions about the system. For instance, if the model traces of the attacker continuously target a device, the IDS can interpret this as a weak point and set a rule to limit this behavior, as this could correspond to the behavior of a real world attacker.

6.2 Data Processing and Standardization

To allow for data to be interpreted by machine learning algorithms it needs to go through a process of standardization. This is often due to categorical non-numeric features or continuous features. The data provided by most if not all internet protocols is categorical (e.g. agent names and method calls). As such, in order to evaluate it we first needed to go through an initial phase of pre-processing. The intent of pre-processing is to render the data machine readable whilst preserving patterns. The process we adapted was the process of binarisation. Binarisation allocates a numeric value to each unique feature for example if dealing with HTTP codes GET would become 0001, POST 0010, DELETE 0100 and PUT 1000. This allows for the features to maintain their patterns and their predictive power and be used normally. This initial step was applied to both the real world dataset and the naive synthetic dataset. This step was however not required for the model dataset as it already produced numeric features rather than categorical ones for efficiency.

6.3 Classifiers

The classifiers we implemented represented the IDSs. We choose to use two separate classifiers to get a better evaluation of the results. Each dataset was used to train two IDSs and then all the IDSs were tested against a new dataset of attack to establish their predictive power and the strength of the datasets.

The first classifier we implemented was Multi Layer Perceptron (MLP) Neural Network. An MLP consists of at least three layers of nodes. Except for the input nodes, each node is a neuron that uses a non-linear activation function [24]. MLP utilizes a supervised learning technique called back propagation for training. Its multiple layers and non-linear activation distinguish MLP from a linear perceptron. A linear perceptron is a function that can decide whether an input, represented by a vector of numbers, belongs to some specific class or not. Combining several together in an MLP and adjusting the functions and weights you build a statistically accurate classifier. The result is a non-linear perceptron that is able to classify non-linear classes.

The second classifier used was a Decision Tree Classifier. A decision tree is a decision support tool that uses a tree-like graph or model of decisions and their possible consequences, including chance event outcomes, resource costs, and utility. It is one way to display an algorithm that only contains conditional control statements [20]. Decision tree learning uses a decision tree (as a predictive model) to go from observations about an item (represented in the branches) to conclusions about the item's target value (represented in the leaves). The rules in the branches are automatically constructed from the training data which is labelled. Using these rules it will be able to take in the test data and run it until it reaches an end node corresponding to a class (either DoS attack or normal behaviour).

7 Results

Following the evaluation criteria in Sect. 5 and recreating the model described in Sect. 4, we generated and tested three model datasets against our benchmarks of the naive dataset and the real world dataset. Beyond the accuracy of the results, we make an argument for feasibility and re usability of our approach. The results were acquired by initially training two classifiers for each dataset, these were trained with 20,000 samples of which 10% were attacks. The classifiers were then evaluated on an unknown and unlabelled real world dataset of 100,000 samples of which 20% were attacks (of two different unknown types). The classifiers then attempted to label the new dataset to predict which ones were attacks.

7.1 Experiment 1 - Results

The neural network trained on the real world dataset proved to be very accurate with a 85.5% prediction accuracy. On the other hand the model dataset trained predictor whilst still high, suffered from some degree of variance ($79.7 \pm 6.3\%$). What was of most interest however was the predictions outputted by the naive dataset of 0.9%. This combined with the relatively inconsistent results of the synthetic dataset ($\pm 6.3\%$) make a case for over fitting. Over fitting is the scenario in which a model is trained so specifically to the training data that it is no longer classifying DoS attacks and normal behaviour of the system but rather focusing solely on the training data and learning on patters unique to the dataset not the system. This is quite common in Neural Networks as they perform best with very large quantities of data [24], which for this part of the experiment we did not have.

The results of the decision tree, contrasting to neural networks do not suffer from the same inadequacy of over fitting and do not necessarily need large amounts of data. This was mirrored by the results, as the model datasets all performed to very similar standards and the added randomness traces which might have disrupted the neural network made for a more ample rule set resulting in near perfect predicting power in the model dataset (98.8 ± 0.6). The real world data which did not look at the possibility of random behaviour only achieved 77% accuracy and the random dataset had a predictive power of near 50% as expected.

7.2 Experiment 2 - Results

We observed that our approach of using non-determinism to recreate attack traces was particularly effective for the rule based classifier however led to disruption during the back-propagation process of the neural network, as non-standardized data can create uneven results. This time using the much larger dataset of 100,000 transitions, the results were a lot more accurate (97.1%) than previously, confirming our hypothesis.

As highlighted by this example our model has one key advantage over the traditional approach. Data generation is fast and efficient. If we wanted to improve the training of the IDS used on the real world dataset to a similar level of accuracy, it would take several days of data collection and consumption of resources (electricity, system downtime etc.). We argue that whilst the initial effort of creating a model might be time consuming and perhaps not as intuitive for a potential system administrator, the phase of dataset generation makes up for this effort both for speed and predicting power of the IDS.

8   Conclusion and Future Work

Our case study and proposed methodology has shown very promising results. We have shown that generating synthetic datasets of DoS attacks in IoT networks through this tool is both effective and efficient. We believe that the ability for this approach to scale easily to multiple devices and protocols in combination with its strong predictive power makes a very good argument for its usage across various IoT networks. Our argument for scalability of this approach is two fold, firstly it scales well in terms of costs as you can make assessment prior to implementing the system and secondly, we can bypass several of the downsides of verification (in terms of state space) as we focus on simulation. Perhaps the most useful feature of our proposed approach is that it allows for the construction of datasets to be very efficient even if a device is added or the system is reconfigured. As this is a prominent concern in dynamic IoT systems this advantage is quite significant.

In this paper we included a case study of a single attack which worked very well. Our future work envisions the ability to model further attacks from a database to create an extensive set of attacks to create a much more predictive dataset. We envision that the ability to relatively easily plug and play any IoT system in combination with implemented corpus of attacks, could turn into a tool that generates synthetic datasets of attacks to train bespoke IDSs for any IoT system.

References

1. Farnell element14, calculating battery life in IoT applications (2017). http://uk.farnell.com/calculating-battery-life-in-iot-applications
2. Hulk, web: server dos tool - confessions of a dangerous mind, February 2013. http://www.sectorix.com/2012/05/17/hulk-web-server-dos-tool/
3. Andova, S.: Probabilistic process algebra. Technische Universiteit Eindhoven (2002)
4. Arnaboldi, L., Morisset, C.: Quantitative analysis of dos attacks and client puzzles in IoT systems. In: Security and Trust Management STM (2017)

5. Baier, C., Katoen, J.P., Larsen, K.G.: Principles of Model Checking. MIT Press, Cambridge (2008)
6. Bhuyan, M.H., Bhattacharyya, D.K., Kalita, J.K.: Network anomaly detection: methods, systems and tools. IEEE Commun. Surv. Tutor. **16**, 303–336 (2014)
7. Böhme, R., Félegyházi, M.: Optimal information security investment with penetration testing. In: Alpcan, T., Buttyán, L., Baras, J.S. (eds.) GameSec 2010. LNCS, vol. 6442, pp. 21–37. Springer, Heidelberg (2010). https://doi.org/10.1007/978-3-642-17197-0_2
8. Buennemeyer, T.K., Gora, M., Marchany, R.C., Tront, J.G.: Battery exhaustion attack detection with small handheld mobile computers. In: Portable Information Devices (2007)
9. Fruth, M.: Formal methods for the analysis of wireless network protocols. Oxford University (2011)
10. Gubbi, J., Buyya, R., Marusic, S., Palaniswami, M.: Internet of Things (IoT): a vision, architectural elements, and future directions. Futur. Gener. Comput. Syst. **29**, 1645–1660 (2013)
11. Guillen, E., Sánchez, J., Paez, R.: Inefficiency of IDS static anomaly detectors in real-world networks. Future Internet **7**(2), 94–109 (2015)
12. Hoare, C.A.R.: Communicating sequential processes. Commun. ACM **21**(8), 666–677 (1978)
13. Kwiatkowska, M., Norman, G., Parker, D.: PRISM: probabilistic symbolic model checker. In: Field, T., Harrison, P.G., Bradley, J., Harder, U. (eds.) TOOLS 2002. LNCS, vol. 2324, pp. 200–204. Springer, Heidelberg (2002). https://doi.org/10.1007/3-540-46029-2_13
14. Liang, L., Zheng, K., Sheng, Q., Huang, X.: A denial of service attack method for an IoT system. In: Information Technology in Medicine and Education, pp. 360–364. IEEE (2016)
15. Mell, P., Hu, V., Lippmann, R., Haines, J., Zissman, M.: An overview of issues in testing intrusion detection systems (2003)
16. Mirkovic, J., Dietrich, S., Dittrich, D., Reiher, P.: Internet Denial of Service: Attack and Defense Mechanisms (Radia Perlman Computer Networking and Security). Prentice Hall PTR, Upper Saddle River (2004)
17. Mukkamala, S., Janoski, G., Sung, A.: Intrusion detection using neural networks and support vector machines. In: Proceedings of the 2002 International Joint Conference on Neural Networks, IJCNN 2002, vol. 2, pp. 1702–1707. IEEE (2002)
18. Roesch, M., et al.: Snort: lightweight intrusion detection for networks. LISA **99**, 229–238 (1999)
19. Roman, R., Zhou, J., Lopez, J.: On the features and challenges of security and privacy in distributed internet of things. Comput. Netw. **57**, 2266–2279 (2013)
20. Safavian, S.R., Landgrebe, D.: A survey of decision tree classifier methodology. IEEE Trans. Syst. Man Cybern. **21**(3), 660–674 (1991)
21. Security, O.: Exploitdb: offensive security's exploit database. Archive (2009). https://www.exploit-db.com/
22. Suo, H., Wan, J., Zou, C., Liu, J.: Security in the internet of things: a review, vol. 3, pp. 648–651. IEEE (2012)
23. Talpade, R., Madhani, S., Mouchtaris, P., Wong, L.: Mitigating denial of service attacks, 29 January 2003. US Patent App. 10/353,527
24. Zhang, G.P.: Neural networks for classification: a survey. IEEE Trans. Syst. Man Cybern. Part C (Appl. Rev.) **30**(4), 451–462 (2000)

Annotated BPMN Models for Optimised Healthcare Resource Planning

Juliana Bowles[1], Ricardo M. Czekster[2(✉)], and Thais Webber[2]

[1] School of Computer Science, University of St Andrews, St Andrews KY16 9SX, UK
jkfb@st-andrews.ac.uk

[2] UNISC - University of Santa Cruz do Sul, Santa Cruz do Sul/RS 96815-900, Brazil
{ricardoc,thaiscs}@unisc.br

Abstract. There is an unquestionable need to improve healthcare processes across all levels of care in order to optimise the use of resources whilst guaranteeing high quality care to patients. However, healthcare processes are generally very complex and have to be fully understood before enhancement suggestions can be made. Modelling with widely used notation such as BPMN (Business Process Modelling and Notation) can help gain a shared understanding of a process, but is not sufficient to understand the needs and demands of resources. We propose an approach to enrich BPMN models with structured annotations which enables us to attach further information to individual elements within the process model. We then use performance analysis (e.g., throughput and utilisation) to reason about resources across a model and propose optimisations. We show the usefulness of our approach for an A&E department of a sizeable hospital in the south of Brazil and how different stakeholders may profit from a richer annotated BPMN-based model.

Keywords: Process modelling · BPMN
Performance analysis · Optimisation · Healthcare

1 Introduction

Managers direct considerable efforts towards process modelling to understand complex behaviours in their application domains. Models, by themselves, are only useful if they enable the extraction of relevant and contextual information that yields process improvements (e.g. task order rearrangements, enhanced allocations, smart schedules, reduction of resources and so on). If not with optimisation in mind, models are mainly used for documentation, describing abstract representations of logical sequences of steps that must be executed in predetermined order to reach specific outcomes. The combination of behavioural modelling with performance evaluation (PE) has recently received interest to handle

This research was partially supported by EPSRC grant EP/M014290/1, RAE grant NRCP1617/5/62 and SFC grant SFC/AN/12/2017.

complex processes in many application domains. PE uses techniques such as monitoring, analytical modelling or simulation to study systems and extract performance indicators (e.g. utilisation or queue length). These techniques help managers to fully understand processes and analyse performance metrics unveiling bottlenecks and more fitting options for resource allocations. One domain where findings can be particularly beneficial is the healthcare domain.

It is common practice today to use model notations such as Business Process Modelling & Notation (BPMN) [18] to gain a better understanding of tasks and assigned resources (both machinery and personnel) required for different purposes across organisations. Although it is possible to apply performance evaluation techniques on such models, this is often not done due to lack of information on required resources for different tasks, inaccurate understanding of processes or simply a lack of knowledge required to understand what is needed as input for a comprehensive performance assessment. In the healthcare domain, the authors in [2] discuss the occurrence of failures when dealing with complex processes due to simple problems related to delivery of care by professionals. This could be avoided if problems were thoroughly analysed for performance problems using standardised notations. Resources (of any kind, e.g., supplies, machines, professionals and so on) are a key issue for maintaining high quality requirements to patients and so they must be addressed with utmost importance, not simply relying on process redesigns/reengineering approaches that permeate huge organisations with unconvincing results. Lack of flexibility in modelling is also a huge challenge for healthcare, since every hospital deals with different constraints and requirements. There must be some degree of adaptability when modelling and inferring performance [6]. However, simulation is sometimes viewed as an intricate technique due to the technical skills required when modelling, executing scenarios, interpreting outputs or making reliable suggestions to other managers or stakeholders. A further source of concern when integrating healthcare domain with performance assessment relates to a communication gap between clinical staff and process analysts [13].

This paper aims to bridge the gap between business process modelling and performance evaluation through task annotations for resource management. The idea is to use text annotations objects in BPMN to automatically fill simulation scenarios with interesting input data. BPMN with structured annotations could be potentially applicable for the automatic generation of simulation models (where analysts could benefit from quantitative evaluation of what-if scenarios, e.g. those maximising throughput or resources utilisation), or even analytical models (where analysts could infer state-based behaviours, performance bottlenecks or possible deadlocks). We propose an easy-to-use structured general-purpose notation format for annotating BPMN models with relevant information for resource planning. In this paper, we apply the notation on a case study describing a simplified healthcare scenario. The critical situation faced by healthcare in Brazil justifies our focus on that domain [10], and hence our aim to improve healthcare processes for hospital management. However, this work can be applied more broadly to different settings and any kinds of processes and simulations. The main goal is a detailed analysis and comparison of resources through simulation with the goal to be able to identify ways of improving processes and reduce resources. In the processes used in hospitals, this can be to reduce the number of staff required at different units at different times of the day, on different days of the week or even to accommodate for needs at different times of the year. High-level stakeholders or non-performance analysts can thus benefit from this annotation structure to help guide performance analysts towards strategic and profitable process configurations. Our case study is based on real processes followed by a hospital located in the south of Brazil (HSB). We have obtained the details of HSB's A&E process through a series of staff interviews and data from the underlying ERP (*Enterprise Resource Planning*) system. Our approach, and the results of the analysis carried out on the scenarios that can be automatically generated from our annotated BPMN models. In this case, we used it to reflect on how to potentially achieve a saving in staff resources required to still guarantee tolerable waiting times.

This paper is structured as follows: Sect. 2 describes general details concerning BPMN modelling and expected performance indices. The work is described in the context of related work in Sect. 3. Section 4 proposes a structured annotation format for domain users to enhance their BPMN models for simulation. Section 5 shows how the annotations can be used in an example of a process followed by one department of hospital HSB. We discuss the scenarios generated automatically from the annotated BPMN model, and the results of their simulation as well as how they can be used for resource planning. Section 6 presents final considerations and ideas for future work.

2   BPMN and Performance Modelling

Enriching models with text annotations for performance analysis is not new and there is a myriad of proposed notations and extensions for coping with model descriptions using *Layered Queueing Networks* (LQN), *Stochastic Petri Nets* (SPN), *Coloured Petri Nets* (CPN), *Performance Evaluation Process Algebra* (PEPA), *Well Formed Networks* (WFN), *Stochastic Automata Networks* (SAN) and so on. Processes, on the other hand, may be modelled using BPMN, Workflows, or *Unified Modelling Language/Activity Diagrams* (UML/AD), among others. The focus of our present research lies on adding simple textual attachments to process elements with performance related data for later analysis (by simulation or other technique), thus offering broader analysis possibilities for stakeholders. The added annotations of BPMN processes may lead to a variety of further possible analyses, where a general view is depicted in Fig. 1.

There is a need to bridge process models with performance models, however, research is lacking on how to perform such integration. The main objective of this work is to discuss how such integration may occur so analysts could use the proposed notation in real world settings helping decisions on resource capacity or other performance metric of interest or *Key Performance Indicator* (KPI) according to the contextual domain of application [14,15].

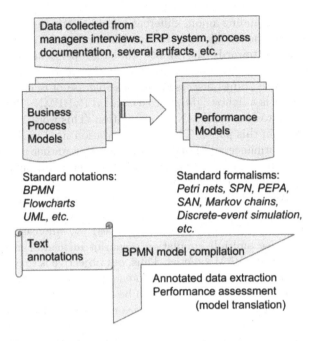

Fig. 1. Interplay between process models and performance models

Discrete Event Simulation (DES) is a well known performance evaluation technique with broad use amidst researchers, modellers, analysts, decision makers and managers in general [12,19,22]. Its scope encompasses different application domains and it is based on building a process model according to a system under study, assign probability distributions to arrivals, tasks durations and amount of needed resources and than execute the model throughout a replication length set up by the modeller. The idea is to compute the usual performance indexes e.g. throughput, utilisation, queue length, waiting time per task or resource and vary parameters for each scenario so comparisons may take place. Simulation is used when available data does not respect restrictions imposed by analytical modelling, for instance, exponential distributions, being more flexible to model patterns of behaviours through the process model [19]. We bring the benefits of this combination into a healthcare domain.

3   The Context and Related Work

Text annotations in business models are not a novel approach to provide more unstructured detail for analysing processes. BPMN in itself uses modelling primitives to convey process behaviours, acting as an effort to document operations for different communities (e.g. managers, factory floor workers, company CEOs and other stakeholders). However, whilst BPMN's standardised notation allows for fast shared understanding among different roles, performance analysis at this level is hampered by the simplicity of the models that can be captured.

Significant efforts towards the ability to blend performance parameters into BPMN models were conducted throughout the years, with considerable advances. For instance [2] has discussed one possible use of richer BPMN models for healthcare. It is a lightweight approach called PyBPMN (Performability-enabled BPMN) that extends BPMN for simulation. This work is the closest to the approach taken in this paper. The textual notation used in [2] to represent *performability* (performance and reliability) is, however, rather unconventional. By contrast, our approach uses a straightforward textual notation, easily understood by managers but rich enough with important parameters for later simulation analysis. Another distinction is that the authors in [2] aimed a model execution using an approach known as eBPMN execution (a domain specific language that retains BPMN's semantic properties) [7], whereas our work has the potential to devise multiple simulation scenarios instead of merely process simulation according to a BPMN model. Thus, our objective is to extend textual annotations to derive simulation scenarios to enable us to understand the effect of varying resources and expected delays and be able to do this dynamically. To the best of our knowledge, this perspective was not discussed in other work.

Other approaches discuss how BPMN could be used to enhance analysis improving automation and dealing with variability, a problem concerning clinical pathways in hospitals [21] and directives on how to combine modelling and simulation altogether [5]. The approach described in [21] discusses that Activity Diagrams (ADs) or BPMN models do not appropriately capture specific clinical requirements, being insufficient and inefficient when addressing performance. To address this, the paper offers an annotation-based approach to deal with those issues, but it presents an unstructured approach with textual data that may or may not be used for further analysis. Conversely, [5] combines BPMN with Business Process Simulation (BPS), a novel approach with considerable limitations. By contrast, our approach uses BPMN to annotate models that can be used in verified and validated simulation software tools such as Arena [19], AnyLogic, ProModel, Simul8, JMT [4], queueing123 GNU/Octave package [17] and so on.

The approach taken by [9] also differs considerably from ours, because it assumes the creation of an intermediary model that stands between the initial AD and the load performance model at the back-end. In their approach, users need to generate another model and fill it with load parameters for stress testing or other quality measures. The model uses a notation similar to extensions provided by UML.

Finally, work using simulation in a healthcare domain has been discussed thoroughly by several authors [3,5,11,12,20]. In particular, Mandahawi [16] has addressed the use of a continuous improvement technique (Six Sigma) and combined it with DES for carrying out waiting time analysis in an A&E department with interesting discussions.

As a standard notation, BPMN provides means to create so called *extensions* with specific sets of descriptions in order to capture elements not anticipated in the original notation core. Our approach, however, does not rely on such extensions because we would like to work with a more structured approach for detailing specific resource related information. Our idea is to define a simple set of elements - which we consider simpler than using extensions - suitable for a broad range of multiple scenario DES analysis and usable by high-level managers and stakeholders (i.e. domain experts) alike.

4   Structured Text Annotation Proposal for Process Models

The key BPMN component used here is the `annotation`, e.g., a textual description allowed by the standard which can be associated to different model elements. These texts are then processed by external tools and used to create a simulation model allowing the composition of multi-parameter, i.e., what-if scenarios. Managers could inspect each scenario outcome and adjust resource capacity or other KPI of interest [15] according to the evaluation needs. Auxiliary tools are used to process the BPMN model extracting useful data suited for DES, e.g., replication length and number of replications, time schedules, mean service time for each resource type, initial simulation conditions (e.g. work in progress), interarrival times, total/maximum amount of entities performing model tasks and so on.

It is worth mentioning that expert opinions are crucial when modelling processes (especially for later simulation prospects), since specific service time distributions should be employed for approximating real settings and yielding valid results. The choice of a probability distribution could profoundly impact analysis and completely change suggestions on resource management, schedules and allocations. For example, using an exponential distribution (one parameter, i.e., average observed value) for inter-arrival times is completely different from using a normal (where parameters are the average and the standard deviation) or a triangular distribution (e.g., a distribution having a minimum value, a mode and a maximum value) which are more suitable for situations characterised by extreme lack of data [19]. This is usually neglected by process modellers, despite being of vital importance for a sound and reliable analysis. The analyst should consult domain experts for the provision of useful statistics that dictates appropriate probability distributions for tasks and events. These measurements are present in ERP databases and logs, sometimes needing extra effort for validating, transforming and extracting relevant information within the vast amounts of textual data that could be available.

Table 1 lists structured text annotations for use in BPMN by managers or analysts, where they could adjust parameters and use diverse processing tools or scripts for generating simulations or analytical models. We stress the fact that our approach contains the least number of parameters for a comprehensive simulation study. In this paper, the main elements for attaching structured annotations are pool/swimlanes, start event, tasks (activities) and exclusive gateways (decisions) according to a standard tag-based BPMN extension proposal. Our

Table 1. Structured annotations for BPMN elements with examples

(a) Per *swimlane*	`SimulationName=<NAME>`
	`SimulationNumberOfReplications=<VALUE>`
	`SimulationReplicationLength=<VALUE>;<UNIT>`
	`SimulationBaseTimeUnit= <UNIT>`
	`<NAME>: string data`
	`<VALUE>: integer value`
	`<UNIT>: seconds|minutes|hours|days`
(b) Per *start* event	`StartEventEntity=<NAME>`
	`StartEventTimeBtwArrivals=<DTYPE>;<PARAMETERS>;<UNIT>`
	`StartEventEntitiesPerArrivals=<VALUE>`
	`StartEventMaxArrivals=<VALUE>`
	`<NAME>: string data`
	`<DTYPE>: triangular|normal|uniform|constant|other`
	`<PARAMETERS>: depends on distribution`
	`<UNIT>: seconds|minutes|hours|days`
	`<VALUE>: integer value`
(c) Per *task* event	`TaskType=<TYPE>`
	`TaskDelayType=<DTYPE>;<PARAMETERS>;<UNIT>`
	`TaskResourceData=<NAME>;<QUANTITY>;<CAPACITY>`
	`<TYPE>: delay|resource-based`
	`<DTYPE>: triangular|normal|uniform|constant|other`
	`<PARAMETERS>: depends on distribution`
	`<UNIT>: seconds|minutes|hours|days`
	`<NAME>: string data`
	`<QUANTITY>: integer value`
	`<CAPACITY>: integer value`
	`<VALUE>: integer value`
(d) Per *decision*	`DecisionData=<TYPE>;<PERCENTAGES>|<CONDITIONS>`
	`<TYPE>: probability|expression (equation)`
	`<PERCENTAGES>: set of comma separated values`
	`<CONDITIONS>: logical expression (equation)`

set of annotations were inspired by the input parameters offered by the DES software Arena [19]. The choice of this particular tool stems from the fact that it is widely used by a large community of practitioners, researchers and modellers.

At this point, we are devising the simulation scenarios from the annotated BPMN model and *manually* creating a process model in Arena. It is our aim, in future research, to incorporate the ability of creating models completely automatically. We have implemented a tool written in Java to support the scenario creation by opening BPMN models (with the annotations mechanism explained here) and parsing its standard XML file. This solution helps stakeholders understand which scenarios are possible as well as to visualise and select the best ones for execution (according to their requirements), using Arena to manually create the simulation model (though other DES could be used).

Table 1 defines the BPMN elements and the proposal of structured text annotations as follows:

(a) The text annotations on pools (or specific swimlanes) specify global parameters related to simulation execution such as the `NumberOfReplications` for confidence intervals, the simulation time characterised by `Replication Length` and `BaseTimeUnit`. The later is an annotation to set the time unit for the calculated results.

(b) The start event element of BPMN models may append text annotations to specify the entities being analysed by their `NAME` (e.g., patients, clients, items). In addition, the simulation execution and the `TimeBtwArrivals` needs to be specified by its probability distribution type (i.e., triangular, exponential, normal, constant, and *other* for different expressions definitions, etc.) and its parameters (values for mean, standard deviation, mode and so on, according to type definitions) along with respective time units for the specified measures.

(c) Tasks are defined by their labels (i.e., `NAME`) and type (`TYPE`), whereby the type can only be `delay` or `resource-based`. If a task is `resource-based`, information about resources must be given in order to map the basic set of parameters for collecting performance indices related to queueing statistics and resource utilisation. A given resource has a label (i.e., an identification name), the quantity needed to perform the specific task and its capacity for the whole process execution (i.e., number of available resources with this label for the process).

(d) Exclusive gateways in the BPMN model representing decisions for taking specific flows can be more detailed using a structured annotation with its `TYPE` (i.e., indicated as `probability` values or an `expression` with logical conditions based on entity attributes, for example). For a `probability` type, a list of $1..(N-1)$ percentage values are needed for output flows of the gateway (where N is the total number of output flows from a gateway).

Generic field names such as `NAME` are reserved for free text input, e.g., strings explaining some specific necessity or commentary describing some important task mention or desired behaviour. Fields containing a `VALUE` are composed of integers depending on the element they are located (in a swimlane, a start event or a task). The `PARAMETERS` found in `StartEventTimeBtwArrivals` and `TaskDelayType` labels indicate the values estimated for the time between arrivals and the average task duration, respectively, following the chosen probability distribution given in the field `DTYPE`.

The proposed format is suitable for models where those explained elements are present so modellers can use annotations to write proper simulation related tags for analysis. These annotations may be inserted in a manual fashion, however, an automatic tool could be effortlessly implemented to help users annotate the elements in a model avoiding mistakes or typos within the tags. Such a tool can save the annotations in the same model format (XML) to be opened and edited later, without interfering with the model's original set of elements and flow. We show how our approach has been used on a case study in the next section.

5   Case Study: Brazilian Hospital Setting

We apply our proposed annotated BPMN to a sizeable hospital HSB located at the southern state of Brazil. It is a hospital with approximately 200,000 occurrences per month (statistics from 2015), with 250 beds and 900 employees. It provides care to both public (under SUS - Brazilian universal public health system) and private patients. The hospital is located in a city with a population of around 160,000 with a further 100,000 living in the surroundings. The hospital is a regional reference for secondary care.

5.1   An A&E Process

The A&E department is viewed by management as the current bottleneck, as the resources are not evenly distributed, causing several delays and loss of revenue, despite dissatisfaction with the service. We have modelled this department using BPMN, and used our annotation mechanism to assign parameters to a future simulation model, where scenarios are to be created to demonstrate to management where the most critical deficiencies are. In addition, it serves as a way to identify further actions that should be implemented to improve the operation, reduce queues and waiting time for patients, as well as reduce costs and resources (balancing the utilisation among different professionals) to augment satisfiability with the service and perhaps increase revenue altogether by reducing unnecessary costs.

Figure 2 contains the initial model for the A&E department. In accordance with our previously introduced annotations, the pool has some general simulation parameters (shown at the top left-hand corner), the initial event (here **Patient arrivals**) has specific annotations related to simulation start rule, and all other tasks have annotations with resource related data. Non-critical patients arrive at A&E and go through an admission registering procedure (note that critical patients bypass this task and go straight to medical care/consultation). After registration, patients are classified according to their condition (Risk assessment process), which is performed by a *Manchester Triage System* trained nurse (with a given duration pattern according to the annotation). We stress the fact that the A&E should be used only in critical cases, however, according to data observations, only 10% are in fact immediate care patients. The hospital management team recognises and is aware of this problem, but are unable to address this since they are obliged to provide care to every patient that arrives at the hospital. After classification patients go to the Medical consultation procedure, where a Clinical decision is made by the medical doctor to send the

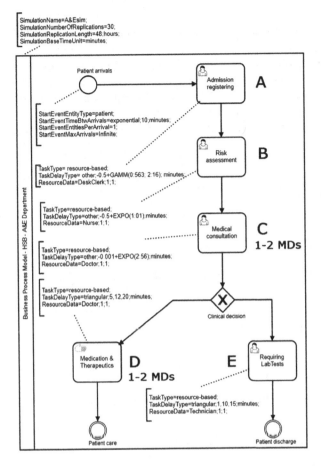

Fig. 2. Annotated BPMN model derived from HSB data for the A&E process.

patient to a Medication & Therapeutics procedure (with some routing probability, e.g. 50%) or to Requiring LabTests procedure for a deeper investigation.
Each possible flow from the exclusive gateway has its specific ending, i.e. patient
discharge or patient care.

Figure 2 also shows some desired scenarios envisaged by the analyst, making
it possible to understand the impact of having different numbers of resources
(such as the number of available medical doctors at a given moment in time)
on performance. We have labelled the figure from A to E, and we have mapped
some resource variations for our purposes, such as having *one* or *two* resources
for tasks C and D (here Medical Doctors – MDs).

As the annotations show, we are mapping resource durations and scenarios
for a simulation, as well as setting some important parameters that could be used
by another (discrete event) simulation tool. It is important to notice that we are
enriching a BPMN model, i.e., the resource-related data was not present in the

original model given to us by hospital staff who are only able to describe the
process flow and activities related to patients that come to the A&E. Instead, we
are proposing a format where data is available for a comprehensive simulation
analysis where modellers are annotating tasks with probability distributions of
interest as well as assigning numbers of resources, task durations and so on, so
multiple scenarios can be automatically created with a reasonable amount of
effort. For the creation of more simulation scenarios, we propose that modellers
could use child annotations, e.g., annotations of annotations, as illustrated in
Fig. 3.

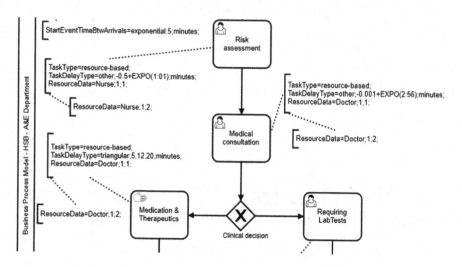

Fig. 3. Example of child annotations usage for deriving possible simulation scenarios.

Introducing yet another notation that modellers should be aware of is problematic and we are aware of this. However, we believe that an auxiliary user
friendly tool could aid modellers specify annotations properly for later processing, as well as making it easier to check the consequences of changes to some
of these annotations. A further advantage is that such a tool can create the
intended set of scenarios for simulation automatically, and the DES tool of choice
can then execute several simulations automatically where performance indices
are calculated for posterior analysis. Going back to the original BPMN model,
making changes to some of the annotations and parameters and rerunning simulations would give users a better understanding of their processes and the effects
of changing resources at different points. Our approach combines strengths of
BPMN and simulation, as it uses a straightforward mechanism to build simulation scenarios using annotations, a simple mechanism already present in the
standard notation.

5.2   Analysis Results

We have used the annotation artifact as source to devise multiple scenarios for analysis. We have extracted the full annotations from the BPMN model by implementing a software written in the programming language Java which used XML APIs for parsing and working with models. The software identified BPMN elements such as pools/swimlanes, start and end events, tasks, sequence flow between tasks and exclusive gateways, and stored the full set of annotations in internal data structures. Then, the annotations are parsed to compute the amount of scenarios that would be created, using the textual variations and other data present in the model. Ideally, the analyst would select just a few scenarios to be executed from the potential high number of possible combinations of options that could be yielded by the user choices. Also, automatically created simulation models could be defined, where specific DES software could run in batch mode, notifying when the process has finished. At the moment, we are taking the scenarios generated by our software, selecting the most interesting ones and then manually creating the simulation models.

According to Fig. 2, the following scenarios are possible to be derived from the basic structured annotations:

- General simulation parameters (annotations at the pool element)
  - Name (SimulationName): `A&Esim`
  - `NumberOfReplications`: 30
  - `ReplicationLength`: 48 h
  - `BaseTimeUnit` (for reporting): minutes

- Start event element (annotations at the `StartEvent` element)
  - `EntityType`: Patient
  - `TimeBtwArrivals`: it follows an exponential distribution with parameter equal to 10 min
  - Further parameters are irrelevant for the present analysis

- Task elements include (annotations at `Task` elements)
  - Admission registering (A), Risk assessment (B), Medical consultation (C), Medication & Therapeutics (D), Requiring LabTests (E). Different parameters are embedded within each annotation, with some variations as to the number of needed resources per task

Looking at the possible scenario variations for this model according to the annotations, we can see that the `ResourceData` parameter is different for some tasks. This represents the amount of resources the manager envisioned to analyse, i.e., the impact of these variations in the performance indices.

In this case, we have four scenarios, where the overall model follows the pattern `Patient Arrival -- Process -- Exit`, where `Patient Arrival` has no variations and `Exit` is just a sink (e.g. where all patients end). Note that we are disregarding the exclusive gateway in this analysis because it has no annotations of type and exit percentages in this example. For simulation purposes we assume 50% chance in the exclusive flows.

The four selected scenarios are as follows (see Fig. 2 – MD stands for *Medical Doctor*):

1. A (1 DeskClerk) – B (1 Nurse) – C (1 MD) – D (1 MD) – E (1 Technician)
2. A (1 DeskClerk) – B (1 Nurse) – **C (2 MDs)** – D (1 MD) – E (1 Technician)
3. A (1 DeskClerk) – B (1 Nurse) – C (1 MD) – **D (2 MDs)** – E (1 Technician)
4. A (1 DeskClerk) – B (1 Nurse) – **C (2 MDs)** – **D (2 MDs)** – E (1 Technician)

Due to observed arrival rates, for this particular analysis we consider Task A to have no concerns, seeming well adjusted according to patient's inflow. In this analysis, we are concerned with investigating the influence on the number of MDs on the performance indices, so our scenarios will vary the amount of doctors at stations C and D. It is worth mentioning that if one resource becomes *idle*, it may be *shared* for better performance – the DES software tool usually implements this behaviour automatically, because in the model we are creating resources of the same *type*, i.e., generic MDs.

It is noticeable that, depending on the choices made by the analyst while defining the annotations, the number of scenarios could be very large. For example, if one selects three distinct inter-arrival times, with a task with one resource associated having two parameter variations and another task with three resource quantities (1, 2 and 4), the number of total scenarios for this case is $3*2*3 = 18$ scenarios, which is a significant amount for a comprehensive analysis. In these cases, the analyst could manually reduce the selected parameter variations or use the tool to generate the full set of scenarios and then select the ones he or she wishes to study more thoroughly (only those would be executed).

Table 2 presents the simulation results for the generated scenarios using Arena [1]. We have extracted the main performance indices for 30 replications, with 48 h duration and interarrival time per patient consisting of 10 min. For this BPMN model, the simulation model conversion was straightforward since no particular Arena element was used. We have used service and arrival times obtained from actual HSB data, with distribution fittings (using Arena's internal tool named *InputAnalyzer*). The tool has yielded the following parameters:

- Time between arrivals: 1 patient, on average, arrives every 10 min (we are modelling the busiest hours, e.g., from 10.00 to 14.00 of a weekday);
- A: Service time $-0.5 + GAMM(0.563, 2.16)$ minutes;
- B: Service time $-0.5 + EXPO(1.01)$ minutes;
- C: Service time $-0.001 + EXPO(2.56)$ minutes;
- D: Service time $TRIA(5, 12, 20)$ minutes;
- E: Service time $TRIA(1, 10, 15)$ minutes.

Waiting Time (W) encompasses the time spent in queue plus the time under service (in Arena, this is called *Total Time*). For this metric, we have computed the average value for all replications.

Utilisation (U) considers the fraction of time that resources remain in *Idle* state (instead of *Busy*, i.e. attending patients), and it is computed internally

Table 2. Results for the simulation scenarios set by the analyst in the annotations.

Scenario	Resource	Utilisation U (%)	Waiting Time W (minutes)	Population N (patients)
1	DeskClerk–A	7.5		
	Nurse–B	6		
	Doctor–C	86.2	48.4	≈2.5 (Consultation)
	Doctor–D	62.6		
	Technician–E	12.4		
2	DeskClerk–A	7.5		
	Nurse–B	7.5		
	Doctor–C	43.9	23.8	*negligible*
	Doctor–D	62.7		
	Technician–E	13		
3	DeskClerk–A	7.5		
	Nurse–B	7.4		
	Doctor–C	85.6	45.8	≈4.1 (Consultation)
	Doctor–D	30.7		
	Technician–E	12.2		
4	DeskClerk–A	7.5		
	Nurse–B	7.6		
	Doctor–C	43.9	19.3	*negligible*
	Doctor–D	31.1		
	Technician–E	13.2		

Throughput: 284 patients (4-h shift) for each scenario (i.e. same interrarrival time)

by Arena. Adding resources would invariably impact performance indices positively (particularly utilisation). For managers, however, it implies additional costs that sometimes are prohibitive, and instead other alternatives should be taken into account (e.g. improving service times or addressing bottlenecks on other stations).

It is worth noticing that Scenario 2 has interesting utilisation levels for the medical doctor resources, i.e., 43.9% for doctor–C–D and 62.7% for doctor–E. It was not clear that this scenario would yield this outcome before our analysis, and it just required one additional resource given the workload required. Also, the waiting time is affected by the number of resources, where Scenario 3 has the worst, despite the increase in terms of medical doctors. For the population metric, for Scenarios 2 and 4, no queueing took place, however, for Scenarios 1 and 3, for the Consultation task, queue lengths of ≈2.5 and ≈4.1 respectively were calculated by the software, which is interesting, because Scenario 3 for instance has had an increase in terms of resources and still has formed significant patient queueing.

Our approach described here allows managers to annotate models and assign parameters for resources (and other measures) in a simple way, yielding performance indices for analysis and scenario comparisons. It would be sufficiently easy to derive parameters as needed, for the same model (e.g. we are considering static models as of now). We chose not to use too many parameter variations due to the number of potential scenarios that could be created. In future work, we will explore how to devise a mechanism to help select a set of *interesting* scenarios.

6   Final Considerations

Performance evaluation directly from BPMN models is not readily available for analysts and stakeholders. At present, process models and performance models are two distinct approaches with separate sets of primitives. This paper tackles this problem by providing an alternative where process models are enriched with textual annotations simple enough to be used by stakeholders with different backgrounds, but still powerful enough to provide interesting information for simulation. The structured annotations that can be attached to process elements include performance data relevant for creating different parameter scenarios, simulation execution, or analytical modelling. If some parameter is missing, our compiler uses predefined values to guarantee an initial analysis. Our approach has been used to tackle resource requirements within complex models to facilitate the informed revision and optimisation of healthcare processes.

In future work, we aim to extend the notation to encompass other advanced modelling and execution as well as devising a scenario report for users where they are able to select scenarios of interest. We will also consider the integration with a simulation package to automatically execute scenarios and generate a graphical report with suggestions.

In another line of work, we are using BPMN to capture clinical guidelines for the treatment of chronic conditions [8]. For patients with multiple ongoing chronic conditions, aka multimorbidity, several guidelines have to be applied simultaneously. We have used constraint solvers to automatically detect inconsistencies between such guidelines and suggest alternatives in accordance to certain parameters. If we can integrate the present BPMN annotations in our BPMN models for clinical guidelines, we may be able to exploit the benefits of both approaches. We will explore this combination in future work.

References

1. Arena simulation. https://www.arenasimulation.com/. Accessed 06 June 2018
2. Antonacci, G., Calabrese, A., D'Ambrogio, A., Giglio, A., Intrigila, B., Ghiron, N.L.: A BPMN-based automated approach for the analysis of healthcare processes. In: Proceedings of the 25th International Conference on Enabling Technologies: Infrastructure for Collaborative Enterprises (WETICE), pp. 124–129. IEEE Computer Society (2016)

3. Baril, C., Gascon, V., Miller, J., Côté, N.: Use of a discrete-event simulation in a Kaizen event: a case study in healthcare. Eur. J. Oper. Res. **249**, 327–339 (2016)
4. Bertoli, M., Casale, G., Serazzi, G.: JMT: performance engineering tools for system modeling. ACM SIGMETRICS Perform. Eval. Rev. **36**, 10–15 (2009)
5. Bisogno, S., Calabrese, A., Gastaldi, M., Ghiron, N.L.: Combining modelling and simulation approaches: how to measure performance of business processes. Bus. Process Manag. J. **22**, 56–74 (2016)
6. Bocciarelli, P., D'Ambrogio, A., Giglio, A., Paglia, E., Gianni, D.A.: Transformation approach to enact the design-time simulation of BPMN models. In: IEEE 23rd International WETICE Conference, pp. 199–204. IEEE Computer Society (2014)
7. Bocciarelli, P., D'Ambrogio, A., Paglia, E.: A language for enabling model-driven analysis of business processes. In: 2nd International Conference on Model-Driven Engineering and Software Development (MODELSWARD), pp. 325–332. IEEE Computer Society (2014)
8. Bowles, J., Caminati, M., Cha, S.: An integrated framework for verifying multiple care pathways. In: Eleventh International Symposium on Theoretical Aspects of Software Engineering (TASE). IEEE Computer Society (2017)
9. Costa, L.T., Czekster, R., de Oliveira, F.M., de M. Rodrigues, E., da Silveira, M.B., Zorzo, A.F.: Generating performance test scripts and scenarios based on abstract intermediate models. In: Proceedings of the 24th International Conference on Software Engineering and Knowledge Engineering (SEKE 2012), pp. 112–117 (2012)
10. Doniec, K., Dall'Alba, R., King, L.: Brazil's health catastrophe in the making. Lancet **392**, 731–732 (2018)
11. Forsberg, H.H., Aronsson, H., Keller, C., Lindblad, S.: Managing health care decisions and improvement through simulation modeling. Qual. Manag. Health Care **20**, 15–29 (2011)
12. Günal, M., Pidd, M.: Discrete event simulation for performance modelling in health care: a review of the literature. J. Simul. **4**, 42–51 (2010)
13. Harper, P.R., Pitt, M.A.: On the challenges of healthcare modelling and a proposed project life cycle for successful implementation. J. Oper. Res. Soc. **55**, 657–661 (2004)
14. Ioan, B., Nestian, A.S., Tita, S.M.: Relevance of key performance indicators (KPIs) in a hospital performance management model. J. East. Eur. Res. Bus. Econ. **2012**, 1–15 (2012)
15. Khalifa, M., Khalid, P.: Developing strategic health care key performance indicators: a case study on a tertiary care hospital. Proc. Comput. Sci. **63**, 459–466 (2015)
16. Mandahawi, N.: Reducing waiting time at an emergency department using design for six sigma and discrete event simulation. Int. J. Six Sigma Competitive Adv. **6**(1/2), 91–104 (2010)
17. Marzolla, M.: The qnetworks toolbox: a software package for queueing networks analysis. In: Al-Begain, K., Fiems, D., Knottenbelt, W.J. (eds.) ASMTA 2010. LNCS, vol. 6148, pp. 102–116. Springer, Heidelberg (2010). https://doi.org/10.1007/978-3-642-13568-2_8
18. OMG: Business Process Model & Notation. v2.0. OMG (2011). http://www.omg.org. Doc. id: formal/2011-01-03
19. Rossetti, M.D.: Simulation Modeling and Arena, 2nd edn. Wiley Press, Hoboken (2010)
20. Shim, S.J., Kumar, A.: Simulation for emergency care process reengineering in hospitals. Bus. Process Manag. J. **16**, 795–805 (2010)

21. Shitkova, M., Taratukhin, V., Becker, J.: Towards a methodology and a tool for modeling clinical pathways. Proc. Comput. Sci. **63**, 205–212 (2015)
22. Sokolowski, J.A., Banks, C.M.: Principles of Modeling and Simulation: A Multi-disciplinary Approach. Wiley, Hoboken (2011)

Using Formal Methods to Validate Research Hypotheses: The Duolingo Case Study

Antonio Cerone$^{(\boxtimes)}$ and Aiym Zhexenbayeva

Department of Computer Science, Nazarbayev University, Astana, Kazakhstan
{antonio.cerone,aiym.zhexenbayeva}@nu.edu.kz

Abstract. In this paper we present a methodology that combines formal methods and informal research methods to validate research hypotheses. We use the CSP (Communicating Sequential Processes) process algebra to model the system as well as some aspects of the user, and PAT (Process Analysis Toolkit) to perform formal verification. We illustrate our methodology on Duolingo, a very popular application for language learning. Two kinds of data are considered: a log of the interaction of the user with the application and the assessment of the user's level of proficiency in the language to be learned (subject profile). The goal is to validate research hypotheses that relate the subject profile to the user's cognitive approach during interaction (cognitive profile). To this purpose, two CSP processes, one modelling the cognitive profile that is associated by the considered research hypothesis to the subject profile and one modelling the interaction log are composed in parallel with the system model. Thus, for each user with the given learner profile and specific interaction log, the verification of the functional correctness of the overall system validates the correlation between cognitive profile and subject profile.

Keywords: Formal methods · CSP process algebra
Process Analysis Toolkit (PAT) · Multimodal interaction
Language learning application

1 Introduction

Almost all people are nowadays routinely running heaps of applications on their mobile devices. There is a large variability of both users, e.g. in terms of age, education and cultural background, and applications, which cover entertainment, learning, personal monitoring, accounting, internet banking, booking and many other domains. Because of this global variability it is essential to understand the different cognitive approaches users may take while interacting with the application and try to address them. However, in order to best adapt the application interface to the user, it is also needed to understand how the user's knowledge and activity within the domain for which the application is created drive a specific cognitive approach.

© Springer Nature Switzerland AG 2018
M. Mazzara et al. (Eds.): STAF 2018 Workshops, LNCS 11176, pp. 163–170, 2018.
https://doi.org/10.1007/978-3-030-04771-9_13

In this paper, we consider a language-learning application, which uses two modalities to present exercises to the user, i.e. audio and printed text, and we observe that the combination of the two modalities within the same exercise may induce some users to make errors. In order to understand what drives the observable user behaviour in interacting with the application, in the specific learning context of our example, we distinguish between the *cognitive profile*, characterising the way the user focuses on a specific presentation modality, and the *subject profile*, characterising the level of proficiency of the user in the foreign language.

We use formal methods, specifically the CSP process algebra [5], to model the application and the cognitive profile and to formally represent the log of the interaction of the user with the application [4,6]. The subject profile is instead defined using social science research methods: tests, questionnaires, interviews, etc. Our approach aims to consider a hypothesis on the relation between given cognitive profile and subject profile and validate it by carrying out, for each user with that subject profile, formal verification on the model of the systems constrained by both the given cognitive profile and a formal representation of the interaction log of the user. We use the model-checking capabilities of the Process Analysis Toolkit (PAT) [2] to perform formal verification.

2   The Problem: Duolingo Application Case Study

Duolingo [1] is the most popular language learning platform. It includes a website and mobile applications. It offers a large number of language courses for both English and non-English speakers.

A lesson is structured as a sequence of exercises of different kinds. After the user completes an exercise, the application provides an assessment as correct or wrong before proceeding to the next exercise or completing the lesson. In this paper we consider the three kinds of exercises illustrated in Fig. 1:

(a)   (b)   (c)

Fig. 1. Duolingo screenshots.

(a) the user hears a sentence in the foreign language and has to type it;

(b) the user reads a sentence in the native language and has to translate it in writing to the foreign language;

(c) the user reads and hears a sentence in the foreign language and has to translate it in writing to the native language.

These three kinds of exercises are representative of the three possible situations in which audio and visual presentation modalities are used separately and in combination.

We carried out some experiments using the Duolingo application and we realised that a common error consists in giving the answer in the wrong language. Typically, the user will tend to ignore the information on the goal of the exercise ("Type what you hear" or "Translate this sentence") and focus instead on the content of the exercise. Furthermore, since the exercise may be proposed using two modalities, audio and printed text, the user may focus on just one of such modalities. For example, when the question involves a translation to the native language, the sentence to translate is proposed in the foreign language using both audio and print modalities. However, the user may actually focus on just one modality. If the user consistently focuses on the audio modality, several repetitions of this kind of exercise will create an automatism whereby the user always tends to translate an audio perception to the foreign language. Therefore, when the exercise requests to type what is heard, a user affected by such acquired automatism would instead translate to the native language, thus giving the wrong answer. We analyse this kind of error in Sects. 4 and 5.

3 CSP Model

In this section we use CSP to model the three kinds of exercises illustrated in Fig. 1. In our abstract model, the only parameter used to discriminate between correct and wrong answer is the language in which the answer is given: native or foreign language. The model is presented in Fig. 2.

```
DuolingoExercise() = exercise -> ( typeWhatYouHear -> CheckTypeWhatYouHear() []
                        translateToForeign -> CheckTranslationToForeign() []
                        translateToNative -> CheckTranslationToNative() );

CheckTypeWhatYouHear() = foreignLang -> correct -> DuolingoExercise() []
                   nativeLang -> wrong -> DuolingoExercise();
CheckTranslationToForeign() = foreignLang -> correct -> DuolingoExercise() []
                   nativeLang -> wrong -> DuolingoExercise();
CheckTranslationToNative() = nativeLang -> correct -> DuolingoExercise() []
                   foreignLang -> wrong -> DuolingoExercise();
```

Fig. 2. System model: exercises and assessment

The DuolingoExercise process presents the three possible kinds of exercises: typeWhatYouHear, translateToForeign and translateToNative. A request to type what is heard in the foreign language (typeWhatYouHear) is checked by the CheckTypeWhatYouHear process, which returns correct if the answer is given in the foreign language (foreignLang) and wrong if it is given in the native language (nativeLang). The other kinds of exercises are checked analogously.

Processes DuolingoAudio and DuolingoPrint in Fig. 3 model the two output modalities used by Duolingo. The requests to translate to the native language (translateToNative) are presented using both audio and printed text, whereas the other two requests are presented using just one modality, printed text for the translation to foreign language (translateToForeign) and audio for request to type what is heard in the foreign language (typeWhatYouHear).

```
DuolingoAudio() = exercise -> ( typeWhatYouHear -> audio -> DuolingoAudio() []
                                translateToNative -> audio -> DuolingoAudio() []
                                translateToForeign -> noAudio -> DuolingoAudio() );

DuolingoPrint() = exercise -> ( typeWhatYouHear -> noPrint -> DuolingoPrint() []
                                translateToNative -> printForeign -> DuolingoPrint() []
                                translateToForeign -> printNative -> DuolingoPrint() );

SessionSystem() = DuolingoExercise() || DuolingoAudio() || DuolingoPrint();
```

Fig. 3. System model: modalities.

```
UserData() = exercise -> typeWhatYouHear -> foreignLang ->
             exercise -> translateToForeign -> foreignLang ->
             exercise -> translateToNative -> nativeLang ->
             exercise -> typeWhatYouHear -> nativeLang -> Stop();

SessionUserData() = SessionSystem() || UserData();
```

Fig. 4. Example of user data.

The overall system is given by process SessionSystem, which is the parallel composition of the three components illustrated above.

Figure 4 shows an example of data (process UserData), consisting of a sequence of four exercises proposed by Duolingo and the corresponding answers given by the user. We can note that, in the last exercise, the user gives the wrong answer by using the native language instead of the foreign language, that is, by translating rather than just typing what is heard.

We may compose the overall system SessionSystem with this specific dataset getting a system behaviour constrained by the data (process SessionUserData). Note that for each exercise the user behaviour starts with an external choice among perception of audio, perception of printing text and user's decision to answer in native or foreign language. In fact, nothing prevents the user from deciding to answer in a language independently of the actual request by the application.

4   Formal Verification

In this section we present how to verify the functional correctness of the model defined in Sect. 3, how to constrain the model with specific user profiles and how to verify whether such user profiles are prone to incur in the error considered at the end of Sect. 2. Functional correctness is characterised by the ability of the system to provide the user with the proper assessment of the answer as correct or wrong for each exercise. We may say that "*always*, if an exercise is presented to the user, then *any further* exercise will *not* be presented to the user *until* the user's answer is assessed as correct *or* wrong". This statement may be refined towards a low-level temporal logical formula as:

"*always*, if there is an **exercise**, then, starting from the *next state* of the system, there will *not* be any **exercise** *until* the user's answer is assessed as **correct** *or* **wrong**".

The temporal logic counterpart of this statement is the formula of the first assertion in Fig. 5. Using PAT we can see that this first assertion is verified as valid. The second assertion, which states that the user gives a correct answer to each exercise, is, instead, verified as invalid. This is obviously due to the fact that, correctly, our model leaves the option that the user may give wrong answers open. We can say that this second assertion formalises a usability property, since it states that the user will not be induced by the system to provide a wrong answer.

In order to analyse the error illustrated at the end of Sect. 2, we consider two cognitive profiles: a user who always focuses on the print modality and a user who always focuses on the audio modality. These two kinds of users, after repeatedly using the application, will be driven towards two different forms of automatism. Figure 6 shows the models for such profiles in terms of the acquired automatism. A user who focuses on the print modality (process UserFocusPrint) realises that:

- if the sentence is not printed, then the answer has to be in the foreign language;
- if the sentence is printed in the native language, then the answer has to be in the foreign language;
- if the sentence is printed in the foreign language, then the answer has to be in the native language.

A user who focuses on the audio modality (process UserFocusAudio) realises that:

- if the sentence is not heard, then the answer has to be in the foreign language.

Therefore the audio modality is less informative than the print modality and gives space to two possible, conflicting forms of automatism. As we have discussed in Sect. 2, the user may interpret the audio either as a request to answer in the foreign language or as request to answer in the native language. The usability property in the first two assertions in Fig. 6 is verified by PAT as valid on process SessionFocusPrint (first assertion) and invalid on process SessionFocusAudio (second assertion). This is consistent with the fact that the automatism developed by the user who focuses on the print modality always leads to the correct answer, but this is not the case for the user who focuses on the audio modality.

```
#assert SessionSystem() |= [] ( exercise -> X (! exercise U ( correct || wrong)) );
#assert SessionSystem() |= [] ( exercise -> (! wrong U (correct)) );
```

Fig. 5. Assertions for functional and usability properties.

```
UserFocusPrint() = noPrint -> foreignLang -> UserFocusPrint() []
                   printNative -> foreignLang -> UserFocusPrint() []
                   printForeign -> nativeLang -> UserFocusPrint();

UserFocusAudio() = audio -> ( foreignLang -> UserFocusAudio() []
                             nativeLang -> UserFocusAudio() ) []
                   noAudio -> foreignLang -> UserFocusAudio();

SessionFocusPrint() = SessionSystem || UserFocusPrint();
SessionFocusAudio() = SessionSystem || UserFocusAudio();

#assert SessionFocusPrint() |= [] ( exercise -> X (! exercise U correct) );
#assert SessionFocusAudio() |= [] ( exercise -> X (! exercise U correct) );

#assert SessionUserData() |= [] ( exercise -> X (! exercise U ( correct || wrong)) );
#assert SessionUserData() |= [] ( exercise -> (! wrong U (correct)) );
```

Fig. 6. User profile model and analysis.

Finally, we may also verify properties of the system behaviour on a specific data set. For example, considering the last two assertions in Fig. 6 with the dataset UserData in Fig. 4, which is consistent with focusing on the audio modality, as component of process SessionUserData, PAT verifies the first assertion (functional property) as valid and the second assertion (usability property) as invalid. Obviously, if we remove the last exercise from UserData, which is the one causing the user error, then the usability property is verified as valid.

5   Hypothesis Formulation and Validation

We formulate two hypotheses to relate a cognitive profile, i.e. which modality the user focus on, to a subject profile, i.e. which level of proficiency the user has in the foreign language.

Hypothesis [H1] *A learner at a beginner level in the foreign language always focuses on the print modality.*

Hypothesis [H2] *A learner at an advanced level in the foreign language always focuses on the audio modality.*

These two hypotheses are suggested by the observation that beginners have difficulty in listening comprehension and need the support of a written text, whereas advanced learners may be able to quickly go through the exercises reacting immediately to the audio without reading the written text.

In order to validate these hypotheses, an extensive user experience evaluation should be conducted at the following two levels:

1. the creation of a log of the interaction of the user with the application, through either natural observation or by using an instrumented version of the application;
2. the assessment of the user's level of proficiency in the foreign language (learner profile), through either a language test or a questionnaire or interviews.

Then, for each subject user, the log is converted into a `UserData` process to be combined with the `UserFocusPrint` or `UserFocusAudio` process depending on whether the user is assessed at the beginner or advanced level of proficiency, respectively.

```
DataModelFocusPrint() = SessionUserData() || SessionFocusPrint();
DataModelFocusAudio() = SessionUserData() || SessionFocusAudio();

#assert DataModelFocusPrint() |= [] ( exercise -> X (! exercise U ( correct || wrong)) );
#assert DataModelFocusAudio() |= [] ( exercise -> X (! exercise U ( correct || wrong)) );
```

Fig. 7. Formal verification for hypothesis validation.

Formal verification is finally carried out as shown in Fig. 7. The two processes, `DataModelFocusPrint` and `DataModelFocusAudio`, combine the data collection at item 1 above, represented by process `SessionUserData`, with the user's assessment at item 2 above, which is associated by our research hypotheses with either process `SessionFocusPrint`, if the user is assessed as a beginner ([**H1**]), or process `SessionFocusAudio`, if the user is assessed as an advanced learner ([**H2**]).

The assertion corresponding to the cognitive profile that one of the research hypotheses associates with the assessed subject profile of the considered user is valid when the behaviour of process `SessionUserData` is consistent with the process that models the cognitive profile, i.e. it does not invalidate the functional correctness. In fact, a mismatch between the considered cognitive profile and the real user data would cause a conflict in some answer assessment as correct or wrong, with a resultant deadlock after the occurrence of `exercise` but before either `correct` or `wrong` may occur, thus invalidating the functional correctness. This is what happens if we verify the first assertion in Fig. 7 on the user data given in Fig. 4, due to the mismatch between a user whose real data is the result of a focus on the audio modality and a cognitive profile constraint modelling a focus on the print modality. Therefore, a research hypothesis is satisfied by a specific user when the assertion on functional correctness is valid. Finally, we can conclude that a research hypothesis is validated when it is satisfied by a statistically significant number of users with the appropriate subject profile.

6   Conclusion and Future Work

The analysis carried out on the Duolingo case study shows that multimodal interaction is not always effective and it is essential to take the user's subject profile into account while choosing whether and how to combine modalities. Furthermore, if our research question is validated, then we may claim that although the Duolingo application is appropriate for learners at the beginner level, in its current state it is not equally effective for learners at the advanced level. In this case, a possible improvement could be the introduction of a learner level, either explicitly set by the user or inferred by the system in some intelligent way. The learner level would then drive the choice of modalities to use for question presentation: multimodality audio and print for a beginner learner and unimodality, either audio or print, for an advanced user.

There are three directions for our future work. First, we would like to validate our research hypotheses for the Duolingo case study on real data as discussed in Sect. 5. Second, we are developing an instrumented language learning application to present a large variety of exercise types, control the order in which they are presented, monitor the interaction for the purpose of data collection and automatically generate formal representations of datasets to be used for hypothesis validation. Finally, we plan to apply our methodology to further, more challenging case studies. In fact, the case study and abstraction level considered in this paper result in very straightforward cognitive profile and system model, with human errors immediately visible on the data model. The purpose of our choice was to test the feasibility of our methodology and easily illustrate it. We now intend to combine this work with our work on cognitive errors [3] and consider system models in which human errors are not easily observable on the data model and emerge because of multiple cognitive causes.

References

1. Duolingo. https://www.duolingo.com
2. PAT: Process Analysis Toolkit. pat.comp.nus.edu.sg
3. Cerone, A.: Towards a cognitive architecture for the formal analysis of human behaviour and learning. In: Mazzara, M., et al. (eds.) STAF 2018 Workshops, LNCS 11176, pp. 216–232 (2018). https://doi.org/10.1007/978-3-030-04771-9_17
4. Dix, A., Finlay, J., Abowd, G., Beale, R.: Human Computer Interaction. Prentice Hall, Upper Saddle River (2004)
5. Hoare, C.A.R.: Communication Sequential Processes. Prentice Hall, Upper Saddle River (2004)
6. van Schooten, B., Donk, O., Zwiers, J.: Modelling interaction in virtual environment using process algebras. In: TWLT15: Interaction in Virtual Worlds, pp. 195–212 (1999)

Personality Gaze Patterns Unveiled via Automatic Relevance Determination

Vittorio Cuculo$^{(\boxtimes)}$ ⑩, Alessandro D'Amelio⑩, Raffaella Lanzarotti⑩, and Giuseppe Boccignone⑩

PHuSe Lab, Department of Computer Science, Università degli Studi di Milano, Milano, Italy
{vittorio.cuculo,alessandro.damelio,raffaella.lanzarotti, giuseppe.boccignone}@unimi.it

Abstract. Understanding human gaze behaviour in social context, as along a face-to-face interaction, remains an open research issue which is strictly related to personality traits. In the effort to bridge the gap between available data and models, typical approaches focus on the analysis of spatial and temporal preferences of gaze deployment over specific regions of the observed face, while adopting classic statistical methods. In this note we propose a different analysis perspective based on novel data-mining techniques and a probabilistic classification method that relies on Gaussian Processes exploiting Automatic Relevance Determination (ARD) kernel. Preliminary results obtained on a publicly available dataset are provided.

Keywords: Eye movement · Gaze · Social interaction
Human behaviour · Gaussian Process · Classification · Personality
Big five

1 Introduction

The Latins would say 'oculus animi index' to refer the amount of personal information provided by a person's eyes. The gaze, indeed, is an important component of social interaction and a crucial non-verbal signal adopted as a basic form of communication [30]. Humans profoundly entrust on gaze cues during social and cooperative tasks with other conspecifics. This effect negatively emerges when referring to persons with autistic-like traits that may have troubles in understanding signals coming from the eye region of the other's face [1].

Eye movements are shown to be relevant and strictly related to the expression and perception of emotional states [2,3,29], cognitive goals [7,13,48], personality traits [12,28,36,41,44] and is known to play a key role in regulatory functions, as conversational turn-taking [20]. In the course of a typical face-to-face interaction, eye contact is an indicator of trustworthiness and attractiveness [6,33], although a long direct gaze could be interpreted as a threat [34].

Neuroimaging studies of face perception confirms that direct eye contact activates specific brain areas involved in human interaction and face processing,

© Springer Nature Switzerland AG 2018
M. Mazzara et al. (Eds.): STAF 2018 Workshops, LNCS 11176, pp. 171–184, 2018.
https://doi.org/10.1007/978-3-030-04771-9_14

namely the superior temporal sulcus (STS) [25]. In particular, the intraparietal sulcus (IPS) appears to specifically support the recognition of another person's gaze direction [14,40]. These results confirm that person perception is increased when gaze is directed toward the viewer.

Having said that, and without going deeper in neurobiological details, it looks obvious that in order to realise effective and 'empathic' computational systems that naturally interacts with humans (HCI) it is necessary to understand or, at least, take into consideration the processes behind human gaze deployment. These could eventually be involved to mediate the interaction with a virtual or physical agent, in particular when dealing with humanoid robots that include eyes (for synthesis) [9], or with ones that gauge the counterpart's gaze (for recognition) [49].

In this work we will focus on the involvement of personality traits as indicator of specific gaze patterns. Personality is an information typically expressed by adopting the Big Five personality traits [23], also known as the five factor model (FFM). The five factors have been defined as agreeableness, conscientiousness, extraversion, neuroticism and openness to experience. These are assessed via standard psychological tests to the participants of an experiment.

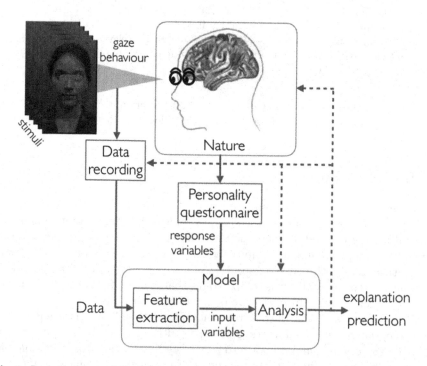

Fig. 1. Investigating subject's personality traits from gaze behaviour in face-to-face interaction (time-varying face stimuli). Full arrows highlight the *Data → Model* road to explanation and prediction; dashed arrows trace the feedback information to meet the quest for suitable predictor variables, model revision and experimental design.

Previous results suggest that personality influences visual information processing and social gazing, but most of these approaches present some drawbacks, such as small dataset size [12], focus on very specific personality traits [28], adoption of non-natural stimulus [44] and in general, for the analysis, they all rely on classical statistical methods applied to spatial and temporal gaze features extracted from raw data.

As to the latter point, here we offer a different perspective. It has been argued [21] that statistical rituals striving for an unthinking "search for statistical significance" have led to "irrelevant theory, questionable conclusions, and has kept statisticians from working on a large range of interesting current problems" [10]. Breiman, in particular has acknowledged that beyond classic data analyses, algorithmic modeling has developed rapidly in realms outside statistics (involving complex prediction problems such as speech recognition, image recognition, nonlinear time series prediction), and it has gained currency since it can be used both on large complex data sets and as a more accurate and informative alternative to data modelling on smaller data sets [10]. In this view the classic data modelling approach starts with assuming a treatable model relating predictor variables to response variables (e.g., a linear regression model) and model validation is performed through classical tests (goodness-of-fit, residual examination, etc). In contrast, machine learning-based modelling relies upon an algorithm that operates on input data (usually in the form of a feature vector) to predict the responses; here, model validation is in terms of measured predictive accuracy. However, these two "cultures" [10] need not be mutually exclusive options. After all statistics starts with data and builds models (cfr. Fig. 1) in order to be able to: (i) forecast what the responses are going to be to future input variables (prediction level); (ii) to derive information about how nature is associating the response variables to the input variables (explanation level). The roots of statistics, as in science, lie in working with data and checking theory against data [10]. If focus is brought back on actually solving the problem, then in many complex and concrete cases this attitude is likely to lead to the adoption of a hybrid methodology. It is worth mentioning that, though algorithmic models can give better predictive accuracy than data models, it is often objected that an emphasis on predictive accuracy leads to complex, uninterpretable models that generalise poorly and offer little explanatory insight. However, the trade-off between predictive accuracy and interpretability is less grievous than deemed [26]. Indeed, it has been shown in the machine learning field that by searching for parsimonious versions of the adopted model (in the Occam's sense), it is possible to achieve predictive performance close to optimal, while gaining explanatory insights into the relevant mechanisms of the phenomenon under consideration [26].

Such a synergistic perspective is the methodological rationale behind the work presented here and it is summarised at a glance in Fig. 1. Techniques coming from different research areas will be adopted, both for feature extraction and classification. In particular, we show how the Automatic Relevance Determination (ARD) approach, which has been originally conceived in the Bayesian machine-learning framework as an effective tool for pruning large numbers of irrelevant features [37], is suitable to lead to a sparse subset of predictor variables. These bear explanatory value, while avoiding cumbersome classic statistical procedures for selecting features, or even more complex machine learning-based approaches (e.g., [5], for the specific case of gaze analysis).

Results obtained on a public dataset [19] acquired during a face-to-face experiment will provide additional levels of explanation of gaze behaviours adopting a probabilistic approach. An overview of the method is given in Sect. 2, while Sect. 3 presents the simulation results, and a conclusive discussion is given in Sect. 4.

2   Method

Gaze shifts are the result of two main oculomotor actions (as shown in Fig. 2): fixations and saccades. The former are concerned with bringing onto the fovea salient objects of a scene, while the latter are rapid transitions of the eye that permit to jump from spotting one location of the viewed scene to another. It is worth noting that the saliency of an object is in principle strictly related to a given task [47]. The study presented here relies on eye-tracking data collected from subjects along a free-viewing (no external task) experiment. Though this choice might be questionable in general [47], in our case the free-viewing condition is suitable for dynamically inferring the history of their "internal" selection goals and motivation, and thus their personal idiosyncrasies, as captured by the resulting attentive behaviour.

Beyond fixations and saccades, in the presence of moving objects (that are likely to occur in dynamic scenes) an additional action arises, called smooth pursuit. This is typically associated with fixations since the focus remain on the same stimulus, but in this case a movement of the eyes is required.

Recent research has shown that the pupil signal from video-based eye trackers contains an additional event, namely post-saccadic oscillations (PSOs). These are very important for a precise temporal classification of the events. PSOs in fact, have shown to influence fixation and saccade durations by at least 20 ms [35].

In the following we will refer to a visual scan path as the result of a stochastic process; namely a time series defined as $\{(r_1, t_1), (r_i, t_i), \cdots\}$, where $r_i = (x_i, y_i)$ identifies a specific gaze location at time t_i in presence of a natural scene $\mathcal{I}$.

$$\mathcal{I} \mapsto \{(r_1, t_1), (r_i, t_i), \cdots\} \tag{1}$$

A classification step [39] is eventually required to distinguish between the four oculomotor actions presented above. This allows to parse the raw data time series into a higher level representation of events: fixations $\mathbf{f} = (r, t^s, t^e)$, saccades $\mathbf{s} = (r^s, r^e, t^s, t^e)$, smooth pursuits $\mathbf{p} = (r^s, r^e, t^s, t^e)$ and PSO $\mathbf{o} = (r^s, r^e, t^s, t^e)$. In the case of saccades, smooth pursuits and PSO, r^s and r^e represent respectively the start and end gaze location. Likewise t^s and t^e stand for start and end time of the event.

2.1 Feature Extraction

Considering a given scan path $\mathcal{W} = \{(\mathbf{f_i}, \mathbf{s_i}, \mathbf{p_i}, \mathbf{o_i})\}_{i=1}^{N}$, with N the number of events, we derive features related to the spatial and temporal properties of specific events. Given the stochastic nature of eye movements, these too can be seen as random variables (RVs) generated by an underlying random process. Such properties include fixation duration, saccade amplitude, saccade direction and event frequency.

Saccade amplitudes and directions are important because lie at the heart of systematic tendencies or "biases" in oculomotor behaviour. These can be thought of as regularities that are common across all instances of, and manipulations to, behavioural tasks [45,46]. One remarkable example is the amplitude distribution of saccades and that typically exhibit a positively skewed, long-tailed shape [45–47]. Other paradigmatic examples of systematic tendencies in scene viewing are: initiating saccades in the horizontal and vertical directions more frequently than in oblique directions; small amplitude saccades tending to be followed by long amplitude ones and vice versa [45,46]. Indeed, biases affecting the manner in which we explore scenes with our eyes are well known in the psychological literature (see [31] for a thorough review), and have been exploited in computational models of eye guidance [4,17,32] providing powerful new insights for unveiling covert strategies about where to look in complex scenes.

As an additional property we also take into consideration the pupil dilation. This information is typically adopted for emotion-related tasks, in particular to assess the level of arousal [8]. To the best of our knowledge, this is the first time pupillometric data are adopted to study personality traits.

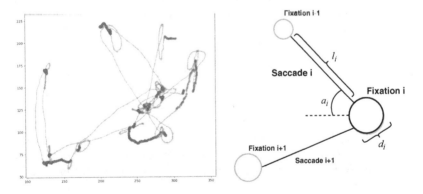

Fig. 2. (Left) visualisation of a typical visual scan path record. (Right) sequence of three fixations with indication of extracted features: fixation duration (d_i), saccade amplitude (l_i) and saccade direction (a_i).

Fixation Duration. The duration of the i-*th* occurrence of the identified fixations measures the time spent spotting a specific location and it is obtained as $d_i =$

$t_i^e - t_i^s$. These durations $D = \{d_i\}_{i=1}^N$ can be seen as gamma-distributed random variables $D \sim \Gamma(a, b)$, whose probability density function (pdf) is defined as

$$f(d \mid a, b) = \frac{1}{b^a \Gamma(a)} d^{a-1} \exp\left(\frac{-d}{b}\right) \tag{2}$$

Here $\Gamma(\cdot)$ is the gamma function; the parameters of shape $D_a = a$, that closely approximates a normal distribution when large, and scale $D_b = b$ are fitted via maximum likelihood estimation (MLE).

Saccade Amplitude. For what concern saccades, one of the properties taken in consideration is their amplitude. This measure the absolute length of the eye movement and is obtained as the Euclidean distance between the start and end locations of each saccade, $l_i = \sqrt{(x_i^s - x_i^e)^2 + (y_i^s - y_i^e)^2}$ where $r_i^s = (x_i^s, y_i^s)$, $r_i^e = (x_i^e, y_i^e)$ and $(r_i^e, r_i^s) \in s_i$. In this case, the amplitudes $L = \{l_i\}_{i=1}^N$ are assumed to be sampled from an α-stable distribution $L \sim f(\xi; \alpha, \beta, \gamma, \delta)$. These form a four-parameter family of continuous probability densities [22], where the parameters are the skewness β (measure of asymmetry), the scale γ (width of the distribution), the location δ and the characteristic exponent α, or index of the distribution that specifies the asymptotic behavior of the distribution as $l^{-1-\alpha}$. Thus, relatively long gaze shifts are more likely when α is small. For $\alpha \geq 2$ the usual random walk (Brownian motion) occurs; if $\alpha < 2$, the distribution of lengths is "broad" and the so called Levy flights take place. Such distributions have been shown to suitably capture the statistical behaviour of gaze shift amplitudes [4,11], and, more generally, brain activities occurring in the attention network [18]. There is no closed-form formula for f, which is often described by its characteristic function $E[\exp(itx)] = \int_{\mathbb{R}} \exp(itx)dF(x)$, F being the cumulative distribution function (cdf). Explicitly,

$$E[\exp(itx)] = \begin{cases} \exp(-|\gamma t|^\alpha (1 - i\beta \frac{t}{|t|}) \tan(\frac{\pi\alpha}{2}) + i\delta t) \\ \exp(-|\gamma t|(1 + i\beta \frac{2}{\pi} \frac{t}{|t|} \ln|t|) + i\delta t) \end{cases}$$

the first expression holding if $\alpha \neq 1$, the second if $\alpha = 1$. Special cases of stable distributions whose pdf can be written analytically, are given for $\alpha = 2$, the normal distribution $f(x; 2, 0, \gamma, \delta)$, for $\alpha = 1$, the Cauchy distribution $f(x; 1, 0, \gamma, \delta)$, and for $\alpha = 0.5$, the Lévy distribution $f(x; 0.5, 1, \gamma, \delta)$; for all other cases, only the characteristic function is available in closed form, and numerical approximation techniques must be adopted for parameter estimation, e.g., [15], which will be used here.

Saccade Direction. The second property obtained from saccades, and usually overlooked, is the direction of successive eye movements. This property, called saccade direction, measures the angular direction between the start and end location of a saccade. Recalling that a saccade is represented as $s_i = (r_i^s, r_i^e, t_i^s, t_i^e)$, we define its angular direction as $a_i = \texttt{arctan2}(y_i^e - y_i^s, x_i^e - x_i^s)$, where $\texttt{arctan2}$ is a function that extends the definition of $\arctan(y/x)$ to the four quadrants $(-\pi, \pi]$, taking in consideration the sign combinations of y and x.

The saccade directions are typically non-uniformly distributed, with most saccades in the horizontal and vertical directions than in oblique [45]. This circular data can be modelled by adopting a von Mises distribution, whose pdf is symmetric and unimodal, and is given by

$$f(a \mid \mu, \kappa) = \frac{\exp(\kappa \cos(a - \mu))}{2\pi I_0(\kappa)}, \tag{3}$$

where $I_0(\cdot)$ is the zero-th order modified Bessel function. Its parameters are the mean direction μ and the dispersion, captured by a concentration parameter κ. For large values of κ, the distribution is concentrated around the μ direction, while for $\kappa = 0$ the pdf is a uniform distribution.

For heterogeneous data, as in the case of saccade directions, a single von Mises distribution does not provide an adequate fit, so it will be discarded in favour of a mixture of two von Mises distributions. Its parameters $A_\mu = [\mu_1, \mu_2]$ and $A_\kappa = [\kappa_1, \kappa_2]$ are estimated using an Expectation-Maximization scheme [27].

Event Frequency. An additional information about the gaze patterns is provided by the frequency of each of the four classified events. These are normalised adopting a classical softmax approach, so that $E_j = \frac{e_j}{(e_1 + \cdots + e_4)}$, with $j = 1, \ldots, 4$.

Pupil Dilation. For what concerns pupil dilation, we consider its absolute percentage variation v_i with respect to the average size in an initial window of 250ms. In this case $V = \{v_i\}_{i=1}^N$ is assumed to be sampled from an half-normal distribution, whose pdf is given by

$$f(v \mid \sigma) = \frac{\sqrt{2}}{\sigma\sqrt{\pi}} \exp\left(-\frac{v^2}{2\sigma^2}\right) \tag{4}$$

and its unique parameter $V_\sigma = \sigma$ estimated via MLE.

Eventually, the gaze behavior of each subject in the dataset is represented by a feature vector,, namely the random vector $\mathcal{X} = [D_a, D_b, L_\gamma, L_\delta, A_\mu, A_\kappa, E, V_\sigma]$ (cfr. Fig. 3). A realisation $\mathcal{X} = \mathbf{x}_i$, summarising the gaze behaviour of subject i on the observed facial stimuli, will represent the observed input of a probabilistic classifier presented below.

2.2   Personality Trait Classification

The classification stage aims at finding a possible nonlinear mapping between a subset of salient features contained in $\mathcal{X}$ and the levels of personality traits $\mathcal{Y}$ acquired in the dataset (the response variables). In the binary case, as the one described in Sect. 3, the model is defined as

$$p(y_i \mid \mathcal{X} = \mathbf{x}_i) = \Phi(y_i f(\mathbf{x_i})), \tag{5}$$

where $\mathbf{x}_i$ represents the realisation of the random vector $\mathcal{X}$ for the i-th subject, and the $y_i \in \{-1, 1\}$ is the result of a *probit regression* approach that maps

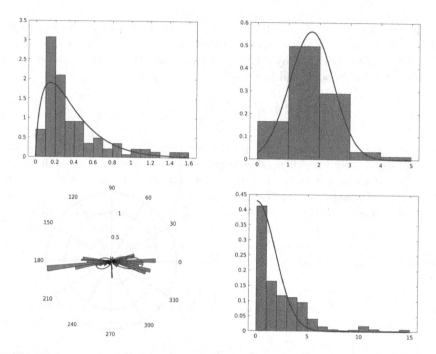

Fig. 3. Fitting of the features extracted from a sample of raw gaze data. (Top) Histogram of fixations durations, fitted via Gamma distribution and saccades amplitudes via the α-stable distribution. (Bottom) Saccade directions fitted with a mixture of von Mises distributions and histogram of pupil dilations overlaid with the half-normal distribution fit.

the output of a regression model into a class probability, namely the cumulative density function of a standard normal distribution $\Phi(z) = \int_{-\infty}^{z} \mathcal{N}(x \mid 0, 1)dx$. The function f in Eq. 5 is sampled from a Gaussian Process,

$$f \sim \mathrm{GP}(\cdot \mid 0, k) \tag{6}$$

that assumes prior probability over functions $p(\mathbf{f}(\mathbf{X})) = p(f(\mathbf{x}_1), \ldots, f(\mathbf{x}_N))$ to be jointly Gaussian with mean function $\mu(\mathbf{x}) = 0$ and covariance matrix $\mathbf{K}$. The latter is usually chosen as a positive definite kernel function $\mathbf{K}_{ij} = k(\mathbf{x}_i, \mathbf{x}_j; \theta)$, θ being the hyperparameters of the kernel function. Such function constrains similar inputs $(\mathbf{x}_i, \mathbf{x}_j)$ to have similar output values (but refer to Rasmussen and Williams [43] for an in-depth and wide introduction).

Often, in going from data to models, there are many possible inputs that might be relevant to predicting a particular output. Thus, we need algorithms that automatically decide which inputs are relevant. In the framework of Gaussian Processes one such tool is naturally provided by automatic relevance determination (ARD) kernels [37].

The adopted ARD kernel is a more general form of the squared exponential kernel for multi-dimensional inputs, that can be defined as

$$k(\mathbf{x}, \mathbf{x}'; \theta) = \sigma^2 \exp\left[-\frac{1}{2}\sum_{d=1}^{D}\left(\frac{x_d - x_{d'}}{w_d}\right)^2\right], \tag{7}$$

with hyperparameters $\theta = \{\sigma^2, w_1 \cdots w_D\}$. Here σ^2 is a scale parameter that determines the variation of function values from their mean. Most important, a different weight w_d, namely the length scale of the function along input dimension d, is assumed for each value x_d of the d-th feature in $\mathcal{X}$. This controls the horizontal length scale over which the function varies. In other terms, w_d determines the relevancy of input feature d to the classification problem: x_d is not relevant if $1/w_d$ is small.

The ARD formulation is usually exploited at the training stage, in terms of an automatic Occam's razor, in order to prune irrelevant dimensions, thus helping towards automatically finding the structure of complex models. In our scenario this will help us identifying predictive features for a specific personality trait.

3 Data Analysis and Results

Analysis has been conducted on a large public available dataset [19]. This includes gaze recordings from 403 participants (202 males, 201 females) watching videos of another person, initially gazing toward the bottom, then gazing up at the participant. A 10-item personality questionnaire based on the Big Five personality inventory [42] has been submitted to each participant, to define values for each of the five classes: agreeableness, conscientiousness, extraversion, neuroticism and openness to experience. They have been assessed through two items, going from 5 to 1, so that the lowest score ($p = 2$) is high in that trait, while highest score ($p = 10$) is low in that trait. It is worth mentioning that to the best of our knowledge this is the only public dataset the provides gaze recordings and personality traits values.

In order to highlight the behavioural differences of each personality trait, a binary classification approach with k-fold cross-validation was adopted ($k = 10$). The classes were formed by separating the highest ($C_1 = \{2 \leq p \leq 5\}$) and the lowest ($C_2 = \{7 \leq p \leq 10\}$) levels of each trait. The neutral value ($p = 6$) has been excluded because considered not relevant.

This partitioning led, in some cases, to unbalanced classes that were treated using the ADASYN oversampling technique [24] inside each fold of the cross-validation, in order to avoid possible overfitting problems. ADASYN is a novel extension of SMOTE [16] method that aims at creating, via linear interpolation, new examples from the minority class next to the bound with the majority one.

Classification results, shown in Fig. 4, include a comparison with a linear discriminant analysis (LDA) and a support vector machine (SVM) with radial basis function kernel. It shows how the GP classifier outperforms, in general, the other two methods and is able to correctly guess the personality class, apart from neuroticism, for the ≥ 73% of cases (chance level is 50%). To provide an overall quantitative evaluation, the mean value of the accuracy and the values of other three metrics for each personality trait, over 10 cross-validation folds of GP classification, are provided in Table 1.

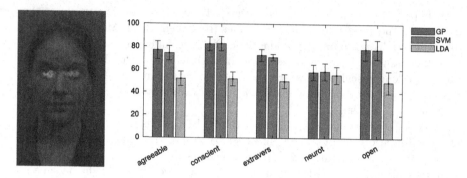

Fig. 4. (Left) heatmap visualisation of fixations recorded from a subject during the experiment. (Right) mean classification accuracy (and standard dev.) for each personality trait obtained with GP classification, SVM with Gaussian kernel and LDA.

Table 1. Mean value (and standard dev.) of the accuracy, precision, recall and F-measure for each personality trait obtained with Gaussian process classifier.

Personality trait	Accuracy	Precision	Recall	F-measure	
Agreeableness	0.77 ± 0.08	0.79	0.96	0.87	GP
	0.74 ± 0.06	0.78	0.93	0.85	SVM
	0.52 ± 0.06	0.78	0.54	0.64	LDA
Conscientiousness	0.82 ± 0.06	0.86	0.94	0.90	GP
	0.82 ± 0.06	0.86	0.94	0.90	SVM
	0.52 ± 0.06	0.86	0.53	0.65	LDA
Extraversion	0.73 ± 0.05	0.74	0.96	0.84	GP
	0.71 ± 0.03	0.75	0.92	0.82	SVM
	0.50 ± 0.06	0.71	0.54	0.62	LDA
Neuroticism	0.58 ± 0.07	0.48	0.44	0.45	GP
	0.58 ± 0.07	0.45	0.14	0.22	SVM
	0.55 ± 0.07	0.45	0.53	0.49	LDA
Openness	0.78 ± 0.09	0.82	0.95	0.88	GP
	0.78 ± 0.08	0.82	0.93	0.87	SVM
	0.49 ± 0.10	0.78	0.53	0.63	LDA

For what concerns the ARD weights learned during the GP training, these have been aggregated adopting a 'winner-takes-all' approach. In other terms, for each fold have been considered only the most prominent feature with respect to each personality trait. Final results are shown in Fig. 5.

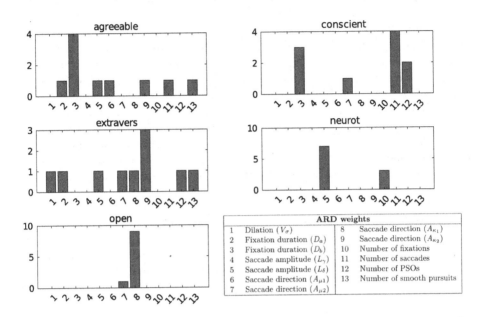

Fig. 5. The ARD weights resulting after training the GP classifiers. The x-axis indicates each of the extracted features $\mathcal{X} = [V_\sigma, D_a, D_b, L_\gamma, L_\delta, A_\mu, A_\kappa, E]$, while y-axis reports the number of 'wins' in the cross-validation.

Beyond the predictive accuracy gained by the model, it is remarkable to note how ARD weights, automatically derived along the training procedure, provide insights with respect to the most relevant features that characterise, according to this analysis, the different personality traits. For example, extraversion and openness to experience are best described in terms of saccade directions; conscientiousness is mostly accounted for by the number of saccades and fixation duration, while the latter is prevalent in explaining agreeablenes. The neuroticism trait, though more difficult to predict than others, is however clearly related to exploratory behaviour represented by saccade amplitude.

4   Discussion

We presented a novel approach for the analysis of gaze patterns in relation to personality traits. We adopted a probabilistic classifier based on Gaussian processes that achieves good results in the recognition of levels of personality traits. In particular, the adoption of an ARD kernel that considers different weights for each feature, allows to automatically detect the most prominent ones in relation to each trait. Indeed, the motivating rationale behind this study was not only to attain predictive performance in terms of classification accuracy, but also to show how machine learning-based modelling could be used for gaining explanatory insights into relevant mechanisms of the studied phenomenon. This explanatory gain could be further exploited in subsequent and more focused refinements of experimental design. For instance, as shown in Fig. 5, it results that the saccades directions, a typically overlooked feature, are a discriminating factor between subject with high and low levels of openness and extraversion.

As a final specific remark, the reasons behind the low accuracy of the neuroticism trait are probably to be found in the nature of the experiment and in the definition of neuroticism. It is not known, in fact, whether the subjects present clinical conditions. This could result into an overlapping between measures of neuroticism addressed via the self-report questionnaire and symptoms of common mental disorders. Moreover, as pointed in [38], does exist a lack of consensus on the optimal conceptualization of neuroticism and they suggest to see it as a mutable score that reflects a person's level of negative affect during a particular period.

Finally, as a general remark, must be kept in mind that, as noted in [19]: *many aspects of the experimental design might have influenced the results [...] The actors we used were all Caucasian between 20 and 40 years old with a neutral expression and did not speak - all factors that could have influenced observers' strategies.*

References

1. Baron-Cohen, S., Campbell, R., Karmiloff-Smith, A., Grant, J., Walker, J.: Are children with autism blind to the mentalistic significance of the eyes? Br. J. Dev. Psychol. **13**(4), 379–398 (1995)
2. Baron-Cohen, S., Wheelwright, S., Hill, J., Raste, Y., Plumb, I.: The reading the mind in the eyes test revised version: a study with normal adults, and adults with asperger syndrome or high-functioning autism. J. Child Psychol. Psychiatry All. Discip. **42**(2), 241–251 (2001)
3. Baron-Cohen, S., Wheelwright, S., Jolliffe, T.: Is there a "language of the eyes"? Evidence from normal adults, and adults with autism or asperger syndrome. Vis. Cognit. **4**(3), 311–331 (1997)
4. Boccignone, G., Ferraro, M.: Ecological sampling of gaze shifts. IEEE Trans. Cybern. **44**(2), 266–279 (2014)
5. Boccignone, G., Ferraro, M., Crespi, S., Robino, C., de'Sperati, C.: Detecting expert's eye using a multiple-kernel relevance vector machine. J. Eye Movement Res. **7**(2), 1–15 (2014)
6. Bolmont, M., Cacioppo, J.T., Cacioppo, S.: Love is in the gaze: an eye-tracking study of love and sexual desire (2014)
7. Borji, A., Itti, L.: Defending yarbus: eye movements reveal observers' task. J. vis. **14**(3), 29 (2014)
8. Bradley, M.M., Miccoli, L., Escrig, M.A., Lang, P.J.: The pupil as a measure of emotional arousal and autonomic activation. Psychophysiology **45**(4), 602–607 (2008)

9. Breazeal, C., Scassellati, B.: A context-dependent attention system for a social robot. rn **255**, 3 (1999)

10. Breiman, L.: Statistical modeling: the two cultures (with comments and a rejoinder by the author). Stat. Sci. **16**(3), 199–231 (2001)

11. Brockmann, D., Geisel, T.: The ecology of gaze shifts. Neurocomputing **32**(1), 643–650 (2000)

12. Broz, F., Lehmann, H., Nehaniv, C.L., Dautenhahn, K.: Mutual gaze, personality, and familiarity: dual eye-tracking during conversation. In: Proceedings - IEEE International Workshop on Robot and Human Interactive Communication, pp. 858–864 (2012)

13. Busswell, G.: How People Look at Pictures: A Study of the Psychology of Perception in Art. Univ. Chicago Press, Oxford (1935)

14. Calder, A.J., et al.: Separate coding of different gaze directions in the superior temporal sulcus and inferior parietal lobule. Curr. Biol. **17**(1), 20–25 (2007)

15. Chambers, J., Mallows, C., Stuck, B.: A method for simulating stable random variables. J. Am. Stat. Ass. **71**(354), 340–344 (1976)

16. Chawla, N.V., Bowyer, K.W., Hall, L.O., Kegelmeyer, W.P.: SMOTE: synthetic minority over-sampling technique. J. Artif. Intell. Res. **16**, 321–357 (2002)

17. Clavelli, A., Karatzas, D., Lladós, J., Ferraro, M., Boccignone, G.: Modelling task-dependent eye guidance to objects in pictures. Cognit. Comput. **6**(3), 558–584 (2014)

18. Costa, T., Boccignone, G., Cauda, F., Ferraro, M.: The foraging brain: evidence of levy dynamics in brain networks. PloS One **11**(9), e0161702 (2016)

19. Coutrot, A., Binetti, N., Harrison, C., Mareschal, I., Johnston, A.: Face exploration dynamics differentiate men and women. J. Vis. **16**(14), 16 (2016)

20. Duncan, S.: Some signals and rules for taking speaking turns in conversations. J. Pers. Soc. Psychol. **23**(2), 283 (1972)

21. Gigerenzer, G.: Mindless statistics. J. Socio-Econ. **33**(5), 587–606 (2004). Statistical Significance

22. Gnedenko, B., Kolmogórov, A.: Limit Distributions for Sums of Independent Random Variables. Addison-Wesley publishing Company, Boston (1954)

23. Goldberg, L.R.: The structure of phenotypic personality traits. Am. psychol. **48**(1), 26 (1993)

24. He, H., Bai, Y., Garcia, E.A., Li, S.: ADASYN: adaptive synthetic sampling approach for imbalanced learning. In: IEEE International Joint Conference on Neural Networks, IJCNN 2008, (IEEE World Congress on Computational Intelligence), pp. 1322–1328. IEEE (2008)

25. Hoffman, E.A., Haxby, J.V.: Distinct representations of eye gaze and identity in the distributed human neural system for face perception. Nat. Neurosci. **3**(1), 80 (2000)

26. Hofman, J.M., Sharma, A., Watts, D.J.: Prediction and explanation in social systems. Science **355**(6324), 486–488 (2017)

27. Hung, W.L., Chang-Chien, S.J., Yang, M.S.: Self-updating clustering algorithm for estimating the parameters in mixtures of von mises distributions. J. Appl. Stat. **39**(10), 2259–2274 (2012)

28. Isaacowitz, D.M.: The gaze of the optimist. Pers. Soc. Psychol. Bull. **31**(3), 407–415 (2005)

29. Isaacowitz, D.M.: Motivated gaze: the view from the gazer. Psychol. Sci. **15**(2), 68–72 (2006)

30. Kingstone, A., Laidlaw, K., Nasiopoulos, E., Risko, E.: Cognitive ethology and social attention. In: Tibayrenc, M., Ayala, F.J. (eds.) On Human Nature, pp. 365–382. Academic Press, San Diego (2017)
31. Le Meur, O., Coutrot, A.: Introducing context-dependent and spatially-variant viewing biases in saccadic models. Vis. Res. **121**, 72–84 (2016)
32. Le Meur, O., Liu, Z.: Saccadic model of eye movements for free-viewing condition. Vis. Res. **116**, 152–164 (2015)
33. Mason, M.F., Tatkow, E.P., Macrae, C.N.: The look of love: gaze shifts and person perception. Psychol. Sci. **16**(3), 236–239 (2005)
34. Mazur, A., Rosa, E., Faupel, M., Heller, J., Leen, R., Thurman, B.: Physiological aspects of communication via mutual gaze. Am. J. Sociol. **86**(1), 50–74 (1980)
35. McConkie, G.W., Loschky, L.C.: Perception onset time during fixations in free viewing. Behav. Res. Methods Instrum. Comput. **34**(4), 481–490 (2002)
36. Mercer Moss, F.J., Baddeley, R., Canagarajah, N.: Eye movements to natural images as a function of sex and personality. PLoS One **7**(11), 1–9 (2012)
37. Neal, R.M.: Bayesian Learning for Neural Networks, vol. 118. Springer, Heidelberg (2012)
38. Ormel, J., Riese, H., Rosmalen, J.G.: Interpreting neuroticism scores across the adult life course: immutable or experience-dependent set points of negative affect? Clin. Psychol. Rev. **32**(1), 71–79 (2012)
39. Pekkanen, J., Lappi, O.: A new and general approach to signal denoising and eye movement classification based on segmented linear regression. Sci. Rep. **7**(1), 1–13 (2017)
40. Pelphrey, K.A., Singerman, J.D., Allison, T., McCarthy, G.: Brain activation evoked by perception of gaze shifts: the influence of context. Neuropsychologia **41**(2), 156–170 (2003)
41. Perlman, S.B., Morris, J.P., Vander Wyk, B.C., Green, S.R., Doyle, J.L., Pelphrey, K.A.: Individual differences in personality predict how people look at faces. PLoS One **4**(6), 2–7 (2009)
42. Rammstedt, B., John, O.P.: Measuring personality in one minute or less: a 10-item short version of the big five inventory in english and german. J. Res. Pers. **41**(1), 203–212 (2007)
43. Rasmussen, C.E., Williams, C.K.: Gaussian Processes for Machine Learning. The MIT Press, Cambridge (2006)
44. Rauthmann, J.F., Seubert, C.T., Sachse, P., Furtner, M.R.: Eyes as windows to the soul: gazing behavior is related to personality. J. Res. Pers. **46**(2), 147–156 (2012)
45. Tatler, B.W., Vincent, B.T.: Systematic tendencies in scene viewing. J. Eye Movement Res. **2**(2), 1–18 (2008)
46. Tatler, B.W., Vincent, B.T.: The prominence of behavioural biases in eye guidance. Vis. Cognit. **17**(6–7), 1029–1054 (2009)
47. Tatler, B., Hayhoe, M., Land, M., Ballard, D.: Eye guidance in natural vision: reinterpreting salience. J. Vis. **11**(5), 5 (2011)
48. Yarbus, A.L.: Eye movements during perception of complex objects. In: Yarbus, A.L. (ed.) Eye movements and vision, pp. 171–211. Springer, Boston (1967). https://doi.org/10.1007/978-1-4899-5379-7_8
49. Yoshikawa, Y., Shinozawa, K., Ishiguro, H., Hagita, N., Miyamoto, T.: The effects of responsive eye movement and blinking behavior in a communication robot, pp. 4564–4569. IEEE (2006)

FormalMiner: A Formal Framework for Refinement Mining

Antonio Cerone$^{(\boxtimes)}$

Department of Computer Science, Nazarbayev University, Astana, Kazakhstan
antonio.cerone@nu.edu.kz

Abstract. Refinement mining has been inspired by process mining techniques and aims to refine an abstract non-deterministic model by sifting it using event logs as a sieve until a reasonably concise model is achieved. FormalMiner is a formal framework that implements model mining using Maude, a modelling language based on rewriting logic. Once the final formal model is attained, it can be used, within the same rewriting-logic framework, to predict the future evolution of the behaviour through simulation, to carry out further validation or to analyse properties through model checking. In this paper we focus on the refinement mining capability of FormalMiner and we illustrate it using a case study from ecology.

Keywords: Formal methods · Model-driven approaches
Rewriting logic · Maude · Process mining
Application to ecosystem modelling

1 Introduction

The use of large repositories to collect data in various domains of social sciences, physical sciences and life sciences offers great opportunities for systematic analysis. *Data mining* aims to extract meaningful information from data and exploit it to describe and understand the processes that have generated such data.

More recently, the scope of data mining enlarged from the description of properties of the data organisation, such as clustering and classification, to the description of the actual process that led to the creation and organisation of the data. *Process mining*, which emerged in the field of business process management (BPM), has been used to extract information from event logs consisting of activities and then produce a graphical representation of the process control flow, detect relations between components involved in the process and infer data dependencies between process activities [20]. This is achieved through either the *discovery* of an *a posteriori* process model or the *extension* of a pre-existing *a priori* model, or the comparison of the *a priori* model with the event logs using a technique called *conformance analysis* [15]. However, these three approaches cannot be automatically integrated, but require the analyst to compare them manually [13]. Therefore, process mining is used for *descriptive* purposes, aiming at the discovery of some aspects of the *past behaviour*, that is, the dynamics that produced the event log.

© Springer Nature Switzerland AG 2018
M. Mazzara et al. (Eds.): STAF 2018 Workshops, LNCS 11176, pp. 185–200, 2018.
https://doi.org/10.1007/978-3-030-04771-9_15

Although there are a number of works in the areas of synthesis of programs [10,17,18] and synthesis of biological and probabilistic systems from data [7,11, 14], to our knowledge, the only attempt to integrate process mining and formal verification is a work by van der Aalst, de Beer and van Dongen's, which aims at verifying whether an event log satisfies a property expressed in linear temporal logic (LTL) [19]. However, such an approach still has a descriptive purpose: the formal characterisation of properties of the event logs from *past behaviour*. The construction of a formal model within a framework equipped with automatic verification tools, instead, enable prediction of *future behaviour*.

In our previous work [5] we have taken a step forward and exploited real data in a *constructive* rather than descriptive way by integrating techniques from the realm of process mining with modelling approaches. The technique we developed, which we called *model mining*, supports the synthesis of a formal model from a dataset and enables the formal analysis of such a model in order to predict the *future behaviour* and characterise its properties. The synthesised model is not a mere representation of the unfolded behaviour, but comprises, instead, a set of formal transition rules for generating the system behaviour, thus supporting powerful predictive capabilities. The set of transition rules can be either inferred directly from the events logs (*constructive mining*) [5] or refined by sifting a plausible *a priori* model using the event logs as a sieve until a reasonably concise model is achieved (*refinement mining*) [4,5]. To this purpose, events are partitioned into two classes, *environmental events*, which allow us to update the system state, and *target events*, which are used in refinement mining to sift a non-deterministic model by possibly invalidating one of its deterministic instances.

We use *equational logic* [9] to define the Model Mining Formal Framework (MMFF) [4,5], which provides a formal description of the events, the system state and the transition rules that change the system state accoding to the event occurrences. *Rewriting logic* [12] is then used to manipulate the data structures defined in MMFF in order to implement the *constructive mining algorithm*, which exploits a list of events to build a set of transition rules, and the *refinement mining algorithm*, which exploits a list of events to refine an *a priori* model consisting of sets of alternative transition rules by reducing the possible alternatives (thus reducing non-determinism) [5].

In this tool paper we introduce *FormalMiner*, which implements MMFF and the two model mining algorithms using the *Maude rewrite system* [8]. Maude is a high-performance modelling and analysis system based on a reflexive language that supports both equational and rewriting logic.

The focus of this paper is the use of FormalMiner in performing refinement mining. Section 2 introduces rewriting logic and Maude and briefly overviews the Maude syntax to enable the reader to understand the examples in this paper and refer them to the Maude code that implements FormalMiner. FormalMiner 1.1, on which this paper is based, and the case study can be downloaded at

https://cs-sst.github.io/faculty/cerone/modellingfromdata.

Sect. 3 presents the architecture of FormalMiner and illustrates the data structures of MMFF and the general functions for manipulating them. Section 4 describes how refinement mining is carried out and introduces the *sifting metric*, which is used to evaluate the validity of alternative instances of the model. Finally, Sect. 5 discusses strategies for carrying out model mining as well as future work.

2   Rewriting Logic and the Maude System

Rewriting logic [12] is based on *rewite rules* of the form $t \implies t'$, with t and t' expressions in a given language. A rewrite rule can be interpreted both *computationally*, as a *local transition* in a concurrent system, and *logically*, as an *inference rule*. Therefore, rewriting logic can be considered both a *computational theory* and a *logical theory*.

Maude [8] is a modelling language based on rewriting logic. It also provides model-checking capabilities, thus supporting the analysis of the modelled system. In this work we only use *Core Maude*, whose syntax we briefly overview in this section. There are two types of modules in Core Maude, *functional modules*, which are restricted to *equational logic* and support declaration of sorts (with keyword sort for one sort, or sorts for many), operations (with keyword op or ops) on them and the definition of such operation using equations (with keyword eq, or ceq in case of conditional equations), and *system modules*, which also support *rewriting logic*, by additionally including the definition of rewrite rules (with keyword rl, or crl in case of conditional rewrite rules). A number of *flags* can be used while defining an operation. For example flag ctor designates the operation as a constructor.

A sort A is specified as a subsort of a sort B by 'subsort A < B'. Keyword subsorts is used in case of multiple subsorts. Variables denote indefinite values for sorts to be used within equations or rewrite rules. They are declared with keyword var or vars. Constants are basically operations with no arguments and are defined through equations. Maude has several predefined sorts for basic values, including the obvious sorts Bool, Nat, Int, Rat, and a sort Qid for *quoted identifiers*, which are sequences of characters starting with the character ' '. All constructs of the Maude language, apart from the toplevel module construct, end with a space followed by a dot ('.').

3   FormalMiner Core: Events, States and Evolution

In order to be successfully processed with the purpose of extracting process control flow information, event logs have first to be semantically interpreted according to the purpose of the model we aim to devise, so that such interpretation can drive their structuring and clustering. Structural and semantical organisation can be attained by applying text mining techniques, in particular semantic indexing, in combination with an appropriate ontology from the given application domain. This approach is commonly used in process mining, which

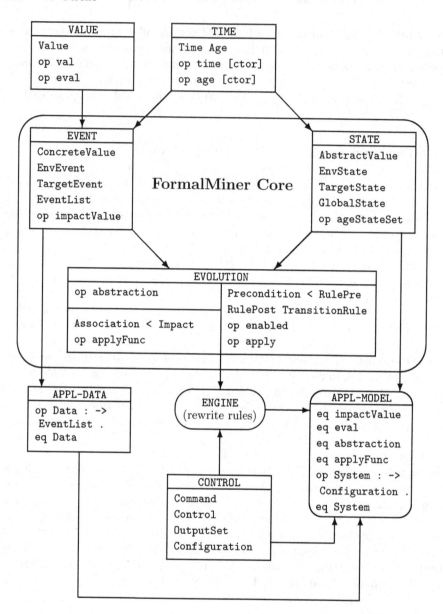

Fig. 1. Architecture of the FormalMiner tool in terms of Maude modules.

is thus applied to a set of *pre-processed* event logs. For the purpose of model mining we assume to have already pre-processed events organised as a sequence of structured entities, which are ordered based on their occurrence times.

In this section we show the basic data structures that make up MMFF and how they are implemented in FormalMiner. For this purpose we refer to the

FormalMiner architecture described in Fig. 1, where squared boxes represent functional modules and oval boxes represent the system modules. An arrow between module M1 and module M2 denotes that M2 imports all declarations and definitions in M1. The FormalMiner Core implements MMFF data structures and the general functions to manipulate them. It consists of three functional modules: EVENT, STATE and EVOLUTION. System module ENGINE, which comprises the rewrite rules that implement the model mining algorithms, and functional module CONTROL, which control FormalMiner output, are also part of the MMFF implementation.

Outside the FormalMiner Core, modules VALUE and TIME contain declarations of generic sorts, whereas constructors and operation declaration and definition are depending on the value and time domains considered for the specific application. Thus, although the structure of these two modules is standard and includes generic sorts Value, Time and Age, such sorts need to be instantiated for each specific application.

Also outside the FormalMiner core, functional module APPL-DATA and system module APPL-MODEL are application specific. Module APPL-DATA contains the dataset, in the form of a defined timed list of events. Module APPL-MODEL contains the definition of the initial configuration, which includes the initial state of the system and the plausible model to refine. The names for these two modules provided here and in Fig. 1 are just placeholders and can be changed to best describe the application. This is consistent with the fact that these two modules are not imported by any other module.

Our goal is to model how environmental events affect a target event. Environmental events act on the system by changing its state and such changes are normally visible through target events. Since the system consists of several components, which we call *domains*, we need to define a local notion of state for each of such domains. We denote such a notion of local state as *domain state*.

3.1 Environmental and Target Events

Environmental and target events are modelled in the EVENT module. An *event* is defined as a triple consisting of

- the *time* at which the event occurs;
- the *event name*;
- a *concrete value* represented as a set $\{t_1(v_1^{V_1}), \ldots, t_n(v_n^{V_n})\}$ of typed basic values, with t_i being the type name and $v_i^{V_i}$ belonging to value domain V_i, for $i = 1 \ldots, n$.

Sorts BasicEvent, EnvEvent (environmental events) and TargetEvent (target events), as well as Event, which comprises the last two as subsorts, and EventList (sequences of events), are declared in Maude together with the definitions of their operations as follows:

```
sorts BasicEvent Event EnvEvent TargetEvent EventList .
subsorts EnvEvent TargetEvent < Event < EventList .
```

```
op [|_,_:_|] : Time Qid ConcreteValue -> BasicEvent [ctor prec 30] .
op env_ : BasicEvent -> EnvEvent [ctor prec 31] .
op target_ : BasicEvent -> TargetEvent [ctor prec 31] .

op noEvents : -> EventList [ctor] .
op _&>_ :  EventList EventList
              -> EventList [ctor assoc prec 32 id: noEvents] .
```

Constructors env and target denote environmental and target events respectively. Constructor &> sequentialises events.

In previous work [1] we modelled the dynamic of a population of *Aedes albopictus*, a mosquito species known as "tiger mosquito", which is endemic in Asian regions, where it is a carrier of dengue fever, and now widespread also in Europe. The model developed in that work is based on biological aspects of the mosquito and considers the impact of changes in the environmental conditions on such biological aspects to simulate the population dynamics. Among relevant environmental conditions are average temperature and rain amount. The simulation made use of data on the size of the mosquito population collected during May–November 2009 in the province of Massa-Carrara (Tuscany, Italy) using CO_2 mosquito traps. We will use this case study throughout the paper to illustrate FormalMiner.

```
eq May = env[| time(1) , 'Temp : 'avg(val(18)) |]     ---   8 May
      &>  target[| time(1) , 'Aedes : 'adult(val(4)) |]
      &>  env[| time(2) , 'Temp : 'avg(val(19)) |]     ---   9 May
  ...
      &>  env[| time(22) , 'Temp : 'avg(val(20)) |]    ---  29 May
      &>  env[| time(23) , 'Temp : 'avg(val(20)) |]    ---  30 May
      &>  env[| time(24) , 'Temp : 'avg(val(22)) |] .  ---  31 May
  ...
eq August = env[| time(96) , 'Temp : 'avg(val(28)) |]  ---  1 August
      &>  env[| time(97) , 'Temp : 'avg(val(31)) |]    ---  2 August
      &>  env[| time(98) , 'Temp : 'avg(val(31)) |]    ---  3 August
      &>  env[| time(99) , 'Temp : 'avg(val(34)) |]    ---  4 August
      &>  env[| time(100) , 'Temp : 'avg(val(33)) |] . ---  5 August

eq Data = May &> June &> July &> August .
```

Fig. 2. Sequence of events describing changes of temperature and sampling of the mosquito population.

Figure 2 shows fragments of a sequence of events over a period of 100 days from 8 May to 5 August 2009. There are only one kind of environmental event, named Temp and describing daily temperature changes, and one kind of target event, named Aedes and describing the sampling of the mosquito population on a specific day. In both kinds of events the concrete value is a singleton describing the average value for temperature changes and the values for the sampling of the mosquito adult population. A richer concrete value for temperature would have also values for minimum and maximum temperature, for example:

```
env[| time(1), 'Temp: 'min(val(13)) 'avg(val(18)) 'max(val(20)) |]
```

3.2 Domain State and Global State

Differently from events, which are concrete entities that accurately represent the reality, states, modelled in module STATE, refer to the model rather than the reality. They are thus abstract entities, whose values are abstract values.

A *domain state* is defined as a quadruple consisting of

- the *domain name*;
- the *set of specifiers* for the domain;
- the *abstract value* that refers to the domain and its specifiers;
- the *state age*, i.e. the amount of time that the state has persisted with unchanged abstract value.

Similarly to events, states may be environmental and target. Environmental states are changed by the occurrence of environmental events (i.e. by the data as event occurrences), whereas target states are changed according to the model (i.e. by the model execution) and will be then validated against the target events. The *global state* of the system we are modelling consists of the *current time* and a set of environmental and target states. The Maude syntax for sorts DomainState, StateSet and GlobalState is

```
op <|_,_,_,_|> : Qid Specifiers AbstractValue Age -> DomainState [...] .
op __ : StateSet StateSet -> StateSet [...] .
op _at_ : StateSet Time -> GlobalState [...] .
```

For example, we may consider four possible abstract values for the size of the adult *Aedes* population: low for low, med for medium, high for high and extr for extreme and the first three also for average temperatures. Then

```
env<| 'Temp,'avg,'med,age(2) |>  target<| 'Aedes,'adult,'med,age(5) |>
at time(0)
```

is the global state describing the initial day (time(0)) in which the average temperature has a medium value (med) that persisted for 2 days (age(2)) and the adult mosquito population has a medium value (med) that persisted for 5 days (age(5)).

3.3 Environment-Driven Evolution

In this section we describe how concrete values of environmental events are mapped to abstract values, which then determine the evolution of environmental states.

Although in our example we have used the same name for corresponding events and states, in general events may be defined with no explicit reference to the affected domains. The evolution of environmental states is described by an *impact relation*, which is implemented by sort Impact, whose elements are sets of impact associations of sort Association. These sorts are declared in module EVOLUTION, where Association < Impact denotes that Association is a subsort of Impact, and defined by the equations in application-specific system module APPL-MODEL.

An impact association defines, under a given condition on the concrete value of the environmental event, which environmental state is affected by the occurrence of the event and how it is affected. The syntax of an impact association

{ ⟨*EventName*⟩ , ⟨*CondLabel*⟩ | ⟨*FuncLabel*⟩ | ⟨*StateName*⟩ , ⟨*Specifiers*⟩ }

defines that an event named ⟨*EventName*⟩

- is associated with a state named ⟨*StateName*⟩ and having ⟨*Specifiers*⟩ as set of specifiers, and
- determines a state transition defined by label ⟨*FuncLabel*⟩, which represents an *evolution function* (not a Maude function!),

when the condition labelled as ⟨*CondLabel*⟩ is true.

The impact relation for our case study consists of the following three impact associations

```
{ 'Temp , 'lowTempCond | 'lowTemp | 'Temp , 'avg }
{ 'Temp , 'medTempCond | 'medTemp | 'Temp , 'avg }
{ 'Temp , 'highTempCond | 'highTemp | 'Temp , 'avg }
```

Actual conditions and model functions are defined by Maude functions `eval` and `applyFunc` in module `APPL-MODEL`. For example, in our case study

```
eq eval('lowTempCond , V) = 0 <= V and V < 20 .
```

defines that condition labelled as `lowTempCond` is true when average temperature is less than 20°, and

```
eq applyFunc('lowTemp , AV ) = 'low .
```

defines that the function represented by label `lowTemp` is the constant function `low`, independently of the previous abstract value `AV` of the average temperature. Actual conditions and evolution functions of the impact relation for our case study are given in Table 1.

Table 1. Conditions and evolution functions of the impact relation for the mosquito case study

State Name	Condition Label CL	Condition Value eval(CL,V)	Function Label CL	Evolution for any AV applyFunc(CL, AV)	Event Name	Concrete Value
Temp	lowTempCond	$0 \leq V < 20$	lowCond	constant low	Temp	avg(V)
	medTempCond	$20 \leq V < 25$	medCond	constant med		
	highTempCond	$25 \leq V < 36$	highCond	constant high		

Although this approach may seem cumbersome for the simple case study we consider in this paper, it supports a general form of modelling. For example,

```
{ 'Rainfall , 'low2medCond | 'low2med | 'Water , 'moisture }
eq eval('low2medCond , amount(A) intensity(I)) = A*K/I>=2 and A*K/I<10 .
eq applyFunc('low2med , 'low ) = 'med .
```

describes the impact of the rain on a soil with permeability characterised by parameter K: a rainfall with amount A in millimetres and intensity I determines an increase of soil moisture from low to medium if $2 \leq A*K/I < 10$. The fact that the higher the intensity of the rainfall the faster water tends to flow and the less it is absorbed, thus resulting in a lower level of soil moisture, is described by A*K/I. Obviously, an environmental event for this example needs two types of basic value, amount and intensity to make a concrete value, for example

```
env[| time(5), 'Rainfall: 'amount(val(13)) 'intensity(val(2)) |]
```

3.4   Model-Driven Evolution

In this section we describe how the plausible model determines the transition of target states. The mapping from concrete values of target events to abstract values of target states is defined by function abstraction declared in functional module EVOLUTION and defined by the equations given in functional module APPL-DATA. For example, the abstraction for our case study, given in Table 2 is defined by

Table 2. Abstract relation for the mosquito case study

Event Name	Typed Basic Value	Condition on Concrete Value V	Abstract Value
Aedes	adult(V)	$0 \leq V < 100$	low
		$100 \leq V < 250$	med
		$250 \leq V < 500$	high
		$V > 500$	extr

```
eq abstraction('Aedes , 'adult , V) =
    if 0 <= V and V < 100 then 'low else
      if 100 <= V and V < 250 then 'med else
        if 250 <= V and V < 500 then 'high else 'extr fi fi fi .
```

The transition of target states is modelled by *transition rules* whose components are declared in module EVOLUTION. The rule precondition is defined by sort RulePre, which is a set of preconditions of sort Precondition, where each precondition states the existence in the global state of an environmental state of given domain and set of specifier such that the age of the abstract value has a given relation with a given threshold. For example

```
( 'Temp , 'avg , 'med | >= age(10) >>)
```

denotes that a medium abstract value of the average temperature has persisted (relation >= between age and threshold) for at least 10 days (threshold expressed by age(10)). The rule postcondition is defined by sort RulePost. For example

```
(<< 'Aedes , 'adult | 'low -- 'increase -> 'med >>)
```

denotes an increase of the mosquito adult population from low to medium. Given an appropriate abstraction of concrete values, it may be obvious that the persistence of a medium temperature for a certain number of days results in an increase of the adult mosquito population from low to medium. However, it is not clear how many days are needed for such an increase. Therefore, we normally need to have, within the same model, distinct transition rules with the same postcondition but preconditions which are not mutually exclusive. A good strategy is to initially include two rules corresponding to what we expect to be reasonable lower and upper bound limits. In our specific case, we may expect the population increase to occur on the same day as the temperature increase or within up to 10 days:

```
( 'Temp , 'avg , 'med | >= age(0) >>)
              => (<< 'Aedes , 'adult | 'low -- 'increase -> 'med >>)
( 'Temp , 'avg , 'med | >= age(10) >>)
              => (<< 'Aedes , 'adult | 'low -- 'increase -> 'med >>)
```

We might even not be sure that the population size can change within these 10 days. Then we also add transition rules

```
( 'Temp , 'avg , 'med | >= age(0) >>)
              => (<< 'Aedes , 'adult | 'low -- 'stable -> 'low >>)
( 'Temp , 'avg , 'med | >= age(10) >>)
              => (<< 'Aedes , 'adult | 'low -- 'stable -> 'low >>)
```

These four rules are grouped together in a set called *option set*, which describes a form of non-determinism, called *option-related non-determinism*, which we expect to be reduced by sifting out those transition rules that are invalidated by the data. Therefore, refinement mining exploits data, in the form of event logs consisting of target events, to reduce option-related non-determinism.

However, not all determinism may be reduced using refinement mining. For example, in ecology, there might be alternative forms of behaviour of individuals which are dictated by their free will. Such alternatives must be modelled by transition rules of distinct option sets. This form of non-determinism, which we call *model-related non-determinism* is intrinsic to the model and cannot be reduced using refinement mining. Finally, the impact of environmental events on environmental states may depend on unknown or only partially known factors. Or it may depend on known factors, which, however, we may have chosen not to model or we cannot model because they depend, in turn, on factors which are either unknown or too complex to include in the model. For example, soil moisture may also depend on desiccation, which, however, we may have chosen not to model or we may not be sure how to model. We call this third form of non-determinism *impact-related non-determinism* and we model it by impact associations whose conditions are not mutually exclusive.

We can thus define a *plausible model* as a set of option sets. The plausible model for our case study is given in Fig. 3. It consists of 10 option sets, numbered 1 to 10. Option set 4 consists of the 4 alternative transition rules

```
[1] < { 1 | ( 'Temp , 'avg , 'low | >= age(0) >>)
             => (<< 'Aedes , 'adult | 'extr -- 'decrease -> 'med >>) } >
[2] < { 1 | ( 'Temp , 'avg , 'low | >= age(0) >>)
             => (<< 'Aedes , 'adult | 'high -- 'decrease -> 'low >>) } >
[3] < { 1 | ( 'Temp , 'avg , 'low | >= age(0) >>)
             => (<< 'Aedes , 'adult | 'med -- 'decrease -> 'low >>) } >
[4] < { 1 | ( 'Temp , 'avg , 'med | >= age(0) >>)
             => (<< 'Aedes , 'adult | 'low -- 'increase -> 'med >>) }
    { 2 | ( 'Temp , 'avg , 'med | >= age(10) >>)
             => (<< 'Aedes , 'adult | 'low -- 'increase -> 'med >>) }
    { 3 | ( 'Temp , 'avg , 'med | >= age(0) >>)
             => (<< 'Aedes , 'adult | 'low -- 'stable -> 'low >>) }
    { 4 | ( 'Temp , 'avg , 'med | >= age(10) >>)
             => (<< 'Aedes , 'adult | 'low -- 'stable -> 'low >>) } >
[5] < { 1 | ( 'Temp , 'avg , 'med | >= age(0) >>)
             => (<< 'Aedes , 'adult | 'high -- 'decrease -> 'med >>) }
    { 2 | ( 'Temp , 'avg , 'med | >= age(4) >>)
             => (<< 'Aedes , 'adult | 'high -- 'decrease -> 'med >>) } >
[6] < { 1 | ( 'Temp , 'avg , 'med | >= age(0) >>)
             => (<< 'Aedes , 'adult | 'extr -- 'decrease -> 'high >>) } >
[7] < { 1 | ( 'Temp , 'avg , 'high | >= age(0) >>)
             => (<< 'Aedes , 'adult | 'low -- 'increase -> 'med >>) }
    { 2 | ( 'Temp , 'avg , 'high | >= age(4) >>)
             => (<< 'Aedes , 'adult | 'low -- 'increase -> 'med >>) } >
[8] < { 1 | ( 'Temp , 'avg , 'high | >= age(0) >>)
             => (<< 'Aedes , 'adult | 'med -- 'increase -> 'high >>) }
    { 2 | ( 'Temp , 'avg , 'high | >= age(4) >>) $\!\!\!\!\!\!\!$
             => (<< 'Aedes , 'adult | 'med -- 'increase -> 'high >>) } >
[9] < { 1 | ( 'Temp , 'avg , 'high | >= age(0) >>)
             => (<< 'Aedes , 'adult | 'med -- 'increase -> 'extr >>) }
    { 1 | ( 'Temp , 'avg , 'high | >= age(16) >>)
             => (<< 'Aedes , 'adult | 'med -- 'increase -> 'extr >>) } >
[10] < { 1 | ( 'Temp , 'avg , 'high | >= age(0) >>)
             => (<< 'Aedes , 'adult | 'high -- 'increase -> 'extr >>) }
    { 2 | ( 'Temp , 'avg , 'high | >= age(2) >>)
             => (<< 'Aedes , 'adult | 'high -- 'increase -> 'extr >>) } >
```

Fig. 3. Plausible model for the mosquito case study.

illustrated above. Some option sets consist of just one transition rules. This is the case for option sets 1–3, due to the belief that a low temperature will always cause a decrease of the adult mosquito population to low on the same day, independently of the size of the initial population. Similar beliefs are that a medium temperature will always cause a decrease of the adult mosquito population from extreme to high on the same day (option set 6). The other option sets (5 and 7–10) consist of two rules corresponding to the same day as the lower bound and what we expect to be a reasonable upper bound.

4   Plausible Model Refinement

In order to check which transition rules are invalidated by the data, each transition rule of an option set has to be consistently checked against the entire dataset. To this purpose, the plausible model is decomposed in all possible *option-free* models, that is, models without option-related non-determinism; each model is then used to perform a simulation, during which the results of simulation steps are compared with the target events. For each option-free model, the model refinement engine records the number of times the model is invalidated by a target event and, for each transition rule used within that model, it also records the number of times the rule is applied through simulation. Finally, the recorded information on the number of times the model is invalidated and its rules are applied is combined into a *sifting metric* that is associated with that specific model in order to provide a measure of model validation.

For each option-free model considered, the refinement mining returns a set Ψ of *option references* representing the selected transition rule for each option set and providing the number of times such a rule is applied. These references are formally defined as follows.

Definition 1. *An **option reference** is defined as a Maude term* $[k \; : \; i(j)]$ *where*

- k *is a reference to the option set whose identification number is k;*
- i *is a reference to the transition rule whose identification number is i within the option set identified by k;*
- j *is the number of times the referred transition rule has been applied during the current simulation.*

For example, in the following list of option references represented as a Maude term

$$
\begin{aligned}
&[1 \; : \; 1(0)] \; [\&> \; [2 \; : \; 1(0)] \; [\&> \; [3 \; : \; 1(1)] \; [\&> \\
&[4 \; : \; 2(1)] \; [\&> \; [5 \; : \; 1(0)] \; [\&> \; [6 \; : \; 1(2)] \; [\&> \\
&[7 \; : \; 1(0)] \; [\&> \; [8 \; : \; 1(1)] \; [\&> \; [9 \; : \; 2(0)] \; [\&> \; [10 \; : \; 1(3)] \quad (1)
\end{aligned}
$$

rule 1 of option set 3, rule 2 of option set 4 and rule 1 of option set 8 are applied once, rule 1 of option set 6 is applied twice and rule 1 of option set 10 is applied three times, whereas all other selected rules are never applied.

4.1   Sifting Metric

Definition 2. *A **model reference** is defined as a Maude term* $\{ \mu, \; \omega \; | \; \Psi \}$, *where*

- $\Psi = [1 \; : \; i_1(j_1)] \; [\&> \; \ldots \; [\&> \; [n \; : \; i_n(j_n)]$ *is a list of n option references, one for each option set;*
- ω *is the number of times the model is invalidated by a target event;*
- μ *is the measure of model validation, which is calculated using the following sifting metric*

$$
\mu = \frac{(1 - c \cdot \frac{\omega}{\eta}) \cdot \sum_{k=1}^{n} j_k}{\sigma}
$$

in which

- η *is the number of target events against which the model is checked during simulation;*
- $c \leq \eta$ *is a positive constant that assigns a fixed weight to all invalidations;*

- σ is the number of environmental state changes due to the occurrences of environmental events.

For example, the model reference corresponding to the list of option references represented as Maude term (1) above is

```
{ 8/17 , 0 | [1 : 1( 0)][&> [2 : 1(0)][&> [3 : 1(1)] [&>
            [4 : 2(1)][&> [5 : 1(0)][&> [6 : 1(2)] [&>
            [7 : 1(0)][&> [8 : 1(1)][&> [9 : 2(0)][&> [10 : 1(3)] }
```

where $\mu = 8/17 \simeq 0.47$ is the value provided by the sifting metric and $\omega = 0$ denotes that the model was never invalidated.

Definition 3. *A **refinement** is a set of model references { μ, ω | Ψ }, such that $\mu > 0$.*

The probability that the model is invalidated by a target event is given by $\frac{\omega}{\eta}$. Thus, for $c = 1$, term $1 - c \cdot \frac{\omega}{\eta}$ gives the probability that the model is not invalidated by a target event. The higher such a value, the more accurate the model. The role of constant c is to take *noise* into account. We choose $c < \eta$ in situations in which noise may invalidate correct models. In this case the higher the noise, the smaller should c be chosen. Unfortunately, the sifting metric cannot help in situations in which noise may validate incorrect models. In the absence of noise we could choose $c = \eta$, which includes in the refinement only the models that are never invalidated, but would exclude possible models invalidated by noise. In our previous work [4] we sifted out a model at the first invalidation. This can be reproduced in our more general framework by choosing $c = \eta$.

Term $(\sum_{k=1}^{n} j_k)$ gives the total number of transition rules applications. Since transition rules are only applied after an environmental state changes due to the occurrence of an environmental event, term $(\sum_{k=1}^{n} j_k)/\sigma$ gives the probability of application of transition rules after an environmental change. This provides a measure of how frequently the model evolves in response to environmental changes. Therefore metric μ combines the fact that the model is validated by the target events (term $1 - c \cdot \frac{\omega}{\eta}$) with the responsiveness of the model to environmental events (term $(\sum_{k=1}^{n} j_k)/\sigma$).

Table 3 shows the results of applying refinement mining to our case study. In absence of noise, for $c = \eta = 10$, the refinement comprises 32 out of 128 option-free models, i.e. all option-free models that are not invalidated ($\omega = 0$). However, for $c = 9 < \eta$, the number of option-free models in the refinement increases to 96 and, for $c = 1 < \eta$, the refinement actually comprises all 128 option-free models, with some models with 1 invalidation ($\omega = 1$) being better ($\mu = 9/17 \simeq 0.529$) than all models with 0 invalidations ($\omega = 0$, $\mu = 8/17 \simeq 0.471$). In fact, the negative effect of ω on metric μ is directly proportional to constant c and inversely proportional to the number η of target events. Thus, in our case study, the small number of target events $\eta = 10$ makes the effect of ω decrease quickly when c decreases: a small η cannot effectively validate the model against noise.

Table 3. Results from applying refinement mining to the plausible model in Fig. 3 (128 option-free models, $\eta = 10$ and $\sigma = 17$).

refinement	no. models	μ	ω	$\sum_{k=1}^{n} j_k$
32	**32**	$8/17 \simeq 0.471$	0	8
models for	64	0	1	8 or 10
$c = 10 = \eta$	32	$-10/17 \simeq -0.588$	2	10
96	**32**	$8/17 \simeq 0.471$	0	8
models for	**32**	$1/17 \simeq 0.059$	1	10
$c = 9 < \eta$	**32**	$4/85 \simeq 0.047$	1	8
	32	$-8/17 \simeq -0.471$	2	10
128	**32**	$9/17 \simeq 0.529$	1	10
models for	**32**	$8/17 \simeq 0.471$	0	8
$c = 1 < \eta$	**32**	$8/17 \simeq 0.471$	2	10
	32	$36/85 \simeq 0.424$	1	8

5   Conclusion and Future Work

In this tool paper we have presented the architecture of FormalMiner and described how refinement mining is carried out on a real case study from ecology. With respect to our previous work [4,5], we emphasised on practical aspects such as the *sifting metric*, which is used to evaluate the validity of alternative option-free instances of the model. In particular, the sifting metric was simplified by removing the dependency from the number of option sets. The definition of refinement was also simplified by removing the notion of a threshold. These simplifications led to a more informative output of FormalMiner, which allows us to improve the refinement mining strategy as discussed below.

In our previous work [5] we discussed the complexity of model mining and presented the results of timing testing. In term of complexity, we observed that the number of transition rule applications grows linearly with respect to the size of the dataset. Moreover, the complexity of the refinement mining algorithm is subquadratic with respect to both the size of the dataset and the number of option-free models.

The main problem is that the total number of option-free models grows exponentially with the number of options per option set. In this sense the complexity is exponential with respect to the level of option-related non-determinism. It is therefore a good strategy to apply refinement mining repeatedly on plausible models which contain only a small number of options per option set. In this way, we may get some ideas on which combinations of transition rules are incompatible and then test them in separate runs of the refinement mining algorithm. In particular, in Sect. 3.4, we suggested to initially include two rules corresponding to what we expect to be reasonable lower and upper bound limits for the persistence of a domain state. In this way, after running refinement mining once, we can select the models that are part of the refinement (those for which $\mu > 0$) and then combine them in a new plausible model such that

1. when only one of the two rules of a pair with lower and upper bound limits was excluded from the refinement, while the other rule was applied at least once, a modified version of the former rule with limit closer to the bound of the latter rule may be introduced;
2. when both rules of a pair with lower and upper bound limits were included in the refinement, the more stringent rule may be eliminated;
3. when both rules of a pair with lower and upper bound limits were excluded from the refinement, either their bound limits may be relaxed or both rules may be eliminated, depending on whether or not we find these two rules consistent with the rest of the plausible model.

Obviously pairs of rules that are included in the refinement but are never applied require further data in order to be validated.

For example, let us consider the option-free model defined by the list of option references reppresented by Maude term (1) in Sect. 4, which is part of the refinement for any choice of constant c. Since rule 2 was included in and rule 1 was excluded from option set 4 in the refinement, following item 1 above, we may make the lower bound closer to the upper bound and run the refinement mining again, thus finding out that for lower bounds between 6 and 9 also rule 1 is included in the refinement. This means that we can replace the two rules of the pairs with just one rule with a persistence of 6 days as a condition. Since both rules 1 and 2 of option set 8 were included in the refinement and applied once, following item 2 above, we may eliminate rule 2, which requires a persistence of 4 days and is therefore more stringent than rule 1. Rules 3 and 4 of option set 4 were both excluded from the refinement. Following item 3 above, they may be eliminated due to their inconsistency with rules 1 and 2 of option set 4. Finally, rules in option sets 5, 7 and 9, which are never applied, require further target events in order to be validated.

In our future work, we intend to automate the combination of option-free models that are comprised by the refinement into a new plausible model. More-over, we are planning to apply refinement mining to other case studies from ecology and from other areas [2], such as human-computer interaction [3,6] and emergency management [16].

References

1. Basuki, T.A., Cerone, A., Barbuti, R., Maggiolo-Schettini, A., Milazzo, P., Rossi, E.: Modelling the dynamics of an aedes albopictus population. In: Proceedings of the AMCA-POP 2010, volume 227 of Electronic Proceedings in Theoretical Computer Science, pp. 37–58 (2010)
2. Cerone, A.: Process mining as a modelling tool: beyond the domain of business process management. In: Bianculli, D., Calinescu, R., Rumpe, B. (eds.) SEFM 2015. LNCS, vol. 9509, pp. 139–144. Springer, Heidelberg (2015). https://doi.org/10.1007/978-3-662-49224-6_12
3. Cerone, A.: A cognitive framework based on rewriting logic for the analysis of inter-active systems. In: De Nicola, R., Kühn, E. (eds.) SEFM 2016. LNCS, vol. 9763, pp. 287–303. Springer, Cham (2016). https://doi.org/10.1007/978-3-319-41591-8_20

4. Cerone, A.: Refinement mining: using data to sift plausible models. In: Milazzo, P., Varró, D., Wimmer, M. (eds.) STAF 2016. LNCS, vol. 9946, pp. 26–41. Springer, Cham (2016). https://doi.org/10.1007/978-3-319-50230-4_3
5. Cerone, A.: Model mining – integrating data analytics, modelling and verification. J. Intell. Inf. Syst. (2017). https://doi.org/10.1007/s10844-017-0474-3
6. Cerone, A.: Towards a cognitive architecture for the formal analysis of human behaviour and learning. In: Mazzara, M., et al. (eds.) STAF 2018 Workshops. LNCS, vol. 11176, pp. 1–17. Springer, Cham (2018). https://doi.org/10.1007/978-3-030-04771-9_17
7. Češka, M., Dannenberg, F., Kwiatkowska, M., Paoletti, N.: Precise parameter synthesis for stochastic biochemical systems. In: Mendes, P., Dada, J.O., Smallbone, K. (eds.) CMSB 2014. LNCS, vol. 8859, pp. 86–98. Springer, Cham (2014). https://doi.org/10.1007/978-3-319-12982-2_7
8. Clavel, M., et al.: The maude 2.0 system. In: Nieuwenhuis, R. (ed.) RTA 2003. LNCS, vol. 2706, pp. 76–87. Springer, Heidelberg (2003). https://doi.org/10.1007/3-540-44881-0_7
9. Gries, D., Scheneider, F.B.: A Logical Approach to Discrete Math. Springer, Heidelberg (1993). https://doi.org/10.1007/978-1-4757-3837-7
10. Gulwani, S.: Automating string processing in spreadsheets using input-output examples. In: Proceedings of the POPL 2011 ACM SIGPLAN Notices, vol. 46, pp. 317–330. ACM (2011)
11. Koksal, A.S., Pu, Y., Srivastava, S., Bodik, R., Fisher, J., Piterman, N.: Automating string processing in spreadsheets using input-output examples. In: Proceedings of the POPL 2013 ACM SIGPLAN Notices, vol. 48, pp. 469–482. ACM (2013)
12. Martí-Oliet, N., Meseguer, J.: Rewriting logic: roadmap and bibliography. Theor. Comput. Sci. **285**(2), 121–154 (2002)
13. Mukala, P.: Process Models for Learning Patterns in FLOSS Repositories. Ph.D. thesis, Department of Computer Science, University of Pisa (2015)
14. Paoletti, N., Yordanov, B., Hamadi, Y., Wintersteiger, C.M., Kugler, H.: Analyzing and synthesizing genomic logic functions. In: Biere, A., Bloem, R. (eds.) CAV 2014. LNCS, vol. 8559, pp. 343–357. Springer, Cham (2014). https://doi.org/10.1007/978-3-319-08867-9_23
15. Rozinat, A., van der Aalst, W.M.P.: Conformance checking of processes based on monitoring real behavior. Inf. Syst. **33**(1), 64–95 (2008)
16. Shams, F., Cerone, A., De Nicola, R.: On integrating social and sensor networks for emergency management. In: Bianculli, D., Calinescu, R., Rumpe, B. (eds.) SEFM 2015. LNCS, vol. 9509, pp. 145–160. Springer, Heidelberg (2015). https://doi.org/10.1007/978-3-662-49224-6_13
17. Solar-Lezama, A., Rabbah, R.M., Bodik, R., Ebcioglu, K.: Programming by sketching for bit-streaming programs. In: Proceedings of the PLDI 2005 ACM SIGPLAN Notices, vol. 40, pp. 281–294. ACM (2005)
18. Srivastava, S., Gulwani, S., Foster, J.S.: From program verification to program synthesis. In: Proceedings of the POPL 2010 ACM SIGPLAN Notices, vol. 45, pp. 313–326. ACM (2010)
19. van der Aalst, W.M.P., de Beer, H.T., van Dongen, B.F.: Process mining and verification of properties: an approach based on temporal logic. In: Meersman, R., Tari, Z. (eds.) OTM 2005. LNCS, vol. 3760, pp. 130–147. Springer, Heidelberg (2005). https://doi.org/10.1007/11575771_11
20. van der Aalst, W.M.P., Stahl, C.: Modeling Business Processes: A Petri Net-Oriented Approach. The MIT Press, Cambridge (2011)

Formal Methods for Interactive Systems (FMIS)

Formal Methods for Interactive Systems: A Research Field in Between HCI, Formal Methods and Software Engineering

Yamine Aït-Ameur[1] and Philippe Palanque[2]

[1]ACADIE-IRIT, ENSEEIHT, France
[2]ICS-IRIT, Université Toulouse III, France
{palanque,yamine}@irit.fr

Abstract. This paper presents the rationale and the content of the Formal Methods for Interactive Systems that was organized alongside Software Technologies: Applications and Foundations (STAF) in Toulouse, in June 2018.

Keywords: Formal methods · Interactive systems · FMIS

1 Introduction and Content

Reducing the likelihood of faults and failures in the development and in the use of interactive systems becomes a more and more inescapable necessity. Indeed the use of such systems is becoming widespread in applications that demand high dependability due to usability, safety or, security requirements while taking into account additional considerations such as User Experience or Learnability. Interactive systems make use of more and more sophisticated electronic devices and are made up by multiple hardware and software components. These systems are in fact large artifacts that are also becoming increasingly ubiquitous and being used in new and more complex situations.

Consequently, the use of formal methods in providing some assurance on the dependability of interactive systems should take into account the wider socio-technical system. The aim of this workshop is to bring together researchers in computer science, human factors, and other areas of HCI, from both academia and industry, who are interested in both formal methods and interactive system design and development.

FMIS 2018 solicited papers that address issues of how formal methods can be applied to interactive system design. It also welcomed papers with a focus on theory provided a link to interactive systems is made explicit. Application areas considered included but were not limited to: mobile devices, embedded systems, safety-critical systems, high-reliability systems, shared control systems, digital libraries, eGovernment, pervasive systems, ubiquitous computing, and computer security applications.

2   Background on FMIS Workshop Series

FMIS workshop organized within STAF 2018 in Toulouse was the seventh of a serie that started in 2016 and was organized as a satellite event of ICFEM 2006. The proceedings of the workshop were published in Electronic Notes of Theoretical Computer Science, Volume 153 [1]. FMIS 2007 was organized immediately after FMIS 2006 and located in Lancaster, UK [2].

After that, FMIS workshops were organized in different places of the world most of the time in conjunction with other main conferences in the are of Software Engineering, Formal Methods or Human-Computer Interaction as for instance FMIS 2012 in conjunction with the international conference of Application and Theory of Command and Control Systems [3].

3   Content of FMIS 2018 Alongside STAF

3.1   Keynote and Papers

FMIS 2018[1] program presented one keynote and a set of 4 long and 2 short papers. The keynote was given by Professor Dominique Mery from Telecom-Nancy, France. The topic was *"Abstraction and Refinement for Managing Features Interactions"* starting the day with deep content and provocative thoughts about the complexity of modeling and verification activities highlighting, in places, the challenges raised by interactive systems.

3.2   Organizers

As FMIS run within STAF 2018, the organizers received extremely useful support from STAF organization committee. In addition, David Chemouil, ONERA, Toulouse, France and Neeraj Kumar Singh, INPT-IRIT, Toulouse, France managed the organizational aspects of the workshop.

The scientific committee was led by Yamine Aït-Ameur, and Philippe Palanque and was composed of the following members:

Matthew Bolton, University at Buffalo, New York, USA
Judy Bowen, University of Waikato, Hamilton, New Zealand
Jose Campos, University of Minho, Braga, Portugal
Antonio Cerone, Nazarbayev University, Astana, Kazakhstan
Horatiu Cirstea, University of Lorraine, Nancy, France
David Chemouil, ONERA, Toulouse, France
Paul Curzon, University of London, UK
Bruno d'Ausbourg, ONERA, Toulouse, France
Michael Harrison, Newcastle University, Newcastle, UK
Kris Luyten, Hasselt University, Hasselt, Belgium
Atif Mashkoor, SCCH, Hagenberg, Austria

---

[1] https://fmis2018.sciencesconf.org/.

Mieke Massink, Institute of Information Science and Technology, Pisa, Italy
Dominique Mery, University of Lorraine, Nancy, France
Charles Pecheur, Université Catholique de Louvain, Louvain, Belgium
Steve Reeves, University of Waikato, Hamilton, New Zealand
Neeraj Kumar Singh, INPT-IRIT, Toulouse, France
Benjamin Weyers, RWTH Aachen University, Aachen, Germany

That committee reviewed and selected the submissions. In addition to the scientific presentations two interactive discussion sessions was organized to exchange ideas and experience on:

- The evolution of interaction techniques and Formal Methods and how can formal approaches for Interactive Systems deal with the rapid evolution of the interaction techniques.
- Properties verification for interactive systems trying to provide answers to the questions "Are we progressing on the verification of properties for interactive systems? Can we define an agenda of items to consider as a priority for future research".

4   Future Events and Perspective

The attendees of the workshop agreed that the topic is worth studying and that there is no other venue that is addressing the topic. ACM SIGCHI conference on Engineering Interactive Computing System (EICS[2]) was mentioned but detailed analysis of published content over the last few years demonstrated that formal aspects of interactive systems is not a subject published there.

It was thus decided to renew the experience in the near future and try to advertise widely the need for more FMIS-related contributions in order to provide users with dependable and usable interactive systems.

References

1. Cerone, A., Curzon, P.: Preface. Electron. Notes Theor. Comput. Sci. **183**(1–2) (2007). ISSN 1571-0661, https://doi.org/10.1016/j.entcs.2007.03.011
2. Cerone, A., Curzon, P., Preface. Electron. Notes Theor. Comput. Sci. **208**(1–3) (2008). ISSN 1571-0661, https://doi.org/10.1016/j.entcs.2008.03.103
3. Bolton, M., Degani, A., Palanque, P.: Proceedings of the Workshop on Formal Methods in Human - Machine Interaction. http://fhsl.eng.buffalo.edu/FormalH/FormalH.2012.Proceedings.pdf

---

[2] https://eics.acm.org/.

Exploring Applications of Formal Methods in the INSPEX Project

Joseph Razavi[1]([⊠]), Richard Banach[1], Olivier Debicki[2], Nicolas Mareau[2], Suzanne Lesecq[2], and Julie Foucault[2]

[1] School of Computer Science, University of Manchester,
Oxford Road, Manchester M13 9PL, UK
{joseph.razavi,richard.banach}@manchester.ac.uk
[2] Commissariat à l'Énergie Atomique et aux Énergies Alternatives,
MINATEC Campus, 17 Rue des Martyrs, 38054 Grenoble Cedex, France
{olivier.debicki,nicolas.mareau,suzanne.lesecq,julie.foucault}@cea.fr

Abstract. As formal methods become increasingly practical, there is a need to explore their use in a variety of domains. Wearable sensing is a rapidly developing area in which formal methods can provide tangible benefits to end users, facilitating the advance of cutting-edge technology where consumer trust is critical. The INSPEX project aims to develop a miniaturized spatial exploration system incorporating multiple sensors and state of the art processing, initially focused on a navigation tool for visually impaired people. It is thus a useful test-case for formal methods in this domain. Applying formal methods in the INSPEX development process entailed adapting to realistic external pressures. The impact of these on the modelling process is described, attending in particular to the relationship between human and tool-supported reasoning.

1 Introduction

The industrial application of formal methods is becoming increasingly common. In safety-critical domains such as aerospace, train systems, and nuclear reactors, it is more and more the case that one can reasonably expect their use [1,3,7,14]. For the design of CPUs, where the financial cost of failures is extreme, formal methods have become standard [22]. This is starting to extend to other types of widely used infrastructure such as operating system components and compilers [16], and famously, in the back-end operations of large web-based companies.[1]

These fields, of course, do not exhaust the range of potential applications. Indeed, a time may come when most software is developed using rigorous techniques, but this future is at present rather remote. Instead, the frontier consists of complex systems whose cost of failure is high, if not quite catastrophic. The development of systems with these characteristics presents an ideal opportunity

---

[1] We have in mind the use by Facebook [11] of behind-the-scenes verification tools, described in [32], and as predicted almost a decade earlier by Meyer in [20].

© Springer Nature Switzerland AG 2018
M. Mazzara et al. (Eds.): STAF 2018 Workshops, LNCS 11176, pp. 205–215, 2018.
https://doi.org/10.1007/978-3-030-04771-9_16

for formal methods researchers and software engineers to engage with each other to make rigorous development more applicable and ubiquitous.

The area of medical devices is evidently one in which the consequences of errors may be permanently debilitating or fatal, and there, system construction is governed by numerous standards, e.g. [17] for software. Adjacent to life-critical devices, there is an expanding area of medical accessories, attempting to enhance the lives of their users in significant if non-critical ways. Among the many specific kinds of device in this category we mention 'assistive technologies' which aim to support users with specific needs to navigate a world principally designed without those needs in mind. If the device functions as it should, the benefit is an increased ability to live independently.

In this paper, we examine the INSPEX system [18], one example of a navigation aid for visually impaired people. Such navigation aids, if they are successful, may help the user to carry out more complex journeys than they would usually feel comfortable undertaking, and with less reliance on others to help them. From this benefit there arises a concomitant cost: if the system should fail, the user may be left stranded in an unfamiliar area which they would otherwise have avoided, perhaps even having to wait for assistance from friends, strangers or emergency services. While such an event would clearly undermine the increased independence which the device should bring, it is not the occurrence but the plausible probability of this kind of problem which is a threat to the system's usefulness: unless users can be reassured that failure is a remote possibility, they can not rely on the technology.

While the most classical navigation aid for visually impaired people, the white cane, is a simple and robust physical tool, the decreasing cost of sensors and increasing ubiquity of portable or wearable computing provides new possibilities to imagine assistive technologies. However, given the high reliability required and the complexity of the technology involved, the issue of correctness presents a barrier to entry for anyone wishing to provide such a product. Indeed, in some jurisdictions, devices of this type are highly regulated, underscoring the challenge to be met.

For these reasons, the development of assistive technologies represents a key area in which the industrial use of formal methods may expand. However, projects in this area are likely to be conducted under significant time pressure, and to be led to a great extent by technology and hardware development. Software components may be re-purposed from previous development efforts which are unlikely to have employed a rigorous methodology. These factors together eliminate two classical approaches for integrating formal methods into a project. A top-down approach becomes impractical, because the desire to leverage new technologies in a timely manner necessitates the use of existing components where possible. On the other hand, an incremental use of static techniques to analyse a system in deployment, as might be used for back-end technologies, is not practical for stand-alone devices which must be highly reliable from the outset.

In this paper, we describe the effects of these constraints on the formal modelling process, based on our experience working on the INSPEX project. In Sect. 2

the INSPEX project is described in more detail. Our experiences with different strategies for modelling under the constraints of the project are discussed in Sect. 3, and the extent to which we have been able to support this activity with existing tools is reported in Sect. 4. Concluding remarks are made in Sect. 5.

2   The INSPEX Project

The INSPEX project [18] aims to construct a wearable spatial exploration system, providing obstacle-detection and warning capabilities. Such systems in themselves are not new, and indeed the traditional white cane used by some visually impaired or blind people constitutes an example. Recently, advances in sensor technologies have made it possible for consumer applications to utilize advanced electronics for this purpose. This leads to enhanced white canes which incorporate range sensors such as ultrasound or LiDAR. While the cane sweeps to detect ground-level obstacles, the sensor can scan a head or body height, and the system can provide a warning beep or buzz if there is an obstacle in its path. A selection of existing or projected systems based around the advanced sensor idea includes Smartcane [28], Ultracane [31], Bawa [5] and Rango [25].

INSPEX will design a small, light device, suitable, in the first instance, to be mounted on a white cane to assist the blind and visually impaired. Further use cases include other low-visibility domains such as fire-fighting in smoke filled environments, or the operation of small airborne drones. INSPEX advances the state of the art for such systems in two ways.

First, incorporating ideas currently used for automotive applications, INSPEX combines readings from multiple sensors into a single statistical model of the environment [15,19,21,27,30]. Specifically, it makes use of a short range LiDAR, a long range LiDAR, an ultra wide-band RADAR, and a MEMS ultrasound sensor. This is a significant improvement over a single-sensor system because each sensor has different characteristics and each performs best under different circumstances. Factors such as light level, fog, rain, snow, reflectivity of the target or its distance and size, impact the accuracy of data from different sensing methods in different ways. Combining these diverse measurements can lead to greater accuracy, and discrepancies between them can reveal properties of environmental objects, such as translucency, which are not possible with one type of reading alone. As part of the INSPEX project, the sensors themselves have to be miniaturized and adapted to function in close proximity to each other. This work is carried out in parallel by the Swiss Center for Electronics and Microtechnology, the French Alternative Energies and Atomic Energy Commission, the Tyndall National Institute Cork, and SensL Technologies.

Second, the INSPEX device integrates a significant amount of processing, so that its output, rather than simple range readings, can consist of more meaningful data such as a depth-map of the scanned environment, or the location of salient obstacles. This saves the data consumer the effort of processing raw readings into a meaningful form. This is significant in human-oriented applications, as traditionally the presence of, or distance to, an obstacle in a particular direction is presented to the user rather directly, in the form of sound or tactile feedback, leaving the user's brain the task of extracting a model of the environment. This will be a familiar experience to those readers who have had to translate the more or less frequent beep of a car reversing sensor into sensible manoeuvres, especially in the presence of small unexpected obstacles. Relieving this cognitive load for users who must make constant use of the data from the sensors is significant, and the processing performed by the INSPEX sensing unit allows a smartphone application, developed with the French startup GoSense, to render the environment in a 3D 'sound picture', presented to the user via binaural headphones.

The system consists of many heterogeneous modules. There is the headset, the smartphone and the environment sensing system. Within the sensing system, which is where the focus of the technological development work is concentrated, the individual sensors are provided by autonomous submodules (capable of being deployed individually in other applications), whose readings are combined using a software processing subsystem for the digital information garnered.

These features make the INSPEX project an ideal test case for the application of formal methods to the class of problems described in the previous section. The success of the device crucially relies on its dependability, making formal methods attractive. However, time constraints, fundamental technological challenges, and the necessary re-use of existing components where possible mean that a pragmatic approach to the formal modelling and verification process must be taken. In what follows, we outline lessons learned from this project about how formal modelling can be incorporated in a development process with these characteristics.

3 Modelling Approaches for INSPEX

As outlined above, when modelling the class of systems of interest in this paper, one must frequently deal with bodies of existing code which have been modified so as to be suitable for the project at hand. In contrast to the ideal application of formal methods, in which formal modelling would be used to derive code from requirements, adding clarity and detail progressively, a more 'bottom up' approach is clearly needed which relates to the existing code as it is, and which acknowledges that requirements are somewhat obscure, encoded implicitly in implementation details and engineers' minds.

In beginning such a modelling exercise, we have found that there are two tempting mistakes which must be avoided. The first is to take 'bottom up' too literally, and attempt to model the low-level of the code in complete detail. Under any plausible constraints on time and personnel, an unmodified interpretation of this is clearly impossible: in a system of any reasonable complexity, there are simply too many low-level events to lead to the extraction of a sensible formal model.

At the level where the functioning of the operating system and libraries is considered to be correct—perhaps leveraging existing work [10,13]—the task has a semblance of achievability, but this quickly turns into a mirage. It rapidly becomes clear that while such a model may be constructible in the time available, there will be little time for anything else. Given that the constructed model would be almost a copy of the code as it is, little value would be added in terms of perception of the intended purpose of the system, at the cost of great effort. Discrepancies would be hard to detect because of the low-level focus, and, since the model would not be independent from the program, they would be vastly more likely to originate in modeller error than to be genuine defects in the system. While existing formalizations of operating system functionality are valuable tools for modellers of higher level systems, the insights contained in them must be more carefully deployed.

It must not be thought that these problems could be overcome by automated means. While models could in principle be extracted from code, ameliorating the issue of the quantity of work, the more fundamental problem of obtaining a copy of the existing low-level artefact would remain. In a system like INSPEX, it would be difficult to analyse such a model, even automatically, for problems more interesting than null pointer dereferences or buffer overruns. For example, the main correctness property we care about for the INSPEX system is liveness: we don't want the system to stop producing output unexpectedly or unreasonably. However, it is clear that there are lots of circumstances under which output is impossible.

In order to perform its analysis, the system requires sufficiently diverse input with sufficient frequency. What exactly is meant by 'sufficiently diverse' and 'with sufficient frequency' is not clear from a high-level point of view without considerable human insight. It crucially depends on implementation details, essentially corresponding to the way memory is managed. Even to understand that the problem can be stated in this form, reducing the number of properties of the implementation to be determined to just two frequencies, a high-level understanding of the code is needed. For the foreseeable future, extracting this kind of conceptual information from a computer program remains an unavoidably human task.

If the desire to start with the details as they exist is problematic, the opposite tendency is equally dangerous. Given that the salient aspects of the code are only visible in the light of a high-level understanding, it is tempting to try to run a traditional formal development, from requirements, through specifications, culminating in implementation-level models. These would then be compared with the existing code for discrepancies. Of course, the likelihood that low level models obtained in this way would match the real code would be remote. Furthermore, it would be a grave mistake to replace the real-world code with something generated by the model, since the real code embodies a wealth of practical experience about the efficient and robust implementation of the system which a modeller is unlikely to be able to replicate, particularly in little time. For this reason, the modeller must keep one eye on the code, though this starts to risk the same problem as the approach above: the specification is no good if it just amounts to saying that the abstract model does whatever the code does and thus the code is correct with respect to the abstract model by default!

A more formidable obstacle is the scale of the problem of going from low-level code to high-level properties suitable for a specification. As described above, coming to understand the precise requirements that the system places on its inputs in order to function properly depends on a detailed understanding of the code. It would be hubristic to imagine that a lengthy cogitation on the details would produce the required perspective for a system of any reasonable complexity.

Both options considered above share the defect that a lot of time and effort is consumed before any actual model results. This is a poor use of resources, as a widely drawn lesson in applied formal methods is that much of their value is derived from the human understanding of the system gained by producing models [4,14]. These models (or from questions driven by constructing them) can be discussed with engineers, revealing points of tension which may imply the presence of inadequate understanding by any of the parties, or of bugs. This interactive process works best if comprehensible models can be produced early in the whole design and implementation activity as it is well known that the cost of fixing defects is roughly exponential in how far along the development route they are discovered [8,23,29].

The resolution of these dilemmas has two aspects. The first is that engineers will already have a conceptual understanding of the code they have produced, which is likely to be at an intermediate level of abstraction. They will be able to provide a description of the functioning of the system at the level of data structures rather than low-level manipulations. A model of this description has the advantage of being at the level engineers already think about the system, facilitating discussion and helping to resolve ambiguities in natural language descriptions. Data structures are likely to be motivated by non-functional considerations such as memory constraints or hardware requirements. In some sense, a description of the system at this level is likely to describe the *practical objectives* met by the code at a level which abstracts from detailed manipulations, but leave the *ultimate purpose* of the system's actions implicit. Therefore, in addition to making explicit how this description connects to the implementation details, the modeller must also extract a specification of correctness with a reasonable degree of independence.

Once this mid-level model is in place, the task of producing high and low level models is dramatically simplified. In a very idealized description, one might imagine working recursively, always attempting to make half-steps in the directions of specification and implementation simultaneously, and filling in the gaps between existing models. The distinctive property of this process of modelling is that refinement relations between models become formalizable all at once, as the end of the process of interpolation is approached. This delays the construction of a formal proof that the system behaves as it should, and prioritizes maximizing the amount of communication with the development team.

In reality, the situation is likely to be a little worse than what has just been stated. Producing models of the entire system, suitable to stand in relations of refinement to each other, becomes increasingly difficult as low-level features are incorporated and get in the way of clean abstraction. Instead, it is advisable to model whatever aspects of the system seem amenable to modelling.

For example, in the INSPEX system, the incoming sensor readings are pre-processed in various ways before being sent to the statistical algorithm which computes a representation of the user's environment. In the course of this processing, they spend time in various internal buffers. In a high-level approximation to the system, one imagines that the message contents themselves move around in these data structures, but in reality only references are manipulated. This generates some subtle requirements. When an abstract object simply disappears, its reference can not disappear: instead it must be used to deallocate the resource referenced. More interestingly, when a piece of abstract data passes from one buffer to another, in reality these buffers may be stored on separate subsystems. In that case, the reference must not be sent. Instead, the data itself must be sent, and the abstract value represented by a new reference to the copy.

In principle, these sorts of details are well captured by refinement, but in practice if the algorithm at an abstract level is already complex, a model incorporating the lower level details can become extremely unwieldy and in particular difficult to discuss with engineers. Instead, the processes implementing individual steps of the low-level memory management procedures can be modelled. The resulting set of models, then, will stand in a variety of relations to each other and to the code, focussing on select aspects of the system chosen by human judgement.

4 Tool Support

Most of the modelling work for INSPEX has been done using Event-B [2] and the Rodin tool [26]. The Event-B style of formal development constructs system models by building state machines, with state spaces (not by any means restricted to finite cardinalities) defined statically, and with the transitions between states defined by guarded events written in a guarded command language. The Rodin tool reasons about the consistency or otherwise of the model defined, by comparing the definition of the model's dynamics against the invariants and other properties that are included in the model's definition.

The choice of Event-B and Rodin was made principally on modelling grounds. We found that Rodin, together with its recently incorporated SAT solving plugins [9] doing the heavy lifting on the proving side, was very convenient for modelling timing-related properties of systems. It performed better for our application, and could be more useful, than tools which focus specifically on time. The reason is that systems such as ours do not fit well the perspective on time that those alternative tools take. By contrast, in many respects Rodin fits very well with the modelling process described here.

Of course, the ability to animate models using the ProB plug-in of Rodin [24] is very useful for communicating the meaning of models to non-specialists. In addition, the semi-interactive style of proof is well-suited to a modelling style in which much of the issue of correctness is left to human discretion. Indeed, we often find that arguments about data structures are often reducible by a combination of human and automated effort into an intuitively obvious statement. This can be marked as 'reviewed' in Rodin, allowing a record of the interplay of human and automated verification.

One might also think that some of the relationships between models alluded to above which do not amount to refinement may be covered by some of the many plug-ins available. Of the plug-ins available, those on model decomposition, and particularly atomicity decomposition [12], seem most likely to be relevant. At present, however, use of these tools presents the problem that one particular formalism out of many possibilities for decomposition must be chosen to represent a relationship between subsystems which is intuitively understood, but may correspond to each of the possibilities only imperfectly. This work only seems justifiable if it is reasonably clear that it would form part of a formal proof of correctness. We may return to this point in future work.

In addition to the relationships between different abstract models, there is also the question of the relationship between these models and the code. For detailed enough models, this relationship can be checked for plausibility by a human being, but this may lead to low-level problems being overlooked. In the INSPEX project, we have made use of the BLAST tool [6] to confirm aspects of our understanding of the code. BLAST was selected as an initial tool to investigate for this purpose because of the availability of tutorial material, and crucially because of its specification language which is conceptually close to the idea of guarded events.

For example, suppose that at a relatively high level of abstraction, we model a sensor process which first allocates slot from a buffer, then fills this slot with a reading from the sensor hardware, and goes back to waiting for free space to be available in the buffer. Schematically, a standard way to model a simple state machine of that kind would be to use a variable for the current state, an abstraction of the control state of the real program. To check that the real code corresponds to the model at this level of abstraction, one might write a BLAST specification in the following way. First, a new variable must be inserted into the code to model the state of the abstract system. To do this the BLAST specification might begin with `global int wait_for_buffer = 1;`. Next, events in the Event-B model are linked to the code by using BLAST events. In the Event-B model, the sensor being allocated space in the buffer would correspond to an event like the following.

$GetBufferSlot$
  WHEN $state = wait\_for\_buffer$
     $available\_slots \geq 1$
  THEN $state := wait\_for\_reading$
     $available\_slots := available\_slots - 1$

In the C code, the event might correspond to calling a function `allocateSlot()`, and the condition that there are available slots in the buffer might be indicated by a pointer, `next_slot` being non-null. Supposing that we are confident that the function `allocateSlot()` does reduce the number of free slots as required, and we only want to check that the control state machine is accurate, we might write a BLAST event as follows.

```
event {
    pattern { buffer_slot = allocateSlot();}
    guard   { wait_for_buffer == 1 &&
              next_slot != NULL }
    action  { wait_for_buffer  == 0; }
}
```

BLAST will check that whenever the 'pattern' in the above specification occurs, the 'guard' is true, and add the 'action' to the code to update the abstract state. This is somewhat like checking a refinement relation between the C code and the Event-B model. However, it relies on assumptions made by the modeller that the functions used behave as expected, and that there are no sources of control flow changes, such as failure to obtain a sensor reading or pre-emption by other threads, which have been ignored. Once these assumptions have been documented, they can be discussed with engineers, or used to guide the development of more detailed refinements of the Event-B models.

5   Conclusions

In this paper, we discussed the lessons learned from our formal modelling work on the INSPEX project about the way in which formal methods can be expanded into domains for which the usual accounts seem difficult to apply.

In particular, by treating formal tools as a way to explicitly represent human intuitions about the system, approximating the process of refinement by describing salient levels of abstraction, as much value can be drawn out of the modelling process as possible in limited time. The drawbacks of this approach are that the partial models constructed can stand in various relationships to each other, which may reduce the applicability of tools and delay the construction of proofs of correctness. In addition, describing the assumptions linking formal models with the real system can become complex. Nevertheless, formal methods can bring tangible benefits to projects where high reliability is important, but practical needs make a process structured around the use of formal methods unworkable.

Acknowledgement. This project has received funding from the European Union's Horizon 2020 research and innovation programme under grant agreement No. 730953. The work was also supported in part by the Swiss Secretariat for Education, Research and Innovation (SERI) under Grant 16.0136 730953. We thank them for their support.

References

1. Abrial, J.R.: Formal methods in industry: achievements, problems future. In: Proceedings ACM/IEEE ICSE 2006, pp. 761–768 (2006)
2. Abrial, J.R.: Modeling in Event-B: System and Software Engineering. CUP (2010)
3. Banach, R. (ed.): Special issue on the state of the art in formal methods. J. Univ. Comput. Sci. **13**(5) (2007)
4. Barnes, J.E.: Experiences in the industrial use of formal methods. Electron. Commun. EASST **46** (2011)
5. Bawa: https://www.bawa.tech/
6. BLAST Tool (2011). https://forge.ispras.ru/projects/blast/
7. Bowen, J., Hinchey, M.: Seven more Myths of formal methods. IEEE Softw. **12**, 34–41 (1995)
8. Braude, E., Bernstein, M.: Software Engineering: Modern Approaches. Wiley, Hoboken (2011)
9. Déharbe, D., Fontaine, P., Guyot, Y., Voisin, L.: SMT solvers for Rodin. In: Derrick, J., et al. (eds.) ABZ 2012. LNCS, vol. 7316, pp. 194–207. Springer, Heidelberg (2012). https://doi.org/10.1007/978-3-642-30885-7_14
10. Divakaran, S., D'Souza, D., Kushwah, A., Sampath, P., Sridhar, N., Woodcock, J.: Refinement-based verification of the FreeRTOS Scheduler in VCC. In: Butler, M., Conchon, S., Zaïdi, F. (eds.) ICFEM 2015. LNCS, vol. 9407, pp. 170–186. Springer, Cham (2015). https://doi.org/10.1007/978-3-319-25423-4_11
11. Facebook: https://en-gb.facebook.com
12. Salehi Fathabadi, A., Butler, M., Rezazadeh, A.: A Systematic approach to atomicity decomposition in Event-B. In: Eleftherakis, G., Hinchey, M., Holcombe, M. (eds.) SEFM 2012. LNCS, vol. 7504, pp. 78–93. Springer, Heidelberg (2012). https://doi.org/10.1007/978-3-642-33826-7_6
13. FreeRTOS: (2017). https://www.freertos.org/
14. Hall, A.: Seven Myths of formal methods. IEEE Softw. **7**, 11–19 (1990)
15. Hall, D.: Mathematical Techniques in Multisensor Data Fusion. Artech House, Norwood (2004)
16. Harrison, J.: Formal proof—theory and practice. Not. AMS **55**, 1395–1406 (2008)
17. IEC 62304: https://webstore.iec.ch/publication/22794
18. INSPEX Homepage: (2017). http://www.inspex-ssi.eu/
19. Kedem, B., De Oliveira, V., Sverchkov, M.: Statistical Data Fusion. World Scientific, Singapore (2017)
20. Meyer, B.: How you will be programming ten years from now. In: ACM SAC-10 Keynote (2010)
21. Moravec, H., Elfes, A.: High resolution maps from wide angle sonar. In: Proceedings IEEE ICRA (1985)
22. Pratt, V.: Anatomy of the Pentium bug. In: Mosses, P.D., Nielsen, M., Schwartzbach, M.I. (eds.) CAAP 1995. LNCS, vol. 915, pp. 97–107. Springer, Heidelberg (1995). https://doi.org/10.1007/3-540-59293-8_189
23. Pressman, R.: Software Engineering: A Practitioner's Approach. McGraw Hill, New York City (2005)
24. ProB Tool: https://www3.hhu.de/stups/prob/
25. Rango: (2018). http://www.gosense.com/rango/
26. RODIN Tool: (2018). http://sourceforge.net/projects/rodin-b-sharp/http://www.event-b.org/

27. Scalise, L., Primiani, V., Russo, P.: Experimental investigation of electromagnetic obstacle detection for visually impaired users: a comparison with ultrasonic sensing. IEEE Trans. Inst. Meas. **61**, 3047–3057 (2012)
28. Smartcane: (2017).   https://www.phoenixmedicalsystems.com/assistive-technology/smartcane/
29. Sommerville, I.: Software Engineering. Pearson, London (2015)
30. Thrun, S., Burgard, W., Fox, D.: Probabilistic Robotics. MIT Press, Cambridge (2005)
31. Ultracane: (2017). https://www.ultracane.com/
32. Verhoef, M.: From documents to models: towards digital continuity. In: SAFECOMP/IMBSA-17 Keynote. https://drive.google.com/file/d/0B9DzO9PFER2xZDRxLUpKVUdYZmM/view?usp=sharing

Towards a Cognitive Architecture for the Formal Analysis of Human Behaviour and Learning

Antonio Cerone[✉]

Department of Computer Science, Nazarbayev University, Astana, Kazakhstan
antonio.cerone@nu.edu.kz
https://cs-sst.github.io/faculty/cerone

Abstract. In this paper we propose a cognitive architecture for the modelling of automatic and deliberate human behaviour as it occurs and evolves in a living environment or in interaction with machine interfaces. Such a cognitive architecture supports the timed modelling of an environment featuring a spatial topology and consisting of an arbitrary number of systems, interfaces and human components. Alternative models of short-term memory can be considered and explored, and long-term memory evolves throughout the time by exploiting experiences and mimicking the creation of expectations as part of mental modelling.

Keywords: Formal modelling · Cognitive architecture
Interactive systems · Rewriting logic · Maude rewrite system

1 Introduction

A *Cognitive architecture* has to be intended as a comprehensive model of the human mind, with a computational power that supports the insilico replication of experiments carried out in cognitive psychology as well as some form of prediction and analysis. A cognitive architecture is based on and implements a *theory of cognition*, which conceptualises the structure of mind in terms of its processing and storage components and the way such components work together to produce human thinking and behaviour [2].

A number of cognitive architectures have been proposed since the 1970s [13], following three approaches: *symbolic* architectures, such as ACT-R [2] and Soar [9], which are based on a set of predefined general rules, *connectionist* architectures, which count on emergent properties of connected processing components (e.g. nodes of a neural network), such as ANNABELL [8], and *hybrid* architectures, such as CLARION [14], which combine the two previous approaches. Although cognitive architectures can mimic many aspects of human behaviour and learning, they never really managed to be easily incorporated in the system and software verification process.

© Springer Nature Switzerland AG 2018
M. Mazzara et al. (Eds.): STAF 2018 Workshops, LNCS 11176, pp. 216–232, 2018.
https://doi.org/10.1007/978-3-030-04771-9_17

In previous work, we have defined a cognitive framework [5], based on the Maude rewrite system [7,11], that provides an approach for the analysis of an abstract overall system consisting of just one machine component and one human component, with a very simple, fixed short-term memory model, which incorporates a minimalist approach to closure but does not address decay and chunking, and a static model of long-term memory, which can statically describe user expectations but does not support the mimicking of learning processes. The cognitive notation defined in such previous work has been used by other researchers in *ad hoc* extensions for modelling human multitasking [3,4].

In this paper we propose a cognitive architecture for the modelling of automatic and deliberate human behaviour as it occurs and evolves in a living environment as well as in interaction with machine interfaces. Our aims are to provide a tool to be used both in human behaviour analysis and system verification, and to overcome the limitations of the cognitive framework presented in our previous work [5].

Section 2 introduces the underlying cognitive model, inspired by the information processing approach, and presents the Human Task Description Language (HTDL), which generalises and enriches the cognitive notation defined in our previous work [5]. Three distinct examples, including a classical Automatic Teller Machine (ATM) case study [5,12,15], are used to illustrate the generality of HTDL. Section 3 describes a rich environment that incorporates models of spatial topology and time scheduling of events, thus supporting the realistic time modelling of a multi-to-multi human-machine interaction. It also provides the semantics of the cognitive description language through a considerable extension of the interaction framework proposed by Abowd and Beale [1], and briefly illustrates the implementation of our cognitive architecture. Section 4 explores the use of the cognitive architecture for modelling learning processes. It illustrates how skill acquisition can be modelled through a transformation of the HTDL terms and how expectations can be built from the models of episodic memory and semantic memory. Finally, Sect. 5 discusses the use of our cognitive architecture and our plans for future work.

2   Cognitive Model and Description Language

Following the *information processing* approach normally used in cognitive psychology, we model human cognitive processes as processing activities that make use of input-output channels, to interact with the external environment, and three main kinds of memory, to store information: *sensory memory, short-term memory (STM)* and *long-term memory (LTM)*. LTM is divided into *declarative memory*, which refers to our knowledge of the world ("knowing what") and consists of the events, experiences (*episodic memory*) and facts (*semantic memory*) that can be consciously recalled, and *procedural memory*, which refers to our skills ("knowing how") and consists of rules and procedures that we unconsciously use to do things, particularly at the motor level.

Input and output occur in humans through senses. We represent input channels in term of *perceptions*, which may be intended in an abstract way, independently of the senses that capture them, or associated with a specific sensory channel. We represent output channels in term of *actions*. Actions are performed in response to perceptions.

Perceptions are briefly stored in the sensory memory and only relevant perceptions are transferred, possibly after some kind of processing, to the STM using *attention*, a selective processing activity that aims to focus on one aspect of the environment while ignoring others. Selective attention may be *explicit*, if it is focussed on goal-relevant stimuli in the environment, or *implicit*, if it is grabbed by sudden stimuli that are associated with the current mental state or carry emotional significance. Inspired by Norman and Shallice [10], we consider two levels of cognitive control:

automatic control
> fast processing activity that requires only implicit attention and is carried out outside awareness with no conscious effort implicitly, using rules and procedures stored in the procedural memory;

deliberate control
> processing activity triggered and focussed by explicit attention, driven by a goal and carried out under the intentional control of the individual, who makes explicit use of facts and experiences stored in the declarative memory and is aware and conscious of the effort required in doing so.

A human *task* consists of *basic activities* which are performed under these two levels of controls. It is modelled in HTDL as $\mathbf{task}(tn, ts, as)$, where tn is the task name, ts is the set of types of entities which the human acts on or interacts with and as is a set of basic activities. We represent in bold HTDL data structure constructors. Note that basic activities were called *basic task* in our previous work [5]. In Sects. 2.1, 2.2 and 2.3 we introduce HTDL and shows its generality using three different examples.

2.1 Modelling Automatic Control

Automatic control is essential in many every-day tasks, such as driving a car. The driver is aware of the high-level tasks that are carried out, but is not aware of low-level activities such as changing gear, using the indicator and reacting to the presence of a traffic light or a zebra crossing, which are performed automatically as a direct response to perceptions, with no involvement of thinking activities. For example, when we see a zebra crossing while driving, this visual perception is transferred from sensory memory to STM through implicit attention and modifies the mental state to be ready to automatically react to pedestrian walking across the road. In order to describe automatic behaviour, it is then necessary to consider a perception, the information in STM that characterise the current mental state, the action to perform and the information to store in STM.

Let Π be a set of perceptions, Σ be a set of actions, Δ a set of pieces of information, with $2^{\Pi \cup \Sigma} \subseteq \Delta$ and Δ closed under set union. We model a *basic activity under automatic control* as

$$info_1 \uparrow perc \overset{d}{\Longrightarrow} act \downarrow info_2$$

where

- $perc \in \Pi$ is a perception;
- $info_1 \in \Delta$ is the information retrieved from the STM;
- $info_2 \in \Delta$ is the information stored in the STM;
- act is a human action;
- d is the delay due to mental processing.

An action act is defined by the operation op and the types st of the systems on which the operation is performed, and is represented as $\mathbf{act}(op, st)$. Delay d only involves the retrieval of information from and storing of information in the STM, but does not concern the physical performance of actions, whose duration depends on the environment with which the human interacts.

The basic activity is *enabled* when $info_1$ is in STM and $perc$ is available in the environment. Its execution results in the removal of $info_1$ from STM, the storage of $info_2$ in STM and the performance of action act.

Information stored in STM includes the perceptions in Π that are selected through attention and the action in Σ whose future execution must be reminded. Cognitive information, represented using constructor $\mathbf{cogn}$, may also be stored in STM to describe the current mental state. We formally denote by $\mathbf{none}$ when an entity of a basic activity is absent (information, perception or action). If the perception is present and the action is not ($act = \mathbf{none}$) then the basic activity models implicit attention. As a shorthand, a singleton of Δ is written as its single element without curly brackets.

The task of driving through a zebra crossing can be thus described by $\mathbf{task}(tn, \{car, ped\}, as)$ where as is the following set of basic activities

$$\mathbf{cogn}(isMov) \uparrow \mathbf{perc}(zebra) \overset{d_1}{\Longrightarrow} \mathbf{none} \downarrow \{\mathbf{cogn}(isMov), \mathbf{perc}(zebra)\} \quad (1)$$

$$\{\mathbf{cogn}(isMov), \mathbf{perc}(zebra)\} \uparrow \mathbf{perc}(ped) \overset{d_2}{\Longrightarrow}$$
$$\mathbf{act}(stop, car) \downarrow \{\mathbf{cogn}(isSta), \mathbf{perc}(ped)\} \quad (2)$$

$$\{\mathbf{cogn}(isSta), \mathbf{perc}(ped)\} \uparrow \overline{\mathbf{perc}}(ped) \overset{d_3}{\Longrightarrow} \mathbf{act}(go, car) \downarrow \mathbf{cogn}(isMov) \quad (3)$$

The mental state during driving is described by $\mathbf{cogn}(isMov)$ when the car is moving and by $\mathbf{cogn}(isSta)$ when the car is static, $\mathbf{perc}$ and $\overline{\mathbf{perc}}$ denote respectively the presence and the absence of a perception ($zebra$ for zebra crossing and ped for crossing pedestrians), and $\mathbf{act}(stop, car)$ and $\mathbf{act}(go, car)$ denote respectively that car car is stopping and going again.

Note that the operation of an action may be described by a mere name, such as $stop$ in $\mathbf{act}(stop, car)$, or by a more complex term. For example, we may describe a rotation of the steering wheel by 30 degree anticlockwise (to the left) by $\mathbf{act}(\mathbf{turn}(-30), car)$.

2.2   Modelling Deliberate Control

Deliberate control is normally driven by a goal, which needs to be achieved by performing the task. A task goal is formally modelled as $\mathbf{goal}(info)$, where $info \in \Delta$ contains the perception and/or the action and/or the cognitive information characterising the achievement of the goal (obviously $info \neq \emptyset$).

Thus we model a *basic activity under deliberate control* as

$$\mathbf{goal}(info) : \; info_1 \uparrow perc \xrightarrow{d} act \downarrow info_2$$

The basic activity is *enabled* when $\mathbf{goal}(info)$ and $info_1$ are in STM and $perc$ is available in the environment. Its execution results in the removal of $info_1$ from STM, the storage of $info_2$ in STM and the performance of action act. Goal $\mathbf{goal}(info)$ is removed from STM only when it is achieved, namely when $info \subseteq \{perc, act\} \cup info_2$. When $info_1 = \mathbf{none}$, the basic activity representation may be shortened as

$$\mathbf{goal}(info) \uparrow perc \xrightarrow{d} act \downarrow info_2$$

If the perception is present and the action is not ($act = \mathbf{none}$) then the basic activity models explicit attention.

Suppose that we need to move a box from one point of a room to another. The box is full of items. If the box is light enough then we just move it, otherwise we have first to empty it, then move it and finally fill in it again. Our explicit attention, driven by the goal of moving the box, will focus on perceiving whether the box is heavy or light. We can abstractly model these two explicit perceptions as $\mathbf{perc}(heavy)$ and $\mathbf{perc}(light)$ independently of the specific senses involved in the perception process. Such explicit attentional activities, which would normally require the same mental processing time d_1, are modeled as

$$\mathbf{goal}(\mathbf{cogn}(movedFull)) \uparrow \mathbf{perc}(light) \xrightarrow{d_1} \mathbf{none} \downarrow \mathbf{perc}(light) \qquad (4)$$

$$\mathbf{goal}(\mathbf{cogn}(movedFull)) \uparrow \mathbf{perc}(heavy) \xrightarrow{d_1} \mathbf{none} \downarrow \mathbf{perc}(heavy) \qquad (5)$$

If the box is light, we can immediately move it using the following basic activity:

$$\mathbf{goal}(\mathbf{cogn}(movedFull)) : \; \mathbf{perc}(light) \uparrow \mathbf{none} \xrightarrow{d_2}$$
$$\mathbf{act}(move, box) \downarrow \mathbf{cogn}(movedFull) \qquad (6)$$

Note that the action of moving the box is a decision based on an already internalised perception (the perception that the box is light transferred from sensory memory to STM by basic activity 4). As a result the perception part of the basic activity model is empty.

If the box is heavy, we need to empty it before moving it. Therefore, we need to create the *subgoal* $\mathbf{goal}(\mathbf{cogn}(empty))$ of emptying the box:

$$\mathbf{goal}(\mathbf{cogn}(movedFull)) : \; heavy \uparrow \mathbf{none} \xrightarrow{d_3} \mathbf{none} \downarrow \mathbf{goal}(\mathbf{cogn}(empty)) \qquad (7)$$

This subgoal can be achieved by emptying the box

$$\mathbf{goal}(\mathbf{cogn}(empty)) \uparrow \mathbf{none} \xrightarrow{d_4} \mathbf{act}(empty, box) \downarrow \mathbf{cogn}(empty) \qquad (8)$$

We can now move the box and then fill in it as follows

$$\textbf{goal}(\textbf{cogn}(movedFull)) : \textbf{cogn}(empty) \uparrow \textbf{none} \xRightarrow{d_5}$$
$$\textbf{act}(move, box) \downarrow \textbf{cogn}(moved) \qquad (9)$$

$$\textbf{goal}(\textbf{cogn}(movedFull)) : \textbf{cogn}(moved) \uparrow \textbf{none} \xRightarrow{d_6}$$
$$\textbf{act}(fill, box) \downarrow \textbf{cogn}(movedFull) \qquad (10)$$

thus achieving the goal.

2.3   Short-Term Memory (STM) and Closure

We model STM as a set of timed information, namely a timestamp is associated with each piece of stored information. The limited capacity of the STM requires the presence of a mechanism to empty it when the stored information is no longer needed. When a goal is achieved, it is removed from the STM and the information used to achieve it may also be removed from the STM, since it is no longer needed. This subconscious removal of information from STM occurs through a process called *closure*. In the example in Sect. 2.2, closure occurs first when sub-goal **goal**(**cogn**(*empty*)) is achieved by reaching cognitive state **cogn**(*empty*) in basic activity 8, then when goal **goal**(**cogn**(*movedFull*)) is achieved by reaching cognitive state **cogn**(*movedFull*) in basic activity 10.

It is not fully understood how closure works. We can definitely say that once the goal is achieved, it is removed from the STM. However, it is not clear what happens to the information that was stored in STM in order to achieve the goal. If we consider a user of an Automatic Teller Machine (ATM) whose goal is to withdraw cash, we can say that the goal is achieved when the user collects the cash from the ATM. However, old ATM interfaces (some still in activity) deliver the cash before returning the card to the user. There is then the possibility that the user collects the cash and, feeling the goal achieved, leaves forgetting to collect the card. This could be explained by assuming that when the user inserts the card in the ATM (**act**(*insert, card*)), some information is stored in STM, as a reminder to collect the card at a later stage (**act**(*collect, card*)), as follows:

$$\textbf{cogn}(useAtm) \uparrow \textbf{perc}(cardR) \xRightarrow{d_1} \textbf{act}(insert, card) \downarrow \textbf{act}(collect, card) \qquad (11)$$

where **cogn**(*useAtm*) is the mental state occurring when using the ATM and **perc**(*cardR*) the perception of the request to insert the card, which is shown on the ATM screen. Note that here the action to be performed in the future (**act**(*collect, card*)) is stored in STM under automatic control; this is different from adding a goal under deliberate control, as we have seen in the example in Sect. 2.2. Collecting the card is not needed to accomplish the goal of withdrawing cash, thus this reminder cannot be added as a subgoal.

When the cash is collected (**act**(*collect, cash*)), both **goal**(**act**(*collect, cash*)) and **act**(*collect, card*) may be removed from the STM, thus disabling the basic activity

$$\textbf{cogn}(useAtm) : \textbf{act}(collect, card) \uparrow \textbf{perc}(cardO) \xRightarrow{d_2}$$
$$\textbf{act}(collect, card) \downarrow \textbf{cogn}(useAtm) \qquad (12)$$

where **perc**(*cardO*) is the perception of the returned card. However, not always cards are forgotten in old ATMs. This means that when closure occurs the STM may not be completely emptied. Our cognitive architecture supports the definition of alternative models of the closure process. If all pieces of information younger than the removed goal (which is in STM since the beginning of the task performance) were also removed, because they are likely to be the no longer needed information used to achieve the goal, then in the old ATM example the card would always be forgotten. But we know that this is not the case. It is instead reasonable to believe that the amount of information removed depends on the load of the STM: the higher the load the more the amount of removed information, in order to reach a minimum of free STM. This explains the fact that when the user's cognitive load is high the likelihood to forget the card is also high. We might actually either assume that the youngest information is removed, since it is likely to be the information used to achieve the goal, or, alternatively, that the oldest information is removed, since it has not been used for a long time. These and many other alternatives may be explored using our cognitive architecture on the same set of real-life examples in order to understand which one appears to best match real data.

Our cognitive architecture also models the decay of STM: we can define at which "age" information disappears from STM. This means that a goal may be removed from the STM before being achieved. In our previous work [5], based on an untimed model of STM, thus with no decay, we proved using model-checking that the user may forgot the card using the old ATM interface (postcompletion error) but will not forget it using the more modern interfaces, in which the card is returned before delivering the cash. Using our new cognitive architecture, however, we identified problems also in the modern ATM interfaces. The removal of the goal (for instance **goal**(**act**(*collect, cash*))) before it is achieved, due to the STM decay, may create confusion to the user when requested to select between different transaction, such as cash withdrawal and statement printing.

3   Environment, Interaction and Communication

The examples presented in Sects. 2.1, 2.2 and 2.3 model tasks whose sets of entity types are not empty. Thus they make sense when the cognitive model describes a human interacting with an environment, either directly or indirectly. In particular, humans interact with systems via interfaces. The *direct interaction* involves humans and interfaces, and occurs through human perceptions and actions. Perceptions may be produced by interfaces (e.g. through messages on the screen) or be the results of the spatial distribution of entities in the environment (e.g. seeing cars or other humans). Human actions are articulated for the specific interface, which converts them to inputs to the system, thus affecting (through *indirect interaction*) the system evolution. Furthermore, humans may indirectly interact with remote systems through a *network*, which support *communication* among systems.

The *observable environment* is the set of entities that can be directly observed by the human and consists of two parts:

- the **spatial distribution** of a *population* of entities of four kinds: *humans, interfaces, systems* and *layout components*, the last two kinds with associated types;
- a set of **events** which may include *timed perceptions, event generators* and a special event *halt(t)*, which terminates the evolution of the overall system at time t;

The *systems* with which the human indirectly interacts, via the interface and the observable environment, is characterised by the current **global state**. The *system environment* consists of

- the **inputs** produced by the interfaces;
- the system **communications** carried out through the network.

The two parts of the observable environment are described in Sects. 3.1 and 3.3, respectively. The interaction and the role of the global state are described in Sect. 3.2.

3.1 Spatial Distributions of Entities

Spatial distribution is described by associating a location with each individual entity. The location of a human or a physical system may be given as an absolute space occupation or be relative to another entity. For example we can say that the location of a car is given by the set of spatial coordinates it occupies while the location of the human driving that car is given by the car itself. For the driving example illustrated in Sect. 2.1 we can consider the spatial distribution of the population { $\text{sys}(car, C, locA), \text{hum}(D, C, T), \text{sys}(ped, P, locB)$ }, where the car C of type *car* is in *locA*, the driver D is a human inside car C, who may perform the tasks whose names are in set T, and the pedestrians P of type *ped* are in *locB*. For the ATM example illustrated in Sect. 2.3 we can consider the spatial distribution of the population

$$\{ \text{sys}(atm, A, locA), \text{hum}(U, locA, T), \text{sys}(card, CD, U),$$

$$\text{sys}(cash, CH, A), \text{int}(Old, A), \text{lay}(screen, SC, Old, locB, io_{screen}),$$

$$\text{lay}(keyboard, K, Old, locC, io_{keyboard}), \text{lay}(cdS, CDS, Old, locD, io_{cdS}),$$

$$\text{lay}(chS, CHS, Old, locE, io_{chS}) \},$$

where both the system A of type *atm* and the user U are in *locA*, the user may perform any task whose name is in T and has card CD of type *card*, the cash CH of type *cash* is in the ATM A, *Old* is the interface of A and layout components K of type *keyboard* (keybord) in location *locB*, SC of type *screen* (screen) in location *locC*, CDS of type *cdS* (card slot) in location *locD* and CHS of type *chS* (cash slot) in location *locE* describe the interface layout. For each layout component l, set io_l contains the perceptions and actions associated with l. Locations of layout components of the interface define their absolute space occupation, which is essential to model the time taken by the user in switching action from one component to the other of the interface, for example using Fitts' law.

As we did for HTDL, we represent in bold also the data structure constructors used in defining the environment. This allows us to distinguish the constructors from the functions that manipulate data structures to model the environment evolution.

3.2 Model of the Interaction

The global state of the system is a set of states, each represented as **state**(sn, n), where sn is a system name and n is the state name. The model of the interaction, which is based on the interaction framework proposed by Abowd and Beale [1] is illustrated in Fig. 1, where values and function arguments are represented in terms of their constructors.

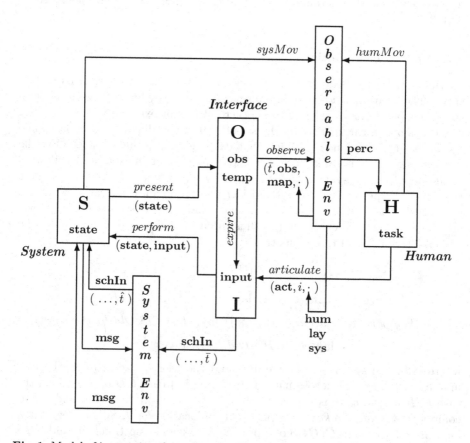

Fig. 1. Model of interaction through an interface with name i. Functions and enabling constructors are represented by arrows with the function/constructor name above and its parameters (if relevant) below. Current time is $\hat{t}$ and scheduling time is $\bar{t}$.

Function *articulate* takes a human action $\mathbf{act}(op, st)$, an interface name i on which the action is performed and an observational environment env as parameters. It returns the set of all possible inputs $\mathbf{input}(op, st, lcn, stn, t)$ for the interface and environment, where stn is a name of a system with interface i, layout component lcn is associated with interface i and t is the time required by a human to perform the action via layout component lcn. Therefore, t may be defined as a function $f(lcn, env)$ of the location of the layout component lcn, which encodes both its position and its size in terms of its spatial distribution, and the location of the acting human component (e.g. this provides distance and size of the target as arguments of Fitts' law). In the ATM example, we model the articulation of the action of inserting a card in the card slot of the ATM using the card slot of the old interface as follows:

$$articulate(\mathbf{act}(insert, card), Old, env) = \{\mathbf{input}(insert, CD, CDS, A, f(CDS, env))\}$$

where CD is the card of type $card$ controlled (specifically "owned") by a human in the environment, CDS is the card slot of interface Old and t is the time the user needs to physically insert the card in the card slot. Inputs for the system may also be autonomously defined by the interface, e.g. independently from the human actions, as we will see below. Once the inputs have been defined, they are scheduled as $\mathbf{schIn}(op, st, lcn, stn, \bar{t})$, in order to be performed by system stn at time $\bar{t} = \hat{t} + t$, where $\hat{t}$ is the current time and t is the time required by the human to perform the action via the interface. This scheduled input becomes available in the system environment.

At time $\bar{t}$ the scheduled input will be performed by the system determining a transition of the system state. Performance is defined by function *perform*, which takes the current state of the system and the appropriate input as parameters and returns a new state. In the ATM example, if the card has not been inserted yet ($\mathbf{state}(A, noCard)$), then, after the card is inserted (as for the input), it is detected by the ATM ($\mathbf{state}(A, cardDetected)$):

$$perform(\mathbf{state}(A, noCard), \mathbf{input}(insert, CD, CDS, A, t)) = \mathbf{state}(A, cardDetected)$$

The time needed for the system to perform the input is given by function pt, which takes the current state and the appropriate input for the interface as parameters and returns the time needed for the transition to the new state.

Function *present* takes a state $\mathbf{state}(sn, n)$ and returns an observable state $\mathbf{obs}(sn, n)$, if the state has to be observable by the user, a temporary state $\mathbf{temp}(sn, n)$, if the state may be changed by the interface, or a special value $\mathbf{noPres}$ otherwise (in this case $\mathbf{state}(sn, n)$ is an internal state of the system).

Function *observe* takes the current time, an observable state, an observable environment and, a mapping $\mathbf{map}(i)$ from pairs consisting of a system type and a state name to the perception observed by the user for a given interface name i, and returns a new observable environment. For example, the old interface of the ATM has mapping

$$\mathbf{map}(Old) = (atm, noCard) \longrightarrow \mathbf{perc}(cardRequest)$$
$$(atm, cardRead) \longrightarrow \mathbf{perc}(pinRequest)$$
$$(atm, cardRead) \longrightarrow 60$$
$$(atm, pinRead) \longrightarrow \mathbf{perc}(selectTransaction)$$
$$\vdots$$

so that, if $\mathbf{obs}(A, cardRead)$ (A is a system of type atm) is one of the observable states presented by A to $\mathbf{int}(Old, A)$, the observable environment returned by *observe* will contain a timed version of perception $\mathbf{perc}(pinRequest)$ that is labelled with its origin (as a location or direction or interface component) and its specific attributes (e.g. intensity). Function *expire* allows the interface to exploits temporary state $\mathbf{temp}(sn, n)$ and the duration of time d (defined by interface i) within which the state must change to define $\mathbf{input}(\mathbf{timeout}, stn, cn, i, d)$. For example, in the ATM example above, the mapping gives to temporary state $\mathbf{temp}(A, cardRead)$ a maximum duration of 60 seconds, within which the user must input the pin to avoid the interaction to be terminated prematurely.

Finally, functions *sysMov* and *humMov* determine changes in the spatial distribution of individuals depending respectively on the state of the system and the goal of the human. Obviously the movement is propagated from the carrier to the carried. Thus, for example, the movement of a car is propagated to the humans carried in it and the movement of an ATM user carrying a card is propagated to the card.

3.3   Events and Event Generators

A perception generated by the interface appears in the environment with a timestamp showing the time when it is generated together with a persistence time, which defines for how long the perception is available in the environment, an origin and specific attributes. For example, for an audio menu, the persistence time of the perception of each item in the menu is very short, whereas for a visual menu it is normally unlimited. Thus persistence time may be used to limit the time span during which the system state should be observable.

In general, we do not want to be forced to have, for each possible perception, a system that generates it. In the driving example in Sect. 2.1 we do not want to model a system that generates perceptions of pedestrians walking across the zebra crossing. Instead, we want to define, in the initial configuration of the overall system, events having future times as timestamps. Possible events are not only perceptions but also goals associated with specific humans. Such events are ignored until the times shown by their timestamps are reached. This is also the case for the special event $halt(t)$, which terminates the evolution of the overall system at time t.

Event generators are special events that generate perceptions. Event generator $\mathbf{iter}(perc, t, d, n)$ generates perception *perc* with persistence time d repeatedly every n time units starting from time t. Generated events may also include the autonomous movement of individuals. Further kinds of event generators may generate random events according to various probabilistic distributions.

Finally, perceptions may be the results of the spatial distribution of individuals in the environment. These spatial perceptions may involve any sense.

3.4 Implementation Using the Maude System

Our cognitive architecture is implemented using the Maude system [7,11]. In this work we only use *Core Maude*, which comprises two types of modules: *functional modules*, which are restricted to *equational logic*, which support the declaration of sorts and operations on them and the definition of such operation using equations, and *system modules*, which also support *rewriting logic*, by additionally including the definition of rewrite rules.

We use the equational logic capabilities of Maude to implement the global state changes as a function of the input produced by the interface and the scheduled communications, and rewrite logic to implement the evolution of observable environment, system environment, STM and the learning processes that modify tasks and knowledge stored in LTM. The implementation of HTDL is immediate, whereas the other parts of the cognitive architecture and its environment require the definition of a several data structure and functions to manipulate them, as illustrated in Sect. 3.1 and 3.2. Rewrite rules are the engine of the cognitive architecture. Furthermore, the model-checking capabilities of Maude support the formal verification of the modelled system.

4   Modelling Human Learning

Human learning is a very complex process, normally evolving over a long time, which can be roughly divided into three phases: (1) understanding, internalising and connecting concepts and notions (learning the theory), (2) practising (putting the theory into practice); (3) experiencing (modifying and expanding the theoretical knowledge). Learning the theory can occur through studying, by observing the reality and abstracting from it or by generalising what is learned in other contexts, but it is not always the most relevant phase. In fact, the importance and duration of these three phases varies from task to task.

For example, in learning to drive a car all three phases are highly important: there is a considerable amount of theory to study and a lot of practice is required but, in the end, only a few people can drive confidently immediately after passing the driving test; most people need to acquire a big deal of experience through the exposure to a large varieties of driving situations and will exploit such experience to improve their driving behaviour (in term of performance, not adherence to the road code), thus achieving full confidence. In learning to bike, instead, the main issue is to acquire balance, which can only be achieved by practicing; there is basically no theory to learn and, once balance is fully acquired, experience will not change our biking behaviour very much. Learning to use an ATM is mainly a matter of acquiring experience with one or more specific interfaces;

the task itself can be easily internalised and does not require much practice. Finally, learning to move a box is for an adult just a matter of applying a few known concepts: it is possible to move only light objects, filled objects can be emptied and emptied objects can be filled in. Children, instead, have to go through all three phases, learning concepts about human physical limitation and object manipulation in various contexts, then putting such concepts into practice by emptying and filling in boxes, and finally exploiting their own experiences of pain to lower the threshold of "heaviness".

In this section we focus on the last two phases: practising makes human behaviour evolve from deliberate to automatic control (*skill acquisition*); experiencing leads to the acquisition of new knowledge about the way the system works (*mental modelling*) and its consequent exploitation to improve the interaction.

4.1 Skill Acquisition

The effect of skill acquisition on tasks is illustrated below and represents the basis for a possible implementation of this form of learning. Following Anderson's ACT^* model [2], *skill acquisition* involves two mechanisms:

proceduralisation determined, as an extension of the ACT^* model, by
> **goal internalisation** which creates a mental state associated with a specific goal and changes attention from explicit to implicit;
> **automatisation** which makes action directly triggered by perception by combining a set of activities under deliberate control, whereby at most one activity of the set has the action specified (the other activities are either attentional or pure mental processing), into a single activity under automatic control;

generalisation which combines several mental states into a general one.

For example if we consider the task of moving a box illustrated in Sect. 2.2, goal internalisation associates a new mental state **cogn**(*movingBox*) with the goal **goal**(**cogn**(*movedFull*)), creates the new basic activity

$$\textbf{goal}(\textbf{cogn}(movedFull)) \uparrow \textbf{none} \overset{d}{\Longrightarrow} \textbf{none} \downarrow \textbf{cogn}(movingBox) \tag{13}$$

and change basic activities 4, 5, 6, 7, 9 and 10 respectively to

$$\textbf{cogn}(movingBox) \uparrow \textbf{perc}(light) \overset{d_1}{\Longrightarrow} \textbf{none} \downarrow \{\textbf{cogn}(movingBox), \textbf{perc}(light)\} \tag{14}$$

$$\textbf{cogn}(movingBox) \uparrow \textbf{perc}(heavy) \overset{d_1}{\Longrightarrow} \textbf{none} \downarrow \{\textbf{cogn}(movingBox), \textbf{perc}(heavy)\} \tag{15}$$

$$\{\textbf{cogn}(movingBox), \textbf{perc}(light)\} \uparrow \textbf{none} \overset{d_2}{\Longrightarrow} \textbf{act}(move, box) \downarrow \textbf{cogn}(movedFull) \tag{16}$$

$$\{\textbf{cogn}(movingBox), \textbf{perc}(heavy)\} \uparrow \textbf{none} \overset{d_3}{\Longrightarrow}$$
$$\textbf{none} \downarrow \{\textbf{cogn}(movingBox), \textbf{goal}(\textbf{cogn}(empty))\} \tag{17}$$

$$\{\textbf{cogn}(movingBox), \textbf{cogn}(empty)\} \uparrow \textbf{none} \overset{d_5}{\Longrightarrow}$$
$$\textbf{act}(move, box) \downarrow \{\textbf{cogn}(movingBox), \textbf{cogn}(moved)\} \tag{18}$$

$$\{\textbf{cogn}(movingBox), \textbf{cogn}(moved)\} \uparrow \textbf{none} \overset{n_6}{\Longrightarrow} \textbf{act}(fill, box) \downarrow \textbf{cogn}(movedFull) \tag{19}$$

thus changing attention from explicit to implicit.

Automatisation combines basic activities 14 and 16 into

$$\textbf{cogn}(movingBox) \uparrow \textbf{perc}(light) \overset{d_7}{\Longrightarrow} \textbf{act}(move, box) \downarrow \textbf{cogn}(movedFull) \quad (20)$$

and basic activities 15 and 17 into

$$\textbf{cogn}(movingBox) \uparrow \textbf{perc}(heavy) \overset{d_8}{\Longrightarrow}$$
$$\textbf{none} \downarrow \{\textbf{cogn}(movingBox), \textbf{goal}(\textbf{cogn}(empty))\} \quad (21)$$

with $d_7 < d_1 + d_2$ and $d_8 < d_1 + d_3$.

Finally, basic activity 20 (and similarly basic activity 21) can be gener-
alised to other objects for which there exist similar basic activities, for example to bags of type bag that can be moved. The mental state changes from
$\textbf{cogn}(movingBox)$ to $\textbf{cogn}(moving)$ and the basic activity becomes

$$\textbf{cogn}(moving) \uparrow \textbf{perc}(light) \overset{d_8}{\Longrightarrow} \textbf{act}(move, s) \downarrow \textbf{cogn}(movedFull) \quad (22)$$

where $s = \{box, bag\}$.

4.2 Mental Modelling: Building Expectations

Humans tend to build mental models of the systems they use. This is an important capability since it allows the human to optimise the interaction and speed
up the task execution, when expectations are met, or to avoid failures after
observing system responses that are inconsistent with expectations. However,
mental models are not always correct and, when the actual system operation
differs from the user's expectations, human errors are likely to occur. In order
to prevent such human errors to occur, it is important to be able to understand
how expectations are build and how they affect human behaviour.

In our cognitive architecture, an *expectation* is a defined as

$$\textbf{exp}(task, g, i, act, perc, ass)$$

where for a given task $task$, goal g, interface i, action act and perception $perc$,
the assessment ass of the expectation equals

success if the goal g is expected to be achieved,
failure if the goal g is not expected to be achieved,
neutral if there is no clear expectation about the achievement of goal g,

when the system response to action act is perceived as perception $perc$, and

novelty when the system response to action act is not expected to be perceived
as perception $perc$.

We model the expectation building by using a representation of the episodic
memory as a mapping that associates each pair consisting of an action and a
perception with a set of pairs, where each pair (t, o) has the time t when the
perception occurred as a response to the action as the first component and the

boolean outcome o in terms of achievement of goal g while interacting with interface i as the second component. We can represent built expectations as information stored in semantic memory as a result of an unconscious analysis of the episodic memory. We can formalise this building process as a function *buildExp* that, given the representation of the episodic memory, a task, a goal, an interface, an action and a perception, returns an expectation.

How to define function *buildExp* is a matter of cognitive psychology theory. Our cognitive architecture aims to provide the infrastructure for exploring alternative theories, as in the case of the alternative closure theories discussed in Sect. 2.3. To illustrate this point we provide below an example of a reasonable *buildExp* definition.

Given action *act*, perception *perc* and an episodic memory *sm* such that $sm(act, perc) = \{(t_1, o_1), (t_2, o_2), \ldots, (t_n, o_n)\}$, where we assume that $t_j < t_{j+1}$ for each $j = 1, \ldots, n - 1$, and defined

$$\bar{\jmath}(ass) = \min\{j \mid \forall k > j.\; k < n \;\rightarrow\; t_k - t_{k-1} \leq \delta \;\wedge\; o_{k-1} = o_n = ass\},$$

buildExp$(sm, task, goal, i, act, perc)$ returns

- **exp**$(task, goal, i, act, perc, \textbf{success})$, if there exists $\bar{\jmath}(\textbf{success})$ such that $n - \bar{\jmath}(\textbf{success}) \geq \eta - 1$;
- **exp**$(task, goal, i, act, perc, \textbf{failure})$, if there exists $\bar{\jmath}(\textbf{failure})$ such that $n - \bar{\jmath}(\textbf{failure}) \geq \eta - 1$;
- **exp**$(task, goal, i, act, perc, \textbf{novelty})$, if $\bar{\jmath}(\textbf{success})$ and $\bar{\jmath}(\textbf{failure})$ do not exist;
- **exp**$(task, goal, i, act, perc, \textbf{neutral})$, otherwise.

This definition of *buildExp* models the building of an expectation assessed as a **success** or **failure**, when the pair action-perception has always led to the same task outcome (respectively in terms of goal achievement or failure) during the last η experiences and the time span between two consecutive of these η experiences does not exceed δ. Obviously the values for δ and η have to be determined empirically for the specific task.

5   Conclusion and Future Work

A partial implementation of the cognitive architecture presented in this paper can be downloaded at

https://cs-sst.github.io/faculty/cerone/formalhci.

Some parts of the cognitive architecture are implemented using different functions with respect to what presented in this paper, due to implementation constraints or optimisations. Timing, spatial distribution and learning processes are currently under implementation.

Our cognitive architecture can be used for modelling and analysing interactive systems. The model-checking capabilities of Maude support the verification of interactive systems for a large range of properties formalised in temporal logic, as shown in our previous work [5]. Moreover, with respect to the simple episodic system model used in our previous work, the final architecture will consider a global system state as a set of local states. This opens the way to high level system modelling using concurrency and communication. As part of our future work we plan to implement such system communication and define translations for directly importing formal models of systems in various formal modelling languages, such as process algebras and Petri nets.

Furthermore, our cognitive architecture aims to be used for exploring alternative cognitive theories, such as different models of the closure phenomenon, using the same set of real-life examples in order to understand which cognitive theory appears to best match real data. Real data can be scheduled as future events, such as goals and perceptions, in the observable environment, so that a simulation can be run and its outcome may be compared with the outcome occurred in the reality. This approach also expands the scope of formal verification to system validation and even to the validation of research hypotheses on cognition [6].

Finally, we remark that our proposed cognitive architecture aims to support modelling at various levels of abstractions. This involves the level of details in perceptions, for which the sensory channel may or may not be specified, actions, in which operations may be defined by abstract names or more accurately specified by enriching the constructor with parameters, and information, which may be structured using a chunking. Furthermore, the topology may vary from one single location to a tridimensional coordinate system and we might wish to create *ad hoc* topologies or, instead, fully abstract from time.

References

1. Abowd, G., Beale, R.: Users, systems and interfaces: a unifying framework for interaction. In: People and Computer VI (HCI 1991), pp. 73–87. Cambridge University Press (1991)
2. Anderson, J.R.: The Architecture of Cognition. Psychology Press, London (1983)
3. Broccia, G., Masci, P., Milazzo, P.: Modelling and analysis of human memory load in multitasking scenarios. In: EICS 2018. ACM (2018)
4. Broccia, G., Milazzo, P., Ölveczky, P.C.: An executable formal framework for safety-critical human multitasking. In: Dutle, A., Muñoz, C., Narkawicz, A. (eds.) NFM 2018. LNCS, vol. 10811, pp. 54–69. Springer, Cham (2018). https://doi.org/10.1007/978-3-319-77935-5_4
5. Cerone, A.: A cognitive framework based on rewriting logic for the analysis of interactive systems. In: De Nicola, R., Kühn, E. (eds.) SEFM 2016. LNCS, vol. 9763, pp. 287–303. Springer, Cham (2016). https://doi.org/10.1007/978-3-319-41591-8_20
6. Cerone, A., Zhexenbayeva, A.: Using formal methods to validate research hypotheses: the Duolingo case study. In: STAF 2018 Workshops (DataMod). LNCS, vol. 11176, pp. 163–170. Springer, Cham (2018)
7. Clavel, M., et al.: The Maude 2.0 system. In: Nieuwenhuis, R. (ed.) RTA 2003. LNCS, vol. 2706, pp. 76–87. Springer, Heidelberg (2003). https://doi.org/10.1007/3-540-44881-0_7

8. Golosio, B., Cangelosi, A., Gamotina, O., Masala, G.L.: A cognitive neural model of executive functions in natural language processing. In: Proceedings of BICA 2015 of Procedia Computer Science, vol. 71, pp. 196–201. Elsevier (2015)
9. Laird, J.E.: The Soar Cognitive Architecture. MIT Press, Cambridge (2012)
10. Norman, D.A., Shallice, T.: Attention to action: willed and automatic control of behaviour. In: Consciousness and Self-Regulation, Advances in Research and Theory, Vol. 4. Plenum Press (1986)
11. Ölveczky, P.C.: Designing Reliable Distributed Systems - A Formal Methods Approach Based on Modeling in Maude. Springer, Heidelberg (2017). https://doi.org/10.1007/978-1-4471-6687-0. Undergraduate Topics in Computer Science
12. Rukšėenas, R., Curzon, P., Blandford, A.: Modelling rational user behaviour as games between an angel and a demon. In: Cerone, A., Gruner, S. (eds.), Proceedings of SEFM 2008, pp. 355–364. IEEE Press (2008)
13. Samsonovich, A.V.: Towards a unified catalog of implemented cognitive architectures. In: Biologically Inspired Cognitive Architectures (BICA 2010), pp. 195–244. IOS Press (2010)
14. Sun, R., Slusarz, P., Terry, C.: The interaction of the explicit and implicit in skill learning: a dual-process approach. Psychol. Rev. **112**, 159–192 (2005)
15. Zhang, M., Wang, F., Yin, J.: A survey on human computer interaction technology for ATM. Intell. Eng. Syst. **6**(1), 20–29 (2013)

Towards Handling Latency in Interactive Software

Sébastien Leriche[✉], Stéphane Conversy, Celia Picard, Daniel Prun,
and Mathieu Magnaudet

ENAC, University of Toulouse, Toulouse, France
{Sebastien.Leriche,Stephane.Conversy,Celia.Picard,Daniel.Prun,
Mathieu.Magnaudet}@enac.fr

Abstract. Usability of an interactive software can be highly impacted by the delays of propagation of data and events and by its variations, i.e. latency and jitter. The problem is striking for applications involving tactile interactions or augmented reality, where the shifts between interaction and representation can make the system unusable. For as much, latency is often taken into account only during the validation phase of the software by means of a value which constitutes an acceptable limit. In this shor paper, we present and discuss an alternative approach: we want to handle the latency at all phases of the life cycle of the interactive software, from specification to runtime adaptation and formal validation for certification purposes. We plan to integrate and validate these ideas into SMALA, our language dedicated to the development of highly interactive and visual user interfaces.

1 Introduction

An interactive software is a computer application which reacts, throughout its execution, to various sources of events. In particular, it produces a perceptible representation of its internal state [1,2]. However, the usability of an interactive application can be appreciably impacted by the delays of propagation of data and events and by its variations, i.e. latency and jitter. The problem is striking for applications involving tactile interactions or augmented reality, where the shifts between interaction and representation can make the system unusable [3,4]. Yet, while latency constraints are expressed at specification, they are often taken into account only very late in the development processes, generally by experimental a posteriori measurements, when the system is fully implemented. For instance, in some air traffic control systems such as radar visualization or remote tower, latency in the visualization of aircrafts position (and the shifts between their real position) is evaluated during experiments. Instead of redesigning the software, this may conduct to dimension the spacing limits between aircrafts [5], with direct consequences on the capacities of air traffic management.

More generally, when focusing on aeronautical software systems, the processes of certifications described in the DO-178C/ED-12C offer an important

© Springer Nature Switzerland AG 2018
M. Mazzara et al. (Eds.): STAF 2018 Workshops, LNCS 11176, pp. 233–239, 2018.
https://doi.org/10.1007/978-3-030-04771-9_18

place to formal checking. We want to take the opportunity to use formal tools and techniques to handle latency in interactive software. We are particularly interested in the SMALA language, dedicated to interactive systems.

2   Djnn and Smala

SMALA[1] is a language that has been designed to effectively support the development of reactive applications. SMALA is built on the top of a set of C libraries named DJNN[2]. DJNN provides a core library that implements the execution engine allowing to run a tree of components [6].

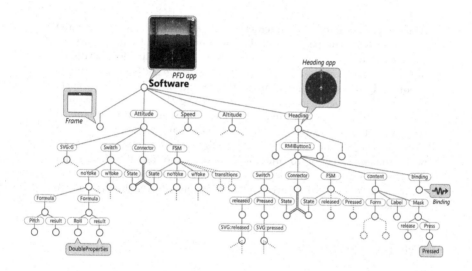

Fig. 1. Tree of DJNN components for an interactive software

Once the tree is loaded and started, the core library starts an event loop that fairly manages the events coming from the environment. On arrival, events are dispatched to the tree components. The control structures contained in this tree specify an activation graph through which the events are propagated Fig. 1.

DJNN provides libraries with various components, ranging from components for arithmetic, logic, finite state machines to graphical shapes, style components, and geometric transformations. Three rendering engines are available, one based on the Qt toolkit, another one based on Cairo, and a third one based on OpenGL.

It is possible to build a tree of components by directly using these libraries and the C language. However the task is akin to those of writing an abstract syntax tree. Thus, we designed SMALA so as to provide a dedicated syntax with specific symbols that helps to visualize the interaction between components.

---

[1] http://smala.io.
[2] http://djnn.net.

SMALA comes with a compiler that transforms the SMALA program into a program written in the C language.

2.1   Smala Applications

Here we describe a part of a demo we developed with Smala to show some interesting points of the language. The objective was to implement a Navigation Display (ND), a standard navigation tool integrated in modern cockpits of airplanes, enhanced with interaction capacities. The ND was designed to be integrated within a full software simulator of an Airbus A320 (Prepar3D/A320 FMGS). In this paper, we will focus on the design of the interaction with a waypoint to show the expressiveness of the smala language.

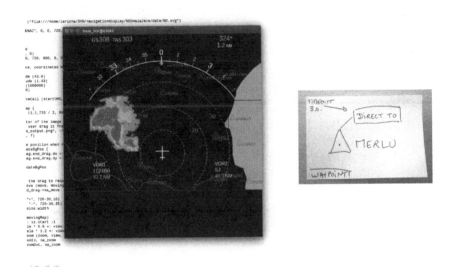

Fig. 2. Navigation Display Experiment and design of interaction with a waypoint

A flight plan mainly consists in a sequence of waypoints specifically selected for a flight before the take off. During the flight, the pilot in command might want to alter the flight plan (e.g. for meteorological reasons) and head the plane directly to another waypoint. We implemented this action on the ND with a touch command that triggers the flight management system to head to the selected waypoint. A sketch of the interaction is shown in Fig. 2: after a touch on a waypoint, a box appears with the text "DIRECT TO", that will stay for 3 seconds. If the pilot touches this box, the command will be send to the flight management system.

The code for the smala component "waypoint" is shown in Fig. 3. This component has two states: when idle (default state) it is represented with a large triangle, including a small square at its exact position and a text label giving its name. When selected, its color must change to green and we add the box with the text "DIRECT TO". The basic graphical components of smala are used (Rectangle, Polygon, Colors...) and a finite state machine (FSM) is explicitly programmed to represent both states and the triggers that change the states. Thus, the component will be selected when a press will be detected inside the triangle (idle.pol.press). It will return to the idle state when either a timeout occurs or if a press is detected inside the "DIRECT TO" box (selected.rdt.press). That last action will trigger the sending of a specific message on the communication bus that links the software to the simulator.

```
1    use core
2    use base
3    use gui
4
5    import TimeOut
6
7    _define_
8    Waypoint (string name, double x_, double y_, Component view, Component frame, Component bus) {
9        Component click
10
11       Rotation r (0,x_,y_)
12       view.heading => r.a
13
14       Translation t (x_, y_)
15       x aka t.tx
16       y aka t.ty
17
18       OutlineColor oc (255, 0, 255)
19       NoFill nf
20       Rectangle p0 (-1,-1,1,1,0,0)    //big pixel center
21       FSM fsm {
22           State idle {
23               Polygon pol {
24                   Point p1 (0,-20)
25                   Point p2 (-20,20)
26                   Point p3 (20,20)
27               }
28           }
29           State selected {
30               FillColor fcg (0, 255, 0) //green
31               Polygon pol {
32                   Point p1 (0,-20)
33                   Point p2 (-20,20)
34                   Point p3 (20,20)
35               }
36
37               FillColor fc (0, 255, 0)
38               OutlineColor oc2 (255, 0, 0)
39               Line l (0,0,20,-20)
40               Rectangle rdt (20,-40,200,30,5,5)
41
42               FillColor fcb (0, 0, 0)
43               Text tdt (30,-20,"DIRECT TO "+name)
44               tdt.width + 20 => rdt.width
45
46               TimeOut to (3)
47               asBusOut = tdt.text =: bus.out :1
48           }
49           idle->selected (idle.pol.press)
50           selected->idle (selected.rdt.press, selected.asBusOut)
51           selected->idle (selected.to.sw.timeout)
52       }
53
54       FillColor fc2 (255, 0, 255)
55       Text label (15, 10, name)
56   }
```

Fig. 3. SMALA code for a waypoint

As a real-world example, we also completely developed the HMI of Volta, the first conventional all-electric helicopter [7]. The HMI has been built concurrently by a programmer and a graphic designer, demonstrating another powerful aspect of our approach: the strict separation of concerns between the design of the visualization and the implementation of interactions.

3 Our Approach to Handle Latency

3.1 Formal Activities Around Djnn/Smala

Although SMALA is still under development, we already could experiment formal techniques for checking properties of SMALA programs. For instance, we exploited the characteristics of the graph of activation [8]. This graph, deduced from the SMALA code, provides all the possible activation relationships following the occurrence of an event. Thus, we managed to formally check attainability properties (i. e., an entry always ends up generating an expected exit or an alarm is always turned off in a certain configuration) or causal activation relationships (i. e., a displayed error message will never be covered by another).

In addition, with the experience gained from previous work on dedicated language and formal validation [9], we experimented in [10] the transformation of SMALA code into Petri nets, with the idea to precisely define an operational semantics for SMALA and to benefit from the associated formal tools and techniques. As a result, the semantics of SMALA is currently under publication in a dedicated paper.

Our medium-term prospects concern the prolongation of the previous studies (based on the graph of activations) and the study of formal proof techniques applied to SMALA code (translation into Caml and use of COQ, translation into Event-B).

3.2 Towards Handling Latency

We want to focus on software layers. Indeed, handling latency can be made at the hardware level with specific tools [11]. However, the end-to-end approaches existing today [12] do not allow to understand the specific issues related to software architecture choices. They are only usable to measure the latency when the system is in its validation phase.

The classical formal approach to handle latency in software systems is to consider their Worst-Case Execution-Time (WCET) [13]. WCET tools and techniques allow to verify timing properties. They are primarily made for real-time systems, and SMALA programs are not. Nevertheless, since the control flow of SMALA programs can be described as a tree, tree-based techniques for computing WCET could be applied. Moreover, the execution engine is being rewritten to comply with the last version of the operational semantics which is a good level to address latency issues [14].

Relying on the operational semantics, we plan to add into SMALA the reification of latency properties. This should allow the programmer to add runtime adaptations (e.g. simplification/enhancement of the visualization to comply with latency constraints) and to optimize the redrawing of the graphical scene.

At last, to limit the known impacts of the operating system on latency, we are experimenting some specific versions of DJNN that can be run on OS-less ('bare') systems. This approach should result in an autonomous and complete software platform to handle latency.

4   Future Work

To achieve these goals, we aim at allowing the developer of interactive software to handle latency as a whole, during each phases of the software life cycle. Thus, this implies the conception of software tools for the measurement, visualization, specification, and formal checking of the different properties. These tools will make possible, during the design time, the objective evaluation of various software architecture solutions. At last, a methodology for designing interactive systems with latency constraints, based on these tools, should be designed.

References

1. Beaudouin-Lafon, M.: Designing interaction, not interfaces. In: Proceedings of the Working Conference on Advanced Visual Interfaces, New York, NY, USA, pp. 15–22 . ACM (2004)
2. Myers, B.A., Rosson, M.B.: Survey on user interface programming. In: Proceedings of the SIGCHI Conference on Human Factors in Computing Systems, New York, NY, USA, pp. 195–202 . ACM (1992)
3. MacKenzie, I.S., Ware, C.: Lag as a determinant of human performance in interactive systems. In: Proceedings of the INTERACT 1993 and CHI 1993 Conference on Human Factors in Computing Systems, New York, NY, USA, pp. 488–493. ACM (1993)
4. Ware, C., Balakrishnan, R.: Reaching for objects in VR displays: lag and frame rate. ACM Trans. Comput.-Hum. Interact. 1(4), 331–356 (1994)
5. Cordeil, M., Dwyer, T., Hurter, C.: Immersive solutions for future air traffic control and management. In: Proceedings of the 2016 ACM Companion on Interactive Surfaces and Spaces, New York, NY, USA, pp. 25–31. ACM (2016)
6. Chatty, S., Magnaudet, M., Prun, D., Conversy, S., Rey, S., Poirier, M.: Designing, developing and verifying interactive components iteratively with djnn. In: proceedings of ERTS 2016, TOULOUSE, France, January 2016
7. Antoine, P., Conversy, S.: Volta: the first all-electric conventional helicopter. In: MEA 2017, More Electric Aircraft, Bordeaux, France, February 2017
8. Chatty, S., Magnaudet, M., Prun, D.: Verification of properties of interactive components from their executable code. In: Proc of EICS 2015, New York, NY, USA, pp. 276–285. ACM (2015)
9. Matougui, M.E.A., Leriche, S.: Validation of COSMOS DSL programs. The 2010 International Conference on Computer Engineering & Systems, pp. 307–313 (2010)
10. Prun, D., Magnaudet, M., Chatty, S.: Towards support for verification of adaptative systems with djnn. Proc. Cogn. (03 2015), 191–194 (2015)
11. Zabolotny, W.M.: Automatic latency balancing in VHDL-implemented complex pipelined systems. CoRR abs/1509.08111 (2015)
12. Casiez, G., Pietrzak, T., Marchal, D., Poulmane, S., Falce, M., Roussel, N.: Characterizing latency in touch and button-equipped interactive systems. In: Proceedings of the 30th Annual ACM Symposium on User Interface Software and Technology, New York, NY, USA, pp. 29–39. ACM (2017)

13. Puschner, P., Burns, A.: Guest editorial: a review of worst-case execution-time analysis. Real-Time Syst. **18**, 115–128 (2000)
14. Asavoae, M., Maiza, C., Raymond, P.: Program semantics in model-based WCET analysis: a state of the art perspective. In: Maiza, C. (ed.) 13th International Workshop on Worst-Case Execution Time Analysis, vol. 30, pp. 32–41. Schloss Dagstuhl-Leibniz-Zentrum fuer Informatik, Wadern, Germany (2013)

Refinement Based Formal Development
of Human-Machine Interface

Romain Geniet[1] and Neeraj Kumar Singh[2(✉)]

[1] Université de Rennes 1, Rennes, France
romain.geniet@laposte.net
[2] INPT-ENSEEIHT/IRIT, University of Toulouse, Toulouse, France
nsingh@enseeiht.fr

Abstract. Human factors have been considered as the most common causes of accidents, particularly for interacting with complex critical systems related to avionics, railway, nuclear and medical domains. Mostly, a human-machine interface (HMI) is developed independently and the correctness of possible interactions is heavily dependent on testing, which cannot guarantee the absence of run-time errors. The use of formal methods in HMI development may assure such guarantee. This paper presents a methodology for developing an HMI using a *correct by construction* approach, which allows us to introduce the HMI components, functional behaviour and the required safety properties progressively. The proposed methodology, generic refinement strategy, supports a development of the *model-view-controller* (MVC) architecture. The whole approach is formalized using Event-B and relies on the Rodin tools to check the internal consistency with respect to the given safety properties, invariants and events. Finally, an industrial case study is used to illustrate the effectiveness of our proposed approach for developing an HMI.

Keywords: Human-machine interface (HMI) · Formal methods
Model-view-controller (MVC) · Refinement and proofs · Event-B
Verification · Validation

1 Introduction

The complexity of critical systems constantly increases and it is important to handle such complexity by addressing several aspects, such as system and user interface, of the system development to reduce the rate of system failure. Note that to design a safe interface that enables a user to interact with system unambiguously may help to reduce the rate of system failure. Developing a human-machine interface (HMI) is a difficult and time-consuming task due to complex system characteristics and user requirements, which allows anticipating human behaviour, system components and operational environment. An interactive system is composed of two main components: *functional core* and *interface*. An interface enables a user to communicate with a system.

© Springer Nature Switzerland AG 2018
M. Mazzara et al. (Eds.): STAF 2018 Workshops, LNCS 11176, pp. 240–256, 2018.
https://doi.org/10.1007/978-3-030-04771-9_19

Our work is focused on the development of HMI for checking the correctness of possible HMI behaviours. There are two main HMI concepts: *user-oriented concepts* and *designer-oriented concepts* [11]. Here, in our work, we use the designer-oriented concepts. In this work, our main objective is to investigate the formal development of HMI using a *correct-by-construction* approach in Event-B, particularly for the MVC architecture. As far as, we know that there is no MVC model in the field of HMI, which is formally developed using a *correct-by-construction* approach.

In this paper, we propose a generic development of HMI based on the MVC architecture in order to design and implement complex HMI progressively and then derive a set of patterns of design and proof that can be used in the HMI development. Here, we begin by formalizing the interaction behaviour and possible modes of an HMI. Then, we formalize the notion of controller and manipulation functions, and finally, we finish by adding the elements of the view component. All these modelling steps are applied progressively through satisfying the required safety properties. Moreover, this development also reflects modelling concepts for handling the problem of communication between HMI components. An incremental development of the MVC architecture for HMI preserves the required behaviour in an abstract model as well as in the refined models. The Event-B language is supported by the Rodin [5] platform, which provides a set of tools for developing, proving and managing the formal specifications. We use the ProB model checker tool [26] to analyse and validate the developed models of HMI.

The remainder of this paper is organized as follows. Section 2 presents the required background. In Sect. 3, we propose a methodology for developing a formal model of HMI based on the MVC architecture. Section 4 presents an overview on the selected case study. In Sect. 5, we present a formal development of the case study in Event-B. In Sect. 6, we discuss the results of our work and Sect. 7 presents the related work. Finally, Sect. 8 concludes the paper with future work.

2   Background

2.1   HMI Architecture

Seeheim and ARCH. Initially, this model was appeared in 1983 [25]. *Seeheim architecture* is a model with four components depicted in Fig. 2. These four components are: **(1) Presentation** - this component handles in/out data from a system; **(2) Dialog control** - this component creates a link between the presentation and interface, and a controller translates a set of interactions of a user in machine instructions; **(3) Interface** - this component allows operations on the data of an application; and **(4) Switch** - this component allows a feedback of that actions which are meaningless for an application.

In 1991, the Seeheim architecture was extended to develop the ARCH architecture [25]. For developing the ARCH architecture (see Fig. 1), two new components are introduced in the Seeheim architecture. These two new components make a link between the three existing components from Seeheim architecture, and the switch is removed in this model. The component presentation logic avoids contradictions between the presentation and dialog controller. The functional core is fully independent of the interface. It makes a link to the machine part of HMI (see Fig. 1). *The main advantage of the ARCH model as compared to Seeheim is the improvement of the decoupling between components thanks to adapter layers* [25]. The adapters enable more flexibility during the evolution of a system, while the other expresses an existence of the functional core for an application.

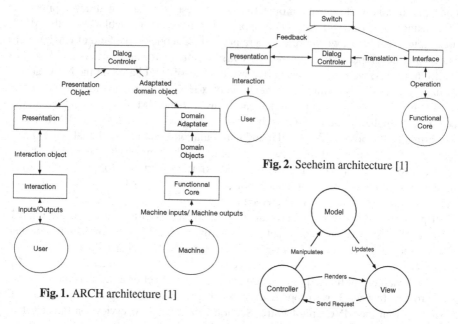

Fig. 1. ARCH architecture [1]

Fig. 2. Seeheim architecture [1]

Fig. 3. MVC architecture

MVC. MVC architecture, proposed in 1979, is the most used architecture in the HMI development (see Fig. 3) [34]. There are three main components of this architecture that are described as follows: **(1) Model -** this is the central component of the MVC architecture that allows the management of data, logic and rules of an application; **(2) View -** this component allows the management of an interface display, and the used data is provided by the model; and **(3) Controller -** this component allows the management of data during an input activity from an interface (such as keyboard, mouse, voice...). In our work, we use this architecture to design an HMI.

2.2 HMI Properties

Usability Principles. According to Dix et al. [20], there are three main categories: **Learnability**-*the easy with which new can begin effective interaction and achieve maximal performance*; **Flexibility**-*the multiplicity of ways the user and system exchange information*; and **Robustness**-*the level of support provided to the user in determining successful achievement and assessment of goal-directed behaviour*. Learnability covers the properties of predictability, synthesizability, familiarity, generalizability, and consistency of possible interactions. Flexibility focuses on the dialog initiative, multi-threading, task migratability, substitutivity, customizability. Finally, Robustness addresses the properties of observability, recoverability, responsiveness and task conformance.

CARE. It is a simple framework for reasoning about the multimodal interaction of HMI from both the system and user perspectives [19,29]. A modality is a way of communication that is used by an interface. For example, an interactive map uses the display modality to communicate information with users. The main four properties are: **Complementarity** - a set of modalities must be used in a complementary way to realize a goal; **Assignation** - there is a unique modality to realize a goal; **Redundancy** - a set of modalities is used redundantly if all the modalities have same expressiveness to realize a goal; and **Equivalence** - a set of modalities is equivalent if anyone modality is sufficient to realize a goal.

2.3 Event-B

The Event-B modelling language is developed by Abrial [4,37], in which most of the constructs are borrowed from the B-method [3]. This modelling language is based on the first-order logic and set theory. The goal of this language is to design a complex system using a *correct-by-construction* approach. The correct-by-construction approach allows us to introduce different system behaviours and properties in successive refinements. The development begins with a very high level of abstraction. The refinement enables us to introduce more detailed behaviour and the required safety properties by transforming an abstract model to a concrete version. The final concrete model can be used to produce the source code in any programming language. Note that the refinement always preserves a relation between an abstract model and its corresponding concrete model. The newly generated proof obligations related to refinement ensures that the given abstract model is correctly refined by its concrete version.

There are two main components of Event-B: *context* and *machine*. A context is composed of several elements, such as *set*, *constant*, and *axiom*. The *set* and *constant* elements are defined to state the type definitions and constant definitions to describe the system behaviour. The *axioms* are some logical propositions that cannot be proved but these axioms are used as the base of mathematical reasoning. A context may be an extension of another context. Note that all the elements of the extended context exist in a new context without being declared. A *context* may also contain some theorems in form of logical properties that can be deducted from the existing axioms.

An Event-B model is characterized by a list of state variables that are modified by a list of events to model the changing behaviour of a system with respect to the given conditions. In general, an event can be described in the following form:

$$e \triangleq \textbf{any } var \textbf{ where } grd \textbf{ then } act \textbf{ end}$$

where var is a list of local variables, grd is a set of guards in form of the conjunction of predicates, and act is a set of parallel actions. Any event can be enabled if the given guards are $true$. If more than one event enables simultaneously then any event can be selected for execution non-deterministically, and if none of the events becomes enabled then the system becomes deadlocked. An event can be always enabled if the event is not guarded. In general, a set of actions of an event is a composition of assignments that execute simultaneously, in which a variable assignment can be either deterministic or non-deterministic. The deterministic assignment can be denoted as $x := \textbf{expr}(var)$, where x is a state variable and **expr**(var) is an expression over the state variable var. The non-deterministic assignment can be denoted as $x :\in S$ or $x : |P(var, x')$, where S is a set of values and $P(var, x')$ is a predicate. In $x :\in S$, x can obtain any value from S and in $x : |P(var, x')$, x can obtain any value that can be satisfied by the predicate $P(var, x')$. Invariants of a machine define the type definition of variables and the required safety properties that must be satisfied during the system execution. In Event-B, there are three type of events: ordinary event, convergent event and anticipated event. The ordinary event has not any constraints. By default, all the events are ordinary events. The convergent event always associates with a variant that models the converging behaviour of a system. An anticipated event is a new event which is not convergent yet but should become convergent in the subsequent refinement.

The foundational semantic of the Event-B language is grounded on *before-after predicates* [4]. The before-after predicate shows a relation between the system states before and after execution of an event. To verify the correctness of an Event-B model, we need to show that the initialization and events preserve the defined invariants. It can be expressed as follows:

$$A(s, c), I(s, c, x), G_e(t, s, c, x), BA_e(t, s, c, x, x') \vdash I(s, c, x')$$

$$A(s, c), BA_{init}(s, c, x') \vdash I(s, c, x')$$

Event-B proof obligations (POs) also allow verifying the event feasibility to show that whenever an event is enabled then there is always a reachable state after the event activation. It can be defined as follows:

$$A(s, c), I(s, c, x), G_e(t, s, c, x) \vdash \exists x'. BA_e(t, s, c, x, x')$$

In the above formulas, $A(s, c)$ is a set of axioms, $I(s, c, x)$ is a set of invariants, $G_e(t, s, c, x)$ is a set of guards and $BA_e(t, s, c, x, x')$ is set of before-after predicates for an event and $BA_{init}(s, c, x')$ is a before-after predicate for the initial event using constants c, carrier sets s and variables x.

To verify the correctness of a refinement step, we need to discharge the generated proof obligations for a refined model. There are several POs, which are detailed in [4]. An abstract model AM with state variable x and invariant $I(x)$ is refined by a concrete model CM with variable y and gluing invariant $J(x, y)$. e and f are events of the abstract model AM and the concrete model CM, respectively, where event f refines event e. $BA_e(t, s, c, x, x')$ and $BA_f(t, s, c, y, y')$ are before-after predicates of events e and f, respectively. The simulation PO (SIM) shows that the new modified action in the refined event is not contradictory to the abstract action and the concrete event simulates the corresponding abstract event. This SIM PO can be defined as follows:

$$A(s, c), I(s, c, x), J(s, c, x, y), G_f(s, c, x, y), BA_f(t, s, c, y, y') \vdash BA_e(t, s, c, x, x')$$

Similarly, in the refined events, we can strengthen the abstract guards to specify more concrete conditions. The generated POs ensure that if a concrete event is enabled then the corresponding abstract event will also be enabled. This PO is defined as follows:

$$A(s,c), I(s,c,x), J(s,c,x,y), G_f(s,c,x,y) \vdash G_e(s,c,x)$$

Rodin [5] is an open source tool based on the Eclipse framework for developing a formal model in the Event-B language. This is the collection of different tools that includes the project management, model development, refinement and proof assistance, model checking and code generation.

3 Methodology

For developing an HMI based on the MVC architecture using a *correct by construction* approach, we propose a generic development depicted in Fig. 4. On the upper part of the figure, we show the classical scheme of MVC with possible interaction protocol. On the bottom part of the figure, we sketch the possible refinement strategy. In this refinement strategy, each triangle corresponds to the formal development of the MVC components, such as *model, controller* and *view*. Note that these triangles are overlapped with each other due to some shared variables and functional behaviours.

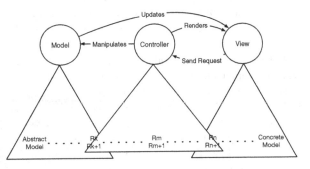

Fig. 4. MVC based refinement strategy

According to the proposed refinement strategy, first, we formalize the *model* components, which describe a very high level of abstraction of HMI in form of system modality. Note that this abstract model can be used in different refinement layers to introduce the complete modality of HMI, and we can also introduce the required safety properties in each refinement level to guarantee the correctness of the modes transitions of HMI. The next step of the development is to introduce the *controller* components and the required controller behaviour. In this phase of the development, we introduce the controller components and their static and dynamic properties. The static properties related to the controller can be defined by extending the context of the model, while the controller components and dynamic properties can be defined by introducing a set of new events and by refining the abstract events. For modelling the controller, we can also use different refinements to reduce the complexity of the controller modelling. All the required safety properties must be introduced in these refinements. The last component of the MVC architecture is *view*, which should be integrated in the previously developed models. In this last phase of the development, we introduce the components and the required properties of the view. The view can also be defined as similar to our previous development in several layers of refinements. By adding the view components, we can prove the correctness of the request functions and responses of the controller. In this step of the development, we implement the behaviours of different elements of HMI. When all the elements are designed and integrated, we introduce the interaction properties for each component to check the correctness of the interaction behaviour of the developing HMI. Note that the formal development related to the view is complex, and we need to add several guards in different events to meet the desired properties of interaction behaviour for each view component of the HMI.

4   Case Study

In this section, we describe an industrial case study of HMI to understand the modelling and designing concepts, and interaction behaviour of different components. Figure 5 depicts a simple HMI that contains a set of graphical components in form of widgets. In this HMI, we have three modes *stop mode*, *limit mode* and *control mode*. These modes always appear on the top left corner of the HMI that shows an actual modality of the physical system. The stop mode indicates that the physical system connected with HMI is stopped, the limit mode represents that the speed of the physical system is limited, and the control mode indicates that the speed of the physical system is controlled. The HMI shows the selected speed, current speed and current mode. The speed of the vehicle is bounded (selected speed and current speed). The selected speed can be modified using widget components like slider and buttons ('+' and '−').

A set of informal requirements of HMI is defined as: R_1: the selected speed is bounded; R_2: the current speed is bounded; R_3: only one button can be pressed at a time; R_4: the slider can be moved only if no button is pressed; R_5: the default mode of HMI is stopped; R_6:

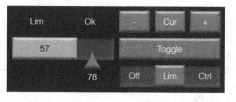

the limit mode and control mode can be active. **Fig. 5.** Graphical view of the case study

5   Formalization of HMI

To develop a formal model of the selected case study, we use the Event-B modelling language [4] that supports an incremental refinement to design a complete system in several layers (i.e. model, controller and view), from an abstract to a concrete specification. Firstly, the initial model captures the basic behaviour of the HMI in an abstract way. Then subsequent refinements are used to formalize the concrete behaviour for the resulting HMI that covers the different elements of the HMI. Note that, in this development, we follow the HMI development similar to our proposed methodology.

5.1 Abstract Model: Model

To model the HMI case study, we choose the MVC architecture. An abstract behaviour of the HMI is depicted in Fig. 6. This figure shows an automaton that models the changing states of the controller. When the system is in the stop mode then it can switch either in the limit mode or in the control mode. There are several possible interactions defined in this abstract automata to describe the model of HMI. In the context of the initial model, we define three enumerated sets: *MODES* - a set of different controller modes; *POWERED* - on and off power states; and *STATUS* - driving status and suspended status.

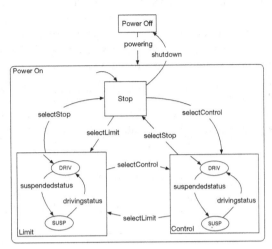

Fig. 6. Automata of an abstract model

$$axm1 : partition(MODES, \{STOPPED\}, \{CONTROL\}, \{LIMIT\})$$
$$axm2 : partition(POWERED, \{ON\}, \{OFF\})$$
$$axm3 : partition(STATUS, \{DRIVING\}, \{SUSPENDED\})$$

An abstract model is used to show the operating modes by observing the system interaction. The machine model formalizes the dynamic behaviour of the HMI. To define the dynamic properties, we introduce three variables *selectedmode*, *powered* and *status*. The variable *selectedmode* represents the current state of the HMI, the next variable *powered* represents the power status of the HMI and the last variable *status* indicates the current status of the system. Four interesting safety properties are defined using safety invariants ($saf1$-$saf4$). The first safety invariant ($saf1$) expresses that the currently selected mode is not in the stopped mode then the power is on. The next safety property ($saf2$) states that if the current mode is stopped then the status is suspended. The next safety property ($saf3$) states that when the system is in driving state then the selected mode is either in the control mode or in the limit mode. The last safety property ($saf4$) states that when the system is off then the system must be in the stopped mode.

$inv1 : selectedmode \in MODES$
$inv2 : powered \in POWERED$
$inv3 : status \in STATUS$
$saf1 : selectedmode \neq STOPPED \Rightarrow powered = ON$
$saf2 : selectedmode = STOPPED \Rightarrow$
    $status = SUSPENDED$
$saf3 : status = DRIVING \Rightarrow selectedmode =$
    $CONTROL \lor selectedmode = LIMIT$
$saf4 : powered = OFF \Rightarrow selectedmode = STOPPED$

EVENT powering
WHEN
    $grd1 : powered = OFF$
THEN
    $act1 : powered := ON$
END

In this abstract model, we introduce seven events: *powering* - to present the power status of the HMI; *shutdown* - to indicate the shutdown status of the HMI; *selectStop* - to select the stop mode; *selectControl* - to select the control mode; *selectLimit* - to select the limit mode; *drivingstatus* - to show the driving status; and *suspendedstatus* - to show the suspended status. The event *powering* specifies the power *on* behaviour of the system. The guard of this event shows that the current power status is OFF and the action of this event sets the current power status as ON.

The next event *selectControl* is used to set the control mode and driving status, when system power is ON and the currently selected mode is not in the *CONTROL* mode. Similarly, the last event *drivingstatus* is also used to set the driving status, when the system power is ON, the currently selected mode is not stopped and the system is in suspended status. Rest of the events are modelled in a similar way, and all these events behave similar to the given abstract level automata (see Fig. 6).

```
EVENT selectControl
  WHEN
    grd1 : powered = ON
    grd2 : selectedmode ≠ CONTROL
  THEN
    act1 : selectedmode := CONTROL
    act2 : status := DRIVING
  END
```

```
EVENT drivingstatus
  WHEN
    grd1 : powered = ON
    grd2 : selectedmode ≠ STOPPED
    grd2 : status = SUSPENDED
  THEN
    act1 : status := DRIVING
  END
```

5.2   First and Second Refinements: Controller

There two different successive refinements for introducing the controller components. In both refinements, we introduce the controller behaviour according to the MVC architecture. In order to design the controller, we introduce the initial speed ($vinit$), maximum speed ($vmax$), and bounded speed ($SPEED$) using axioms ($axm1$ - $axm4$) in the first refinement. Note that the axiom $axm3$ states that the maximum speed must be greater than the initial speed.

In the first refinement, we only introduce a new variable *SelectedSpeed*, which is defined as $SelectedSpeed \in SPEED$. In this refinement, we introduce a new event *ChangeSpeed* for modifying the selected speed non-deterministically. This event will be refined in the next refinement to add more precise controller behaviour of the system.

```
axm1 : vinit ∈ ℕ
axm2 : vmax ∈ ℕ
axm3 : vmax ≥ vinit
axm4 : SPEED = 0..vmax
```

```
EVENT ChangeSpeed
  WHEN
    grd1 : powered = ON
  THEN
    act1 : SelectedSpeed :∈ SPEED
  END
```

In the second refinement, we introduce a new constant $STEP$ defined as $STEP \in \mathbb{N}$. This constant is used in the refined model to change the selected speed through interacting several HMI components, such as buttons and sliders. In this second refinement, we introduce two new events, *IncreaseSpeed* - to increase a value of the selected speed; and *DecreaseSpeed* - to decrease a value of the selected speed, which are the refinements of the abstract event *ChangeSpeed*. The guards of the *IncreaseSpeed* state that the system power is ON, the choice of step value (x) is either 1 or default STEP, and the sum of the selected speed and the choice of step value (x) must be less than or equal to the maximum speed ($vmax$). The action of this event states that the selected speed increases by the step value (x).

EVENT IncreaseSpeed REFINES ChangeSpeed
ANY x
  WHEN
    grd1 : $powered = ON$
    grd2 : $x = 1 \lor x = STEP$
    grd3 : $SelectedSpeed + x \leq vmax$
  THEN
    act1 : $SelectedSpeed := SelectedSpeed + x$
END
	EVENT DecreaseSpeed REFINES ChangeSpeed
	ANY x
	  WHEN
	    grd1 : $powered = ON$
	    grd2 : $x = 1 \lor x = STEP$
	    grd3 : $SelectedSpeed - x \geq vmax$
	  THEN
	    act1 : $SelectedSpeed := SelectedSpeed - x$
	END

The event *DecreaseSpeed* is also formalised similar to the event *IncreaseSpeed*. The guards of the *DecreaseSpeed* state that the system power is ON, the choice of step value (x) is either 1 or default STEP, and the subtraction of the choice of step value (x) from the selected speed must be greater than or equal to the maximum speed ($vmax$). The action of this event states that the selected speed decreases by the step value (x).

5.3 Third and Fourth Refinements: View

This is the last phase of our development according to our proposed methodology, which allows us introducing the view components of the MVC architecture using several refinements. In the third refinement, we introduce a set of HMI elements, such as buttons and slider, and possible interactions between HMI components, for example, *click* and *dblclick* operations of buttons, and *moving* and *sliding* operations of slider. In order to design the selected case study, we introduce a slider and two buttons ('+' and '−') to modify the selected speed. In this development, we also introduce a set of buttons to represent the *Toggle, Lim, Ctrl, Curr* and *Off* buttons. We introduce three enumerated sets *SLIDERMODE, SLIDERDIRECTION* and *PRESSED* in axioms ($axm1 - axm3$). A set of axioms ($axm4 - axm5$) is defined to represent the possible slider positions according to the changing speed of the system. An additional axiom ($axm6$) is defined to state that the maximum speed is equivalent to the maximum value of the slider position. It means that whenever the speed changes, the slider position also updates accordingly.

$axm1 : partition(SLIDERMODE, \{YES\}, \{NO\})$
$axm2 : partition(SLIDERDIRECTION, \{NONE\}, \{INCR\}, \{DECR\})$
$axm3 : partition(PRESSED, \{NOTPRESS\}, \{YESPRESS\})$
$axm4 : POSITION = 0 .. xmax$
$axm5 : speed \in POSITION \rightarrow SPEED \land speed = id$
$axm6 : xmax \in \mathbb{N} \land vmax = speed(xmax)$

In this refinement, we introduce ten new variables using invariants ($inv1 - inv5$). All these variables represent the different states of the HMI components in form of $PRESSED, SLIDERMODE$ or $SLIDERDIRECTION$.

$inv1 : pressedPlus \in PRESSED \land pressedMinus \in PRESSED$
$inv2 : pressedCur \in PRESSED \land pressedToggle \in PRESSED$
$inv3 : pressedOff \in PRESSED \land pressedLim \in PRESSED$
$inv4 : pressedCtrl \in PRESSED \land slidermode \in SLIDERMODE$
$inv5 : sliderdirection \in SLIDERDIRECTION \land sliderposition \in POSITION$

Several new safety properties ($saf1-saf10$) are introduced in this development. The first safety property ($saf1$) states that when the button ('+') is pressed then the rest of the buttons are not pressed. Similar to the first safety property, next eight safety properties ($saf2 - saf9$) are introduced, which always guarantee that if the selected button is pressed then the other buttons are not pressed. The next safety property ($saf10$) states that when the slider direction is NONE then the sliding mode is active. The last safety property is a gluing invariant to establish a relation between abstract variable *selectedspeed* and concrete speed function *speed*.

$saf1 : pressedPlus = YESPRESS \Rightarrow (pressedLess = NOTPRESS \wedge$
$\qquad pressedToggle = NOTPRESS \wedge pressedOff = NOTPRESS \wedge$
$\qquad pressedLim = NOTPRESS \wedge pressedCtrl = NOTPRESS)$
$saf2 : ...,$
$...$
$...$
$saf9 : ...$
$saf10 : sliderdirection \neq NONE \Rightarrow slidermode = YES$
$glu1 : \forall p \cdot p \in POSITION \wedge p = sliderposition) \Rightarrow selectedspeed = speed(p)$

In this development, we introduce 14 new events to describe the functional behaviour of the different HMI components. A new event *pressPlus* is defined to show the functional behaviour of the button ('+'). The guards of this event state that the power is ON, slider mode is not active, current button *pressedPlus* is not pressed and the other remaining buttons are also not pressed. If all the given guards are true then the action states that the current button can be pressed. The next event *unpressPlus* is defined to model the button ('+') when this button is no more active to press. The guards of this event state that the power is on, the button is in the press state and the slider position is greater than the maximum speed. The action of this event states that the button will be switched in the $NOTPRESS$ mode. The other events are used in similar fashion to model the rest of the HMI components. Note that we have also introduced extra guards in other events to model the desired behaviour of the HMI.

EVENT pressPlus
  WHEN
    $grd1 : powered = ON \wedge slidermode = NO \wedge pressedPlus = NOTPRESS$
    $grd2 : pressedMinus = NOTPRESS \wedge pressedCur = NOTPRESS \wedge$
        $pressedToggle = NOTPRESS \wedge pressedOff = NOTPRESS \wedge$
        $pressedLim = NOTPRESS \wedge pressedCtrl = NOTPRESS$
  THEN
    $act1 : pressedPlus := YESPRESS$
  END

The fourth refinement is also the part of view component according to the MVC architecture. In this refinement, we introduce the current speed of the system which is produced by the physical system and its application. The development of the main physical system is beyond the scope of this work because we are mainly interested to design an HMI using a *correct by construction* technique. However, we introduce a new variable *currentspeed* as $currentspeed \in SPEED$ and a new event to model an interface between the HMI and physical system. The current speed is defined as similar to the selected speed. The new event *updatecurrentspeed* is defined to capture the current actual speed of the system.

```
EVENT unpressPlus
  WHEN
    grd1 : powered = ON
    grd3 : pressedPlus = Y ESP RESS
    grd4 : sliderposition + ST EP > vmax∨
           sliderposition + 1 > vmax
  THEN
    act1 : pressedPlus := NOT P RESS
  END
```

```
EVENT updatecurrentspeed
  ANY v
  WHEN
    grd1 : v ∈ SP EED
    grd2 : v ≠ currentspeed
    grd3 : powered = ON
  THEN
    act1 : currentspeed := v
  END
```

A complete formal development of the HMI case study is available on our website[1].

5.4   Model Validation and Analysis

This section summarises the proof statistics of the generated proof obligations in each refinement. The Event-B supports mainly *consistency checking* and *model analysis*. The consistency checking shows that all the events always preserve the defined safety properties, and the refinement checking checks the correctness of the refinement process.

The model analysis is performed using ProB [26] model checker, which can be used to explore traces of Event-B models. The ProB tool supports *automated consistency checking, constraint-based checking* and it can also detect the possible deadlocks. Table 1 summarises the generated proof obligations for each refinement steps.

Table 1. Proof statistics

Model	Total number of POs	Automatic proof	Interactive proof
Abstract model	25	25(100%)	0(0%)
First refinement	5	5(100%)	0(0%)
Second refinement	3	3(100%)	0(0%)
Third refinement	233	219(94%)	14(6%)
Fourth refinement	31	25(81%)	6(19%)
Total	297	277(94%)	20(6%)

The stepwise development results in 297(100%) proof obligations, in which 277(94%) are proved automatically, and the remaining 20(6%) are proved interactively using the different Rodin provers, such as SMT solvers and standard B prover. Note that the third refinement has the highest number of proof obligations because, in this development, we introduce all the HMI components with required functional behaviour. To validate the developed HMI model, we use the ProB tool for animating the models. This validation approach refers to gaining confidence that the developed models are consistent with requirements. The ProB animation helps to identify the desired behaviour of the HMI model in different scenarios. In particular, this tool assists us in finding potential problems, and to improve the guard predicates of events. Moreover, we have also used the ProB tool as a model checker to prove the absence of errors (no counterexample exists) and deadlock-free. It should be noted that the ProB uses all the described safety properties during the model checking process to report any violation of safety properties against the formalized system behaviour.

In this development, the main derived properties from the usability principles, such as consistency, observability and task conformance, are considered. A set of invariants in form of safety properties is introduced equivalent to the subset of the HMI usability principles. Note that these properties are also validated using ProB model checker through animation. For example, in the abstract model, we check the behaviour of the

---

[1] http://singh.perso.enseeiht.fr/Conference/FMIS2018/HMI_Models.zip.

model components; in the second and third refinements, we check the behaviour of the *controller* components; and in the last third and fourth refinements, we check the behaviour of the *view* components.

6   Discussion

Stepwise refinement played an important role in our work for developing the HMI progressively. A stepwise refinement is a suggestive approach from a long time in order to design a complex system. As we have mentioned before that the refinement is a core concept in Event-B development. It is crucial, how to decide on what to introduce in a new refinement level. There may be no universally 'correct' pattern to follow. However, building on experience in HMI development we identified the order of: (1) Introduce the *model* components of MVC (possible modes of HMI); (2) Introduce the *controller* components of MVC; (3) Introduce the *view* components of MVC.

Note that the adopted notion of MVC allows us to build a complex HMI model systematically and this approach also allows us to do reasoning steps systematically considering usability principles. Due to the complex nature of HMI, we do not claim that the proposed modelling approach (see Fig. 4) can be a standard approach for handling any HMI. In fact, our results showed that the proposed modelling approach can be used to model most of the HMI models. To demonstrate the practicality of the identified modelling pattern based on the MVC (see Fig. 4), we have developed the selected HMI case study using a *correct by construction* approach. We described the system requirements using set-theoretical notations abstractly, that can be further refined incrementally to reach a concrete level similar to code. Event-B has a very good tool support that allows us to prove the given properties (mostly) automatically. Other formal modelling tools like VDM, Z, Alloy can be used in place of the Event-B modelling language.

As far as we know, there is no work related to the formal development of HMI based on the MVC architecture using progressive refinement. We used informal descriptions of the MVC architecture as a basis for this work. We also identified a list of safety properties in the refinement process to verify the correctness of overall formalized system behaviour, including newly introduced features. These safety properties guarantee that all possible executions of the system are safe if the generated proof obligations are successfully discharged – and if our list of safety properties is correct and complete. We have considered only the main safety properties related to modes and interaction of the view components. These properties are derived from the usability principles, such as learnability, flexibility and robustness. We can introduce the additional HMI properties in form of safety properties in different refinements to meet the goal of usability principles. Note that the presented case study does not cover the whole set of usability principles. In particular, the current work is focused on consistency, observability and task conformance. In addition, the use of the model checker allows us the validate the developed model with respect to the given safety properties. In summary, we can conclude that the some of the interesting critical properties of the HMI are proved and checked but other remaining properties can be checked during the testing process.

7 Related Work

There are several works related to the formal development of HMI, but most of them use different methods such as Petri net [31], process algebra [22] and model checking [2]. Bowen et al. [15] present a refinement approach for designing UI, and [14] describes models and techniques to incorporate the design artefacts into a formal development process of HMI to specify the system behaviour. [35] describes a refinement process to demonstrate that the given requirements of a device must be satisfied by the specification. Compos et al. [16] propose a framework for checking the HMI system for a given set of generic properties using model checkers. Combefis et al. [18] present a formal approach based on bisimulation to analyse the HMI mechanism. Navarre et al. [30] propose a framework for analysing the interactive systems, particularly for the combined behaviour of user task models and system models to check whether a user task is supported by the system model. [27] describes an approach for generating formal designs of HMI behaviour from task-analysis models and then the results are demonstrated through different case studies. [17] presents the use of formal techniques for the analysis of human-machine interactions. Michael et al. [23] present a formal approach and methodology for the analysis and generation of user interfaces. Palanque et al. [32,33] propose the development of HMI using Interactive Cooperative Objects (ICO) formalism, in which the object-oriented framework and possible functional behaviour are described with high-level Petri-nets. Bolton et al. [12,13] propose a framework to analyse human errors and system failures by integrating the task models and erroneous human behaviour with formal techniques to check the required safety properties.

Ameur et al. [8,9] propose an incremental development of an interactive system using B methods. The proposed approach targets the important problems of HMI related to reachability, observability and reliability. A global development approach for developing a software for human-computer interaction is proposed in [6,7] that can be used from the abstract model to the code generation. Silva et al. [36] propose an approach to generate user interface software, particularly in Java, from a declarative description in the Teallach MB-UIDE. CARE properties are defined using the first order logic in [10]. A new tool-supported approach from specification to the implementation is proposed in [24]. This approach is based on CAV architecture, which is a hybrid model of the MVC and PAC models. The Event-B language is also used for developing the multi-model interactive system using a correct by construction approach in [10]. The ARCH architecture [29] is used during the development of the multi-model interactive system. In addition, several safety properties are introduced to verify the required multi-model interactive behaviour.

In this paper, our approach is different from existing works. The proposed approach allows us to develop a formal model of an HMI based on the MVC architecture using a *correct by construction* approach by analysing the system requirements, modes and interaction mechanism. The use of refinement approach helps to introduce several properties in a progressive way and to verify the correctness of the HMI model under the given safety properties, which can be derived from the usability principles. Moreover, we can use progressive reasoning step in a complex model to cover the different HMI properties. In addition, the progressively developed model can be used for validating the specified system requirements using the model checker and animation. Note that the final concrete model of the HMI can be used to generate source code in many programming languages using EB2ALL [21,28] in a prototype development or simulating a user interface.

8   Conclusion

This paper presents a generic methodology for developing a formal model of HMI using incremental refinement. In particular, the proposed methodology focused on the MVC architecture of HMI to analyze an interactive behaviour of a system under the given safety properties. We used the Event-B modelling language, together with its associated tools, to develop the proof-based formal model of HMI using a *correct by construction* approach. Our incremental development of HMI based on the MVC architecture reflects the complexity and modelling challenges in the area of HMI.

The proposed methodology is a generic solution of the HMI development that can help to certify the HMI software. Our goal is to integrate formal models in the development of HMI for verifying the desired behaviour under the relevant safety properties and be able to guarantee the correctness of the functional behaviour. The proposed generic methodology is used to develop the HMI case study for designing a safe interface progressively and checking the correctness of interactive behaviour.

Our future work intends on the proof of specification and their logical translation in order to create templates to conceive and prove the development of HMI in Event-B. Note that the current work does not cover the several HMI properties and CARE properties, so we plan to include these properties in the process of HMI development. Another important goal of this work is to validate the possible interaction using an interface. Thus, our new challenges in the future will be to develop a set of patterns like Dwyer's pattern in order to validate the model through animation and tests. Moreover, we plan to develop a set of libraries of HMI components in Event-B using ontology relations, so that it can be used later in the development of HMI.

References

1. https://tel.archives-ouvertes.fr/file/index/docid/48279/filename/2_2modelesinterface_referen.html
2. Abowd, G.D., Wang, H.M., Monk, A.F.: A formal technique forautomated dialogue development. In: Proceedings of the 1st Conference on Designing Interactive Systems: Processes, Practices, Methods, & Techniques, DIS 1995, pp. 219–226. ACM, New York (1995)
3. Abrial, J.R.: The B-Book: Assigning Programs to Meanings. Cambridge University Press, New York (1996)
4. Abrial, J.R.: Modeling in Event-B: System and Software Engineering, 1st edn. Cambridge University Press, New York (2010)
5. Abrial, J.R., Butler, M., Hallerstede, S., Hoang, T.S., Mehta, F., Voisin, L.: Rodin: an open toolset for modelling and reasoning in event-b. Int. J. Softw. Tools Technol. Transf. **12**(6), 447–466 (2010)
6. Ameur, Y.A.: Cooperation of formal methods in an engineering based software development process. In: 2000 Proceedings Second International Conference Integrated Formal Methods, IFM 2000, Dagstuhl Castle, Germany, 1–3 November, pp. 136–155 (2000)

7. Ameur, Y.A., Aït-Sadoune, I., Mota, J., Baron, M.: Validation et vérification formelles de systèmes interactifs multi-modaux fondées sur la preuve. In: Proceedings of the 18th International Conference of the Association Francophone d'Interaction Homme-Machine, Montreal, Quebec, Canada, 18–21 April 2006, pp. 123–130 (2006)

8. Ameur, Y.A., Girard, P., Jambon, F.: A uniform approach for specification and design of interactive systems: the B method. In: Design, Specification and Verification of Interactive Systems 1998, Supplementary Proceedings of the Fifth International Eurographics Workshop, 3–5 June 1998, Abingdon, United Kingdom, pp. 51–67 (1998)

9. Ameur, Y.A., Girard, P., Jambon, F.: Using the B formal approach for incremental specification design of interactive systems. In: Engineering for Human-Computer Interaction, IFIP TC2/TC13 WG2.7/WG13.4 Seventh Working Conference on Engineering for Human-Computer Interaction, Heraklion, Crete, Greece, 14–18 September, pp. 91–109 (1998)

10. Ameur, Y.A., Sadoune, I.A., Baron, M.: Etude et comparaison de scénarios de développements formels d'interfaces multi-modales fondés sur la preuve et le raffinement. RSTI- Ingénierie des Systèmes d'Informations **13**(2), 127–155 (2008)

11. Baron, M., Lucquiaud, V., Autard, D., Scapin, D.L.: K-made: Unenvironnement pour le noyau du modèle de description del'activité. In: Proceedings of the 18th Conference onL'Interaction Homme-Machine, IHM 2006, pp. 287–288. ACM, New York (2006)

12. Bolton, M.L., Siminiceanu, R.I., Bass, E.J.: A systematic approach to model checking human - automation interaction using task analytic models. IEEE Trans. Syst. Man Cybern. - Part A: Syst. Hum. **41**(5), 961–976 (2011)

13. Bolton, M.L., Bass, E.J.: Building a formal model of a human-interactive system: insights into the integration of formal methods and human factors engineering. In: First NASA Formal Methods Symposium - NFM, California, USA, 6–8 April, pp. 6–15 (2009)

14. Bowen, J., Reeves, S.: Formal models for user interface design artefacts. Innov. Syst. Softw. Eng. **4**(2), 125–141 (2008)

15. Bowen, J., Reeves, S.: Refinement for user interface designs. Electron. Notes Theor. Comput. Sci. **208**, 5–22 (2008)

16. Campos, J.C., Harrison, M.D.: Systematic analysis of control panel interfaces using formal tools. In: Graham, T.C.N., Palanque, P. (eds.) DSV-IS 2008. LNCS, vol. 5136, pp. 72–85. Springer, Heidelberg (2008). https://doi.org/10.1007/978-3-540-70569-7_6

17. Combéfis, S., Giannakopoulou, D., Pecheur, C., Feary, M.: Learning system abstractions for human operators. In: Proceedings of the International Workshop on Machine Learning Technologies in Software Engineering, MALETS 2011, pp. 3–10. ACM, New York City (2011)

18. Combéfis, S., Pecheur, C.: A bisimulation-based approach to the analysis of human-computer interaction. In: Proceedings of the 1st ACM SIGCHI Symposium on Engineering Interactive Computing Systems, EICS 2009, pp. 101–110. ACM, New York (2009)

19. Coutaz, J., Nigay, L., Salber, D., Blandford, A., May, J., Young, R.M.: Four easy pieces for assessing the usability of multimodal interaction: the care properties. In: Nordby, K., Helmersen, P., Gilmore, D.J., Arnesen, S.A. (eds.) Human-Computer Interaction. IFIP Advances in Information and Communication Technology, pp. 115–120. Springer, Boston (1995). https://doi.org/10.1007/978-1-5041-2896-4_19

20. Dix, A., Finlay, J.E., Abowd, G.D., Beale, R.: Human-Computer Interaction, 3rd edn. Prentice-Hall Inc., Upper Saddle River (2003)

21. EB2ALL: An automatic code generation tool from Event-B (2011). http://eb2all.loria.fr/

22. Eijk, P.V., Diaz, M. (eds.): Formal Description Technique Lotos: Results of the Esprit Sedos Project. Elsevier Science Inc., New York (1989)

23. Heymann, M., Degani, A.: Formal analysis and automatic generation of user interfaces: approach, methodology, and an algorithm. Hum. Factors **49**(2), 311–330 (2007)

24. Jambon, F.: From formal specifications to secure implementations. In: Proceedings of the Fourth International Conference on Computer-Aided Design of User Interfaces III, Valenciennes, France, 15–17 May 2002, pp. 51–62 (2002)
25. Lecrubier, V.: A formal language for designing, specifying and verifying critical embedded human machine interfaces. Theses, INSTITUT SUPERIEUR DE L'AERONAUTIQUE ET DE L'ESPACE (ISAE); UNIVERSITE DE TOULOUSE, June 2016. https://hal.archives-ouvertes.fr/tel-01455466
26. Leuschel, M., Butler, M.: ProB: a model checker for B. In: Araki, K., Gnesi, S., Mandrioli, D. (eds.) FME 2003. LNCS, vol. 2805, pp. 855–874. Springer, Heidelberg (2003). https://doi.org/10.1007/978-3-540-45236-2_46
27. Li, M., Wei, J., Zheng, X., Bolton, M.L.: A formal machine-learning approach to generating human-machine interfaces from task models. IEEE Trans. Hum.-Mach. Syst. **47**(6), 822–833 (2017)
28. Méry, D., Singh, N.K.: Automatic code generation from event-b models. In: Proceedings of the Second Symposium on Information and Communication Technology, SoICT 2011, pp. 179–188. ACM, New York (2011)
29. Mohand Oussaïd, L.M.O.: Formal modelling and verification of multimodal human computer interfaces : output multimodality. Theses, ISAE-ENSMA Ecole Nationale Supérieure de Mécanique et d'Aérotechique - Poitiers, December 2014. https://tel.archives-ouvertes.fr/tel-01127547
30. Navarre, D., Palanque, P., Paternò, F., Santoro, C., Bastide, R.: A tool suite for integrating task and system models through scenarios. In: Johnson, C. (ed.) DSV-IS 2001. LNCS, vol. 2220, pp. 88–113. Springer, Heidelberg (2001). https://doi.org/10.1007/3-540-45522-1_6
31. Palanque, P., Bastide, R., Sengès, V.: Validating interactive system design through the verification of formal task and system models. In: Bass, L.J., Unger, C. (eds.) EHCI 1995. IFIP Advances in Information and Communication Technology, pp. 189–212. Springer, Boston (1996). https://doi.org/10.1007/978-0-387-34907-7_11
32. Palanque, P.A., Bastide, R.: Petri net based design of user-driven interfaces using the interactive cooperative objects formalism. In: Paternó, F. (ed.) Interactive Systems: Design, Specification, and Verification Focus on Computer Graphics (Tutorials and Perspectives in Computer Graphics), pp. 383–400. Springer, Berlin (1995). https://doi.org/10.1007/978-3-642-87115-3_23
33. Palanque, P., Bastide, R.: Verification of an interactive software by analysis of its formal specification. In: Nordby, K., Helmersen, P., Gilmore, D.J., Arnesen, S.A. (eds.) Human—Computer Interaction. IFIP Advances in Information and Communication Technology, pp. 191–196. Springer, Boston (1995). https://doi.org/10.1007/978-1-5041-2896-4_32
34. Reenskaug, T.M.H.: The original MVC reports (1979)
35. Ruksenas, R., Masci, P., Harrison, M.D., Curzon, P.: Developing and verifying user interface requirements for infusion pumps: a refinement approach. ECEASST, 69 (2013). ISSN: 1863-2122
36. Pinheiro da Silva, P., Griffiths, T., Paton, N.W.: Generating user interface code in a model based user interface development environment. In: Proceedings of the Working Conference on Advanced Visual Interfaces, AVI 2000, pp. 155–160. ACM, New York (2000)
37. Singh, N.K.: Using Event-B for Critical Device Software Systems. Springer, Heidelberg (2013)

Using Abstraction with Interaction Sequences for Interactive System Modelling

Jessica Turner[✉], Judy Bowen, and Steve Reeves

University of Waikato, Hamilton, New Zealand
jdt11@students.waikato.ac.nz, {jbowen,stever}@waikato.ac.nz

Abstract. Interaction sequences can be used as an abstraction of an interactive system. We can use such models to consider or verify properties of a system for testing purposes. However, interaction sequences have the potential to become unfeasibly long, leading to models which are intractable. We propose a method of reducing the state space of such sequences using the *self-containment* property. This allows us to hide (and subsequently expand) some of the model describing parts of the system not currently under consideration. Interaction sequences and their models can therefore be used to control the state space size of the models we create as an abstraction of an interactive system.

Keywords: Interaction sequences · Interactive system testing
Formal methods

1 Introduction

As part of a sound software engineering development process, interactive systems should be tested thoroughly to ensure behaviour is as expected. In the process of developing and maintaining safety-critical interactive systems (systems in which failure can lead to serious injury or even fatalities [12,15]) this is particularly important. Models and model-based testing are useful techniques to employ when testing interactive systems as they focus on different aspects of the system, the functionality or the usability, which provides flexibility when designing tests.

In order to model the system behaviour, interaction sequences can be used as a simple abstraction. An interaction sequence is the series of steps a user can take to perform a certain task or arbitrarily explore an interactive system. We can derive these sequences at different points in the development life-cycle, for example from formal specifications, system prototypes or from implementations. Interaction sequences can take many different forms depending on the specific technique being used and the required level of abstraction. In our work we describe the sequences in terms of system states, widgets of the user interface (UI), user tasks, or combinations of these. We formalise these sequences using Presentation Models (PM) (see [4]) and Finite State Automata (FSA).

© Springer Nature Switzerland AG 2018
M. Mazzara et al. (Eds.): STAF 2018 Workshops, LNCS 11176, pp. 257–273, 2018.
https://doi.org/10.1007/978-3-030-04771-9_20

Regardless of how the sequences are formalised, conceptually we can think of them as never-ending and they can also be combined in an inexhaustible number of ways. This is reflected in the models of sequences as an increased number of states which can lead to intractably large models—the state explosion problem. The main contribution of this paper is an approach using abstraction of parts of a sequence to address this problem. We define the property of *self-containment* and use this to abstract parts of the model into an *abstract state*, consequently reducing the state space. By abstracting sequences using this property we are able to hide certain parts of the model, however we can also retrieve this information if required by expanding the abstract state without loss of information. Therefore, we may be able to reduce and expand the state space using the self-containment property, providing the ability to constrain the size of the model.

2   Background and Related Work

In this research, our focus is on modelling interaction sequences, specifically task-widget based sequences (we will discuss different types of sequences in more depth later). Several approaches to modelling interaction sequences in the domain of interactive system testing exist. A common theme between different approaches is how to constrain or limit the models so that they remain tractable. We discuss the most relevant techniques to our work here.

The use of directed graphs is a popular visualisation for many of the techniques we will discuss here, such as Event Flow Graphs (EFG) [10], FSA (used here interchangeably with Finite State Machines (FSM)) [1,7,8,13,16,18,19], and hierarchical Task Models [2,5,11]. Directed graphs establish specific paths through a graph which allow us to traverse specific orderings. They allow us to view and easily understand how we can generate sequences of varying lengths.

There are different ways in which state explosion in directed graphs can be managed. One approach is to limit by sequence length, which is utilised by Nguyen *et al.* in the creation of their testing tool GUITAR [10]. They utilise interaction sequences to describe systems using EFGs. All sequences of a given length (such as two) are then generated and they systematically explore these sequences. Constraining sequences to a defined length gives control over the state space size, however, it does also potentially hide behaviours that could be exposed by longer sequences, or combinations of longer sequences.

Finite state automata, or more specifically Mealy machines, are used to model systems for testing purposes by making certain assumptions about the System Under Test (SUT), and modelling the system based on input/output pairs [18]. To address the state explosion problem an extended finite state machine (EFSM) is used which has variables to store important information. For example, a time-out counter variable can be used instead of three duplicated timeout states. This reduces the number of states required to model the SUT and restricts the length of the sequences. It is possible to have lengthy sequences with no duplication and using an EFSM does not guarantee constraining models to a tractable size.

Interaction sequences are also used in some testing approaches where well-known traversal algorithms, or variations of these, are used to explore their models. This is another approach which focuses on restricting the sequence length to those generated by specific traversal algorithms. For example, Salem presents an approach where an FSA is converted so they can be explored using the UPPAAL model checker, this method allows them to avoid direct state-explosion [13]. In [7] Huang *et al.* use weight based methods to calculate paths of a specified length to traverse through the models. Essentially these approaches, and others like them, allow the traversal algorithm to "trim" the model. For example, a weighted strategy only traverses sequences which are more likely to occur based on probability metrics. This type of strategy only works under certain conditions for specific types of software (such as GUI-based applications as in [7]) and further abstraction is often required to reduce the model's complexity.

The symmetry property is introduced in [8] by Ip and Dill, which can be applied to directed graphs to simplify them. They argue if a series of states results in the same output, it does not matter which path is taken, as the result is the same. This use of symmetry could, "help to reduce even infinitely long graphs", and as a consequence reduce the overall sequence length. However, we found that symmetry is not common in interaction sequences. Complete Interaction Sequences (CIS) are a way to model the responsibilities (what the system should allow the user to perform) of an interface rather than the user actions [19]. Using FSA to model these responsibilities still results in the state explosion problem. In order to reduce the number of states, strongly connected components, or symmetric components, are identified and abstracted into a 'super' state. This gives a significant reduction in the number of sequences, as well as their length. While these interaction sequences differ from those we present (they consider sequences at a higher level of abstraction) the identification of specific components as the basis for abstraction is relevant to our work and has informed our approach.

Another way of constraining interaction sequences is to focus on specific tasks. This allows us to consider only sequences aimed at satisfying specific goals (although many different sequences may satisfy the same task). Since the sequences used are based on tasks and widgets, the extensive literature on task modelling is relevant. Particularly those based around tools for modelling interactive systems such as CTT [11] and HAMSTERS [2]. These task models focus on the set of steps a user takes to complete a certain task, and in this respect form the basis for own approach. The main point of difference from the modelling perspective is that while task models typically view the system relationships at a higher level and hierarchically decompose tasks into smaller and smaller steps, we use the task as a mechanism for composing user actions into specific groupings, which enables us to limit interaction sequence length (combining the two methods of length and tasks). We link these task definitions to system actions specifically via the widget descriptions.

3 Interaction Sequences

We have identified three perspectives which can be used as the basis for interaction sequences, these are state-based; task-based; and widget-based. We can use these individually, or in combination with each other to build sequences.

State-based sequences are created by identifying the different states (which may relate to composite states, windows, dialogs or modes) available in a system and how the user is able to transition between these states. Task-based sequences are created by taking a goal (as a task description) the user wishes to achieve, and then listing the interactions (or set of interactions) it takes to achieve that goal. Lastly, widget-based sequences are created by identifying the different widgets that are available in the system and the actions associated with those widgets.

Our larger goal for modelling interaction sequences is to adapt them for interactive system testing purposes. This leads to the following requirements for our sequences (we discuss each of these requirements next):

1. We must be able to automatically generate sequences of varying lengths so that the testing process is faster.
2. We must be able to constrain the sequence length in order to avoid the state explosion problem.
3. The sequences must allow us to clearly identify why the system did not behave as expected, for example by producing counter-examples.

3.1 Automatic Generation

We can already automatically generate interaction sequences of varying lengths using the Presentation Models (PM) of the SUT. PMs provide us with an abstract view of the interactive component of an interactive system with widgets described as triples of the form: "$((WidgetName, WidgetCategory, (Behaviour(s)))$". To build sequences we begin by modelling the PMs of the SUT, taking into account the widgets and their related actions, for example "Button1" has the action "Press". In order to be able to build these models and their respective sequences, we must have a thorough understanding of the system. It is expected in a good engineering design process this knowledge is readily available from task models, user-centred design artefacts, specifications etc. We make assumptions about the sequence based on internal values of the system (for example, we may want to generate a sequence where a counter variable is 10) and generate steps of the form: "$<action><widget><number\ of\ interactions>$". Once we have a generated sequence we can then model this as an FSA.

We use FSA to model the sequences due to their simplicity and the advantage of being able to draw on existing, well-defined, theory (other approaches have used FSA to model interaction systems see [1,5,16] for similar advantages). This enables us to manipulate FSA using standard techniques, such as removal of non-determinism or minimisation. We can easily combine multiple FSA by making use of task ordering knowledge and techniques, such as union or concatenation.

We can generate subsequences of any given sequence by traversing its FSA via different traversal algorithms. When sequences are adapted for testing this is a useful characteristic of the sequence models, as it allows us to explore variations of particular tasks and exploring such variations is more likely to expose errors. This also mimics users' behaviour, in that they typically do not always follow a pre-defined sequence for a particular task if there are several alternatives.

It is typical in interaction sequences to focus mainly on either direct (see [3,17]) or response (see [9,14]) actions. Direct actions are the literal actions performed by the user, for example "Press Ok 1". Response actions are the actions that the user will perform in response to a change in the system, for example "Observe Display". In this work we use both direct and response actions to create a complete set of actions for our sequences.

3.2 Constraining Sequence Length

The focus of this paper is to address this second requirement, that is to lessen the state explosion problem by constraining sequence length. When we first began using interaction sequences for larger and more complex interactive systems we found that using existing theory, such as removal of non-determinism and minimisation, was not enough alone to ensure tractability. Using these techniques resulted in a loss of information in the models, and thus the meaning of the behaviour of the sequence changed. Therefore, we needed a technique which would allow us to hide information, or rather abstract it.

Our first attempt to solve this was to focus solely on task-widget based sequences. Widgets allow us to divide the sequence into steps based on the interactions with those widgets, this allow us to describe sequences consistently. The simplest way to constrain a sequence which "never ends" is to limit the length of that sequence, tasks allow us to do this as every task has a defined "end point" or "goal". From experimentation with different types of models and sequences we found this did not provide a solution. The reason for this being that it resulted in a loss of information about the interaction sequence and its behaviour. The use of FSA to model task-widget based sequences reduces the sequence length further, as it constrains us to subsets of sequences for specific tasks, but it is still not enough to fully solve the state explosion problem. The contribution of this paper is, therefore, a method to address this.

3.3 Using Interaction Sequences for Testing

This requirement further influenced the choice of sequences to task-widget based. The task-based sequences on their own were too "restrictive" in the sense that they did not allow for easy generation while the widget-based sequences were too "free" (allowing for never ending sequences), hence the need for the combination. The state-based sequences have the potential to unintentionally hide widgets of the system which do not have an observable effect on state, resulting in poor coverage of the system behaviour, and for this reason would not be appropriate to use either alone or in combination with the other types. Requirement three will be addressed in future work and we do not discuss this further beyond the implications it has for the work we describe.

4   Definitions

In this research FSA are used to model interaction sequences. Our purpose is to make these models more tractable and therefore we introduce 'the self-containment property'. In what follows we define: the machines as a variation of traditional FSA (Definition 1); the self-containment property (Definition 4); abstraction (Definition 7); and expansion of these machines (Definition 8) also supporting definitions for: paths (Definition 2); connectedness (Definition 3); alphabet function (Definition 5); override function (Definition 6). We follow this in the next section with lemmas (and their proofs) to show that these definitions have the useful properties we expect and that they have captured the properties necessary to address the state explosion problem.

Definition 1. *A finite state automaton (FSA) is of the form* $M \stackrel{def}{=} (Q, \Sigma, \delta, S, F)$ *where:*

1. *Q is a finite set of states,*
2. *Σ is a finite set of symbols, the alphabet accepted by M,*
3. *δ is a finite set of triples which defines the transitions of machine M, i.e. given states $q, q' \in Q$, input $x \in \Sigma$, we can denote each transition as (q, x, q'),*
4. *S is the set of start states and $S \subseteq Q$,*
5. *F is the set of final (accepting) states and $F \subseteq Q$.*

Definition 2. *Given a finite state automaton $M = (Q, \Sigma, \delta, S, F)$, a path ρ from $q \in Q$ to $q' \in Q$ is a sequence of transitions from δ such that ρ is the empty sequence $< >$, or ρ has first element $(q, x, q'') \in \delta$ and the remainder of ρ is a path from q'' to q'.*

If a path exists between two states $q, q' \in Q$ we say that q' is reachable from q.

Definition 3. *A FSA is connected iff every state is reachable from a start state.*

Definition 4. *Given machine $M = (Q, \Sigma, \delta, S, F)$ we define a machine $M_s \stackrel{def}{=} (Q_s, \Sigma_s, \delta_s, S_s, F_s)$ which is self-contained with respect to M iff:*

1. *$Q_s \subseteq Q$, $\Sigma_s \subseteq \Sigma$, $\delta_s \subseteq \delta$,*
2. *M_s is closed with respect to M, which means that if any transition in δ starts and ends in Q_s then it is in δ_s too: $\delta_s = \{(q_s, x, q'_s) | (q_s, x, q'_s) \in \delta \wedge q_s, q'_s \in Q_s\}$,*
3. *The only transitions of M that start outside M_s and end inside M_s are those that end in start states of M_s: for all $(q, x, q') \in \delta$, if $q \in Q \setminus Q_s$ and $q' \in Q_s$ then $q' \in S_s$,*

4. *The only transitions of M that start inside M_s and end outside M_s are those that start in final states of M_s: for all $(q, x, q') \in \delta$, if $q \in Q_s$ and $q' \in Q \setminus Q_s$ then $q \in F_s$.*

Definition 5. *There is an alphabet function such that, for any machine $M = (Q, \Sigma, \delta, S, F)$ we have $\alpha(\delta) \stackrel{def}{=} \{x | (q, x, q') \in \delta\}$.*

Definition 6. *For any machine $M = (Q, \Sigma, \delta, S, F)$ we can override its set of transitions δ as follows with the override function:*

$$\substack{P \\ p'} \delta \substack{Q \\ q'} \stackrel{def}{=} \left\{ \begin{cases} (p'x, r'), & \text{if } r \in P \\ (r, x, r'), & \text{otherwise} \end{cases} \middle| (r, x, r') \in \delta' \right\}$$

where

$$\delta' \stackrel{def}{=} \left\{ \begin{cases} (r, x, q'), & \text{if } r' \in Q \\ (r, x, r'), & \text{otherwise} \end{cases} \middle| (r, x, r') \in \delta \right\}.$$

Note: In what follows, we are dealing specifically with interaction sequences, thus a FSA will always be connected, however, the proofs do not rely on this. We also assume that a FSA's alphabet is exactly the set of symbols that label its transitions, i.e. for all FSAs $(Q, \Sigma, \delta, S, F)$ we have $\alpha(\delta) \stackrel{def}{=} \Sigma$. **End note.**

Definition 7. *Given machine $M = (Q, \Sigma, \delta, S, F)$ where $S \neq \emptyset$ and $F \neq \emptyset$ (we call M the machine abstracted on), machine $M_s = (Q_s, \Sigma_s, \delta_s, S_s, F_s)$ where M_s is self-contained with respect to M, and an abstract state x where $x \notin Q, Q_s$ then an abstract machine $M_a \stackrel{def}{=} (Q_a, \Sigma_a, \delta_a, S_a, F_a)$ where:*

1. $Q_a = (Q \setminus Q_s) \cup \{x\}$,
2. $\Sigma_a \subseteq \Sigma$,
3. $\delta_a = \substack{F \\ x}(\delta \setminus \delta_s)\substack{S \\ x}$,
4. $(S \cap Q_s = \emptyset \implies S_a = S) \wedge (S \cap Q_s \neq \emptyset \implies S_a = \{x\})$,
5. $(F \cap Q_s = \emptyset \implies F_a = F) \wedge (F \cap Q_s \neq \emptyset \implies F_a = \{x\})$.

The abstract machine is essentially the original machine we started with except with the removal of the self-contained machine. However, this would result in a machine which is not connected, indicating a non-connected interaction sequence. This would be a confusing model of a sequence as it would be unclear how to process a path through the states which were originally connected to the self-contained machine. Therefore, we introduce the abstract state to indicate that an abstraction has taken place and at which point this occurred. The transitions that originally finished and started in the the self-contained machine start and final states are then overridden to reflect this change.

Definition 8. *Given abstract machine $M_a = (Q_a, \Sigma_a, \delta_a, S_a, F_a)$ with abstract state $x \in Q_a$ and any machine $M = (Q, \Sigma, \delta, S, F)$ with $x \notin Q$, there is a machine M_b, which we call the expansion of M_a with respect to M, and $M_b \stackrel{def}{=} (Q_b, \Sigma_b, \delta_b, S_b, F_b)$ where:*

1. $\Sigma_b = \Sigma_a \cup \Sigma$,
2. $Q_b = (Q_a \backslash \{x\}) \cup Q$,
3. $\delta_b = \delta \bigcup_{s \in S, f \in F} (_f^{\{x\}}(\delta_a)_s^{\{x\}})$, *which is to say x as a "from" state in a transition is replaced by the final states of M, and x as the "to" state in any transition is replaced by the start states of M,*
4. *If S_a contains only x then S_b contains only s. Otherwise $S_b = S_a$,*
5. *If F_a contains only x then F_b contains only f. Otherwise $F_b = F_a$.*

At some point we may wish to explore the sequence in the self-contained machine, therefore we needed a way to expand the abstract state. Definition 8 shows how we can correctly expand this state, allowing us to reconstruct our original machine. As a result we can reduce and expand the state space.

5   Results

In this section we will prove some results that give some evidence that our definitions correctly capture our intuitions.

Lemma 1. *For any machine $M = (Q, \Sigma, \delta, S, F)$ with $s, f \notin Q$, there is an equivalent machine $M_c \overset{def}{=} (Q_c, \Sigma_c, \delta_c, S_c, F_c)$ where:*

1. *S is not a singleton set and*
   (a) $Q_c = Q \cup \{s\}$,
   (b) $\Sigma_c = \Sigma \cup \{\epsilon\}$ *where ϵ is the blank symbol,*
   (c) $\delta_c = \delta$ *and for all $(q, x, q') \in \delta_c$, if $q \in S$ then $\delta_c = \delta_c \cup (s, \epsilon, q)$,*
   (d) $S_c = \{s\}$,
   (e) $F_c = F$.
2. *F is not a singleton set and*
   (a) $Q_c = Q \cup \{f\}$,
   (b) $\Sigma_c = \Sigma \cup \{\epsilon\}$,
   (c) $\delta_c = \delta$ *and for all $(q, x, q') \in \delta_c$, if $q' \in F$ then $\delta_c = \delta_c \cup (q', \epsilon, f)$,*
   (d) $S_c = S$,
   (e) $F_c = \{f\}$.

Proof: Section 2.2 [6, p. 26] states that a string w with ϵs (ϵ representing the blank symbol) in is equivalent to w. Therefore, by Theorem 3.8 from [6, p. 65] the new machine is equivalent to M as it accepts the same language.   □

Task-widget based interaction sequences have a defined single start and end point to the sequence due to the nature of tasks, and thus have singleton start and final state sets. However, we could have machines which do not. Lemma 1 shows that for any machine there is an equivalent machine with singleton start and final state sets, thus we do not have to include this as a restriction.

Lemma 2. *Given a machine $M = (Q, \Sigma, \delta, S, F)$, M is self-contained with respect to itself.*

Proof:

1. Immediate.
2. Immediate.
3. There are no states of M outside M, therefore implication is true (since false implies anything, *ex falso quod libet*).
4. Similarly to 3.

□

Lemma 2 proves that for any given machine it is self-contained with respect to itself. This addresses the state explosion problem in the most extreme case as we can now take any machine and reduce the state space to exactly one state, the abstract state. However, this also results in loss of all information for that machine as it is hidden inside this abstract state. While this solves the state explosion problem, it is not particularly useful or interesting, especially not in consideration of adapting the sequences and their consequent models for testing.

Our main result is that, under certain circumstances, we can take a machine M, abstract it with respect to machine M_s (where M_s is self-contained with respect to M) to get abstract machine M_a, and then expand M_a with respect to M_s to get machine M again. While we have all of the component parts in the definitions above, there is still a crucial relationship amongst the various machines that we are missing, and this is that we have, of course, to be able to re-connect the start and final states as originally intended when expanding the abstract machine. The definitions so far, while allowing re-connection, lose crucial information about start and final states. The property that we require for our main result ensures that this information can be recovered. The property is that if *any* state of the self-contained machine M_s is also a start state of the machine M it is self-contained with respect to, then the start states of the self-contained machine *must be* the start states of the original machine. Essentially we need this as we use the start and final states as "markers" to show how the various machines fit together properly when we do the expansion. It turns out that this also requires that all the machines involved have singleton start and final state sets, but we already know (by Lemma 1) that this is not a restriction.

All this leads to needing the following:

Definition 9. *Given machine* $M = (Q, \Sigma, \delta, S, F)$ *and machine* $M_s = (Q_s, \Sigma_s, \delta_s, S_s, F_s)$ *which is self-contained with respect to* M, *then* M *and* M_s *have the SF property iff: if any state of* M_s *is also a start state* M, *then the start states of* M_s *must be the start states of* M, *i.e.*

$$Q_s \cap S \neq \emptyset \implies S_s = S$$

and similarly for final states

$$Q_s \cap F \neq \emptyset \implies F_s = F$$

Note that in our case where we can assume all machines have singleton start and final state sets, these conditions simplify to

$$s \in Q_s \implies s_s = s$$

and

$$f \in Q_s \implies f_s = f$$

because $S = \{s\}, F = \{f\}, S_s = \{s_s\}$ *and* $F_s = \{f_s\}$.

Lemma 3. *Let* $M = (Q, \Sigma, \delta, \{s\}, \{f\})$ *be any machine for modelling inter-action sequences and* $M_s = (Q_s, \Sigma_s, \delta_s, \{s_s\}, \{f_s\})$ *be a self-contained machine with respect to* M. *We are assuming without loss of generality that machines* M *and* M_s *have singleton start and final sets, by Lemma 1. We require that* M *and* M_s *have the SF property (Definition 9). Further, let* $M_a = (Q_a, \Sigma_a, \delta_a, S_a, F_a)$ *be an abstract machine with abstract state* $x \notin Q, Q_s$, *where* M_s *is the machine abstracted on. Finally, we assume a machine* $M_b = (Q_b, \Sigma_b, \delta_b, S_b, F_b)$ *which is the expansion of* M_a *with respect to* M_s. *Then our result is that machine* M_b *is equivalent to machine* M.

Proof

We have

$$\delta_a = {}^{\{f_s\}}_x(\delta \setminus \delta_s)^{\{s_s\}}_x \qquad \text{from Definition 7} \qquad (1)$$

and

$$
\begin{aligned}
\delta_b &= \delta_s \cup \; {}^{\{x\}}_{f_s}(\delta_a)^{\{x\}}_{s_s} & \text{from Definition 8} \quad (2) \\
&= \delta_s \cup \; {}^{\{x\}}_{f_s}(\; {}^{\{f_s\}}_x(\delta \setminus \delta_s)^{\{s_s\}}_x)^{\{x\}}_{s_s} & \text{substituting from 1} (3) \\
&= \delta_s \cup (\delta \setminus \delta_s) & \text{over-riding and then reversing} (4) \\
&= \delta & \delta_s \subseteq \delta \text{ from Definition 4 and set theory} \\
& & (5)
\end{aligned}
$$

So also

$$
\begin{aligned}
\Sigma &= \alpha(\delta) & \text{by our Note above} & \quad (6) \\
&= \alpha(\delta_b) & \text{by substitution and (2)-(5)} & \quad (7) \\
&= \Sigma_b & \text{by our Note above} & \quad (8)
\end{aligned}
$$

Then

$$
\begin{aligned}
Q_b &= (Q_a \setminus \{x\}) \cup Q_s & \text{by Definition 8} & \quad (9) \\
&= (((Q \setminus Q_s) \cup \{x\}) \setminus \{x\}) \cup Q_s & \text{by Definition 7} \, Q_a = (Q \setminus Q_s) \cup \{x\} & \\
& & & (10) \\
&= (Q \setminus Q_s) \cup Q_s & \text{by Definition 7} \, x \notin Q, Q_s & \quad (11) \\
&= Q & Q_s \subseteq Q \text{ from Definition 4 and set theory} & \\
& & & (12)
\end{aligned}
$$

Turning to the start states, recall from Definition 8 if S_a contains only x then S_b contains only s_s. Otherwise $S_b = S_a$. Within those cases each has to consider whether or not $s \in Q_s$. We proceed by nested cases.

$$\text{Assume } S_a \text{ contains only } x, \text{ so } S_a = \{x\}. \qquad (13a)$$

Now we have further cases depending on $s \in Q_s$.

$$\text{Assume} s \in Q_s \tag{13ba}$$
$$\{s\} = \{s_s\} \qquad \text{by Definition of 9 and 13ba} \tag{13bb}$$
$$= S_b \qquad \text{by consequence of 13a and Definition 8} \tag{13bc}$$

$$\text{Assume} s \notin Q_s \tag{13ca}$$
$$\{s\} = S_a \qquad \text{by Definition 7, since 13ca means } S \cap Q_s = \emptyset \tag{13cb}$$
$$= \{x\} \qquad \text{by 13a} \tag{13cc}$$
$$contradiction \qquad \text{Definition 7 requires } x \notin Q \text{ but } s \in Q \tag{13cd}$$

$$\text{Assume } S_a \neq \{x\} \tag{13d}$$

Now we have further cases depending on $s \in Q_s$

$$\text{Assume } s \in Q_s \tag{13ea}$$
$$S_a = \{x\} \qquad \text{by Definition 7 and 13ea} \tag{13eb}$$
$$contradiction \qquad \text{by 13d} \tag{13ec}$$

$$\text{Assume } s \notin Q_s \tag{13fa}$$
$$\{s\} = S_a \qquad \text{by 13fa and Definition 7} \tag{13fb}$$
$$= S_b \qquad \text{by 13d and Definition 8} \tag{13fc}$$

$$\text{By cases (twice) we conclude that } S_b = \{s\} \tag{13g}$$

Finally to the final states, recall that Definition 8 gives if F_a contains only x then F_b contains only f_s. Otherwise $F_b = F_a$. Within those cases each has to consider whether or not $f \in Q_s$. We proceed by nested cases.

$$\text{Assume } F_a \text{ contains only } x, \text{ so } F_a = \{x\}. \tag{13h}$$

Now we have further cases depending on $f \in Q_s$.

$$\text{Assume } f \in Q_s \tag{13ia}$$
$$\{f\} = \{f_s\} \qquad \text{by Definition of 9 and 13ia} \tag{13ib}$$
$$= F_b \qquad \text{by consequence of 13 h and Definition 8} \tag{13ic}$$

$$\text{Assume } f \notin Q_s \tag{13ja}$$
$$\{f\} = F_a \qquad \text{by Definition 7, since 13ja means } F \cap Q_s = \emptyset \tag{13jb}$$
$$= \{x\} \qquad \text{by 13h} \tag{13jc}$$
$$contradiction \qquad \text{Definition 7 requires } x \notin Q, \text{ but } f \in Q \tag{13jd}$$

$$\text{Assume } F_a \neq \{x\} \tag{13k}$$

Now we have further cases depending on $f \in Q_s$

$$\text{Assume } f \in Q_s \tag{13la}$$

$$F_a = \{x\} \qquad \text{by Definition 7 and 13la} \tag{13lb}$$

$$contradiction \qquad \text{by 13k} \tag{13lc}$$

$$\text{Assume } f \notin Q_s \tag{13ma}$$

$$\{f\} = F_a \qquad \text{by 13ma and Definition 7} \tag{13mb}$$

$$= F_b \qquad \text{by 13k and Definition 8} \tag{13mc}$$

$$\text{By cases (twice) we conclude that } F_b = \{f\} \tag{13n}$$

We have, in 2–5, 6–8, 9–12, 13g and 13n, that $M = M_b$ as required.   □

6   Infusion Pump Example

In this example we illustrate our main result as proven in Lemma 3 specifically for interaction sequences, in this case for a simplified infusion pump, created in reference to the Alaris GP Volumetric Pump (see Fig. 1). This simplified version has the functionality to set up an infusion based on duration, time and pump type; start, pause or stop an infusion; and view settings and check the battery life. In total it has six widgets which allow the user to perform different actions, these are the Up, Down, YesStart, NoStop, OnOff buttons, and Display.

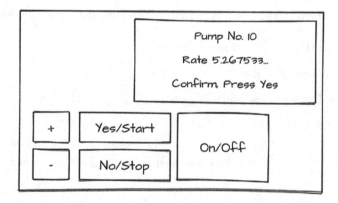

Fig. 1. Wireframe of: simplified medical infusion pump

We create a task-widget-based sequence for this device. The tasks are: setting up an infusion; starting the infusion; checking the settings; pausing and then stopping the infusion. Note that a task-based sequence does not need to be based on a single task, as in practice it is common to combine tasks to create more meaningful sequences. To generate the interaction sequence we must make a few assumptions, this is to ensure that the sequence is reproducible and has no ambiguity. In this example we assume that all initial values are set to 0; we begin in the initial state of the system; volume is set to 4ml and duration is set to 2 hours. Using the PM for this example we generate the following sequence.

1. Click YesStart 1.	7. Observe Display 1.	13. Observe Display 1.
2. Observe Display 1.	8. Click YesStart 1.	14. Click YesStart 1.
3. Click Up 4.	9. Observe Display 1.	15. Observe Display 1.
4. Observe Display 1.	10. Click YesStart 1.	16. Click YesStart 1.
5. Click YesStart 1.	11. Observe Display 1.	17. Observe Display 1.
6. Click Up 2.	12. Click YesStart 1.	18. Click NoStop 2.

We can now convert this sequence to an FSA. This involves using Definition 1 to construct a well-formed machine $M = \{Q, \Sigma, \delta, S, F\}$. For machine M, Q is the set of widgets used in the sequence and Σ is the set of interactions. δ represents the transitions of the machine in the form (q, x, q') where q is the widget from the previous step, x is the interaction of the current step, and q' is the widget from the current step. If a widget is interacted with more than once, for example "Click Up 4", then this step also has the transition (q', x, q'). The start set S is a singleton set comprising of the state "Initialise" which is a "place holder" to ensure that we have included the initial action performed on the YesStart as a triple in δ. The final set F is a singleton set including the final widget of the final step. Therefore, machine M is as follows:

$Q = \{Initialise, Display, NoStop, YesStart, Up\}$
$\Sigma = \{Click, Observe\}$
$\delta = \{(Initialise, Click, YesStart), (Display, Click, NoStop), (Display, Click,$
$YesStart), (Display, Click, Up), (NoStop, Click, NoStop), (YesStart, Click, Up),$
$(YesStart, Observe, Display), (Up, Click, Up), (Up, Observe, Display)\}$
$S = \{Initialise\}$
$F = \{NoStop\}$

Note that in FSA M we assume that the device is already switched on prior to any interaction. The FSA allows us to generate sequences of varying lengths for a specific task based on the assumptions. This has helped in reducing the number of sequences we explore due to the use of the task to constrain the sequence and consequently the model, in other words the FSA of the sequence.

We now apply the definition of self-containment (Definition 4) to this machine to construct machine $M_s = \{Q_s, \Sigma_s, \delta_s, S_s, F_s\}$:

$Q_s = \{Display, YesStart, Up\}$
$\Sigma_s = \{Click, Observe\}$
$\delta_s = \{(Display, Click, YesStart), (Display, Click, Up), (YesStart, Click, Up), (Yes$
$Start, Observe, Display), (Up, Click, Up), (Up, Observe, Display)\}$

$S_s = \{YesStart\}$
$F_s = \{Display\}$

M_s is not the only self-contained machine we can construct using Definition 4. As proven in Lemma 2 every machine is self-contained with respect to itself and in fact each single state could be a self-contained machine, however as stated previously this would not be particularly useful in terms of the state explosion problem. If we inspect M_s it contains all the widgets associated with setting up and starting the infusion. We are left with a sequence which we assume sets up and begins an infusion correctly, then explicitly pauses and stops that infusion.

To perform the abstraction we create a new FSA $M_a = \{Q_a, \Sigma_a, \delta_a, S_a, F_a\}$ as per Definition 7:

$Q_a = \{Initialise, \Omega_0, NoStop\}$
$\Sigma_a = \{Click\}$
$\delta_a = \{(Initialise, Click, \Omega_0), (\Omega_0, Click, NoStop), (NoStop, Click, NoStop)\}$
$S_a = \{Initialise\}$
$F_a = \{NoStop\}$

In this machine we have added an abstract state "Ω_0" representing M_s. In Lemma 3 the machine we are abstracting must have singleton start and final states in order to preserve equivalence, in this case M_s satisfies this condition. If required, we could apply Lemma 1 to M_s to ensure that this is true.

The abstract sequence for the same task is reduced from 18 steps to two. It is important to remember that this reduction comes from being able to not only contain the other 16 steps in a self-contained machine, but also from specifying a focus for later testing purposes. If we wish to test the setup and start of the infusion we could focus on the self-contained machine M_s, ignoring the last two steps of the original sequence, however the reduction here is significantly smaller.

Using Definition 8 we can reconstruct our original machine M by expanding the abstract state. The input transitions to the abstract state are re-directed to the start state of the sub-machine, and the output transitions are now output transitions of the final state of the sub-machine.

The new machine $M_b = \{Q_b, \Sigma_b, \delta_b, S_b, F_b\}$ as per Definition 8:

$Q_b = \{Initialise, Display, NoStop, YesStart, Up\}$
$\Sigma_b = \{Click, Observe\}$
$\delta_b = \{(Initialise, Click, YesStart), (Display, Click, NoStop), (Display, Click, Yes$
$Start), (Display, Click, Up), (NoStop, Click, NoStop), (YesStart, Click, Up),$
$(YesStart, Observe, Display), (Up, Click, Up), (Up, Observe, Display)\}$
$S_b = \{Initialise\}$
$F_b = \{NoStop\}$

As expected from Lemma 3 M and M_b are equivalent machines. This result illustrates that even in a small example we can significantly reduce the number of states in a machine of the form in Definition 1, thus addressing the state explosion problem. Furthermore, should we wish to revisit the original machine we are able to expand the abstract state, this allows us to hide, rather than lose, information, which may become important when adapting the sequences for testing purposes. More importantly, this gives control over the size of the state space to reduce and expand as required.

To demonstrate the use of our technique, in this example we show machine M and then build the corresponding abstract machine. However, in practical use we envision that machines will be constructed with abstract states to hide certain parts of an interactive system, which can be modelled later (or not at all). For example, in a safety-critical interactive system we may wish to focus specifically on the safety-critical aspects of that system, we may construct an abstract machine which hides the non-safety-critical aspects in abstract states. We will then be able to use this technique to expand the abstract state if required.

7 Future Work and Conclusions

In this paper we have introduced a new technique for abstracting and expanding states in an FSA representing interaction sequences to provide more control over the state space. We described how we use tasks and widgets to describe interaction sequences and how we formalise them using PMs and FSA. We discussed sequence length and tasks to constrain sequences to avoid intractable models. We also highlighted how this in combination with existing techniques such as FSA minimisation was not enough to address the state explosion problem.

This led to further investigation into abstraction within models to address this problem. The main contribution of this paper was to define the self-containment property and how this is used to further abstract and constrain sequences. Furthermore, we showed how we could expand the abstract state to include the hidden information, allowing us to reduce and expand the state space as required. This not only addressed the state explosion problem but also provided us with greater control over the state space and results in more tractable models.

Our modelling approach is not without limitations, the major concern being we could have a model which contains no self-contained sub-models (beyond the trivial case of abstracting to a single state). In this instance we are not be able to abstract the model further using this method. It is possible that this could occur in a highly inter-connected system and further investigation is required.

Furthermore, while we can use the self-containment property to construct the abstract machine automatically, we cannot know if this abstraction will be useful or not (in terms of adapting the sequences for testing purposes). Keeping in mind that we can abstract an entire machine to a single abstract state, we leave it to human reasoning to determine if abstracting a self-contained machine provides benefits or not from a testing perspective. Future work will involve investigations into adapting this approach for testing and the implications of the abstraction in the testing environment.

References

1. Banu-Demergian, I.T., Stefanescu, G.: Towards a formal representation of interactive systems. Fundam. Inform. **131**(3–4), 313–336 (2014)
2. Barboni, E., Ladry, J.F., Navarre, D., Palanque, P., Winckler, M.: Beyond modelling: an integrated environment supporting co-execution of tasks and systems models. In: Proceedings of the 2nd ACM SIGCHI Symposium on Engineering Interactive Computing Systems, pp. 165–174. ACM (2010)
3. Bauersfeld, S., Vos, T.E.: GUItest: a Java library for fully automated GUI robustness testing. In: Proceedings of the 27th IEEE/ACM International Conference on Automated Software Engineering, pp. 330–333. ACM (2012)
4. Bowen, J., Reeves, S.: Formal models for user interface design artefacts. Innov. Syst. Softw. Eng. **4**(2), 125–141 (2008)
5. Campos, J.C., Fayollas, C., Gonçalves, M., Martinie, C., Navarre, D., Palanque, P., Pinto, M.: A more intelligent test case generation approach through task models manipulation. Proc. ACM Hum.-Comput. Interact. **1**(1), 9 (2017)
6. Hopcroft, J.E.: Introduction to Automata Theory, Languages, and Computation. Pearson Education, London (1979)
7. Huang, C.Y., Chang, J.R., Chang, Y.H.: Design and analysis of GUI test-case prioritization using weight-based methods. J. Syst. Softw. **83**(4), 646–659 (2010)
8. Ip, C.N., Dill, D.L.: Better verification through symmetry. Form. Methods Syst. Des. **9**(1–2), 41–75 (1996)
9. Martinie, C., Palanque, P., Winckler, M.: Structuring and composition mechanisms to address scalability issues in task models. In: Campos, P., Graham, N., Jorge, J., Nunes, N., Palanque, P., Winckler, M. (eds.) INTERACT 2011. LNCS, vol. 6948, pp. 589–609. Springer, Heidelberg (2011). https://doi.org/10.1007/978-3-642-23765-2_40
10. Nguyen, B.N., Robbins, B., Banerjee, I., Memon, A.: GUITAR: an innovative tool for automated testing of GUI-driven software. Autom. Softw. Eng. **21**(1), 65–105 (2014)
11. Paternò, F., Zini, E.: Applying information visualization techniques to visual representations of task models. In: Proceedings of the 3rd Annual Conference on Task Models and Diagrams, pp. 105–111. ACM (2004)
12. Porrello, A.M.: Death and denial: the failure of the THERAC-25, a medical linear accelerator. Website (ND). http://users.csc.calpoly.edu/~jdalbey/SWE/Papers/THERAC25.html. Accessed 27 July 2015
13. Salem, P.: Practical programming, validation and verification with finite-state machines: a library and its industrial application. In: Proceedings of the 38th International Conference on Software Engineering Companion, pp. 51–60. ACM (2016)
14. Spano, L.D., Fenu, G.: IceTT: a responsive visualization for task models. In: Proceedings of the 2014 ACM SIGCHI Symposium on Engineering Interactive Computing Systems, pp. 197–200. ACM (2014)
15. The Economist: When code can kill or cure, June 2012. http://www.economist.com/node/21556098. Accessed 9 Dec 2015
16. Thimbleby, H.: Contributing to safety and due diligence in safety-critical interactive systems development by generating and analyzing finite state models. In: Proceedings of the 1st ACM SIGCHI Symposium on Engineering Interactive Computing systems, pp. 221–230. ACM (2009)

17. Thimbleby, H.: Action graphs and user performance analysis. Int. J. Hum.-Comput. Stud. **71**(3), 276–302 (2013)
18. Utting, M., Legeard, B.: Practical Model-Based Testing: A Tools Approach. Morgan Kaufmann-Elsevier Inc., Burlington (2010)
19. White, L., Almezen, H., Alzeidi, N.: User-based testing of GUI sequences and their interactions. In: Proceedings of 12th International Symposium on Software Reliability Engineering, ISSRE 2001, pp. 54–63. IEEE (2001)

Formal Modelling as a Component of User Centred Design

Michael D. Harrison[1]([✉])(iD), Paolo Masci[2](iD), and José Creissac Campos[2](iD)

[1] School of Computing, Newcastle University, Urban Sciences Building,
Newcastle upon Tyne, UK
michael.harrison@ncl.ac.uk
[2] HASLab/INESC-TEC and Department Informatics/University of Minho,
Campus de Gualtar, Braga, Portugal
paolo.masci@inesctec.pt, jose.campos@di.uminho.pt

Abstract. User centred design approaches typically focus understanding on context and producing sketch designs. These sketches are often non functional (e.g., paper) prototypes. They provide a means of exploring candidate design possibilities using techniques such as cooperative evaluation. This paper describes a further step in the process using formal analysis techniques. The sketch design of a device is enhanced into a specification that is then analysed using formal techniques, thus providing a systematic approach to checking plausibility and consistency during early design stages. Once analysed, a further prototype is constructed using an executable form of the specification, providing the next candidate for evaluation with potential users. The technique is illustrated through an example based on a pill dispenser.

1 Introduction

User centred design approaches are designed to satisfy Gould and Lewis's guiding principles [7]: (i) to focus on user tasks early and throughout the design process; (ii) to measure usability empirically; (iii) to design and test iteratively. These approaches are important where devices can be used in a variety of different contexts by different users with different backgrounds and where the consequences of misuse can compromise safety. A variety of techniques exist that satisfy these principles to a greater or lesser extent. Contextual design [1] and scenario based design [5] are examples. Contextual design aims to understand the context through observation to identify what would help improve the situation in which the proposed design is to be used. This process involves focussing on user needs and tasks, asking questions of the following type (taking a medical example): *"Who enters patient, medicine and prescription details in the medical device, and where do these activities happen? How and where are reminders produced and how does the patient access the dose?"*. Contextual design and scenario based design techniques use *scenarios* that capture typical or exceptional situations in which a possible design would be used.

© Springer Nature Switzerland AG 2018
M. Mazzara et al. (Eds.): STAF 2018 Workshops, LNCS 11176, pp. 274–289, 2018.
https://doi.org/10.1007/978-3-030-04771-9_21

The *sketch designs* developed as a result of this process are often initially non-functional (for example it could be a simple PowerPoint presentation or a paper storyboard). They are developed and evaluated by letting end users interact with the sketch design in selected scenarios of use. Think aloud techniques such as cooperative evaluation [13] are typically used to collect feedback that is useful to improve the design and judge whether a further iteration would be appropriate.

The focus of this paper is *the nature of the sketch design and the process of development of the final design*. This paper briefly explores integration of the informal, though structured, approach typical of contextual design and scenario based design with formal techniques. An example based on an automated pill box for dispensing drugs to patients at specific times is used throughout the paper to present the approach.

In the following sections, first we describe how the initial sketch design was developed (Sect. 3.1). Then, an enhanced design is presented that fills various gaps observed of the initial design (Sect. 3.2). This design is checked for plausibility (Sect. 4) and against use-related requirements. The first use-related requirements are designed to check the consistency of the actions offered by the enhanced design (Sect. 5.1). Requirements also consider the reversibility of scrolling behaviour (Sect. 5.2). The iteration of the design (Sect. 6) is then described with a discussion of comparable approaches and further work (Sect. 7).

Contributions of the paper are: (1) an illustration and discussion of how existing formal tools could be used as part of a user centred design process; (2) a case study using a pill dispenser design as focus.

2   The Approach

The aim is to integrate the formal modelling process with user centred design. We do this through five steps.

Step 1: An initial interactive sketch design is created that demonstrates the different screens of the system, either as a storyboard or a non functional prototype. This provides the first candidate for evaluation with potential end users.

Step 2: Once evaluated, a revised design is created based on a formal model developed from the prototype. This initial formal specification includes details of modes, actions, and fields of each screen. This model is assessed for *plausibility*. The specification is plausible if it correctly reflects the designer's intention. This can be demonstrated through exploration of the executable form of the specification and also achieved by demonstrating that the design exhibits intended functional properties.

Step 3: The formal specification is iterated as a result of the assessment of step 2. The new version of the specification is analysed using formal verification technologies to explore inconsistencies and gaps in the proposed design.

Step 4: An executable formal specification, developed as a result of the analysis of step 3, provides the next candidate for evaluation with potential users.

Step 5: The process (steps 2–4) is repeated.

The steps of the method use the following tools provided by the PVSio-web toolkit: PVS [16] to develop and analyse the model; PVSio [15] to check its plausibility; the PVSio-web Storyboard Editor [18] to develop the initial sketch; the PVSio-web Prototype Builder [12] to produce an interactive prototype based on the PVS model. PVSio-web is a web-based environment that enables the creation of interactive prototypes based on executable PVS specifications. The toolkit supports the creation of both *storyboard-based prototypes* using mockup pictures of different screens of the system under development, and *high-fidelity prototypes* that can closely resemble the visual appearance and behaviour of a final product. The interactive prototype, so constructed, can be evaluated with end-users. The PVS language builds on higher-order logic, and provides an extensive library of constructs for representing complex system behaviours and datatypes. PVSio is a tool that extracts Common Lisp code from PVS executable specifications. This makes it possible to test the functionality of PVS specifications by evaluating ground expressions representing user actions performed on the system state.

3   Designing a Pill Dispenser

A pill dispenser is a medical device that provides doses of drugs to patients at specified times. While such devices are often designed for individual use, the considered example was designed to be used by groups of patients, perhaps in a care home common room or a hospital ward. The proposed initial design suggests a device that caters for the multiple and complex requirements of patients. While this service was initially sketched by engineers, it would be expected that, as part of a user centred approach, the initial design would have been informed by developing an understanding of the context in which the design is to be situated. The device as envisaged in early sketches alerts the patient when medicine is due and the patient responds and obtains their dose using a thumb print to ensure they are receiving the medication intended for them. The device maintains a database of patients who have been subscribed to the system as well as a database of medicines. The pill dispenser supports "columns" of pills from which the patient can obtain their required dose.

3.1   The Starting Point: The Sketch Design

A video was provided to the authors of an early prototype of the device. A storyboard was produced from this video (see Fig. 1). The display designs were sketched and transitions between displays indicated. The initial prototype was the sketch design. A state transition diagram described the transitions between displays (see Fig. 2). PVSio-web uses a graphical state transition language (emucharts a simplified version of Statecharts [9]) to describe the flow of the storyboards. The sketch screens are linked to nodes of the emuchart which can be translated automatically into PVS as illustrated in Listing 1.1. Figure 3 indicates a phase of the creation of the interactive storyboard in PVSio-web. Green areas on the left hand side of the sketch design represent interactive buttons that can be used to navigate to a different screen. The full list of screens used to develop the sketch design is shown at the bottom-left corner of the figure.

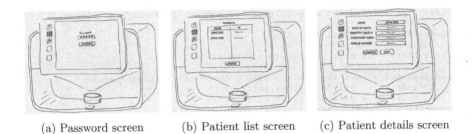

| (a) Password screen | (b) Patient list screen | (c) Patient details screen |

Fig. 1. Example display images produced for the initial prototype.

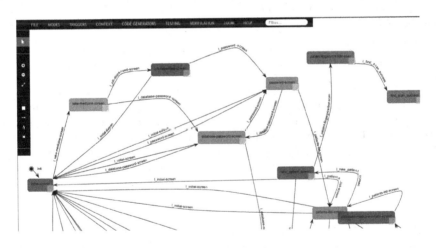

Fig. 2. The initial sketch: state transition diagram

The initial sketch design, as represented in the video, illustrated three user pathways. *The first pathway* allows entry, or modification, of patient details. This requires use of a password and involves the nurse or carer responsible for setting up patient details. New patient information can be entered, including the patient's thumb print for validation purposes, or a list of existing patients in the database is displayed which can be scrolled up or down to allow access to all patients for selection. Details of the patients can be changed. Each patient has up to five prescriptions (in this version of the prototype). A prescription can be added or removed and includes details of time and frequency of each drug prescribed. *The second pathway*, also protected by password, allows access by carers or nurses or doctors who are able to enter details of medicines. This pathway allows entry or editing of medicines. In a similar way the medicine pathway allows medicines to be listed or displayed and modified.

```
pill_dispenser: THEORY BEGIN
  %-- operating modes
  Mode: TYPE = { initial_screen, password_screen, patients_list_screen, ...}
  %-- state attributes
  State: TYPE = [# mode: Mode #]
  %-- init function
  init: State = (# mode := initial_screen #)
  %-- transition functions
  per_password_screen(st: State): bool = (mode(st) = initial_screen)
    OR (mode(st) = pill_dispensed_screen)
    OR (mode(st) = database_password_screen)
  password_screen(st: (per_password_screen)): State =
    COND
      mode(st) = initial_screen
      -> LET st = leave(initial_screen)(st)
           IN enter(password_screen)(st),
      mode(st) = pill_dispensed_screen
      -> LET st = leave(pill_dispensed_screen)(st)
           IN enter(password_screen)(st),
      mode(st) = database_password_screen
      -> LET st = leave(database_password_screen)(st)
           IN enter(password_screen)(st)
    ENDCOND
  %-- ...more transition functions omitted
END pill_dispenser
```

Listing 1.1. PVS specification generated from the emuchart

The third pathway was not provided in the video and further information would be required to complete it. As is common in design approaches of this kind the current version of the design is partial. Further iteration will flesh out the details of the design. This pathway identifies and alerts the patient who is required to take their medicine. The patient's thumbprint is required to access the dose. The paper focuses on the two pathways that were illustrated in the original video.

3.2   The Enhanced Model

Additional details about modes, actions and field types present in each screen are now added to the initial model and the model is restructured. The full specification of the illustrated case study may be found at our repository[1]. This model of the design is based on actions that are invoked when the user presses a control that is visible on the display. The revised model provides more detail of the interaction: which actions are available; which fields must be entered before an action can be completed. Actions of selecting and entering fields are included as well as, in some cases, concrete examples of information in the pillbox (e.g., patient names, content of prescription charts, and so on). The pill dispenser screen is assumed to be a touch screen but for present purposes the details of how the pressing takes place is not a concern. These actions cause transitions between modes. Further transitions are caused by selecting fields and entering values.

---

[1] http://hcispecs.di.uminho.pt/m/8.

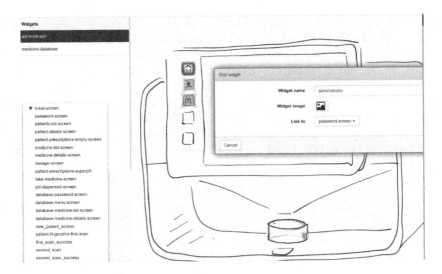

Fig. 3. Phase of the creation of the initial sketch design using PVSio-web.

These transitions do not change mode. They add to the set of fields that have been entered and also add the values entered to temporary records of patients, their prescriptions or medicines (depending on mode). Modes, actions and fields are represented using `mode_type` (lines 1–2 of Listing 1.2), `actions_type` (line 3) and `fields_type` (line 5).The availability or visibility of actions and fields is made explicit using boolean functions, for example (in the case of actions) `available_actions_type` (line 4). The state of the device is represented by a type `state`, a fragment of the definition is illustrated in line 7–12.

```
1  mode_type: TYPE = { initial, pwd, db_pwd, db_menu, patient_list,
2                      db_med_list, new_patient_details, ... }
3  actions_type : TYPE = { key1, key2, key3, confirm, create, ... }
4  available_actions_type : TYPE = [ actions_type -> boolean ]
5  fields_type : TYPE = { password, dob, dosage, id_card, mob, carer, ... }
6  fields_set: TYPE = [ fields_type -> boolean ]
7  state: TYPE = [# mode: mode_type,
8                   vis_field: fields_set,
9                   sel_field: fields_set,
10                  ent_field: fields_set,
11                  action: available_actions_type,
12                  ... #]
```

Listing 1.2. Types used in the model of the first sketch

A PVS function is now illustrated that specifies the behaviour of the pill dispenser when the operator enters new patient details (Listing 1.3). The specification of the function includes identification of the actions that are visible (lines 5–7), the fields that are visible (lines 16–18), the fields that are selected (none in this case, see line 19) and the field that is entered (line 20). Within the mode, specified by the **mode** attribute of **state**, fields can be entered (as discussed below, and see definition of **enter** in Listing 1.5). In the initial state of this mode, described here, only one field is represented as entered, namely the patient name. For reasons of simplicity the name is taken to be generated automatically in this initial model (see definition of np in line 2).

Each time a field is entered the temporary patient record (temp_patient) is updated. In the initial transition (new_patient_details_screen) all fields are empty since this is a new patient except for the patient name. The temporary patient record (temp_patient, lines 8–11) is also set with the patient name (p_name, line 8) set to np, and the rest of the patient record set to null. Further temporary elements are set to null: temp_script (which identifies prescriptions associated with the patient) and temp_med (which is used when setting up the record for a medicine).

```
1  new_patient_details_screen(st: state): state =
2    LET np = next_pid(st`p_max)
3    IN clear_screen(st) WITH
4       [ mode := new_patient_details,
5         action := LAMBDA(x: actions_type):
6                   (x = key1) OR (x = key2) OR (x = key3) OR
7                   (x = confirm) OR (x = quit),
8         temp_patient := (# p_name := np,
9                            p_fields :=  LAMBDA(x: fields_type): FALSE,
10                           scripts_index := s_null,
11                           scripts := LAMBDA (s: s_index): nil_script #),
12        temp_script := nil_script,
13        temp_med := nil_med,
14        m_current := m_null,
15        p_current := np,
16        vis_field := LAMBDA(x: fields_type):
17                     (x = name) OR (x = dob) OR (x = id_card) OR
18                     (x = carer) OR (x = mob),
19        sel_field := LAMBDA(x: fields_type): FALSE,
20        ent_field := LAMBDA(x: fields_type): x = name ]
```

Listing 1.3. The specification of the new patient details screen

The patient database (Listing 1.4), is specified by type patient_db_type. This type describes a list of patient records. Patient records include fields associated with date of birth, carer and so on as well as the prescriptions that are associated with them (scripts). There is a limit to the number of scripts that can be associated with a patient as defined by type s_index.

```
1  list_script_type: TYPE = [s_index -> script_type]
2  patient_type: TYPE = [# p_name : p_index,
3                          p_fields : fields_set,
4                          scripts_index: s_index,
5                          scripts: list_script_type #]
6  patient_db_type: TYPE = list[patient_type]
```

Listing 1.4. Patient database types

Patient fields can be entered in mode new_patient_details. Entry of a field requires two pre-conditions. The field must be visible. Hence in Listing 1.3 (lines 16–18), name, dob, id_card, carer and mob are fields that are visible. A field must also be selected (only one field is selected at a time and selection is lost when the field is entered). Hence in line 19, no fields are selected. Two actions select and enter specify selection and entry of fields. Selection also specifies selection of actions. The function enter is illustrated in Listing 1.5. Entering a field first checks that the field is selected (line 2). It then updates temporary database fields. These are: `temp_script` (lines 4–6), `temp_patient` (lines 7–9) and `temp_med` (lines 10–12). These updates depend on whether the mode relates to entry of values to these temporary records. In all cases the entered field is added to the set of entered fields (line 13), and the selection of the field necessary prior to entry is set to false (line 14).

```
enter(f: fields_type, st: state): state =
    IF sel_field(st)(f)
    THEN st WITH [
            temp_script := IF per_enter_patient_script(f, st)
                           THEN enter_script_field(f, st`temp_script)
                           ELSE st`temp_script ENDIF,
            temp_patient := IF per_enter_patient_field(f,st)
                            THEN enter_patient_field(f, st`temp_patient)
                            ELSE st`temp_patient ENDIF,
            temp_med := IF per_enter_med_field(f, st)
                        THEN enter_med_field(f, st`temp_med)
                        ELSE st`temp_med ENDIF,
            ent_field := LAMBDA(x: fields_type): x = f OR st`ent_field(x),
            sel_field := LAMBDA(x: fields_type): FALSE ]
    ELSE st ENDIF
```

Listing 1.5. Entering a field

4 Plausibility

Once the specification has been developed, and before further analysis of the implications of the design, it is clearly necessary to be assured that the model is a plausible reflection of the envisaged design. This checking process is iterative. The design is developed by fleshing out interaction detail and adding functionality. It is not conventional formal refinement because at each step the design is in flux, open to change as a result of evaluation and discussion with potential users. The plausibility of the specification of the design is explored in two ways. Firstly, PVSio is used to explore grounded versions of the specified functions. This allows a form of direct interaction with the model to exercise the available actions and observe their effect on the state of the system. It makes it possible to explore some situations in which actions do not have the expected behaviour. Inevitably using PVSio does not allow exhaustive analysis in the sense that model checking (see for example [2]) does. The goal at this stage however is to establish a first impression about the model and flush out any obvious problems, before more exhaustive analysis is carried out. Secondly, PVS theorems are constructed to demonstrate that actions change state as expected. Here the aim is to demonstrate that for all states (not just the states generated through execution of the ground functions), the behaviour of actions is as expected. The use of PVSio, to explore plausibility is now considered in more detail.

4.1 Using *PVSio* to Check plausibility

PVSio [15] makes it possible to *test* the model. Although the model is of a half-formed sketch design, testing can be sufficient to check that the model meets the designer's intentions. An example of how PVSio can be used to check plausibility now follows. The following shows the last steps of a sequence that builds a database of patients. The sequence shows the last few actions of a much longer sequence including selecting (i.e., pressing) *key2*, selecting the password field, entering the password, and then pressing *confirm*. The sequence that produces the state `editmdpnp2` constructs the elements of the database. In fact the analysis of the specification involved checking that each step of the sequence had the desired effect.

```
susdmdnp2minus: state = LET st = editmdnp2,
                            st = select(key2, st),
                            st = select(password, st),
                            st = enter(password, st)
                        IN act(confirm, st)
```

PVSio shows the effect of this long sequence on the state of the pill dispenser (see Listing 1.6). There is only space to show a small part of the state that is produced. At the end of the action sequence the mode is `patient list` (line 1 in Listing 1.6). This mode shows a list of up to five (five is the limit for the screen) patients. There are no visible fields associated with this mode, but there are visible actions: *key1*, *key2*, *key3* and *create* (line 3). The state attribute `patient_id_line` shows the list of patients (identified by `p_name`) that are visible in the list (line 4). The listing also shows one element of the patient database (`patients_db`) with `p_name` equal to 1 (lines 5–24). This patient entry shows that fields `dob`, `id_card`, `mob` and `carer` have been entered as well as the prescriptions that have been entered. The patient entry allows for five prescriptions. Only elements l(0) and l(1) have been entered.

```
1  (# mode := patient_list,
2     vis_field := {  }, sel_field := {  }, ent_field := {  },
3     action := { key1, key2, key3, create },
4     patient_id_line := { 1(4):=5, 1(3):=4, 1(2):=3, 1(1):=2, 1(0):=1 },
5     patients_db := (:
6        (# p_name := 1,
7           p_fields := { dob id_card mob carer  }, scripts_index := 2,
8           scripts := { 1(4) := (# med_name := 0, s_fields := {  },
9                                    s_period := period_null,
10                                   quant := 0, t1 := 0, t2 := 0 #)
11                        1(3) := (# med_name := 0, s_fields := {  },
12                                   s_period := period_null,
13                                   quant := 0, t1 := 0, t2 := 0 #)
14                        1(2) := (# med_name := 0, s_fields := {  },
15                                   s_period := period_null,
16                                   quant := 0, t1 := 0, t2 := 0 #)
17                        1(1) := (# med_name := 2,
18                                   s_fields := { dosage prescription },
19                                   s_period := daily,
20                                   quant := 5, t1 := 7, t2 := 0 #)
21                        1(0) := (# med_name := 1,
22                                   s_fields := { dosage prescription },
23                                   s_period := bidaily,
24                                   quant := 3, t1 := 3, t2 := 5 #) } #),
25       (# p_name := 2, %... details omitted #) } #),
26    %-- ...further entries and structures omitted #)
```

Listing 1.6. Displaying the effect of a sequence

The information provided by PVSio therefore makes it possible to check the effect of sequences of actions. It is possible to use sequences of this kind to demonstrate that in a particular context, as defined in a sequence of ground functions, an action (or sequence of actions) will have a desired effect. An example that was explored demonstrates that, after the execution of a sequence for creating more than five patients in the database (five is the limit of patients that can be displayed at a time), scrolling down the patient list in the relevant mode, followed by scrolling it up, produced the same display as before the scrolling actions were taken. Listing 1.7 shows the sequence that was explored. The context for the exploration is the state susdmdnp2minus produced by the sequence mentioned above. The sequence of actions considered is Listing 1.7. The result of performing the sequence is shown in Listing 1.6. The patient_id_line is unchanged and the line indexed by 0 points to p_name = 1.

PVSio therefore makes it possible to test the model to check that the behaviour coincides with the expected behaviour insofar as it is represented in the sketch model. In Sect. 5 we consider template properties [10] that are designed to check use-related properties of the emerging design. In Sect. 5.2 we prove that the patient list scrolling actions are inverses of each other.

```
scrolldscrollu: state = LET st = susdmdnp2minus ,
                            st = scroll_down_patient_list(st)
                        IN scroll_up_patient_list(st)
```

Listing 1.7. Adding scroll down followed by scroll up

4.2   From Plausibility Checks to Plausibility Theorems

PVS theorems can be used to demonstrate that the model has consistent and desirable behaviour thus providing confidence in its plausibility. An example illustrates the process. Consider for example the mode that allows the entry of patient details. Based on our understanding, actions *key1*, *key3*, *confirm*, *prescriptions* and *quit* are visible inviting the user to take one of these actions. The PVS theorem (see Listing 1.8) aims to prove that these actions have the desired effect, producing the relevant mode displays and updating the patient database appropriately. Thus it can be demonstrated that one step behaviours are consistent with those suggested of the sketch design for all states of the pill dispenser. As an example, consider *quit*. The sketch indicates that the action takes the pill dispenser to a mode where a list of patients, taken from the patient database, is shown (see line 26) and takes no further action.

On the other hand pressing *confirm* also updates the patient database (if any changes have been made in the patient details screen) and produces the patient list screen (see lines 7–18). Furthermore the sketch indicates that the *confirm* action is only permitted if all the relevant fields have been selected and entered. In this case the patient database is updated with the temporary patient record (st2'temp_patient) using the function p_insert which inserts the patient into the database (lines 16–18). The database is ordered and the insertion either replaces an existing record or inserts the record in the right place in the list.

In the case of prescriptions the database is updated with the temporary patient and a transition is made to the current list of prescriptions for that patient. A collection of PVS theorems like check212 demonstrates that expected transitions take place and have been verified using the PVS theorem proving assistant.

```
check212: THEOREM FORALL (st: state):
 ((p_current(st) < p_max(st)) AND (p_max(st) < plimit))
    IMPLIES
  LET st1 = patient_details_screen(st)
  IN ((select(key1, st1) = init_screen(st)) AND
      (select(key3, st1) = db_menu_screen(st)) AND
      %-- set up the state for the confirm action
      (LET st2 = enter(name, select(name, st1)) IN
      (LET st2 = enter(dob, select(dob, st2)) IN
      (LET st2 = enter(id_card, select(id_card, st2)) IN
      (LET st2 = enter(carer, select(carer, st2)) IN
      (LET st2 = enter(mob, select(mob, st2)) IN
      %-- the effect of the confirm action
        (select(confirm, st2) =
            patient_list_screen(st2 WITH [
                patients_db := p_insert(st2`p_current,
                                        st2`temp_patient,
                                        st2`patients_db) ])))))))) AND
      %-- the effect of the prescriptions action (sets up scripts list)
      (select(prescriptions, st1) =
        LET tp = p_find(st`p_current, st`patients_db),
            stx = st WITH [ patients_db := p_insert(st`p_current, tp,
                                                    st`patients_db),
                            temp_patient := tp ]
        IN script_list_screen(stx)) AND
        (select(quit, st1) = patient_list_screen(st)))
```

Listing 1.8. Plausible actions from the patient details screen

5   Proving Properties

Once a plausible model has been developed it is possible to do further exploration. This includes user evaluation of a realistic prototype, but it also makes it possible to analyse the behaviour of the modelled prototype against use-centred requirements [10]. These requirements may include safety requirements that are used in the software safety analysis required by the regulatory authorities. This step therefore enables a more exhaustive analysis of the emerging design than would be possible with the functional prototype typically used in use-centred design. It also supports software engineering of the system using a spiral model, and the mapping of a requirements specification including use-centred requirements [17]. The approach is demonstrated by considering two use-centred requirements: consistency and reversibility.

5.1 Consistency

Action Consistency

$$\forall a \in Act, s \in S, m \in MS :$$
$$guard(s, m) \wedge$$
$$pre\_filter(s, m) \; \varphi \; post\_filter(a(s), m) \tag{1}$$

The action consistency property is formulated as a property of either a single action, or of a group of actions (we will refer to them as Act) which may exhibit similar behaviours. A relation $\varphi : C \times C$ connects a filtered state, before an action occurs (captured by $pre\_filter : S \times MS \rightarrow C$), with a filtered state after the action (captured by $post\_filter : S \times MS \rightarrow C$).

There are many properties of the model of the sketch design that relate to its consistency. It is relatively common that actions are inconsistent in some detail. Consider, for example $quit$ as represented in the storyboard. A first consideration of prototype material indicates that $quit$ consistently changes mode without changes to either the patient or meds database. The action consistency template can be instantiated to a theorem that makes this assumption. The theorem fails to be true because there is a special case during the patient's thumb print registration sequence when $quit$ is used to exit the sequence and the patient database is changed. The consistency template instantiation is reformulated to include a guard that excludes this feature. The formulation of the theorem is as follows: it uses a simple guard (`mode(st) /= creation_success`), and the filters extract the attributes that specify the patient database and the medicine database:

```
quit_consistency_thm: THEOREM FORALL (st: state):
  mode(st) /= creation_success
    IMPLIES
  LET st1 = select(quit, st)
    IN (st`meds_db = st1`meds_db AND st`patients_db = st1`patients_db)
```

5.2 Reversibility

When testing plausibility using PVSio we considered the reversibility of scroll actions. The testing that was done inevitably considered only specific states of the patient database that generated the patient listing (see Sect. 4.1). A general reversibility property, which proves this requirement for all states, is identified in the reversibility template as follows. This template is formulated for a group of actions $Act \subset S \rightarrow S$ using $guard : S \rightarrow B$, and a $filter : S \rightarrow C$ relevant to the entry mode. For each $a \in Act$, there corresponds a $b \in Act$ such that:

Reversibility

$$\forall s \in S : guard(s) \Longrightarrow$$
$$filter(b(a(s)) = filter(s)) \tag{2}$$

This template can be used to prove that scrolling actions have required characteristics. Consider two actions `scroll_up_patient_list` and `scroll_up_med_list` and their inverses `scroll_down_patient_list` and `scroll_down_med_list`. The guards require that respective list screens are visible. The theorem is expressed using a function that instantiates the template and is proved using structural induction. Structural induction assumes that the property is true of an initial state and then proves that as a consequence it is true of any state that can be reached by the actions supported of the device. The verification of the theorem as formulated succeeds, i.e., the formulated property is true of the design.

```
%-- reversibility of scroll actions
confirm_ud_scroll_fn(st: state): boolean =
  (mode(st) = patient_list
    IMPLIES scroll_down_patient_list(scroll_up_patient_list(st)) = st)
  AND (mode(st) = db_med_list
        IMPLIES scroll_down_med_list(scroll_up_med_list(st)) = st)
%-- reversibility theorem, formulated using structural induction
confirm_ud_scroll_thm: THEOREM
  FORALL (pre, post: state):
    init?(pre) IMPLIES confirm_ud_scroll_fn(pre)
      AND (state_transitions(pre, post) AND
              confirm_ud_scroll_fn(pre) IMPLIES confirm_ud_scroll_fn(post))
```

6   Iterating the Prototype

Once properties are proved of this version of the PVS model, a further prototype can be developed for co-operative evaluation with end users. The visual appearance of the prototype is based on a concept design image created, for example, using a photo-editing tool. PVSio-web is then used to create hotspot areas over the picture and link them to the PVS model. Hotspots over buttons represent input widgets of the prototype, and they are linked to transition functions defined in the PVS model. Hotspot areas over display elements are used to render the value of state variables so that the visual appearance of the prototype closely resembles that of the real system in the corresponding states.

Figure 4 shows a screenshot of the developed prototype. It uses 17 widgets to model different elements in the various screens of the pillbox. Listing 1.9 shows a snippet of JavaScript code necessary for creating the *home* button of the prototype. `TouchscreenButton` is the widget constructor. The `new` operator is used to create a new object of type TouchscreenButton. The created widget is stored in a variable `key1`. The *first argument* of the constructor is a string defining the widget identifier. The PVSio-web toolkit uses this string as a basis for deriving the name of the transition function in the PVS model to be linked to the widget. The full name of the transition function is constructed by concatenating the user action that activates the widget with the widget identifier.

For example, when the user clicks on the button, the transition function that will be evaluated is `act(key1, st)`. The *second argument* is a structure defining the coordinates and size of the widget. This is necessary to create an interactive overlay area of the correct size for the image used as a basis for the visual appearance of the prototype, and to position the interactive area in the correct place, that is the left side of the screen. The *third argument* provides information about the callback function to be invoked for refreshing the visual appearance

Fig. 4. Pillbox prototype based on concept design image.

of the prototype when the evaluation of the transition function associated with the button generates a new system state, as well as information on the visual appearance of the touchscreen button (label, colour, font).

The visual aspect of all widgets is refreshed each time the PVS specification is evaluated in PVSio. The evaluation of the specification occurs either when the user interacts with an input widget (e.g., presses a button), or periodically (if the device has internal timers that are ticking).

```
var key1 = new TouchscreenButton("key1", {
    top: 216, left: 230, height: 64, width: 64
}, {
    softLabel: "home",
    backgroundColor: "green",
    fontsize: 16,
    callback: render
});
```

Listing 1.9. Creation of a touchscreen button using PVSio-web.

This enhanced version of the prototype benefits from improved look and feel. The results of the evaluation with end users is then used to iterate the design process.

7   Related Work and Conclusions

While there is relatively little literature concerned with development techniques that combine informal representations of design with formal models, there are many activities that combine different formal descriptions of visual, functional and task elements. Bowen and Reeves [4] explore the relation between display and functional models. Their work also focuses on specifications of sketch designs and aims to enable analysis of these designs. We are not, however, aware of development of executable versions of their models. Haesen and others [8] integrate models and informal design knowledge. Their focus is also the role of formal task models and abstract user interfaces in user centred design. They use personas, scenarios and related task models in their models. Graphical models of storyboards are produced along with constraints on these models. Bolton and others [3], Paterno and others [14] and Fields [6] combine task and functional models. Palanque and others [11] combine visual, functional and task elements.

An important challenge in developing the approach described in this paper was not to reduce the value of user centred design. A criticism often levelled at formal techniques is that they can have the effect of limiting the scope of the analysis, ignoring important broader issues. We believe that our analysis, as an adjunct to the techniques and approaches of user centred centred design, responds to these criticisms. A further concern is that the effort and knowledge involved in producing the models and performing the analysis are not cost effective. It is true that these are techniques that are not typically found in the toolkit of a development team, particularly the small teams that often design and implement medical devices. However the safety of medical devices, in particular, is crucial and a thorough analysis of usability issues is a key contribution ensuring safety.

An important future dimension of our work, currently under development, is to simplify and automate some of these processes. Tools for presenting and instantiating property templates are being developed. Heuristics are being developed to automate the proof of PVS theorems. We are also simplifying the process of using PVSio-web to construct prototypes from models. The aim is to make these techniques accessible to a wider group of developers.

Acknowledgement. We are grateful to Nuno Rodrigues, João Vilaça and Nuno Dias from IPCA (Polytechnic Institute of Cavado and Ave) who developed the first prototype of the pill dispenser. José C. Campos, Paolo Masci and Michael Harrison were funded by project NORTE-01-0145-FEDER-000016, financed by the North Portugal Regional Operational Programme (NORTE 2020), under the PORTUGAL 2020 Partnership Agreement, and through the European Regional Development Fund (ERDF).

References

1. Beyer, H., Holtzblatt, K.: Contextual Design: Defining Customer-centred Systems. Morgan Kaufmann, Burlington (1998)
2. Bolton, M.L., Bass, E., Siminiceanu, R.: Using formal verification to evaluate human-automation interaction, a review. IEEE Trans. Syst., Man, Cybern., Part A: Syst. Hum. **99**, 1–16 (2013)
3. Bolton, M., Jiménez, N., van Paassen, M., Trujillo, M.: Automatically generating specification properties from task models for the verification of human-automation interaction. IEEE Trans. Hum. Mach. Syst. **44**(5), 561–575 (2014)

4. Bowen, J., Reeves, S.: Combining models for interactive system modelling. In: Weyers, B., Bowen, J., Dix, A., Palanque, P. (eds.) The Handbook of Formal Methods in Human-Computer Interaction. HIS, pp. 161–182. Springer, Cham (2017). https://doi.org/10.1007/978-3-319-51838-1_6

5. Carroll, J. (ed.): Scenario Based Design: Envisioning Work and Technology in System Development. Wiley, Hoboken (1995)

6. Fields, R.E.: Analysis of erroneous actions in the design of critical systems. Ph.D. thesis, Department of Computer Science, University of York, Heslington, York, YO10 5DD (2001)

7. Gould, J.D., Lewis, C.: Designing for usability: key principles and what users think. Commun. ACM **28**(3), 300–311 (1985)

8. Haesen, M., et al.: Using storyboards to integrate models and informal design knowledge. In: Hussmann, H., Meixner, G., Zuehlke, D. (eds.) Model-Driven Development of Advanced User Interfaces. SCI, pp. 87–106. Springer, Heidelberg (2011). https://doi.org/10.1007/978-3-642-14562-9_5

9. Harel, D.: Statecharts: a visual formalism for complex systems. Sci. Comput. Program. **8**, 231–274 (1987)

10. Harrison, M., Masci, P., Campos, J.: Verification templates for the analysis of user interface software design. IEEE Trans. Softw. Eng. (2018). epub ahead of print

11. Martinie, C., et al.: Formal tasks and systems models as a tool for specifying and assessing automation designs. In: Proceedings of the 1st International Conference on Application and Theory of Automation in Command and Control Systems, ATACCS 2011, pp. 50–59, IRIT Press, Toulouse, France (2011)

12. Masci, P., Oladimeji, P., Zhang, Y., Jones, P., Curzon, P., Thimbleby, H.: PVSio-web 2.0: Joining PVS to HCI. In: Kroening, D., Păsăreanu, C.S. (eds.) CAV 2015. LNCS, vol. 9206, pp. 470–478. Springer, Cham (2015). https://doi.org/10.1007/978-3-319-21690-4_30

13. Monk, A., Wright, P., Haber, J., Davenport, L.: Improving Your Human-computer Interface: A Practical Technique. Prentice-Hall, Upper Saddle River (1993)

14. Mori, G., Paternò, F., Santoro, C.: CTTE: support for developing and analyzing task models for interactive system design. IEEE Trans. Software Eng. **28**(8), 797–813 (2002)

15. Muñoz, C.: Rapid prototyping in PVS. Technical Report, NIA Report No. 2003–03, NASA/CR-2003-212418, National Institute of Aerospace (2003)

16. Owre, S., Rushby, J.M., Shankar, N.: PVS: a prototype verification system. In: Kapur, Deepak (ed.) CADE 1992. LNCS, vol. 607, pp. 748–752. Springer, Heidelberg (1992). https://doi.org/10.1007/3-540-55602-8_217

17. Sommerville, I.: Software Engineering. Addison-Wesley, Boston (2010)

18. Watson, N., Reeves, S., Masci, P.: Integrating user design and formal models within PVSio-Web. In: Workshop on Formal Intergrated Development Environment (F-IDE-18). Electronic Proceedings in Theoretical Computer Science (EPTCS) (2018)

Foundations of Coordination Languages and Self-adaptative Systems (FOCLASA)

FOCLASA 2018 Organizers' Message

Being distributed, concurrent and mobile, modern information systems often involve the composition of heterogeneous components as well as standalone services. Theoretical models, languages and tools for coordinating, composing and adapting services are required. They can indeed simplify the development of complex distributed service-based systems, enable functional correctness proofs and improve reusability and maintainability of such systems. In this context, the goal of the FOCLASA series of workshop is to gather researchers and practitioners of the aforementioned fields, to share their best practices and experiences, to identify common problems, and to devise general solutions in the context of coordination languages, service orchestration, and self-adaptive systems.

The 16th International Workshop on Foundations of Coordination Languages and Self-Adaptative Systems (FOCLASA 2018) was held in Toulouse, France, on June 26th 2018, as a satellite event of the federated STAF/SEFM conferences. The Program Committee (PC) of Foclasa 2018 consisted of 26 prominent researchers from 14 different countries. Thirtheen submissions were received. Each submission was reviewed by three independent referees. The review process included an in-depth discussion phase during which the merits of all the papers were discussed. Based on quality, originality, clarity and relevance criteria, the PC finally selected six contributions. The program was further enhanced by two invited talks given by Stefano Mariani from the UniMore University (Italy) on the Coordination of Complex Socio-technical Systems, and by Antonio Brogi from the University of Pisa (Italy) on Micro-Service.

Many people contributed to the success of FOCLASA 2018. We first would like to thank the authors for submitting high-quality papers. We also thank the Program Committee members for their effort and time to read and discuss the paper and we equally acknowledge the help of additional external reviewers who evaluated submissions in their area of expertise. We wish also to thank Stefano Mariani and Antonio Brogi, our invited speakers, for their keynotes.

It is also our pleasure to thank Marc Pantel, the general chair of STAF/SEM as well as Manuel Mazzara, Julian Ober and Gwen Salaun, the workshops chairs. We also like to thank the providers of the EasyChair conference management system, whose facilities greatly helped us to run the review process and facilitate the preparation of the proceedings. Finally, we are endebted to the workshop attendees for keeping the FOCLASA research community lively and interactive, and ultimately ensuring the success of this workshop series.

September 2018

Jean-Marie Jacquet
Jacopo Soldani

Organization

FOCLASA 2018 - Steering Commmittee

Farhad Arbab	CWI, The Netherlands
Antonio Brogi	University of Pisa, Italy
Carlos Canal	University of Málaga, Spain
Jean-Marie Jacquet	University of Namur, Belgium
Ernesto Pimentel	University of Málaga, Spain
Gwen Salaün	University of Grenoble Alpes, France

FOCLASA 2018 - Program Committee

Gul Agha	University of Illinois at Urbana-Champaign, USA
Pedro Alvarez	Universidad de Zaragoza, Spain
Farhad Arbab	CWI, The Netherlands
Simon Bliudze	Inria Lille – Nord Europe, France
Radu Calinescu	University of York, UK
Javier Camara	Carnegie Mellon University, USA
Flavio De Paoli	University of Milano Bicocca, Italy
Francisco J. Durán	Universidad de Malaga, Spain
Erik de Vink	Eindhoven University of Technology, The Netherlands
Schahram Dustdar	TU Wien, Austria
Letterio Galletta	IMT Lucca, Italy
Eva Kuhn	Vienna University of Technology, Austria
Alberto Lluch Lafuente	Technical University of Denmark, Denmark
Sun Meng	Peking University, China
Hernan C. Melgratti	University of Buenos Aires, Argentina
Mohammad Mousavi	Halmstad University, Sweden
Pascal Poizat	Université Paris Ouest, France
Jose Proenca	INESC TEC & Universidade do Minho, Portugal
Gwen Salaün	University of Grenoble, France
Michael Sheng	University of Adelaide, Australia
Marjan Sirjani	Reykjavik University, Iceland
Carolyn Talcott	SRI International, USA
Massimo Tivoli	University of L'Aquila, Italy
Emilio Tuosto	University of Leicester, UK
Lina Ye	CentraleSupélec, France
Gianluigi Zavattaro	University of Bologna, Italy

FOCLASA 2018 - Additional Reviewers

Maryam Bagheri	Sharif University of Technology, Iran
Narges Khakpour	Linnaeus University, Sweden
Colin Paterson	York University, UK

Coordination of Complex Socio-Technical Systems: Challenges and Opportunities

Stefano Mariani[✉][iD]

Department of Sciences and Methods for Engineering,
Università degli Studi di Modena e Reggio Emilia, Reggio Emilia, Italy
stefano.mariani@unimore.it

Abstract. The issue of coordination in Socio-Technical Systems (STS) mostly stems from "humans-in-the-loop": besides software-software we have software-human interactions to handle, too. Also, a number of peculiarities and related engineering challenges make a socio-technical gap easy to rise, in the form of a gap between what the computational platform provides, and what the users are expecting to have. In this paper we try to shed some light on the issue of engineering coordination mechanisms and policies in STS. Accordingly, we highlight the main challenges, the opportunities we have to deal with them, and a few selected approaches for specific STS application domains.

Keywords: Coordination · Socio-technical systems · MoK
Speaking objects · $\mathcal{A}rgo\mathcal{R}ec$ · Self-organisation · BIC · Argumentation

1 Introduction

Modern society is a growing interconnection of (sub)systems, such as healthcare, transportation networks, supply chain, etc. Its complexity thus stems from both the inherent complexity of each subsystem, and the added complexity of *interactions* amongst subsystems. The same can be said for modern IT systems, where managing interactions among components is at least as complex as designing the computational function of each component itself.

Furthermore, IT systems and the society rarely are isolated systems: rather, the latter relies on the former for many vital services and functionalities, giving birth to the so-called *Socio-technical Systems* (STS). There, "humans-in-the-loop" [20] are the norm rather than the exception, thus management of interactions further complicates: besides software-software, we now have software-human interactions to account for, too.

STS, in fact, arise when cognitive and social interaction is mediated by information technology rather than by the natural world (alone) [52]. As such, STS include people, processes, etc., which are inherent parts of the system. An example of STS is a Smart City, a social network, a Computer Supported Collaborative Work platform, any Internet of Things (IoT) deployment featuring human users—i.e. assisted living, smart homes, retail applications, etc.

M. Mazzara et al. (Eds.): STAF 2018 Workshops, LNCS 11176, pp. 295–310, 2018.
https://doi.org/10.1007/978-3-030-04771-9_22

STS are technically difficult to design, mostly because social activity is flexible and multi-faceted [1]. Also, a number of peculiarities and related engineering challenges have been highlighted by various research works [1,12,25]. Failing to recognise any one of the above facets, therefore missing to deal with the related issue, leads to a *socio-technical gap* in the STS, that is, a gap between what the computational platform provides, and what its users are expecting to have.

In this paper we try to shed some light on the issue of engineering coordination mechanisms and policies in STS. Accordingly, Sect. 2 highlights the main challenges to be faced in the process, Sect. 3 discusses promising approaches dealing with each of them, and Sect. 4 describes a few research contributions putting these approaches in practice in specific STS application domains.

2   Socio-Technical Systems: Challenges

Unsurprisingly, the challenges to be faced when engineering STS are twofold: technical, and socio-cognitive ones. Among the former, we can put any issue concerned with how to design the STS so that it serves at best its users' needs. Among the latter, we can include issues related to how users interact with the STS as well as to how they perceive it—in psychological terms. The remainder of this section somewhat follows this distinction, first by focussing on STS technical requirements such as self-organisation and adaptation, then by analysing the mindset humans have when dealing with STS, and finally by discussing how they perceive their computational ("algorithmic") part. Please, notice that the latter two issues pose their own technical requirements, too.

2.1   Emergence, Adaptation, Awareness

In [1] the distinguishing properties of STS are discussed. Among the many, the following are particularly interesting in the context of this paper:

- STS have emergent properties, which therefore cannot be attributed to individual parts of the system, but rather stem from the dependencies between system components. Given this complexity, these properties can be evaluated only once the system has been tested and deployed, not at design time
- *awareness*, that is, knowing who is present, and peripheral awareness, that is, monitoring of others' activity, are fundamental in STS [21], because visibility of information flow – thus observability of dependencies – enables learning and improves efficiency [22]
- people *adapt* to the systems they use, but also strive to adapt those systems to best meet their needs [35,37]

Emergent properties of a STS may be modelled and analysed, for instance by exploiting agent-based modelling and simulation frameworks [34]. Nevertheless, actual deployment of the STS inevitably has differences w.r.t. the "synthetic" version – i.e. unpredictability of human behaviour vs. predictability of software agents – thus cannot exactly predict the actual STS dynamics. Supporting awareness may seem more feasible, but enabling observability of actions, interactions, and dependencies among activities – namely, anything that can happen in a STS – poses serious scalability and privacy issues which have no silver bullet available, yet—just look at the Cambridge Analytica scandal [40]. Adaptation received a lot of attention from computer scientists, there included the FOCLASA community—i.e. see [48]. What is most challenging here, unsurprisingly, is taking into account unpredictability of human behaviour: adaptations may solicit unexpected reactions in users, which may begin "fighting" against the system, possibly because they ignore the reason for adaptation and/or the expected benefits.

Dealing with each of the facets above is challenging on its own, let alone conceiving and designing a system successfully tackling all of them.

2.2   Goals and Assertions vs. Actions and Perceptions

In [24] further considerations about peculiarities of STS are made, in the specific context of a novel approach to engineering Social Internet of Things applications, that is, applications in which IoT devices and software must have social interactions to achieve the goals of the system, between both themselves and human users [3]. The proposed Speaking Objects approach puts emphasis on two traits of human interaction which sharply contrast with device-to-device interaction:

- humans better reason in terms of *goals* to be achieved, rather than by directly thinking at the actions needed to achieve them. Accordingly, they usually interact by expressing their own goals, not by explicitly commanding others what to do
- humans also better reason in terms of complex situations, state of affairs holding in the past, at present, or desired for the future, rather than by thinking at all the specific perceptions of their surroundings which make up a situation. Accordingly, they usually interact by exchanging *assertions* about those situations and their properties, not by debating over specific measurements of them

This is quite the opposite of what sensors and actuators do: they simply provide perceptions, which are then composed by someone else (usually, ad-hoc machine learning algorithms), and react to explicit commands for undertaking specific actions. Thus, their interaction is a mere exchange of measurements, sampling a specific facet of a complex situation, and commands about what to do (not what to achieve).

It is therefore quite difficult for humans and devices to fruitfully communicate and interact unless either humans learn "the language of devices", or devices learn to think more like humans, in terms of goals and assertions—instead of actions and perceptions.

2.3   Algocracy and Trust

As clearly witnessed by statements such as the ACM "Statement on Algorithmic Transparency and Accountability" [2] we are living in an *algocracy*, that is, in a society in which increasingly pervasive, complex, and delicate aspects of our everyday lives are decided, or at least influenced, by computer algorithms [12]. A typical example is the filter bubble effect [38], caused, i.e., by the ranking algorithms running behind the news feed of social networks such as Facebook, or by more subtle ones, which are ultimately everywhere—for instance, algorithms regulate stock-trading, access to healthcare and insurance, employment chances, and much more [31,33].

While living in an algocracy does not necessarily represent an issue on its own, the lack of *transparency* and *accountability* does: if users of a STS have no clue of what is going on "behind the scenes", and who is to blame when something goes wrong, they are likely to lose trust of the system—to eventually stop using it. The path toward making algorithms accountable and transparent is full of challenges and open issues, and often heavily depends on the specific scenario where the STS is deployed [14,18].

3   Coordination: Opportunities

As for Sect. 2, the approaches to coordination in STS may focus more on the technical side or on the socio-cognitive one. In the remainder of this section we discuss both: we start with the latter, by summarising the evolution from stigmergic to observation-based coordination, then proceed with the technical side by analysing how self-organisation can be engineered, and finally go back to the socio-cognitive facet of STS by briefly discussing how argumentation may alleviate the issue of trust and the fear of algocracy.

3.1   Observation-Based Coordination

Observation-based coordination captures the idea of coordinating an ensemble of agents by enabling them to observe each other's actions, or the traces that those actions leave in the environment where they happen [41].

The most well known example of observation-based coordination is *stigmergy*. The term has been originally introduced to define the coordination approach of a specific species of termites in collectively building their nest, communicating and synchronising their activities through the environment rather than by directly communicating [19]. Then, throughout the years, it undergone many generalisations/specialisations/extensions [36,39,43]. Here, we refer to a generic set of coordination mechanisms mediated by the environment. Accordingly, stigmergic coordination requires that:

- agents act on the environment leaving some traces, or markers, which can then be *locally* perceived by others—and, possibly, affect their behaviour

- all interactions among agents are mediated by the environment, through traces—like ants' pheromones
- emission of traces is generative, namely, once they are produced their lifecycle is independent of their producer's one
- evolution of traces over time (and in space) may depend on the environment—as in the case of pheromone diffusion, aggregation, and evaporation in ant colonies

The interplay between these requirements produces *self-organisation*: whereas actions occur on a local basis – i.e. termites assemble soil locally, and ants sort broods locally – their effect is global in terms of the structures and behaviours they originate system-wide, by emergence [45]—as in the case of termites' nests, or ants' brood sorting.

Stigmergy is not confined to the world of insects: research in cognitive sciences emphasises the fundamental role that stigmergy plays also within human societies [44,47]—hence in STS, too. There, stigmergy provides novel opportunities, because traces become amenable of human interpretation within a conventional system of signs, thus may be exploited by the cognitive abilities of the interacting agents to better coordinate. Along this line, [43] introduces the notion of *cognitive stigmergy* as the evolution of stigmergic coordination in those contexts where agents are capable of symbolic reasoning, as in the case of humans.

As such, cognitive stigmergy is a key enabler of *awareness*: through traces, in fact, agents may perceive what others are doing, and if traces are amenable of symbolic interpretation, they may even try to infer their intentions and goals. In turn, awareness is a pre-condition for *adaptation*: in order to plan actions aimed at improving the current situation, one must know what the current situation is, there including what others are doing. Then, emergent behaviours are likely to arise from the interplay between adaptation and awareness [6].

Both stigmergy and cognitive stigmergy are mostly concerned with traces of actions left in a shared environment, rather than on actions themselves. Also, they do not consider the effect that awareness of observability of actions and their traces have on the acting agent: if an agent knows that its actions could be observed, it may decide to act in a given way just to communicate something. This is where *Behavioural Implicit Communication* (BIC) [11] enters the picture, as a further generalisation of cognitive stigmergy embracing actions in their own right, too.

BIC is a cognitive theory of communication fostering the idea that practical behaviour can be used as a means for communicating, even without any additional specialised signal. On the contrary, communication actions are normally carried on by specialised behaviours (e.g., speech acts). BIC has been already taken as a reference for observation-based coordination, mostly based on a list of "tacit messages" that practical behaviours may convey. For instance, the "presence" tacit message communicates that "agent A is here", by the fact that whichever is the action that A made, it is evident now for who observed it that A exists. Or tacit message "intention", which communicates that "A plans to do action β", by the fact that actions may (partially) reveal the plan behind them, such as in the case where agents follow a pre-determined workflow therefore observing action α may reveal at which point of the workflow A is—thus the next action it has to commit to. The complete list of tacit messages and many illustrative examples can be found in [10].

BIC clearly represents a step forward on the path laid by stigmergy and cognitive stigmergy, enabling further forms of observation-based coordination based on practical behaviour rather than on dedicated communication acts, and on a process of signification of the intentions, conditions, and opportunities behind actions [9].

It is worth emphasising that existence of a suitable environment, where actions take place and their traces are recorded, is a necessary pre-condition for BIC, because it is the environment that enables and constrains observation of actions and their traces—in a computational world, in the physical one, and in the mixed world of STS. Also, it should be noted that BIC is a key enabler in raising the abstraction level within a STS, by allowing designers to think in terms of *intentions* and *goals* behind actions, and agents as well as interaction mechanisms to be designed accordingly.

3.2   Self-organisation

Given the importance of awareness and observability as witnessed by stigmergy and BIC, one could be tempted to adopt a centralised approach to coordination in STS, where a single component (the coordinator) has complete knowledge of the state of the system, and accordingly schedules others' actions globally so as to guarantee absence of unwanted interference and efficient collaboration. Nevertheless, *decentralisation* is one of the keys enabling self-organisation, which is a sort of holy grail for coordination models and languages: the ability of a system as a whole to *autonomously* (re-)configure itself in face of change, without any global supervision but rather relying on locally available information solely [17]. Besides self-* properties, decentralisation enables greater scalability, efficiency, and fault-tolerance w.r.t. centralised approaches, usually at the price of the complexity of implementation.

Awareness is apparently in contrast with decentralisation, since the latter explicitly avoids gathering of complete information by any component of the STS. Nevertheless, decentralisation often implies that computations depend on the context local to the executing component, that is, on what the component locally perceives about the state of the system, and on how it can act on its local portion of the computational environment to carry out its duties. Awareness is thus conveniently re-defined on a local basis in place of a global one, not lost. And there, *situatedness* plays a crucial role, as the property of actions (computation) and interactions (coordination) of being deeply intertwined with the environment they are immersed in [46]: on the one hand, they are affected by it, as it enables and constrains what agents can and cannot do, can and cannot perceive (thus, be aware of); on the other hand, they can affect it in turn, by changing its properties and structure (thus, possibly, also the admissible actions and perceptions).

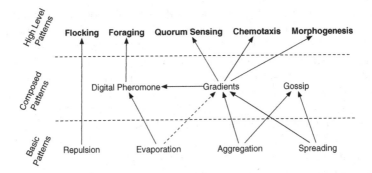

Fig. 1. Design patterns according to [16]. (Dashed) Arrows indicate (optional) composition.

Decentralised approaches to self-organisation have been widely studied, as regards both computation [4,32] and coordination [13,16], and already proved to be effective in dealing with the many issues of distributed computing in general [53]. In [16], for instance, the authors surveyed the literature regarding nature-inspired self-organising mechanisms, with the goal of compiling a catalogue of design patterns to promote reusability—pretty much like object-oriented design patterns do. As a result, the patterns depicted in Fig. 1 are detected, and related to each other in a compositional hierarchy consisting of three layers:

Basic Patterns – can be used to form more complex patterns, but cannot be further decomposed into smaller ones

Composed Patterns – obtainable as a composition of some basic mechanisms, and which in turn can serve as building blocks for higher level ones

High Level Patterns – patterns directly supporting complex self-organising emergent behaviours, showcasing how to exploit basic and composed patterns

For instance, gradients compose spreading and aggregation (optionally evaporation, too) to dynamically build routing paths inspired by force fields in physics [26], whereas flocking exploits repulsion as birds and schools of fishes do to maintain a given structure despite disruption.

All of the patterns may be implemented in a decentralised way, and leverage situatedness of interacting components to achieve self-organisation.

3.3   Argumentation

As just discussed, self-organisation is undoubtedly a desirable property to have for any given system, also because it alleviates the developers' burden of explicitly intervene on the system to manually adapt its functionalities and behaviour upon need. Nevertheless, self-organisation comes at a price: for instance, it makes it more difficult to deterministically guarantee what the configuration or behaviour of the system would be in any given situation, due to the lack of a global supervisor or strict design-time rules [20]. Although many approaches have been proposed to help engineers correctly design self-organisation, either through model-checking of desired safety and liveness properties [23], run-time verification of expected behaviour [7], or by construction [51], an important issue is still open: understanding what exactly went wrong in case of abnormal behaviour. The reason being that self-organisation is by definition a (partially) *opaque* process, where it is not always clear how to attribute a given global behaviour to the locally programmed rules—the so-called "local-to-global" issue [27].

Here, an intriguing opportunity is represented by *argumentation*, as the inter-disciplinary research field studying dialogues and debates to understand their dynamics and the corresponding reasoning process [49]. In particular, computational argumentation exploits computational techniques to automatically analyse and build arguments and their relationships, there including generating explanations and justifications of decision making [8]. For instance, argumentation-based negotiation applies argumentation principles to negotiation-based coordination in multi-agent systems [42]. There, in fact, negotiation mechanisms are usually blind with respect to the strategy adopted by the agents participating in the protocol, that is, to their motivations in performing bids. By adding argumentation, instead, agents can disclose the reason why they are taking a given stance, thus improving the odds of reaching an agreement by collectively reasoning on conflicting goals and motivations. In the case of self-organisation, having components being able to explain why they performed a given action is a potentially effective way of promoting *accountability*, that is, exactly the practice of identifying someone or something as the cause of an effect.

Argumentation has therefore the great advantage of promoting trustability in a STS: if users can get justifications about the decision making undergoing "behind the scenes", they are likely to increase their confidence in the capabilities of the system. In this respect, it is worth emphasising that striving to provide trustability and accountability is an increasingly hot topic well beyond coordination in STS, but in many fields of AI – from big data [33] to algorithms in general [31] – as witnessed by the recent "transparency initiative" endorsed by many organisations worldwide[1].

4   Selected Applications and Proposed Approaches

With the aim of showing how the research works described in Sect. 3 can be actually exploited in the real-world to tackle the challenges discussed in Sect. 2, the remainder of this section reports on three promising yet novel proposals each integrating some of the approaches in its own unique way: the $\mathcal{M}$olecules of $\mathcal{K}$nowledge model blends self-organisation with BIC, the Speaking Objects vision focusses on giving to users the right level of abstraction when interacting with technical systems while leveraging situatedness and argumentation, $\mathcal{A}$rgo$\mathcal{R}$ec is

---

[1] http://www.transparency-initiative.org/.

mostly concerned with promoting trust and fighting algocracy through argumentation and awareness.

4.1   Self-organising Knowledge Management with $\mathcal{MoK}$

The $\mathcal{M}$olecules of $\mathcal{K}$nowledge model [29] ($\mathcal{MoK}$) fosters a novel way to engineer computational platforms supporting knowledge management in STS, according to which the software exploits users' interactions to continuously and spontaneously (self-)organise information. $\mathcal{MoK}$ is built around the integration of a biochemical metaphor [50] and BIC [11]: the former defines how to carry out computations, while the latter how to manage interactions.

Accordingly, a $\mathcal{MoK}$ system is a network of *compartments* (representing information repositories), where *seeds* (sources of information) continuously and spontaneously inject *atoms* (atomic information), which may then aggregate into *molecules* (composite information), diffuse to other compartments, gain/lose relevance, and so on. These processes are enacted by $\mathcal{MoK}$ *reactions* (the coordination laws dictating how the system evolves) executing within compartments, and influenced by *enzymes* (the reification of agents' actions) and *traces* (their side effects). Both enzymes and traces are left within compartments by *catalysts* (the agents) while performing their activities.

Reactions leverage decentralisation and situatedness to promote self-organisation: first, they rely only on information local to their compartment and can only affect neighbours, at most; second, they are scheduled according to dynamic rate expressions inspired by natural chemical reactions, which are sensitive to the contextual information (possibly) affecting their own outcomes. Enzymes and traces instead fully exploit the BIC theory for enabling awareness and observation-based coordination: by reifying actions themselves as well as their traces, in fact, they make agents aware of what others are doing, and thus enable their coordination. For a description of each reaction, enzyme, and trace, as well as their relationships, the interested reader is referred to [28].

In [30], a citizen journalism scenario is taken as a case study: there, users share a $\mathcal{MoK}$-coordinated IT platform for retrieving, assembling, and publishing news stories. They use the $\mathcal{MoK}$ middleware for a number of actions such as searching for relevant information and working on these information to shape their own news stories. While they carry out their activities, users release enzymes and traces within their working space (a compartment), which ends up attracting similar information from other compartments through $\mathcal{MoK}$ reactions. Namely, the $\mathcal{MoK}$ middleware exploits users' (local) interactions to improve the (global) spatial organisation of information (Fig. 2): whenever users implicitly manifest interest in information, $\mathcal{MoK}$ interprets their intention of exploiting information, and the opportunity for others to exploit it as well, by attracting similar information toward the compartment where the action took place.

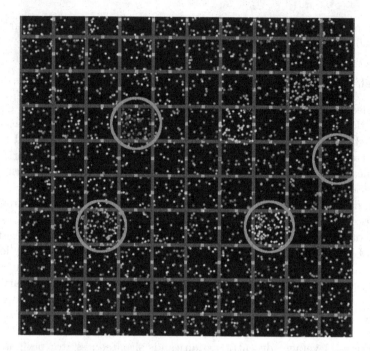

Fig. 2. Clusters of similar information appearing in *MoK by emergence*, as a result of users' interactions (image from [30]).

4.2   Traffic Control with Speaking Objects

In [25] the novel concept of Speaking Objects is presented as a brand new way to conceive and design distributed systems in general, with a particular emphasis on the Internet of Things vision. There, the core idea is that in a few years sensor and actuator devices will no longer simply provide measurements of pre-defined metrics and react to simple commands for affecting the state of the local environment. Rather, they will become able to assert complex situations about the state of the world and to *autonomously* pursue *goals* ascribed to users or explicitly designed for the system itself. Essentially, this amounts at transitioning from actions and perceptions to goals and assertions. Key enabler of such a paradigm shift is the increasing computational power that can be embedded in everyday objects, along with advancements in machine learning techniques, which, for instance, are making it possible to analyse data locally [5].

In such a setting, coordination becomes the capability of *argumenting* about the current "state of affairs", and of triggering *conversations* to collectively decide how to act in order to achieve the desired future ones. Besides support-ing decentralised coordination by leveraging opportunities for negotiation [53], argumentation also embraces humans-in-the-loop by enabling users to interact in natural language [8], and deals with the issues of trust and algocracy by making explanations and justifications of decision making available and amenable of inspection and interpretation by human supervisors.

In [24], a traffic control scenario is taken as a case study. There, vehicles approaching an intersection are supposed to be equipped with an array of speaking and hearing objects, as the intersection itself—i.e., cameras, traffic lights, etc. As they get closer to the intersection, vehicles start argumenting with the traffic light about who has the right of way and who should instead stop and wait (Fig. 3). After a negotiation phase where vehicles try to persuade the traffic light to decide in their favour, the dispute is settled when the argumentation process finds a solution for which no vehicle has to stop.

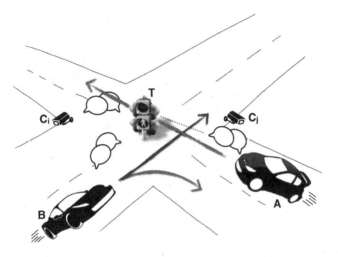

Fig. 3. Argumentation-based intersection management (image from [24]).

4.3   Personalised Medicine with $\mathcal{A}$rgo$\mathcal{R}$ec

In [15] another example of fighting the fear of algocracy by promoting trust and interpretability with argumentation can be found. There, a recommender system named $\mathcal{A}$rgo$\mathcal{R}$ec is introduced, whose distinctive feature is to rely on *argumentation* to provide *justifiable* and *personalised* recommendations. In fact, on the one hand argumentation empowers $\mathcal{A}$rgo$\mathcal{R}$ec with explanatory power regarding why and how recommendations are provided, while, on the other hand, argumentation improves the user experience of patients thanks to natural language generation.

In particular, $\mathcal{A}$rgo$\mathcal{R}$ec adopts a simple framework for structured argumentation—depicted in Fig. 4 as an argumentation graph: arguments (shaded boxes) are made up of claims (darker nodes) and their premises (lighter ones), and put together by attack (solid arrows) and support relations (dashed arrows). Attacks may be rebuttals (darker arrows) or undercuts (lighter ones),

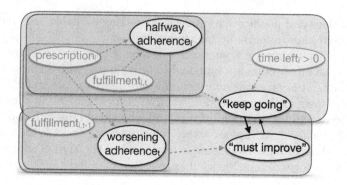

Fig. 4. Example of argumentation graph exploited by $\mathcal{A}$rgo$\mathcal{R}$ec [15].

that is, contradictory claims or premises, respectively. All relations have a strength represented by a numeric weight (thickness of the line).

In $\mathcal{A}$rgo$\mathcal{R}$ec, recommendations are interpreted as arguments composed by a claim and its supporting premises: the former is, for instance, the suggestion to keep going with the current activities, while the latter could be the fact that the patient has a good compliance with the prescriptions assigned by the medical staff. Attack relations are the consequence of the fact that patients' compliance is monitored through automated tools – such as wearable devices – which provide raw measurements, which are unaware of the goal behind the prescription, nor of the history of the patient, nor of any other contextual information. The argumentation process enacted by $\mathcal{A}$rgo$\mathcal{R}$ec, instead, is aware of all the different measurements available, as well as of the status and history of the patient, thus exploits this awareness to both produce justifiable and personalised recommendations: the former by tracking the argumentation graph, the latter by generating sentences tailored to the patient (i.e. calling him/her by name, recalling the time left to complete a prescription, informing him/her on the current compliance, etc.).

For instance, in Fig. 4 recommendation "keep going" is the strongest argument: although comparison of latest event ($fulfillment_{i,t}$) with previous one ($fulfillment_{i,t-1}$) suggests to warn the patient (recommendation "must improve") since her/his adherence to prescriptions is worsening, the fact that there is still time left to complete prescription ($prescription_i$) makes recommendation "keep going" win the dispute.

5   Conclusion and Outlook

Engineering socio-technical systems is a complex task, and this comes at no surprise: the technical perspective is usually quite different from the socio-cognitive one, thus adopting either standpoint easily leads to a socio-technical gap. Nevertheless, there exist approaches attempting to integrate these two facets, by carefully linking socio-cognitive theories with technical solutions, as in the case of the three research proposals described in Sect. 4. There, for instance, $\mathcal{MoK}$ attempts to integrate decentralised computations with stigmergic coordination in the same framework, so as to achieve a sort of user-driven self-organisation—as happens with the clustering emergent phenomenon depicted in Fig. 2. Speaking Objects, instead, focuses on integrating goal-orientation with argumentation-based negotiation, so as to provide more flexible coordination schemes in distributed scenarios, while also increasing the abstraction level. All of this with the ultimate goal of shrinking the socio-technical gap arising when engineering STS as much as possible.

It is thus apparent that *integration* is the key here: as scientists and engineers, we need to find a way to include socio-cognitive aspects in our technical solutions since the very beginning of the design phase by using proper models and theories, not as an orthogonal dimension to be added later on, or dealt with in an ad-hoc way.

Accordingly, the three approaches discussed in Sect. 4 are not to be seen as mutually-exclusive solutions to the same problem, but rather as *complementary* one to each other as focussed on a different layer or perspective of the STS at hand. For instance, $\mathcal{MoK}$ is perfectly suited at working as the information handling layer in a Smart City deployment adopting the Speaking Objects vision. Just think of a Smart City as a large-scale STS: speaking and hearing objects are scattered throughout the city to compose the IT infrastructure with which human users constantly and seamlessly interact in their everyday activities. All the information recorded in this urban STS continuously and spontaneously evolves according to the $\mathcal{MoK}$ vision, and is made available to speaking and hearing objects as they need premises to either support or attack each other arguments. There, even $\mathcal{ArgoRec}$ could be added to the picture, for instance as an approach to build personal digital assistants offering guidance and assistance regarding. i.e., public transportation services, touristic attractions, interaction with the local administration, etc.

In this paper, we tried to shed some light on the possible paths to follow in order to make such an integration happen, with the aim of providing fertile ground for further discussion and research on the matter.

Acknowledgement. This work has been partially supported by the CONNECARE (Personalised Connected Care for Complex Chronic Patients) project (EU H2020-RIA, Contract No. 689802).

References

1. Ackerman, M.S.: The intellectual challenge of CSCW: the gap between social requirements and technical feasibility. Hum.-Comput. Interact. **15**(2–3), 179–203 (2000)
2. ACM, US Public Policy Council: statement on algorithmic transparency and accountability, January 2017. https://www.acm.org/binaries/content/assets/public-policy/2017_usacm_statement_algorithms.pdf

3. Atzori, L., Iera, A., Morabito, G., Nitti, M.: The social internet of things (SIoT)-when social networks meet the internet of things: concept, architecture and network characterization. Comput. Netw. **56**(16), 3594–3608 (2012)
4. Babaoglu, O., et al.: Design patterns from biology for distributed computing. ACM Trans. Auton. Adapt. Syst. (TAAS) **1**(1), 26–66 (2006)
5. Bourzac, K.: Millimeter-scale computers: now with deep-learning neural networks on board, February 2017. https://goo.gl/sciVTC
6. Brun, Y., et al.: Engineering self-adaptive systems through feedback loops. In: Cheng, B.H.C., de Lemos, R., Giese, H., Inverardi, P., Magee, J. (eds.) Software Engineering for Self-Adaptive Systems. LNCS, vol. 5525, pp. 48–70. Springer, Heidelberg (2009). https://doi.org/10.1007/978-3-642-02161-9_3
7. Calinescu, R., Ghezzi, C., Kwiatkowska, M., Mirandola, R.: Self-adaptive software needs quantitative verification at runtime. Commun. ACM **55**(9), 69–77 (2012)
8. Caminada, M.W., Kutlak, R., Oren, N., Vasconcelos, W.W.: Scrutable plan enactment via argumentation and natural language generation. In: Proceedings of the 2014 International Conference on Autonomous Agents and Multi-agent Systems, AAMAS 2014, pp. 1625–1626. International Foundation for Autonomous Agents and Multiagent Systems, Richland (2014)
9. Castelfranchi, C.: Modelling social action for AI agents. Artif. Intell. **103**(1–2), 157–182 (1998)
10. Castelfranchi, C., Pezzullo, G., Tummolini, L.: Behavioral implicit communication (BIC): communicating with smart environments via our practical behavior and its traces. Int. J. Ambient. Comput. Intell. **2**(1), 1–12 (2010)
11. Castlefranchi, C.: From conversation to interaction via behavioral communication: for a semiotic design of objects, environments, and behaviors. In: Theories and Practice in Interaction Design, pp. 157–79 (2006)
12. Danaher, J.: The threat of algocracy: reality, resistance and accommodation. Philos. Technol. **29**(3), 245–268 (2016)
13. De Wolf, T., Holvoet, T.: Design patterns for decentralised coordination in self-organising emergent systems. In: Brueckner, S.A., Hassas, S., Jelasity, M., Yamins, D. (eds.) ESOA 2006. LNCS (LNAI), vol. 4335, pp. 28–49. Springer, Heidelberg (2007). https://doi.org/10.1007/978-3-540-69868-5_3
14. Diakopoulos, N.: Accountability in algorithmic decision making. Commun. ACM **59**(2), 56–62 (2016)
15. Fernández, J.M., et al.: Towards argumentation-based recommendations for personalised patient empowerment. In: Elsweiler, D., et al. (eds.) Proceedings of the 2nd International Workshop on Health Recommender Systems co-located with the 11th International Conference on Recommender Systems (RecSys 2017). CEUR Workshop Proceedings, Como, Italy, 31 August 2017, vol. 1953, pp. 2–5. CEUR-WS.org (2017)
16. Fernandez-Marquez, J.L., Di Marzo Serugendo, G., Montagna, S., Viroli, M., Arcos, J.L.: Description and composition of bio-inspired design patterns: a complete overview. Nat. Comput. **12**(1), 43–67 (2013)
17. Di Marzo Serugendo, G., Karageorgos, A.: Self-organisation and emergence in MAS: an overview. Informatica **30**(1), 45–54 (2006)
18. Goodman, B., Flaxman, S.: European Union regulations on algorithmic decision-making and a "right to explanation". ArXiv e-prints, June 2016
19. Grassé, P.P.: La reconstruction du nid et les coordinations interindividuelles chez Bellicositermes natalensis et Cubitermes sp. la théorie de la stigmergie: Essai d'interprétation du comportement des termites constructeurs. Insectes Sociaux **6**(1), 41–80 (1959)

20. Hillston, J., Pitt, J., Wirsing, M., Zambonelli, F.: Collective adaptive systems: qualitative and quantitative modelling and analysis (Dagstuhl Seminar 14512). Dagstuhl Rep. **4**(12), 68–113 (2015)
21. Hudson, S.E., Smith, I.: Techniques for addressing fundamental privacy and disruption tradeoffs in awareness support systems. In: Proceedings of the 1996 ACM Conference on Computer Supported Cooperative Work, CSCW 1996, pp. 248–257. ACM, New York (1996)
22. Hutchins, E.: Cognition in the Wild. MIT Press, Cambridge (1995)
23. Latella, D., Loreti, M., Massink, M.: On-the-fly PCTL fast mean-field approximated model-checking for self-organising coordination. Sci. Comput. Program. **110**, 23–50 (2015)
24. Lippi, M., Mamei, M., Mariani, S., Zambonelli, F.: An argumentation-based perspective over the social IoT. IEEE Internet Things J. **5**, 1 (2017)
25. Lippi, M., Mamei, M., Mariani, S., Zambonelli, F.: Coordinating distributed speaking objects. In: 2017 IEEE 37th International Conference on Distributed Computing Systems (ICDCS), pp. 1949–1960, June 2017
26. Mamei, M., Zambonelli, F., Leonardi, L.: Co-fields: towards a unifying approach to the engineering of swarm intelligent systems. In: Petta, P., Tolksdorf, R., Zambonelli, F. (eds.) ESAW 2002. LNCS (LNAI), vol. 2577, pp. 68–81. Springer, Heidelberg (2003). https://doi.org/10.1007/3-540-39173-8_6
27. Mariani, S.: On the "local-to-global" issue in self-organisation: chemical reactions with custom kinetic rates. In: 8th IEEE International Conference on Self-Adaptive and Self-Organizing Systems Workshops, SASOW 2014, pp. 61–67. IEEE CS, London, September 2014
28. Mariani, S.: Coordination of Complex Sociotechnical Systems - Self-organisation of Knowledge in MoK. Artificial Intelligence: Foundations, Theory, and Algorithms. Springer, Cham (2016). https://doi.org/10.1007/978-3-319-47109-9
29. Mariani, S., Omicini, A.: Molecules of knowledge: self-organisation in knowledge-intensive environments. In: Fortino, G., Badica, C., Malgeri, M., Unland, R. (eds.) IDC 2012. SCI, vol. 446, pp. 17–22. Springer, Heidelberg (2013). https://doi.org/10.1007/978-3-642-32524-3_4
30. Mariani, S., Omicini, A.: Anticipatory coordination in socio-technical knowledge-intensive environments: behavioural implicit communication in *MoK*. In: Gavanelli, M., Lamma, E., Riguzzi, F. (eds.) AI*IA 2015. LNCS (LNAI), vol. 9336, pp. 102–115. Springer, Cham (2015). https://doi.org/10.1007/978-3-319-24309-2_8
31. Medsker, L.: Algorithmic Transparency and Accountability - AI Matters (2017) https://sigai.acm.org/aimatters/blog/2017/06/01/algorithmic-transparency-and-accountability/
32. Nagpal, R.: A catalog of biologically-inspired primitives for engineering self-organization. In: Di Marzo Serugendo, G., Karageorgos, A., Rana, O.F., Zambonelli, F. (eds.) ESOA 2003. LNCS (LNAI), vol. 2977, pp. 53–62. Springer, Heidelberg (2004). https://doi.org/10.1007/978-3-540-24701-2_4
33. Nature: More accountability for big-data algorithms. Nature **537**(7621), 449–449 (2016)
34. Nikolai, C., Madey, G.: Tools of the trade: a survey of various agent based modeling platforms. J. Artif. Soc. Soc. Simul. **12**(2), 2 (2009)
35. O'Day, V.L., Bobrow, D.G., Shirley, M.: The social-technical design circle. In: Proceedings of the 1996 ACM Conference on Computer Supported Cooperative Work, pp. 160–169. ACM (1996)

36. Omicini, A.: Agents writing on walls: cognitive stigmergy and beyond. In: Paglieri, F., Tummolini, L., Falcone, R., Miceli, M. (eds.) The Goals of Cognition. Essays in Honor of Cristiano Castelfranchi, Tributes, vol. 20, Chap. 29, pp. 543–556. College Publications, London, December 2012

37. Orlikowski, W.J.: The duality of technology: rethinking the concept of technology in organizations. Organ. Sci. **3**(3), 398–427 (1992)

38. Pariser, E.: The Filter Bubble: What the Internet is Hiding From You. Penguin, Harmondsworth (2011)

39. Dyke Parunak, H.: A survey of environments and mechanisms for human-human stigmergy. In: Weyns, D., Van Dyke Parunak, H., Michel, F. (eds.) E4MAS 2005. LNCS (LNAI), vol. 3830, pp. 163–186. Springer, Heidelberg (2006). https://doi.org/10.1007/11678809_10

40. Persily, N.: Can democracy survive the internet? J. Democr. **28**(2), 63–76 (2017)

41. Piunti, M., Castelfranchi, C., Falcone, R.: Anticipatory coordination through action observation and behavior adaptation. In: Proceedings of AISB (2007)

42. Rahwan, I., Ramchurn, S.D., Jennings, N.R., Mcburney, P., Parsons, S., Sonenberg, L.: Argumentation-based negotiation. Knowl. Eng. Rev. **18**(4), 343–375 (2003)

43. Ricci, A., Omicini, A., Viroli, M., Gardelli, L., Oliva, E.: Cognitive stigmergy: towards a framework based on agents and artifacts. In: Weyns, D., Parunak, H.V.D., Michel, F. (eds.) E4MAS 2006. LNCS (LNAI), vol. 4389, pp. 124–140. Springer, Heidelberg (2007). https://doi.org/10.1007/978-3-540-71103-2_7

44. Schmidt, K., Wagner, I.: Ordering systems: coordinative practices and artifacts in architectural design and planning. Comput. Support. Coop. Work. (CSCW) **13**(5–6), 349–408 (2004)

45. DI Marzo Serugendo, G., et al.: Self-organisation: paradigms and applications. In: Di Marzo Serugendo, G., Karageorgos, A., Rana, O.F., Zambonelli, F. (eds.) ESOA 2003. LNCS (LNAI), vol. 2977, pp. 1–19. Springer, Heidelberg (2004). https://doi.org/10.1007/978-3-540-24701-2_1

46. Suchman, L.A.: Situated actions. In: Plans and Situated Actions: The Problem of Human-Machine Communication, Chap. 4, pp. 49–67. Cambridge University Press, New York (1987)

47. Susi, T., Ziemke, T.: Social cognition, artefacts, and stigmergy: a comparative analysis of theoretical frameworks for the understanding of artefact-mediated collaborative activity. Cogn. Syst. Res. **2**(4), 273–290 (2001)

48. Usman Iftikhar, M., Weyns, D.: A case study on formal verification of self-adaptive behaviors in a decentralized system. ArXiv e-prints, August 2012

49. Van Eemeren, F.H., Grootendorst, R., Johnson, R.H., Plantin, C., Willard, C.A.: Fundamentals of Argumentation Theory: A Handbook of Historical Backgrounds and Contemporary Developments. Routledge, London (2013)

50. Viroli, M., Casadei, M.: Biochemical tuple spaces for self-organising coordination. In: Field, J., Vasconcelos, V.T. (eds.) COORDINATION 2009. LNCS, vol. 5521, pp. 143–162. Springer, Heidelberg (2009). https://doi.org/10.1007/978-3-642-02053-7_8

51. Viroli, M., Damiani, F.: Type-based self-stabilisation for computational fields. Log. Methods Comput. Sci. **11** (2015)

52. Whitworth, B.: Socio-technical systems. In: Encyclopedia of Human Computer Interaction, pp. 533–541 (2006)

53. Zambonelli, F., et al.: Developing pervasive multi-agent systems with nature-inspired coordination. Pervasive Mob. Comput. **17**, 236–252 (2015). Special Issue "10 years of Pervasive Computing" In Honor of Chatschik Bisdikian

Reo Coordination Model for Simulation of Quantum Internet Software

Ebrahim Ardeshir-Larijani[1,2(✉)] and Farhad Arbab[3,4]

[1] Department of Computer and Data Science, Faculty of Mathematical Sciences,
Shahid Beheshti University (SBU), Tehran, Iran
[2] School of Computer Science, Institute for Research in Fundamental Sciences (IPM),
Tehran, Iran
e.a.larijani@ipm.ir
[3] Centrum Wiskunde and Informatica (CWI), Amsterdam, Netherlands
[4] Leiden University, Leiden, Netherlands
farhad.arbab@cwi.nl

Abstract. The novel field of quantum technology is being promoted by academia, governments and industry. Quantum technologies offer new means for carrying out fast computation as well as secure communication, using primitives that exploit peculiar characteristics of quantum physics. While building quantum computing devices remains a challenge, the area of quantum communication and cryptography has been successful in reaching industrial applications. In particular, recently, plans for building quantum internet have been put into action and expected to be launched by 2020 in the Netherlands. Quantum internet uses quantum communication as well as quantum entanglement along with classical communication. This makes design of software platform for quantum networks very challenging and a daunting task. Seamless design and testing of platforms for quantum software, thus, becomes a necessity to develop complex simulators for this kind of networks. In this short paper, we argue that using coordination models such as Reo can significantly simplify the development of software applications for quantum internet. Moreover, formal verification of such quantum software becomes possible, thanks to the separation of concerns, compositionality, and reusability of Reo models. This paper introduces an extension of a recently developed simulator for quantum internet (SimulaQron) by incorporating Reo models extended with quantum data and operations, along with classical data. We explain the main concepts and our plan for implementing this extension as a new tool: SimulaQ(reo)n.

Keywords: Quantum communication · Quantum information
Quantum networks · Reo Coordination Model

The first author is supported in part by a grant from the School of Computer Science, Institute for Research in Fundamental Sciences (IPM), Iran.

M. Mazzara et al. (Eds.): STAF 2018 Workshops, LNCS 11176, pp. 311–319, 2018.
https://doi.org/10.1007/978-3-030-04771-9_23

1   Introduction

As quantum technologies emerge rapidly, designing reliable hardware and software for hybrid quantum/classical systems poses significant challenges both theoretically and experimentally. Nevertheless, specific quantum networks have been built in various cities around the world and already a satellite has been launched to provide secure quantum communication. Using such networks demands rigorous analysis and verification before they can be trusted in safety- and security-critical applications. One way to achieve this goal is to develop a dedicated simulation toolset before actual quantum devices get deployed. SimulaQron [2] is an example of such a tool that is able to model the behaviour of local simulators or even actual quantum devices in a hybrid quantum/classical network which is called quantum internet [4]. The tool itself can be thought of as a platform for developing software applications for quantum internet, and is designed to offer ease-of-use and clarity in that regard. However, simulating complex interactions in quantum networks needs incorporation of coordination models for the same reasons as in the case of classical networks (e.g., compositionality and reusability), even more strongly so, because in quantum networks, primitives with non-local (entanglement) effects play a critical role. Currently, the majority of research in quantum programming focuses on sequential programs and efficient simulation of sequential quantum algorithms (e.g., see [10]).

In this short paper we pursue two objectives: first, to bring the problem of coordination in quantum internet to the attention of the computer science community, especially those active in the field of coordination models [15]. Second, we explain the principles of extending Reo [3, 13, 14] coordination model and language to support modeling of the behaviour of quantum networks. One milestone toward our second objective consists of automatic generation of executable code for protocols over quantum internet. To this end, the current Reo compiler has to be modified in order to support quantum data types, operations and primitives, as we explain later in this paper. To our knowledge this paper presents the first work on coordination of quantum software components.

The rest of this paper is organized as follows. In Sect. 2, we present the necessary background on quantum information processing. In Sect. 3, we review the Reo coordination concepts. We describe the SimulaQron tool in Sect. 4. In Sect. 5, we present the principles of extension of Reo to support coordination in the quantum setting, particularly in connection with SimulaQron. Finally, we conclude the paper in Sect. 6 with plans for future work.

2   Quantum Information

This section provides a concise introduction to quantum information processing (QIP). For more details, we refer to [1]. The basic unit of quantum information is a *qubit* (quantum bit). A qubit can be in a *basis* state, represented by $|0\rangle$ or $|1\rangle$. These basis states correspond to the classical states 0 and 1. However, a qubit may be in a *superposition* of states, described by $\alpha|0\rangle + \beta|1\rangle$, with $|\alpha|^2 + |\beta|^2 =$

1 where α and β are complex numbers called *amplitudes*. More generally, we consider a state of n qubits, whose general form is $|\psi\rangle = \alpha_0|00\ldots0\rangle + \ldots + \alpha_{2^n-1}|11\ldots1\rangle$ with $\Sigma_i|\alpha_i|^2 = 1$.

The state of a single qubit is an element of a two-dimensional complex vector space, called *Hilbert space*. Multi-qubit state spaces can be constructed by tensor products, e.g., $|0\rangle \otimes |0\rangle \otimes \cdots \otimes |0\rangle$ defines an n-qubit basis state $|00\ldots0\rangle$.

There are two kinds of operations on quantum states: unitary operations and measurements. A unitary transformation is an invertible linear operation on the Hilbert space. In a two dimensional Hilbert space, measurement randomly projects the state onto one of a pair of orthogonal subspaces, with a probability determined by the amplitudes. A measurement, thus, produces classical information as a result. For example, if the state $\alpha|0\rangle + \beta|1\rangle$ is measured in the standard basis, then the classical result is 0 with probability $|\alpha|^2$ or 1 with probability $|\beta|^2$. Moreover, measurement of a quantum state (in the standard basis) permanently changes it to $|0\rangle$ or $|1\rangle$, respectively.

An important phenomenon in quantum physics is *entanglement*. A multi-qubit state is entangled if it cannot be decomposed as a tensor product of simpler states. An example is the two-qubit state $\frac{1}{\sqrt{2}}(|00\rangle + |11\rangle)$, which is known as an EPR pair. This pair is one of a set of four important two-qubit entangled states, termed *Bell states*. In this state, if the first qubit is measured in the standard basis, then the overall state collapses to either $|00\rangle$ or $|11\rangle$, which also determines the state of the second qubit. Therefore, there is a correlation between the two entangled qubits even when they are separated by a distance.

3   Reo Coordination Model

Reo [3] is a language for exogenous coordination of software components, wherein protocols are defined as graphs of primitives called channels. In Reo, graphs of channels, called connectors, are defined compositionally. Recently, a new textual syntax together with a versatile compiler for this syntax have been added to the set of Reo tools [9]. The simplest form of connectors are channels that connect two ends by defining a relation on the observable data exchanged at those ends. This relation imposes a constraint on the flow of data between those end points. Channels constitute the edges of Reo connector graphs on whose nodes channel ends coincide. Reo allows arbitrary user-defined channel types, but only two types of channel ends can exist: a source end through which data enters into a channel, and a sink end through which data leaves a channel. Compositions of these two types of channel ends yields only three types of nodes: source, sink, and mixed. A source node consists of one or more source channel ends; a sink node consists of one or more sink channel ends; and a mixed node consists of one or more source and one or more sink channel ends. Components can perform I/O operations on only source and sink (but not mixed) nodes of a connector. A data item written to a source node gets replicated to every source channel end of the node, only when all of them are able to accept; a source node, thus, performs a form of synchronous broadcast of its incoming data-flow stream onto its outgoing data-flow streams. A take operation on a sink node non-deterministically selects a data item available at one of the sink channel ends of the node and leaves the others intact; a sink node, thus, performs a non-deterministic merge of its incoming data-flow streams onto its outgoing data-flow stream. A mixed node repeatedly performs an atomic operation that combines the behaviour of a sink and a source node: in each iteration, it non-deterministically selects a data item from one of its sink channel ends and replicates it onto all of its source channel ends, all in one atomic operation.

We now informally explain the behaviour of some of the channels in terms of constraints that they impose on data-flow. For formal definition of constraint automata as operational semantics of Reo language, see [3]. The $Sync(a, b)$ channel, gets data items trough its end a and synchronously (i.e., atomically) outputs them through its end b. Similarly, the $LossySync(a, b)$, accepts data through its end a and atomically, either loses the data or outputs them through its end b. A $FIFO(a, b)$ channel synchronously accepts a data item, d, through its channel end a and stores it in its internal buffer, which has the capacity to hold a single data item. The channel then offers the data item in its buffer through its channel end b and clears its buffer when b dispenses the data item. A $Filter[P](a, b)$ channel behaves almost exactly as a $Sync(a, b)$ channel, except that it passes only those data items from a to b that match its pattern parameter, P. The channel accepts any data item that it receives through a, and either loses the data item if it does not match P, or passes it through b if it does match P. A $Transformer[f](a, b)$ channel behaves like a $Sync$ channel, except that it applies the unary function f to every data item that it passes from a to b. The channel silently loses all data items taken from a that are not in the domain of f.

We use two specific variants of the $Transformer$ channel to express quantum computing protocols, where instead of the function f we use either a unitary operation U_f that operates on qubits, or a projective measurement operator. In the latter case, we get a classical bit as an outcome, and a distorted qubit (depending on the outcome). Thus, evaluating a function by a unitary operator is a reversible action, whereas measuring qubits, is irreversible.

4   SimulaQron

Motivated by the plan to establish a prototype for quantum internet, researchers have proposed SimulaQron [2] as a platform for developing quantum internet software. With SimulaQron it is possible to simulate the behaviour of a quantum network, where each node may have a share of a quantum entanglement as well as the ability to perform quantum operations on qubits. The back-end of the SimulaQron at each node of the network consists of two main entities: a virtual node and a CQC (classical and quantum combiner) interface. The virtualization of nodes allows us to use different quantum simulators on the network. A virtual node a quantum register, simulated qubits and virtual qubits. A quantum register interacts with the local simulator. Simulated qubits are objects that enable us to manipulate qubits without interacting with quantum registers directly. Finally, virtual qubits are objects with pointers to simulated qubits, some of which may be owned by other virtual nodes, i.e., their pointers may refer to simulated qubits in other virtual nodes. To model entanglement, which excludes the possibility to simulate qubits separately, SimulaQron allows merging virtual nodes in such a way as to place all simulated qubits that are entangled together, in one virtual node. The quantum registers of the merged virtual nodes must be merged as well.

The CQC back-end is an interface for specification of interaction with a quantum network. It enables simulation of sending and receiving qubits to/from a quantum network, command type messages, and information for entanglement management. Figure 1, illustrates the position of the CQC interface in the overall architecture of SimulaQron. For more details see reference [2].

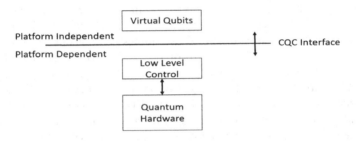

Fig. 1. CQC interface

5   Extension: SimulaQ(reo)n

Since quantum entanglement cannot be simulated locally, interdependence of qubits becomes implicit in current models and languages used to express quantum computing. Reo connectors can serve as a middleware that explicitly expresses entanglement, quantum and classical communications, and the protocol for their coordination, all in one structure. Extending Reo with quantum computing primitives can offer a high-level tool for simulating complex interactions among nodes in the quantum networks introduced in the previous section.

In this work we propose the design of a special coordination layer for quantum components, which relates Reo type connectors with the CQC back-end. To realize this coordination layer, we must extend Reo to support quantum data and operations. However, quantum extension seems incompatible with the semantics of some primitives in classical Reo. For example, Fig. 2 shows two instances of a simple Reo connector, called *replicator*. A replicator consists of three *Sync* channels and its behaviour in the classical data domain is to replicate data that arrive on node C atomically through nodes A and B. However, the no-cloning theorem [1] in quantum mechanics states that no physical process can duplicate a quantum state. Therefore, when qubits arrive at C, two cases need carefull consideration.

Consider a replicator with a fan-out of 2, (similar to the replicators in Fig. 2), we describe the behaviour of this replicator in terms of a quantum operation that is called controlled-NOT $(CNOT)$.[1] For $d \in \{0,1\}$, when a qubit in the state $|d\rangle$ arrives at the source node of this replicator, the replicator creates a qubit in the initial state $|0\rangle$, and subsequently performs the controlled-NOT operation $CNOT(|d\rangle|0\rangle)$. This results in a two qubit system in the state $|dd\rangle$, which is a separable state. Thus, each of the channel ends A and B in the Fig. 2(a), receives a qubit in the state $|d\rangle$, which allows the local "downstream" simulators to manipulate their corresponding qubits separately. On the other hand, if the incoming qubit is in a superposition state, e.g., $|d\rangle = \frac{1}{\sqrt{2}}(|0\rangle \pm |1\rangle)$, the $CNOT$ operation creates an entangled state, e.g., the EPR state $\frac{1}{\sqrt{2}}(|00\rangle \pm |11\rangle)$. Entangled states are not separable, meaning that we cannot assign local states to the qubits arriving at channel ends A and B, in Fig. 2(b). Instead, if at later stage, one measures either of the qubits coming out of nodes A and B, the observed outcome of either $|00\rangle$ or $|11\rangle$ will be the same (correlated) at both ends. This instance of replication demonstrates that local "downstream" quantum simulators cannot always operate on quantum states in a distributed manner: such cases require an entanglement/virtualization management layer.

The idea of using the $CNOT$ operation is taken from the work of Altenkirch [5] in quantum functional programming. To implement the replicator of Fig. 2 in Reo, we place a filter channel before every source node in order to distinguish between classical and quantum data. For every quantum data item, we create a qubit in the initial state $|0\rangle$ and add a transformer channel to perform the $CNOT$.

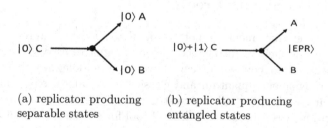

(a) replicator producing   (b) replicator producing
separable states   entangled states

Fig. 2. Replicator connector

Quantum Key Distribution (QKD) is an example of an industrialized quantum protocol, which can be integrated into a classical network. We now analyze a version, introduced by Ekert [11], where Alice and Bob share classical keys

---

[1] This two qubits operation consists of a control and a target qubit. If the control gate is set in the state $|1\rangle$, a quantum flip operation (also known as the Pauli X) is applied to target qubit. [1].

using entanglement. In this protocol Alice and Bob share pairs of entangled qubits. Then each party randomly decides on applying quantum measurement in standard basis (S) or X basis (where bases are entangled EPR states) on its share. For those bases that both parties agree, measurement outcomes are in fact shared keys. We illustrate this protocol using Reo connectors in Fig. 3. These connectors use quantum channels (depicted as double line arrows) to produce entangled pairs. The symbol $\otimes$ represents Reo's standard exclusive router. Two kinds of transformers, X and S represent quantum measurements in different bases. If we are interested only in sharing keys without external observation, Fig. 3(a), specifies the necessary interaction between parties. However, we often need to know the statistics of cases of agreement between Alice and Bob. To obtain this information, we compose the connector in Fig. 3(a) with a simple circuit that "taps" the flow of data in the protocol circuit and diverts it to a monitor, as in Fig. 3(b). Here $\oplus$ represents a component that merely monitors the number of agreements between Alice and Bob. This composition of an external monitor is a desirable feature in the sense that components (Alice and Bob) do not need to be modified while exogenously, we are able to count the number of times they agree on their choices of quantum measurement.

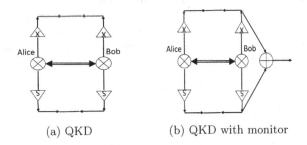

(a) QKD   (b) QKD with monitor

Fig. 3. Connectors in Reo

It is also possible to consider local quantum simulations as web services provided to the network, by adopting Reo based orchestration techniques introduced in [6], in the quantum setting. Here the goal would be to develop and implement proxies between Reo connectors (e.g., Fig. 3(b)) and network nodes (e.g., CQC back-end).

Similar to classical Reo, the formal semantics of quantum primitives may be described by (an extension of) constraint automata, where the data domain is extended to include a quantum data type (qubits). The set of states in this case, may include description of quantum states. This is in particular important in the case of *FIFO* channels. The constraint on the data-flow in this channel type is specified by the value in its memory, which may be a quantum state. However, in the generalization of this channel, e.g., $FIFO^n$, where the memory has n cells, we may have both quantum and classical data types. We leave the exact definition of quantum constraint automata and its composition for future work.

There are several case studies at the frontline of implementation of a distributed quantum networks such as quantum leader election, quantum byzantine agreement, and quantum dining philosophers. These are examples where quantum solutions are often faster and simpler (e.g., deterministic) compared with their classical counterparts. For instance, dining philosophers (DP) is a classic problem in distributed system [8] where the effectiveness of exogenous coordination can be neatly demonstrated (see Sect. 7 of [7]). In the quantum version of the DP problem [12], an entangled state $|0^n\rangle + |1^n\rangle$ gets distributed among n parties (this can be done by each philosopher sending an EPR pair to its neighbours). Then each party needs to do internal quantum operations and measurements to (I) run a fair leader election, and (II) form two groups for breaking symmetry. We envisage that adding a Reo connector to generate a coordination layer, separating it from internal actions of each party, simplifies the implementation of quantum DP on quantum internet infrastructure.

6   Future Work and Conclusion

In this short paper we argued that using a coordination model to implement quantum internet software can play an important role in realizing such technology in near future. We explained how Reo coordination concepts can be extended to the setting of the so-called quantum internet. The main line for future work is to formally define the coordination layers for quantum components, and to express its (operational) semantics in an extended version of constraint automata. This must be followed by automatic code generation using an extension of the current Reo compiler [9] to generate executable code for the CQC back-end of the SimulaQron tool. Generating code for this back-end raises the question of existence of specific optimization methods for the Reo compiler, given the non-locality of quantum primitives in a distributed system.

It is also crucial to collaborate with experimental teams to accurately incorporate their requirements and levels of abstractions needed for coordination of quantum software components.

Using formal verification schemes developed for coordination formalisms such as Reo in distributed quantum programming presents an important line for future work. Full implementation of quantum algorithms for dining philosophers and Byzantine agreement on SimulaQron using the extension presented in this paper is an interesting line of future work.

References

1. Nielsen, M.A., Chuang, I.L.: Quantum Computation and Quantum Information. Cambridge University Press, Cambridge (2000)
2. Dahlberg, A., Wehner, S.: SimulaQron - A simulator for developing quantum internet software. Quantum Sci. Technol. **4**(1) (2019). https://doi.org/10.1088/2058-9565/aad56e
3. Arbab, F.: Reo: a channel-based coordination model for component composition. Math. Struct. Comput. Sci. **14**(3), 329–366 (2004)

4. Castelvecchi, D.: The entangled web. Nature **554**, 289–292 (2018)
5. Altenkirch, T., Grattage, J.: A functional quantum programming language. In: 20th Annual IEEE Symposium on Logic in Computer Science, LICS 2005, pp. 249–258 (2005)
6. Jongmans, S.-S.T.Q., Santini, F., Sargolzaei, M., Arbab, F., Afsarmanesh, H.: Automatic code generation for the orchestration of web services with Reo. In: De Paoli, F., Pimentel, E., Zavattaro, G. (eds.) ESOCC 2012. LNCS, vol. 7592, pp. 1–16. Springer, Heidelberg (2012). https://doi.org/10.1007/978-3-642-33427-6_1
7. Arbab, F.: Composition of interacting computations. In: Goldin, D., Smolka, S.A., Wegner, P. (eds.) Interactive Computation, pp. 277–321. Springer, Heidelberg (2006). https://doi.org/10.1007/3-540-34874-3_12
8. Dijkstra, E.W.: Hierarchical ordering of sequential processes. Acta Informatica **1**, 115–138 (1971)
9. ReoLanguage   GitHub   repository.   https://github.com/ReoLanguage/Reo. Accessed 23 Mar 2018
10. Microsoft Quantum Dev Kit (2018). https://www.microsoft.com/en-us/quantum/
11. Ekert, A.K.: Quantum cryptography based on Bell's theorem. Phys. Rev. Lett. **67**, 661–663 (1991)
12. Aharonov, D., Ganz, M., Magnin, L.: Dining Philosophers, Leader Election and Ring Size problems, in the quantum setting. arXiv: 1707.01187 (2017)
13. Arbab, F.: Puff, the magic protocol. In: Agha, G., Danvy, O., Meseguer, J. (eds.) Formal Modeling: Actors, Open Systems, Biological Systems. LNCS, vol. 7000, pp. 169–206. Springer, Heidelberg (2011). https://doi.org/10.1007/978-3-642-24933-4_9
14. Arbab, F.: Proper protocol. In: Ábrahám, E., Bonsangue, M., Johnsen, E.B. (eds.) Theory and Practice of Formal Methods. LNCS, vol. 9660, pp. 65–87. Springer, Cham (2016). https://doi.org/10.1007/978-3-319-30734-3_7
15. Arbab, F.: What do you mean, coordination? In: Bulletin of the Dutch Association for Theoretical Computer Science, NVTI, pp. 11–22 (1998)

Computing the Parallelism Degree
of Timed BPMN Processes

Francisco Durán[1], Camilo Rocha[2], and Gwen Salaün[3(✉)]

[1] University of Málaga, Málaga, Spain
[2] Pontificia Universidad Javeriana, Cali, Colombia
[3] Univ. Grenoble Alpes, CNRS, Grenoble INP, Inria, LIG, 38000 Grenoble, France
`gwen.salaun@inria.fr`

Abstract. A business process is a combination of structured and related activities that aim at fulfilling a specific organizational goal for a customer or market. An important measure when developing a business process is the *degree of parallelism*, namely, the maximum number of tasks that are executable in parallel at any given time in a process. This measure determines the peak demand on tasks and thus can provide valuable insight on the problem of resource allocation in business processes. This paper considers *timed* business processes modeled in BPMN, a workflow-based graphical notation for processes, where execution times can be associated to several BPMN constructs such as tasks and flows. An encoding of timed business processes into Maude's rewriting logic system is presented, enabling the automatic computation of timed degrees of parallelism for business processes. The approach is illustrated with a simple yet realistic case study in which the degree of parallelism is used to improve the business process design with the ultimate goal of optimizing resources and, therefore, with the potential for reducing operating costs.

1 Introduction

A business process is a collection of structured activities or tasks that produce a specific product and fulfill a specific organizational goal for a customer or market. A process aims at modelling activities, and their causal and temporal relationships by defining specific business rules that process executions have to comply with. The Business Process Model and Notation (BPMN) [10] is a graphical modeling language for specifying business processes. BPMN was published as an ISO standard in 2013 and has become the common notation for designing business processes.

Business process optimization is a strategic activity in organizations because of its potential to increase profit margins and reduce operating costs. Resource allocation is one of the main challenges in order to maximize resource usage, improve sharing, and detect bottlenecks with the final goal of optimizing processes. An important metric when modelling and developing a business process is its degree of parallelism, which is defined as the maximum number of tasks that are executable in parallel in the process. The degree of parallelism determines the

M. Mazzara et al. (Eds.): STAF 2018 Workshops, LNCS 11176, pp. 320–335, 2018.
https://doi.org/10.1007/978-3-030-04771-9_24

peak demand on tasks and provides a valuable guide for the problem of resource allocation in business processes [20]. Examples of such resources include physical objects, goods, robots, and employees.

This paper presents a solution for computing the degree of parallelism of business processes modeled in the BPMN notation. The focus here is on a subset of the BPMN notation that supports the main constructs of the language, including start/end events, sequence flows, tasks, and gateways. This subset also takes time features into account, making possible the association of timing attributes (e.g., duration) to sequence flows and tasks. A formal specification of this BPMN subset is provided in Maude's rewriting logic infrastructure [3], resulting in a formal timed semantics of the language under consideration. The automatic computation of the parallelism degree is achieved by using tools available from the Maude formal environment itself. A given BPMN process is encoded into Maude and all reachable states are automatically traversed to find the states with the maximum number of tokens: a token is the usual mechanisms employed for identifying a specific execution instance in the BPMN semantics. This approach has been applied to several real-world processes for validation purposes. In this paper, it is illustrated with a case study in which the degree of parallelism is used to optimize a process.

The organization of the rest of the paper is as follows. Section 2 introduces the BPMN notation with time features. Section 3 overviews the Maude rewriting logic framework. Section 4 presents the encoding of the BPMN subset considered in this work into Maude's rewriting logic. Section 5 focuses on the computation of the parallelism degree. Section 6 introduces a case study and shows how the approach can be used to optimize a BPMN process. Section 7 surveys related work and Sect. 8 concludes the paper.

2   BPMN with Time

This section explains the subset of BPMN considered in this paper, which focuses on behavioral aspects (start/end events, tasks, flows, gateways) enriched with time. The timed extension of BPMN was originally presented in [7].

A BPMN process is a directed graph with nodes as vertices and sequence flows as directed edges. A node is a start or end event, a task, or a gateway. Start and end events are used to initialize and terminate processes, respectively. A task represents an atomic activity, and has exactly one incoming and one outgoing flow. A gateway is used to control the split patterns (i.e., flow divergence) and merge patterns (i.e., flow convergence) of execution in a process. In this paper, a process is considered to have exactly one start event and at least one end event. The three main gateways available in BPMN are considered, namely, exclusive, parallel, and inclusive gateways. An exclusive gateway chooses one out of a set of mutually exclusive alternative incoming or outgoing branches. A parallel gateway creates concurrent flows for all its outgoing branches or synchronizes concurrent flows for all its incoming branches. In an inclusive gateway, any number of branches among all its incoming or outgoing branches may be taken. Looping behaviors and unbalanced structure of the process (no strict correspondence between split and merge gateways) are supported in this work.

In addition to these classic BPMN constructs, time can be associated to tasks and flows. In this paper, time is interpreted as a duration of a task or a flow. When a flow has a duration d greater than zero, it means that the destination node is triggered after d units of time. If the duration is zero, that node is immediately triggered. Similarly, a task triggers its outgoing flow at once for a duration equal to zero and waits for d units of time when a duration d greater than zero is associated to that task.

Figure 1 summarizes the syntax of BPMN supported in this work, including examples of the timing constructs. In this paper, we assume that BPMN processes are syntactically correct. This can be enforced using existing works, e.g., [8], or using a BPMN engine, e.g., the Activiti BPM platform, Bonita BPM, or the Eclipse BPMN Designer.

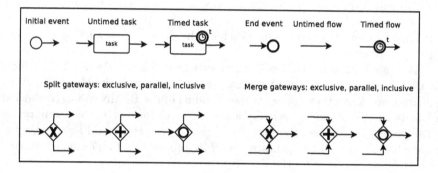

Fig. 1. BPMN syntax with time features

The informal semantics of BPMN is described in official documents [10,18] and some attempts have been made to formalize it (e.g., [5,16,19,21]). The execution semantics of BPMN is usually given by means of tokens representing how the execution of the process evolves over time. At the beginning of the process execution, there is exactly one token at the start event. A token can move along sequence flows. A token can also enter and leave a task by following the flow associated to that task. When a token arrives at a gateway, the execution behaves differently depending on the kind of gateway encountered. When a token arrives at a parallel split gateway, the token is consumed and one token is generated for every outgoing flow of the split gateway. When a token is consumed at an exclusive split gateway, only one token is created and assigned to one of its outgoing flows. In the case of an inclusive split gateway, when a token is consumed, some new tokens are generated and assigned to the outgoing flows. For the inclusive split gateway, the choice of outgoing branches to be activated depends on data-based conditions (e.g., "$x > 50$" is associated to one outgoing flow and "$x \leq 50$" is associated to the other flow) that can be evaluated to true or false. In this work, we preferred to abstract away those data conditions and consider that all branches can be executed (we enumerate all possible combinations). Merge gateways usually act as synchronization points and can be triggered when all expected tokens have arrived. A process finishes its execution when all tokens have reached an end event.

3   Maude in a Nutshell

Rewriting logic [15] is a semantic framework that unifies a wide range of models of concurrency. Specifications in rewriting logic are called rewrite theories and they can be executed in Maude [3]. A rewrite logic theory is a tuple $(\Sigma, E \cup A, R)$, where $(\Sigma, E \cup A)$ is a membership equational logic [2] theory with Σ its signature, E a set of conditional equations, A a set of equational axioms (e.g., associativity, commutativity and identity) so that rewriting is performed modulo A, and R is a set of labeled conditional rules.

In rewriting logic, a distributed system is axiomatized by an equational theory describing the set of states as an algebraic data type and a collection of conditional rewrite rules specifying the concurrent transitions. Rewrite rules are written as crl $[l]$: $t => t'$ if C, with l a label, t and t' terms, and C a guard or condition. Rules describe the local, concurrent transitions that are possible in the system, i.e., when a part of the system state fits the pattern t, then it can be replaced by the corresponding instantiation of t'. The guard C acts as a blocking precondition in the sense that a conditional rule can only be fired if its condition is satisfied. Rules may be given without label or condition. Unlabelled and unconditional rules may be written as rl $t => t'$.

Conditions are either a Boolean expression or a conjunction of equalities $u_i = v_i$, membership axioms $u_i:s_i$ or matching equations of the form $p_i := u_i$, where u_i and v_i are terms, p_i are pattern terms (irreducible terms with variables), and s_i are sorts. In its simplest form, pattern terms are just variables, with a functionality equivalent to *where* statements in typical functional programs.

In the Maude language, object-oriented systems can be specified by object-oriented modules in which classes and subclasses are declared. A class is declared with syntax class $C \mid a_1 : S_1, \ldots, a_n : S_n$, where C is the name of the class, a_i are attribute identifiers, and S_i are the sorts of the corresponding attributes. The objects of a class C are then record-like structures of the form $<O : C \mid a_1 : v_1, \ldots, a_n : v_n>$, where O is the name of the object and v_i are the current values of its attributes. An object-oriented system, such as the one presented in this paper, evolves as the result of applying the rewrite rules on collections of objects in the system states.

4   Encoding into Rewriting Logic

In this section, the encoding of the subset of BPMN with time information is presented as a Real-Time Maude [17] specification. This Maude specification consists of two parts: the encoding of the process structure and the description of the semantics of our BPMN subset using rewrite rules. In this section, the two parts of the encoding are surveyed. The interested reader is referred to [7] for a more in-depth presentation of this encoding and to [1] for the complete Maude specification, which includes all the rules and examples of BPMN processes.

As we will see in the rest of this section, the declarative style of Maude allowed us to encode BPMN execution semantics in a quite simple and elegant way. Moreover, Maude's formal environment is equipped with a large variety of analysis tools. The computation of the timed degree of parallelism relies on some of them as we will see in Sect. 5.

4.1 Process Encoding

Each BPMN process is translated into Maude for its analysis. This transformation is automated by applying a Python script we implemented as plugin of the VBPMN platform [12]. A BPMN process is represented in Maude as a set of flows and a set of nodes. A flow is represented as a term $\mathsf{flow}(\mathsf{sf}_i, t)$, with sf_i an identifier and t a duration (zero if there is no delay associated to that flow). There are different kinds of nodes: start, end, task, split, and merge. A start (end, resp.) node consists of an identifier and an output (input, resp.) flow identifier. A task node involves an identifier, a task description, two flow identifiers (input and output), and a duration (zero if no duration is associated to this task). A split node includes a node identifier, a gateway type (exclusive, parallel, or inclusive), an input flow identifier, and a set of output flow identifiers. A merge node includes a node identifier, a gateway type, a set of input flow identifiers, and an output flow identifier.

4.2 Execution Semantics

The execution semantics of BPMN constructs is usually described using tokens, which are associated to tasks and flows. The tokens circulate along those flows and tasks, and this evolution of tokens specifies the way a process executes. This token-based semantics is represented in rewriting logic using rewrite rules. We define one or several rewrite rules for each BPMN construct introduced in Sect. 2, modelling the different actions that may occur in the system, e.g., a token enters a task, a token moves along a flow, a token goes throw a gateway, etc. The rewrite rules are encoded once and for all and do not depend on the process specification.

Each rewrite rule applies on systems composed of a process object and a simulation object. The process object represents the BPMN process, and it does not change. The simulation object keeps information on the execution of the process: a set of tokens and a global time described using a natural number (discrete time). Each token is defined by the identifier of the flow or task it is associated to as well as a time corresponding to a duration. The simulation object may consist of several tokens at some point because parallel or inclusive split patterns generate several tokens as output given one token as input.

```
class Process | nodes : Set{Node}, flows : Set{Flow} .
class Simulation | tokens : Set{Token}, gtime : Time .
```

A tick rule is used to simulate the time evolution. This rule increases the global time and decreases all tokens' timers. The timing semantics forces the execution of actions by moving tokens in the process to a scheduler. The time cannot elapse when timers have reached zero time units, meaning that actions need to be triggered in the process.

We give now an informal introduction to the rewrite rules axiomatizing the process transitions for the BPMN subset considered in this work. As far as start/end events are concerned, it is assumed that the simulation object includes an initial token. The start rule (Fig. 2) is triggered when this token is available (node identifier NId, line 6). When the startProc rule is applied, the initial token is consumed and another one is added to the set of current tokens (note lines 6 and 13), which indicates that the flow outgoing from the start event has been activated (FId). The time assigned to this new token is the duration of the flow FId (line 11).

```
1  rl [startProc] :
2    < PId : Process |
3        nodes : (start(NId, FId), Nodes),
4        flows : (flow(FId, T), Flows) >
5    < SId : Simulation |
6        tokens : (token(NId, 0), Tks),        --- init token available
7        Atts >
8    =>
9    < PId : Process |
10       nodes : (start(NId, FId), Nodes),
11       flows : (flow(FId, T), Flows) >
12   < SId : Simulation |
13       tokens : (token(FId, T), Tks),        --- token for FId with duration
14       Atts > .
```

Fig. 2. Start event rule

The end event rule is triggered when there is a token for the incoming flow with zero time duration. This token is consumed, terminating this flow's execution.

A task execution is encoded with two rules expressing the possibility that a task may take time if a duration is associated to it. An initiation rule activates the task when a token representing the incoming flow is available. In this case, a new token with the task identifier and the task duration is generated. A second rule is used for representing the task completion. This rule is triggered when there is a token for that task with time zero. In that case, this token is consumed and a new one is generated for the outgoing flow.

As far as gateways are concerned, the rewrite rules are different depending on the gateway. The exclusive and parallel gateways used in Sect. 6 for the case study are presented below (refer to [7] for details about inclusive gateways).

The semantics of exclusive gateways is encoded with two rules. The rule for the exclusive split gateway executes when a token with time zero is available in the input flow and non-deterministically generates a token for one of the output branches. The exclusive merge gateway executes when there is one token for one of the incoming flows. In this case, the token is consumed and a token is generated for the merge outgoing flow.

The parallel split gateway rule is triggered when a token corresponding to the input flow is available. If so, the token is consumed and one token is added for each outgoing flow. The merge rule for the parallel gateway (Fig. 3) is executed when there is a token for each incoming branch (function allTokensParallel in Fig. 3, line 12). In that case, these tokens are removed (function removeTokensParallel, line 11) and a new token is generated for the outgoing flow.

```
1  crl [mergeParallelGateway] :
2    < PId : Process |
3        nodes : (merge(NId, parallel, FIds, FId), Nodes),
4        flows : (flow(FId, T), Flows) >
5    < SId : Simulation | tokens : Tks, Atts >
6    =>
7    < PId : Process |
8        nodes : (merge(NId, parallel, FIds, FId), Nodes),
9        flows : (flow(FId, T), Flows) >
10   < SId : Simulation |
11       tokens : (token(FId, T), removeTokensParallel(FIds, Tks)), Atts >
12   if allTokensParallel(FIds, Tks) .    ---- all incoming flows activated
```

Fig. 3. Parallel merge gateway rule

5 Computing the Parallelism Degree with Maude

The encoding of the BPMN semantics in Maude can be used to simulate process executions. By using Maude's meta-programming capabilities, an interesting repertory of different measures related to the degree of parallelism of a process can be offered. The reader is referred to [3] for details on Maude and its reflective capabilities.

For the computation of the degree of parallelism, there is special interest in the search command: the process of searching for a term satisfying some conditions starting from an initial term is metarepresented by the built-in function metaSearch. This function takes as arguments the metarepresentation of a module, the metarepresentation of the starting term for search, the metarepresentation of the pattern to search for, the metarepresentation of a condition to be satisfied, the metarepresentation of the kind of search to carry on (the quoted identifier '* for a search involving zero or more rewrites), a bound value (maximum depth of the search), and a natural number indicating the solution of interest. In order to explore all possible reachable states, an algorithm has been implemented in Maude for iterating over all possible values of this solution number until the metasearch function fails to find any more states.

```
op metaSearch :
     Module Term Term Condition Qid Bound Nat ~> ResultTriple?
```

The parDegree function in Fig. 4 computes the number of states and the (timed) degree of parallelism. Specifically, given a module M with the representation of the BPMN process to analyze, an initial state given by a term T, and a bound B, parDegree(M, T, B) will return a pair (N, PD) where N is the number of (different) reachable states up to the specified depth, and PD is the maximum degree of parallelism for that process.

Notice that given the representation of process states, in the presence of a loop there is the issue of nontermination. Therefore, the analysis is bounded up to some given depth, so that termination is always guaranteed. Theoretically, this bound may have an impact on the result because by missing executions an erroneous degree of parallelism could be computed. In practice, a large bound is chosen (100 for instance for the example presented in Sect. 6) in order to avoid such faulty results.

The parDegree function is implemented using an homonym function with three additional arguments: the target term (a variable of sort Configuration, so that any reachable state is considered), an index with the solution number to consider, and the provisional maximum degree of parallelism (zero at the beginning and updated every time a greater value is found). For each solution number N, the metaSearch operation is invoked. If the operation returns failure, the pair (N, PD) is returned with PD the maximum degree of parallelism. Notice the use of the getTerm operation to obtain the term component of the tuple returned by metaSearch and metaReduce, and the use of metaReduce to evaluate the auxiliary function getNumberOfTokens on the metaterm obtained as result of the search operation.

```
1   op parDegree : Module Term Bound -> Tuple{Nat, Nat} .
2   op parDegree : Module Term Term Bound Nat Nat -> Tuple{Nat, Nat} .
3
4   eq parDegree(M, T, B) = parDegree(M, T, 'St:Configuration, B, 0, 0) .
5   ceq parDegree(M, T, T', B, N, N1)
6     = if RT == failure
7       then (N, N1)
8       else parDegree(M, T, T', s N,
9             max(N1, downTerm(
10                 getTerm(
11                   metaReduce(M,
12                     'getNumberOFTokens[getTerm(RT)]))), INF)))
13       fi
14   if RT := metaSearch(M, T, T', nil, '*, B, N) .
```

Fig. 4. Degree of parallelism: the parDegree function

Complementarily to the maximum degree of parallelism, the minimum degree can be computed. Both values may help in scheduling the minimum and maximum amount of resources required for the execution of the process over time. To do so, the parDegreeTrace function in Fig. 5 computes a map associating to each moment of time a pair (min, max) with the minimum and the maximum number of tokens seen at that time. The function is similar to the above parDegree function. The main difference is that in this case the function produces a mapping that assigns a pair (min, max) to each instance of time, collecting the minimum and maximum numbers of tokens in each of the visited states with that time as current time. Pairs (min, max) are represented as elements of sort Tuple{Nat, Nat}, defined with constructor (_,_) and projection operations p1_ and p2_. Maude's built-in maps are defined as a set of pairs, with empty as empty mapping, and operations _[_] and insert to, respectively, consult and update values. Given a variable TMMM of sort Map{Time, Tuple{Nat, Nat}}, we can consult the value associated to some time G with TMMM[G]. If the map TMMM does not associate a value to a given key G, TMMM[G] will return the value undefined.

```
1  op parDegreeTrace : Module Term Term Bound -> Map{Time,Tuple{Nat,Nat}} .
2  op parDegreeTrace : Module Term Term Bound Nat Map{Time,Tuple{Nat,Nat}}
3       -> Map{Time,Tuple{Nat,Nat}} .
4  op parDegreeTrace : Module Term Term Bound Nat Map{Time,Tuple{Nat,Nat}}
5       Term -> Map{Time,Tuple{Nat,Nat}} .
6
7  eq parDegreeTrace(M, T, T', B) = parDegreeTrace(M, T, T', B, 0, empty) .
8  ceq parDegreeTrace(M, T, T', B, N, TMMM)
9     = if RT:ResultTriple? == failure
10        then TMMM
11        else parDegreeTrace(M, T, T', B, N, TMMM, getTerm(RT:ResultTriple?))
12        fi
13     if RT:ResultTriple? := metaSearch(M, T, T', nil, '*, B, N) .
14  ceq parDegreeTrace(M, T, T', N, TMMM, T'')
15     = parDegreeTrace(M, T, T', s N,
16         if TMMM[G] == undefined
17         then insert(G, (D, D), TMMM)
18         else if D < p1 (TMMM[G])
19              then insert(G, (D, p2 (TMMM[G])), TMMM)
20              else if D > p2 (TMMM[G])
21                   then insert(G, (p1 (TMMM[G]), D), TMMM)
22                   else TMMM
23                   fi
24              fi
25         fi)
26     if D := downTerm(getTerm(metaReduce(M, 'getNumberOFTokens[T''])), INF)
27     /\ G := downTerm(getTerm(metaReduce(M, 'getTime[T''])), INF) .
```

Fig. 5. Degree of parallelism along execution: the parDegreeTrace function

6   Case Study

Figure 6 presents the case study used in this paper to illustrate the proposed approach. It is a simplified version of an employee hiring process in a company. This process focuses on the different tasks to be carried out once the employee has successfully passed the interview. The process thus starts by some paperwork that has to be accomplished by the employee. (S)He has to see the doctor for medical check-up. If the employee needs visa, (s)he should also apply for working visa. If all the submitted documents are not satisfactory, the company may ask for them again. If everything is fine, all documents are accepted as is. In some cases, the company can validate the files but asks the employee to provide additional documents or information. The employee is then added to the personnel database and, in parallel, Human Resources (HR) anticipate wage payment while an assistant prepares the welcome kit (office, badge, keys, etc.). Finally, all provided documents are archived properly by HR.

It is worth noting that this process exhibits different kinds of gateways (exclusive and parallel), looping behaviors, and time associated to tasks. The rest of this section focuses on the timed degree of parallelism by analyzing how this measure can be used to optimize the workflow in terms of execution time.

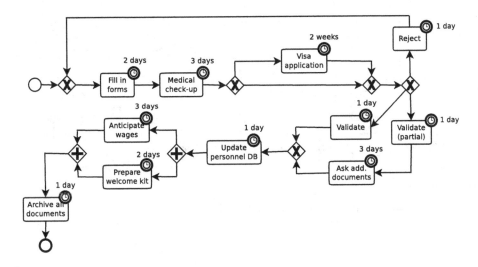

Fig. 6. BPMN process for employee hiring

The degree of parallelism for this example, obtained by using the approach presented in the previous sections, is 2.

```
reduce parDegree(upModule('VERIF, false),
          'initSystem.Configuration, 'St:Configuration, 100) .
result Tuple{Nat,Nat}: (1710,2)
```

This comes from the final part of the process where a parallel split/merge is used. If a closer look is taken at this part of the process, it can be seen that it takes 5 days to compute the final four activities. However, these tasks involve different people: the assistant is in charge of preparing the welcome kit, the technical staff updates the DB, and HR are in charge of the two other activities (anticipate wages, archive all documents). So this final part of the process could be organized differently. The employee information can be stored in the DB (prerequisite to other tasks), and then "anticipate wages" and "prepare welcome kit" tasks are performed in parallel. Archiving all documents is independent and could be achieved in another parallel branch. A second version of the process is given in Fig. 7.

When applying the computation of the timed degree of parallelism to the second version of this process, the degree is 3. This is because, although archiving all documents are completed before the internal parallel split is triggered, that token waits at the parallel merge level for the other branch to complete.

Related to that, the two tasks carried out by HR (anticipate wages and archive all documents) do not overlap and the execution time of this part of the workflow is reduced by one day (going from 5 days in the original version of the process to 4 days in this new version). It is worth observing that execution times can be automatically computed with the approach proposed in this paper too.

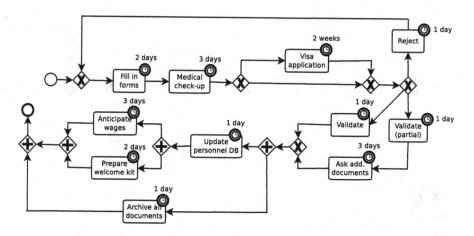

Fig. 7. BPMN process for employee hiring (V2)

In the initial part of the workflow, the first three activities involve the employee. These tasks are quite time-consuming because of the appointment with a doctor (3 days in average in our model) and the visa application (2 weeks in average). However, most of the time the employee is available, (s)he is just waiting due to external constraints. Therefore, those 3 activities could be executed in parallel as shown in Fig. 8. In this case, the degree of parallelism for that part of the process jumps to 3 and the execution time goes from 19 days to 14 days. More generally, the degree of parallelism of this third version (Fig. 8) is 3 for the top part and 3 for the bottom part.

One can wonder whether the bottom part could be improved a little bit more by increasing the degree of that part if the used resources allows it. This is actually the case, because the "ask additional documents" task is achieved by the employee and is independent of the rest of this part of the process. In its current form, this task even delays the execution of the final part of the workflow. A possible optimization is to execute this task in parallel with the rest of the final activities. This makes the degree of parallelism, in this part of the workflow, increase to 4, resulting in saving 3 days with respect to the former version of the process. Figure 9 gives the resulting process after the three optimizations. Assuming that the documents are not rejected, note that the overall maximum

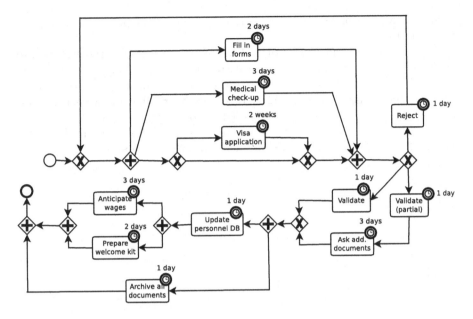

Fig. 8. BPMN process for employee hiring (V3)

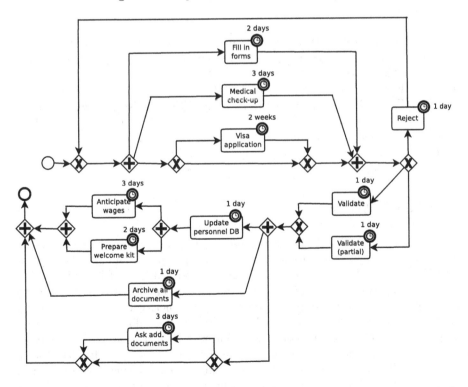

Fig. 9. BPMN process for employee hiring (V4)

execution time was of 28 days in the original version of the process and drops to 19 days in the final version.

The variation of the minimum and maximum degree of parallelism is also worth looking at in order to better allocate required resources over time. By using the parDegreeTrace function, a sequence of these values can be computed for each execution time (discrete time). Figure 10 shows the graphical representation for the last version of the running example (the process depicted in Fig. 9). In this process, it can be observed how the maximum degree of parallelism fluctuates between 3 and 4, whilst the minimum degree varies from 0 to 3.

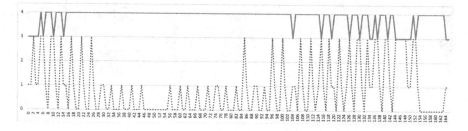

Fig. 10. Max-Min degree for the employee hiring process (V4)

Last but not least, we made experiments to see how our approach scales. The main factor of explosion regarding the computation time is not the number of tasks in the process but the number of gateways, which increases the parallelism of the process and thus the number of possible executions that need to be explored. We applied our approach to large examples consisting of more than 20 gateways, including multiple nested parallel and inclusive gateways. For those examples, it took several minutes to compute the degree of parallelism. It is worth saying that we built these examples for evaluation purposes, but we have never seen a real-world process with so many nested gateways.

7   Related Work

Two categories of related work are surveyed: (i) those proposing solutions for computing the degree of parallelism of BPMN processes, and (ii) those using rewriting logic and Maude for specification and verification of BPMN processes.

The degree of parallelism for BPMN can be computed by reasoning on Petri net models and determining the bound of a Petri net, which is the maximum number of tokens in a marking of the net. However, to do so, the reachability graph for the net should be constructed entirely. The reachability problem for some specific Petri nets, such as conflict-free Petri nets and 1 safe live free-choice nets [9], is NP-complete. Note that for arbitrary Petri nets, this problem is much harder [14]. This is probably the reason why, to the best of authors' knowledge, there is no work on degree computation with Petri nets in the literature.

In [20] several algorithms are proposed for directly calculating the degree of parallelism of a BPMN process without transforming it to another model. In this work, a duration constraint is associated to each task, i.e., a task is required to be completed within a certain time frame. Furthermore, a task must begin immediately after the completion of its precedent task. Without considering inclusive gateways, they deal with three special cases of BPMN processes: with only one type of gateways; without split exclusive gateway nor cycles; with only two types of gateways. Each case is treated with a different algorithm. The solution proposed in this paper focuses on BPMN processes with time too, and allows for the automatic computation of the degree of parallelism for complex BPMN structures, i.e., combining different gateways and cycles, without imposing restrictions on the structure of processes.

In [13], the authors propose an approach to automatically measure the degree of parallelism for BPMN processes. They rely on a formal model for BPMN processes defined in terms of Labelled Transition Systems, obtained through process algebra encodings. The degree of parallelism is then computed by using model checking techniques and dichotomic search. The main difference with respect to the approach presented in this work is that the subset of BPMN considered in [13] does not support timing features.

Several research contributions have used rewriting logic and Maude to formalyze and analyze BPMN processes. El-Saber and Boronat [8] propose a translation of BPMN into rewriting logic with a special focus on data-based decision gateways. They provide mechanisms to avoid structural issues in workflows such as flow divergence by introducing the notion of "well-formed" BPMN process. Kheldoun et al. [11] propose high-level Petri nets and to use Maude's LTL model checker for, respectively, specifying BPMN processes and analyzing behavioral properties. Both works do not support time features. Corradini et al. [4] present BProVe, a tool for the verification of business processes modeled in BPMN. The tool accepts BPMN processes in standard notation and can perform checks of soundness and safeness on them, as defined in [22] and [5], respectively, using Maude's LTL model checker.

In a previous work [7], the idea of specifying BPMN with time using Maude's rewriting logic was introduced by some of the authors of the present paper. However, little attention was paid to the degree of parallelism. This is the focus of the current paper, which presents how the parallelism degree of timed BPMN processes can be automatically computed, and how it can be used as a measure to improve and optimize a process in practice. In the present paper, it is also shown how to compute the variation between the minimum and maximum degree of parallelism of timed BPMN processes. More recently, the authors have developed a rewriting logic executable specification of BPMN with time and probabilities supporting the automatic analysis of stochastic properties via statistical model checking [6].

8 Concluding Remarks

This paper contributed a mechanical approach to the key question of business process optimization. Business processes are described using a subset of BPMN supporting the main behavioral constructs (including, start/end events, flows, tasks, gateways) and time features. This BPMN subset was formalized using rewriting logic, resulting in a formal and executable semantics of the language. In a second step, the timed degree of parallelism has been computed. This measure can be useful for better understanding a business process and for improving the execution time of a process. The parallelism degree is computed automatically using Maude's metaprogramming capabilities. A realistic case study has been used to illustrate the approach, which can in general guide process refactoring tasks with optimization purposes in mind.

As far as future work is concerned, a first perspective is to integrate an explicit description of the resources (e.g., HR, assistant, and employee in the case study in Sect. 6) at the BPMN model level. To enable the automatic computation of new metrics, such as resource occupancy and average execution time, the verification framework would need to be extended for considering multiple concurrent executions of a process. A second perspective could focus on the thorough automation of the approach presented here. It is true that in its current form, the refactoring task is guided by the parallelism degree results, but it is ultimately manually applied. Measuring the degree of parallelism could be part of a more general methodology where other measures and additional information (e.g., regarding the resources) would drive the entire automated refactoring of the process for optimization purposes.

Acknowledgments. The authors would like to thank the anonymous reviewers for their valuable comments on an earlier draft of this paper. F. Durán has been partially supported by Spanish MINECO/FEDER project TIN2014-52034-R. The work of C. Rocha was partially supported by CAPES, Colciencias, and Inria via the STIC AmSud project "EPIC: EPistemic Interactive Concurrency" (Proc. No 88881.117603/2016-01), and by Capital Semilla 2017, project "SCORES: Stochastic Concurrency in Rewrite-based Probabilistic Models" (Proj. No. 020100610).

References

1. http://maude.lcc.uma.es/MaudeBPMN/
2. Bouhoula, A., Jouannaud, J.-P., Meseguer, J.: Specification and proof in membership equational logic. Theor. Comput. Sci. **236**(1), 35–132 (2000)
3. Clavel, M., Durán, F., Eker, S., Lincoln, P., Martí-Oliet, N., Meseguer, J., Talcott, C.: All About Maude - A High-Performance Logical Framework, How to Specify, Program and Verify Systems in Rewriting Logic. LNCS, vol. 4350. Springer, Heidelberg (2007). https://doi.org/10.1007/978-3-540-71999-1
4. Corradini, F., Fornari, F., Polini, A., Re, B., Tiezzi, F., Vandin, A.: BProVe: a formal verification framework for business process models. In: Proceedings of ASE, pp. 217–228. IEEE Computer Society (2017)

5. Dijkman, R., Dumas, M., Ouyang, C.: Semantics and analysis of business process models in BPMN. Inf. Softw. Technol. **50**(12), 1281–1294 (2008)
6. Durán, F., Rocha, C., Salaün, G.: Stochastic analysis of BPMN with time in rewriting logic. Sci. Comput. Program. **168**, 1–17 (2018)
7. Durán, F., Salaün, G.: Verifying timed BPMN processes using Maude. In: Jacquet, J.-M., Massink, M. (eds.) COORDINATION 2017. LNCS, vol. 10319, pp. 219–236. Springer, Cham (2017). https://doi.org/10.1007/978-3-319-59746-1_12
8. El-Saber, N., Boronat, A.: BPMN formalization and verification using Maude. In: Proceedings of BM-FA 2014, pp. 1–8. ACM (2014)
9. Esparza, J.: Reachability in live and safe free-choice Petri nets is NP-complete. Theor. Comput. Sci. **198**, 211–224 (1998)
10. ISO/IEC. International Standard 19510, Information technology - Business Process Model and Notation (2013)
11. Kheldoun, A., Barkaoui, K., Ioualalen, M.: Specification and verification of complex business processes - a high-level Petri net-based approach. In: Motahari-Nezhad, H.R., Recker, J., Weidlich, M. (eds.) BPM 2015. LNCS, vol. 9253, pp. 55–71. Springer, Cham (2015). https://doi.org/10.1007/978-3-319-23063-4_4
12. Krishna, A., Poizat, P., Salaün, G.: VBPMN: automated verification of BPMN processes (tool paper). In: Polikarpova, N., Schneider, S. (eds.) IFM 2017. LNCS, vol. 10510, pp. 323–331. Springer, Cham (2017). https://doi.org/10.1007/978-3-319-66845-1_21
13. Mateescu, R., Salaün, G., Ye, L.: Quantifying the parallelism in BPMN processes using model checking. In: Proceedings of CBSE 2014, pp. 159–168. ACM (2014)
14. Mayr, E.: An algorithm for the general Petri net reachability problem. SIAM J. Comput. **13**(3), 441–460 (1984)
15. Meseguer, J.: Conditional rewriting logic as a unified model of concurrency. Theor. Comput. Sci. **96**(1), 73–155 (1992)
16. Morales, L.E.M., Capel, M.I., Pérez, M.A.: Conceptual framework for business processes compositional verification. Inf. Soft. Technol. **54**(2), 149–161 (2012)
17. Ölveczky, P.C., Meseguer, J.: Semantics and pragmatics of real-time Maude. High.-Order Symbolic Comput. **20**(1–2), 161–196 (2007)
18. OMG. Business Process Model and Notation (BPMN) - Version 2.0, January 2011
19. Poizat, P., Salaün, G.: Checking the realizability of BPMN 2.0 choreographies. In: Proceedings of SAC 2012, pp. 1927–1934. ACM Press (2012)
20. Sun, Y., Su, J.: Computing degree of parallelism for BPMN processes. In: Kappel, G., Maamar, Z., Motahari-Nezhad, H.R. (eds.) ICSOC 2011. LNCS, vol. 7084, pp. 1–15. Springer, Heidelberg (2011). https://doi.org/10.1007/978-3-642-25535-9_1
21. Wong, P.Y.H., Gibbons, J.: A process semantics for BPMN. In: Liu, S., Maibaum, T., Araki, K. (eds.) ICFEM 2008. LNCS, vol. 5256, pp. 355–374. Springer, Heidelberg (2008). https://doi.org/10.1007/978-3-540-88194-0_22
22. Wynn, M.T., Verbeek, H.M.W., van der Aalst, W.M.P., ter Hofstede, A.H.M., Edmond, D.: Business process verification - finally a reality!. Bus. Process Manag. J. **15**(1), 74–92 (2009)

ReoLive: Analysing Connectors in Your Browser

Rúben Cruz[1,2] and José Proença[1,2(✉)]

[1] HASLab, INESC TEC, Braga, Portugal
rubenamcruz@gmail.com
[2] Dep. Informatics, Universidade do Minho, Braga, Portugal
jose.proenca@di.uminho.pt

Abstract. Connectors describe how to combine independent components by restricting the possible interactions between their interfaces. In this work, connectors are specified using an existing calculus of connectors for Reo connectors. Currently there are no tools to automatically analyse these connectors, other than a type-checker for a embedded domain specific language. A collection of tools for different variations of Reo connectors exists, but most use a heavy Eclipse-based framework that is not actively supported.

We propose a set of web-based tools for analysing connectors—named ReoLive—requiring only an offline Internet browser with JavaScript support, which also supports a client-server architecture for more complex operations. We also show that the analysis included in ReoLive are correct, by formalising the encoding of the connector calculus into Port Automata and into mCRL2 programs. We include extensions that generate such automata, mCRL2 processes, and graphical representations of instances of connectors, developed in the Scala language and compiled into JavaScript. The resulting framework is publicly available, and can be easily experimented without any installation or a running server.

1 Introduction

Proença and Clarke [9] investigated how one can specify and combine connector families, and how to check if the interfaces of these families match. Their core calculus is a monoidal category, where connectors are morphisms composed sequentially with the morphism composition ';', and in parallel with the tensor operator '⊕'. This calculus was formalized with a tile semantics that describes the behaviour of a connector, and how to combine tiles between two connectors.

We pursue this work by building tools to analyse and verify a calculus of Reo connectors, focusing on its subset without variability. More concretely, we build a framework—ReoLive—that draws instances of connectors, and encodes connectors into automata and into a process algebra used by the mCRL2 model checker. This paper formally shows the correctness of these encodings, closely following the encoding of Reo connectors (seen as Constraint Automata) into mCRL2 by Kokash et al. [7].

© Springer Nature Switzerland AG 2018
M. Mazzara et al. (Eds.): STAF 2018 Workshops, LNCS 11176, pp. 336–350, 2018.
https://doi.org/10.1007/978-3-030-04771-9_25

Consider the connector in Fig. 1, known in the literature as the exclusive router. The left side presents its usual graphical representation, while the right side uses its representation in the calculus of connectors used in this paper, c.f. [9]. Intuitively, each basic element of the calculus is a primitive connector with a fixed sequence of source and sink ports, composed sequentially with ';' and composed in parallel with ⊕. More details on this calculus will be given in the next section.

The key challenges of this paper consist of presenting a framework to analyse connectors specified in this calculus, providing a set of different *widgets* that help the developer understand the graphical structure and its semantics. More specifically, the ReoLive framework receives algebraic specifications of connectors and (1) calculates and depicts a graphical representation with a easy-to-understand layout, (2) calculates and depicts an automata representing its semantics, based on constraint automata [2] without data constraints, and (3) produces a mCRL2 specification [5] that can be used for model checking with external tools. While the first contribution is less scientific and mainly technical, the other two contributions include correctness proofs, based on the formalisation of the encodings into automata and mCRL2.

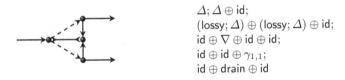

$\Delta; \Delta \oplus$ id;
(lossy; Δ) $\oplus$ (lossy; Δ) $\oplus$ id;
id $\oplus \nabla \oplus$ id $\oplus$ id;
id $\oplus$ id $\oplus \gamma_{1,1}$;
id $\oplus$ drain $\oplus$ id

Fig. 1. The exclusive router connector: its graphical representation (left) and its algebraic representation using the calculus of Reo connectors (right).

Section 2 formalises Reo connectors using this calculus of connector. Section 3 translates the calculus into port automata, and Sect. 4 into mCRL2, following the work by Kokash et al. [7]. Section 5 describes the ReoLive framework for our calculus of connector, and Sect. 6 concludes and discusses future work.

2   Calculus of Reo Connector (CRC)

The input of our ReoLive framework are Reo connectors [1] specified using a calculus of connectors, following Proença and Clarke [9]. We start by describing this calculus, disregarding the notion of families presented originally, and will later show that they are indeed equivalent to two other existing semantic models: Port Automata (Sect. 3) and mCRL2 programs (Sect. 4).

2.1   Syntax

The syntax of a core connector is given by the grammar in Fig. 2. We use a simplified version from our previous publication [9] by using natural numbers for the input and output interfaces, where the tensor is the sum. This makes the category of our connectors more specific—a Prop category with traces [8]. This simplification has been made also in our previous work, when describing the implementation of a type-inference algorithm.

Figure 3 depicts some examples of connectors. Each box contains (1) a connector on top, (2) its interfaces in the middle, and (3) its visual representation below depicting inputs on the left and outputs on the right. Intuitively, each connector has a sequence of input ports and a sequence of output ports, which we number incrementally from 1. Composing two connectors sequentially $c_1; c_2$ means connecting the i-th sink port c_1 to the i-th source port of c_2, for every sink port of c_1 and source port of c_2; composing connectors in parallel $c_1 \oplus c_2$ means combining all source and sink ports of both c_1 and c_2; wrapping a connector c by a trace over n means connecting the last n sink ports of c to its last n source ports. The semantics of Reo connectors, written using this calculus, uses the Tile Model [4], following the original publication of this calculus [9].

The sintax and semantics of the calculus of connector families is not introduced in this document, as it is not refered throughout the document (except in Sect. 5). In [9] we can find a more detailed description of this calculus.

$$
\begin{array}{llll}
c ::= \text{id}_n & \text{identities} & p \in \mathcal{P} ::= \Delta_n & \text{duplicator into } n \text{ ports} \\
\mid \gamma_{n,m} & \text{symmetries} & \mid \nabla_n & \text{merger of } n \text{ inputs} \\
\mid p \in \mathcal{P} & \text{primitive connectors} & \mid \text{drain} & \text{synchronous drain} \\
\mid c_1 ; c_2 & \text{sequential composition} & \mid \text{fifo} & \text{buffer} \\
\mid c_1 \oplus c_2 & \text{parallel composition} & \mid \ldots & \text{user-defined connectors} \\
\mid \text{Tr}_n(c) & \text{traces (feedback loops)} & &
\end{array}
$$

Fig. 2. Grammar for core connectors, where $n, m \in \mathbb{N}$.

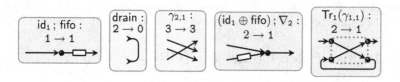

Fig. 3. Connectors, their interfaces, and their visualisation.

2.2   Tile Semantics

Each connector in the Tile Model consists of a set of tiles, one for each possible behaviour, as defined in Fig. 4. Each of these tiles contains at most 4 morphisms between shared objects, belonging to two different categories over the same objects: natural numbers, which we call $\mathcal{H}$ for the a *horizontal category* and $\mathcal{V}$ for a *vertical category*. The horizontal category $\mathcal{H}$ is the category of connectors used for the our connector calculus—with a tensor, symmetries, and traces. The vertical category $\mathcal{V}$ is a new category with the same objects $\mathbb{N}$, and with only the morphisms $fl : 1 \to 1$ and $nofl : 1 \to 1$, also with a tensor product, where $nofl$ acts as the identity and the composition is represented by '$\circ$'.

$$id_1 = \left\{ id_1 \xrightarrow[fl]{fl} id_1 \,,\, id_1 \xrightarrow[nofl]{nofl} id_1 \right\}$$

$$\gamma_{1,1} = \left\{ \gamma_{1,1} \xrightarrow[nofl\oplus fl]{fl\oplus nofl} \gamma_{1,1} \,,\, \gamma_{1,1} \xrightarrow[fl\oplus nofl]{nofl\oplus fl} \gamma_{1,1} \,,\, \gamma_{1,1} \xrightarrow[fl\oplus fl]{fl\oplus fl} \gamma_{1,1} \,,\, \gamma_{1,1} \xrightarrow[nofl\oplus nofl]{nofl\oplus nofl} \gamma_{1,1} \right\}$$

$$\Delta_2 = \left\{ \Delta_2 \xrightarrow[fl\oplus fl]{fl} \Delta_2 \,,\, \Delta_2 \xrightarrow[nofl\oplus nofl]{nofl} \Delta_2 \right\}$$

$$\nabla_2 = \left\{ \nabla_2 \xrightarrow[fl]{fl\oplus nofl} \nabla_2 \,,\, \nabla_2 \xrightarrow[fl]{nofl\oplus fl} \nabla_2 \,,\, \nabla_2 \xrightarrow[nofl]{nofl\oplus nofl} \nabla_2 \right\}$$

$$drain = \left\{ drain \xrightarrow[fl]{fl} drain \,,\, drain \xrightarrow[nofl]{nofl} drain \right\}$$

$$lossy = \left\{ lossy \xrightarrow[fl]{fl} lossy \,,\, lossy \xrightarrow[nofl]{fl} lossy \,,\, lossy \xrightarrow[nofl]{nofl} lossy \right\}$$

$$fifo = \left\{ fifo \xrightarrow[nofl]{fl} fifofull \,,\, fifo \xrightarrow[nofl]{nofl} fifo \right\}$$

$$fifofull = \left\{ fifofull \xrightarrow[fl]{nofl} fifo \,,\, fifofull \xrightarrow[nofl]{nofl} fifofull \right\}$$

Fig. 4. Behaviour of primitive connectors using tiles.

Composing Tiles. Tiles can be composed in three ways: in parallel with '$\oplus$', horizontally with '$;$', and vertically with '$\circ$'.

$$c_1 \xrightarrow[v]{v_1} c_2 \,;\, c_1' \xrightarrow[v_2]{v} c_2' \;=\; (c_1; c_1') \xrightarrow[v_2]{v_1} (c_2; c_2') \qquad \text{(horizontal)}$$

$$c_1 \xrightarrow[v_2]{v_1} c \circ c \xrightarrow[v_2']{v_1'} c_2 \;=\; c_1 \xrightarrow[v_2 \circ v_2]{v_1' \circ v_1} c_2 \qquad \text{(vertical)}$$

$$c_1 \xrightarrow[v_2]{v_1} c_2 \oplus c_1' \xrightarrow[v_2']{v_1'} c_2' \;=\; c_1 \oplus c_2 \xrightarrow[v_2 \oplus v_2']{v_1 \oplus v_1'} c_1' \oplus c_2' \qquad \text{(parallel)}$$

For example, the tiles $t_l = lossy \xrightarrow[fl]{fl} lossy$ and $t_f = fifo \xrightarrow[nofl]{fl} fifofull$ can be composed horizontally producing the new tile $t_l; t_f = (lossy; fifo) \xrightarrow[nofl]{fl} (lossy; fifofull)$. This new tile captures data going through the lossy and into the fifo. Similarly, t_l can be composed vertically with the tile $t_l' = lossy \xrightarrow[nofl]{fl} lossy$ yielding the new tile $t_l \circ t_l' = lossy \xrightarrow[fl \circ nofl]{fl \circ fl} lossy$, which captures two steps of the same lossy: first by having data flowing from its source to its sink, and later by having dataflow only on its source end.

3   Connectors as Port Automata

The semantics of the calculus of Reo connectors (CRC) is given by a set of tiles. This section encodes the tile semantics of CRC as Port Automata [6], which can be regarded as data-agnostic Constraint Automata [2], showing this encoding is correct.

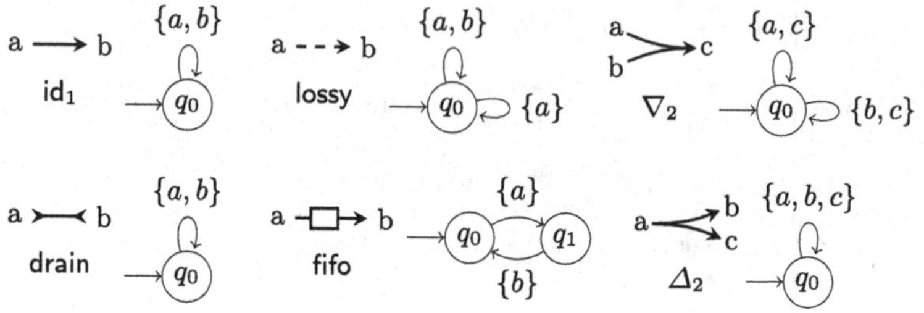

Fig. 5. Port Automata of primitive connectors.

3.1   Port Automata (PA)

Following Koehler and Clarke [6], composing two automata is done by the *product* operation $\bowtie$, forcing shared ports to occur together, while hiding ports from a connector removes them from the transitions, disallowing further communications. We define *port substitution* of a by b in an automaton $\mathcal{A}$ as the automaton $\mathcal{A}\{a\mapsto b\} = (Q, N\{a\mapsto b\}, \dashrightarrow, q_0)$, where $q_i \overset{X\{a\mapsto b\}}{\dashrightarrow} q_j$ iff $q_i \overset{X}{\rightarrow} q_j$, and $X\{a\mapsto b\}$ denotes the set X replacing a by b.

For simplicity, we write $q_i \overset{N}{\rightarrow} q_j$ to denote $\rightarrow (q_i, N, q_j)$. Figure 5 depicts examples of a set of primitive automata commonly found in the literature, including also the corresponding notation in our calculus.

3.2   Encoding CRC into Port Automata

The semantics of CRC is given by the Tiles Model, where a tile $c_1 \overset{src}{\underset{snk}{\longrightarrow}} c_2$ means that the connector c_1 can evolve to a new state given by the connector c_2, by firing its source ports based on src and its sink ports based on snk. Here src and snk are morphisms built by composing simpler morphisms fl and nofl, indicating which ports have flow and no-flow.

The encoding of a connector c into a PA is written as $\mathcal{PA}(c)$, defined below. Each port is a pair (n, s) where $n \in \mathbb{N}$ is the order number of its source or sink node, and $s \in \{\mathsf{sr}, \mathsf{sk}, \mathsf{mx}\}$ is a constant that marks it as being a source (sr) or a sink (sk) port, or temporarily marking it as a mixed port during composition.

Definition 1 (Tiles of a connector). *Given a core connector c, we write $T(c)$ to represent all tiles for c and for the reachable states from c. Formally, $T(c)$ is the smallest set such that, for every tile $t = \left(c \xrightarrow[sk]{sr} c' \right)$ we have that $t \in T(c)$ and $T(c') \subseteq T(c)$.*

Definition 2 (Reachable connectors). *Given a connector c, we write $Reach(c)$ to represent all reachable connectors from c, i.e., $Reach(c)$ is the smallest set such that $c \in Reach(c)$, and for every tile $c \xrightarrow[sk]{sr} c'$ we have that $Reach(c') \subseteq Reach(c)$.*

Definition 3 (Encoding $\mathcal{PA}(c)$). *Let c be a connector from n to m. Its port automaton $\mathcal{PA}(c)$ is $(Q, N, \rightarrow, q_0)$ where*

- $Q = Reach(c)$
- $N = \{(i, sr) \mid i \in \{1 \dots n\}\} \cup \{(j, sk) \mid j \in \{1 \dots m\}\}$
- $q \xrightarrow{X_{sr} \cup X_{sk}} q' \Leftrightarrow \exists t \in T(c) : t = c_1 \xrightarrow[snk]{src} c_2 \ \wedge$

  $X_{sr} = \{(i, sr) \mid src = v_1 \oplus \cdots \oplus v_n, i \in \{1 \dots n\}, v_i = fl\}$
  $X_{sk} = \{(i, sk) \mid snk = v_1 \oplus \cdots \oplus v_m, j \in \{1 \dots m\}, v_j = fl\}$

For example, the fifo channel can be encoded as $\mathcal{PA}(\text{fifo}) = (\{\text{fifo}, \text{fifofull}\}, \{(1, sr), (1, sk)\}, \rightarrow, \text{fifo})$, where

$$\text{fifo} \xrightarrow{(1, sr)} \text{fifofull} \qquad \text{fifofull} \xrightarrow{(1, sk)} \text{fifo} \qquad \text{fifo} \xrightarrow{\emptyset} \text{fifo} \qquad \text{fifofull} \xrightarrow{\emptyset} \text{fifofull}.$$

3.3 Correctness of $\mathcal{PA}(\cdot)$

We defined how to encode any connector c into a PA $\mathcal{PA}(c)$. We say this encoding is correct with respect to an automaton A if $\mathcal{PA}(c)$ is **strongly bisimilar** to A, written $\mathcal{PA}(c) \approx A$. I.e., there exists a bisimulation relation R between states such that any transition from $\mathcal{PA}(c)$ can be matched by a transition in A leading to states in R (and its dual for transitions from A). For simplicity, we ignore all reflexive transitions with empty sets as labels in $\mathcal{PA}(c)$, which must exist for all primitive connectors – because the Port Automata semantics assumes that connectors can decide not to have dataflow and remain in the same state.

We show that this definition is correct using an inductive argument. We show that (1) the encodings of primitive channels from Sect. 2 are correct with respect to the automata from Sect. 3, and (2) the encoding of a connector built with the sequential, parallel, or trace operators is correct with respect to the automata of their parts after composing the appropriate ports. Note that γ and id_n are regarded here as primitive connectors.

Lemma 1 (Correctness of primitive's encodings). *Any primitive from Fig. 4 is correct w.r.t. its corresponding automaton from Fig. 5, after renaming ports in the latter to follow the same convention as in the encoding (e.g., $(1, sr)$ instead of a).*

Proof. We will only show that this lemma holds for one of the connectors, the fifo, because the other connectors can be shown in a similar way. Recall that after Definition 3 we defined $\mathcal{PA}(\text{fifo})$ as an example. The resulting automaton has 4 transitions, and after ignoring the reflexive and empty transitions only two remain. Recall also the port automaton of the fifo in Fig. 5. It is enough to observe that $R = \{\langle\text{fifo}, q_0\rangle, \langle\text{fifofull}, q_1\rangle\}$ is a strong bisimulation between the two automata, after replacing a by $(1, \text{sr})$ and b by $(1, \text{sk})$.

Lemma 2 (Correctness of $\mathcal{PA}(c_1; c_2)$). *If $\mathcal{PA}(c_1)$ and $\mathcal{PA}(c_2)$ are correct with respect to A_1 and A_2, respectively, and $c_1; c_2$ is well-typed, then $\mathcal{PA}(c_1; c_2)$ is correct with respect to $(A_1\sigma_1 \bowtie A_2\sigma_2)\backslash X$, where σ_1, σ_2 and X define port renamings and hiding of ports that mimic the connecting of ports from c_1 to c_2:*

$$\sigma_1 = \{(i, \text{sk}) \mapsto (i, \text{mx}) \mid (i, \text{sk}) \in N_1\}$$
$$\sigma_2 = \{(i, \text{sr}) \mapsto (i, \text{mx}) \mid (i, \text{sr}) \in N_2\} \qquad X = \{(i, \text{mx}) \mid (i, \text{sk}) \in N_1\}$$

Proof. We provide only a sketch of the proof. This proof follows in two phases. First, by considering a transition $(p, q) \xrightarrow{K} (p', q')$ in $(A_1\sigma_1 \bowtie A_2\sigma_2)\backslash X$, one can conclude by performing a case analysis that $\exists (p; q) \xrightarrow{K'} (p'; q')$ in $\mathcal{PA}(c_1; c_2)$. Second, by verifying that the dual also holds.

Lemma 3 (Correctness of $\mathcal{PA}(c_1 \oplus c_2)$). *If, for $i \in \{1, 2\}$, $\mathcal{PA}(c_i)$ is correct with respect to $A_i = (Q_i, N_i, \rightarrow_i, q_{0,i})$, $c_i : n_i \rightarrow m_i$, and $c_1 \oplus c_2$ is well-typed, then $\mathcal{PA}(c_1 \oplus c_2)$ is correct with respect to $A_1 \bowtie (A_2\sigma)$, where σ defines port renamings:*

$$\sigma = \{(i, \text{sr}) \mapsto (i + n_1, \text{sr}) \mid (i, \text{sr}) \in N_2\}$$
$$\cup \{(j, \text{sk}) \mapsto (j + m_1, \text{sr}) \mid (j, \text{sk}) \in N_2\}$$

Proof. We provide only a sketch of the proof. This proof follows the same strategy as the proof for the sequential composition. Start by considering a transition $(p, q) \xrightarrow{K} (p', q')$ in $(A_1 \bowtie A_2)\sigma$. By analysing the possible cases, it is possible to conclude that $\exists (p \oplus q) \xrightarrow{K'} (p' \oplus q')$ in $\mathcal{PA}(c_1 \oplus c_2)$ that mimics this transition. A similar argument for its dual can also be made.

Theorem 1 (Correctness of $\mathcal{PA}$). *Given a well-typed connector c, $\mathcal{PA}(c)$ is correct with respect to some port automaton A built by composing the automata of the primitive connectors within c.*

Proof. This result follows by induction on the structure of connectors, whereas the base case is captured by Lemma 1, and the inductive steps are captured by Lemmas 2 and 3, and by the fact that the trace operation can also be shown correct with respect to some port automaton – due to space restrictions, and because the proof follows similar steps to Lemma 2, we omit here that proof.

4   Connectors as mCRL2 Specifications

The mCRL2 toolset consists of a collection of tools to analyse systems specified in a dedicated process algebra of communicating processes. In a given mCRL2 model, the atomic element of processes are actions. By defining and combining actions we create processes. We describe the core subset of the mCRL2 specification language, focusing on the relevant constructs to understand the encoding of our calculus to mCRL2. A process can be one of the following.

- $a_1|\ldots|a_n$. P – *atomic execution* of n actions (a_1 until a_n), where $n \geq 1$, followed by the execution of P;
- $P + Q$ – *non-deterministic choice* between two processes P and Q;
- $P \parallel Q$ – *parallel execution* of a process P and a process Q (interleaved or at the same time);
- $\delta_H(P)$ – *encapsulation*, blocking the actions in H when executing P;
- $\Gamma_C(P)$ – *communication* of ports, where C is a mapping from groups of atomic actions $a_1|\ldots|a_n$ to another action b (with $n \geq 2$), replacing all groups of actions $a_1|\ldots|a_n$ by b in the execution of P.
- *Reference* to a process name P defined in the scope of the process.

An *mCRL2 program* consists of a pair (P, π) with a process P and a mapping π from process names to process definitions (with possibly recursive definitions), as described above.

The full language is rich enough to capture aspects such as data types and parametrised actions, which we do not explore here. Given a specification in mCRL2 one can, for example, compile and visualise its corresponding labelled transition system, and can verify properties in a dedicated dynamic calculus with fix points.

4.1   Encoding CRC into mCRL2 Programs

We adapt the translation by Kokash et al. [7]. Although the authors encode different connector semantics into mCRL2 programs, we focus on their encoding into constraint automata, for which they have a correctness proof (which ignores data constraints, similarly to CRC).

Table 1 presents the mCRL2 process definitions for the primitives used in Fig. 5. These can be combined in parallel to produce more complex connectors, as exemplified below.

Table 1. mCRL2 processes of primitives, for some actions a, b, c.

id_1	$Id1 = a|b$. $Id1$	lossy	$Lossy = (a + a|b)$. $Lossy$
fifo	$Fifo = a$. b . $Fifo$	Δ_2	$Dupl = a|b|c$. $Dupl$
drain	$Drain = a|b$. $Drain$	∇_2	$Merger = (a|c + b|c)$. $Merger$

Example 1. Consider the connector $c = \mathsf{id}_1; \Delta_2; (\mathsf{fifo} \oplus \mathsf{lossy})$. Each channel in the connector maps to the following processes:

$$Id_1 = (a|b) \cdot Id_1 \qquad\qquad Fifo = f \cdot g \cdot Fifo$$
$$Dupl = c|d|e \cdot Dupl \qquad\qquad Lossy = (h + h|i) \cdot Lossy$$

Let π_c be the set of definitions above. A program for c can be built by placing these definitions in parallel, by imposing communication with Γ, and by encapsulating internal ports with δ. For example, the program (P_c, π_c), with P_c defined below, provides a (naive) encoding of the behaviour of c, which only exposes the ports a, g, and i.

$$P_c = \delta_{\{b,c,d,e,f,h\}}$$
$$(\Gamma_{\{b|c \to bc, d|f \to df, e|h \to eh\}}(Sync \parallel Dupl \parallel Fifo \parallel Lossy))$$

This naive approach to combine connectors leads to an exponential increase of combinations of actions as the connector grows, which quickly becomes untreatable by the mCRL2 tools. This problem is addressed by performing communication and encapsulation as soon as possible, i.e., everytime a new primitive is connected to a connector [7]. Our encoding follows the same ideas, performing encapsulation as soon as possible.

Definition 4 (Encoding $\mathcal{MC}$). *The encoding $\mathcal{MC}$ follows a similar approach to $\mathcal{PA}$, where actions follow the pattern $(n, \mathsf{sr})_\ell$, $(n, \mathsf{sk})_\ell$, or $(n, \mathsf{mx})_\ell$ to indicate that n-th source, sink, or mixed port, using the unique identifier ℓ to distinguish between actions from different basic automata. We start by defining auxiliary functions Block, Hide, and Com, used to describe ports that are blocked, are hidden, and communicate. $N_{i,\ell}$ is the name we give to processes denoting nodes that connect pairs of ports.*

$$Block(n, \ell_1, \ell_2) = \bigcup_{1 \leq i \leq n} \{(i, \mathsf{sk})_{\ell_1}, (i, \mathsf{sr})_{\ell_2}\} \qquad Hide(n, \ell_1) = \bigcup_{1 \leq i \leq n} \{(i, \mathsf{mx})_{\ell_1}\}$$
$$Com(n, \ell_1, \ell_2, \ell) = \bigcup_{1 \leq i \leq n} \{(i, \mathsf{sk})_{\ell_1} | (i, \mathsf{sr})_{\ell_2} \to (i, \mathsf{mx})_\ell\}$$

Given a connector c and a unique identifier ℓ, $\mathcal{MC}(c)_\ell$ is defined below.

$$\mathcal{MC}(p)_\ell = (P_\ell, \{P_\ell = Primitive(p, \ell)\})$$
$$\text{where } Primitive(p, \ell) \text{ is the process of primitive } p \ (c.f. \ Table \ 1),$$
$$\text{using the proposed notation for actions marked by } \ell.$$
$$\mathcal{MC}(c_1; c_2)_\ell = (P_\ell, \{P_\ell = \tau_{Hide(n,\ell)}(\partial_{Block(n,\ell_1,\ell_2)}(\Gamma_{Com(n,\ell_1,\ell_2,\ell)}$$
$$(P_1 \| P_2)))\} \cup \pi_1 \cup \pi_2)$$
$$\text{where } c_1 : n_1 \to n \quad c_2 : n \to n_2$$
$$(P_1, \pi_1) = \mathcal{MC}(c_1)_{\ell_1} \quad (\ell_1 \text{ is fresh})$$
$$(P_2, \pi_2) = \mathcal{MC}(c_2)_{\ell_2} \quad (\ell_2 \text{ is fresh})$$

$$\mathcal{MC}(c_1 \oplus c_2)_\ell = (P_\ell\ ,\ \{P_\ell = (P_1 \parallel P_2)\} \cup \pi_1 \cup \pi_2')$$

$$where\ c_1 : n_1 \rightarrow m_1 \quad c_2 : n_2 \rightarrow m_2$$

$$(P_1, \pi_1) = \mathcal{MC}(c_1)_\ell$$

$$(P_2, \pi_2) = \mathcal{MC}(c_2)_{\ell_2} \quad (\ell_2\ is\ fresh)$$

$$\pi_2' = \pi_2\, \{(i, \mathsf{sr})_{\ell_2} \mapsto (i + n_1, \mathsf{sr})_\ell \mid 1 \leq i \leq n_2\} \cup$$

$$\{(j, \mathsf{sk})_{\ell_2} \mapsto (j + m_1, \mathsf{sk})_\ell \mid 1 \leq j \leq m_2\}$$

The definition of $\mathcal{MC}(\mathsf{Tr}_n(c))_\ell$ is omitted here, and follows a similar structure to the encoding of $\mathcal{MC}(c_1; c_2)_\ell$.

We illustrate this encoding using a simplified version of Example 1.

Example 2. Let $x = \Delta_2$; (fifo $\oplus$ lossy) and a, b, c, d, e be unique identifier:

$$\mathcal{MC}(\mathsf{fifo} \oplus \mathsf{lossy})_a = (P_a, \pi_a)$$

$$\pi_a = \{P_a = Fifo_a \parallel Lossy_a$$

$$, Fifo_a = (1, \mathsf{sr})_a | (1, \mathsf{sk})_a\ .\ Fifo_a$$

$$, Lossy_a = ((2, \mathsf{sr})_a + (2, \mathsf{sr})_a | (2, \mathsf{sk})_a)\ .\ Lossy_a\}$$

$$\mathcal{MC}(x)_b = (P_b, \pi_b)$$

$$\pi_b = \{P_b = \tau_{\{(1,\mathsf{mx})_b, (2,\mathsf{mx})_b\}} (\delta_{\{(1,\mathsf{sk})_c, (1,\mathsf{sr})_a, (2,\mathsf{sk})_c, (2,\mathsf{sr})_a\}}$$

$$(\Gamma_{\{(1,\mathsf{sk})_c | (1,\mathsf{sr})_a \rightarrow (1,\mathsf{mx})_b, (2,\mathsf{sk})_c | (2,\mathsf{sr})_a \rightarrow (2,\mathsf{mx})_b)\}}$$

$$(\Delta_{2,c} \parallel P_a)))$$

$$, \Delta_{2,c} = (1, \mathsf{sr})_c | (1, \mathsf{sk})_c | (2, \mathsf{sk})_c\ .\ \Delta_{2,c}\} \cup \pi_a$$

4.2 Correctness of $\mathcal{MC}_\ell(\cdot)$

Kokash et al. [7] have shown the correctness of a similar encoding from Port Automata (which they call data-agnostic Constraint Automata) to mCRL2. We claim that the correctness of our encoding follows from the correctness of CRC with respect to Port Automata, and from the correctness by Kokash et al. regarding mCRL2 specifications, as depicted in Fig. 6. We defined the encoding $\mathcal{MC}$ from CRC—and not from the PA model—to preserve the parallel structure of the communicating components, which would be lost if our starting point would be the (flatten) tile semantics followed by the $\mathcal{PA}$ encoding.

Figure 6 highlights the two correctness results, via bisimulations, between the connector calculus, the PA semantcs, and mCRL2 programs. Note that we do not formally show that our encoding matches precisely the encoding from Kokash et al. [7], and only explain that our encoding follows the same ideas as the previous encoding to mCRL2.

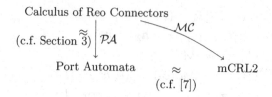

Fig. 6. Relation between CRC, PA, and mCRL2.

5 ReoLive Framework

The ReoLive framework combines tools that analyse connectors and families of connectors under a single web-based front-end. The project and a compiled snapshot can be found online in https://github.com/ReoLanguage/ReoLive. This section focuses on what the framework currently offers, and gives less how to extend it with new plug-ins. More concretely, it describes how to specify connectors and how to visualise it and analyse it using the Port Automata and the mCRL2 encodings.

5.1 Architecture

This project combines software artefacts in more than one programming languages. The core tools to parse and analyse connectors are implemented in Scala by the Preo project,[1] which is either compiled into JavaScript, using the Scala.js compiler,[2] or into a client-server pair of programs. In the latter, the client is compiled also into JavaScript and the server is based on the Play framework,[3] and is compiled into Java binaries. Furthermore, both JavaScript programs use the D3 JavaScript libraries[4] to produce the graph layouts, which manipulate SVG-based diagrams.

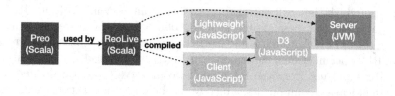

Fig. 7. Architecture of the ReoLive implementation.

The overall architecture is summarised in Fig. 7. The code can be compiled in two different ways: by producing a *standalone* JavaScript library (bottom

---

[1] https://github.com/ReoLanguage/Preo.
[2] https://www.scala-js.org.
[3] https://www.playframework.com.
[4] https://d3js.org.

right rectangle), or by producing a *client-server* architecture (top right rectangle). The former has the advantage of being easier to distribute (a snapshot of our implementation can be found online), while the latter has the advantage of being more powerful and complete (currently using an SMT solver for more complex families of connectors, but the server has to be compiled and executed locally). The ReoLive project website keeps a snapshot of a recent version of the standalone version, depicted in Fig. 8. This web front-end is subdivided into different containers we call *widgets*: (1) where the user specifies connectors, (2) displays the connector's type, (3) displays a concrete instance and its type, (4) presents example connectors to help knowing the syntax, (5) depicts graphically the instance from 3, (6) depicts the Port Automata of that instance (c.f. Sect. 3), and (7) outputs the mCRL2 program (c.f. Sect. 4), ready to be analysed by mCRL2 tools.

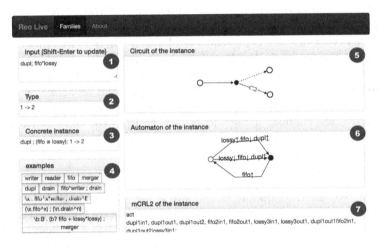

Fig. 8. Screenshot of the standalone version of ReoLive's website.

5.2   The Preo Language

The Preo language is a concrete language for the calculus described in [9], given by the grammar below.

$$c = p \in \mathcal{P} \mid \texttt{id} \mid \texttt{sym}(n_1, n_2) \mid c;c' \mid c*c' \mid \texttt{Tr}(n)(c) \mid c^{\wedge}n \mid ...$$

The rest of the syntax, corresponding to the ellipsis, concern families of connectors, i.e., how to define and restrict parameters that, once instantiated, lead to different connectors of a same family. This is out of the scope of this paper. Furthermore, the language includes the **reader** and **writer** constructs, describing Reo reader and writer components, and supports the definition of named *subconnectors*. The set of primitives $\mathcal{P}$ include mergers, duplicators, fifo channels, lossy channels, and synchronous drains, but others can be easily included. The complete list of primitives can be found by exploring the examples in widget (4) from Fig. 8. Our running example in widget (1) "dupl;fifo*lossy" corresponds to the connector Δ_2; (fifo $\oplus$ lossy), also used in Example 2.

5.3 Interconnecting Widgets

The content of the website is subdivided into *widgets*, as highlighted in Fig. 8. Internally a widget is a statefull object that can interact with the user, and produces a value when *fired*, possibly using values produced by other widgets. Each widget defines its own firing behaviour: the *Type* widget (2) produces a typed connector and its type from the value of the *Input* widget (1); the *Instance* widget (3) calculates a concrete instance *con* based on the connector from the *Type* widget; the *Circuit* widget (5) calculates and depicts a graph structure of *con* in the *Instance* widget; the *Automaton* widget (6) calculates and depicts a Port Automaton of *con*, as described in Sect. 3; and the *mCRL2* widget (7) calculates and displays the mCRL2 program of *con*, as described in Sect. 4.

A special event may trigger a sequence of firings—in our case, pressing shift-enter triggers the firing of all widgets in order except widget (4). More complex orchestration mechanisms of widgets, based on the concept of reactive programming, are left for future work. Furthermore, widgets can be *active* or *inactive*; to toggle between these one only needs to press the header of the widget, and when inactive the content of the widget is not displayed. Only active widgets are fired, and when a widget is fired when it becomes active. In the client-server architecture widgets can further possess a callback function with a dedicated firing behaviour triggered by the server.

Example 3. We use the example in Fig. 8 to guide a more detailed explanation of each widget. The user starts by specifying the connector "dupl;fifo*lossy" in the Input widget. When pressing Shift-Enter, the Input Widget stores the string internally, so that other widgets can access it. The Type widget accesses this string, parses it, produces the connector Δ_2; fifo $\oplus$ lossy, and type checks it. The resulting type $1 \mapsto 2$ is depicted, and the connector is stored and made available to other widgets.

The Instance widget simplifies this connector, removing some syntactic sugar – if the connector had parameters, not addressed in this paper, it would search for valid assignments for this parameters, replacing them by the assignment found. This widget then stores and displays the simplified connector alongside its type. In the client-server architecture the Type and Instance widgets are combined: the server receives the string from the Input widget, producing both a type and an instance and sending this information to the corresponding widget.

All the 3 right widgets access the connector stored in the Instance widget. The Circuit widget generates a graph containing a Reo representation of this connector. Some simplifications from the original connector are made, e.g., removing redundant Sync channels, or combining nested mergers into a single merger. The Automaton widget depicts the associated port automaton, using the rules explained in Sect. 3 to generate the automaton. This widget uses an abstraction of the names for readability, using only the name of the primitives they refer to enhanced with a downward arrow depicting the entry of data into the primitive, an upward arrow depicting data leaving the primitive, and a double arrow to depict both cases. Finally, the mCRL2 widget contains the mCRL2 model of the connector, following the encoding from Sect. 4. In this model each action is identified by the name and a unique identifier of the primitive it refers to, as well as information about the type of port. For example, the action `fifo2in1` refers to the first source (input) port of the fifo, and 2 is the unique identifier of that fifo primitive connector.

5.4 Towards Verification of Connector Families

The Preo language, as well as the full version of the connector calculus from Proença and Clarke [9], describe families of connectors. In this paper we did not consider the families aspect, although the existing tools to type-check Preo connectors are included in ReoLive.

We experimented on how to verify the full calculus of connector families using the mCRL2 toolset, following the ideas from Beek and de Vink [3]. Unfortunately, mCRL2 requires the number of processes running in parallel to be fixed and known upfront, limiting the analysis to only a bounded set of families. The latest experiments consist of generating a small number of instances of a connector and include them in a single mCRL2 model, which can be used for model checking. However, we did not find a satisfactory approach to either select an interesting set of candidates for instances, or to give some control over the instances being selected. Furthermore, modelling families of connectors can easily produce a state explosion that is hard to control. Hence we left these experiments out of the existing framework, although they can be found in experimental branches on our GitHub project. Future work will involve providing some control over the instances that could be of interest when analysing families of connectors, and investigating a suitable (modal) logic to describe properties over families of connectors.

6 Conclusion and Future Work

This paper describes a semantic model for the connector calculus using the port automata. Based on this model we encode our connector calculus into mCRL2, following Kokash et al. [7]. These two encodings are included in the ReoLive framework, animating our calculus with our web framework which implements the calculus, the port automata semantics, and the mCRL2 of each connector.

Our future work is many-fold. We expect to extend the portfolio of available modules; for example, add support for a dedicated modal logic to verify connectors, analyse different semantics of Reo connectors other than Port Automata (incorporation of the IFTA tools is planned soon),[5] and add support for the Treo language to specify connectors.[6]

---

[5] https://github.com/haslab/ifta.
[6] https://github.com/ReoLanguage/Reo.

Orthogonally, we also plan to improve the client-server version of ReoLive, by taking advantage of the server capabilities. For example, we plan on automatically processing the mCRL2 model encoded, which the user may download, or use to verify the dedicated modal logic for connectors.

Acknowledgements. This work is financed by the ERDF – European Regional Development Fund through the Operational Programme for Competitiveness and Internationalisation – COMPETE 2020 Programme and by National Funds through the Portuguese funding agency, FCT – Fundação para a Ciência e a Tecnologia, within projects POCI-01-0145-FEDER-016692 (first author) and POCI-01-0145-FEDER-029946 (second author).

References

1. Arbab, F.: Reo: a channel-based coordination model for component composition. Math. Struct. Comput. Sci. **14**(3), 329–366 (2004)
2. Baier, C., Sirjani, M., Arbab, F., Rutten, J.J.M.M.: Modeling component connectors in Reo by constraint automata. Sci. Comput. Program. **61**(2), 75–113 (2006)
3. ter Beek, M.H., de Vink, E.P.: Using mCRL2 for the analysis of software product lines. In: Proceedings of the 2nd FME Workshop on Formal Methods in Software Engineering, FormaliSE 2014, pp. 31–37. ACM, New York (2014)
4. Gadducci, F., Montanari, U.: The tile model. In: Proof, Language, and Interaction, pp. 133–166. MIT Press (2000)
5. Groote, J.F., Mathijssen, A., Reniers, M., Usenko, Y., van Weerdenburg, M.: The formal specification language mCRL2. In: Methods for Modelling Software Systems (MMOSS), Dagstuhl Seminar Proceedings (2007)
6. Koehler, C., Clarke, D.: Decomposing port automata. In: Proceedings of SAC 2009, pp. 1369–1373. ACM, New York (2009)
7. Kokash, N., Krause, C., de Vink, E.P.: Reo + mCRL2: a framework for model-checking dataflow in service compositions. FAC **24**(2), 187–216 (2012)
8. MacLane, S.: Categorical algebra. Bull. Am. Math. Soc. **71**(1), 40–106 (1965)
9. Proença, J., Clarke, D.: Typed connector families and their semantics. Sci. Comput. Program. **146**, 28–49 (2017)

Multi-agent Systems with Virtual Stigmergy

Rocco De Nicola[1], Luca Di Stefano[2(✉)], and Omar Inverso[2]

[1] IMT School of Advanced Studies, Lucca, Italy
[2] Gran Sasso Science Institute (GSSI), L'Aquila, Italy
luca.distefano@gssi.it

Abstract. We introduce a simple language for multi-agent systems that lends itself to intuitive design of local specifications. Agents operate on (parts of) a decentralized data structure, the stigmergy, that contains their (partial) knowledge. Such knowledge is asynchronously propagated across local stigmergies. In this way, local changes may influence global behaviour. The main novelty is in that our interaction mechanism combines stigmergic interaction with attribute-based communication. Specific conditions for interaction can be expressed in the form of predicates over exposed features of the agents. Additionally, agents may access a global environment. After presenting the language, we show its expressiveness on some illustrative case studies. We also include some preliminary results towards automated verification by relying on a mechanizable symbolic encoding that allows to exploit verification tools for mainstream languages.

1 Introduction

Multi-agent systems are collections of autonomous agents that operate according to local rules and limited mutual awareness. They are a convenient formalism for representing several classes of complex systems, and can help reasoning about them. A fundamental demand that frequently arises when considering multi-agent systems is to determine whether a global property of interest emerges from the combination of the local behaviours of multiple agents. Being inherently distributed and asynchronous, multi-agent systems are characterized by considerably large state spaces. Therefore, techniques for automated verification that complement simulation-based approaches should be considered essential.

In this paper, we introduce a simple language for multi-agent systems that lends itself to intuitive design of local specifications. The language is simple yet versatile enough to model several interesting classes of systems. It combines stigmergic interaction [15,18] with attribute-based communication [1]. A key concept of the language is the *stigmergy*, a distributed data structure that models the global knowledge of the system. Each agent operates only on its own local copy of the stigmergy, that stores his own (partial) knowledge of the system. Knowledge is asynchronously propagated across local stigmergies. Thus, changes by an agent may indirectly affect the behaviour of another.

© Springer Nature Switzerland AG 2018
M. Mazzara et al. (Eds.): STAF 2018 Workshops, LNCS 11176, pp. 351–366, 2018.
https://doi.org/10.1007/978-3-030-04771-9_26

In the originally proposed version of the stigmergy, agents are concrete entities having their own position in space, and the propagation of the information is restricted to neighbours. To increase expressiveness, we generalise stigmergic interaction to arbitrary *predicates* over exposed features, referred to as *attributes*, of the agents. In fact, our language has no explicit concept of position, and thus of neighbours, for agents. An agent can have instead local attributes, and predicates over these attributes can express the conditions for two components to be allowed to exchange knowledge. Movement is no longer seen as a specific action; components may update the attribute that encodes their position by performing a standard action.

The above generalisation of stigmergic interaction makes the language more flexible and allows us to model a wider class of systems. However, it is still insufficiently rich to model several other classes of multi-agent systems where the global *environment* plays a crucial role [9]. To address this shortcoming, we extend our language with tailored primitives to explicitly model the actions of the agents on the environment.

The rest of the paper is organized as follows. In Sect. 2 we present the formal semantics of the core language, allowing us to define systems where agents interact indirectly through a virtual stigmergy. In Sect. 3 we present the environment-oriented primitives of the richer language and their semantics. In Sect. 4 we demonstrate the features of the language by modeling a selection of simple case studies. As part of the discussion on the case studies, we include some preliminary results towards automated verification of one of the presented systems, by means of a mechanizable symbolic encoding that allows to re-use general-purpose verification tools for mainstream languages. Finally, in Sect. 5, we draw conclusions and discuss related and future work.

2   The LAbS language

In this section we introduce LAbS (Language with Attribute-based Stigmergy), a language for multi-agent systems. LAbS is inspired by a specific form of stigmergic interaction originally proposed with the Buzz language [15] and generalises it to attribute-based communication [1].

A key concept in our language is the *virtual stigmergy*, a distributed data structure that models the global knowledge of the system. Each agent maintains a local copy of (part of) this data structure, that contains his own (partial) knowledge of the system. We call these copies *local stigmergies*. An agent reads from and writes to his local stigmergy only. Silently, knowledge is then asynchronously propagated across local stigmergies. This way, indirect agent interaction is achieved. Formally, local stigmergies $L \in \mathcal{L}$ are partial functions that map keys to timestamped values: $\mathcal{L} = \mathcal{K} \hookrightarrow \mathcal{V} \times \mathbb{N}$, where $\mathcal{K}, \mathcal{V}$ are the sets of allowed keys and values, respectively. We use natural numbers to represent timestamps. If $(x, v, t) \in L$, we say that v is the *value* of x and that t is its *timestamp* in the local stigmergy L. We refer to these as $value(L, x)$ and $time(L, x)$, respectively. We write $L(x) = \bot$ whenever $\forall v. \forall t. (x, v, t) \notin L$.

The operations on the stigmergy and the propagation mechanism are the following. When an agent *writes* a key-value pair into its local stigmergy, a timestamp is retrieved from a global clock and bound to the pair. If the local stigmergy contains an entry with the same key, it is substituted by the new one. The new data is then automatically (though asynchronously) propagated to its neighbours. For agents in the neighbourhood that already have a value bound to the same key but with a newer timestamp, the propagation has no effect; all the others update their local stigmergy, and in turn propagate the new value. This process allows information to be spread throughout the whole system, eventually. Conversely, each time an agent *reads* from its local stigmergy, a key confirmation request is sent to the neighbourhood to confirm whether the data just accessed was up-to-date. This will in turn cause any more recent information from other local stigmergies nearby to be propagated, or older entries to be updated, and then propagated as well.

Insertion of a tuple in a local stigmergy is a function $\oplus : \mathcal{L} \times (\mathcal{K} \times \mathcal{V} \times \mathbb{N}) \longrightarrow \mathcal{L}$ defined as the smallest relation that satisfies the rules in Table 1, where we denoted by $L[x \mapsto (v,t)]$ the partial function L' such that $L'(x) = (v,t)$ and $L'(x') = L(x') \ \forall x' \neq x$. Note that by defining the insertion in such a way, only new tuples are considered. A tuple is new if its key is missing from the local stigmergy, or if it has a more recent timestamp than the existing one.

Table 1. Operations on the virtual stigmergy.

$$\frac{L(x) = \bot}{L \oplus (x,v,t) = L[x \mapsto (v,t)]} \ (\text{ADD}) \qquad \frac{t > time(L,x)}{L \oplus (x,v,t) = L[x \mapsto (v,t)]} \ (\text{UPDATE})$$

$$\frac{t \leq time(L,x)}{L \oplus (x,v,t) = L} \ (\text{DISCARD})$$

An example of stigmergic interaction is shown in Fig. 1. Here, agents intend to move following the direction stored in the virtual stigmergy. Initially (a), two agents, c_1 and c_2, are moving in opposite directions. When c_1 moves (b), it accesses the stigmergy to read its own direction: therefore, it asks its neighbours if a newer direction is available (c), and receives a more up-to-date value from c_2 (d). Note the dashed circle that represents the communication range of c_1, which has radius δ (b); the dotted arrows indicate stigmergic communication. We should stress that these protocols are transparent to the designer of the individual behaviour, who only needs to specify read and write operations on the agent's local copy of the data structure.

The above description slightly deviates from the Buzz language in a few points. First, while Buzz agents can communicate through multiple stigmergies, in our language there is a unique stigmergy. Multiple stigmergies however can be replicated by adding different prefixes to each stigmergy key. Moreover, Buzz

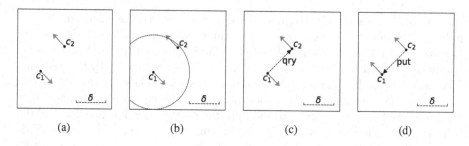

| (a) | (b) | (c) | (d) |

Fig. 1. A possible evolution of a system in the presence of stigmergic interaction.

stigmergies are based on Lamport timestamps [11] and rely on unique component identifiers to break ties, which may occur when the same timestamp is used multiple times; this cannot happen in our language, since we assume the existence of a global clock. Finally, differently from Buzz, in our core language there is no explicit message passing between components. Components can only interact via the stigmergy or the environment. We introduced the above assumptions for the sake of simplicity and homogeneity. We might reconsider them in future version of our language, if demanded by applications.

However, our calculus generalises some of the concepts related to the virtual stigmergies of Buzz. Most importantly, in our language the ability of exchanging information through the stigmergy is not directly constrained by spatial vicinity. In fact, there is no explicit concept of an agent's position at all. Rather, we rely upon local properties of the agents to define when they are allowed to communicate.

The syntax of LAbS is described in Table 2. When introducing **expressions**, we assume that $v \in \mathcal{V}$, $x \in \mathcal{K}$; and that $\diamond$ stands for a binary operator over $\mathcal{V}$, such as $(+, -, \times \ldots)$. When introducing **guards**, $\bowtie$ denotes comparison relations over $\mathcal{V} \cup \{\bot\}$, namely $(=, <, >)$.

Table 2. LAbS syntax. Assume K to be taken from a set of named processes.

$$P ::= \ 0 \mid \sqrt{} \mid \alpha \mid P; P \mid P + P \mid b \rightarrow P \mid P|P \mid K \qquad \text{process}$$
$$\alpha ::= \ I(x) := e \mid L(x) := e \qquad \text{elementary actions}$$
$$e ::= \ v \mid L(x) \mid I(x) \mid e \diamond e \qquad \text{expression}$$
$$b ::= \ true \mid e \bowtie e \mid \neg b \mid b \wedge b \qquad \text{guard}$$
$$c ::= \ \langle I, L, P, Z_c, Z_p \rangle \qquad \text{component}$$
$$S ::= \ c \mid S \| S \qquad \text{system}$$

A **system** is the parallel composition of a number of components; while a **component** is a 5-ple $\langle I, L, P, Z_c, Z_p \rangle$ where:

- $I : \mathcal{K} \hookrightarrow \mathcal{V}$ (*interface*) contains key-value pairs (attributes); the set of all interfaces is denoted by $\mathcal{I}$.
- $L \in \mathcal{L}$ is the component's *local stigmergy*.
- P is a *process* describing the component's behaviour.
- Z_c is the set of keys that the component has to confirm.
- Z_p is the set of keys that the component must propagate.

Thus, each component is equipped with a local stigmergy and an *interface*, which is a dynamic set of key-value pairs (*attributes*). Attributes can be specified at initialization and modified at runtime and represent either a variable in the component's memory, or a physical property of the agent (for instance, its position). Similarly, events that change those physical properties are not seen as a different kind of action. For instance, a component may move by updating the attribute that encodes its position. In addition, attributes are used to determine whether two agents are able to communicate. Namely, it is assumed that the user of the language can specify a custom, attribute-based predicate that, given two interfaces, determines whether the corresponding components are able to communicate. This is an important source of flexibility, as attributes can be used to model different means of communication available to each agent. The ability of components to change their own attributes at any time means that connections among components can be dynamically established or removed.

2.1 Processes and Expressions

A **process** within a component models the behaviour of the component. The elementary processes are the *idle* or deadlocked process 0, the successfully terminated process $\sqrt{}$, and those denoted by α:

- the update of one of the attributes of the component with the result of the evaluation of an expression,
- the update of a stigmergy key with the result of the evaluation of an expression.

The sequential composition of two processes, $P; Q$, is the process that behaves as P until it terminates and behaves as Q afterwards. On the other hand, the nondeterministic choice $P + Q$ can behave either as P or Q. The guarded process $b \rightarrow P$ can only continue as P if the guard b is satisfied. The parallel composition of processes is a process $P \mid Q$ where the executions of P and Q are interleaved. Nondeterministic choice and parallel composition are both commutative operators. Recursion is modeled through named process invocations: we assume there is a set of *process constants* $K \triangleq P$, where P is a process expression that follows the syntax of Table 2 and may contain references to K itself and to other process constants.

Expressions may contain constants, refer to the value of local attributes or stigmergy keys, or binary operators involving sub-expressions. A guard may either be the *true* predicate, which is always satisfied, or a comparison between

Table 3. Semantics of processes. λ denotes a generic transition label (either an α or $\sqrt{}$).

$$\frac{}{\sqrt{} \overset{\sqrt{}}{\longmapsto} 0} \text{ (TICK)} \qquad \frac{}{\alpha \overset{\alpha}{\longmapsto} \sqrt{}} \text{ (ACT)} \qquad \frac{P \overset{\lambda}{\longmapsto} P'}{P + Q \overset{\lambda}{\longmapsto} P'} \text{ (CHOICE-L)} \qquad \frac{Q \overset{\lambda}{\longmapsto} Q'}{P + Q \overset{\lambda}{\longmapsto} Q'} \text{ (CHOICE-R)}$$

$$\frac{P \overset{\alpha}{\longmapsto} P'}{P;Q \overset{\alpha}{\longmapsto} P';Q} \text{ (SEQ1)} \qquad \frac{P \overset{\sqrt{}}{\longmapsto} P' \quad Q \overset{\lambda}{\longmapsto} Q'}{P;Q \overset{\lambda}{\longmapsto} Q'} \text{ (SEQ2)} \qquad \frac{P \overset{\lambda}{\longmapsto} P' \quad K \triangleq P}{K \overset{\lambda}{\longmapsto} P'} \text{ (CON)}$$

$$\frac{P \overset{\alpha}{\longmapsto} P'}{P \mid Q \overset{\alpha}{\longmapsto} P' \mid Q} \text{ (PAR1)} \qquad \frac{P \overset{\sqrt{}}{\longmapsto} P' \quad Q \overset{\lambda}{\longmapsto} Q'}{P \mid Q \overset{\lambda}{\longmapsto} Q'} \text{ (PAR2)} \qquad \frac{P_1 \mid P_2 \overset{\lambda}{\longmapsto} P'}{P_2 \mid P_1 \overset{\lambda}{\longmapsto} P'} \text{ (PARCOMM)}$$

two expressions. Guards can also be negated ($\neg b$) or composed through the conjunction operator, $\wedge$. The semantics of processes and expressions is reported in Tables 3 and 4, respectively. We also provide a function $\mathcal{K}[\![\cdot]\!]$ to compute the set of stigmergy keys that have to be read in order to evaluate an expression. This function is instrumental to formalize the mechanisms of virtual stigmergies. We allow the semantic function of expressions $\mathcal{E}[\![\cdot]\!]$ to return the undefined value $\bot$, for instance when the expression reads an undefined value or applies an operator to incompatible values (e.g. adding a number to a string).

Table 4. Semantics of expressions.

$$\mathcal{E}[\![\cdot]\!] : Expr \longrightarrow (\mathcal{I} \times \mathcal{L} \to \mathcal{V} \cup \{\bot\}) \qquad\qquad \mathcal{K}[\![\cdot]\!] : Expr \longrightarrow 2^{\mathcal{K}}$$
$$\mathcal{E}[\![v]\!] = \lambda(I, L).v \qquad\qquad \mathcal{K}[\![v]\!] = \emptyset$$
$$\mathcal{E}[\![I(x)]\!] = \lambda(I, L).I(x) \qquad\qquad \mathcal{K}[\![I(x)]\!] = \emptyset$$
$$\mathcal{E}[\![L(x)]\!] = \lambda(I, L).value(L, x) \qquad\qquad \mathcal{K}[\![L(x)]\!] = \{x\}$$
$$\mathcal{E}[\![e_1 \diamond e_2]\!] = \lambda(I, L).\mathcal{E}[\![e_1]\!](I, L) \diamond \mathcal{E}[\![e_2]\!](I, L) \qquad\qquad \mathcal{K}[\![e_1 \diamond e_2]\!] = \mathcal{K}[\![e_1]\!] \cup \mathcal{K}[\![e_2]\!]$$
$$\mathcal{E}[\![e \diamond \bot]\!] = \mathcal{E}[\![\bot \diamond e]\!] = \lambda(I, L).\bot$$

The *satisfaction* of a guard b is formalized as a relation $I, L \models b$ (Table 5). A necessary condition for satisfaction is that b must be *well-defined* with respect to interface I and stigmergy L, i.e. all the sub-expressions of b must only refer to defined attributes and stigmergy keys (defined as $\vdash$ in Table 6). Notice that $\bot$ belongs only to exactly one $\bowtie$ relation, namely $\bot = \bot$. In both tables, it is assumed that $v \in \mathcal{V}$, $x \in \mathcal{K}$; $\diamond$ and $\bowtie$ are the same as for Table 2.

2.2   Link Predicates

Our semantics is parametric to a *link predicate* φ that, given two interfaces, holds if the corresponding components are able to communicate. This predicate

Table 5. Satisfaction of guards.

$$I, L \models true$$
$$I, L \models \neg b \iff I, L \not\models b \text{ and } I, L \vdash b$$
$$I, L \models e_1 \bowtie e_2 \iff \mathcal{E}[\![e_1]\!](I, L) \bowtie \mathcal{E}[\![e_2]\!](I, L) \text{ and } I, L \vdash e_1 \text{ and } I, L \vdash e_2$$
$$I, L \models b_1 \wedge b_2 \iff I, L \models b_1 \text{ and } I, L \models b_2 \text{ and } I, L \vdash b_1 \text{ and } I, L \vdash b_2$$

Table 6. Well-definedness of expressions and guards.

$$I, L \vdash v \qquad\qquad\qquad\qquad\qquad I, L \vdash true$$
$$I, L \vdash I(x) \iff I(x) \neq \bot \qquad\qquad I, L \vdash \neg b \iff I, L \vdash b$$
$$I, L \vdash L(x) \iff value(L, x) \neq \bot \qquad I, L \vdash e_1 \bowtie e_2 \iff I, L \vdash e_1 \text{ and } I, L \vdash e_2$$
$$I, L \vdash e_1 \diamond e_2 \iff I, L \vdash e_1 \text{ and } I, L \vdash e_1 \qquad I, L \vdash b_1 \wedge b_2 \iff I, L \vdash b_1 \text{ and } I, L \vdash b_2$$

generally depends on the scenario one wants to describe. We say that two agents are *neighbours* if they satisfy such predicate. This is useful, for instance, in the case of multi-robot systems, where more complex predicates allow to effectively model different sensors and capabilities for each robot. The syntax is identical to that of guards, but sub-expressions η are defined over two interfaces.

$$\varphi ::= \quad true \mid \eta \bowtie \eta \mid \neg \varphi \mid \varphi \wedge \varphi \qquad\qquad \text{predicate}$$
$$\eta ::= \quad v \mid I_1(x) \mid I_2(x) \mid \eta \diamond \eta \qquad\qquad \text{expression}$$

We use $\mathcal{H}[\![\cdot]\!]$ to denote the semantic function of expressions η. We omit a formal definition, as it is nearly identical to the function $\mathcal{E}[\![\cdot]\!]$ described in Table 3. The only difference is that $\mathcal{H}[\![\cdot]\!]$ maps an expression to a function of two interfaces, rather than an interface and a local stigmergy. Similarly, we assume the definitions of satisfaction $(I_1, I_2 \models \varphi)$ and well-definedness $(I_1, I_2 \vdash \varphi)$ closely follow the ones introduced for guards. The ability of combining link predicates offers an intuitive way to model different communication modes for agents. For instance, the predicate below, where $\|\cdot\|$ denotes the Euclidean norm, states that two agents can communicate if their positions are closer than a constant δ or if they both possess a long-range networking device.

$$\|I_1(pos) - I_2(pos)\| \leq \delta \vee (I_1(LongRange) = \text{``true''} \wedge I_2(LongRange) = \text{``true''})$$

2.3 Components and Systems

Component-level transitions define what happens when a component performs an execution step; they are modelled in Table 7, there it is assumed that $v = value(L, x)$, $t = time(L, x)$, and $l = I(loc)$. For instance we have that, when a component performs an attribute update $I(x) := e$, the result of expression e is bound to attribute x, and the stigmergy keys used to evaluate e are added to the set of keys to be confirmed.

Stigmergy updates are defined in rule (LSTIG) and result in the insertion of a tuple in the local stigmergy of the component. Here we use $now()$ to represent the timestamp, obtained from a global clock, which is assigned to the new tuple. Since the newly inserted tuple must be propagated, its key is added to Z_p; Z_c may also be updated, like for the attribute update case. Rule (AWAIT) specifies that a guarded process $b \to P$ can only proceed if the guard b is satisfied. λ denotes a generic transition label. The above transitions are labelled ε to denote they are internal to each components, i.e. they are invisible from the point of view of the system.

Table 7. Semantics of components.

$$
\frac{P \xrightarrow{I(x):=e} P' \quad \mathcal{E}[\![e]\!]\,(I,L) = v \quad I[x \mapsto v] = I' \quad Z_c = Z_p = \emptyset}{\langle I, L, P, Z_c, Z_p \rangle \xrightarrow{\varepsilon} \langle I', L, P', Z_c \cup \mathcal{K}[\![e]\!], Z_p \rangle} \text{ (ATTR)}
$$

$$
\frac{P \xrightarrow{L(x):=e} P' \quad \mathcal{E}[\![e]\!]\,(I,L) = v \quad t = now() \quad Z_c = Z_p = \emptyset}{\langle I, L, P, Z_c, Z_p \rangle \xrightarrow{\varepsilon} \langle I, L \oplus (x,v,t), P', Z_c \cup \mathcal{K}[\![e]\!], Z_p \cup \{x\} \rangle} \text{ (LSTIG)}
$$

$$
\frac{I, L \models b \quad \langle I, L, P, Z_c, Z_p \rangle \xrightarrow{\lambda} \langle I', L', P', Z'_c, Z'_p \rangle}{\langle I, L, b \to P, Z_c, Z_p \rangle \xrightarrow{\lambda} \langle I', L', P', Z'_c, Z'_p \rangle} \text{ (AWAIT)}
$$

On the other hand, system-level transitions formalize the management of the shared knowledge inside the virtual stigmergy (Table 8). Rule (PAR) simply states that parallel subsystems interleave their internal actions. The symmetrical rule to (PAR) has been omitted. Rules (COMM) and (ASSOC) describe that parallel composition is commutative and associative. Rule (PROPAGATE) states that a component can always propagate the tuple corresponding to a key in its own Z_p set. When this happens, the key of the propagated tuple is removed from the set. Rule (CONFIRM) specifies that the same can happen with Z_c keys. The different nature of the messages is reflected by different transition labels (put for propagation; qry for confirmation). The (PUT) rule allows tuples to spread to other components. When a subsystem performs a put (I', x, v, t) transition, a neighbouring component (that is, one with an interface I that satisfies the predicate φ) with an outdated value will update its local stigmergy and add x to the keys to propagate. Notice that x is also removed from Z_c, as it is assumed that the new value does not need to be confirmed anymore. Notice that a composite system evolves by emitting the same transition label as its subsystem. This means that the rule is recursively applied until all neighbours perform their stigmergy update.

The rules for confirmation messages are quite similar, but the action of components depend on the current state of their local stigmergy. Rule (QRY$_1$) says that a component with an older entry will react to a query transition qry (I', x, v, t) by updating its own stigmergy and propagating the value afterwards. On the other hand, a component that has a more up-to-date value will just update Z_p to propagate it, while discarding the received entry (rule QRY$_2$).

Please, notice that component-level rules (ATTR) and (LSTIG) are also guarded by the condition $Z_c = Z_p = \emptyset$. This means that system-level rules have a higher priority: components have to propagate or confirm all pending keys before they are able to continue their execution.

Table 8. Semantics of systems. Assume λ to be a generic transition label.

$$\frac{S \xrightarrow{\varepsilon} S'}{S\|T \xrightarrow{\varepsilon} S'\|T} \text{ (PAR)} \qquad \frac{S_1\|S_2 \xrightarrow{\lambda} S'}{S_2\|S_1 \xrightarrow{\lambda} S'} \text{ (COMM)} \qquad \frac{(S_1\|S_2)\|S_3 \xrightarrow{\lambda} S'}{S_1\|(S_2\|S_3) \xrightarrow{\lambda} S'} \text{ (ASSOC)}$$

$$\frac{S \xrightarrow{\mathsf{put}(I',x,v,t)} S' \quad I',I \models \varphi \quad L \oplus (x,v,t) \neq L}{S\|\langle I,L,P,Z_c,Z_p\rangle \xrightarrow{\mathsf{put}(I',x,v,t)} S'\|\langle I,L \oplus (x,v,t),P,Z_c \setminus \{x\}, Z_p \cup \{x\}\rangle} \text{ (PUT)}$$

$$\frac{S \xrightarrow{\mathsf{qry}(I',x,v,t)} S' \quad I',I \models \varphi \quad time(L,x) < t}{S\|\langle I,L,P,Z_c,Z_p\rangle \xrightarrow{\mathsf{qry}(I',x,v,t)} S'\|\langle I,L \oplus (x,v,t),P,Z_c \setminus \{x\}, Z_p \cup \{x\}\rangle} \text{ (QRY1)}$$

$$\frac{S \xrightarrow{\mathsf{qry}(I',x,v,t)} S' \quad I',I \models \varphi \quad time(L,x) \geq t}{S\|\langle I,L,P,Z_c,Z_p\rangle \xrightarrow{\mathsf{qry}(I',x,v,t)} S'\|\langle I,L,P,Z_c,Z_p \cup \{x\}\rangle} \text{ (QRY2)}$$

$$\frac{x \in Z_c \quad L(x) = (v,t)}{\langle I,L,P,Z_c,Z_p\rangle \xrightarrow{\mathsf{qry}(I,x,v,t)} \langle I,L,P,Z_c \setminus \{x\}, Z_p\rangle} \text{ (CONFIRM)}$$

$$\frac{x \in Z_p \quad L(x) = (v,t)}{\langle I,L,P,Z_c,Z_p\rangle \xrightarrow{\mathsf{put}(I,x,v,t)} \langle I,L,P,Z_c,Z_p \setminus \{x\}\rangle} \text{ (PROPAGATE)}$$

3   Modeling the Environment

Many real-world scenarios rely on the interaction between agents and the physical environment they are operating in [21, 22]. This kind of interaction enjoys some specific features that are difficult to express with the constructs introduced in Sect. 2.

We define an *environment* to be a partial function from keys to values, like interfaces. A *situated system* is a pair (E, S) where E is an environment and S is a LAbS system.

Components can now perform two new basic actions that we call *situated actions* to differentiate those interacting with the environment from those interacting with components. Situated actions can write the result of an expression into the environment - $E(x) := e$, or can store an environmental value into an attribute - $I(y) := E(x)$ (Table 9). We therefore introduce additional transition rules and labels to the semantics of components: $v \triangleright x$ denotes the willingness of a component to update the environmental key x to value v, while $y \triangleleft x$ denotes the intention of retrieving the value of $E(x)$ and binding it to attribute y.

The semantics of the new actions is defined in Table 10. To define the semantics of situated systems, in Table 11 we introduce an unlabeled transition relation

($\rightarrowtail$); there the rule symmetrical of (PARE) is omitted. Rule (READ) states that the action $I(y) := E(x)$ results in assigning the value $E(x)$ to attribute y of the component. In the rules we use $c[I'/I]$ to refer to a component that is identical to c except for the interface, which is instead I'. Due to the condition $E(x) \neq \bot$, a situated read action may block a process when the requested key is undefined. Rule (WRITE) states that the write action induces a change in the environment. Rule (LSTIG) simply states that the actions related to stigmergic communications only affect the system and leave the environment unchanged. Finally, rule (PARE), which is commutative, states that the parallel composition of two systems affects the environment in an interleaved fashion.

Table 9. Basic processes in situated systems.

$$\alpha ::= \quad I(x) := e \mid L(x) := e \mid E(x) := e \mid I(y) := E(x)$$

Table 10. Semantics of situated actions.

$$\frac{P \xrightarrow{E(x):=e} P' \quad \mathcal{E}[\![e]\!]\,(I, L) = v \quad Z_c = Z_p = \emptyset}{\langle I, L, P, Z_c, Z_p \rangle \xrightarrow{v \triangleright x} \langle I, L, P', Z_c \cup \mathcal{K}[\![e]\!], Z_p \rangle} \quad (\text{ENV1})$$

$$\frac{P \xrightarrow{I(y):=E(x)} P' \quad Z_c = Z_p = \emptyset}{\langle I, L, P, Z_c, Z_p \rangle \xrightarrow{y \triangleleft x} \langle I, L, P', Z_c, Z_p \rangle} \quad (\text{ENV2})$$

Table 11. Semantics of situated systems ($\mu \in \{\mathsf{qry}, \mathsf{put}\}$). Assume c to be a component $\langle I, L, P, Z_c, Z_p \rangle$.

$$\frac{c \xrightarrow{y \triangleleft x} c' \quad E(x) = v \neq \bot}{(E, c) \rightarrowtail (E, c'[I\,[y \mapsto v]/I])} \quad (\text{READ}) \qquad \frac{c \xrightarrow{v \triangleright x} c'}{(E, c) \rightarrowtail (E[x \mapsto v], c')} \quad (\text{WRITE})$$

$$\frac{S \xrightarrow{\mu(I, x, v, t)} S'}{(E, S) \rightarrowtail (E, S')} \quad (\text{LSTIG}) \qquad \frac{(E, S) \rightarrowtail (E', S')}{(E, S\|T) \rightarrowtail (E', S'\|T)} \quad (\text{PARE})$$

4   Case Studies

In this section we introduce a selection of LAbS systems that model popular scenarios in the multi-robot and multi-agent literature.

4.1   Flocking

A system of mobile agents exhibits flocking behaviour when its agents start from a state of incoherent motion (i.e. in different directions or at different velocities) but eventually manage to move coherently in a single direction. This behaviour is thought to emerge from simple individual mechanisms, such as remaining close to one's neighbours (while avoiding collisions) and matching their velocity [17].

We model a flocking system as follows. Our swarm is a group of N robots distributed on a square grid (*arena*) of size $G \times G$. We store the position of each robot as a local attribute *pos*, and its direction in its local stigmergy. To model the limited range of the sensor, we define a link predicate that is true if and only if the distance between the two robots is less than or equal to a constant δ:

$$\varphi \equiv \|I_1(pos) - I_2(pos)\| \leq \delta$$

where by $\|\cdot\|$ we denote the Euclidean norm. The movement process is defined as

$$\textsc{Move} \triangleq I(pos) := I(pos) + L(dir) \mod G; \textsc{Move}$$

Here we use the mod G notation to describe what happens when a robot reaches the borders of the arena. For the sake of simplicity we have assumed that our arena represents a torus: so, for instance, a component at position $(x, G-1)$, by moving in direction $(0, 1)$, will reach $(x, 0)$.

Assume that D is the set of allowed directions. Then the process executed by each robot is just

$$\textsc{Flock} \triangleq \sum_{(i,j) \in D} L(dir) := (i, j); \textsc{Move}$$

where the *generalized choice* construct $\sum_{x \in \{x_1, x_2, \ldots, x_n\}} P(x)$ denotes the process $P[x_1/x] + P[x_2/x] + \ldots + P[x_n/x]$. This means that each robot chooses an arbitrary direction from D and assigns it to the stigmergy key *dir*; It then moves in that direction by calling the recursive process $\textsc{Move}$. When two robots are close enough to satisfy φ, they will agree on the direction with the most recent timestamp.

For this specific case study, we experimented with automated verification of LAbS programs. We translated the specifications into a C program. We then instrumented the program for symbolic execution by introducing nondeterministic variables to model the system's initial configuration and the process interleaving. By restricting the nondeterminism of these variables, we encoded fairness guarantees in the translation, so that each robot executes a transition in a round-robin fashion. Interleaving of stigmergy transitions was also partially constrained, by compressing the propagation of the messages to all neighbours into a single execution step. Eventually, we used a general-purpose bounded model checking tool [7] to automatically analyse the instrumented program. Note that our translation consists in a direct encoding of the SOS rules presented in Sect. 2 and is therefore straightforwardly mechanizable. Once automated, the translation would be totally transparent to the user of the language.

By following the above procedure, we verified whether a swarm of N robots could reach a consensus on the direction after a finite number B of execution steps. For our analysis we considered swarms of 3,4,6, and 8 agents in a $16 \times$

16 arena. The experimental results and verification times are summarized in Table 12. In particular, we proved that, for *any possible initial position* of the agents on the arena, for a sensor range $\delta = 21$ the system reaches the consensus within 12 steps. We also proved that with smaller sensor range, or larger swarms, there exist some initial configuration for which the same number of steps is no longer sufficient for the agent to agree on the same direction.

Table 12. Verification results for the flocking case study.

N	B	δ	Result	Time (s)
3	12	20	Fail	74
3	12	21	Pass	388
4	12	21	Fail	213
6	12	21	Fail	352
8	12	21	Fail	112

4.2 Opinion Formation

In opinion formation protocols, each agent starts with a certain *opinion* taken from a set of possible *options*, and dynamically changes it if certain conditions are met. The voter model is an elementary example of opinion formation: each agent can inspect the opinion of a random neighbour and copy it [12]. Stigmergies are not suitable in this scenario, as opinions would only propagate according to their attached timestamps. Opinion formation protocols, on the other hand, might have additional goals, such as encouraging the spread of the option initially held by a majority of agents.

What follows is a LAbS encoding of a voter model supported by the environment primitives introduced in Sect. 3. Each agent can either "talk", by writing its opinion to the environment, or listen to the opinion of another agent and copy it.

$$\textsc{Listen} \triangleq I(opinion) := E(opinion); \textsc{Listen}$$
$$\textsc{Talk} \triangleq E(opinion) := I(opinion); \textsc{Talk}$$
$$\textsc{Voter} \triangleq \textsc{Talk} \mid \textsc{Listen}$$

We could similarly model more complex protocols, such as the k-unanimity rule. In this case, an agent only changes its opinion to some option if it perceives that k other agents agree on that option [19]. We can use k environment keys to store opinions. We use a generalized choice to describe that, whenever an agent "talks", it writes its own opinion into one of the k environment keys. Guarded processes and nondeterministic choice can be combined to recreate an "if-then-else" construct.

$$unanimity \equiv \bigwedge_{i=2}^{k} I(1) = I(i)$$
$$\text{LISTEN}_k \triangleq I(1) := E(1); I(2) := E(2); \dots ; I(k) := E(k);$$
$$(unanimity \rightarrow I(opinion) := I(1)) + (\neg unanimity \rightarrow \sqrt{});$$
$$\text{LISTEN}_k$$
$$\text{TALK}_k \triangleq \sum_{i=1}^{k} E(i) := I(opinion); \text{TALK}_k$$
$$\text{VOTER}_k \triangleq \text{TALK}_k \mid \text{LISTEN}_k$$

In these examples, each agent can talk and listen to any other agent. This is not the case in most research on opinion formation, where agents can only communicate with a set of neighbours. However, we can model these scenarios by adding more environment keys and letting agents interact with different subsets of said keys.

4.3 Foraging

Foraging is a popular case study in distributed robotics, as it can model many other scenarios, such as *waste retrieval* and *search and rescue* [6]. In this scenario, a swarm of robots explores the arena with the goal of finding and collecting items. We can store these items in the environment and interact with them through the primitives introduced in Sect. 3. First, let us assume that robots perform a *random walk* to explore the arena. Like in the flocking case study, we assume the arena is a torus and that D is the set of directions a robot can take. A step in a random walk can be modeled by the following process:

$$\text{STEP} \triangleq \sum_{(i,j) \in D} I(pos) := I(pos) + (i,j)$$

Now suppose that there are m items, and that the environment key $E(i)$ stores the position of the i-th item. If the item has been collected, $E(i)$ instead contains the string *"taken"*.

Then a robot can check if it has found the i-th item, and possibly collect it, by executing the process CHECK_i:

$$\text{CHECK}_i \triangleq I(i) := E(i);$$
$$(I(pos) = I(i) \rightarrow E(i) := \text{"taken"}) + (\neg I(pos) = I(i) \rightarrow \sqrt{})$$

If we denote by $\prod_{x_i \in X} P(x)$ the parallel composition of all processes in the form $P[x_i/x]$, then the behaviour that checks for the presence of a generic item is a composition of one CHECK_i processes for each item. Thus, the foraging behaviour is just a recursive sequence of movements and checks.

$$\text{FORAGER} \triangleq \text{STEP}; \prod_{i=1}^{m} \text{CHECK}_i; \text{FORAGER}$$

This model has some limitations. Since the environmental operations can be fully interleaved, two robots would be able to reach the position of a given food item and collect it twice (by writing *"taken"* into the environment). Introducing atomic operations on the environment, such as compare-and-set, could be a way to overcome this drawback.

5   Conclusion, and Related and Future Work

We have introduced LAbS, a core language for multi-agent systems which relies on a shared data structure for all inter-component communication. This data structure is based on the concept of virtual stigmergies. Agents can only directly access their local copy of the stigmergy; however, changes are transparently propagated through the system, leading to indirect agent interaction. Rather than restricting the exchange of messages to physical neighbours, our representation comes with a flexible mechanism of communication based on components attributes, and is well suited to describe and reason about swarms of robots and other kinds of distributed systems. In the case of multi-robot systems, our language can naturally model different kinds of robots equipped with multiple sensors. We have then extended LAbS with an external environment, acting as a shared memory for components. Our design choices were driven by the analysis of different languages available in the multi-robot and multi-agent literature [9]. Finally, we have modelled with LAbS frequently used case studies to highlight the main features of the language and its expressive power.

In the near future we plan to investigate the need of additional primitives to describe more complex individual behaviour. Examples include alternative communication models between components and atomic interaction with the environment. Future research might also include the study of logical formalisms to conveniently describe key properties of LAbS systems, and the implementation of mechanized translations from LAbS to other formalisms to facilitate automated verification of such properties.

Related Work. Most works in both swarm robotics and multi-agent systems research follow a bottom-up approach, also known as behaviour-based design [6]: designers iteratively alter the behaviour of individual agents and verify if the desired properties emerge on a global level. In addition, most of the swarm robotics literature provides ad-hoc solutions to specific tasks, which can be classified in a few broad categories such as robot aggregation; flocking; object foraging; construction; and swarm deployment (e.g. for surveillance, distributed sensing, or signal relaying) [5].

Swarm-oriented languages could help research in the field by providing adequate primitives that can be combined to solve many of the tasks described above. For instance, Buzz [15] follows object-oriented principles and is based upon communication between neighbors, team management, and consensus achievement; another example is Proto/Protoswarm [3,4], a functional language where individual agents are seen as part of a virtual *spatial computer*. Higher-level formalisms can also ease the design process by expressing individual behaviour in an intuitive way while avoiding ambiguity [16]. Languages that provide a notion of an environment as part of their semantics include ISPL [13] and the PALPS process calculus [14]. Languages equipped with a formal semantics could allow for a more general and automated approach to system verification. Efforts in this direction include both formalizations of existing languages, such as a calculus based on Proto [8], as well as calculi that are given a formal specification at the design stage, such as SCEL [10].

Verification of multi-robot systems has offered general results for a simple model where robots have identical behaviour and repeatedly perform three actions: store the position of other robots in their local memory (*Look*); decide if and where it should move (*Compute*); and finally apply the decision (*Move*). Depending on the synchronicity of these steps and on the shape of the arena, possibility or impossibility results have been proved for tasks related to pattern formation [20] or consensus achievement in the presence of Byzantine robots [2]. However, the requirements on the behaviour of robots mean that these results cannot be automatically extended to heterogeneous systems.

References

1. Abd Alrahman, Y., De Nicola, R., Loreti, M.: On the power of attribute-based communication. In: Albert, E., Lanese, I. (eds.) FORTE 2016. LNCS, vol. 9688, pp. 1–18. Springer, Cham (2016). https://doi.org/10.1007/978-3-319-39570-8_1
2. Auger, C., Bouzid, Z., Courtieu, P., Tixeuil, S., Urbain, X.: Certified impossibility results for byzantine-tolerant mobile robots. In: Higashino, T., Katayama, Y., Masuzawa, T., Potop-Butucaru, M., Yamashita, M. (eds.) SSS 2013. LNCS, vol. 8255, pp. 178–190. Springer, Cham (2013). https://doi.org/10.1007/978-3-319-03089-0_13
3. Bachrach, J., Beal, J., McLurkin, J.: Composable continuous-space programs for robotic swarms. Neural Comput. Appl. **19**(6), 825–847 (2010)
4. Bachrach, J., McLurkin, J., Grue, A.: Protoswarm: a language for programming multi-robot systems using the amorphous medium abstraction. In: 7th International Joint Conference on Autonomous Agents and Multiagent Systems (AAMAS), vol. 3, pp. 1175–1178. IFAAMAS (2008)
5. Bayındır, L.: A review of swarm robotics tasks. Neurocomputing **172**(442), 292–321 (2016)
6. Brambilla, M., Ferrante, E., Birattari, M., Dorigo, M.: Swarm robotics: a review from the swarm engineering perspective. Swarm Intell. **7**(1), 1–41 (2013)
7. Clarke, E., Kroening, D., Lerda, F.: A tool for checking ANSI-C programs. In: Jensen, K., Podelski, A. (eds.) TACAS 2004. LNCS, vol. 2988, pp. 168–176. Springer, Heidelberg (2004). https://doi.org/10.1007/978-3-540-24730-2_15
8. Damiani, F., Viroli, M., Beal, J.: A type-sound calculus of computational fields. Sci. Comput. Program. **117**, 17–44 (2016)
9. De Nicola, R., Di Stefano, L., Inverso, O.: Toward formal models and languages for verifiable multi-robot systems. Front. Robot. AI **5**, 1–15 (2018). https://doi.org/10.3389/frobt.2018.00094. Article no. 94
10. De Nicola, R., et al.: The SCEL language: design, implementation, verification. In: Wirsing, M., Hölzl, M., Koch, N., Mayer, P. (eds.) Software Engineering for Collective Autonomic Systems. LNCS, vol. 8998, pp. 3–71. Springer, Cham (2015). https://doi.org/10.1007/978-3-319-16310-9_1
11. Lamport, L.: Time, clocks, and the ordering of events in a distributed system. Commun. ACM **21**(7), 558–565 (1978)
12. Liggett, T.M.: Interacting Particle Systems. CM. Springer, Heidelberg (2005). https://doi.org/10.1007/b138374

13. Lomuscio, A., Qu, H., Raimondi, F.: MCMAS: an open-source model checker for the verification of multi-agent systems. Int. J. Softw. Tools Technol. Transfer **19**(1), 9–30 (2017)
14. Philippou, A., Toro, M., Antonaki, M.: Simulation and verification in a process calculus for spatially-explicit ecological models. Sci. Ann. Comput. Sci. **23**(1), 119–167 (2013)
15. Pinciroli, C., Beltrame, G.: Buzz: an extensible programming language for heterogeneous swarm robotics. In: IEEE/RSJ International Conference on Intelligent Robots and Systems (IROS), pp. 3794–3800. IEEE (2016)
16. Pitonakova, L., Crowder, R., Bullock, S.: Behaviour-data relations modelling language for multi-robot control algorithms. In: IEEE/RSJ International Conference on Intelligent Robots and Systems (IROS), pp. 727–732. IEEE (2017)
17. Reynolds, C.W.: Flocks, herds and schools: a distributed behavioral model. In: 14th Annual Conference on Computer Graphics and Interactive Techniques (SIGGRAPH), vol. 21, pp. 25–34. ACM (1987)
18. Ricci, A., Omicini, A., Viroli, M., Gardelli, L., Oliva, E.: Cognitive stigmergy: towards a framework based on agents and artifacts. In: Weyns, D., Parunak, H.V.D., Michel, F. (eds.) E4MAS 2006. LNCS (LNAI), vol. 4389, pp. 124–140. Springer, Heidelberg (2007). https://doi.org/10.1007/978-3-540-71103-2_7
19. Scheidler, A., Brutschy, A., Ferrante, E., Dorigo, M.: The k-unanimity rule for self-organized decision-making in swarms of robots. IEEE Trans. Cybern. **46**(5), 1175–1188 (2016)
20. Suzuki, I., Yamashita, M.: Distributed anonymous mobile robots: formation of geometric patterns. SIAM J. Comput. **28**(4), 1347–1363 (1999)
21. Weyns, D., Holvoet, T.: A formal model for situated multi-agent systems. Fundamenta Informaticae **63**(2–3), 125–158 (2004)
22. Weyns, D., Schumacher, M., Ricci, A., Viroli, M., Holvoet, T.: Environments in multiagent systems. Knowl. Eng. Rev. **20**(02), 127 (2006)

Towards a Hybrid Verification Approach

Nahla Elaraby[1,2(✉)], Eva Kühn[1], Anita Messinger[1],
and Sophie Therese Radschek[1]

[1] Faculty of Informatics, TU Wien, Argentinierstr. 8, Vienna, Austria
{ne,ek,ahm,str}@complang.tuwien.ac.at
[2] Canadian International College – CIC, Cairo, Egypt
http://www.complang.tuwien.ac.at/eva

Abstract. Verification methods have limitations rooted in their methodological approach. Different methods can be more appropriate in verifying some type of properties than others. We propose a "Hybrid Verification" scheme that verifies different properties using different verification methods and supports a unified specification interface, based on a suitable coordination model. Identifying appropriate verification methods for each property to be verified is a necessary prerequisite for this approach. This work introduces a categorization of properties to be verified and a corresponding mapping to suitable verification methods in accordance with and discussing existing literature. A unified modeling methodology for various assertions based on a coordination model is presented. A generic use cases from the railway domain is used to show the applicability of the proposed Hybrid Verification scheme.

Keywords: System verification · Hybrid verification scheme
Distributed systems · Coordination

1 Introduction

Formal models incorporated in the design process lead to more robust systems. The verified models ensure the correctness of the system under design in the early design stages. A broad range of modeling and verification tools is investigated in research aiming for higher confidence in the system functionality. The verification process is mainly to explore a model investigating the correctness of functional requirements expressed as formal properties. However, there is no general solution that can be used to verify all desired properties of a model since all verification methods have limitations rooted in their methodological approach. Varying methods can be more appropriate in verifying some type of properties than others. Our thesis is that a "Hybrid Verification" approach can allow developers to get more confidence in their models through the possibility to apply different formal methods to the same model. In order to achieve a unified modeling methodology, we propose to use a unified modeling tool, in our case we use a coordination modeling tool termed the Peer Model [32,35]. The

© Springer Nature Switzerland AG 2018
M. Mazzara et al. (Eds.): STAF 2018 Workshops, LNCS 11176, pp. 367–386, 2018.
https://doi.org/10.1007/978-3-030-04771-9_27

modeling tool provides an assertion notation [37]. It serves as the interface for developers, and behind it – beyond its built-in runtime assertion mechanism – several different formal methods can be integrated.

In this work, a categorization of properties to be verified and a mapping of them to suitable verification methods is presented. While the categories and mappings are not new, as they are (implicitly) used in literature, they pose the foundation of the proposed approach and their collection and discussion is a major stepping stone towards the development of the Hybrid Verification method. The development and evaluation of the proposed Hybrid Verification idea is carried out based on examples and experiences of the authors with the railway domain[1]; however, the approach is applicable to all kinds of coordination problems, as the Peer Model is an extensible coordination model that has proved useful in different domains. The use case selected for the evaluation is a generic pattern, where messages are sent via an unreliable wireless communication link, and where this link is supervised by controller components in order to allow its integration into a safety-critical system.

All properties to be verified are modeled with the Peer Model. Based on the classification, the assertions can be verified with different formal methods and tools. So far, Event-B [1] has been integrated into the Peer Model [36]; in future work we plan to underpin the proposed Hybrid Verification approach with other formal methods, following the proposed idea.

The paper is structured as follows: Sect. 2 discusses limitations of important verification methods used in the railway domain. Section 3 presents the Hybrid Verification approach starting with a proposed classification for properties to be verified, followed by a mapping to the most appropriate verification methods for each class, and finally explaining the verification scheme. Section 4 describes a generic use case from the railway domain and uses it to define a list of relevant system properties to be verified, which are classified according to the proposed classes. Section 5 shows how the proposed approach can be integrated into the Peer Model and evaluates the feasibility of the unified modeling tool by means of the use case from Sect. 4. Section 6 summarizes the new ideas and gives an outlook to future work.

2   Related Work

Verification of railway systems is a well explored task and therefore will be used as motivation and explanation of the proposed approach. A variety of scientific work explores the specification and verification of e.g., signaling and interlocking or ERTMS/ETCS[2]. The most striking limitation of such approaches is that of the formal method and specification language used. It limits the type of system properties that can be specified and verified directly through language limitations or indirectly by infeasibility, leading to partial or multiple system models. Two of the most powerful formal methods – Model Checking and the B Method – are

---

[1] http://www.loponode.org, funded by the Austrian Federal Railways (ÖBB Infra).
[2] http://www.era.europa.eu/core-activities/ertm.

discussed by way of examples from the railway domain to show the limitations of single formal methods.

Model Checking [13] approaches are powerful, as they can be used to verify temporal logic formulas, but face the problems of indeterministic state transitions without timing information, and state explosion (even with symbolic model checking). Different approaches deal with state explosion in various ways: E.g., [26] manage the state explosion by keeping to the limited language of ladder diagrams using only boolean variables and by using slicing and SAT-Solving. In [47], the authors propose to work on a minimal model of the system. [11] note problems with larger systems and hints at trying to solve them by changing the system representation. The common weakness of these and similar strategies is that they are highly application and representation dependent, leading to abstract models of the system either in a given development or conceptualization stage. In [19], the authors even claim that general purpose model checkers (SPIN and NuSMV) cannot be used for large interlocking systems. To tackle the problem of timing information, there are combined tools such as Verus [9,10], which provides a syntax and verification kit for real-time systems.

Other approaches (e.g., using UPPAAL [30]) rely on Timed Automata instead of Finite State Machines as a representation of the system, which are also very restricted in their expressiveness and lead to large systems.

The B Method [2], a specification and verification technique for the entire development cycle, has been shown to be useful in train application development [5,8]. However, natively, the approach only supports invariant and variant proofs. Proofs of temporal logic properties or real-time property specification is not supported. The ProB model checker [38] is an attempt to provide the B Method with Model Checking, but due to the different representation of states and state space, different optimization problems arise than in classical Model Checking.

Due to these limitations, a major challenge lies in bridging the gap between complex systems and various properties to be verified and the different limited verification techniques and methods. Relevant approaches combine an appropriate modeling interface or front-end and different verification techniques.

For example [24] extends Model Checking verification through combining symbolic trajectory evaluation with either Symbolic Model Checking or SAT-based Model Checking; while [6] presents an approach for the verification of embedded software with hardware dependencies using a mixed bottom-up/top-down algorithm with optimized static parameter assignment (SPA). These algorithms and methodologies like SPA and counterexample guided simulation are used to combine simulation-based and formal verification in a new way. SPA offers a way to interact between dynamic and static verification approaches based on an automated ranking heuristics of possible function parameters according to the impact on the model size.

The hybrid verification method presented in [4] is based on numerical static analysis and verification condition generation. The method aims to preserve the proof obligations of source codes to be evident on compiled programs.

The Statemate Verification Environment (STVE) [7] is an extension to the STATEMATE industrial specification and verification tool based on state charts [23]. It allows refinement based modeling and provides code generation, simulation and formal verification using Symbolic Model Checking. E.g. [15] successfully model and verify properties of a case study proposed by the German Railway Company. State charts are widely used as a modeling language in safety related development but lack the framework of a well-defined coordination model.

[25] propose the OnTrack verification toolset to model and verify railway applications. Their approach is similar to ours in such that it provides one frontend (also with graphical representation) and multiple verification tools behind it. The toolset is enhanceable. The approach is specifically tailored to railway systems, which has the advantage that specific train and railway related problems can be explicitly modeled and verified, but the disadvantage is that it cannot be used in other domains without major adaptations. Using a coordination language that is enhanceable and not restricted one domain overcomes this disadvantage.

3   Proposed Approach

3.1   Classification of Properties to Be Verified

Properties to be verified are the essential system requirements obligatory for proper system operation. The choice of model together with verification method determines whether or not a certain property can be expressed and verified. In this paper we investigate limitations of widely used verification methods, made evident by system properties that cannot be verified with enough confidence using the method. Researches investigating verification methods are concerned with a certain set of properties that are the most critical for the application. Types of properties that are highly concerned were chosen so that the classification is aligned with literature, however it can be refined in future work. The classification is a prerequisite for our Hybrid Verification method that aims to provide researchers with suitable methods for respective property classes. We classify system properties into 5 categories: Safety, Reliability, Availability, Timing and Security. Some properties are classifiable into more than one category. Choice and fine-tuning of classification is up to the user and poses one of the inputs for future machine learning to better classify properties and recommend suitable formal methods for their verification.

Safety. Safety requirements are essential for most systems, as they define how to avoid system hazards. The work in [43] provides a specification and formal verification of safety properties in point automation for railway system. In this research safety properties are defined as a list of requirements that leads to a safe train journey. In [12] the authors formally define the safety properties as a particular variable p that is supposed to be always true for all possible scenarios. For a given combinational circuit C, a safety property p is valid, if $s(p) = 1$, for all solutions s of C. For a sequential circuit (C, D), a safety property p is valid, if for all k, for all solution paths $(s_1, \ldots, s_k)$ of (C, D), and for all $1 \leq i \leq k$, $s_i(p) = 1$. [29] considers safety properties to be those that when incorrectly specified or violated lead to considerable property damage and/or human casualties. Accordingly, in this paper we define safety properties as system requirements that are essential to prevent hazards.

Reliability. Reliability is known as a measure of the probability that a system or system components will function as intended for a specified interval under certain conditions. [39] adds the Scale domain to the Hyperball abstraction to increase the accuracy in verifying reliability properties and increase the system failure vulnerability. The challenging problem of how to ensure the high reliability of electrical devices and software that may fail randomly in The Flight Control Systems is investigated in [46]. [18] analyzes the complex properties of the Chinese high-speed rail networks. The work simulates the performance of network vulnerability when the stations fail. The survivability and rationality of three networks are compared to study the dynamic change of network vulnerability. We define reliability properties as requirements for failure vulnerability.

Availability. Availability is the probability that a system or a system component will be operational at any random time and can be measured as: Uptime/(Uptime + Downtime). The framework proposed in [17] verifies the availability of services by injecting faults into different components of Open-Stack. Beside injection service indicators such as downtime are monitored. The requirements are verified by comparing the monitored metrics against the provided service level agreement. [28] presents a prediction for the trend in radio resource availability in cognitive radio. We define the set of availability properties as those requirements measuring the time in which the system is running.

Timing. Timing information is important in many systems. Verifying timing requirements is heavily investigated in literature. In [44] a temporal logic framework is proposed for modeling and verification of timing properties. Timing properties are expressed as axioms controlling temporal variables that are either true or false over a certain time interval. [16] analyzes timing properties of real time prototypes which consist of timing constraints that must be satisfied at any given time and time-series constraints that must be satisfied over a period of time are verified through proposed scheme. MARTE (Modeling and Analysis of Real-Time and Embedded Systems) [42] is an industrial standard built to align with UML 2.0, offering a range of capabilities needed to model RT/ES including discrete/dense and chronometric/logical time. Since it deals with quantitative time information, timing mechanisms (clocks, timers) and services, it is used to describe events in time (timed events), instants and duration, timed elements, time values, observation (of time passing) and a form of timing constraints. [45] applies it to verify security and timing properties in UML Models. We define timing properties as relative and/or absolute timing constraints.

Security. Security policies including authenticity, authorization, secrecy, integrity, freshness and fair exchange [45] are enforced within a system when security must be verified. UMLsec [27] is a comprehensive profile for developing secured software applications offering recurring security requirements, such as secrecy, integrity, and authenticity as specification elements. [40] introduces a verification method of security-critical systems based on cryptographic protocols. Standard security properties such as secrecy or authenticity are investigated beside application-specific security properties to give better guarantees. We define security properties as all aspects related to the confidentiality of system data.

3.2 Mapping of Verification Methods

This section explores the strengths and limitations of verification methods and suggests which methods are suitable for a class and which are not. The mapping is done according to the definitions of property classes given in the previous section. It is not a 1:1 mapping between verification method and property classes, but is a discussion of the applicability and suitability of formal methods and concepts to the property classes identified. It is a summary of well known facts and poses a starting point for a recommendation system to support users in the choice of appropriate methods to verify certain system properties.

Model Checking (MC) tools unroll the state space of the system model to verify that none of the reachable states violates the properties. Verification using MC is simple, always terminates with a clear result of yes or no, and is widely used in both software and hardware systems, but suffers from the so-called state space explosion problem that is when the number of states is so large in a way that its creation and exploration take exponential time. MC is not suitable for verifying real time systems in general because of the state explosion problem. However MC greatly fits verification problems of safety properties. Safety properties are critical and must be verified in a clear deterministic way, accordingly MC can be well applied to safety properties as it provides a decisive way with clear termination of the problem and counterexamples.

Finite State Machines (FSM) describe purely discrete systems (i.e. systems without real time properties) that can be checked using MC. They are widely used in industrial development and most tool suites rely on them as a modeling tool, but for complex systems models tend to become large (even with modularization and edge synchronization) and there are no intrinsic mechanisms (other than edge synchronization) to describe distributed and concurrent systems. Since FSM describe purely discrete systems, they can not be used for verifying timing properties. FSM are the most suitable for security properties, as they describe discrete features of a system.

Hybrid Automata (HA) describe discrete systems in continuous environments but they are undecidable in general and models tend to become large. Verification tools based on HA are limited to (efficiently) decidable sub-sets or give only a confidence measurement for truth values, so they are the most suitable for reliability properties.

Timed Automata (TA) are a decidable sub-set of hybrid automata, providing timing information. They are restricted in their expressiveness. In some implementations, transitions are allowed, supporting stochastic models. Since TA are restricted in their expressiveness, they are not appropriate for safety properties. However they are the most suitable for timing properties class.

B Method (B) is an approach not only for verifying but also for modeling and developing a system from scratch. It is based on the formal method theorem proving and was selected in this survey as one representative of such methods that has been useful in industrial development. It is refinement based and provides a methodology and tool set for all stages of the development cycle from specification of coarse properties to an implementation level description to be translated into code. One disadvantage of B is the state-transition style system specification. While it is more concise than the definition of FSM and allows for invariant proofs instead of MC to verify safety properties, the expressiveness is the same. B is suitable for more than one class of properties. It can be used for availability properties as the requirements are automatically deduced from the model in a way that give high confidence needed to check these properties. B is also appropriate for reliability class of properties. But due to the lack of efficient real time representation it is not suitable for timing properties.

3.3   Proposed Hybrid Verification Approach

Formal verification is a part of the design process to ensure the correctness of a system in the early design stages. Correctness of a system is identified by satisfying a set of properties. Verification approaches are evaluated through the applicability to formal models and the level of confidence in verification results. We propose to use different methods to verify properties of systems. The motivation is to keep each method pure and lean and use it to verify the most suited set of properties, in contrast with other approaches based on extending or customizing a method for a certain application or domain. Excessive extension means to add features to the formal method that are driven by ad-hoc use case requirements and/or to technically integrate two conceptually different formal techniques – which would also add unnecessary complexity. We propose to support the verification methods Model Checking, Finite State Machines, Hybrid Automata, Timed Automata, and B Method (to start with) in a single tool that can match the most suitable verification method to property type. The idea is to use a powerful model as an interface for developers and to allow the generation of formal models for each method based on the system specification they provide. All classes of properties can be proved with the most appropriate method and the approach can be applied to any application domain. Further verification methods can be included without impeding the existing ones and the goal is to build on the mentioned classification and keep refining it to best provide a good verification scheme for all properties.

4 Use Case Based Analysis of Verification Requirements

In this section we describe the properties to be verified for the selected generic use case pattern, where two controllers communicate through an unreliable linking channel (cf. the "Black Channel" principle [22]). The range and diversity of the properties makes the need of our Hybrid Verification approach evident. The System (see Fig. 1) consists of Controller A, unreliable Radio Frequency based Communication Link (RFCL), and Controller B. The System is integrated into a Host A and Host B. There are many concrete use cases where this pattern occurs, e.g., in ERTMS/ECTS for the communication between on-board unit and track-side; e.g. for the communication between a train detection sensor and a level crossing (see Sect. 5.1). The System general setup can be defined as follows:

- Host A must always know the status of Host B; i.e. the actual status information of Host B must be transmitted correctly and timely to Host A.
- The system is not symmetric.
- Photo Voltaic (PV) modules are used for energy harvesting.
- The RFCL is a Wireless Sensor Network (WSN) consisting of 2 or more motes; i.e. 2 end motes and 0, 1, 2, ... forwarder motes.
- The end motes are connected with the respective controllers via cable.
- System consists of hardware and of software controlling hardware operation.

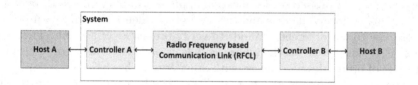

Fig. 1. System to be verified.

The use case requirements classified according to Sect. 3.1 are:

Safety Properties

1. Status messages sent via RFCL from Host B to Host A must be correct
2. If Host A does not receive a status messages from Host B at least every K_1 ms by using the RFCL, it must put Host A into a safe state. K_1 depends on the concrete use case; e.g. in the level crossing use case (see Sect. 5.1) on speed of train and distance of sensor from level crossing.
3. A failure in the transmission medium must be detected after maximum K_2 ms. K_2 depends on the concrete use case; e.g. for level crossing use case: $K_2 = 2$ IMT (Inter Message Time) + WCEDT (Worst Case Event Detection Time) ≤ 1 s.

Reliability Properties

1. Battery must support mote operation for at least K_3 days without charging
2. Condensed water must not build up inside the casing, as it may damage the hardware. Therefore, the mote casing must not be airtight.
3. High reliability of connection $\geq K_4\%$ success rate for transmission using RFCL; K_4 depends on the number of motes.
4. Allowed number of failures: less than K_5 failures per year for RFCL.

Availability Properties

1. The PV modules must be protected from mechanical damages. Resilient materials must be used resisting hailstones with a diameter of up to 15 mm.
2. The surface of the PV module must be protected against buildup of dirt and snow via suitable coatings that do not reduce transparency of the surface.
3. The PV modules must provide more power than consumed by the Printed Circuit Board (PCB) for its regular operation in order to enable charging of the battery.
4. The solar cells have to be oriented in a way that provides extended periods of direct sunlight. Multiple solar cells in several directions, which cover at least 180°, shall be used.
5. The tilt angle of the PV modules shall be adapted to the altitude of the sun, around 60°.
6. Motes must support harsh weather conditions (low/high temperatures, snow/ rain/hail etc.).
7. Hardware (incl. all components) must support temperature range from -40 up to $+85\,^\circ$C.
8. Hardware must survive at least for 5 years.
9. Motes must be able to power themselves for any relevant location.
10. Due to possibly curved tracks, a rather wide angle for the antennas beam is envisaged, i.e. about 45° to the left and right of the main direction.
11. The casing design must consider the radio characteristics of the motes.
12. Continuous transmission of data from Controller B to Controller A.

Timing Properties

1. Receive messages from the sensor (= Controller B) every 500 ms.
2. Messages are forwarded from mote to the next through every K_6 ms.
3. Message is sent 2 times on 2 different channels (frequencies) to avoid losing messages.
4. Status messages are sent from Controller B to the Controller A every K_7 ms.
5. The clocks of the single motes must not drift more than K_6 ms, i.e. a synchronization to compensate for drifting clocks is needed.

Security Properties

1. Received message at Host A must be from Host B.
2. Fake messages must be recognized and ignored.
3. Messages cannot be read and decoded by external observers of the system.

The kind of property that can be proved within a system model strongly depends on the choice of modeling perspective and tool.

5 Integration and Evaluation

In this section, the proposed Hybrid Verification approach is evaluated by integrating it into a concrete modeling tool, and by applying it to a concrete use case. The Peer Model has been chosen for the integration because it is a coordination model that has been applied already to several use cases. Appendix A contains an explanation of the Peer Model concepts and terminology used to understand the use case. Its focus is to simplify the development of complex distributed systems and to improve the reusability by abstracting the coordination parts in form of patterns [32,35]. The reason for the choice of a coordination model is that the coordination problem is a complex one that exhibits all/most of the analyzed classes of properties. Also the Hybrid Verification approach needs a unified powerful notation that can map different methods and express assertions in the same notation so that users do not need to go through different formal notations. The Peer Model was developed by our group and provides a language for the specification of assertions. It is capable of representing diverse properties of systems, allows for a user defined line of separation between application and coordination logic. So far, the Event-B method has been integrated with the Peer Model [36]. In this case, the properties of the Peer Model in general are provided as an abstract model and the concrete model is generated as a refinement from the meta model of the system specification, leaving only the proof obligations of use case specific properties to be tackled at runtime. This way Peer Model based models can be verified with the Event-B tools. A similar approach will be pursued for other formal methods relying on the respective offered mechanisms.

5.1 Evaluation by Means of the Level Crossing Use Case

We investigate the feasibility of using the Peer Model as a facade for the Hybrid Verification approach by means of the level crossing use case (see Fig. 2). We define concrete values for the K_i-parameters in the generic pattern, and select software properties to be verified from Sect. 4. The Proof-of-Concept foresees to present a formal model by means of the Peer Model and to specify the properties as assertions. Figure 4 shows the time-triggered communication protocol of the RFCL; in the example four motes (M_1, ..., M_4) are used. M_1 is the end mote that is connected to Controller A (which is integrated into Host A) via RS232, M_4 is the end mote that is connected to Controller B (which is integrated into Host B) via RS232, and M_2 and M_3 are forwarder motes. We use 8 time slots. RX stands for receiving and TX for sending. The time-triggered wiring mechanism of the Peer Model is used to specify the RFCL. It includes also a piggy-backed clock synchronization protocol.

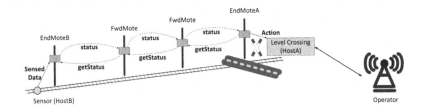

Fig. 2. Concrete use case: Level Crossing (LC).

The Model: The most relevant part of the model in graphical Peer Model notation can be found in Appendix B. All motes, the operator and both controllers are modeled as peers. The up-stream messages are represented by entries of type "getStatus", and the down-stream messages by entries of type "status". The latter have the following property fields: "txT" (time when the entry was sent), "rxT" (time when the entry was received). Controller A regularly sends getStatus via M_1 to M_4 (up-stream), sets a local watchdog and waits for a status message to be received from Controller B (down-stream) within the required 960 ms. If the status message says train is coming, it closes the LC. If it does not receive a valid status message within this time period, it sends a failure entry to the Operator, and enters a fail safe state by closing and shutting down the LC. Controller B signs all messages it sends with its private key. More precisely, it sets a property termed "sig" in the status entry it sends back as response to a getStatus message, where sig is the signature of the `fid` (flow identifier, a system-defined property [32] used to correlated messages) of getStatus. Within a TX slot, a mote sends each message on 2 different radio channels to other motes. It reports in entries of type "sentDown" resp. "sentUp" on which channel a message was sent. The end mote at site A keeps a local "report" entry counting the ok and not ok message rounds.

In order to be able to check a property, a respective entry (with needed properties) must be modeled and written to a container in the model, because the entries in containers reflect the entire system state, to which assertions refer.

Properties. The following list summarizes software related properties to be verified (cf. Sect. 4) and gives concrete values for all parameters. Host A is a Level Crossing System (LC), Host B is a Train Detection Sensor.

SAF-1: Status messages received by Controller A must be correct.

SAF-2: If Contr. A receives no status message for 960 ms, shut down Host A.

REL-1: 99% success rate for RFCL transmission.

REL-2: Less than 2 RFCL failures per year.

AVA-1: Continuous transmission of sensor data to Controller A.

TIM-1: ControllerA must receive status message every 960 ms.

TIM-2: Mote to mote latency ≤100 ms.

TIM-3: Redundancy through sending on 2 different channels (within one slot).

TIM-4: Clock drift between motes must be ≤10 ms.

SEC-1: Status message received by Controller A must be from Controller B.

SEC-2: Fake status messages must be recognized and ignored.

Assertions. All selected assertions could be represented by the Peer Model assertion language. Their informal description is:

SAF-1 is modeled by SEC-1.

SAF-2 specifies that if there is at least one peer of type ControllerA, in which HIC a sendStatus entry can be found, but for which no response (i.e. status entry) was received after max. 960 ms, then in the PIC of the Operator peer there must exist at least one failure entry.

REL-1 specifies that for all peers of type EndMoteA there must be a report entry indicating that the success rate of the RFCL is at least 99%.

REL-2 specifies that for all peers of type ControllerA it must hold that the Operator peer at most 2 entries of type failure must exist, and which are not older than 1 year, and which are from the same Controller A. Note that failure entries are never cleared, so the PIC can be used instead of the HIC.

AVA-2 specifies that for all peers of type ControllerA within 960 ms eventually at least one status message is received in its PIC.

TIM-1 specifies that for all peers of type ControllerA it must hold that if a getStatus entry existed, then within max. 960 ms there must be a status entry (response to getStatus) be received in its PIC.

TIM-2a–d specify for the different mote types (FwdMote, EndMoteA, End-MoteB) that time drift of status/getStatus messages is less than 100 ms.

TIM-3a specifies that for all peers of type EndMoteA, if they have sent a message down (reflected by sentDown entry), then after max. 60 ms there must be yet another sentDown entry which has another channel set.

TIM-3b1–2 specify the same for the forwarder motes (in both directions).

SEC-1 specifies for all ControllerA peers, if a status entry is in the PIC then its "sig" is a valid signature of Controller B. I.e. if decoded with the public key of site B, the result is the original flow id (fid) of the status entry.

SEC-2 is subsumed by SEC-1.

The formal representation of the assertions is:

SAF-1:	(* see SEC-1 *)
SAF-2:	[≥1] ⟨ControllerA⟩ {{HIC{getStatus} AND (NOT PIC$^{[0;960]}$ {status})}} → ⟨Operator⟩ PIC {{failure[≥1]}}
REL-1:	[ALL] ⟨EndMoteA⟩ {PIC {report [[nok/(ok+nok) ≤ 0,01]]}}
REL-2:	[ALL] $CA IN ⟨ControllerA⟩ → [ALL] ⟨Operator⟩ {PIC {failure[0;2] [[t≥(time()−1y)]] AND lc == $CA}}
AVA-1:	[ALL] ⟨ControllerA⟩ {PIC$^{[0;960]}$ {status[≥1]}}
TIM-1:	[ALL] ⟨ControllerA⟩ {HIC {getStatus} → PIC$^{[0;960]}$ {status}}
TIM-2a:	[ALL] ⟨FwdMote⟩ {PIC {getStatus} <$txT=txT, $rxT=rxT> → [[($txT + 100) > $rxT]]}
TIM-2b:	[ALL] ⟨FwdMote⟩ {PIC {status} <$txT=txT, $rxT=rxT> → [[($txT + 100) > $rxT]]}
TIM-2c:	[ALL] ⟨EndMoteA⟩ {PIC {status} <$txT=txT, $rxT=rxT> → [[($txT + 100) > $rxT]]}
TIM-2d:	[ALL] ⟨EndMoteB⟩ {PIC {getStatus} <$txT=txT, $rxT=rxT> → [[($txT + 100) > $rxT]]}
TIM-3a:	[ALL] ⟨EndMoteA⟩ {PIC {sentDown <$chan = chan>} → PIC$^{[0;60]}$ {sentDown [[chan ≠ $chan]]}}
TIM-3b1:	[ALL] ⟨FwdMote⟩ {PIC {sentDown <$chan = chan>} → PIC$^{[0;60]}$ {sentDown [[chan ≠ $chan]]}}
TIM-3b2:	[ALL] ⟨FwdMote⟩ {PIC {sentUp <$chan = chan>} → PIC$^{[0;60]}$ {sentUp [[chan ≠ $chan]]}}
SEC-1:	[ALL] ⟨ControllerA⟩ {PIC {status} → [[fid == decode(sig, $PUBKEY_B)]]}
SEC-2:	(* see SEC-1 *)

The assertions can be verified by means of the built-in runtime assertions mechanism (except of those using the future container). Beyond that, depending on their category (Safety, Reliability, Availability, Timing or Security) and according to the proposed Hybrid Verification approach, they can be verified by all formal methods integrated into the Peer Model.

6 Conclusion and Future Work

There is no "silver bullet" that can be used to verify all desired properties of a system. Our thesis is that a Hybrid Verification approach can allow users to get more confidence in their models through application of different formal methods. In addition, we have presented a systematic classification of properties to be verified which is the prerequisite for selecting suitable formal methods for a given set of properties to be verified. In order to achieve an integrated modeling methodology, we propose to use a unified modeling tool, in our case a coordination modeling tool termed the Peer Model, as the front end for developers. This modeling tool provides an assertion notation. Behind this usable interface for developers, a built-in runtime assertion mechanism and several different formal methods can be used. The evaluation was carried out as a proof-of-concept with a railway use case. All properties of all categories were modeled with the Peer Model, showing that it can successfully be used as user interface.

The next steps of our future work comprise: Based on the classification, the assertions shall be verified with respective formal methods tools. We plan to underpin the proposed Hybrid Verification approach with many other suited formal methods beyond Event-B by means of automatic translations from existing Peer Model specifications. A recommendation system shall be implemented based on the mapping of properties to formal methods and tools. Application of the Hybrid Verification approach to other (coordination) modeling languages and tools will also be investigated.

Appendix A: Peer Model/Graphical Notation in a Nutshell

The following is a brief overview – assembled from [31, 33, 37] – of the features of the Peer Model needed for the use case presented in this paper. The Peer Model is a coordination model that relies on known foundations like shared tuple spaces [20, 21, 34], Actor Model [3], and Petri Nets [41]. It separates coordination logic from business logic and is intended to model reusable coordination solutions. A peer relates to an actor in the Actor Model [3]. It is an autonomous worker with a name; it receives entries (representing messages, events etc.) in an incoming mailbox termed "peer input container" (PIC). Optionally it also possesses a "peer output container" (POC). A container is a tuple space that stores entries that are written, read, or taken (i.e., read and removed) in local transactions. Entries are the units of information passed between peers. An entry has system- and application-defined properties. The coordination behavior of a peer is explicitly modeled with wirings, which have some similarity with Petri Net transitions [41]. A wiring has guards that retrieve entries from containers, and actions that write entries to containers or send them to other peers. In addition, a wiring may call a service which encapsulates application logic. All wirings run concurrently. The arrival of entries in containers triggers the execution of wirings.

Property $prop = (label, val)$. $label$ is a name, and val denotes a value. The property is named after its label.

Entry $e = \mathbb{E}prop$. $\mathbb{E}prop$ is a set of properties $\{prop_1, prop_2, \ldots, prop_n\}$.

Container $c = (cid, \mathbb{E}, \mathbb{C}oord, \mathbb{C}prop)$. A container stores entries. cid is a unique name, $\mathbb{E}$ a set of entries, $\mathbb{C}oord$ a set of coordinators (see Query below), and $\mathbb{C}prop$ a set of system properties. A container relates to an XVSM container [34]. We differentiate between space containers and internal containers. The former ones support transactions and blocking behavior. Entries are retrieved by a query that necessarily requires the coordination type of the entry.

Query $q = (type, cnt, \mathbb{S}el)$. $type$ is an entry coordination type. cnt is a number, a range, or the keyword ALL or NONE, determining the amount of entries to be selected; default is 1. $\mathbb{S}el$ is a sequence of AND/OR connected selectors. A selector is lent from the XVSM query mechanism [14]. It refers to a container coordinator (e.g. `fifo`, `key`, `label`, `any`) or is a selection expression involving entry properties, variables and system functions.

Link $l = (c_1, c_2, op, q, \mathbb{E}xpr, \mathbb{L}prop)$. c_1 refers to a source and c_2 to a target container. op possibilities are[3]: `create` (creates new entries and writes them to c_2), `read` (reads entries from c_1 and writes them to c_2), `take` (reads and deletes entries from c_1 and writes them to c_2), `delete` (reads and deletes entries from c_1), and `test` (checks entries in c_1). All operations must fulfill the query q, if it is not empty, on c_1. $\mathbb{E}xpr$ is a sequence of expressions that set or get properties of selected entries and/or of variables. $\mathbb{L}prop$ is a set of system properties, like e.g. using flow correlation.

Wiring $w = (wid, \mathbb{G}, \mathbb{S}, \mathbb{A}, wic, \mathbb{W}prop)$. wid is a unique name, $\mathbb{G}$ is a sequence of guard links, $\mathbb{S}$ is a sequence of service links to external services, $\mathbb{A}$ is a sequence of action links, wic is the id of an internal container, and $\mathbb{W}prop$ is a set of system properties. All links are numbered, specifying an execution order which has impact on concurrency and performance. Entries selected by guards are written into wic. Then w calls the services in the specified sequence. Finally, the wiring executes the action links. c_2 of a guard and c_1 of an action link is wic. There is one dedicated wiring in a peer termed init wiring with its first guard having the identifier "*"; it is fulfilled exactly once, namely when the peer is activated.

Service $s = (sid, app)$. sid is the name of the service and app a reference to the implementation of its application logic (method). A service gets entries from its wiring's wic as input and emits result entries there (via service links).

Peer $p = (pid, pic, poc, \mathbb{W}id, \mathbb{S}pid, \mathbb{P}prop)$. pid is a unique name, pic and poc are the ids of incoming and outgoing space containers where p receives and delivers entries, $\mathbb{W}id$ is a set of wiring ids, $\mathbb{S}pid$ is a set of ids of sub-peers, and $\mathbb{P}prop$ is a set of system properties.

Peer Model $PM = (\mathbb{P}, \mathbb{W}, \mathbb{C})$. $\mathbb{P}$ is the set of all peers including sub-peers, $\mathbb{W}$ is the set of all wirings, and $\mathbb{C}$ is the set of all containers in the system.

Runtime Assertion Mechanism: In [37], invariant assertions for the Peer Model have been introduced. They are statements about container states. They consist of *intra-peer assertions* connected to a logic formula by NOT, AND, OR and →. Intra-peer assertions contain a *context* and a *statement* part. The context defines number, type and properties of peers for which the statement must be fulfilled. The statement is a logic formula of *container assertions* connected by NOT, AND, OR and →. Container assertions refer to a *container* where they must hold and a *container statement*. The container can be the PIC or the POC. The container statement basically is a query on the respective container which may involve local variables (written with a starting $ character). Clearly, due to the nature of runtime assertions, it cannot be guaranteed that all failures are detected. If a strict verification is need, a so-called "history container" HIC can be involved which remembers all events. The mechanism allows for asynchronous distributed runtime reasoning about distributed states with small messaging

---

[3] `read` is also denoted as `copy`, and `take` as `move`.

overhead. The Peer Model supports also the specification of timing properties, but the assertions as presented in [37] cannot yet define constraints on them.

The here proposed Hybrid Verification approach relies on this assertion language to formulate properties and to verify them with respective integrated verification methods. For this, we extend the assertion language by a "future container", which is a similar concept like the history container. The difference is that assertions using the future container refer to future system states. It is denoted by $PIC^{[t1;t2]}$. This way assertions can refer to entries in the PIC between current time plus t1 and current time plus t2. The implementation of future runtime assertion checking for assertions is part of our future work.

Real-Time Wirings: The Peer Model supports the combination of event- and time-triggered coordination. For the latter, time-triggered wirings and real-time exceptions are defined (see [31] for more details). Time triggered wirings are activated at a specified absolute time (`tt.start`), and have a defined period (`tt.period`) and duration(`tt.duration`).

Graphical Notation: The graphical representation of the Peer Model is shown in Fig. 3, outlining one peer with one wiring that has two links and calls one service (the depiction of service links is skipped in Fig. 3). The guard link connects the peer's *pic* with the wirings's *wic*, and the action link connects the wiring's *wic* with the peer's *poc*. Note that the source space container of a guard can also be the peer's *poc* or the *poc* of a sub-peer. Analogously the target space container of an action link can also be the peer's *pic* or the *pic* of a sub-peer. A wiring can have many links that are numbered with $G_1, ..., G_k, S_1, ..., S_m, A_1, ..., A_n$ (the link ids are not depicted in Fig. 3). A peer can have many wirings.

Sub-wirings that are called as synchronous sub-transactions [33] are denoted with dashed lines.

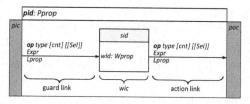

Fig. 3. Example peer [33].

	slot₁	slot₂	slot₃	slot₄	slot₅	slot₆	slot₇	slot₈
M₁ (EndMoteA)	RX	TX					RX	TX
M₂ (FwdMote)		RX	TX			RX	TX	
M₃ (FwdMote)			RX	TX	RX	TX		
M₄ (EndMoteB)				RX	TX			

msg direction = down   msg direction = up

Fig. 4. Time triggered protocol in general.

Appendix B: Excerpt from Railway Use Case Model

(See Fig. 5).

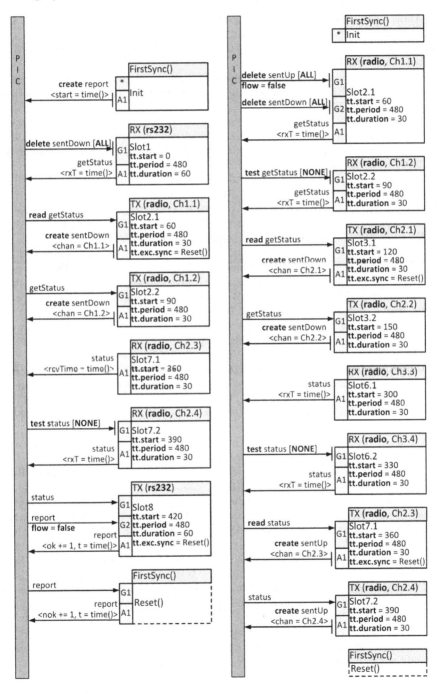

Fig. 5. EndMoteA M_1 (left) and FwdMote M_2 (right) models (see Fig. 4).

References

1. Abrial, J.R.: Modeling in Event-B: System and Software Engineering. Cambridge University Press, Cambridge (2010)
2. Abrial, J.R., Abrial, J.R.: The B-Book: Assigning Programs to Meanings. Cambridge University Press, Cambridge (2005)
3. Agha, G.A.: ACTORS: A Model of Concurrent Computation in Distributed Systems. MIT Press, Cambridge (1990)
4. Barthe, G., et al.: Preservation of proof obligations for hybrid verification methods. In: 6th IEEE International Conference on Software Engineering and Formal Methods, pp. 127–136 (2008)
5. Behm, P., Benoit, P., Faivre, A., Meynadier, J.-M.: Météor: a successful application of B in a large project. In: Wing, J.M., Woodcock, J., Davies, J. (eds.) FM 1999. LNCS, vol. 1708, pp. 369–387. Springer, Heidelberg (1999). https://doi.org/10.1007/3-540-48119-2_22
6. Behrend, J., et al.: Optimized hybrid verification of embedded software. In: 15th Latin American Test Workshop (LATW), pp. 1–6 (2014)
7. Bienmüller, T., Damm, W., Wittke, H.: The STATEMATE verification environment. In: Emerson, E.A., Sistla, A.P. (eds.) CAV 2000. LNCS, vol. 1855, pp. 561–567. Springer, Heidelberg (2000). https://doi.org/10.1007/10722167_45
8. Butler, M.: A system-based approach to the formal development of embedded controllers for a railway. Des. Autom. Embed. Syst. **6**(4), 355–366 (2002)
9. Campos, S., et al.: Verus: a tool for quantitative analysis of finite-state real-time systems. In: ACM SIGPLAN 1995 Workshop on Languages, Compilers and Tools for Real-time Systems. LCTES, pp. 70–78 (1995)
10. Campos, S., Clarke, E.: The verus language: representing time efficiently with BDDs. In: Bertran, M., Rus, T. (eds.) ARTS 1997. LNCS, vol. 1231, pp. 64–78. Springer, Heidelberg (1997). https://doi.org/10.1007/3-540-63010-4_5
11. Cimatti, A., Giunchiglia, F., Mongardi, G., Romano, D., Torielli, F., Traverso, P.: Model checking safety critical software with SPIN: an application to a railway interlocking system. In: Ehrenberger, W. (ed.) SAFECOMP 1998. LNCS, vol. 1516, pp. 284–293. Springer, Heidelberg (1998). https://doi.org/10.1007/3-540-49646-7_22
12. Claessen, K.: Safety property verification of cyclic synchronous circuits. Electron. Notes Theor. Comput. Sci. **88**, 55–69 (2004)
13. Clarke, E.M., Schlingloff, B.H.: Model checking. In: Handbook of Automated Reasoning, pp. 1635–1790. Elsevier (2001)
14. Craß, S., Kühn, E., Salzer, G.: Algebraic foundation of a data model for an extensible space-based collaboration protocol. In: International Database Engineering and Applications Symposium (IDEAS), pp. 301–306. ACM (2009)
15. Damm, W., Klose, J.: Verification of a radio-based signaling system using the STATEMATE verification environment. Formal Methods Syst. Des. **19**(2), 121–141 (2001)
16. Drusinky, D., Shing, M.T.: Verification of timing properties in rapid system prototyping. In: 14th IEEE International Workshop on Rapid System Prototyping, pp. 47–53 (2003)
17. Du, Q., et al.: High availability verification framework for OpenStack based on fault injection. In: 11th International Conference on Reliability, Maintainability and Safety (ICRMS), pp. 1–7 (2016)

18. Feng, C., et al.: Complexity and vulnerability of high-speed rail network in China. In: 236th Chinese Control Conference (CCC), pp. 10034–10039 (2017)
19. Ferrari, A., Magnani, G., Grasso, D., Fantechi, A.: Model checking interlocking control tables. In: Schnieder, E., Tarnai, G. (eds.) FORMS/FORMAT 2010, pp. 107–115. Springer, Heidelberg (2011). https://doi.org/10.1007/978-3-642-14261-1_11
20. Gelernter, D.: Generative communication in linda. ACM Trans. Program. Lang. Syst. (TOPLAS) **7**(1), 80–112 (1985)
21. Gelernter, D., Carriero, N.: Coordination languages and their significance. Commun. ACM (CACM) **35**(2), 96–107 (1992)
22. Glosser, R.J., et al.: Black channel communications apparatus and method, US Patent, WO2016039737, GE Intelligent Platorms Inc. (2016)
23. Harel, D., Politi, M.: Modeling Reactive Systems with Statecharts: The STATE-MATE Approach. McGraw-Hill, New York City (1998)
24. Hazelhurst, S., et al.: A hybrid verification approach: getting deep into the design. In: Design Automation Conference (IEEE Cat. No. 02CH37324), pp. 111–116 (2002)
25. James, P., Moller, F., Nguyen, H.N., Roggenbach, M., Treharne, H., Wang, X.: OnTrack: the railway verification toolset. In: Margaria, T., Steffen, B. (eds.) ISoLA 2016. LNCS, vol. 9953, pp. 294–296. Springer, Cham (2016). https://doi.org/10.1007/978-3-319-47169-3_21
26. James, P., Roggenbach, M.: Automatically verifying railway interlockings using SAT-based model checking. ECEASST **35** (2010)
27. Jrjens, J.: Secure Systems Development with UML. Springer, Heidelberg (2005). https://doi.org/10.1007/b137706
28. Kaneko, S., et al.: Experimental verification on the prediction of the trend in radio resource availability in cognitive radio. In: IEEE 66th Vehicular Technology Conference, pp. 1568–1572 (2007)
29. Kang, K.C., Ko, K.I.: Formalization and verification of safety properties of statechart specifications. In: Asia-Pacific Software Engineering Conference, pp. 16–27 (1996)
30. Khan, U., et al.: Real time modeling of interlocking control system of Rawalpindi Cantt train yard. In: 13th International Conference on Frontiers of Information Technology (FIT), pp. 347–352. IEEE (2015)
31. Kühn, E.: Peer Model White Paper. Technical report, TU Wien (2012–2018)
32. Kühn, E.: Reusable coordination components: reliable development of cooperative information systems. Int. J. Coop. Inf. Syst. (IJCIS) **25**(4) (2016)
33. Kühn, E.: Flexible transactional coordination in the peer model. In: Dastani, M., Sirjani, M. (eds.) FSEN 2017. LNCS, vol. 10522, pp. 116–131. Springer, Cham (2017). https://doi.org/10.1007/978-3-319-68972-2_8
34. Kühn, E., et al.: Introducing the concept of customizable structured spaces for agent coordination in the production automation domain. In: 8th International Conference on Autonomous Agents and Multiagent System (AAMAS), IFAAMAS, pp. 625–632 (2009)
35. Kühn, E., Craß, S., Joskowicz, G., Marek, A., Scheller, T.: Peer-based programming model for coordination patterns. In: De Nicola, R., Julien, C. (eds.) COORDINA-TION 2013. LNCS, vol. 7890, pp. 121–135. Springer, Heidelberg (2013). https://doi.org/10.1007/978-3-642-38493-6_9
36. Kühn, E., Radschek, S.T.: An initial user study comparing the readability of a graphical coordination model with Event-B notation. In: Cerone, A., Roveri, M.

(eds.) SEFM 2017. LNCS, vol. 10729, pp. 574–590. Springer, Cham (2018). https://doi.org/10.1007/978-3-319-74781-1_38

37. Kühn, E., Radschek, S.T., Elaraby, N.: Distributed coordination runtime assertions for the peer model. In: Di Marzo Serugendo, G., Loreti, M. (eds.) COORDINATION 2018. LNCS, vol. 10852, pp. 200–219. Springer, Cham (2018). https://doi.org/10.1007/978-3-319-92408-3_9

38. Leuschel, M., Butler, M.: ProB: a model checker for B. In: Araki, K., Gnesi, S., Mandrioli, D. (eds.) FME 2003. LNCS, vol. 2805, pp. 855–874. Springer, Heidelberg (2003). https://doi.org/10.1007/978-3-540-45236-2_46

39. Lidman, J., Mckee, S.A.: Verifying reliability properties using the hyperball abstract domain. ACM Trans. Program. Lang. Syst. **40**(1), 3:1–3:29 (2017)

40. Moebius, N., Stenzel, K., Reif, W.: Formal verification of application-specific security properties in a model-driven approach. In: Massacci, F., Wallach, D., Zannone, N. (eds.) ESSoS 2010. LNCS, vol. 5965, pp. 166–181. Springer, Heidelberg (2010). https://doi.org/10.1007/978-3-642-11747-3_13

41. Petri, C.A.: Kommunikation mit Automaten. Ph.D. thesis, Technische Hochschule Darmstadt (1962)

42. Ribeiro, F.G.C., et al.: Guidelines for using MARTE profile packages considering concerns of real-time embedded systems. In: 15th International Conference on Industrial Informatics (INDIN), pp. 917–922 (2017)

43. Sener, I., et al.: Specification and formal verification of safety properties in point automation system by using timed-arc Petri nets. In: 19th IFAC World Congress. IFAC Proceedings Volumes, vol. 47, no. 3, pp. 12140–12145 (2014)

44. Stothert, A., MacLeod, I.: Modelling and verifying timing properties in distributed computer control systems. In: 13th IFAC Workshop on Distributed Computer Control Systems (DCCS). IFAC Proceedings Volumes, vol. 28, no. 22, pp. 25–30 (1995)

45. Thapa, V., Song, E., Kim, H.: An approach to verifying security and timing properties in UML models. In: 15th IEEE International Conference on Engineering of Complex Computer Systems, pp. 193–202 (2010)

46. Wang, L., Cai, F.: Reliability analysis for flight control systems using probabilistic model checking. In: 8th IEEE International Conference on Software Engineering and Service Science (ICSESS), pp. 161–164 (2017)

47. Winter, K., et al.: Tool support for checking railway interlocking designs. In: Tenth Australian Workshop on Safety-Related Programmable Systems (SCS). CRPIT, ACS, vol. 55, pp. 101–107 (2005)

Using Reinforcement Learning to Handle the Runtime Uncertainties in Self-adaptive Software

Tong Wu, Qingshan Li$^{(\boxtimes)}$, Lu Wang, Liu He, and Yujie Li

Software Engineering Institute, Xidian University, Xi'an 710071, China
qshli@mail.xidian.edu.cn

Abstract. The growth of scale and complexity of software as well as the complex environment with high dynamic lead to the uncertainties in self-adaptive software's decision making at run time. Self-adaptive software needs the ability to avoid negative effects of uncertainties to the quality attributes of the software. However, existing planning methods cannot handle the two types of runtime uncertainties caused by complexity of system and running environment. This paper proposes a planning method to handle these two types of runtime uncertainties based on reinforcement learning. To handle the uncertainty from the system, the proposed method can exchange ineffective self-adaptive strategies to effective ones according to the iterations of execution effects at run time. It can plan dynamically to handle uncertainty from environment by learning knowledge of relationship between system states and actions. This method can also generate new strategies to deal with unknown situations. Finally, we use a complex distributed e-commerce system, Bookstore, to validate the ability of proposed method.

Keywords: Self-adaptive software · Runtime uncertainty
Reinforcement learning · Self-adaptive planning method

1 Introduction

The growth of software scale increases the costs of the operation and maintenance for software. This has driven the development of self-adaptive software (SAS). SAS can automatically adjust its attributes or artifacts by self-adaptive (SA) strategies in order to adapt to changes and improve the quality attributes (QAs) of software [1]. The process that selects suitable strategies called self-adaptive planning. However, the increase of software complexities brings challenges to the SA planning, which is mainly reflected in the following two aspects: First, the complex internal structure and components relationship of software make it difficult to know the execution effects of the strategies. Second, the running environment of software gradually tends to open, dynamic and complex such as Internet environment. Software changes occur frequently so that it is difficult to define SA strategies for each change. These uncontrollable and unpredictable factors may cause the result that SAS fail to adapt to software changes at run time. Therefore, SAS needs to handle the runtime uncertainties in the planning process to better ensure the QAs of the software.

© Springer Nature Switzerland AG 2018
M. Mazzara et al. (Eds.): STAF 2018 Workshops, LNCS 11176, pp. 387–393, 2018.
https://doi.org/10.1007/978-3-030-04771-9_28

We discuss the uncertainties caused by two aspects mentioned above. On one hand, the uncertainty caused by the complexity of the system leads to the difference of the actual execution effects and expected effects of the strategies. For example, developers define a strategy to improve the response time of a web page in the system, but it does not achieve desired effect. The planning method needs to adjust decision making at run time to handle this situation. On the other hand, open, dynamic and complex running environments also make it difficult for developers to consider all possible changes. This will cause the result that system can only deal with the predefined changes. The system does not have the ability to handle unknown situations.

Scholars have tried many methods to handle runtime uncertainties in SAS, including modeling uncertainties and machine learning, etc. However, most methods cannot solve the uncertainties from both two aspects. Rainbow framework [2] calculates the average of observations to simply deal with the uncertainty from environment. POISED [3] models uncertainties and adjust by refactoring components. However, it can only deal with the defined uncertain situations. FUSION [4] and Mao's team [5] handle uncertainties through machine learning. FUSION adjusts strategies online through a learning loop with a learning model. So it need to train the model before system runs and cannot deal with the unknowns. Mao's team use reinforcement learning (RL) to plan dynamically. This method can solve a part of unknowns through existing strategies. But it ignored that existing strategies cannot solve all the unknown situations.

This paper proposes a planning method to handle runtime uncertainties from two aspects in SAS, using RL. RL [6] will learn the relationship between system states and actions. It will give the feedback on the execution effects of SA strategies and adjust decision making through the feedback when strategies are ineffective. So it can plan at run time and work in changeable environment. This can handle the uncertainty caused by complex internal structure and component relationship. And the proposed method can select strategies for unknown situations through learning knowledge. Meanwhile, it can also generate strategies to solve unknowns that existing strategies can't solve. In addition, in order to improve the efficiency of the algorithm, this paper adds heuristic information into feedback.

2 Proposed Method

We use an agent to implement a learning unit. It can interact with the environment to get system states and plan according to the current state. The proposed method records the feedback on execution effects of strategies as rewards and add heuristic information into it. This method selects suitable strategies by learning knowledge and generates new strategies by strategy combinations for unknowns.

2.1 Learning Unit

We use Event-Condition-Action rules to model SA strategies. Events represent software changes. Condition is a part of the system state that strategies need to meet when executing. Action is one or a set of adjustments on system defined as follows.

$$Action = \{Aid,\ AName,\ AObject,\ AOperation\} \tag{1}$$

Aid and AName is denote the identification and the name of this action. AObject denotes the specific object of adjustment in this action. AOperation is the specific opration of adjustment. A strategy is the dynamic mapping among them.

We implement a learner with an agent including a sensor, a planning maker and an executor (see Fig. 1).

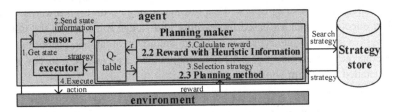

Fig. 1. The structure of a learner realized by an agent.

The sensor interacts with the environment to get system states and tells if system needs SA adjustments. Then the planning maker selects strategies according to the planning method and sends it to the executor. After this strategy was executed, the state changes. Next, the agent gets the feedback of strategies by the change of states. This can help SAS to handle the uncertainty from the complex system. We use a value called reward to express the feedback of strategies and define a function to calculate it. Planning method will put rewards into Q-table as the basis of planning. It can also generate new strategies to handle unknowns through these learning knowledge.

2.2 Reward with Heuristic Information

We calculate rewards to evaluate effects of strategies. It will be positive if the system state becomes better after a strategy was executed. Compared to common reward definition in RL, we add heuristic information into it. The heuristic information can add prior knowledge in planning. We use the change of QAs to express effects of strategies. Besides, we consider the overhead of them. Therefore, we consider above two as heuristic information. And we defined a function as follows to calculate its values.

$$H_t = \sum_{i=0}^{n} (Q_i(S_{t+1}) - Q_i(S_t)) + \rho \tag{2}$$

$Q_i(S_t)$ is the value of the ith QA in current system state S_t; S_{t+1} is the next state after the strategies are executed. ρ represents the inverse of the overhead.

2.3 Detailed Planning Method

RL records the feedback of effects of SA strategies in Q-table. This method plans according to actual effects of strategies. RL has the ability to plan at run time, it can make decisions while learn. So it can adjust decision making to handle uncertain execution effects from the complex system in changeable environment. To handle uncertainty from complex environment, the proposed method learns the relationship between system states and actions. Proposed method make decisions depend on a semi-random algorithm. When agents do not have enough learning experience, it will try some new strategies. Otherwise, it will exploit the strategy with high rewards. Agents will select effective strategies based on learning knowledge to deal with the unknown situations. If existing strategies cannot solve the unknown situations, proposed method will generate new strategies by strategy combinations and add it into SA strategy library. Detailed algorithm shows as follows:

Algorithm 1 Runtime uncertainties handling method based on reinforcement learning

For each item in Q-table, initialize $Q(s, a) \leftarrow 0$

Repeat

    If current state S_t is a new state

        Get executable actions of S_t and initialize Q-value

    End If

    Repeat

        Take action a_t with strategy selection method

        Execute action a_t and add action at into action sequence a

        Get next state S_{t+1}, reward r and update Q-table

        Current state $S_t \leftarrow S_{t+1}$

    Until S_t is a normal state

    If action sequence a is a new action for S_0

        Add action sequence a into the set of executable actions and update Q-table;

    End If

Until Q-table is convergent

---

a_t expresses the selected action in current decision-making process. Software change occurs at the initial state S_0 and planning maker starts to select strategies. A SA process starts from the initial state until the system is back to normal. During each planning process, proposed method will tell if the sequence of actions executed is contained in the action space. Then it will add the new action sequences into action space as new strategies. When the accumulations of rewards tend to be stable, algorithm is convergent. Agents can get optimal strategy through learning knowledge.

3   Experiment

To validate our method, we use an e-commerce system selling books called Bookstore as the case study. It has high demands for QAs but it runs in an open, dynamic network environment. We design SA scenarios for it to test our method.

Bookstore system has a complex distributed architecture. It has four mainly function modules, including the commodity module, the shopping module, the recommendation module and the user module. And it has four pages related to the four function modules, including a homepage, a search page, a books page and a details page (see Fig. 2).

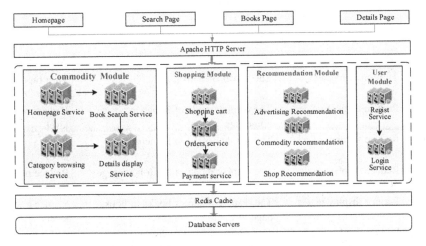

Fig. 2. The structure of Bookstore system.

We deploy the four function modules of Bookstore distributed. Each module has several servers and Bookstore supports to adjust the number of servers. In addition, it provides different display modes and numbers of books. And Bookstore can dynamically adjust these modes and methods to adapt to changes.

Due to a huge amount of requests on Bookstore, the response time of four pages frequently times out. Bookstore will periodically record the average response time of each page and tell if it is timeout. And we use the response time (RT) of four pages as the system state, shown as follows:

$$\{Homepage\,RT,\ Search\,page\,RT,\ Books\,page\,RT,\ Details\,page\,RT\,\} \quad (3)$$

We express response time of pages by number 0 to 5. The RT difference between every two numbers is one second. The Bookstore can dynamically adjust the display mode of books, the number of books, servers and advertisement, etc. These adjustments can help Bookstore system to improve performance. We defined several strategies for timeout. They have different overhead and effects. Table 1 gives a part of SA strategies of timeout scenarios.

Table 1. The self-adaptive strategies of timeout scenarios.

State	Event	Condition	Action
S2111	Homepage timeout	Has free server	001 Turn on homepage server
		Display mode > 0	002 Reduce display mode
		Ad number > 0	003 Reduce ad number
		Ad display mode > 0	004 Reduce ad display mode
S1121	Books page time out	Display mode > 0	005 Reduce display mode
		Display number > 5	006 Reduce display number

Table 2 describes the detailed definitions of actions in Table 1.

Table 2. The detailed definitions of actions.

Aid	AName	AObject	AOperation
001	Turn on homepage server	The server of homepage	Turn on one
002	Reduce display mode	The display mode of books in homepage	Reduce one level
003	Reduce number of ad	The number of ad in homepage	Reduce one level
004	Reduce display mode of ad	The display mode of ad in homepage	Reduce one level
005	Reduce display mode	The display mode of books in books page	Reduce one level
006	Reduce display number	The number of books displayed in books page	Reduce one level

We use Apache JMeter to simulate http requests. We use 60 threads to send 60 http requests per second. When sensor perceives the response timeout of four pages, it will trigger adaptive adjustment. This method will select decisions to adapt to the change of software. The algorithm iterates the feedback information in the Q-value and record information of the feedback shown in Table 3. It reflects the actual effects of strategies.

According to the Q-value of these strategies, the action 003 and the action 006 performs best in the book display page timeout event. In addition, there are some new strategies generated by strategy combinations. When existing strategies cannot deal with software changes, the proposed method will continue planning until system back to normal. Table 1 shows an undefined event. Its state is 2121 which means the response time of the homepage and the commodity display page are both time out. The proposed method combines actions in both two timeout events to solve the undefined timeout event. Then it will try these action sequences to find the best strategies. And the action 011 which action sequence is 003,005 performs better in this event.

Table 3. Adjustment information and Q-table

State	Event	Action	Q-value
S2111	Homepage timeout	001 Turn on homepage server	5.3882
		002 Reduce display mode	4.8248
		003 Reduce ad number	7.8719
		004 Reduce ad display mode	7.0198
S1121	Books page time out	005 Reduce display mode	7.9375
		006 Reduce display number	7.9847
S2121	Undefined event	011 Combine 003 and 005	9.8787
		012 Combine 005 and 004	8.541
		013 Combine 001 and 006	6.63

4   Conclusion and Future Work

This paper discusses two types of runtime uncertainties from the complex environment and system in SAS. We propose a method to handle them based on RL. But with the increase of software scale, more knowledge is needed to learn. In the future, we will try to storage the feedback with a non-table form to accelerate learning. Meanwhile, we will consider the influence of other agents in SAS and have a try on credit assignment.

Acknowledgement. This work is supported by the Projects (61672401) supported by the National Natural Science Foundation of China; Projects (315***10101, 315**0102) supported by the Pre-Research Project of the "Thirteenth Five-Year-Plan" of China.

References

1. Krupitzer, C., Roth, F.M., Vansyckel, S., et al.: A survey on engineering approaches for self-adaptive systems. Pervasive Mob. Comput. **17**(PB), 184–206 (2015)
2. Cheng, S.W., Garlan, D.: Handling uncertainty in autonomic systems. In: International Workshop on Living with Uncertainties (2007)
3. Esfahani, N., Kouroshfar, E., Malek, S., et al.: Taming uncertainty in self-adaptive software. In: 13th European conference on Foundations of Software Engineering, pp. 234–244. ACM (2011)
4. Elkhodary, A., Esfahani, N., Malek, S., et al.: FUSION: a framework for engineering self-tuning self-adaptive software systems. In: 18th ACM SIGSOFT International Symposium on Foundations of Software Engineering, pp. 7–16. ACM (2010)
5. Mao, X., Dong, M., Liu, L., et al.: An integrated approach to developing self-adaptive software. J. Inf. Sci. Eng. **30**(4), 1071–1085 (2014)
6. Amoui, M., Salehie, M., Mirarab, S., et al.: Adaptive action selection in autonomic software using reinforcement learning. In: International Conference on Autonomic and Autonomous Systems, pp. 175–181. IEEE Computer Society (2008)

Graph Computation Models (GCM)

Ninth International Workshop on Graph Computation Models (GCM 2018)

Hans-Jörg Kreowski

Department of Computer Science, University of Bremen, Bibliothekstr. 5,
28359 Bremen, Germany
kreo@informatik.uni-bremen.de

Abstract. This preface describes the objectives and scope of the series of International Workshops on Graph Computation Models (GCM) and provides a short report on the ninth edition in 2018.

Keywords: Graph computation · Graph modeling · Graph transformation

Objectives and Scope

Graphs are common mathematical structures that are visual and intuitive. They constitute a natural and seamless way for system modeling in science, engineering and beyond, including computer science, biology, business process modeling, etc. Graph computation models constitute a class of very high-level models where graphs are first-class citizens. They generalize classical computation models based on strings (e.g., Chomsky grammars) or on trees (e.g., term rewrite systems). Their mathematical foundation, in addition to their visual nature, facilitates the specification, validation and analysis of complex systems. A variety of computation models have been developed using graphs and rule-based graph transformation. These models include features of programming languages and systems, paradigms for software development, concurrent calculi, local computations and distributed algorithms, as well as biological or chemical computations. Thus, GCM aims at foundational research and applications of state-of-the-art graph computation models, especially to the areas of modeling and software engineering. GCM solicits papers in all areas of graph computation models including but not limited to the following topics of interest.

Foundations: Models of graph transformation; Parallel, concurrent, and distributed graph transformation; Term graph rewriting; Formal graph modeling; Logics on graphs and graph transformation; Formal graph languages; Analysis and verification of graph transformation systems; Foundations of specification and programming languages.

Applications: Software architecture; Software validation; Software evolution; Visual programming; Security models; Implementation of specification and programming languages; Rule-based systems; Workflow and business processes; Model-driven engineering; Service-oriented applications; Bioinformatics and system biology; Social network analysis; Case studies.

The aim of the series of the International Workshops on Graph Computation Models (GCM) is to bring together researchers interested in all aspects of computation models based on graphs and graph transformation. It promotes the cross-fertilizing exchange of ideas and experiences among senior and young researchers from the different communities interested in the foundations, applications, and implementations of graph computation models and related areas. Previous editions of the GCM series were held in Natal, Brazil (GCM 2006), in Leicester, UK (GCM 2008), in Enschede, The Netherlands (GCM 2010), in Bremen, Germany (GCM 2012), in York, UK (GCM 2014), in L'Aquila, Italy (GCM 2015), in Wien, Austria (GCM 2016), and in Marburg, Germany (GCM 2017).

The GCM workshop series is closely related to the International Conferences on Graph Transformation (ICGT) being part of the STAF conferences for some years. In previous years, authors of selected papers were invited to submit revised and extended versions after the workshop. Until GCM 2015, accepted selected contributions were published in special issues of the international journal *Electronic Communications of the EASST*. Previous issues of ECEASST dedicated to GCM include Volume 39 (2011), Volume 61 (2013), Volume 71 (2015), and Volume 73 (2016). Since 2016, GCM has joined other STAF workshops in collecting the final versions of the best papers in a joint volume.

Short Report on GCM 2018

GCM 2018 was a full-day event on 27 June 2018 after the two days of ICGT 2018. In all three sessions, about 20 participants took part in the lively discussions. The program consisted of nine presentations that are documented on the workshop website https://www.gcm2018.uni-bremen.de. Six of them were proposed for the joint STAF 2018 post-proceedings.

I would like to thank the members of the Program Committee I had the pleasure to chair for their competent and deeply committed work: Andrea Corradini (University of Pisa, Italy), Rachid Echahed (LIG Lab., Grenoble, France), Stefan Gruner (University of Pretoria, South Africa), Annegret Habel (University of Oldenburg, Germany), Dirk Janssens (University of Antwerp, Belgium), Barbara König (University of Duisburg-Essen, Germany), Mohamed Mosbah (University of Bordeaux, France), Detlef Plump (University of York, UK), and Leila Ribeiro (Universidade Federal do Rio Grande do Sul, Brazil). I am also very grateful to Timothy Atkinson, Aaron Lye, Christoph Peuser, and Christian Sandmann who served as subreviewers.

From my point of view, GCM 2018 worked very well and provided interesting and excellent talks. Therefore, it proved to be another link of the successful workshop series GCM.

Model Based Development of Data Integration in Graph Databases Using Triple Graph Grammars

Abdullah Alqahtani$^{(\boxtimes)}$ and Reiko Heckel

Department of Informatics, University of Leicester, Leicester, UK
{aqa2,rh122}@le.ac.uk
http://www2.le.ac.uk

Abstract. Graph databases such as neo4j are designed to handle and integrate big data from heterogeneous sources. For flexibility and performance they do not ensure data quality through schemata but leave it to the application level. In this paper, we present a model-driven approach for data integration through graph databases with data sources in relational databases. We model query and update operations in neo4j by triple graph grammars and map these to Gremlin code for execution. In this way we provide a model-based approach to data integration that is both visual and formal while providing the data quality assurances of a schema-based solution.

Keywords: Data integration · Graph databases
Model-based development · Triple graph grammars

1 Introduction

Data integration is the process of combining data from heterogeneous sources in a unified and consistent way [12]. In changing market conditions businesses have to be flexible, able to merge, cooperate with or acquire other businesses [10]. To work together effectively, such newly related businesses will have to integrate at least some of their data. As with application integration in general, approaches to data integration should support flexibility of future evolution and allow to share data while retaining ownership. For example, two businesses may agree to share their customer, product and supplier data but keep their internal processes separate. In such scenarios, data integration should be loose and partial to guarantee sustainability in the face of changing business goals [23].

Business data is often high in volume and velocity of change [12]. Data sources may be too large to replicate or merge fully and both data and data models may undergo changes at different rates. Keeping data loosely coupled or linked, it is easier to maintain integration [32]. Unfortunately, legacy data integration concepts do not address these requirements. Graph databases (GDB) such as neo4j [28] provide a scalable semi-structured data store based on a simple and flexible

© Springer Nature Switzerland AG 2018
M. Mazzara et al. (Eds.): STAF 2018 Workshops, LNCS 11176, pp. 399–414, 2018.
https://doi.org/10.1007/978-3-030-04771-9_29

graph data model. They are able to store large data sets [22] and query them efficiently using navigational query languages such as `Cypher` and `Gremlin` [15]. Triple graph grammars (TGG) are a declarative language to relate heterogeneous data through a relational structure. They support uni- and bidirectional transformations as well as linking existing data [26]. TGGs have originally been developed for model transformation, integration and synchronisation [11,18].

In this paper, we present an approach using TGG as data integration language on top of a GDBs. This is supported by the generation of code from TGG rules for GDB query and update operations. The overall architecture is shown in Fig. 1. Data integration is specified at a model layer, describing sources using UML models and the links to be created between them using TGG rules. This also allows to maintain the consistency of links and to update them when the source data changes. To implement the data integration, TGG rules are translated to the agnostic GDB query language `Gremlin` [25]. Then, the relevant data is imported to the GDB through source adapters, such that the `Gremlin` code can be executed.

Advantages of this approach are (i) the level of abstraction is increased due to the use of model-driven technology, (ii) the use of a GDB to maintain the link structure supports scalability, (iii) schema safety is maintained due to the use of typed TGG rules at model level and their correct translation to `Gremlin`, (iv) the visual nature of the model will allow business experts to understand and support the development of the integration.

In particular, correctness and scalability will be evaluated experimentally.

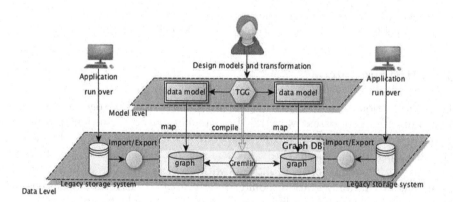

Fig. 1. Presenting TGG and UML models for data integration in graph databases.

The remainder of the paper is organised as follows: Sect. 2 motivates the problem by an integration scenario. Section 3 introduces the overall approach. Model-level data integration using TGGs is discussed in Sect. 4. Section 5 defines the mapping from TGGs to `Gremlin` while Sects. 6 and 7 present the evaluation of the approach and related work respectively. Section 8 concludes the paper and discusses future work.

2   Application Scenario

The domain of business data provision is used as a running example throughout paper. CompaniesHouse (CH) and CompanyCheck (CC) are two well-known UK business data providers. Both are responsible for filing data of all limited companies in the UK providing data on four million companies to be accessed online or downloaded [1]. However, the data provided by both sources is generally not consistent, differing in what data is provided per company but also in the semantics of apparently shared fields. In general, data can be incomplete or missing.

To mitigate these problems and benefit from the full extent of the data provided, we would like to link corresponding records in both databases and support mutual updates in both directions. More precisely, the requirements for integration are as follows:

① Bidirectional Integration: In this scenario data may be moved from CH to CC or vice versa. In case either side are missing data, they should be updated accordingly while retaining independent ownership.

② Scalability: Data is provided for millions of companies, so scalability of the integration process is important.

③ Visual Integration: Business data integration requires input by domain experts. This should be supported by visualising the integration components and rules.

④ Agile Integration: To be able to evolve our understanding of the integration incrementally, we have to support partial integration and existing rules and models should be easy to modify [16].

⑤ Heterogeneity: Both domains structure their data differently. Data representing the same objects are described using different names. Thus integration should be able to map heterogeneous representations into a shared consolidated structure.

3   Model Driven Approach to Data Integration

Our approach is based on data modelling and model transformation rules to be compiled into GDB code for execution. The two levels are briefly discuss below.

3.1   Model Level

This layer describes the integration at a high level of abstraction by representing source data models using UML class diagrams. This provides a platform-independent in terms of common modelling features such as classes, attributes, associations, etc. Relations between source data models are described using TGG rules, which can be used to link, synchronise and map data between the different models [13,19]. TGG rules are created by Eclipse Modelling Framework (EMF) and eMoflon [2,27]. In particular, eMoflon is a metamodelling tool for creating and executing TGG rules.

TGGs are used to create and maintain relations between source and target elements [13, 20]. Such relations can be used to update their constituents incrementally thus supporting data evolution. Therefore, despite their origins in meta modelling, TGGs can be used as a data integration and mapping language at the application level. Model transformation using TGGs to support data integration in GDBs has been suggested for these reasons. First, TGGs provide a solution to link heterogeneous components, establishing correspondences between elements that describe or share similar information, hence supporting requirement ⑤. They can copy and update such data if needed, e.g., to react incrementally to changes on either side in the integration, supporting requirement ④. Second, TGGs are a visual query language for GDBs, meeting requirement ③. Third, TGGs support bidirectional transformations, meeting requirement ①.

3.2 Implementation Level

UML models and TGG rules are mapped into `noe4j` property graphs and `Gremlin` queries. This allows us to leave the execution to the GDB. UML models are mapped to `neo4j` using the `NeoEMF` framework [4]. The mapping from TGGs to `Gremlin` is implemented using the `Acceleo` tool [24]. Data sources are imported via CSV files, loaded to `neo4j` using the `neo4j-shell` commands [17]. Such commands are modified based on the model mapping using `NeoEMF`.

Due to the scalability of `neo4j`, its use together with `Gremlin` to execute the integration helps us meet requirement ②. In addition to the incremental development of TGG rules, the flexibility of schemaless data in the GDB also supports requirement ④.

4   Model-Level Data Integration Using TGGs

Declarative TGG rules describe how two models are related, however, these relations can be translated to perform batch transformation. The derived rules are needed to copy data back and forth between sources. In addition, translation of TGG can also be used to relate elements at different sources which describe the same phenomena without moving data across. Such different translations depend on the same TGG specification between the sources [13]. Therefore, we derive three types of which are forward, backward, and consistency checking rules (see [13]). However, due to lack of space we will only show an example of forward transformation in Sect. 5.

Figure 2 shows the class diagrams for both domains, CompaniesHouse (CH) in Fig. 2(a) and CompanyCheck (CC) in 2(b). CH contains the main Company class as well as information such as the registered address (RegAddress) of the company, Account, Managers, and Trading classes. In the CC domain most information is similar in content but differently structured and named. This mismatch needs to be resolved conceptually, using the declarative TGG rules to relate corresponding concepts, as well as operationally by deriving the relevant TGG data transformation rules.

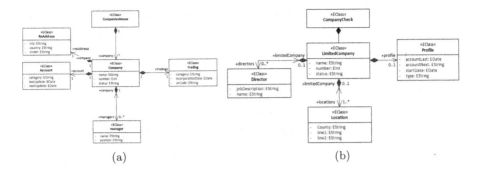

Fig. 2. (a) CompaniesHouse model and (b) CompanyCheck model

Figure 3 presents six TGG rules. Rules are created using the TGG tool in eMoflon. Rule 3(a) creates a pair of classes, CH and CC, without any preconditions (i.e., an empty left-hand side). This type of rule refers to as an axiom, and it is applicable before and independently of any other rule. Rule 3(b) relates the Company and LimitedCompany classes. It requires the pattern created by 3(a) as precondition (left-hand side). This is denoted by black elements while the elements newly generated are shown in green. Rules 3(c), (d) and (f) are used to create consistent pairs of Trading with Profile, RegAddress with Location, and Manager with Director classes. They can all be applied independently since they do not depend on each other but only on Rule 3(b).

In rule 3(e), the Account class is created and linked to the Profile class from rule 3(d). The left-hand side includes the precondition pattern of 3(d) and the class Profile. The right-hand side only adds the Account class from the source domain and the AccountToProfile class from the correspondence domain. This rule presents a good example of how backward transformation can be derived from a TGG specification, E.g., a new element is created in one domain that relates to an existing elements of the other domain.

5   Mapping TGGs to Graph Databases

GDBs are based on a simple graph model known as *property graph*. It is defined by sets of nodes N and relationships R, attributed by key-value pairs known as properties. The NeoEMF framework [4] has been used to map EMF objects manipulated by TGG rules to corresponding neo4j nodes and edges.

We only map a subset of TGGs, which does not include all features such as negative application conditions. Mapping derives directed (operational) TGG rules for forward, backward and consistency transformation from the same declarative TGG rules. The left-hand side of a TGG operational rule is implemented using the pattern matching capability of Gremlin. If the Gremlin query is successful, the graph will be updated according to mutation statements derived from the right-hand side. Nodes and edges of a specific domain are created based on the type of the operational rule from given context elements.

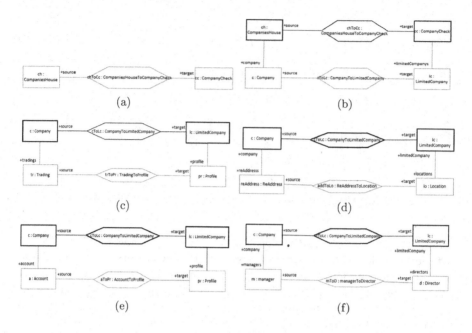

Fig. 3. TGG rules of running example

The concepts of `Gremlin` and TGGs can be aligned to demonstrate the mapping of rules into queries. TGG concepts are categorised based on the types of elements used in the transformation and their binding type, for instance objects and links. There are three types of bindings of TGG elements within rules: (1) check, (2) create, and (3) destroy [29]. The check type states a precondition of the TGG rule, requiring objects and/or links to be present to apply the rule. The create type is instructing objects or links to be created. In our mapping, we only consider check and create bindings. According to each binding type, elements and nodes are translated into the logic of `Gremlin` statements. Table 1 presents the mapping of concepts between TGGs and `Gremlin` based on the binding types of links and objects.

For illustration of the mapping, we focus on a forward transformation rule derived from TGG rule depicted in 3(b) of Fig. 3. In such a rule, correspondence and target elements are created from given source and context elements. Figure 4 shows the forward rule, whose left-hand side is denoted by black elements and the new elements in the right-hand side are denoted by green elements. Our mapping example only uses directed rules for forward and backward translation. However, as discussed previously, from the same symmetric TGG productions we can generate consistency checking translation rules.

We implemented the mapping using `Acceleo`, a general EMF-based tool to generate text from models [24]. In our translation, we rely on the TGG meta-model defined by `eMoflon` [29]. The metamodel is fed to the `Acceleo` genera-

Table 1. Mapping of TGG rules to Gremlin

TGG elements	GDB elements	Semantics	
		TGG	Gremlin expression
TGG object	Neo4j Vertex	Check only binding (LHS)	- graph.v(VertexName) for single vertex matching
			- graph .V(VertexName).as('x').out (EdgeLabel).as('y')
			- graph .V(VertexName).outE (EdgeLabel). inV(VertexName)
			For multi-vertices matching
		Create binding (RHS)	graph.AddVertex(Properties)
TGG link	Neo4j Edge	Check only binding (LHS)	- graph.e(EdgeId) For single edge matching
			- graph.v(VertexName).bothE
			For multi-edges matching of a specific vertex
		Create binding (RHS)	- graph.AddEdge(Properties)

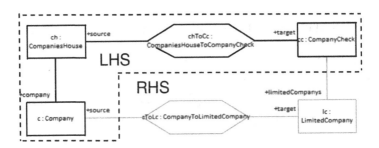

Fig. 4. Compact representation of forward transformation rule derived from Fig. 3(b) in Fig. 3

tor which uses metamodel elements based on designated templates to generate Gremlin code.

Pattern Matching (LHS). This phase involves matching entities of the left-hand side pattern graph with corresponding elements in the property graph. That means, the pattern is interpreted as a query. Pattern matching is the most expensive part of executing graph transformations [5]. One of the features of Gremlin is to provide efficient techniques for complex pattern matching regardless of the size of the graph. Therefore, we use Gremlin to implement pattern matching. For example, the left-hand side of the rule in Fig. 4 is encoded by the Gremlin query in Listing 1.1, showing how context elements are retrieved and matched using *out* and *as* steps, and how the result is stored and returned in the form of a *table*.

Listing 1.1. Gremlin query for LHS of forward rule in Fig. 4

```
t= new  Table ()
g.v('name', chToCc).as('x').
    out(target).as('y').table(t).loop('x')
=> [x : v(5) , y: v(8)]
g.v('name', chToCc).as('x').
    out(source).as('y').table(t).loop('x')
=> [x : v(5) , y: v(6)]
g.v(name, c)
=> v(7)
```

In the above `Gremlin` code we first find all target nodes of the outgoing *target* and *source* edges from the *chToCc* node. The table step selects the 1st and 2nd edge of the all paths that reach the nodes and inserts them into the table *t* as rows. The loop step is used for recursive matching, i.e., if there are any multiply connected nodes with the same link label. Finally, the query returns the node of the source model *c* of type *Company*.

Graph Manipulation (RHS). This phase executes the creation and deletion of nodes and edges of the target graph. We implement these operations using `Gremlin` methods and statements. Data methods to update the graph are implemented within a transactional block to ensure that each transformation step is atomic [31]. Methods include `graph.addVertex()` and `graph.addEdge()` for node and edge creation and `graph.removeVertex, graph.removeEdge()` for node and edge deletion. However, for operational rules derived from TGGs, deletion operations are not needed. Referring to our forward rule in Fig. 4, its righ-hand side is implemented using the following `Gremlin` code using the query defined in Listing 1.1.

Listing 1.2. Gremlin code for RHS of forward rule in Fig 4

```
1 graph.tx().onReadWrite(Transaction)
2 g.addVertex('name',cToLc )
3 g.addVertex('name', lc )
4 g.addEdge( cToLc , c, source)
5 g.addEdge( cToLc, lc , target)
6 g.addEdge(cc, lc , limitedCompanys)
7 graph.tx ().commit()
```

The above code creates nodes *cToLc* in Line 2 and *lc* in line 3. Edges of type *source, target* from correspondence to source and target nodes are created in Lines 4 and 5. Line 6 shows the creation of a *limitedCompanys* edge required for conformance to the CC class diagram.

6   Experimental Evaluation

The queries generated by `Acceleo` from TGG rules in `eMoflon` are evaluated for correctness and performance.

6.1   Correctness

To evaluate correctness of our approach, we need to ensure that the generated `Gremlin` queries implement the same behaviour of TGGs. We generate test cases based on the TGG specification, and map them to `neo4j` using the `NeoEMF` framework [4]. Then, `Gremlin` queries are applied using the blueprint interface. TGG transformations result in consistent pairs of source and target models. Based on the direction of transformation, source or target model serves as test inputs and transformation implemented by `Gramlin` is System Under Test (SUT). The target model of the TGG transformation represents the expected output [34]. The *test generator* [34] is implemented in `eMoflon` and uses TGG specification to generate valid and adequate test suits (pairs of test models and valid outputs based on TGG rules). The tool automatically generates test cases either for all TGG rules (large test cases) or individual TGG rules (small test cases). It is based on a grammar-based generation approach and uses auxiliary functions to support *traversal strategy* and *stop criterion*. It also passes the generated tests to a component that evaluates the quality of test cases based on gathered coverage data from the TGG metamodel and applicable rules and produces a quality report accordingly.

The generated test suit of each rule consists of five test cases. The stop criterion is based on the size of the sample model. The minimum size of tests is 20 elements, and the maximum size is 7,000 elements. They cover the structural features of the source model, as well as its classes, attributes and associations *w.r.t* applicable TGG rules. The number of objects in each test case and the selection of TGG rules are manually encoded before the generation. Then, we generate the test cases for the complete transformation. The traversal strategy of the applicable rules is parameterised based on the interdependency of the rules to meet a certain application sequence, i.e. in our running example, we have six rules (r(a), r(b), * r(c) * r(d) * r(e) * r(f)), such that r(a) is the axiom or initial rule, and r(b) depends on the application of r(a). The * means that the remaining rules can be randomly applied. We limited the number of applications of the axiom rule to one to ensure that we have one root element for every test graph. Each generated EMF object graph (test case) is mapped into a `neo4j` graph [4].

Table 2 presents a summary of the generated test cases and the applications of the rules (the elements of each rule). It is presented to demonstrate the quality of generated test cases. Each test case is bounded in size, as shown in the first row (numbers within brackets). The number of generated elements for each rule out of the defined upper bound is presented for each test case. Note that the test cases also cover the edges required by the TGG rules.

Table 2. Summary of applications for each rule of generated test cases

Rules	#$Test_1$(20)	#$Test_2$(200)	#$Test_3$(1000)	#$Test_4$(3000)	#$Test_5$(7000)
r(a)	1/20	1/200	1/1000	1/3000	1/7000
r(b)	5/20	43/200	205/1000	602/3000	1358/7000
r(c)	4/20	42/200	189/1000	580/3000	1426/7000
r(d)	2/20	31/200	201/1000	611/3000	1398/7000
r(e)	4/20	42/200	197/1000	539/3000	1382/7000
r(f)	4/20	41/200	207/1000	613/3000	1435/7000

To compare the result of the execution of the queries with the expected output based on the TGG specification we have to establish a graph isomorphism between output graphs G_{neo} generated by Gremlin in neo4j with EMF graphs G_{emf} generated by the original TGG rules in eMoflon.

In the initial mapping to the GDB, we maintain consistency of identifiers of input model elements. This is ensured by running EMFCompare [30], a tool for comparing two EMF models, to match corresponding elements, creating a partial isomorphism that covers all elements retained from the given object graph. However, the newly created elements by Gremlin are not known to NeoEMF resource which makes it impossible to use EMFCompare to complete the test.

In addition to manual testing for small test cases via visualising the graphs using Gephi [3], a graph visualisation tool, we implemented the isomorphism test after each transformation step using the igraph package, employing a standard graph isomorphism algorithm [6]. Igraph implements the VF2 isomorphism algorithm in Python. The VF2 algorithm is a simple isomorphism check based on tree search and backtracking [21].

This is done incrementally after each application of a query. A TGG model transformation $G_{emf} \xrightarrow{*} G_{emf}\prime$ breaks down into individual steps $G_{emf} = G_{emf_0} \xrightarrow{r_1} \ldots \xrightarrow{r_n} G_{emf_n} = G_{emf}\prime$ with rules $r_1, \ldots, r_n$.

The same structure can be identified in the neo4j transformation $G_{neo} \xrightarrow{*} G_{neo}\prime$ as $G_{neo} = G_{neo_0} \xrightarrow{q_1} \ldots \xrightarrow{q_n} G_{neo_n} = G_{neo}\prime$ with queries $q_1, \ldots, q_n$ derived from the rules above.

In order to be correct, the execution should result in isomorphic graphs $G_{neo}\prime \cong G_{emf}\prime$. Based on the NeoEMF mapping we can assume $G_{neo} \cong G_{emf}$. Then, the isomorphism of $G_{emf_{i+1}}$ and $G_{neo_{i+1}}$ is obtained by the correspondence of r_{i+1} and q_{i+1} from isomorphic graphs G_{emf_i} and G_{neo_i}. By induction this ensures $G_{neo}\prime \cong G_{emf}\prime$.

We follow an iterative process to update Acceleo templates for preserving the behaviour of the TGG rules. We manually mutate the mapped inputs for some of the test cases (e.g. by inverting the directions of some edges or by changing the names of nodes) before the application of Gremlin, in which the application fails during the matching pattern phase for respective queries posed against the modified structure; therefore, no updates were made as we instructed our implemented GDB application. The reason for the mutation step is to ensure that the modified graphs cannot be executed by the generated `Gremlin`. Therefore, we produce invalid graphs as a part of the testing because the tool only generates valid pairs of source and target models.

Both G_{neo}' and G_{emf}' are incrementally sent to the `igraph` function, which returns the isomorphism of the valid generated graphs (after attempts of corrections) and the *non-isomorphism* for mutated graphs. To correct the errors in the `Acceleo`, we relied on small test cases to visualise the graphs and compare them manually because the `igraph` does not manifest the differences for the given graphs. Most of the errors were `Gremlin` based, hence scripts were updated without changing the main mapping rules. We run the function after each correction attempt until we ensured that the given (valid) graphs are isomorphic. We complete our test by successfully covering all generated test cases.

6.2 Performance

We conducted an experiment to compare execution times of TGGs using `eMoflon` and of the translated `Gremlin` queries using `neo4j`. Results show that the GDB engine provides a highly scalable platform, executing our queries on large graphs. Using the six rules discussed in Sect. 4 we execute a complete forward transformation from CH to CC. Source models of various size have been automatically generated using model generators based on the TGG rules. These provide the input EMF graphs G_{emf} which are mapped to `neo4j` using `NeoEMF` into property graphs G_{neo}. Then, TGG rules are applied using `eMoflon` and `Gremlin` queries are applied using `neo4j` and the times for both executions are measured. The experiment has been conducted on Macintosh machine with a 2.5 GHz Intel Core i7 processor and 16 GB 1600 MHz DDR3 RAM memory. The results show that `neo4j` outperforms the execution using `eMoflon`, especially with larger graphs of more than 100,000 elements. Figure 5 plots execution times in seconds.

In our application scenario discussed in Section 2, information of 200,000 companies requires one million data objects which have been executed in 180 s which was the largest information that can be transformed using `eMoflon` using our example.

CompaniesHouse provides data of approximately four million companies. For this purpose, we execute the `Gremlin` queries alone to evaluate the scalability of the approach w.r.t real-world examples. Memory configurations of `neo4j` were modified to set the parameters of the heap size that is responsible for query execution and caching transactions as per `neo4j` recommendations. Based on the same hardware specification, the result shown in Fig. 6 indicates that the approach scales up to transform information of 1.5 million companies, and can be executed in 1388 s. Due to memory overhead on the virtual machine, an error was thrown when transforming graphs consist of more than 8 million nodes.

To recap, the evaluation shows unsurprisingly that our approach achieves better performance than current implementation of `eMoflon` due to the use of GDB as the underlying storage and engine. Also, the approach can scale to large data, beyond the ability of the current EMF-based transformation tools.

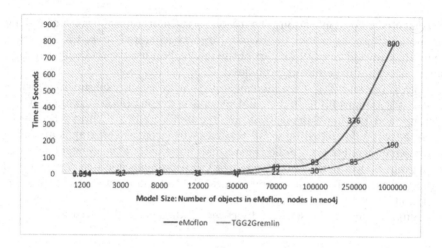

Fig. 5. Execution times of eMoflon and Neo4j

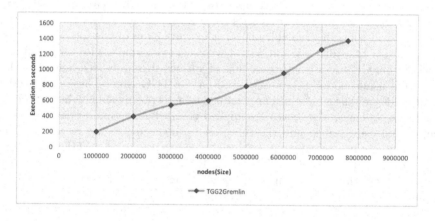

Fig. 6. Stand alone execution of Neo4j

6.3 Threats to Validity

There are some features that might threaten the validity of experimental evaluation. We discuss them briefly as follows: The limited number of TGG rules makes it difficult to generalise the conclusion. Only six TGG rules of a single transformation are tested. There is no firm conclusion on the effect of TGG complexity on execution time. e.g. there are other scenarios which require transformations where the individual rules may be large and complex. Although we only demonstrated an example of forward transformation, this threat is mitigated via maintaining non-functionality through code generation of backward transformation from the same specification. Thus, we rely on bidirectional behaviour of TGGs in general rather than reducing complexity of the TGG design. We also rely on the fact of existence of similar integration examples especially in small and medium size businesses.

7 Related Work

We distinguish between the use of non-relational databases as scalable solutions for the implementation of MDE tools and as a scalable persistence layer for data-driven applications.

In [9], the authors propose mappings of UML models to GDBs in two stages. First, a model transformation is defined between the UML metamodel and the graph metamodel. Second, a framework is designed to generate Java code that can access the GDB. Our approach shares with this framework the concept mapping from class diagrams to the property graph model. However, we define a new mapping of TGG rules to native GDB code rather than access it by Java.

Mogwai [8] presents a lightweight model query language using the Object Constraint Language (OCL), extending the NeoEMF [4] mapping. They translates OCL into Gremlin expressions and compute queries on GDB representations of models. The approach uses model-to-model transformation from OCL to Gremlin. Instead, our approach uses model-to-text transformations based on Acceleo and supports side effects arising from update operations of translated TGG rules. Such implementation of Acceleo produces valid Gremlin queries w.r.t TGG rule without the need to establish a complex metamodel for Gremlin language.

In the second category, BXE2E [14] is a bidirectional approach to support import and export of electronic medical records. The study focusses on defining a mapping between the OSAR and E2E medical record systems based on embedding TGG rules that relate both data models. The implementation of BXE2E is based on Java code to support native operations of data transformation. To reduce execution costs, the design of the TGG rules does not use pattern matching, but encapsulates complex queries with lenses operations. Although this approach exploits TGGs for data-driven applications, it works with a restricted form of TGG rules which does not permit to use the full power of TGGs as a declarative language. Moreover, TGG rules do not describe bidirectional data integration for data-driven, schema-less applications.

Recent work [7] describes a model transformation engine based on NoSQL databases. The essence of the approach is based on mappings of ATL transformation rules into the Gremlin query language via M2M transformations. The approach defines mappings from the ATL metamodel into a subset of the Gremlin domain metamodel, called Gremlin Traversal. Since the approach considers ATL rules to accomplish the transformation, the approach is unidirectional. Moreover, the approach does not directly contribute to building data-driven solutions or data integration systems.

GRAPE [33] presents as scalable graph transformation engine based on neo4j. It employs Coljure as domain-specific language for the textual syntax of rewriting rules and GraphViz for rule visualisation. Unidirectional rule operations such as addition, deletion and matching operations are compiled into the

Cypher query language. This compilation utilises the pattern matching capability of Cypher on neo4j graphs. The engine provides persistence backtracking facilities based on the property graph model and transaction features of neo4j. Despite the fact that the transformation engine is built on top of neo4j, imperative and unidirectional transformations are compiled into Cypher and do not avoid vendor lock-in since Cypher runs only on neo4j.

In our approach, TGGs are formally translated to an agnostic GDB query language to execute data operations for scalable performance. We compare our approach with aforementioned related work in terms of the requirements in Sect. 2. Agility is compared based on incremental development of TGGs to support evolving requirements. We also refer to the use of GDBs as a persistence and computation engine. Table 3 shows a summary of the comparison.

Table 3. General comparison of relevant approaches based on discussed requirement in Sect. 2

Approach	Bidirectional	GDB support	Agility	Visual query	Heterogeneity support
Mogwai	✗	✓	✗	✗	✗
UMLtoGraphDB	✗	✓	✗	✓	✗
Grape	✗	✓	✗	✓	✗
BXE2E	✓	✗	✓	✓	✗
ATL2Gremlin	✗	✓	✗	✗	✗
TGG2Gremlin	✓	✓	✓	✓	✓

8   Conclusion and Future Work

In this paper, we show a how graph databases and model-driven development tools can work together to build data integration solutions. Concepts and techniques of both technologies can lead to advantages at both design and execution level. As future work, we plan to enhance our mapping to cover most features and useful extensions of TGG such as negative application conditions in order to provide more options for data integration designers. Multi-data sources integration will be investigated. This task involves extending the current specification of TGGs to cope with multi-models. The bidirectionality of the approach is to be extended to cover incremental and synchronisation features of TGGs. eMoflon has already implemented parsing strategies that are built in its execution model. We plan to study the mapping of these parsing strategies into neo4j to perform the synchronisation.

References

1. Companieshouse (2011). https://assets.publishing.service.gov.uk/government/uploads/system/uploads/attachment_data/file/247006/0284.pdf
2. Anjorin, A., Lauder, M., Patzina, S., Schürr, A.: eMoflon: leveraging EMF and professional CASE tools. In: 3 Workshop Methodische Entwicklung von Modellierungswerkzeugen (MEMWe 2011) (2011)
3. Bastian, M., Heymann, S., Jacomy, M., et al.: Gephi: an open source software for exploring and manipulating networks. ICWSM **8**, 361–362 (2009)
4. Benelallam, A., Gómez, A., Sunyé, G., Tisi, M., Launay, D.: Neo4EMF, a scalable persistence layer for EMF models. In: Cabot, J., Rubin, J. (eds.) ECMFA 2014. LNCS, vol. 8569, pp. 230–241. Springer, Cham (2014). https://doi.org/10.1007/978-3-319-09195-2_15
5. Bergmann, G., Horváth, Á., Ráth, I., Varró, D.: A benchmark evaluation of incremental pattern matching in graph transformation. In: Ehrig, H., Heckel, R., Rozenberg, G., Taentzer, G. (eds.) ICGT 2008. LNCS, vol. 5214, pp. 396–410. Springer, Heidelberg (2008). https://doi.org/10.1007/978-3-540-87405-8_27
6. Csardi, M.G.: Package 'igraph' **3**(09), 214–217 (2013)
7. Daniel, G., Jouault, F., Sunyé, G., Cabot, J.: Gremlin-ATL: a scalable model transformation framework. In: 2017 32nd IEEE/ACM International Conference on Automated Software Engineering (ASE), pp. 462–472, October 2017
8. Daniel, G., Sunyé, G., Cabot, J.: Mogwaï: a framework to handle complex queries on large models. In: International Conference on Research Challenges in Information Science (RCIS 2016), Grenoble, France, June 2016. https://hal.archives-ouvertes.fr/hal-01344019
9. Daniel, G., Sunyé, G., Cabot, J.: UMLtoGraphDB: mapping conceptual schemas to graph databases. In: Comyn-Wattiau, I., Tanaka, K., Song, I.-Y., Yamamoto, S., Saeki, M. (eds.) ER 2016. LNCS, vol. 9974, pp. 430–444. Springer, Cham (2016). https://doi.org/10.1007/978-3-319-46397-1_33
10. Fensel, D., et al.: Product data integration in B2B e-commerce. IEEE Intell. Syst. **16**(4), 54–59 (2001)
11. Giese, H., Hildebrandt, S.: Efficient model synchronization of large-scale models. No. 28, Universitätsverlag Potsdam (2009)
12. Halevy, A., Rajaraman, A., Ordille, J.: Data integration: the teenage years. In: Proceedings of the 32nd International Conference on Very Large Data Bases, pp. 9–16. VLDB Endowment (2006)
13. Hermann, F., Ehrig, H., Golas, U., Orejas, F.: Formal analysis of model transformations based on triple graph grammars. Math. Struct. Comput. Sci. **24**(04), 240408 (2014)
14. Ho, J., Weber, J., Price, M.: BXE2E: a bidirectional transformation approach for medical record exchange. In: Guerra, E., van den Brand, M. (eds.) ICMT 2017. LNCS, vol. 10374, pp. 155–170. Springer, Cham (2017). https://doi.org/10.1007/978-3-319-61473-1_11
15. Holzschuher, F., Peinl, R.: Performance of graph query languages: comparison of cypher, gremlin and native access in Neo4j. In: Proceedings of the Joint EDBT/ICDT 2013 Workshops, pp. 195–204. ACM
16. Hughes, R.: Agile Data Warehousing: Delivering World-Class Business Intelligence Systems Using Scrum and XP. IUniverse, Bloomington (2008)
17. Hunger, M.: Neo4j-shell tools. GitHub repository (2013). https://github.com/jexp/neo4j-shell-tools

18. Kindler, E., Rubin, V., Wagner, R.: An adaptable TGG interpreter for in-memory model transformation. In: Proceedings of the 2nd International Fujaba Days 2004, Darmstadt, Germany. Technical report, vol. tr-ri-04-253, pp. 35–38. University of Paderborn, September 2004

19. Knigs, A., Schrr, A.: Tool integration with triple graph grammars - a survey. Electron. Notes Theor. Comput. Sci. **148**(1), 113–150 (2006). http://www.sciencedirect.com/science/article/pii/S1571066106000454. proceedings of the School of SegraVis Research Training Network on Foundations of Visual Modelling Techniques (FoVMT 2004)

20. Leblebici, E., Anjorin, A., Schürr, A.: A catalogue of optimization techniques for triple graph grammars. Modellierung **19**, 21 (2014)

21. Levendovszky, T., Charaf, H.: Pattern matching in metamodel-based model transformation systems. Period. Polytech. Electr. Eng. **49**(1–2), 87–107 (2006)

22. Miller, J.J.: Graph database applications and concepts with Neo4j. In: Proceedings of the Southern Association for Information Systems Conference, Atlanta, GA, USA, 23rd–24th March (2013)

23. Münch, T., Buchmann, R., Pfeffer, J., Ortiz, P., Christl, C., Hladik, J., Ziegler, J., Lazaro, O., Karagiannis, D., Urbas, L.: An innovative virtual enterprise approach to agile micro and SME-based collaboration networks. In: Camarinha-Matos, L.M., Scherer, R.J. (eds.) PRO-VE 2013. IAICT, vol. 408, pp. 121–128. Springer, Heidelberg (2013). https://doi.org/10.1007/978-3-642-40543-3_13

24. Musset, J., et al.: Acceleo user guide, vol. 2 (2006). http://acceleo.org/doc/obeo/en/acceleo-2.6-user-guide.pdf

25. Rodriguez, M.A., De Wilde, P.: Gremlin (2011). https://github.com/tinkerpop/gremlin/wiki

26. Schürr, A.: Specification of graph translators with triple graph grammars. In: Mayr, E.W., Schmidt, G., Tinhofer, G. (eds.) WG 1994. LNCS, vol. 903, pp. 151–163. Springer, Heidelberg (1995). https://doi.org/10.1007/3-540-59071-4_45

27. Steinberg, D., Budinsky, F., Merks, E., Paternostro, M.: EMF: Eclipse Modeling Framework. Pearson Education, London (2008)

28. The Neo4j Team: (2018). https://neo4j.com. Neo4j Graph Database Platform

29. eMoflon team, T.: An introduction to metamodelling and graph transformations with eMoflon. Technical report, TU Darmsadt (2014)

30. Toulmé, A., Inc., I.: Presentation of EMF compare utility. In: Eclipse Modeling Symposium, pp. 1–8

31. Varró, G., Friedl, K., Varró, D.: Graph transformation in relational databases. Electron. Notes Theor. Comput. Sci. **127**(1), 167–180 (2005). Proceedings of the International Workshop on Graph-Based Tools (GraBaTs 2004)

32. Wasserman, A.I.: Tool integration in software engineering environments. In: Long, F. (ed.) Software Engineering Environments. LNCS, vol. 467, pp. 137–149. Springer, Heidelberg (1990). https://doi.org/10.1007/3-540-53452-0_38

33. Weber, J.H.: GRAPE – a graph rewriting and persistence engine. In: de Lara, J., Plump, D. (eds.) ICGT 2017. LNCS, vol. 10373, pp. 209–220. Springer, Cham (2017). https://doi.org/10.1007/978-3-319-61470-0_13

34. Wieber, M., Anjorin, A., Schürr, A.: On the usage of TGGs for automated model transformation testing. In: Di Ruscio, D., Varró, D. (eds.) ICMT 2014. LNCS, vol. 8568, pp. 1–16. Springer, Cham (2014). https://doi.org/10.1007/978-3-319-08789-4_1

Short-Cut Rules

Sequential Composition of Rules Avoiding Unnecessary Deletions

Lars Fritsche[1](✉)[iD], Jens Kosiol[2](✉)[iD], Andy Schürr[1][iD], and Gabriele Taentzer[2][iD]

[1] TU Darmstadt, Darmstadt, Germany
{lars.fritsche,andy.schuerr}@es.tu-darmstadt.de
[2] Philipps-Universität Marburg, Marburg, Germany
{kosiolje,taentzer}@mathematik.uni-marburg.de

Abstract. Sequences of rule applications in high-level replacement systems are difficult to adapt. Often, replacing a rule application at the beginning of a sequence, i.e., reverting a rule and applying another one instead, is prevented by structure created via rule applications later on in the sequence. A trivial solution would be to roll back all applications and reapply them in a proper way. This, however, has the disadvantage of being computationally expensive and, furthermore, may cause the loss of information in the process. Moreover, using existing constructions to compose the reversal of a rule with the application of another one, in particular the concurrent and amalgamated rule constructions, does not prevent the loss of information in case that the first rule deletes elements being recreated by the second one. To cope with both problems, we introduce a new kind of rule composition through 'short-cut rules'. We present our new kind of rule composition for monotonic rules in adhesive HLR systems, as they provide a well-established generalization of graph-based transformation systems, and motivate it on the example of Triple Graph Grammars, a declarative and rule-based bidirectional transformation approach.

Keywords: Rule composition · Amalgamated rule
E-concurrent rule · Triple graph grammars

1 Introduction

High-level replacement (HLR) systems [2,3] are a useful generalization for transforming various kinds of high-level structures, such as graphs, in a rule-based manner. Transformation processes consist of sequences of rule applications. These sequences effectively de-/construct and modify structures, yet, they also implicitly create dependency relationships: an earlier rule application may be the precondition for a later one. Often, these relationships prevent rule applications at the beginning of a sequence to be replaced by another one, as reverting

© Springer Nature Switzerland AG 2018
M. Mazzara et al. (Eds.): STAF 2018 Workshops, LNCS 11176, pp. 415–430, 2018.
https://doi.org/10.1007/978-3-030-04771-9_30

the former would destruct preconditions used for transformations later in the sequence. A trivial solution would be to roll back all applications that depend on each other, until reaching the one that is to be replaced, and reapply them in a proper way. However, rolling back and recreating these sequences has the disadvantage of being computationally expensive and, furthermore, may cause the loss of information in the process. Thus, it would be highly beneficial to replace rule applications in a – preferably also rule-based – way that preserves the remaining sequence. Existing approaches to rule composition, namely the parallel, concurrent, and amalgamated rule constructions [1–3], are not apt to deal with that kind of dependency.

Hence, we introduce a novel kind of rule composition through *short-cut rules* whose applications serve as an alternative to possibly long chains of replacement actions. A short-cut rule composes the reversal of a monotonic rule, i.e., of a rule which only creates structure, with the application of a second one. Yet, doing this, the short-cut rule identifies elements, deleted by reverting the first rule, with elements, created by the second one, hereby preserving them. This preservation allows for applications of short-cut rules even in situations where the reversal of the first rule itself is impossible. We accomplish this by pair-wisely comparing the rules of a given HLR system searching for common substructures. Consequently, we exploit this information for creating short-cut rules that preserve those common substructures. While the approach is formalized for monotonic rules in HLR systems in general, we use Triple Graph Grammars (TGGs) [10] as example for demonstration purposes. TGGs are an established formalism for the declarative description of complex consistency relationships between two modelling languages with graph-like representations. They are especially useful for efficiently checking and restoring the consistency of a given pair of models [9] or for generating possible combinations of consistent pairs of models; unfortunately, they do not offer adequate means for the specification of arbitrarily complex editing operations that directly transform one consistent pair of models into another consistent pair of models. With our contribution we are able to solve a common problem of TGGs by using our novel rule composition scheme to take a set of TGG rules as input and produce a set of short-cut rules as output. The rule composition scheme guarantees that any combination of inverse and normal applications of TGG rules can be replaced by short-cut rules and may even be executed in several situations where the inverse application is impossible. They have the additional advantage of preserving some graph elements which otherwise would be deleted by the corresponding inverse application of a TGG rule and be recreated by the corresponding normal application of a TGG rule.

The main contributions of this paper are as follows: We illustrate the use of short-cut rules in the context of TGGs (Sect. 2). We formalize the construction of short-cut rules and prove the Short-Cut Theorem (Theorem 7), settling the synthesizability of applications of monotonic rules into an application of a short-cut rule and the analysability of applications of a short-cut rule into applications of monotonic rules (Sect. 4). We formally compare our new kind of rule composition with existing ones (Sect. 5). Furthermore, in Sect. 3 we recall transformation rules and HLR systems. Section 6 concludes the paper and points to some future work. For most of the proofs we refer to a long version of this paper [4].

2   Introductory Example

The construction and use of short-cut rules is motivated at the example of consistency between a simplified class diagram and a custom documentation structure. It is an excerpt of, and based on the example provided by Leblebici et al. [8], yet, in a simplistic form to show the basic idea of our approach. Thus, it contains no (propagation of) attributes, which will be covered in future work. Our example is an excerpt from a consistency specification between a class diagram and a documentation structure using Triple Graph Grammars (TGGs). It thus consists a *Package* structure containing *Classes* on the one side and a *Folder* structure containing *Doc-Files* on the other.

TGGs [10] are a declarative, rule-based bidirectional transformation approach proposed by Schürr. Given two input meta-models, a TGG specification defines consistency between instances of both. To this end, it consists of a finite set of graph grammar rules that define how consistent pairs of both models co-evolve. In order to relate elements from both sides, TGGs introduce a third meta-model, which is referred to as the correspondence meta-model. It is used to connect elements of both sides such that they become correlated and thus traceable.

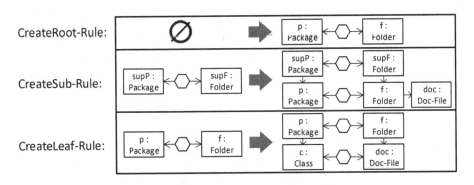

Fig. 1. A TGG to co-evolve class diagram and documentation structure

Figure 1 shows the rule set for our example consisting of three TGG rules. The first rule depicts the base TGG rule of the given rule set. Since its left-hand side (LHS) L is empty, and thus no precondition exists, it can always and arbitrarily often create a root *Package* together with a root *Folder* and a correspondence link between both. Given the context from the LHS, the second rule creates a *Package* and *Folder* hierarchy where every sub-folder has a *Doc-File* that may contain the documentation of the corresponding *Package*. Finally, the third

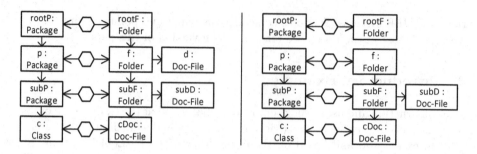

Fig. 2. Two examples for consistent triples

rule creates a *Class* together with a corresponding *Doc-File* analogously to the *Package* and *Folder* of the previous rule.

Given these rules, one can create consistent graph triples, such as those shown in Fig. 2. The exemplary triple on the left consists of a hierarchy of three *Packages* on the left side which are correlated to a similar hierarchy of *Folders* via correspondence links. However, the *Folders* f and subF additionally contain their own *Doc-File*. Thus, the triple was created via four consecutive applications of TGG rules by applying first *CreateRoot-Rule*, followed by *CreateSub-Rule* twice and finally *CreateLeaf-Rule*.

An important point about this transformation sequence is that it creates entities for both the class diagram and the documentation structure simultaneously, but the resulting model does not contain any information about the contents of the created elements. This means that, in practical applications, the user may add data manually which is not correlated to the other side, like layout information for the class diagram or textual descriptions as the contents of *Doc-Files*. Due to this lack of correlation, one has to be careful on how to change models in order to avoid unnecessary data loss. Given the model on the left side of Fig. 2, a reasonable example for such a change would be the separation of the first two hierarchy levels making the former sub-elements p and f to be root elements by effectively deleting the connection to their former root elements (and the superfluous *Doc-File*) as is depicted on the right side of Fig. 2. However, no rule of the current grammar is able to perform such a change and to modify the triple by hand is a tedious and error-prone task that can create triples which do not longer comply with the TGG language. To solve this issue and to create a triple graph which contains *Package* p and *Folder* f as additional roots (and is unmodified otherwise) we have to proceed as follows: We have to roll back all rule applications except the first one (*CreateRoot-Rule*) and recreate the deleted parts of the graph triple from scratch again – despite the fact that the intended modification affects only a small portion of the graph triple. Executing this strategy with large hierarchies has two major disadvantages. First, it is tedious and might be computationally expensive for complex models. Second, one may loose a large amount of manually added data.

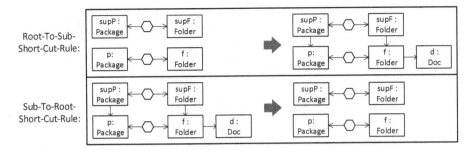

Fig. 3. Two examples for short-cut rules (interface K of rules given implicitly as $L \cap R$)

However, when studying the TGG rules of Fig. 1 in detail, we see that *CreateRoot-Rule* and *CreateSub-Rule* have common substructures, i.e., we can find nodes and edges of the same type arranged in the same way in left- and right-hand sides of both rules. In our example, such a common substructure of their right-hand sides (RHS) R stems from the fact that both rules create a *Package* and a *Folder* together with a correspondence link between those two elements. It consists of the *Folders* f and *Packages* p but does not include the *Doc-File* only contained by *CreateSub-Rule*.

Taking a closer look at our example in Fig. 2, one can see how this insight propagates to the model level and that the only difference between a root-*Folder* and a sub-*Folder* is that the latter one possesses an additional *Doc-File* and has an incoming hierarchy edge. Hence, one might want to exploit this knowledge by replacing a TGG rule application somewhere in a sequence of rule applications by another similar rule application such that formerly created elements are possibly preserved and the need to roll back sub-sequences does not arise. In the current case this would mean to preserve all elements that are contained in the **root** elements by changing the *CreateSub-Rule*-application to become a *CreateRoot-Rule*-application. Therefore, we have to use the common parts of both rules to create a new rule which directly transforms the left to the right graph triple depicted in Fig. 2, which again is an element of the language of the TGG of Fig. 1. Thus, the result of the application of such a 'short-cut rule' looks like the composition of the effects of the reverse application of *CreateSub-Rule* followed by the application of *CreateRoot-Rule*. Implicitly, the application of the short-cut rule operates as a kind of meta-rule on sequences of TGG rule applications as it replaces an occurrence of a rule with the occurrence of another rule in an arbitrarily long sequence of rule applications. Figure 3 depicts two short-cut rules that enable to replace *CreateRoot-Rule* with *CreateSub-Rule* and vice versa. In our example, *Sub-To-Root-Short-Cut-Rule* replaces an occurrence of *CreateSub-Rule* with an occurrence of *CreateRoot-Rule* as shown in Fig. 4. Note, however, that short-cut rules extend the set of rules rather than replace it.

It, thus, preserves the consistency of the graph triple of Fig. 2 by selecting the elements p and f as new root elements and by deleting the now superfluous

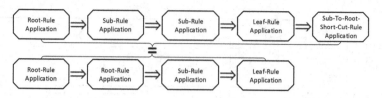

Fig. 4. Example: application of short-cut rule

d element associated with f as well as the edges connecting `rootP` and `rootF` to
p and f, respectively. This singular application of one short-cut rule stands in
contrast to the deletion and recreation of the affected triple graph from scratch.

3   Preliminaries

Since adhesive categories [6] provide a suitable formal framework generalizing
many instances of rule-based rewriting of graph-like structures (including triple
graphs), we present our work in that setting. This section shortly recalls the
definition of rule-based transformation systems. For a short recapitulation of
adhesive categories and some of their properties and most of the proofs, we refer
to the long version of this paper [4].

Rules are a declarative way to define transformations of objects. They consist
of a left-hand side (LHS) L, a right-hand side (RHS) R, and a common subobject
K, the interface of the rule. In case of (typed) triple graphs, application of a rule
p to a graph G amounts to choosing an image of the rule's LHS L in G, deleting
the image of $L \setminus K$ and adding a copy of $R \setminus K$. This procedure can be formalized,
also in the more general setting of adhesive categories, by two pushouts. Rules
and their application semantics are defined as follows.

Definition 1 (Rules and adhesive HLR systems). *Given an adhesive category C, a rule (or production) p consists of three objects L, K, and R, called left-
hand side, interface (or gluing object), and right-hand side, and two monomor-
phisms $l : K \hookrightarrow L, r : K \hookrightarrow R$. Given a rule $p = (L \xleftarrow{l} K \xrightarrow{r} R)$, the inverse
rule p^{-1} is defined as $p^{-1} = (R \xleftarrow{r} K \xrightarrow{l} L)$. A rule $p = (L \xleftarrow{l} K \xrightarrow{r} R)$ is called
monotonic (or non-deleting) if $l : K \hookrightarrow L$ is an isomorphism. In that case we
just write $r : L \hookrightarrow R$.*

*A subrule p' of a rule $p = (L \xleftarrow{l} K \xrightarrow{r} R)$ is a
rule $p' = (L' \xleftarrow{l'} K' \xrightarrow{r'} R')$ with monomorphisms
$u : L' \hookrightarrow L, w : K' \hookrightarrow K, v : R' \hookrightarrow R$ such that both
squares in the diagram to the right are pullbacks and
a pushout complement for $u \circ l'$ exists.*

$$
\begin{array}{ccccc}
L' & \xleftarrow{\;\;l'\;\;} & K' & \xhookrightarrow{\;\;r'\;\;} & R' \\
{\scriptstyle u}\downarrow & & {\scriptstyle w}\downarrow & & \downarrow{\scriptstyle v} \\
L & \xleftarrow{\;\;l\;\;} & K & \xhookrightarrow{\;\;r\;\;} & R
\end{array}
$$

A common kernel rule p for rules p_1 and p_2 is a common subrule of both.

*An adhesive high-level replacement system (or HLR system for short) con-
sists of an adhesive category C and a set of rules P in that category.*

Figure 3 and 1 depict rules in the category of triple graphs. The first are monotonic, the second set includes a general rule. Together they form an HLR system.

For the construction of short-cut rules, we are mainly interested in common kernel rules of monotonic rules, which we will denote by $k : L_\cap \hookrightarrow R_\cap$. They are necessarily monotonic themselves. Note that, in adhesive categories with strict initial object, i.e., with initial object $\emptyset$ where each morphism into $\emptyset$ is an isomorphism, the *trivial common kernel rule* $id_\emptyset : \emptyset \hookrightarrow \emptyset$ is a common kernel rule for any two monotonic rules r_1 and r_2. Such strict initial objects exist, e.g., in the categories of sets, graphs, and triple graphs.

The next definition determines the semantics of the application of a rule.

Definition 2 (Transformation).
In an adhesive category $\boldsymbol{C}$, *given a rule* $p =$
$(L \xleftarrow{l} K \xrightarrow{r} R)$, *an object* G, *and a monomor-phism* $m : L \hookrightarrow G$, *called* match, *a (direct) transformation* $G \Rightarrow_{p,m} H$ *from* G *to* H *via* p *at match* m *is given by the diagram to the right where both squares are pushouts.*

$$
\begin{array}{ccccc}
L & \xleftarrow{\;\;l\;\;} & K & \xhookrightarrow{\;\;r\;\;} & R \\
m \uparrow & & \uparrow & & \uparrow n \\
G & \longleftarrow & D & \hookrightarrow & H
\end{array}
$$

A rule p *is called* applicable *at match* m *if the first pushout square above exists, i.e., if* $m \circ l$ *has a pushout complement. When applying a rule* p *to an object* G, *the arising object* D *is called the* context *object of the transformation.*

4 Construction Process

In this section, we formalize the construction of short-cut rules. As explained in Sect. 2, a short-cut rule is a composition of a monotonic rule r_2 with the inverse rule r_1^{-1} of a monotonic rule r_1. The composition is done in such a way that the short-cut rule may preserve certain elements which an inverse application of r_1 would delete and an application of r_2 would recreate. The extent to which preservation of elements takes place is flexible, depending on a chosen common kernel rule of the two rules. In the following, we first present the construction of a short-cut rule given a common kernel rule. Afterwards, we prove the correctness of the construction and discuss its merits.

We use common kernel rules to construct short-cut rules. Given a common kernel rule k of monotonic rules r_1 and r_2, their short-cut rule $r_1^{-1} \ltimes_k r_2$ arises by gluing r_1^{-1} and r_2 along k. The LHS of k contains the information how to glue r_1^{-1} and r_2 to receive the LHS L and the RHS R of the short-cut rule $r_1^{-1} \ltimes_k r_2$. I.e., $r_1^{-1} \ltimes_k r_2$ is constructed in such a way, that a match for it consists of matches for r_1^{-1} and r_2 which intersect in the LHS of k. The RHS of k contains the information how to construct the interface K of the short-cut rule $r_1^{-1} \ltimes_k r_2$. In case of (triple) graphs, elements of $R_\cap \setminus L_\cap$ are included in K, i.e., $R_\cap \setminus L_\cap$ specifies exactly those elements that would have been deleted by r_1^{-1} and recreated by r_2. Hence, they are to be preserved when applying the short-cut rule.

Definition 3 (Short-cut rule). *In an adhesive category C, given two monotonic rules $r_i : L_i \hookrightarrow R_i$, $i = 1, 2$, and a common kernel rule $k : L_\cap \hookrightarrow R_\cap$ for them, the short-cut rule $r_1^{-1} \ltimes_k r_2 := (L \overset{l}{\hookleftarrow} K \overset{r}{\hookrightarrow} R)$ is computed by executing the following steps:*

1. *The union $L_\cup$ of L_1 and L_2 along $L_\cap$ is computed as pushout (2) in Fig. 5.*
2. *The LHS L of the short-cut rule $r_1^{-1} \ltimes_k r_2$ is constructed as pushout (3a) in Fig. 5.*
3. *The RHS R of the short-cut rule $r_1^{-1} \ltimes_k r_2$ is constructed as pushout (3b) in Fig. 5.*
4. *The interface K of the short-cut rule $r_1^{-1} \ltimes_k r_2$ is constructed as pushout (4) in Fig. 6.*
5. *Morphisms $l : K \to L$ and $r : K \to R$ are obtained by the universal property of K.*

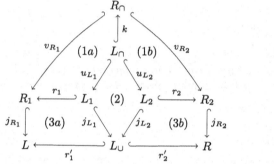

Fig. 5. Construction of LHS and RHS of short-cut rule $r_1^{-1} \ltimes_k r_2$

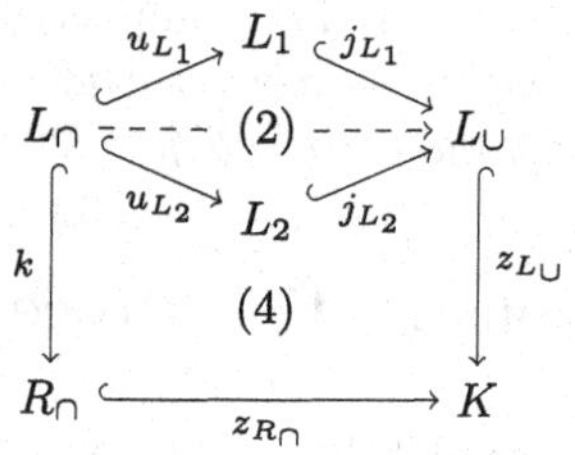

Fig. 6. Construction of interface K of $r_1^{-1} \ltimes_k r_2$

Example 4. We illustrate the construction of short-cut rules with a detailed example. First, *CreateRoot-Rule* is a (non-trivial) common kernel rule for *CreateSub-Rule* and itself, as depicted in Fig. 7. Here, and in the following figures, morphisms are indicated by the names of the nodes; the mapping of edges follows unambiguously. Hence, *CreateRoot-Rule* is embedded into itself via the identity morphism and its RHS is mapped to nodes p of type *Package* and f of type *Folder* in the RHS of *CreateSub-Rule*; the morphism between the LHSs is the unique empty map.

Next, computation of $L_\cup$ and the LHS and RHS of the short-cut rule is done by computing the three pushouts as depicted in Fig. 8. It is a concrete instantiation of the lower part of the diagram depicted in Fig. 5. The two pushouts to the left and in the middle are pushouts along the empty triple graph, i.e., the respective objects are just copied next to each other. The pushout to the right is a pushout along an isomorphism, hence the resulting morphism to the very right is an isomorphism as well.

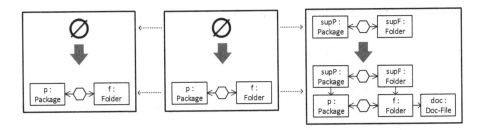

Fig. 7. *CreateRoot-Rule* as common kernel rule for *CreateSub-Rule* and itself

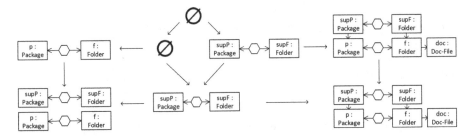

Fig. 8. Construction of LHS and RHS of a short-cut rule for *CreateRoot-Rule* and *CreateSub-Rule*

Lastly, the interface of the short-cut rule is calculated as pushout as depicted in Fig. 9. It is a concrete instantiation of the diagram depicted in Fig. 6. As pushout along the empty triple graph, again, the resulting triple graph consists of copies of the two triples at the lower left and the upper right. The monomorphisms from the interface into the LHS and RHS computed above, are, again, indicated by the names of the nodes. Thus, the resulting short-cut rule is *Root-To-Sub-Short-Cut-Rule* as displayed in Fig. 3 or in the upper part of Fig. 12.

The following lemma ensures that short-cut rules are rules in the sense of Definition 1, i.e., that the morphisms from the interface to the LHS and RHS are monomorphisms. (Such rules are also called *linear* rules.)

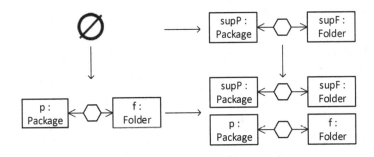

Fig. 9. Construction of the interface of a short-cut rule

Lemma 5 (Linearity of short-cut rule). *In an adhesive category C, given two monotonic rules $r_i : L_i \hookrightarrow R_i$, $i = 1, 2$, and a common kernel rule $k : L_\cap \hookrightarrow R_\cap$ for them, the induced morphisms $l : K \to L$ and $r : K \to R$ in the short-cut rule $r_1^{-1} \ltimes_k r_2$ are monomorphisms.*

The next definition relates common kernel rules for rules r_1, r_2 with sequences of applications of r_1^{-1} and r_2.

Definition 6 (Compatibility).
Given a sequence $G_1 \Rightarrow_{r_1^{-1}, m_1}$ $G \Rightarrow_{r_2, m_2} G_2$ of rule applications, where rules r_1 and r_2 are monotonic, and a common kernel rule $k : L_\cap \hookrightarrow R_\cap$ for these rules, then k is called compatible with the application sequence *if the resulting square (5) in the diagram to the right is a pullback.*

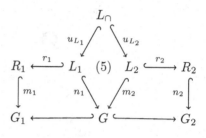

Compatibility as defined above ensures the existence of a unique morphism $h : L_\cup \hookrightarrow G$ such that $n_1 = h \circ j_{L_1}$ and $m_2 = h \circ j_{L_2}$ (compare pushout square (2) in Fig. 5). Moreover, in adhesive categories h is a monomorphism. Note that, given a sequence of rule applications, a compatible common kernel rule can always be obtained by computing $L_\cap$ and the corresponding embeddings into L_1, L_2 as pullback and setting $R_\cap = L_\cap$ (with the embedding being the identity).

The following Short-cut Theorem is our main result. Its synthesis part states that an inverse application of a monotonic rule followed by an application of a monotonic rule may indeed be replaced by an application of a short-cut rule. Its analysis part states that the application of a short-cut rule may be split into the reverse application of a monotonic rule followed by the application of a second one if the reverse application of the first rule is possible at all. Its proof makes use of a technical lemma, stating the equivalence of the existence of certain pushout complements, whose statement we postpone towards the end of this section. If analysis is possible then synthesis and analysis are inverse to each other.

Theorem 7 (Short-cut Theorem). *In an adhesive category C, let $r_i : L_i \hookrightarrow R_i$, $i = 1, 2$, be two monotonic rules, $k : L_\cap \hookrightarrow R_\cap$ a common kernel rule for them, and $r_1^{-1} \ltimes_k r_2$ the corresponding short-cut rule. Then the following holds:*

1. **Synthesis:** *For each transformation sequence $G_1 \Rightarrow_{r_1^{-1}, m_1} G \Rightarrow_{r_2, m_2} G_2$ compatible with k there exists a direct transformation $G_1 \Rightarrow_{r_1^{-1} \ltimes_k r_2, m_1'} G_2$ with context object G' and a monomorphism $g : G \hookrightarrow G'$, s. t. $m_1' \circ j_{R_1} = m_1$.*
2. **Conditional Analysis:** *Given a direct transformation $G_1 \Rightarrow_{r_1^{-1} \ltimes_k r_2, m_1'} G_2$ with context object G' such that a pushout complement for $m_1 \circ r_1 : L_1 \hookrightarrow G_1$ exists, where $m_1 = m_1' \circ j_{R_1}$, then there exists a transformation sequence $G_1 \Rightarrow_{r_1^{-1}, m_1} G \Rightarrow_{r_2, m_2} G_2$ compatible with k. Moreover, a monomorphism $g : G \hookrightarrow G'$ exists.*

3. **Correspondence:** *In those cases, where the pushout complement necessary for the analysis construction exists, the synthesis and analysis constructions are inverse to each other (up to isomorphism).*

Proof. 1. Let a transformation $G_1 \Rightarrow_{r_1^{-1}, m_1} G \Rightarrow_{r_2, m_2} G_2$ be given. The outer square in Fig. 10 is the pushout given by the application of r_1^{-1} with match m_1 and (3a) is the pushout used to define L. Since the transformation sequence is compatible with k, a unique monomorphism $h : L_\cup \hookrightarrow G$ with $n_1 = h \circ j_{L_1}$ exists. Since (3a) is a pushout, $m_1' : L \hookrightarrow G_1$ exists. In an adhesive category, it is a monomorphism since $G \hookrightarrow G_1$ and $m_1 : R_1 \hookrightarrow G_1$ are monomorphisms. By pushout decomposition, the resulting square (6)+(7a) is a pushout. Define (6) again by taking the pushout. Like above, the resulting map $G' \hookrightarrow G_1$ is a monomorphism and square (7a) is a pushout by pushout decomposition. Thus, rule $r_1^{-1} \ltimes_k r_2$ is applicable at G_1 with match m_1' and G' is the context object of the resulting transformation. Moreover, G embeds into G' by $g : G \hookrightarrow G'$.

Comparing Fig. 11, an analogous argument shows that G_2 is the pushout of $r : K \hookrightarrow R$ and $n_1' : K \hookrightarrow G'$. Altogether, the resulting transformation, applying $r_1^{-1} \ltimes_k r_2$ at match m_1', consists of (7a) and (7b).

2. Let a direct transformation $G_1 \Rightarrow_{r_1^{-1} \ltimes_k r_2, m_1'} G_2$ with context object G' be given. Defining $m_1 = m_1' \circ j_{R_1}$ gives a match for r_1^{-1} in G_1. By assumption, the rule r_1^{-1} is applicable at that match, i.e., a pushout complement for $m_1 \circ r_1 : L_1 \hookrightarrow G_1$ exists (compare again Fig. 10). Lemma 9 states that the existence of such a pushout complement is equivalent to the existence of a pushout complement for $n_1' \circ z_{L_\cup} : L_\cup \hookrightarrow G'$ (with arising objects being isomorphic). Therefore, application of r_1^{-1} at match m_1 results in an object G with morphism $g : G \to G'$ to the context object of the transformation $G_1 \Rightarrow_{r_1^{-1} \ltimes_k r_2, m_1'} G_2$. The morphism g is a monomorphism, since pushout (6) is a pushout along the monomorphism $z_{L_\cup}$.

Define $m_2 := h \circ j_{L_2} : L_2 \hookrightarrow G$ as match for r_2 in G (compare again Fig. 11). Then, since (3b), (6), and (7b) are pushouts, the outer square is also a pushout, and hence G_2 is the result of applying r_2 with match m_2 at G. Moreover, by definition of m_2, the resulting transformation sequence is compatible to k.

3. If the analysis construction is possible, the synthesis and analysis constructions are inverse to each other because pushout complements along monomorphisms and pushouts are unique (up to isomorphism) in adhesive categories.   □

The following lemma states that, generally, the monomorphism $g : G \hookrightarrow G'$, arising in both the synthesis and the analysis construction above, is not an isomorphism. Thus, in case of (triple) graphs, applying a short-cut rule instead of the original rules actually preserves elements, namely the elements of $G' \setminus G$.

Lemma 8 (Preservation). *In an adhesive category C, let $r_i : L_i \hookrightarrow R_i$, $i = 1, 2$, be two monotonic rules and $k : L_\cap \hookrightarrow R_\cap$ a common kernel rule for them. Let $g : G \hookrightarrow G'$ be a monomorphism arising by synthesis of a transformation sequence $G_1 \Rightarrow_{r_1^{-1}, m_1} G \Rightarrow_{r_2, m_2} G_2$ or by analysis of a transformation*

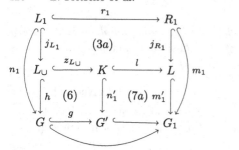
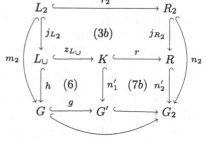

Fig. 10. Synthesis and analysis: formation of context object G'

Fig. 11. Synthesis and analysis: result of rule application

$G_1 \Rightarrow_{r_1^{-1} \ltimes_k r_2, m_1'} G_2$ *(compare Theorem 7, especially Figs. 10 and 11). Then g is an isomorphism iff k is.*

Before concluding this section with a discussion of the value of short-cut rules, we state the lemma used in the proof of Theorem 7.

Lemma 9 (Characterization of PO-complements). *In any adhesive category with initial pushouts, given a commutative diagram like Fig. 10 where (3a) and (7a) are pushouts, a pushout complement object G for $m_1 \circ r_1 : L_1 \hookrightarrow G_1$ is a pushout complement object for $n_1' \circ z_{L_\cup} : L_\cup \hookrightarrow G'$ and vice versa. Particularly, a pushout complement for $m_1 \circ r_1 : L_1 \hookrightarrow G_1$ exists iff a pushout complement for $n_1' \circ z_{L_\cup} : L_\cup \hookrightarrow G'$ exists.*

Benefits and Limitations of Short-Cut Rules. We motivated the use of short-cut rules twofold. (1) That the application of short-cut rules generally preserves elements instead of deleting and recreating them, as stated in Lemma 8. (2) That the application of a short-cut rule may actually amount to a 'short-cut' which is due to the asymmetry of synthesis and analysis in the Short-Cut Theorem. Applications of the short-cut rules *Sub-To-Root-Short-Cut-Rule* and *Root-To-Sub-Short-Cut-Rule* (Fig. 3) with the obvious matches transform between the two consistent triples depicted in Fig. 2. But in either case, dangling edges prevent the analysis of the short-cut rule's application into a sequence of two rule applications. Thus, the subsequent applications of rules in the upper transformation chain in Fig. 4 would need to be revoked first, before a reverse application of the respective second rule application is possible in the first place.

However, not every application of a short-cut rule, that may not be analyzed, is a 'short-cut'. For example, applying the short-cut rule *Root-To-Sub-Short-Cut-Rule* to the left instance in Fig. 2, but with nodes `rootP` and `subP` of type *Package* and `rootF` and `subF` of type *Folder* as match instead, creates additional container edges for nodes `subP` and `subF` and a second *Doc-File* inside of node `subF`. This instance is not an element of the language defined by the original TGG (Fig. 1). This stems from the fact that the short-cut rule *Root-To-Sub-Short-Cut-Rule* revokes an application of the rule *CreateRoot*, while the elements chosen to be revoked by the match have actually been created using the rule *CreateSub*.

A first possible strategy to resolve that issue is the development of application conditions [5] for short-cut rules ensuring that a short-cut rule is only applicable at matches on which it revokes the proper rule. For example, the short-cut rule *Root-To-Sub-Short-Cut-Rule* could be equipped with an application condition forbidding the existence of incoming edges to nodes p and f, respectively. Another possible strategy is the use of marked TGGs and trace information [7] to the same end, i.e., to only allow those matches for a short-cut rule where the rule that was actually used to create the structure is revoked. We plan to further elaborate and compare between both strategies as future work. Our aim is to arrive at short-cut rules whose application does not divert from the language defined by the HLR system from which the short-cut rules were derived.

5   Related Work: Comparison to Other Formalisms of Rule Composition

In the literature, there exist several formalisms for composition of rules, most importantly *parallel, concurrent*, and *amalgamated rules* [1–3]. We relate our construction of short-cut rules to these other formalisms. A common difference to short-cut rules is that the parallel, concurrent, and amalgamated rule constructions are defined for general rules, whereas our construction of short-cut rules is restricted to the case of monotonic rules for now. Therefore, in this section, we first recall the relevant constructions generally and then relate these to our construction of short-cut rules in the special case of monotonic rules.

The parallel rule of two rules combines their respective actions into one rule. Two independent direct transformations arising by applications of these rules may alternatively be replaced by an application of their parallel rule [2].

Definition 10 (Parallel rule). *Given an adhesive category $\boldsymbol{C}$ with binary coproducts, the parallel rule $p_1 + p_2$ of two rules $p_i = (L_i \xleftarrow{l_i} K_i \xrightarrow{r_i} R_i)$, $i = 1, 2$, is defined by $p_1 + p_2 = (L_1 + L_2 \xleftarrow{l_1 + l_2} K_1 + K_2 \xrightarrow{r_1 + r_2} R_1 + R_2)$, where $+$ denotes the coproduct or the induced morphism, respectively.*

In categories with strict initial object (explained in Sect. 3) short-cut rules along the trivial common kernel rule are the same as parallel rules. This is, e.g., the case in the category of (triple) graphs, where the empty (triple) graph is the (only) strict initial object.

Proposition 11 (Relation to parallel rule). *Let two monotonic rules r_i : $L_i \hookrightarrow R_i$, $i = 1, 2$, in an adhesive category $\boldsymbol{C}$ with strict initial object $\emptyset$ be given. Then, for the trivial common kernel rule $id_\emptyset : \emptyset \hookrightarrow \emptyset$, the short-cut and the parallel rule coincide, i.e., $r_1^{-1} + r_2 = r_1^{-1} \ltimes_{id_\emptyset} r_2$.*

Like the parallel rule, a so-called E-concurrent rule combines the action of two rule applications into the application of one rule. But here, the rule applications may be sequentially dependent [2]. An E-dependency relation encodes this possible dependency. The definition of E-dependency relations and E-concurrent rules assumes a given class $\mathcal{E}$ of pairs of morphisms with the same codomain.

Definition 12 (*E*-dependency relation and *E*-concurrent rule). *Given two rules* $p_i = (L_i \xleftarrow{l_i} K_i \xrightarrow{r_i} R_i)$, $i = 1, 2$, *an object E with morphisms* $e_1 : R_1 \to E$ *and* $e_2 : L_2 \to E$ *is an E-dependency relation for p_1 and p_2 if* $(e_1, e_2) \in \mathcal{E}$ *and the pushout complements (8a) and (8a) over* $K_1 \xrightarrow{r_1} R_1 \xrightarrow{e_1} E$ *and* $K_2 \xrightarrow{l_2} L_2 \xrightarrow{e_2} E$ *as depicted below exist.*

Given an E-dependency relation $(e_1, e_2) \in \mathcal{E}$ *for rules p_1, p_2, the E-concurrent rule $p_1 *_E p_2$ is defined by* $p_1 *_E p_2 := (L \xleftarrow{lok_1} K \xrightarrow{rok_2} R)$ *as shown below, where (9a) and (9b) are pushouts and (10) is a pullback.*

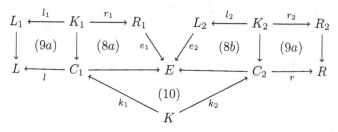

The amalgamated rule combines the actions of two, maybe parallel dependent, rule applications into one rule [1,3].

Definition 13 (Amalgamated rule).

Given a common subrule $p = (L \xleftarrow{l} K \xrightarrow{r} R)$ *of rules* $p_i = (L_i \xleftarrow{l_i} K_i \xrightarrow{r_i} R_i)$, $i = 1, 2$, *the amalgamated rule* $p_1 \oplus_p p_2 = (L' \xleftarrow{l'} K' \xrightarrow{r'} R')$ *is constructed by taking the three pushouts depicted to the right, where morphisms* l', r' *are given by the universal property of pushout object K'.*

We now relate short-cut rules to *E*-concurrent and amalgamated rules of rules, where the first rule only deletes and the second rule only creates. Further, we take $\mathcal{E}$ to be the class of pairs of morphisms which are jointly epimorphic and where both morphisms are monomorphisms, i.e., the following statements for concurrent rules hold under that assumption. To begin, both concurrent and amalgamated rules "degenerate" in that setting. They are merely constructed as sums over constant rules.

Lemma 14 (Degeneration). *Let two monotonic rules $r_i : L_i \hookrightarrow R_i$, $i = 1, 2$, in an adhesive category C be given. Then the classes of E-concurrent rules and amalgamated rules for r_1^{-1} and r_2 coincide. In particular, they both coincide with $C := \{r_1^{-1} \oplus_p r_2 \,|\, p = (X_1 \xleftarrow{x_1} X \xrightarrow{x_2} X_2)$, x_1, x_2 isomorphisms, and p common subrule of $r_1, r_2\}$, i.e., the class of rules amalgamated along a common constant subrule of r_1^{-1} and r_2.*

As a consequence of the above lemma, in our context every E-concurrent or amalgamated rule can be constructed as a short-cut rule. On the contrary, concrete examples show that short-cut rules exist which cannot be constructed as E-concurrent or amalgamated rule (and hence neither as parallel rule).

Proposition 15 (Subsumption). *Let two monotonic rules $r_i : L_i \hookrightarrow R_i$, $i = 1, 2$, in an adhesive category C be given. Then every E-concurrent or amalgamated rule for r_1^{-1} and r_2 coincides with a short-cut rule for them, but generally not the other way around, i.e., generally the class C of E-concurrent and amalgamated rules for r_1^{-1} and r_2 (Lemma 14) is properly contained in the class $C' := \{r_1^{-1} \ltimes_k r_2 \mid k : L_\cap \hookrightarrow R_\cap$ is a common kernel rule for $r_1, r_2\}$ of short-cut rules for r_1^{-1} and r_2.*

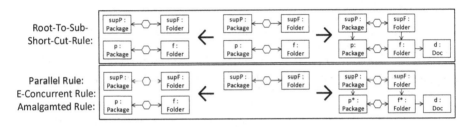

Root-To-Sub-Short-Cut-Rule:

Parallel Rule:
E-Concurrent Rule:
Amalgamted Rule:

Fig. 12. Relating short-cut rule to other formalisms of rule composition

Idea of Proof. To show the containment relationship, it suffices to check that $r_1^{-1} \oplus_p r_2 = r_1^{-1} \ltimes_p r_2$ for a common constant subrule p of r_1^{-1} and r_2 (in particular, p is a common kernel rule for r_1 and r_2).

As stated in Example 4, *Root-To-Sub-Short-Cut-Rule* is the short-cut rule for the inverse rule of *CreateRoot-Rule* and *CreateSub-Rule* along *CreateRoot-Rule* as common kernel rule. Their parallel rule and the only possibility for an amalgamated or E-concurrent rule is the second rule depicted in Fig. 12, which differs from the short-cut rule in its interface graph.   □

6   Conclusion

In this paper, we formally introduced short-cut rules for monotonic rules in adhesive HLR systems, a novel kind of rule composition. We proved that short-cut rules preserve information instead of deleting elements and recreating them again, when revoking a transformation and applying another one instead. Additionally, we gave examples using a TGG where applying short-cut rules spares us rolling back whole chains of transformations, thus providing 'short-cuts' when revising those. Moreover, we proved short-cut rules to differ from the already established formalizations for composition of rules, i.e., the parallel, concurrent, and amalgamated rules.

Besides developing language-preserving short-cut rules (as already discussed at the end of Sect. 4), we plan to develop a construction of short-cut rules for general rules, also, and advance the theory of short-cut rules by respecting possible application conditions of the involved rules. On the practical side, we plan to operationalize short-cut rules stemming from TGGs to enhance model synchronization.

Acknowledgments. This work was partially funded by the German Research Foundation (DFG), project "Triple Graph Grammars (TGG) 2.0".

References

1. Boehm, P., Fonio, H.R., Habel, A.: Amalgamation of graph transformations. A synchronization mechanism. J. Comput. Syst. Sci. **34**(2), 377–408 (1987). https://doi.org/10.1016/0022-0000(87)90030-4
2. Ehrig, H., Ehrig, K., Prange, U., Taentzer, G.: Fundamentals of Algebraic Graph Transformation. Monographs in Theoretical Computer Science. Springer, Heidelberg (2006). https://doi.org/10.1007/3-540-31188-2
3. Ehrig, H., Golas, U., Habel, A., Lambers, L., Orejas, F.: $\mathcal{M}$-adhesive transformation systems with nested application conditions. Part 1: parallelism, concurrency and amalgamation. Math. Struct. Comput. Sci. **24**(4), 240406 (2014). https://doi.org/10.1017/S0960129512000357
4. Fritsche, L., Kosiol, J., Schürr, A., Taentzer, G.: Short-cut rules. Sequential composition of rules avoiding unnecessary deletions: extended version. Technical report, Philipps-Universität Marburg (2018). https://www.uni-marburg.de/fb12/arbeitsgruppen/swt/forschung/publikationen/2018/FKST18-TR.pdf
5. Habel, A., Pennemann, K.H.: Correctness of high-level transformation systems relative to nested conditions. Math. Struct. Comput. Sci. **19**(2), 245–296 (2009). https://doi.org/10.1017/S0960129508007202
6. Lack, S., Sobociński, P.: Adhesive and quasiadhesive categories. Theor. Inf. Appl. **39**(3), 511–545 (2005). https://doi.org/10.1051/ita:2005028
7. Leblebici, E., Anjorin, A., Fritsche, L., Varró, G., Schürr, A.: Leveraging incremental pattern matching techniques for model synchronisation. In: de Lara, J., Plump, D. (eds.) ICGT 2017. LNCS, vol. 10373, pp. 179–195. Springer, Cham (2017). https://doi.org/10.1007/978-3-319-61470-0_11
8. Leblebici, E., Anjorin, A., Schürr, A., Taentzer, G.: Multi-amalgamated triple graph grammars: formal foundation and application to visual language translation. J. Vis. Lang. Comput. **42**, 99–121 (2017). https://doi.org/10.1016/j.jvlc.2016.03.001
9. Leblebici, E., Anjorin, A., Schürr, A.: Inter-model consistency checking using triple graph grammars and linear optimization techniques. In: Huisman, M., Rubin, J. (eds.) FASE 2017. LNCS, vol. 10202, pp. 191–207. Springer, Heidelberg (2017). https://doi.org/10.1007/978-3-662-54494-5_11
10. Schürr, A.: Specification of graph translators with triple graph grammars. In: Mayr, E.W., Schmidt, G., Tinhofer, G. (eds.) WG 1994. LNCS, vol. 903, pp. 151–163. Springer, Heidelberg (1995). https://doi.org/10.1007/3-540-59071-4_45

Graph Repair by Graph Programs

Annegret Habel and Christian Sandmann[(✉)]

Universität Oldenburg, Oldenburg, Germany
{habel,sandmann}@informatik.uni-oldenburg.de

Abstract. Model repair is an essential topic in model-driven engineering. We consider the problem of graph repair: Given a graph constraint, we try to construct a graph program, such that the application to any graph yields a graph satisfying the graph constraint. We show the existence of terminating repair programs for a number of satisfiable constraints.

1 Introduction

In model-driven software engineering the primary artifacts are models, which have to be consistent wrt. a set of constraints (see e.g. [EEGH15]). To increase the productivity of software development, it is necessary to automatically detect and resolve inconsistencies arising during the development process, called model repair (see, e.g. [NEF03, MGC13, NKR17]). Since models can be represented as graph-like structures [BET12], in this paper, we consider the problem of *graph repair*: Given a graph constraint, we try to construct a graph program, called *repair program*, such that the application to any graph yields a graph satisfying the graph constraint.

Repair problem

> **Given:** A graph constraint d.
> **Task:** Find a graph program P: $\forall G \Rightarrow_P H$. $H \models d$.

More specifically, we look for repair programs that are terminating and maximally preserving, meaning that an input graph is preserved as long as there is no requirement for non-existence of items.

Our general aim is to construct repair programs for all satisfiable conditions. In this paper, we show that there are terminating repair programs for a large class of satisfiable conditions (without conjunctions and disjunctions), for

This work is partly supported by the German Research Foundation (DFG), Grants HA 2936/4-2 and TA 2941/3-2 (Meta-Modeling and Graph Grammars: Generating Development Environments for Modeling Languages).

M. Mazzara et al. (Eds.): STAF 2018 Workshops, LNCS 11176, pp. 431–446, 2018.
https://doi.org/10.1007/978-3-030-04771-9_31

conjunctions $d_1 \wedge d_2$ provided that there are terminating repair programs for the subconditions and one program preserves the other constraint, and for disjunctions $d_1 \vee d_2$ provided that there are terminating repair program for some subcondition.

The structure of the paper is as follows. In Sect. 2, we review the definitions of graphs, graph conditions, and graph programs. In Sect. 3, we present repair programs for "proper" conditions, i.e., conditions with alternating quantifiers ending with **true** or of the form $\exists (A, \nexists C)$, without conjunctions and disjunctions. In Sect. 4, we collect some results for the conjunction and disjunction of constraints. In Sect. 5, we present some related concepts. In Sect. 6, we give a conclusion and mention some further work.

2   Preliminaries

In the following, we recall the definitions of directed, labelled graphs, graph conditions, rules, and graph programs [EEPT06, HP09].

A directed, labelled graph consists of a set of nodes and a set of edges where each edge is equipped with a source and a target node and where each node and edge is equipped with a label.

Definition 1 (graphs & morphisms). A *(directed, labelled) graph* (over a label alphabet $\mathcal{L}$) is a system $G = (V_G, E_G, s_G, t_G, l_{V,G}, l_{E,G})$ where V_G and E_G are finite sets of *nodes* (or *vertices*) and *edges*, $s_G, t_G \colon E_G \to V_G$ are total functions assigning *source* and *target* to each edge, and $l_{V,G} \colon V_G \to \mathcal{L}$, $l_{E,G} \colon E_G \to \mathcal{L}$ are labeling functions. If $V_G = \emptyset$, then G is the *empty graph*, denoted by $\emptyset$. A graph is *unlabelled* if the label alphabet is a singleton. Given graphs G and H, a *(graph) morphism* $g \colon G \to H$ consists of total functions $g_V \colon V_G \to V_H$ and $g_E \colon E_G \to E_H$ that preserve sources, targets, and labels, that is, $g_V \circ s_G = s_H \circ g_E$, $g_V \circ t_G = t_H \circ g_E$, $l_{V,G} = l_{V,H} \circ g_V$, $l_{E,G} = l_{E,H} \circ g_E$. The morphism g is *injective* (*surjective*) if g_V and g_E are injective (surjective), and an *isomorphism* if it is injective and surjective. In the latter case, G and H are *isomorphic*, which is denoted by $G \cong H$. An injective morphism $g \colon G \hookrightarrow H$ is an *inclusion morphism* if $g_V(v) = v$ and $g_E(e) = e$ for all $v \in V_G$ and all $e \in E_G$.

Graph conditions are nested constructs, which can be represented as trees of morphisms equipped with quantifiers and Boolean connectives. Graph conditions and first-order graph formulas are expressively equivalent [HP09].

Definition 2 (graph conditions). A *(graph) condition* over a graph P is of the form (a) **true** or (b) $\exists (a, c)$ where $a \colon P \hookrightarrow C$ is a proper inclusion morphism[1] and c is a condition over C. For conditions c, c_i ($i \in I$ for some finite index set I) over P, $\neg c$ and $\wedge_{i \in I} c_i$ are conditions over P. Conditions over the empty graph $\emptyset$ are called *constraints*. In the context of rules, conditions are called *application conditions*.

---

[1] Without loss of generality, we may assume that the conditions are *proper*, i.e., for all inclusion morphisms $a \colon P \hookrightarrow C$ in the condition, P is a proper subgraph of C.

Graph conditions may be written in a more compact form: $\exists a$ abbreviates $\exists (a, \mathtt{true})$, $\mathtt{false}$ abbreviates $\neg\mathtt{true}$ and $\forall(a, c)$ abbreviates $\nexists (a, \neg c)$. The expressions $\vee_{i \in I} c_i$ and $c \Rightarrow c'$ are defined as usual. For an inclusion morphism $a \colon P \hookrightarrow C$ in a condition, we just depict the codomain C, if the domain P can be unambiguously inferred. Conditions of the form $\exists C$ and $\nexists C$ are *positive* and *negative*, respectively. Conditions of the form $\forall(A, \exists C)$ are $\forall\exists$-*conditions*.

Definition 3 (semantics). Any injective morphism $p \colon P \hookrightarrow G$ satisfies $\mathtt{true}$. An injective morphism p *satisfies* $\exists (a, c)$ with $a \colon P \hookrightarrow C$ if there exists an injective morphism $q \colon C \hookrightarrow G$ such that $q \circ a = p$ and q satisfies c.

$$\exists (\; P \overset{a}{\hookrightarrow} C, \; c \;)$$

An injective morphism p *satisfies* $\neg c$ if p does not satisfy c, and p *satisfies* $\wedge_{i \in I} c_i$ if p satisfies each c_i $(i \in I)$. We write $p \models c$ if p satisfies the condition c (over P). A graph G *satisfies* a constraint c, $G \models c$, if the morphism $p \colon \emptyset \hookrightarrow G$ satisfies c. $\llbracket c \rrbracket$ denotes the class of all graphs satisfying c. A constraint c is *satisfiable* if there is a graph G that satisfies c.

Two conditions c and c' over P are *equivalent*, denoted by $c \equiv c'$, if for all graphs G and all injective morphisms $p \colon P \hookrightarrow G$, $p \models c$ iff $p \models c'$. A condition c *implies* a condition c', denoted by $c \Rightarrow c'$, if for all graphs and all injective morphisms $p \colon P \hookrightarrow G$, $p \models c$ implies $p \models c'$.

Definition 4 (conditions with alternating quantifiers). Conditions of the form $Q(A_1, \overline{Q}(A_2, Q(A_3, \ldots)))$ with $Q \in \{\forall, \exists\}$, $\overline{\forall} = \exists$, $\overline{\exists} = \forall$ ending with $\mathtt{true}$ or $\mathtt{false}$ are conditions with *alternating quantifiers*. A condition with alternating quantifiers ending with $\mathtt{true}$ is *pure* and *proper* if it is pure or of the form $\exists(A, \nexists C)$.

Fact 1 (alternating quantifiers). For every condition (without conjunctions and disjunctions), an equivalent condition with alternating quantifiers can be constructed.

Proof. Given a condition d, by a normal form result, an equivalent condition d' in normal form can be constructed. Applying the rule $\nexists (a, \neg c) \equiv \forall(a, \exists c)$ as long as possible to d', yields an equivalent condition with alternating quantifiers. □

Fact 2. Proper conditions are satisfiable.

Proof. A proper condition is $\mathtt{true}$, ends with a condition of the form $\exists (x, \mathtt{true}) \equiv \exists x$ or $\forall(x, \mathtt{true}) \equiv \mathtt{true}$, or is of the form $\exists(A, \nexists C)$. Thus, it is satisfiable. □

Rules are specified by a pair of inclusion morphisms. For restricting the applicability of rules, the rules are equipped with a left application condition. Such a rule is applicable with respect to an injective "match" morphism from the left-hand side of the rule to a graph, if, and only if, the underlying plain rule is applicable and the match morphism satisfies the left application condition.

Definition 5 (rules and transformations). A *rule* $\varrho = \langle p, \mathrm{ac} \rangle$ consists of a *plain rule* $p = \langle L \hookleftarrow K \hookrightarrow R \rangle$ with inclusion morphisms $K \hookrightarrow L$ and $K \hookrightarrow R$ and an application condition ac over L. It is *increasing* if $L \cong K$ and *decreasing* or *deleting* if $L \supset K$. A rule $\langle p, \mathtt{true} \rangle$ is abbreviated by p.

$$
\begin{array}{ccccc}
\mathrm{ac} \blacktriangleright & L & \longleftarrow K \longrightarrow & R \\
& g \downarrow & (1) \quad d\downarrow \quad (2) & \downarrow h \\
& G & \longleftarrow D \longrightarrow & H
\end{array}
$$

A *direct transformation* from a graph G to a graph H applying rule ϱ at an injective morphism g consists of two pushouts[2] (1) and (2) as below where $g \models \mathrm{ac}$.

Notation. A rule $\langle L \hookleftarrow K \hookrightarrow R \rangle$ sometimes is denoted by $L \Rightarrow R$ where indexes in L and R refer to the corresponding nodes.

Graph programs are made of sets of rules with application conditions, sequential composition, the if-then-else statement, and as-long-as possible iteration. The presentation is based on [PP12].

Definition 6 (graph programs). *(Graph) Programs* are defined inductively: Every finite rule set $\mathcal{R}$ is a program. Given a condition c and programs P and Q, then $\langle P; Q \rangle$, $P \downarrow$, and $\mathtt{if}\ c\ \mathtt{then}\ P\ \mathtt{else}\ Q$ are programs. The construct $\mathtt{Skip}$ denotes the rule set with empty rule $\langle \emptyset \hookleftarrow \emptyset \hookrightarrow \emptyset \rangle$, ϱ abbreviates the rule set $\{\varrho\}$, and $\mathtt{if}\ c\ \mathtt{then}\ P$ abbreviates $\mathtt{if}\ c\ \mathtt{then}\ P\ \mathtt{else}\ \mathtt{Skip}$.

The semantics is given in the style of structural operational semantics. Inference rules inductively define a small-step transition relation $\rightarrow$ on configurations.

Definition 7 (semantics). A *configuration* is a tuple $\langle P, G \rangle$ of a program P and a graph G (unfinished computation) or a graph H (finished computation). The figure below shows the inference rule for the core constructs[3].

$$[\mathrm{Call}_1]\ \frac{G \Rightarrow_{\mathcal{R}} H}{\langle \mathcal{R}, G \rangle \rightarrow H} \qquad\qquad [\mathrm{Call}_2]\ \frac{G \not\Rightarrow_{\mathcal{R}}}{\langle \mathcal{R}, G \rangle \rightarrow \mathrm{fail}}$$

$$[\mathrm{Seq}_1]\ \frac{\langle P, G \rangle \rightarrow \langle P', H \rangle}{\langle\langle P; Q \rangle, G \rangle \rightarrow \langle\langle P'; Q \rangle, H \rangle} \qquad [\mathrm{Seq}_2]\ \frac{\langle P, G \rangle \rightarrow H}{\langle\langle P; Q \rangle, G \rangle \rightarrow \langle Q, H \rangle}$$

$$[\mathrm{Seq}_3]\ \frac{\langle P, G \rangle \rightarrow \mathrm{fail}}{\langle\langle P; Q \rangle, G \rangle \rightarrow \mathrm{fail}}$$

$$[\mathrm{If}_1]\ \frac{\langle c, G \rangle \rightarrow G}{\langle \mathtt{if}\ c\ \mathtt{then}\ P\ \mathtt{else}\ Q, G \rangle \rightarrow \langle P, G \rangle} \quad [\mathrm{If}_2]\ \frac{\bar{c}\ \text{finitely fails on}\ G}{\langle \mathtt{if}\ c\ \mathtt{then}\ P\ \mathtt{else}\ Q, G \rangle \rightarrow \langle Q, G \rangle}$$

$$[\mathrm{Alap}_1]\ \frac{\langle P, G \rangle \rightarrow^+ H}{\langle P\downarrow, G \rangle \rightarrow \langle P\downarrow, H \rangle} \qquad [\mathrm{Alap}_2]\ \frac{P\ \text{finitely fails on}\ G}{\langle P\downarrow, G \rangle \rightarrow G}$$

A command sequence P *finitely fails* on a graph G if (1) there does not exist an infinite sequence $\langle P, G \rangle \rightarrow \langle P_1, G_1 \rangle \rightarrow \ldots$ and (2) for each terminal[4]

---

[2] For definition & existence of pushouts in the category of graphs see e.g. [EEPT06].

[3] $\bar{c}$ stands for the empty rule with the application condition c. $\rightarrow^+$ denotes the transitive closure of $\rightarrow$.

[4] A configuration γ is *terminal* if there is no configuration δ such that $\gamma \rightarrow \delta$.

configuration γ such that $\langle P, G \rangle \Rightarrow^* \gamma$, $\gamma =$ fail. For $\langle P, G \rangle \rightarrow^* H$, we also write $G \Rightarrow_P H$. Two programs P, P' are *equivalent*, denoted $P \equiv P'$, if for all transformations $G \Rightarrow_P H$, there is a transformation $G \Rightarrow_{P'} H$ and vice versa. A program P is *terminating* if the relation $\rightarrow$ is terminating.

Conditions can be "shifted" over morphisms and rules.

Lemma 1 (Shift, Left, Pres). There are constructions Shift, Left, and Pres such that the following holds. For each condition d over P and injective morphisms $b \colon P \hookrightarrow R, n \colon R \hookrightarrow H$, $n \circ b \models d \iff n \models \text{Shift}(b, d)$. For each rule $p = \langle L \hookleftarrow K \hookrightarrow R \rangle$ and each condition ac over R, for each $G \Rightarrow_{p,g,h} H$, $g \models \text{Left}(p, \text{ac}) \iff h \models$ ac. For each rule ϱ and each constraint c, a condition ac $= \text{Pres}(\varrho, c)$ can be constructed such that for all $G \Rightarrow_{\langle \varrho, \text{ac} \rangle} H$, $G \models c$ implies $H \models c$.

Construction 1. The Construction is as follows[5],[6].

$$
\begin{array}{ccc}
P & \overset{b}{\hookrightarrow} & R \\
{\scriptstyle a}\downarrow & (0) & \downarrow{\scriptstyle a'} \\
C & \overset{b'}{\dashrightarrow} & R' \\
\Delta & & \Delta \\
c & &
\end{array}
$$

$\text{Shift}(b, \text{true}) := \text{true}.$
$\text{Shift}(b, \exists(a, d)) := \bigvee_{(a', b') \in \mathcal{F}} \exists(a', \text{Shift}(b', d))$ where
$\mathcal{F} = \{(a', b') \mid b' \circ a = a' \circ b, \ a', b' \text{ inj}, \ (a', b') \text{ jointly surjective}\}$
$\text{Shift}(b, \neg d) := \neg \text{Shift}(b, d), \ \text{Shift}(b, \wedge_{i \in I} d_i) := \wedge_{i \in I} \text{Shift}(b, d_i).$

$$
\begin{array}{ccc}
R & \hookleftarrow K \hookrightarrow & L \\
{\scriptstyle a}\downarrow \ \ (1) & \downarrow \ \ (2) & \downarrow{\scriptstyle a'} \\
R' & \hookleftarrow K' \hookrightarrow & L' \\
\Delta & & \Delta \\
\text{ac} & &
\end{array}
$$

$\text{Left}(p, \text{true}) := \text{true}.$
$\text{Left}(p, \exists(a, \text{ac})) := \exists(a', \text{Left}(p', \text{ac}))$ if p^{-1} is applicable w.r.t. the morphism a, $p' := \langle L' \hookleftarrow K' \hookrightarrow R' \rangle$ is the *derived* rule, and false, otherwise.
$\text{Left}(p, \neg \text{ac}) := \neg \text{Left}(p, \text{ac}), \quad \text{Left}(p, \wedge_{i \in I} \text{ac}_i) := \wedge_{i \in I} \text{Left}(p, \text{ac}_i).$

$\text{Pres}(\varrho, c) := \text{Shift}(\emptyset \hookrightarrow L, c) \Rightarrow \text{Left}(\varrho, \text{Shift}(\emptyset \hookrightarrow R, c)).$

3 From Graph Conditions to Repair Programs

In this section, we construct terminating repair programs for proper conditions with alternating quantifiers.

A repair program for a constraint is a graph program with the property that any application to a graph yields a graph satisfying the constraint. More specific, we look for maximally preserving repair programs where items are preserved whenever possible (A formal definition can be found in [HS18]).

---

[5] A pair (a', b') is *jointly surjective* if for each $x \in R'$ there is a preimage $y \in R$ with $a'(y) = x$ or $z \in C$ with $b'(z) = x$.

[6] For a rule $p = \langle L \hookleftarrow K \hookrightarrow R \rangle$, $p^{-1} = \langle R \hookleftarrow K \hookrightarrow L \rangle$ denotes the *inverse* rule. For $L' \Rightarrow_p R'$ with intermediate graph K', $\langle L' \hookleftarrow K' \hookrightarrow R' \rangle$ is the *derived* rule.

Definition 8 (repair programs). A *repair program* for a constraint d is a graph program P such that, for all transformations $G \Rightarrow_P H$, $H \models d$. A *repair program* for a condition ac over A is a graph program P such that, for all transformations $G_A \Rightarrow_{P_A} H_A$, $H_A \models ac_A$.

The construction of the repair programs is based on the construction for the basic conditions $\exists (A \hookrightarrow C)$ and $\nexists (A \hookrightarrow C)$. Given an inclusion morphism $a \colon A \hookrightarrow C$, we construct rule sets $\mathcal{R}_a$, and $\mathcal{S}_a$. The rules in $\mathcal{R}_a$ are increasing and of the form $B \Rightarrow C$ where $A \subseteq B \subset C$ and an application condition requiring that no larger subgraph B' of C occurs and the shifted condition $\nexists a$ is satisfied. By the application condition, each rule can only be applied iff the constraint is not satisfied and no other rule whose left-hand side includes B and is larger can be applied. The rules in $\mathcal{S}_a$ are decreasing and of the form $C \Rightarrow B$ where $A \subseteq B \subset C$ such that, if the number of edges in C is larger than the one in A, they delete one edge and no node, and delete a node, otherwise. By $B \subset C$, both rule sets do not contain identical rules.

Construction 2. For a proper inclusion morphism $a \colon A \hookrightarrow C$, let

$$\mathcal{R}_a = \{\langle B \Rightarrow C, ac \wedge ac_B \rangle \mid A \subseteq B \subset C\}$$
$$\mathcal{S}_a = \{\langle C \Rightarrow B \rangle \mid C \supset B \supseteq A \text{ and } (*)\}$$

where $ac = \text{Shift}(A \hookrightarrow B, \nexists a)$, $ac_B = \bigwedge_{B'} \nexists B'$, $\bigwedge_{B'}$ ranges over B' with $B \subset B' \subseteq C$, and $(*)$ if $|E_C| > |E_B|$ then $|V_C| = |V_B|$, $|E_C| = |E_B| + 1$ else $|V_C| = |V_B| + 1$.

Example 1. Consider the constraint $\exists a$ with $a \colon \; \overset{\circ}{{}_1} \; \hookrightarrow \; \overset{\circ}{{}_1}\rightleftarrows\circ$. The rule set $\mathcal{R}_a$ is as follows:

$$\mathcal{R}_a = \begin{cases} \varrho_1 = \langle \overset{\circ}{{}_1} \quad\Rightarrow\; \overset{\circ}{{}_1}\rightleftarrows\circ\,, \nexists \; \circ \quad \circ \rangle \\[4pt] \varrho_2 = \langle \overset{\circ}{{}_1} \quad \overset{\circ}{{}_2} \Rightarrow \overset{\circ}{{}_1}\rightleftarrows\overset{\circ}{{}_2}\,, \nexists \; \overset{\circ}{{}_1}{\rightarrow}\overset{\circ}{{}_2} \wedge \nexists \; \overset{\circ}{{}_1}{\leftarrow}\overset{\circ}{{}_2} \wedge \nexists \; \overset{\circ}{{}_1}\rightleftarrows\circ \; \overset{\circ}{{}_2} \rangle \\[4pt] \varrho_3 = \langle \overset{\circ}{{}_1}{\rightarrow}\overset{\circ}{{}_2} \Rightarrow \overset{\circ}{{}_1}\rightleftarrows\overset{\circ}{{}_2}\,, \nexists \; \overset{\circ}{{}_1}\rightleftarrows\overset{\circ}{{}_2} \wedge \nexists \; \circ\rightleftarrows\overset{\circ}{{}_1}{\rightarrow}\overset{\circ}{{}_2} \rangle \\[4pt] \varrho_4 = \langle \overset{\circ}{{}_1}{\leftarrow}\overset{\circ}{{}_2} \Rightarrow \overset{\circ}{{}_1}\rightleftarrows\overset{\circ}{{}_2}\,, \nexists \; \overset{\circ}{{}_1}\rightleftarrows\overset{\circ}{{}_2} \wedge \nexists \; \overset{\circ}{{}_1}{\leftarrow}\overset{\circ}{{}_2}\rightleftarrows\circ \rangle \end{cases}$$

The first rule requires a node and attaches a 2-cycle, i.e., two edges in opposite direction, provided that there do not exist two nodes. The second rule requires two nodes and attaches a 2-cycle provided there is no edge from the image of node 1 to the image of node 2, no edge from the image of 2 to the image of 1, no 2-cycle at the image of node 1. The third and forth rule are similar. The rule set $\mathcal{R}_a$ is used, e.g., for the repair program of the constraint $\forall (\circ, \exists \; \circ\rightleftarrows\circ)$ (see Construction 3).

Example 2. For the condition $\nexists a$ with $a \colon \circ \hookrightarrow \circ\rightleftarrows\circ$, $\mathcal{S}_a = \{\overset{\circ}{{}_1}\rightleftarrows\overset{\circ}{{}_2} \Rightarrow \overset{\circ}{{}_1}{\rightarrow}\overset{\circ}{{}_2}\}$. For the constraint $\nexists a'$ with $a' = \emptyset \hookrightarrow \circ \; \circ$, $\mathcal{S}_a = \{\overset{\circ}{{}_1} \; \circ \Rightarrow \overset{\circ}{{}_1}\}$.

For existential constraints $\exists (A, c)$, we have the idea of marking: we select or mark an occurrence of A, apply the marked program for the subcondition c, and, finally, unmark the occurrence.

Definition 9 (marked version). Let G be a graph and $g\colon A \hookrightarrow G$ be an injective morphism. Then G_A denotes the A-*marked* version of G, i.e., the graph in which all items in the subgraph $g(A) \subseteq G$ are additionally labelled by the name of the item. For an injective morphism $A \hookrightarrow K$ and a rule $\varrho = \langle L \hookleftarrow K \hookrightarrow R, \mathrm{ac} \rangle$, $\varrho_A = \langle L_A \hookleftarrow K_A \hookrightarrow R_A, \mathrm{ac}_A \rangle$ is the *marked* rule where ac_A denotes the *marked* application condition where the subgraph A is marked in all components. For a rule set $\mathcal{R}$ and a graph A, $\mathcal{R}_A = \{\varrho_A \mid \varrho \in \mathcal{R}\}$. For programs P, Q, conditions c, and a graph A, $\langle P; Q \rangle_A = \langle P_A; Q_A \rangle$, $P{\downarrow}_A = P_A{\downarrow}$, and $(\text{if } c \text{ then } P \text{ else } Q)_A = \text{if } c_A \text{ then } P_A \text{ else } Q_A$.

Theorem 1 (Repair). For proper conditions, a terminating repair program can be constructed.

Construction 3. For a proper condition d over A, the program P_d for d is constructed inductively as follows.

(1) For $d = \text{true}$, $P_d = \text{Skip}$.
(2) For $d = \exists\, a$, $P_d = \text{if } \nexists\, a \text{ then } \mathcal{R}_a$ ($\mathcal{R}_a$ as in Construction 2).
(3) For $d = \nexists\, a$, $P_d = \mathcal{S}'_a \downarrow$ ($\mathcal{S}_a$ as in Construction 2).
(4) For $d = \exists\, (a, c)$, $P_d = \langle P_{\exists\, a}; \text{Select}_C; (P_c)_C; \text{Unselect}_C \rangle$.
(5) For $d = \forall(a, c)$, $P_d = \langle \text{SelectVio}_C; (P_c)_C; \text{Unselect}_C \rangle \downarrow$

where $a\colon A \hookrightarrow C$ and c is a condition over C, $\text{Select}_C = \langle C_A \Rightarrow C_C \rangle$, $\text{SelectVio}_C = \langle \text{Select}_C, \neg c_A \rangle$, P_c is a repair program for the condition c, and Unselect_C is the inverse of Select_C. $\mathcal{S}'_a = \{\varrho^{\mathrm{dg}} \mid \varrho \in \mathcal{S}_a\}$ (see below).

Remark. In the double-pushout approach, the *dangling condition* for a rule $\varrho = \langle L \Rightarrow R \rangle$ and an injective morphism $g\colon L \hookrightarrow G$ requires: "No edge in $G - g(L)$ is incident to a node in $g(L - K)$". The dangling condition can be expressed as negative application condition $\mathrm{dg} = \bigwedge_{L' \in \mathcal{L}} \nexists\, L'$ where $\mathcal{L}$ denotes the set of all graphs obtained from the graph L by adding an outgoing edge, an incoming edge or a loop. The program $\varrho^{\mathrm{dg}} = \langle \text{Select}_L; \text{Prog}(\mathrm{dg}); \varrho; \text{Unselect}_R \rangle$ selects an occurrence of L, removes the dangling edges by the repair program of dg, applies the rule ϱ, and unselects R. In this way, one can simulate the single-pushout approach [Löw93] for rules with injective matching.

Fact 3. For edge-increasing morphisms[7] a, $\mathcal{S}_a \equiv \mathcal{S}'_a$.

Example 3. For the condition $d = \exists\, a$ with $a\colon \overset{\circ}{{}_1} \hookrightarrow \overset{\circ}{{}_1}\!\rightleftarrows\!\circ$, $P_d = \text{if } \nexists\, a \text{ then } \mathcal{R}_a$ is a repair program with $\mathcal{R}_a$ as in Example 1. For $d = \nexists\, a$ with $a\colon \emptyset \hookrightarrow \circ\ \circ$, $P_d = \mathcal{S}'_a \downarrow$ with $\mathcal{S}_a = \{\overset{\circ}{{}_1}\ \circ \Rightarrow \overset{\circ}{{}_1}\}$ is a repair program for d. The program selects an occurrence, deletes the dangling edges, and applies the rule of $\mathcal{S}_a$, as long as possible. For the constraint $d = \exists\,(\overset{\circ}{{}_1}, \nexists\, \overset{\circ}{{}_1}\!\rightleftarrows\!\circ)$ meaning there exists a node without 2-cycle, $P_d = \text{if } \nexists\, a \text{ then } \mathcal{R}_a; \langle \text{Select}_C; \mathcal{S}'_c\downarrow; \text{Unselect}_C \rangle$ where $a\colon \emptyset \hookrightarrow \overset{\circ}{{}_1}$, $c = \nexists\, \overset{\circ}{{}_1} \hookrightarrow \overset{\circ}{{}_1}\!\rightleftarrows\!\circ$, $C = \circ$ and $\mathcal{S}_c = \{\overset{\circ}{{}_1}\!\rightleftarrows\!\overset{\circ}{{}_2} \Rightarrow \overset{\circ}{{}_1}\!\rightarrow\!\overset{\circ}{{}_2}\}$.

---

[7] A morphism $a\colon A \hookrightarrow C$ is *edge-increasing*, if $|E_C| > |E_A|$.

The program checks whether there exists a node, and if not, it creates one. It selects a node and, if there are two edges in opposite directions, it deletes one. The check of existence is done one time, the deletion as long as possible. For the constraint $d = \forall(\,\overset{\circ}{\underset{1}{}},\exists\;\overset{\circ}{\underset{1}{}}\!\rightleftarrows\!\circ\,)$, meaning that, for every node, there exists a 2-cycle, $P_d = \langle \texttt{SelectVio}_C; (P_c)_C; \texttt{Unselect}_C\rangle \downarrow$ is a repair program for d, $P_c = \texttt{if } \nexists a \texttt{ then } \mathcal{R}_a$ the repair program for $c = \exists\;\overset{\circ}{\underset{1}{}} \hookrightarrow \overset{\circ}{\underset{1}{}}\!\rightleftarrows\!\circ$, and $\mathcal{R}_a$ is as in Example 1. The repair program selects a node without 2-cycle, e.g. the third node from left (see below), applies the rule ϱ_4, and unselects the selected part. Afterwards all nodes possess a 2-cycle.

$$\circ\!\rightleftarrows\!\circ\rightarrow\circ \quad\underset{\texttt{SelectVio}_C}{\Rightarrow}\quad \circ\!\rightleftarrows\!\circ\rightarrow\bullet \quad\underset{\varrho_4}{\Rightarrow}\quad \circ\!\rightleftarrows\!\circ\!\rightleftarrows\!\bullet \quad\underset{\texttt{Unselect}_C}{\Rightarrow}\quad \circ\!\rightleftarrows\!\circ\!\rightleftarrows\!\circ$$

For the pure constraint $d = \exists\,(\,\circ\,,\forall(\,\circ\!\rightarrow\!\circ\,,\exists\;\circ\!\rightarrow\!\circ\!\circlearrowright\,)\,)$ with inclusion morphism $a\colon \emptyset \hookrightarrow \circ$ and subcondition c, we obtain the following repair program:

$$P_d = \langle P_{\exists a}; \texttt{Select}_C; (P_c)_C; \texttt{Unselect}_C\rangle \text{ with } C = \circ$$
$$P_c = \langle \texttt{SelectVio}_D; (\mathcal{R}_a)_D; \texttt{Unselect}_D\rangle \downarrow \text{ with } D = \circ\!\rightarrow\!\circ$$
$$\mathcal{R}_a = \{\langle \overset{\circ}{\underset{1}{}}\!\rightarrow\!\overset{\circ}{\underset{2}{}} \Rightarrow \overset{\circ}{\underset{1}{}}\!\rightarrow\!\circ\!\circlearrowright_{2}, \nexists\;\overset{\circ}{\underset{1}{}}\!\rightarrow\!\circ\!\circlearrowright_{2}\rangle\}$$

For an input graph G, we check the condition $\nexists a$ and repair it, select a node (C), apply P_c on the selected node, i.e., we select an outgoing edge (D) for which there is no loop at the target, and repair it (add one), unselect the outgoing edge. This is done as long as possible. Finally, we unselect the selected node (C).

Fact 4 (repair).
1. $(P_c)_A \equiv \langle \texttt{Select}_C, (P_c)_C, \texttt{Unselect}_C\rangle$.
2. If P_c is a repair program for c, then $(P_c)_A$ is a repair program for c_A.
3. $\langle P_{\exists A}; (P_c)_A\rangle$ is a repair program for $\exists\,(a,c)$.

Fact 5 (termination).
1. Finite rule sets are terminating.
2. If P is terminating, then P_A is terminating.
3. If programs P, Q are terminating, then $\langle P; Q\rangle$ is terminating.
4. If a rule set S is deleting, then $S\downarrow$ is terminating.

Proof (of Theorem 1).
P_d **is correct: By induction on the structure of** d.
Let d be a proper condition and P_d the program as in Construction 3.

(1) Let $d = \texttt{true}$ and $P_d = \texttt{Skip}$. By the semantics of $\texttt{Skip}$, for every transformation $G \Rightarrow_{\texttt{Skip}} H \cong G \models \texttt{true}$, i.e., $\texttt{Skip}$ is a repair program for d.
(2) Let $d = \exists a$ and $P_d = \texttt{if } \nexists a \texttt{ then } \mathcal{R}_a$ with $\mathcal{R}_a$ as in Construction 2. If $G \models \nexists a$, then, for every transformation $G \Rightarrow_{\mathcal{R}_a} H$, there is a rule $B \Rightarrow C$ in $\mathcal{R}_a$ and an injective morphism $h\colon B \hookrightarrow H$ for which the application condition $\texttt{ac} = \texttt{Shift}(b, \nexists a)$ is violated, i.e., $\texttt{Shift}(b, \exists a)$ is satisfied. By the Shift Lemma 1, there is an injective morphism $p = h \circ b\colon A \hookrightarrow H$ (see the figure below), satisfying the application condition $\exists a$.

$$\exists\, h\colon B \hookrightarrow H.h \not\models \mathrm{Shift}(b, \nexists\, a)$$
$$\Leftrightarrow \exists\, h\colon B \hookrightarrow H.h \models \mathrm{Shift}(b, \exists\, a)$$
$$\Leftrightarrow \exists\, p\colon A \hookrightarrow H.p \models \exists\, a$$

If $G \models \exists\, a$, then, by the semantics of if-then-, $G \Rightarrow H \cong G \models \exists\, a$. (3) Let $d = \nexists\, a$ and $G \Rightarrow_{\mathcal{S}'_a\downarrow} H$. By the semantics of $\downarrow$, the program $\mathcal{S}'_a$ is not applicable to H. Then, for every injective morphism $h\colon A \hookrightarrow H$ and every rule $\langle C \Rightarrow B \rangle$ in $\mathcal{S}_a$, there is no injective morphism $q\colon C \hookrightarrow H$, such that $q \circ a = h$, i.e., $h \models \nexists\, a$. Thus, $H \models \nexists\, a$. (4) Let $d = \exists\, (a,c)$ and $G \Rightarrow_{P_d} H$. By (2), $P_{\exists\, a}$ is a repair program for $\exists\, a$. By induction hypothesis, P_c is a repair program for c, by Fact 4, the program $(P_c)_A = \langle \mathrm{Select}_C; (P_c)_C; \mathrm{Unselect}_C \rangle$ is a repair program for c_A, and $P_d = \langle P_{\exists\, a}; (P_c)_A \rangle$ is a repair program for $\exists\, (a,c)$. (5) Let $d = \forall(a,c)$ and $G \Rightarrow_{P_d} H$. By definition of P_d, the transformation is of the form $G \Rightarrow_{\mathrm{SelectVio}_A} G_A \Rightarrow_{(P_c)_A} H_A \Rightarrow_{\mathrm{Unselect}_A} H$. By induction hypothesis, P_c is a repair program for c, and, by Fact 4, $(P_c)_A$ is a repair program for c_A. By the semantics of $\downarrow$, no rule is applicable to H_A resp. H, thus $H \models \nexists\, (a, \neg c) \equiv \forall(a,c)$.

P_d is terminating: By induction on the structure of P_d.
For simplicity, we prove the statement for unlabelled graphs. (For labelled graphs it is similar.) Let d be a proper condition, P_d be the corresponding program, $G \Rightarrow_{P_d} H$, $n = \max(m, |V_G|)$ is the maximal number of nodes in d, m the number of nodes of the largest graph of d, and k is the maximal number of parallel edges in d. Let K_n^{rk} denote the complete graph with n nodes and, for each pair of nodes $\langle v_1, v_2 \rangle$, there are k parallel edges from v_1 to v_2. We show: $H \sqsubseteq K_n^k$ (i.e., there is an injective morphism from H into K_n^k.) From this immediately it follows that P_d is terminating.

(1) For $d = \mathtt{true}$, $P_d = \mathtt{Skip}$, and $H \cong G \sqsubseteq K_n^k$.
(2) For $d = \exists\, a$, $\mathcal{R}_a$ is a rule set, $P_d = \mathtt{if}\ \nexists\, a\ \mathtt{then}\ \mathcal{R}_a$, and $H \sqsubseteq K_n^k$. This may be seen as follows: Let $G \Rightarrow_\varrho H$ be a direct transformation through the rule $\varrho = \langle B \Rightarrow C, \mathrm{ac}_B \wedge \mathrm{ac} \rangle$ in $\mathcal{R}_a$. If $|V_G| < |V_C|$, then $|V_B| = |V_G|$ and, by the application condition ac_B (there is no larger B' with $B \subset B' \sqsubseteq C$), $|V_H| = |V_C|$. If $|V_G| \geq |V_C|$, then $|V_B| \leq |V_C|$ and $|V_H| = |V_G|$. Thus $|V_H| = \max(m, |V_G|) = n$. Moreover, by the application condition ac_B, $|E_H| \leq k \cdot |V_H| \times |V_H|$ where k is the maximal k parallel edges in $\mathcal{R}_a$.
(3) For $d = \nexists\, a$, $\mathcal{S}_a$ is deleting, $P_d = \mathcal{S}'_a\downarrow$, and $H \sqsubseteq K_n^k$.
(4) For $d = \exists\, (a,c)$. Then, for all transformations $G \Rightarrow_{P_{\exists\, a}} G'$, $G' \sqsubseteq K_n^k$. By induction hypothesis, for all transformations $G' \Rightarrow_{P_c} H \sqsubseteq K_n^k$. Thus, by Fact 4, $P'_c = \langle \mathrm{Select}_A; (P_c)_A; \mathrm{Unselect}_A \rangle$ is terminating and, for all transformations $G \Rightarrow_{P_d} H \sqsubseteq K_n^k$.
(5) For $d = \forall(a,c)$. By induction hypothesis P_c is terminating, by Fact 5, $P'_c = \langle \mathrm{SelectVio}_A; (P_c)_A; \mathrm{Unselect}_A \rangle$ is terminating and for all transformations $G_i \Rightarrow_{P'_c} G_{i+1} \Rightarrow_{P'_c} \ldots \Rightarrow_{P'_c} H \sqsubseteq K_n^k$. By pureness, the condition d ends with

true and the program P_d is increasing. Suppose $\rightarrow$ is not terminating. Then, there must be a graph with infinite number of nodes or edges. Contradiction to $H \subseteq K_n^k$. By SelectVio$_A$, it is not possible to apply at a repaired position. Consequently, P_d is terminating.   □

Remark. For proper conditions, we have shown that there are terminating repair programs. Our aim is to construct repair programs for satisfiable conditions. The condition $\forall(\, \underset{1}{\circ}\, , \exists\, \underset{1}{\circ}\overset{}{\rightleftarrows}\underset{2}{\circ}\, , \nexists\, \underset{1}{\circ}\overset{}{\rightleftarrows}\underset{2}{\circ}\leftarrow\circ\,)$ is satisfiable, but, up to now, we have no repair program for it.

4 Conjunctive and Disjunctive Constraints

In this section, we consider constraints with conjunctions and disjunctions. Our approach is based on the divide and conquer method: Given a constraint, transform it into a normal form and test it on satisfiability, construct repair programs for the subconstraints, and compose the repair programs for the subconstraints to a repair program for the more complex constraint.

4.1 Conjunctive Constraints

First, we recall the definition of constraint preservation [HP09] and show that repair programs P_1, P_2 for constraints d_1, d_2 can be sequentially composed to a repair program $\langle P_1; P_2 \rangle$ for $d_1 \wedge d_2$ provided that the program P_2 preserves the constraint d_1. Beyond this general result, we present a result for the case where the repair program of one constraint does not preserve the other constraint.

Definition 10 (preservation). For a constraint d, a program P is d-*preserving* if for every transformation $G \Rightarrow_P H$, $G \models d$ implies $H \models d$.

Lemma 2 (Repair). If P_i is a repair program for d_i $(i = 1, 2)$ and P_2 is d_1-preserving, then $\langle P_1; P_2 \rangle$ is a repair program for $d_1 \wedge d_2$. If P_i is terminating, then $\langle P_1; P_2 \rangle$ is terminating.

Proof. Let $\langle P_1; P_2 \rangle$ and $d = d_1 \wedge d_2$. Since P_i is a repair program for d_i $(i = 1, 2)$ and P_2 is d_1-preserving, for every transformation $G \Rightarrow_{P_1} H \Rightarrow_{P_2} M$, $H \models d_1$ and $M \models d_1 \wedge d_2$, i.e., $\langle P_1; P_2 \rangle$ is a repair program for $d_1 \wedge d_2$. By termination of P_1 and P_2, $\langle P_1; P_2 \rangle$ is terminating.   □

Example 4. Consider the constraints $d_1 = \nexists\, \circ\!\rightarrow\!\circ\!\leftarrow\!\circ$ and $d_2 = \forall(\, \circ\, , \exists\, \circ\overset{}{\rightleftarrows}\circ\,)$. The repair programs $\mathcal{R}_1 \downarrow, \mathcal{R}_2 \downarrow$ are based on $\mathcal{R}_1 = \{\langle\, \underset{1}{\circ}\!\rightarrow\!\underset{2}{\circ}\!\leftarrow\!\underset{3}{\circ}\, \Rightarrow\, \underset{1}{\circ}\!\rightarrow\!\underset{2}{\circ}\ \ \underset{3}{\circ}\, \rangle\}$ and $\mathcal{R}_2 = \mathcal{R}_a$ in Example 1. By Lemma 2, neither $\langle \mathcal{R}_1\downarrow; \mathcal{R}_2 \downarrow\rangle$ nor $\langle \mathcal{R}_2 \downarrow; \mathcal{R}_1\downarrow\rangle$ is a repair program for $d_1 \wedge d_2$. On the other hand, the constraint $d_1 \wedge d_2$ is satisfiable by graphs of the form K_2^n $(n \geq 0)$ where K_2^n denotes the n-fold disjoint union of the complete graph with two nodes (K_2):

$$\circ\overset{}{\rightleftarrows}\circ,\ \circ\overset{}{\rightleftarrows}\circ\ \circ\overset{}{\rightleftarrows}\circ,\ \circ\overset{}{\rightleftarrows}\circ\ \circ\overset{}{\rightleftarrows}\circ\ \circ\overset{}{\rightleftarrows}\circ,\ldots.$$

In the following, we try to handle Example 4 and similar examples. The investigations are based on the idea of constraint preservation and the repair of conditions. In [HP09], it is shown that, for every rule ϱ and every constraint d_1, an application condition $\text{Pres}(\varrho, d_1)$ can be constructed such that the rule together with the application condition is d_1-preserving. The set of d_1-preserving rules preserves the constraint d_1, but, in general, the corresponding program is no longer a repair program for d_2. The reason for this is that the applicability of the rules is restricted. By Theorem 1, for every rule ϱ and every satisfiable application condition ac, effectively a repair program $\text{Prog}(ac)$ can be constructed. The application of the program modifies the input graph in such a way that, at a selected occurrence of the left-hand side of the rule, the application condition $ac = \text{Pres}(\varrho, d_1)$ becomes satisfied.

Assumption. Let d_1, d_2 be constraints with repair programs $\mathcal{R}_1\downarrow, \mathcal{R}_2\downarrow$.

Theorem 2 (Repair). For constraints d_1, d_2 with satisfiable conjunction d, a repair program for d can be constructed provided that

1. d_1 is positive and d_2 pure,
2. d_1, d_2 are negative,
3. $d_1 = \exists C_1$, $d_2 = \nexists C_2$ with $C_1 \subset C_2$,
4. d_1 is negative and $d_2 = \forall(A, \exists C)$ with $A \neq \emptyset^8$.

Construction 4. A repair program P_d for d is constructed as follows.

1. For positive d_1 and pure d_2, and
2. For negative d_1, d_2, $P_d = \langle \mathcal{R}_1\downarrow; \mathcal{R}_2\downarrow \rangle$.
3. For $d_1 = \exists \bar{C}_1$, $d_2 = \nexists C_2$ with $C_1 \subset C_2$, $P_d = \langle \mathcal{R}_1\downarrow; \text{Pres}(\mathcal{R}_2, d_1)\downarrow \rangle$.
4. For a negative d_1 and $d_2 = \forall(A, \exists C)$ with $A \neq \emptyset$,

$$P_d = \langle \mathcal{R}_1\downarrow; \mathcal{R}_2^{d_1}\downarrow; \mathcal{D}\downarrow \rangle$$

where $\mathcal{R}_2^{d_1} = \{\varrho^{d_1} \mid \varrho \in \mathcal{R}_2\}$, $\mathcal{D} = \langle \text{SelectVio}_A; (P_{\nexists A})_A \rangle$, and $P_{\nexists A}$ is the repair program for $\nexists A$. For $\varrho = \langle B \Rightarrow C, ac_0 \rangle \in \mathcal{R}_2$ and a constraint d_1, $\varrho^{d_1} = \langle \text{SelectVio}_A; P(\varrho); \text{Unselect}_A \rangle$ where

$$P(\varrho) = \langle \text{SelectVio}_B; \text{Prog}(ac)_B; \langle \varrho, ac \rangle_B; \text{Unselect}_B \rangle$$

where $a: A \hookrightarrow C$, $\text{SelectVio}_A = \langle A \Rightarrow A_A, \nexists a \rangle$, $\text{SelectVio}_B = \langle B_A \Rightarrow B_B, \text{Shift}(A \hookrightarrow B, \nexists a) \rangle$. $\text{Prog}(ac)$ is the repair program for the condition $ac = \text{Pres}(\varrho, d_1)$ if ac is satisfiable and Skip, otherwise. $\langle \varrho, ac \rangle$ is the d_1-preserving rule. Unselect_B and Unselect_A are the inverse rules of Select_B and Select_A, respectively.

---

[8] The requirement $A \neq \emptyset$ in Theorem 2 cannot be deleted: for the unsatisfiable constraint $\nexists C \wedge \exists C$, there is no repair program.

Remark. The first idea is to construct for every rule $\varrho \in \mathcal{R}_2{}^9$ and the constraint d_1, the d_1-preserving rule ϱ with application condition ac $= \mathrm{Pres}(\varrho, d_1)$ [HP09]. The second idea is to construct - if possible - for each application condition ac, the repair program $\mathrm{Prog}(\mathrm{ac})$. This allows to modify the input graph such that the d_1-preserving rule $\langle \varrho, \mathrm{ac} \rangle$ becomes applicable. This is done as long as possible. Afterwards, if the condition is violated, we use the repair program $P_{\sharp A}$ to delete the remaining occurrences of A violating $\exists\, a$.

Example 5. We continue with Example 4. By construction, $\mathcal{R}_1\!\downarrow$ is a repair program for d_1. By Construction 1, for every rule $\varrho \in \mathcal{R}_2$, the application condition $\mathrm{Pres}(\varrho, d_1)$ can be constructed.

$$\mathrm{Pres}(\varrho_1, d_1) = \nexists\ \circ{\longrightarrow}\!\underset{1}{\circ}$$

$$\mathrm{Pres}(\varrho_2, d_1) = \nexists\ \circ{\longrightarrow}\!\underset{1}{\circ}\ \underset{2}{\circ} \wedge \nexists\ \underset{1}{\circ}\ \underset{2}{\circ}{\longleftarrow}\circ$$

$$\mathrm{Pres}(\varrho_3, d_1) = \nexists\ \circ{\longrightarrow}\!\underset{1}{\circ}{\longrightarrow}\!\underset{2}{\circ} \wedge \nexists\ \circ{\longrightarrow}\!\underset{1}{\circ}{\longleftarrow}\!\underset{2}{\circ}$$

$$\mathrm{Pres}(\varrho_4, d_1) = \nexists\ \circ{\longrightarrow}\!\underset{1}{\circ}{\longleftarrow}\!\underset{2}{\circ} \wedge \nexists\ \underset{1}{\circ}{\longleftarrow}\!\underset{2}{\circ}{\longleftarrow}\circ$$

Unfortunately, the d_1-preserving program $\{\langle \varrho, \mathrm{Pres}(\varrho, d_1)\rangle \mid \varrho \in \mathcal{R}_2\}\!\downarrow$ is not a repair program for d_2: The normal form $\circ\rightleftarrows\!\circ\,{\overset{\frown}{\rightarrow}}\circ$ does not satisfy d_2. Then, we construct the repair programs for $\mathrm{ac}_i = \mathrm{Pres}(\varrho_i, d_1)$, given below.

$$\mathrm{Prog}(\mathrm{ac}_1) = \langle\, \underset{1}{\circ}{\longrightarrow}\!\underset{2}{\bullet} \Rightarrow \underset{1}{\circ}\ \ \underset{2}{\bullet}\,\rangle \downarrow$$

$$\mathrm{Prog}(\mathrm{ac}_2) = \{\langle\, \underset{1}{\circ}{\longrightarrow}\!\underset{2}{\bullet}\ \underset{3}{\bullet} \Rightarrow \underset{1}{\circ}\ \ \underset{2}{\bullet}\ \underset{3}{\bullet}\,\rangle, \langle\, \underset{1}{\bullet}\ \underset{2}{\bullet}{\longleftarrow}\!\underset{3}{\circ} \Rightarrow \underset{1}{\bullet}\ \underset{2}{\bullet}\ \underset{3}{\circ}\,\rangle\} \downarrow$$

$$\mathrm{Prog}(\mathrm{ac}_3) = \{\langle\, \underset{1}{\circ}{\longrightarrow}\!\underset{2}{\bullet}{\cdots}{\rightarrow}\!\underset{3}{\bullet} \Rightarrow \underset{1}{\circ}\ \underset{2}{\bullet}{\cdots}{\rightarrow}\!\underset{3}{\bullet}\,\rangle, \langle\, \underset{1}{\bullet}{\cdots}{\rightarrow}\!\underset{2}{\bullet}{\longleftarrow}\!\underset{3}{\circ} \Rightarrow \underset{1}{\bullet}{\cdots}{\rightarrow}\!\underset{2}{\bullet}\ \underset{3}{\circ}\,\rangle\} \downarrow$$

$$\mathrm{Prog}(\mathrm{ac}_4) = \{\langle\, \underset{1}{\circ}{\longrightarrow}\!\underset{2}{\bullet}{\longleftarrow}{\cdots}\underset{3}{\bullet} \Rightarrow \underset{1}{\circ}\ \underset{2}{\bullet}{\longleftarrow}{\cdots}\underset{3}{\bullet}\,\rangle, \langle\, \underset{1}{\bullet}{\longleftarrow}{\cdots}\underset{2}{\bullet}{\longleftarrow}\!\underset{3}{\circ} \Rightarrow \underset{1}{\bullet}{\longleftarrow}{\cdots}\underset{2}{\bullet}\ \underset{3}{\circ}\,\rangle\} \downarrow$$

The $\mathtt{SelectVio}_B$ rules are as follows.

$$\mathtt{SelectVio}_{B_1} = \langle\, \underset{1}{\circ} \Rightarrow \underset{1}{\bullet}, \nexists\ \circ\ \ \circ\,\rangle$$

$$\mathtt{SelectVio}_{B_2} = \langle\, \underset{1}{\circ}\ \underset{2}{\circ} \Rightarrow \underset{1}{\bullet}\ \underset{2}{\bullet}, \nexists\ \underset{1}{\circ}{\longrightarrow}\!\underset{2}{\circ} \wedge \nexists\ \underset{1}{\circ}{\longleftarrow}\!\underset{2}{\circ} \wedge \nexists\ \underset{1}{\circ}\rightleftarrows\!\underset{2}{\circ}\,\rangle$$

$$\mathtt{SelectVio}_{B_3} = \langle\, \underset{1}{\circ}{\longrightarrow}\!\underset{2}{\circ} \Rightarrow \underset{1}{\bullet}{\cdots}{\rightarrow}\!\underset{2}{\bullet}, \nexists\ \underset{1}{\circ}\rightleftarrows\!\underset{2}{\circ} \wedge \nexists\ \underset{1}{\circ}\rightleftarrows\!\underset{2}{\circ}{\longrightarrow}\!\circ\,\rangle$$

$$\mathtt{SelectVio}_{B_4} = \langle\, \underset{1}{\circ}{\longleftarrow}\!\underset{2}{\circ} \Rightarrow \underset{1}{\bullet}{\longleftarrow}{\cdots}\underset{2}{\bullet}, \nexists\ \underset{1}{\circ}\rightleftarrows\!\underset{2}{\circ} \wedge \nexists\ \circ\rightleftarrows\!\underset{1}{\circ}{\longleftarrow}\!\underset{2}{\circ}\,\rangle$$

After the application of $\mathcal{R}_1\!\downarrow$, $\mathcal{R}_2^{d_1}\!\downarrow$ works as follows: By $\mathtt{SelectVio}_B$, we select an occurrence of B, where $\mathrm{Shift}(A \hookrightarrow B, \exists\, a)$ is violated. For the (left) graph below, the only edge, where $\mathtt{SelectVio}_{B_3}$ is applicable, is the rightmost. $\mathrm{Prog}(\mathrm{ac}_3)$ deletes the incoming edge, the d_1-preserving rule $\langle \varrho_3, \mathrm{ac}_3 \rangle$ becomes applicable and is applied, finally, we unmark B. In this way, we obtain a graph satisfying the constraint $d_1 \wedge d_2$.

---

[9] For a rule $\varrho = \langle L \Rightarrow R, \mathrm{ac}_0 \rangle$, $\langle \varrho, \mathrm{ac} \rangle$ denotes the rule $\langle p, \mathrm{ac}_0 \wedge \mathrm{ac} \rangle$.

$\circ \rightleftarrows \circ \rightarrow \circ \rightarrow \circ \Rightarrow_{\mathtt{SelectVio}_{B_3}} \circ \rightleftarrows \circ \rightarrow \bullet \cdots \rightarrow \bullet \Rightarrow_{\mathtt{Prog(ac_3)}} \circ \rightleftarrows \circ \quad \bullet \cdots \rightarrow \bullet$

$\Rightarrow_{\langle \varrho_3, \mathrm{ac}_3 \rangle} \circ \rightleftarrows \circ \quad \bullet \rightleftarrows \bullet \Rightarrow_{\mathtt{Unselect}_B} \circ \rightleftarrows \circ \quad \circ \rightleftarrows \circ$

However, there are examples, where $\mathrm{Prog(ac)}$ is not applicable; without violating $\exists a$. This is reflected by $\mathtt{SelectVio}_B$. Consider, for example, the graph below. The first two nodes have a 2-cycle. By $\mathrm{Shift}(A \hookrightarrow B, \exists a)$, the third node cannot be selected either, thus, $\mathcal{R}_2^{d_1}$ is not applicable. Since d_2 is violated (the third node does not have a 2-cycle), with $(P_{\sharp}A)_A$ we delete this node.

$\circ \rightleftarrows \circ \rightarrow \circ \not\Rightarrow_{\mathcal{R}_2^{d_1}} \Rightarrow_{\mathtt{SelectVio}_A} \circ \rightleftarrows \circ \rightarrow \bullet \Rightarrow_{(P_{\sharp}A)_A} \circ \rightleftarrows \circ$

Lemma 3. Let $\mathcal{R}_1{\downarrow}, \mathcal{R}_2{\downarrow}$ be repair programs for a negative d_1, $d_2 = \forall(A, \exists C)$.

1. $\mathcal{R}_2^{d_1} \equiv \mathcal{R}_2$ provided that $\mathcal{R}_2$ is d_1-preserving.
2. $\mathcal{R}_2^{d_1}$ is a repair program for $\exists a$ and d_1-preserving.
3. $\mathcal{D}$ is a repair program for d_2 and d_1-preserving.

Proof. 1. Let $\mathcal{R}_2$ be d_1-preserving. Then, for all transformations $H \Rightarrow_{\mathcal{R}_2{\downarrow}} M$, $H \models d_1$ implies $M \models d_1$. For all rules $\varrho \in \mathcal{R}_2$, $\mathrm{ac} = \mathrm{Pres}(\varrho, d_1) \equiv \mathtt{true}$, $\mathrm{Prog(ac)} = \mathtt{Skip}$, and $\mathcal{R}_2^{d_1} \equiv \mathcal{R}_2$. 2. By construction, the rules $\langle \varrho, \mathrm{ac} \rangle$ are d_1-preserving. By $d_1 = \sharp C_1$, the programs $\mathrm{Prog(ac)}$ and $\mathcal{D}$ are deleting, and, thus, d_1-preserving. Let ϱ^{d_1} be as in Construction 4. Given an occurrence of A such that $\sharp a$ is satisfied and an extension B of A such that $\mathrm{Shift}(A \hookrightarrow B, \sharp a)$ is satisfied, then $\mathrm{Prog(ac)}$ is $\exists a$ preserving and, by Theorem 1, $\langle \varrho, \mathrm{ac} \rangle$ is a repair program for $\exists a$. 3. By $\mathcal{D}$, one occurrence of A, violating the condition $\exists a$ is selected and repaired. Thus, for a step $H \Rightarrow_{\mathcal{D}} M$, the number of violated occurrences of A decreases, i.e. $\mathrm{vio}(A)_H > \mathrm{vio}(A)_M$. By the semantics of ${\downarrow}$, $\mathtt{SelectVio}_A$ is not applicable, thus for all occurrences of A, $\exists a$ is satisfied, i.e. $M \models d_2$. Since $\mathcal{D}$ is deleting, it is d_1-preserving. Consequently, $M \models d_1 \wedge d_2$. $\square$

Proof (of Theorem 2). 1. For a pure constraint d_2, $\mathcal{R}_2$ is increasing and, thus, d_1-preserving. By Lemma 2, P_d is a repair program for d. 2. For negative constraints d_1, d_2, $\mathcal{R}_2$ is d_1-preserving, and, by Lemma 2, P_d is a repair program for d. 3. For $d_1 = \exists C_1$ and $d_2 = \sharp C_2$ with $C_1 \subset C_2$, the program $\mathrm{Pres}(\mathcal{R}_2, d_1)$ is d_1-preserving, by $C_1 \subset C_2$, $\mathrm{Pres}(\mathcal{R}_2, d_1)$ is a repair program for d_2, and, by Lemma 2, P_d is a repair program for d. 4. Let d_1 negative, $d_2 = \forall(A, \exists C)$ with $A \neq \emptyset$ and $G \Rightarrow_{P_d} M$. By definition of P_d, $G \Rightarrow_{\mathcal{R}_1{\downarrow}} H \Rightarrow_{\mathcal{R}_2^{d_1}{\downarrow}} M \Rightarrow_{\mathcal{D}} N$. Since $\mathcal{R}_1{\downarrow}$ is a repair program for d_1, $H \models d_1$. By Lemma 3, $\mathcal{R}_2^{d_1}$ is a repair program for $\exists a$ and d_1-preserving, i.e., $H \models d_1$. By Lemma 3, $\mathcal{D}$ is a repair program for d_2 and d_1-preserving. Thus, the program P_d repairs d_1, repairs as many as possible occurrences of A in a d_1-preserving way, and finally, removes all remaining occurrences of A violating $\exists A$. Since $\mathcal{D}$ is deleting, it is d_1-preserving. Thus, $N \models d_1 \wedge d_2$. $\square$

4.2 Disjunctive Constraints

Every repair program for a conjunctive constraint is also a repair program for the corresponding disjunctive constraint.

Lemma 4 (Repair)

1. If P is a repair program for d and $d \Rightarrow d'$, then P is a repair program for d'.
2. Every repair program for d_1 is repair program for $d_1 \vee d_2$.

Proof. 1. If P is a repair program for d and $d \Rightarrow d'$, then for every transformation $G \Rightarrow_P H$, $H \models d \Rightarrow d'$, i.e., P is a repair program for d'. 2. By $d_1 \Rightarrow d_1 \vee d_2$ and statement 1, P_1 is a repair program for $d_1 \vee d_2$.   □

5 Related Concepts

In this section, we present some related concepts of rule-based programs generated from a constraint. We compare proven correctness, completeness, in the sense that for all first-order constraints a program can be automatically generated, and termination of the program for all cases.

In Pennemann [Pen09], an algorithm is given that generates for each graph condition c a non-deterministic program $\texttt{SeekSat}(c)$, which will find a valid graph for every satisfiable condition. Starting from the empty graph, the algorithm adds items, progressing to a valid graph which satisfies the constraint. Since negative conditions are refuted, the program needs backtracking. The algorithm is correct and complete, but it is not guaranteed to terminate in general. For the non-nested fragment of conditions, $\texttt{SeekSat}$ is guaranteed to terminate.

In Nassar et al. [NKR17], a rule-based approach to support a modeler in automatically trimming and completing EMF models and thereby resolving their cardinality violations is proposed. For that, repair rules are automatically generated from multiplicity constraints imposed by a given meta-model.

The control flow of the algorithm consists of two main phases:

(1) Model trimming eliminates supernumerous model elements.
(2) Model completion adds required model elements.

It is shown that both of the algorithms are correct, and, for fully finitely instantiable type graphs, the model completion algorithm terminates. The rules are designed to respect EMF constraints, which are in general not expressible with nested conditions.

In Nentwich et al. [NEF03] a repair framework for inconsistent distributed UML documents is presented. Given a first order formula, the algorithm automatically creates a set of repair actions from which the user can choose, when an inconsistency occurs. These repair actions can either delete, add or change a model document. It can be shown, that the repair actions are correct and complete. The problem of repair cycles is left for future work. Since, in general, it is undecidable, if a constraint is satisfiable, the algorithm may not terminate.

In Puissant et al. [PSM15], a regression planner is used to automatically generate sequences of repair actions that transform a model with inconsistencies to a valid model. The initial state of the planner is the invalid model, represented as logical formula, the accepting state is a condition specifying the absence of inconsistencies. Then, a recursive best-first search is used to find the best suitable plan for resolving the inconsistencies. The correctness of the algorithm is not proven, but the approach is evaluated through tests on different UML models.

The semantics of graph programs is a simplified version of the one by Poskitt and Plump [PP13]. One may get fail whenever the program is of the form $\ldots; \mathcal{R};\ldots$. In our programs, we cannot get fail because our programs are of the forms $\mathcal{R} \downarrow$ or $\texttt{if} - \texttt{then}$.

In this paper, we focus on the repair, not on the satisfaction of constraints. For the satisfaction of constraints, the constraint solver of Schneider et al. [SLO18] can be used.

6   Conclusion

In this paper, we have focused on arbitrary constraints and have presented terminating repair programs

(1) for proper conditions (Theorem 1).
(2) for conjunctions $d_1 \wedge d_2$ provided that there are terminating repair programs for d_i ($i = 1, 2$) and one program preserves the other condition (Lemma 2) as well as specific constraints without the requirement of constraint preservation (Theorem 2).
(3) for disjunctions $d_1 \vee d_2$ provided that there is a terminating repair program for some d_i (Lemma 4).

Further topics are

(1) Repair programs for all satisfiable conditions.
(2) Repair programs for typed attributed graphs.
(3) Repair programs for EMF-models. (EMF-models are typed, attributed graphs satisfying some constraints, e.g., no containment cycles [NKR17].)

Acknowledgements. We are grateful to Berthold Hoffmann, Marius Hubatschek, Jens Kosiol, Nebras Nassar, Okan Özkan, Christoph Peuser, Detlef Plump, Gabriele Taentzer, and the anonymous reviewers for their helpful comments to this paper.

References

[BET12] Biermann, E., Ermel, C., Taentzer, G.: Formal foundation of consistent EMF model transformations by algebraic graph transformation. Softw. Syst. Model. **11**(2), 227–250 (2012)

[EEGH15] Ehrig, H., Ermel, C., Golas, U., Hermann, F.: Graph and Model Transformation - General Framework and Applications. Monographs in Theoretical Computer Science. Springer, Heidelberg (2015). https://doi.org/10.1007/978-3-662-47980-3

[EEPT06] Ehrig, H., Ehrig, K., Prange, U., Taentzer, G.: Fundamentals of Algebraic Graph Transformation. EATCS Monographs of Theoretical Computer Science. Springer, Heidelberg (2006). https://doi.org/10.1007/3-540-31188-2

[HP09] Habel, A., Pennemann, K.-H.: Correctness of high-level transformation systems relative to nested conditions. Math. Struct. Comput. Sci. **19**, 245–296 (2009)

[HS18] Habel, A., Sandmann, C.: Graph repair by graph programs. In: Graph Computation Models (GCM 2018), Electronic Pre-Proceedings (2018). https://www.gcm2018.uni-bremen.de/assets/gcm_2018_paper_5.pdf

[Löw93] Löwe, M.: Algebraic approach to single-pushout graph transformation. Theor. Comput. Sci. **109**, 181–224 (1993)

[MGC13] Macedo, N., Guimarães, T., Cunha, A.: Model repair and transformation with echo. In: Automated Software Engineering (ASE 2013), pp. 694–697. IEEE (2013)

[NEF03] Nentwich, C., Emmerich, W., Finkelstein, A.: Consistency management with repair actions. In: Software Engineering, pp. 455–464. IEEE Computer Society (2003)

[NKR17] Nassar, N., Kosiol, J., Radke, H.: Rule-based repair of EMF models: formalization and correctness proof. In: Graph Computation Models (GCM 2017) (2017). https://www.uni-marburg.de/fb12/arbeitsgruppen/swt/forschung/publikationen/2017/NKR17.pdf

[Pen09] Pennemann, K.-H.: Development of correct graph transformation systems. Ph.D. thesis, Universität Oldenburg (2009)

[PP12] Poskitt, C.M., Plump, D.: Hoare-style verification of graph programs. Fundamenta Informaticae **118**(1–2), 135–175 (2012)

[PP13] Poskitt, C.M., Plump, D.: Verifying total correctness of graph programs. Electron. Commun. EASST **61** (2013)

[PSM15] Puissant, J.P., Van Der Straeten, R., Mens, T.: Resolving model inconsistencies using automated regression planning. Softw. Syst. Model. **14**(1), 461–481 (2015)

[SLO18] Schneider, S., Lambers, L., Orejas, F.: Automated reasoning for attributed graph properties. Int. J. Softw. Tools Technol. Transf. **20**, 705–737 (2018)

Double-Pushout Rewriting in Context

Michael Löwe$^{(\boxtimes)}$

FHDW Hannover, Freundallee 15, 30173 Hannover, Germany
michael.loewe@fhdw.de

Abstract. Double-pushout rewriting (DPO) is the most popular algebraic approach to graph transformation. Most of its theory has been
developed for linear rules, which allow deletion, preservation, and addition of vertices and edges only. Deletion takes place in a careful and
circumspect way: a double pushout derivation does never delete vertices
or edges which are not in the image of the applied match. Due to these
restrictions, every DPO-rewrite is invertible. In this paper, we extend
the DPO-approach to non-linear and still invertible rules. Some model
transformation examples show that the extension is worthwhile from the
practical point of view. And there is a good chance for the extension of
the existing theory. In this paper, we investigate parallel independence.

1 Introduction

Double-pushout rewriting (DPO) is the most popular algebraic approach to
graph and model transformation [3,4]. It can be formulated on a purely categorical level.

Definition 1 (DPO-rewriting). *A rule $\varrho = (l : K \rightarrowtail L, r : K \rightarrowtail R)$ is a span
of monomorphisms. A match $m : L \rightarrow G$ for rule ϱ in an object G is a morphism
from ϱ's left-hand side to G. Rule ϱ can be applied at match m, if there are two
pushout diagrams as depicted in Fig. 1, i.e., (m, g) and (p, h) are pushouts of
(l, n) and (r, n) resp. The two pushouts constitute a* direct derivation.

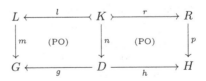

Fig. 1. Double-pushout rewrite

By definition, every direct derivation is reversible in the following sense: If
$\varrho^{-1} = (r, l)$ denotes the inverse rule for a rule $\varrho = (r, l)$, we obtain for every

M. Mazzara et al. (Eds.): STAF 2018 Workshops, LNCS 11176, pp. 447–462, 2018.
https://doi.org/10.1007/978-3-030-04771-9_32

direct derivation from G to H using rule ϱ, that there is a direct derivation using ϱ^{-1} from H to G.

Furthermore, the pushout complement object D constructed as the intermediate object in a direct derivation is unique (up to isomorphism) in suitable categories.[1] This uniqueness property is lost, if the rule's left-hand sides are not restricted to monomorphisms, i.e., if we allow so-called *non-linear* left-hand sides. An example in the category of graphs is depicted in Fig. 2. The morphism $l : K \to L$ is a rule's left-hand side which is not monic and splits a vertex into two particles. The depicted match $m : L \to G$ allows 8 different pushout complements and 3 pairwise non-isomorphic variants.[2] The concrete distribution of the adjacent edges of the split vertex is not specified by the rule and can be chosen arbitrarily by the direct derivation. Thus, the effect of the rule is underspecified.

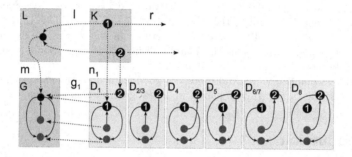

Fig. 2. Indeterministic double-pushout rewrite

For a deterministic effect of such rules, we have to specify how the context (adjacent objects) of split items shall be handled. We can do this, if we address the context explicitly in the rule itself and specify exactly where the context shall be attached to. Two of such specifications for the example of Fig. 2 are depicted in Fig. 3. In the left part of Fig. 3, the context specification in K and L (thick grey arrows without source or target vertex) states that all incoming *and* all outgoing context edges shall be attached to the split-particle "1". Thus, the corresponding direct derivation picks D_1 (compare Fig. 2) from the choice of possible pushout complements. In the right part of Fig. 3, the context specification in K' and L (again thick grey arrows) states that all incoming context edges shall be attached to split-particle "2" whereas all outgoing context edges shall be attached to the split-particle "1". Thus, the corresponding direct derivation picks D_4 (compare Fig. 2) from the choice of possible pushout complements.

---

[1] Adhesive categories, details see below.

[2] The pushout complements D_2 and D_3 as well D_6 and D_7 produce isomorphic objects but differ in the assignments of edges to G, i.e., $g_2 \neq g_3$ and $g_6 \neq g_7$. The complement pairs D_1 and D_8, D_4 and D_5, as well as $D_{2/3}$ and $D_{6/7}$ are isomorphic and can only be distinguished if we fix the embedding of K.

The context handling we introduced on the intuitive level in Fig. 3 cannot single out each derivation (all the possible pushout complements) of Fig. 2, since all incoming context edges as well as all outgoing context edges of a split vertex are handled in an uniform way. For the sample situation of Fig. 2, we can only distinguish rewrites picking the complements D_1, D_4, D_5, and D_8. As we will see in the sample Sect. 4, this is not a major drawback wrt. applicability.

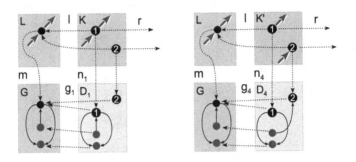

Fig. 3. Handling of context

The context specification cannot copy context items or distribute them indeterministically. If we specified in the example that all outgoing edges shall be attached to particle "1" and all incoming edges shall be attached to both particles "1" *and* "2", there are two possible interpretations: (1) incoming edges shall be 'copied' to both particles or (2) incoming edges can be attached arbitrarily. In the first case, there is no suitable pushout complement (compare possibilities D_1 – D_8 in Fig. 2); in the second case, the rewrite is underspecified again, since D_1 and D_4 are non-isomorphic pushout complements satisfying the specification.

But not only non-linear left-hand sides of rewrite rules cause problems in the double-pushout approach. We obtain some indeterminism as well, if we admit non-linear right-hand sides, i.e., if we do not restrict the rules' right-hand sides to monomorphisms. These problems are not concerned with the rewrite itself, since pushouts are uniquely determined (up to isomorphism) for arbitrary pairs of morphisms. The inverse rule (r, l) for a rule (l, r) with non-monic r, however, has a non-linear left-hand side and produces the sort of indeterminism which we observed above for example in Fig. 2.

For a rewrite example with a non-linear right-hand side see Fig. 4: the vertices "1" and "2" are mapped to the same vertex by the rule's right-hand side r : $K \rightarrow R$. A direct derivation with that rule merges the two matched vertices and connects *all* edges (incoming and outgoing) of these vertices ("1" and "2" in D_1) to the merged result vertex in H, compare morphism $h_1 : D_1 \rightarrow H$ in Fig. 4.

If we apply the inverse rule (r, l) at the induced co-match $p : R \rightarrow H$, we again obtain several different pushout complements as in Fig. 2. Among these pushout complements is the "original" one, namely D_1, that was used in the derivation that lead to the co-match p. But if we forgot the derivation structure and remembered the resulting co-match only, we are not able to choose the correct inverse derivation (among the 8 possible choices). This means that the information about the merging that took place in the derivation step is stored in the direct derivation only. Knowing the rule and the induced co-match is not sufficient to construct the compensating inverse derivation.

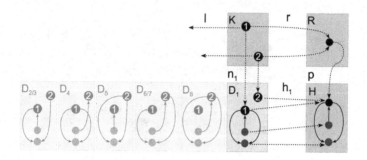

Fig. 4. Indeterministic inverse rewrite

Again, an explicit specification of context handling can help making rules and their inverse rules deterministic. The information about the merging that took place in Fig. 4 can be stored in the rule itself, if we use the context specification of K in the left part of Fig. 3. With this 'context decoration', the rule and the induced co-match carry enough information to uniquely determine D_1 as the intermediate object for the compensating inverse derivation.

In this paper, we formalise the sort of context specification which we informally introduced above in Fig. 3. For this purpose, we borrow and specialise constructions and mechanisms from AGREE-rewriting [1] and from rewriting in span categories [12] in Sect. 2. In Sect. 3, we show that the new rewrite construction is a conservative extension of double-pushout rewriting with left- and right-linear rules. Section 4 demonstrates the applicability of the introduced rewrite mechanism in the field of model transformation. Section 5 provides first theoretical results wrt. parallel independence which demonstrates that theoretical results for the DPO-approach are very likely to carry over to the extended rewrite mechanism. Finally, the conclusion provides a preview of future research.

2   DPO-Rewriting in Context

The theory for double-pushout rewriting has been formulated in adhesive categories [3,11]. We adopt this basic requirement for the constructions and results presented below for double-pushout rewriting in context, which we call DPO-C.

Definition 2 (Adhesive category). *A category is adhesive if*

1. it has all pullbacks and

2. *it has pushouts along monomorphisms which are all van-Kampen squares.*

A pushout $(f' : B \to D, g' : C \to D)$ *of a span* $(g : A \to B, f : A \to C)$ *is a van-Kampen square, if, for every commutative diagram as depicted in the left part of Fig. 5 in which sub-diagrams* (2) *and* (3) *are pullbacks, the following compatibility of pushouts and pullbacks is satisfied: the pair* (f'_h, g'_h) *is pushout of the span* (g_h, f_h), *if and only if sub-diagrams* (4) *and* (5) *are pullbacks.*

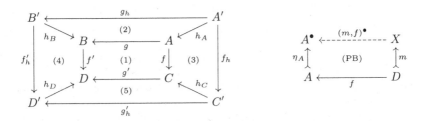

Fig. 5. Adhesivity, hereditariness, and partial arrow classifier

As we said in the introduction, DPO-C borrows major ingredients from AGREE-rewriting. A central issue is the existence of partial arrow classifiers.

Definition 3 (Partial arrow classifiers). *A category has* partial arrow clas-sifiers, *if there is monic* $\eta_A : A \rightarrowtail A^\bullet$ *for every object A satisfying: For every pair* $(m : D \rightarrowtail X, f : D \to A)$ *of morphisms with monic m, there is a unique morphism* $(m, f)^\bullet : X \to A^\bullet$ *such that* (m, f) *is the pullback of* $(\eta_A, (m, f)^\bullet)$, *compare right part of Fig. 5. In the following, the unique morphism* $(m, f)^\bullet$ *is also called* totalisation *of* (m, f). *We abbreviate* $(m, \mathrm{id}_A)^\bullet$ *by* $m^\bullet$ *and obtain for this special case where* $m : A \rightarrowtail X$ *is monic and* $f = \mathrm{id}_A : A \to A$: $m^\bullet \circ m = \eta_A$.

Fact 4 (Classifier). *There are well-known facts for partial arrow classifiers:*

1. *If* $f : D \rightarrowtail A$ *is monic,* $(\eta_D, f)^\bullet$ *is monic.*
2. *If* $c : C \rightarrowtail B$, $b : B \to A$, *and* $a : C \rightarrowtail A$ *are morphisms with monic c and a, then* (c, id_C) *is pullback of* (a, b) *and* $b \circ c = a$, *if and only if* $c^\bullet = a^\bullet \circ b$.
3. *All pushouts are hereditary:*[3] *Pushout* (f', g') *of* (g, f) *in sub-diagram* (1) *of Fig. 5 is hereditary, if all commutative situations as in the left part of Fig. 5 where sub-diagrams* (2) *and* (3) *are pullbacks and* h_B *and* h_C *are monic satisfy:* (f'_h, g'_h) *is pushout of* (g_h, f_h), *if and only if sub-diagrams* (4) *and* (5) *are pullbacks and* h_D *is monic.*

Almost all categories which are used in graph transformation are adhesive and possess partial arrow classifiers. Examples are graphs, i.e., algebras and homomorphisms wrt. the signature G depicted in Fig. 6, and the simplified object-oriented class models, i.e., algebras and homomorphisms wrt. the signature M depicted in Fig. 6, which we use for the sample transformations in Sect. 4.

---

[3] Compare [10].

```
G(raph) = sorts V(ertex) [painted as: ●], E(dge) [painted as: →]
          opns  s(ource), t(arget): E ⟶ V

M(odel) = sorts T(ype) [painted as: □],
                I(nheritance) [painted as: ─▶],
                A(ssociation) [painted as: ──▶]
          opns  c(hild), p(arent): I ⟶ T
                o(wner), t(arget): A ⟶ T
```

Fig. 6. Graphs and simple object-oriented models

Figure 7 depicts three sample partial arrow classifiers in G: (1) for a single vertex, (2) for a discrete graph with two vertices, and (3) for a graph with two vertices, a loop, and an edge between the vertices. The graph A that is classified is painted black, the grey parts are added by the classifier $A^\bullet$, and the classifying monomorphism is the inclusion. The classifier provides the additional structure that is needed to uniquely map the objects that are not in the image of m in arbitrarily given pair $(m : D \rightarrowtail X, f : D \rightarrow A)$. Note that the additional structure that the classifier adds to a classified graph does not differ, if we change the number of edges only, compare (2) and (3) in Fig. 7.

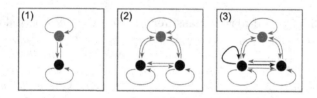

Fig. 7. Sample partial arrow classifiers in the category G

Figure 8 shows two sample classifiers in M: (S) for a model with a single type C and (P) for a model with a pair of types C and C'.[4] Again, the classified models are painted black, the structure added by the classifier is painted grey, and the classifier is the inclusion homomorphism. (Arrows with two heads abbreviate two arrows, namely one in each direction.)

According to Definition 3, the classifying M-homomorphism $\eta_S : S \rightarrowtail S^\bullet$ in Fig. 8 can be interpreted as follows: For any M-algebra A and an assignment f for a subset T of the types in A to the classified type C in S, i.e., $f : T \rightarrow S$ and $\subseteq_T : T \hookrightarrow A$, there is a unique way to extend this assignment to a homomorphism $f^\bullet : A \rightarrow S^\bullet$, namely by mapping all types outside T to the 'grey' type and all inheritance relations and association to the uniquely available suitable

---

[4] Inheritance relations and associations in the classified model do not change the structure that is added by the classifier. The classifier structure depends on the (number of) types only.

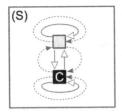
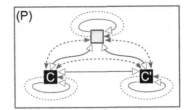

Fig. 8. Sample partial arrow classifiers in the category M

'grey' relations in S. Therefore, S provides the *sufficient* and *necessary* structure to map the *context* of $\mathcal{T}$ to S. And this extension of f to $f^\bullet$ [or more precisely to $(\subseteq_{\mathcal{T}}, f)^\bullet$] has the property that the pair $(\subseteq_{\mathcal{T}}, f)$ is pullback of $(\eta_S, f^\bullet)$. This additional property/requirement of partial arrow classifiers is essential. It prevents that, for the special case that $\mathcal{T} = \emptyset$ and f is the empty mapping, some type in A is mapped to the type C in S by $(\emptyset, \emptyset)^\bullet$.

The partial arrow classifier for given M-algebra A is constructed as follows: (1) Add a Type-element $\perp$. (2) For every pair (t, t') of T-elements, add a I-element $^I\!\perp_{t'}^t$ with $t' = \mathsf{c}(^I\!\perp_{t'}^t)$ and $t = \mathsf{p}(^I\!\perp_{t'}^t)$ and A-element $^A\!\perp_{t'}^t$ with $t' = \mathsf{o}(^A\!\perp_{t'}^t)$ and $t = \mathsf{t}(^A\!\perp_{t'}^t)$. The added type $\perp$ is called the *undefined* type and the I- and A-loop added on this type are called *completely undefined* I- and A-edge respectively.

Assumption 5 (Basic category). For the rest of the paper, we assume an adhesive category with partial arrow classifiers.

For this sort of categories, we know the following facts [11]:

Fact 6 (Properties of the underlying category).

1. *Pushouts along monomorphisms are pullbacks.*
2. *Pushouts preserve monomorphisms.*
3. *Pushout of intersection is union: If $(x : X \rightarrowtail Z, y : Y \rightarrowtail Z)$ is a cospan of monomorphisms, $(x' : I \rightarrowtail Y, y' : I \rightarrowtail X)$ its pullback span, and $(x^* : X \rightarrowtail U, y^* : Y \rightarrowtail U)$ the pushout of (x', y'), then the unique morphism $u : U \rightarrowtail Z$ with $u \circ x^* = x$ and $u \circ y^* = y$ is monic, compare Fig. 9.*

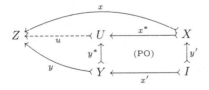

Fig. 9. Union of intersection

Partial arrow classifier constructions have been successfully applied in AGREE-rewriting [1] in order to control the deletion and copy process of context items in a rewrite which can be stipulated by non-linear left-hand sides of rules. For a double-pushout semantics, we need to restrict the AGREE-rewriting mechanism: context items must not be copied nor deleted, they can only be distributed to split particles, compare motivating examples in the introduction.

Definition 7 (DPO-C-rule). *A rule $(l : K \to L, c : K \rightarrowtail C, r : K \to R)$ is a triple of morphisms such that the context specification c is monic and, given the pushouts $(c_l : L \rightarrowtail L_C, l_c : C \to L_C)$ and $(c_r : R \rightarrowtail R_C, r_c : C \to R_C)$ of (l, c) and (r, c) respectively, the morphisms $c_l^\bullet$ and $c_r^\bullet$ are monic, compare Fig. 10.*[5]

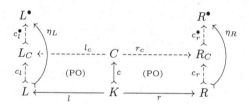

Fig. 10. DPO-C rule

DPO-C rules are special AGREE-rules. The special rule format makes sure that items in L_C which are not in L, have a 'unique preimage' under l_c. In the category G of graphs for example, we cannot choose $C = K^\bullet$ and $c = \eta_K$, if there are vertices $v_1 \neq v_2$ with $l(v_1) = l(v_2)$. In this case, the pushout of l and η_K results in a graph with at least 4 context loops on $l(v_1)$ and this graph is not a sub-graph of $L^\bullet$, which has a one loop only, compare (1) and (2) in Fig. 7. The symmetric restriction of the right side will ensure reversibility of rewrites.

Definition 8 (DPO-C-match and -derivation). *Given rule $\sigma = (l : K \to L, c : K \rightarrowtail C, r : K \to R)$, a monomorphism $m : L \rightarrowtail G$ is a match, if the following match condition is satisfied: The morphism $m^\bullet : G \to L^\bullet$ factors through L_C, i.e., there is $m' : G \to L_C$ such that $c_l^\bullet \circ m' = m^\bullet$.*

A derivation with rule σ at match m is constructed as follows, compare Fig. 11:

1. *Construct pullback $(g : D \to G, n' : D \to C)$ of $(m' : G \to L_C, l_c : C \to L_C)$.*
2. *Let $n : K \rightarrowtail D$ be the unique mediating morphism for this pullback for $(m \circ l, c)$. By pullback decomposition and Fact 6(1) for pushout (l_c, c_l), (l, n) is pullback of (g, m). Since pullbacks preserve monomorphisms, n is monic.*
3. *Construct pushout $(h : D \to H, p : R \rightarrowtail H)$ of $(n : K \rightarrowtail D, r : K \to R)$. The morphism p is monic by Fact 6(2).*

---

[5] The pushout morphisms c_l and c_r are monic by Fact 6(2).

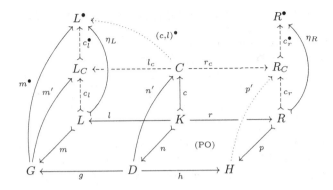

Fig. 11. DPO-C match and derivation

Remarks. Note that we restrict matches to monomorphisms.[6] The morphism m' which satisfies the matching condition is unique, if it exists, since $c_l^\bullet$ is monic. The morphism n can be constructed in Step 2 of Definition 8, since $c_l^\bullet \circ m' \circ m = m^\bullet \circ m = \eta_L = c_l^\bullet \circ c_l$ implies $m' \circ m = c_l$ due to $c_l^\bullet$ being monic.

The match condition in Definition 8 formulates a negative application condition as in [8]. Especially the *dangling condition* of double pushout rewriting in the category G of graphs [9] is reformulated this way: if the rule's left-hand side $l : K \to L$ is not epic on vertices, there is vertex v without pre-image under l. Since L_C is pushout, this means that $c_l(v)$ can only have adjacent edges that have pre-images under c_l. If there is an edge adjacent to $m(v)$ without pre-image under m, this edge 'is' not in L and not in L_C, it is *dangling*, and it cannot be mapped by m' to any edge in L_C in order to satisfy the match condition.

The rewrite mechanism in Definition 8 is a special case of AGREE-rewriting: If (g, h) is DPO-C trace of DPO-C rule (l, c, r) at match m, then it is also AGREE trace of AGREE rule (l, c, r) at m.[7] The rule restriction of Definition 7 and the match condition of Definition 8, however, tame the 'AGREE-tiger' such that (1) items outside the match cannot be deleted nor copied and (2) irreversible merging is avoided.

3 Analysis of DPO-C Derivations

In this section, we analyse the properties of DPO-C-derivations. Especially, we investigate reversibility and show that the DPO-C-approach is a conservative extension of the DPO-approach with left- and right-linear rules at monic matches.

---

[6] Therefore, the *identification condition* for rule applicability [9] does not matter here.
[7] Since (id_L, c_l) and (c, l) are pullbacks of $(\eta_L, c_l^\bullet)$ resp. (l_c, c_l) by Fact 6(1) and, therefore, (l, c) is pullback of $(c_l^\bullet \circ l_c, \eta_L)$, we have that $c_l^\bullet \circ l_c = (c, l)^\bullet$. Since $c_l^\bullet$ is monic, (id_G, m') is pullback of $(c_l^\bullet, m^\bullet)$ and (n', g) is pullback of $(m^\bullet, c_l^\bullet \circ l_c)$.

Proposition 9 (Determinism). *DPO-C-rewrites are deterministic.*

Proof. The pullback and pushout constructed in Step 1 resp. 3 of Definition 8 are unique up to isomorphism. So given two trace and co-match pairs $((g_1, h_1), p_1)$ and $((g_2, h_2), p_2)$ for two derivations with rule σ at the same match m, there are isomorphisms i_g and i_h such that $i_g \circ g_1 = g_2$, $i_h \circ h_1 = h_2 \circ i_g$, and $i_h \circ p_1 = p_2$.

This result justifies the following notation:

Notation 10 (Deterministic rewrite). *In a derivation with rule σ at match m as in Definition 8, the result H is denoted by $\sigma@m$, the span (g, h) is called the trace, written $\sigma \langle m \rangle$, and morphism p constitutes the co-match, written $m \langle \sigma \rangle$.*

Proposition 11 (Rewrite properties). *Consider a derivation with rule $\sigma = (l, c, r)$ at match $m : L \rightarrowtail G$ as depicted in Fig. 11. The participating sub-diagrams have the following properties:*

1. *(m, id_L) and (n, id_K) are pullback of (m', c_l) and (n', c) respectively.*
2. *(m, g) and (m', l_c) are pushouts of (l, n) and (g, n') respectively.*
3. *If $p' : H \to R_C$ is the unique morphism for pushout (p, h) providing $p' \circ p = c_r$ and $p' \circ h = r_c \circ n'$, then*
   (a) *(h, n') and (p, id_R) are pullbacks of (r_c, p') and (p', c_r) respectively and*
   (b) *(r_c, p') is pushout of (n', h).*

Proof. (1) We know that (m, id_L) is pullback of $(m^\bullet, \eta_L)$ and, since $c_l^\bullet$ is monic, that (m', id_G) is pullback of $(m^\bullet, c_l^\bullet)$. Since $c_l^\bullet \circ c_l = \eta_L$ and $m' \circ m = c_l$, pullback decomposition provides (m, id_L) as pullback of (m', c_l). Now (m, id_L) is pullback of (m', c_l) and we always have that (id_K, l) is pullback of (id_L, l). Thus, pullback composition provides $(\mathrm{id}_K, m \circ l)$ as pullback of $(m', c_l \circ l)$. Since $c_l \circ l = l_c \circ c$ and $m \circ l = g \circ n$, $(\mathrm{id}_K, g \circ n)$ is pullback of $(m', l_c \circ c)$. Since (g, n') has been constructed as pullback of (m', l_c), pullback decomposition guarantees that (n, id_K) is pullback of (n', c).

(2) Adhesivity (compare Definition 2 van-Kampen property if-part) guarantees that (g, m) is pushout of (l, n), since the pushout (l_c, c_l) of (l, c) is a pushout along monomorphism c and surrounded by 4 pullbacks, namely (i) (id_K, n) of (n', c), (ii) (id_K, l) of (id_L, l), (iii) (id_L, m) of (m', c_l), and (iv) (n', g) of (m', l_c). Now, pushout decomposition provides (m', l_c) as pushout of (g, n').

(3a) Adhesivity (compare Definition 2 van-Kampen property only-if-part) guarantees the desired pullback properties, since (r_c, c_r) is pushout of (r, c) along monic c, (p, h) is pushout of (r, n) by the construction of the derivation, (id_K, n) is pullback of (n', c) by (1) above, and (id_K, r) is trivially pullback of (id_R, r).

(3b) Pushout decomposition provides that (r_c, p') is pushout of (n', h).

Thus, every square in Fig. 11 is pushout *and* pullback. Therefore, DPO-C-rewriting could also be called *triple* double-pushout transformation.

Corollary 12 (Reversibility). *Every DPO-C-rewrite is reversible: if (g, h) is trace and p co-match of the application of rule (l, c, r) at match m, then (h, g) is the trace and m the co-match of applying the inverse rule (r, c, l) at match p.*

Proof. Consider the derivation in Fig. 11. We are done, if the pair (p, p') is match for the inverse rule, since, by Proposition 11, (n', h) is pullback of (r_c, p') and (g, m) is pushout of (l, n). Thus, it remains to show that $c_r^\bullet \circ p' = p^\bullet$, i.e., that (id_R, p) is pullback of $(\eta_R, c_r^\bullet \circ p')$. We know by Proposition 11 (3a) that (p, id_R) is pullback of (p', c_r) and, since $c_r^\bullet$ is monic, that (p', id_H) is pullback of $(c_r^\bullet \circ p', c_r^\bullet)$. Since $c_r^\bullet \circ c_r = \eta_R$, pullback composition provides the desired result.

We close this section by showing that standard DPO-rewriting with left- and right-linear rules is a special case of DPO-C-derivations.

Definition 13 (DPO-simulation). *The DPO-C-simulation of left- and right-linear DPO-rule $\varrho = (l : K \rightarrowtail L, r : K \rightarrowtail R)$ is the triple $\sigma_\varrho = (l, \eta_K, r)$.*

Proposition 14 (DPO-simulation). *DPO-C-simulations are DPO-C-rules.*

Proof. We have to show the conditions of Definition 7. For this purpose, consider Fig. 12, where u_l and u_r are the unique morphisms providing (i) $u_l \circ c_l = \eta_L$, (ii) $u_l \circ l_c = (\eta_k, l)^\bullet$, (iii) $u_r \circ c_r = \eta_R$, and (iv) $u_r \circ r_c = (\eta_k, r)^\bullet$. By Fact 4(1), $(\eta_k, l)^\bullet$ and $(\eta_k, r)^\bullet$ are monic and, by Fact 6(3), u_l and u_r are monic. Equations (i) and (iii) and u_l and u_r being monic implies that (c_l, id_L) and (c_r, id_R) are pullbacks of (u_l, η_L) and (u_r, η_R) respectively. Thus, $u_l = c_l^\bullet$ and $u_r = c_r^\bullet$.

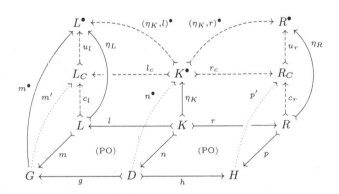

Fig. 12. DPO-rule simulation

Theorem 15 (DPO-extension). *If $\varrho \langle m \rangle$ and $m \langle \varrho \rangle$ are trace and co-match of a DPO-derivation with linear rule ϱ, then $\sigma_\varrho \langle m \rangle = \varrho \langle m \rangle$ and $m \langle \sigma_\varrho \rangle = m \langle \varrho \rangle$.*

Proof. Consider Fig. 12 where the two bottom pushouts constitute a DPO-derivation with left- and right-linear rule (l, r). Then there is $n^\bullet : D \to K^\bullet$ such that (n, id_K) is pullback of $(n^\bullet, \eta_K)$ and especially $n^\bullet \circ n = \eta_K$. Since (m, g) is pushout, we obtain morphism $m' : G \to L_C$ making the diagram commutative. Given pullbacks (n, id_K) of $(n^\bullet, \eta_K)$ and (l, id_K) of (id_L, l) and the given pushouts (m, g) and (l_c, c_l) together with the van-Kampen property of Definition 2, guarantee that $(g, n^\bullet)$ is pullback of (m', l_c) and (m, id_L) is pullback of (m', c_l). This last pullback property and u_l being monic such that (m', id_G) is pullback of $(u_l, u_l \circ m')$ implies that $u_l \circ m' = m^\bullet$ by pullback composition and uniqueness of totalisations. Since $(n^\bullet, g)$ is pullback of (m', l_c) and (h, p) is pushout of (r, n), $\sigma_\varrho \langle m \rangle = \varrho \langle m \rangle$ and $m \langle \sigma_\varrho \rangle = m \langle \varrho \rangle$.

4   Model Refactorisation - Some Sample Rules

In this section, we demonstrate the applicability of double-pushout rewriting in context by some sample rules for object-oriented system refactoring [7]. To keep the examples simple, we use the simplified meta-model M for object-oriented models defined in Fig. 6.

Figure 13 depicts two first sample rules. The mapping of the morphisms is indicated by number correspondence. For easy notation, we identify the undefined type of each partial arrow classifier (grey boxes in Fig. 8) with the framing box which surrounds the respective graphical visualisation of the algebra. We also implicitly assume that the two (completely undefined) loops on the undefined type are contained in and preserved by the context specification of all rules. An edge which connects a type inside a picture with the frame is some context inheritance relation or association, i.e., belongs to L_C, C, or R_C.

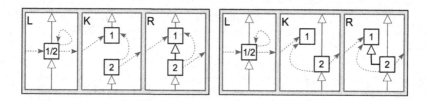

Fig. 13. Extracting abstract type

Figure 13 depicts variants for extracting an abstract type out of a given type. The first variant on the left refines the inheritance hierarchy by splitting the matched type "1/2" into an abstract particle "1" and a concrete particle "2" in the intermediate structure K. The context relations of the split type are distributed as follows: All target-roles of associations and child-roles of inheritance relations are attached to the abstract particle, all other roles are connected with the concrete particle. Note the explicit handling of association loops which also follows this rule wrt. owner- and target-roles. Finally, the rule's right-hand side R adds the needed inheritance relation between the two particles. The difference of the second variant is that the new abstract type is not integrated into the existent inheritance hierarchy.

Note that both rules formulate a negative application condition, namely that there are no Inheritance-loops on the refactored type. This shall be true in all reasonable object-oriented models where the inheritance relation is hierarchical.

The rules in Fig. 13 read from right to left specify the elimination of superfluous types. For these elimination rules to work correctly, the type "1" shall be abstract. This is a feature that must be added to the model signature in Fig. 6. We do not describe the details here due to space limitations.

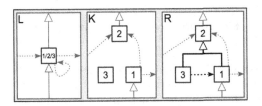

Fig. 14. Introducing proxy

Figure 14 depicts a rule that puts indirection into an object-oriented model by introducing some proxy-objects [6]. Again the context is distributed as in Fig. 13, the refactored type, however, is split into *three* particles, namely "1" which further manages the resources of the type, "2" which provides abstract access to 'objects' of type "1", and "3" which can be interpreted as an approximation of the original type. The rule's right-hand side adds the needed inheritance relations and the association which allows 'proxy' objects to delegate to 'real' objects.

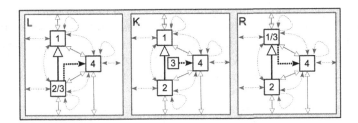

Fig. 15. Pulling-up association

Figure 15 describes the shift of the **owner**-role of an association to a more abstract type.[8] This rule is neither left- nor right-linear. The standard DPO-solution for this purpose is a linear rule that deletes the association on the left-hand side and adds a *new* association on the right-hand side. This rule has the same effect on the model level. But if there were **instanceOf**-relations from the object level to the model level that point to this association,[9] the rule in Fig. 15 preserves all these links while the linear rule deletes them and introduces a new 'empty' association without any links. For details compare also [13].

---

[8] Double-headed context arrows represent a pair of arrows one in each direction.

[9] This feature needs to be added in the model signature in Fig. 6.

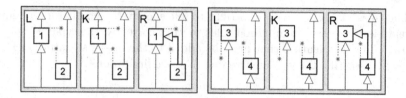

Fig. 16. Preserving inheritance hierarchy

Figure 16 demonstrates a useful application of the application conditions which are built-in in DPO-C-rewriting. These two rules add inheritance relations carefully, i.e., they keep the inheritance hierarchy cycle-free: A type "2" can only become new sub-type of type "1" if it has no sub-types itself and a type "3" can only become new super-type of type "4" if it has no super-types itself. Since the association context is not important here and the rules are linear, the asterisk-notation we used in Fig. 16 indicates *complete association contexts*.[10]

These examples demonstrate the DPO-C-rewriting can be useful in practical applications and that it is worthwhile to elaborate more complex case studies.

5   Parallel Independence

In this section, we show that DPO-C-rewriting is not only useful from the practical point of view. Also from the theoretical perspective, it is promising, since most results for the DPO-approach [3] are very likely to carry over to DPO-C. We start here by providing first results wrt. parallel independence.

Parallel independence analysis investigates the conditions under which two rewrites of the same object can be performed in either order and produce the same result. Essential for the theory is the notion of *residual match*: Under which conditions are two matches $m_G : L \rightarrowtail G$ and $m_H : L \rightarrowtail H$ for a rule's left-hand side L *the same match*, if there is a trace $(g : D \rightarrow G, h : D \rightarrow H)$? The DPO-answer is: m_G and m_H are the same, if there is $m_D : L \rightarrowtail D$ with $g \circ m_D = m_G$ and $h \circ m_D = m_H$, compare [9]. This answer is not sufficient for DPO-C, since we need to take the context matches into account as well, i.e., $m_G^\bullet$, $m_D^\bullet$, and $m_H^\bullet$ shall classify the 'same objects' the same way. This means that we must require $m_G^\bullet \circ g = m_D^\bullet$ and $m_H^\bullet \circ h = m_D^\bullet$ which, by Fact 4(2), is equivalent to requiring that (id_L, m_D) is pullback of (m_G, g) and (m_H, h).[11,12]

Definition 16 (Residual). *Let $(g : D \rightarrow G, h : D \rightarrow H)$ be a trace of a direct derivation and m match for rule σ in G. A match m^{gh} for σ in H is the residual of m for trace (g, h), if there is morphism m_D from the left-hand side L of σ to D such that (id_L, m_D) is pullback of (m, g) and (m^{gh}, h), compare Fig. 17.*

---

[10] *Complete association contexts* means e.g., for type "1" in Fig. 16 that there 'are' 2 adjacent association pairs from and to type "2" and from and to the undefined type.

[11] This condition is identical to the one in [2].

[12] In case of a monic trace (g and h are monic), $g \circ m_D = m_G$ and $h \circ m_D = m_H$ implies that (id_L, m_D) is pullback of (m_G, g) and (m_H, h).

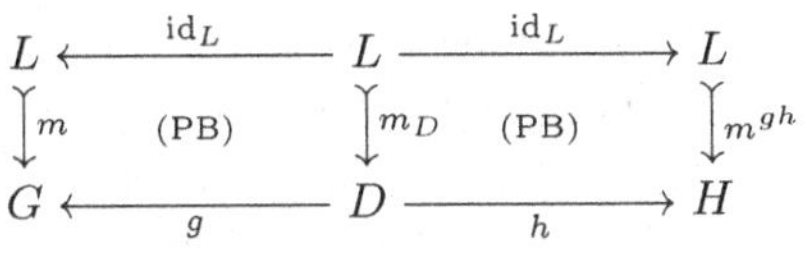

$$L \xleftarrow{\mathrm{id}_L} L \xrightarrow{\mathrm{id}_L} L$$

$$\downarrow m \quad (\mathrm{PB}) \quad \downarrow m_D \quad (\mathrm{PB}) \quad \downarrow m^{gh}$$

$$G \xleftarrow{g} D \xrightarrow{h} H$$

Fig. 17. Residual

The pullback properties uniquely determine *the* residual, if it exists. Two derivations of the same object are called independent, if they have mutual residuals.

Definition 17 (Parallel independence). *Two direct derivations with rules σ_1 and σ_2 at matches m_1 and m_2 resp. rewriting the same object are parallel independent, if m_1 has a residual for $\sigma_2 \langle m_2 \rangle$ and m_2 has a residual for $\sigma_1 \langle m_1 \rangle$.*

The following theorem shows that parallel independent derivations with rules σ_1 and σ_2 *commute* in the following sense: First applying σ_1 at its match and then applying σ_2 at the residual results in the same trace as first applying σ_2 at its match and then applying σ_1 at the residual.

Theorem 18 (Confluence). *If derivations with rules σ_1 and σ_2 at matches m_1 and m_2 are parallel independent, then the derivations with the mutual residuals $m_1^{\sigma_2 \langle m_2 \rangle}$ and $m_2^{\sigma_1 \langle m_1 \rangle}$ produce the same result, i.e., $\sigma_1 @ m_1^{\sigma_2 \langle m_2 \rangle} \approx \sigma_2 @ m_2^{\sigma_1 \langle m_1 \rangle}$, and the same trace, i.e., $\sigma_2 \left\langle m_2^{\sigma_1 \langle m_1 \rangle} \right\rangle \circ \sigma_1 \langle m_1 \rangle = \sigma_1 \left\langle m_1^{\sigma_2 \langle m_2 \rangle} \right\rangle \circ \sigma_2 \langle m_2 \rangle$.*[13]

6 Conclusion

We introduced a conservative extension of linear DPO-rewriting which we call DPO-C. The "C" indicates that the extension allows explicit handling of the context of a match. The context specification allows non-linear rules with deterministic and reversible rewrites: Given a match $m : L \to G$ for rule σ with left-hand side L and right-hand side R, the rewrite with σ at m produces a uniquely determined result H and provides a co-match $p : R \to H$ such that the rewrite with the inverse rule σ^{-1} at p results in an object isomorphic to G.

The deterministic and reversible behaviour of DPO-C allows to extend well-known theoretical results. We started the analysis of parallel independence in this paper. And the explicit handling of context improves the applicability of the rewrite approach in situations where 'unknown context' must be checked (by some negative application conditions), distributed, or merged. We demonstrated this mechanism by some examples from system refactoring. Thus, a further development of DPO-C seems worthwhile from the practical *and* theoretical point of view. Future research can address the following issues:

- Characterising conditions for parallel independence.

---

[13] For a detailed proof, see [14].

- Extension of the theory for example with respect to sequential independence, concurrency, critical pair analysis, parallelism, and amalgamation.
- Comparison of the DPO-C-built-in negative application conditions to the well-known negative application conditions from the literature, e.g., [8].
- Comparison of DPO-C to other reversible approaches e.g., [2].
- Development of a clear and handy visual notation for the rules especially for the context specification.
- Elaboration of bigger case studies e.g., in the field of model transformation.

References

1. Corradini, A., Duval, D., Echahed, R., Prost, F., Ribeiro, L.: AGREE – algebraic graph rewriting with controlled embedding. In: Parisi-Presicce, F., Westfechtel, B. (eds.) ICGT 2015. LNCS, vol. 9151, pp. 35–51. Springer, Cham (2015). https://doi.org/10.1007/978-3-319-21145-9_3
2. Danos, V., Heindel, T., Honorato-Zimmer, R., Stucki, S.: Reversible sesqui-pushout rewriting. In: Giese, H., König, B. (eds.) ICGT 2014. LNCS, vol. 8571, pp. 161–176. Springer, Cham (2014). https://doi.org/10.1007/978-3-319-09108-2_11
3. Ehrig, H., Ehrig, K., Prange, U., Taentzer, G.: Fundamentals of Algebraic Graph Transformation. MTCSAES. Springer, Heidelberg (2006). https://doi.org/10.1007/3-540-31188-2
4. Ehrig, H., Ermel, C., Golas, U., Hermann, F.: Graph and Model Transformation - General Framework and Applications. MTCSAES. Springer, Heidelberg (2015). https://doi.org/10.1007/978-3-662-47980-3
5. Ehrig, H., Rensink, A., Rozenberg, G., Schürr, A. (eds.): ICGT 2010. LNCS, vol. 6372. Springer, Heidelberg (2010). https://doi.org/10.1007/978-3-642-15928-2
6. Gamma, E., et al.: Design Patterns: Elements of Reusable Object-Oriented Software. Addison-Wesley, Boston (1994)
7. Fowler, M.: Refactoring - Improving the Design of Existing Code. Addison Wesley Object Technology Series. Addison-Wesley, Boston (1999)
8. Habel, A., Heckel, R., Taentzer, G.: Graph grammars with negative application conditions. Fundam. Inform. **26**(3/4), 287–313 (1996)
9. Habel, A., Müller, J., Plump, D.: Double-pushout graph transformation revisited. Math. Struct. Comput. Sci. **11**(5), 637–688 (2001)
10. Heindel, T.: Hereditary pushouts reconsidered. In: Ehrig et al. [5], pp. 250–265 (2010)
11. Lack, S., Sobocinski, P.: Adhesive and quasiadhesive categories. ITA **39**(3), 511–545 (2005)
12. Löwe, M.: Graph rewriting in span-categories. In: Ehrig et al. [5], pp. 218–233 (2010)
13. Löwe, M.: Refactoring information systems: association folding and unfolding. ACM SIGSOFT Softw. Eng. Notes **36**(4), 1–7 (2011)
14. Löwe, M.: Double pushout rewriting in context. Technical report 2018/02, Fachhochschule für die. Wirtschaft, Hannover (2018)

From Hyperedge Replacement Grammars to Decidable Hyperedge Replacement Games

Christoph Peuser[✉]

Carl von Ossietzky Universität Oldenburg, Oldenburg, Germany
peuser@informatik.uni-oldenburg.de

Abstract. We consider correctness of hyperedge replacement grammars *under adverse conditions*. In contrast to existing approaches, the influence of an adverse environment is considered in addition to system behaviour. To this end, we construct a hyperedge replacement game where rules represent the moves available to players and a temporal condition specifies the desired properties of the system. In particular, the construction of parity pushdown games from hyperedge replacement grammars results in a decidable class of games.

Keywords: Context-free graph grammars · Game theory
Hyperedge replacement grammars · Pushdown games · Parity games

1 Introduction

Graph transformation systems and graph grammars [5] offer a graphical, yet precise formalism for modeling a system. The system state is a graph and state changes are modeled by graph transformations. There are a number of approaches to proving the correctness of a graph transformation system relative to conditions, e.g. for nested conditions [8,14] or the μ-calculus [3].

We consider system correctness under *adverse conditions*, such as interference from the environment. Once we consider actions of the system and environment seperately, we require more control over the relative frequency with which system or environment may act. By modeling system and environment as players of a game, we limit the number of moves a player is allowed to make.

Games are a natural model for processes under the influence of an adverse environment and there are many results for solving these games, see e.g. [6]. In particular, solutions to parity games cover a variety of interesting properties and can be solved both in the case of finite state spaces and for some infinite state spaces, such as those that can be represented by a pushdown process [16], i.e. a pushdown automaton without acceptance features.

This work is supported by the German Research Foundation through the Research Training Group (DFG GRK 1765) SCARE (www.scare.uni-oldenburg.de).

© Springer Nature Switzerland AG 2018
M. Mazzara et al. (Eds.): STAF 2018 Workshops, LNCS 11176, pp. 463–478, 2018.
https://doi.org/10.1007/978-3-030-04771-9_33

Graph grammars have an infinite state space in general and games defined over infinite state spaces are not generally decidable.

In this paper, we restrict ourselves to context-free hypergraph grammars, or more specifically hyperedge replacement (HR) grammars, and construct hyperedge replacement (HR) games to use the decidability result for parity pushdown games from Walukiewicz [16].

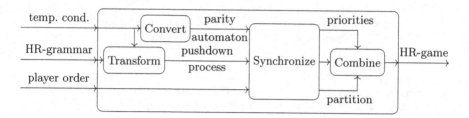

Fig. 1. Construction of a HR game

This process is illustrated in Fig. 1: Given an "ordered" HR-grammar, a temporal graph condition and a player order, we construct a HR-game as follows:

1. **Transform** the ordered HR-grammar and the temporal graph condition to a pushdown process, such that the states of the pushdown process are labelled with the atomic conditions of the temporal graph condition.
2. **Convert** the temporal graph condition into a parity automaton.
3. **Synchronize** the pushdown process with the player order and the parity automaton.
4. **Combine** the resulting pushdown process, partition function and priority function to form a HR-game.

The system is said to be correct, if there is a winning strategy for the system player. By the results of Walukiewicz [16], we can find such a strategy, if the HR-game is a parity pushdown game.

The remainder of the paper is structured as follows: Sect. 2 introduces ordered hyperedge replacement grammars and temporal graph conditions. Section 3 provides a definition for pushdown processes and parity pushdown games. Section 4 presents the transformation of an ordered hyperedge replacement grammar and a temporal graph condition to a pushdown process. In Sect. 5 a hyperedge replacement game is constructed from the pushdown process by integrating the player order and generating a priority function from the temporal graph condition. Moreover the main result is presented: HR-games are decidable. Section 6 covers related work and the paper is concluded in Sect. 7.

Due to space limitations, the proof for Theorem 2 has been omitted. It can be found in [12].

2   HR-Grammars and Temporal Graph Conditions

In this section, we define hyperedge replacement grammars [4,7] and introduce temporal graph conditions, i.e. graph conditions [8] equipped with temporal operators. The basis are hypergraphs and hypergraph morphisms. Hypergraphs are a generalization of graphs where hyperedges are allowed to have a number of tentacles instead of one source and one target.

Assumption. Let Σ be a finite, ranked alphabet and $N \subseteq \Sigma$ be a subset of *nonterminal* symbols where $rank \colon \Sigma \to \mathbb{N}^1$ assigns to each symbol $a \in \Sigma$ its rank $rank(a)$.

Definition 1 (Hypergraph & Hypergraph Morphism). A *hypergraph* over Σ is a tuple $G = (V, E, att, lab, ext)$, consisting of a set of *nodes* V, a set of *hyperedges* E, an *attachment function* $att \colon E \to V^{*2}$, a labelling function $lab \colon E \to \Sigma$ and a (possibly empty) sequence $ext \in V^*$ of pairwise disjoint *external nodes*. For $e \in E$, we set $rank(e) = rank(lab(e))$ and require $|att(e)| = rank(e)^3$. A hypergraph is *finite* if the sets of nodes and edges are finite. We denote the empty graph as $\emptyset$. The components of a hypergraph G are denoted as $V_G, E_G, att_G, lab_G, ext_G$, respectively. Furthermore, $E_G^N = \{e | e \in E_G : lab(e) \in N\}$ denotes the set of *nonterminal hyperedges* of G, i.e. hyperedges labelled with nonterminal symbols.

Given two hypergraphs G, H, a *hypergraph morphism* $f \colon G \to H$ consists of functions $f_V \colon V_G \to V_H$ and $f_E \colon E_G \to E_H$, such that $f_V^*(att(e)) = att(f_E(e))^4$ and $lab(e) = lab(f_E(e))$, i.e., morphisms preserve attachments and labels. A morphism is *injective*, *surjective* or an *isomorphism*, if f_V and f_E are, respectively, injective, surjective or both.

We use hypergraphs to define rules which replace a hyperedge by a hypergraph and connect them along the nodes connected to the hyperedge and the external nodes of the hypergraph.

Definition 2 (Hyperedge Replacement). A *hyperedge replacement rule* $r \colon X ::= R$ consists of a nonterminal label $X \in N$ and a hypergraph R over Σ where $rank(X) = |ext_R|$.

Let G, H be hypergraphs, $r \colon X ::= R$ a rule and $e \in E_G$ a nonterminal hyperedge with $rank(e) = |ext_R|$ and $lab(e) = X$. A *derivation* or *hyperedge replacement* from G to H by the rule r applied to e, written $G \Rightarrow_{r,e} H$ or $G \Rightarrow_r H$, is the substitution $H = G[R/e]$ of a hyperedge $e \in E_G$ by R, i.e.,

- $V_H = V_G \uplus (V_R \setminus [ext_R])^5$

---

[1] $\mathbb{N}$ is the set of all natural numbers, including 0.

[2] V^* is the collection of all finite sequences over V, including the empty sequence ϵ.

[3] $|att(e)|$ denotes the length of a sequence $att(e)$.

[4] For a function $f \colon A \to B$, the free symbolwise extension $f^* \colon A^* \to B^*$ is defined by $f^*(a_1...a_n) = f(a_1)...f(a_n)$.

[5] $\uplus$ denotes the disjoint union, $\setminus$ the difference of sets and $[ext_R]$ denotes the set of elements of ext_R.

- $E_H = (E_G \setminus \{e\}) \uplus E_R$
- $att_H = att_G|(E_G \setminus \{e\}) \cup att_R; mod^6$
- $lab_H = (lab_G|(E_G \setminus \{e\})) \cup lab_R$
- $ext_H = ext_G$

where mod matches external nodes of R to the attachments of e, i.e. $mod = id_{V_H} \cup \{[ext_R(1) \rightarrow att_G(e)(1), ..., ext_R(rank(e)) \rightarrow att_G(e)(rank(e))]\}$.

Definition 3 (Hyperedge Replacement Grammar). A *hyperedge replacement (HR-)grammar* is a tuple $\mathfrak{G} = (G_0, \mathcal{R})$ where G_0 is the *start hypergraph* and $\mathcal{R}$ is a finite set of rules.

We extend hyperedge replacement grammars to *ordered* ones to obtain an analogue of left-most derivations [9]. For this purpose, we consider *ordered hypergraphs* in which the set of nonterminal hyperedges is ordered.

Definition 4 (Ordered Hyperedge Replacement Grammar). An *ordered* hyperedge replacement grammar is a hyperedge replacement grammar with an ordered start graph and a set of ordered rules.

An *ordered* hypergraph (G, o) consists of a hypergraph G together with a bijective function $o: E_G^N \rightarrow [1, n]^7$ (or equivalently a sequence $o = e_1, e_2, ..., e_n$) where E_G^N denotes nonterminal hyperedges in G and $n = |E_G^N|$ is the number of elements in the set.

An *ordered hypergraph morphism* from (G, o_G) to (H, o_H) is a hypergraph morphism $f: G \rightarrow H$ that *respects the order*, i.e., for all $e, e' \in E_G$, $o_G(e) < o_G(e')$ implies $o_H(f(e)) < o_H(f(e'))$.

A rule $r : X::= (R, o)$ is *ordered*, if (R, o) is an ordered hypergraph.

An *ordered derivation* from an ordered hypergraph (G, o_G) to an ordered hypergraph (H, o_H) by an ordered rule $r : X::= (R, o_R)$ is a derivation from G to H in which the first nonterminal hyperedge in the order is replaced. The order of the resulting hypergraph H is obtained by substituting the hyperedge e_1 in the order o_G by the order o_R.

Notation. For an ordered hypergraph G with $o = e_1 e_2 ... e_n$ and a natural number $i \leq n$, by the hyperedge e_i we refer to the edge at position i in o and $\mathbf{str}(G)$ produces the sequence of nonterminal labels in the graph in the reverse order of its hyperedges, i.e. $\mathbf{str}(G) = X_n X_{n-1} ... X_1$ where $X_i = lab(e_i)$.

In the following we write *graph, edge, rule* and *grammar* instead of ordered hypergraph, hyperedge, ordered rule and ordered hyperedge replacement grammar and G, H, R are always ordered hypergraphs.

Example 1 (Ordered Hyperedge Replacement Grammar). Consider the grammar $\mathfrak{G} = (G_0, \mathcal{R})$ with the start graph G_0 and rules $\mathcal{R} = \{extend, wait, switch, delete,$

---

^{6} The function $f|S$ is the restriction of f to a set S. The symbol ; denotes forward composition of functions, i.e. $f; g(x) = f(g(x))$.

^{7} $[1, n]$ denotes the set of natural numbers from 1 to n.

fix} as shown below. The position of a hyperedge in the respective order is marked by a label $\langle i \rangle$ with $i \in \mathbb{N}$. Unless otherwise specified, we assume both the attachment function and the order of hyperedges proceed left to right.

Definition 5 (Temporal Graph Condition). A *positive condition* is of the form $\exists(a : \emptyset \hookrightarrow C)$, where $a : \emptyset \hookrightarrow C$ is a morphism into a graph C, short $\exists(C)$. A positive condition c is *satisfied* by a graph G, written $G \models c$, if there exists an injective morphism q, such that for the morphism $i_G : \emptyset \hookrightarrow G$, we have $a; q = i_G$.

Temporal graph conditions are propositional LTL-formulas [13] where positive conditions are the *atomic conditions*. We use the usual abbreviations of *always* ($\square$) and *eventually* ($\lozenge$) operators. For a temporal graph condition ϕ, the set of all atomic conditions is $At(\phi)$.

For the definition of the semantics of temporal graph conditions, we define labelled transition systems in the sense of [11] and *graph transition systems* analogously to [3].

A *labelled transition system* over some alphabet consists of a, potentially infinite, labelled graph with a designated start node and edges labelled over the alphabet. We refer to the nodes of a transition system as *states* and the edges as *transitions*. A *run* over a transition system is a sequence $\sigma = \sigma_0 \sigma_1 \sigma_2 ...$ of states along transitions of the transition system beginning with the start node that is either infinite or must end in a state without outgoing transitions.

Definition 6 (Graph Transition System). The *graph transition system* $\mathcal{T} = (T, s_0)$ of a grammar $\mathfrak{G} = (G_0, \mathcal{R})$ is a labelled transition system where T is a tree[8] with root node s_0 and $lab(s_0) = G_0$ where every state $s \in V_T$ is labelled with a graph, every transition $t \in E_T$ is labelled with a rule, and there exists a transition $s \xrightarrow{r} s'$ for states $s, s' \in E_T$ and $r \in \mathcal{R}$, if $lab(s) \Rightarrow_r lab(s')$.

Notation. Where it is clear from context, we speak of *transition systems*, rather than labelled transition systems or graph transition systems.

Satisfaction of temporal graph conditions is defined over graph transition systems, where atomic conditions are evaluated over state labels.

Example 2 (Temporal Graph Condition). In the following, we use the temporal graph condition $\phi = \square \neg c$ with the atomic condition $c = \exists(\bullet \!\!-\!\!\!\rightarrow\!\bullet \ \ \rightarrow\!\bullet)$.

---

[8] A *tree* is a connected, cycle free graph with a designated root node.

3 Parity Pushdown Games

In this section, we recall the definition of parity pushdown games [16]. We consider two player games, in which one player sys represents actions of a system and the other player env represents interference from the environment. Pushdown games are defined over pushdown processes, i.e. pushdown automata without acceptence features. We label the transitions of pushdown processes with rules and define transition systems of pushdown processes as counterparts to graph transition systems.

Definition 7 (Pushdown Process). Let $\mathcal{R}$ be a set of hyperedge replacement rules. A *pushdown process* over $\mathcal{R}$ is a tuple $\mathcal{P} = (Q, \Gamma, q_0, w_{init}, \delta)$, where Q is a finite set of *states*, Γ is a finite *stack alphabet*, q_0 is the start state, $w_{init} \in \Gamma^{+9}$ is the *initial stack content*, and $\delta \subseteq Q \times \Gamma \times \mathcal{R} \times Q \times \Gamma^*$ is the *transition relation*. A *configuration* is a pair (q, s), where $q \in Q$ is a state and $s \in \Gamma^+$ is the word called the *stack content*. The *initial configuration* is (q_0, w_{init}).

The *transition system* $\mathcal{T}(\mathcal{P}) = (T, s_0)$ of a pushdown process $\mathcal{P}$ is a labelled transition system where T is a tree with root s_0, $lab(s_0) = (q_0, w_{init})$ and there exists an edge $(q_i, s \cdot X, r) \xrightarrow{e} (q_j, s \cdot w)^{10}$ with $lab(e) = (r, X, w)$, $q_i, q_j \in E_T$, if there is a corresponding transition $(q, r, X) \rightarrow (q', w)$ with $q, q' \in Q$ in the pushdown process $\mathcal{P}$.

A *pushdown transducer* $\mathcal{PT}$ is a pushdown process with additional input and output alphabets Σ_i, Σ_o and a partial output function $\lambda \colon Q \rightarrow \Sigma_o$.

Notation. We order elements on the stack from left to right, such that the rightmost element is at the top of the stack.

Lemma 1 (Pushdown Store Languages are Regular [2]). Given a pushdown process with a set of *final states*, the *pushdown store language*, i.e. the language of words over Γ on the stack in a final state, is regular.

Given a pushdown process, every priority function induces a parity condition.

Definition 8 (Parity Condition). Given a pushdown process $\mathcal{P}$ with state set Q and a *priority function* $pri \colon Q \rightarrow \mathbb{N}$, the condition $Par(pri)$, with $Par(pri) \models \sigma$ if and only if the least priority $pri(\sigma_i)$ occurring infinitely often is even for a run $\sigma = \sigma_0 \sigma_1 \sigma_2 ...$ over $\mathcal{T}(\mathcal{P})$, is called *parity condition*.

A pushdown process along with a partition of its states and a priority function constitute a parity pushdown game.

Definition 9 (Parity Pushdown Game [16]). A *parity pushdown game* $\mathcal{G} = (\mathcal{P}, part, pri)$ consists of a pushdown process $\mathcal{P}$ along with a *partition function* $part \colon Q \rightarrow \{\text{sys}, \text{env}\}$ and a priority function $pri \colon Q \rightarrow \mathbb{N}$. A *run* over the transition system of $\mathcal{P}$ is *won* by player sys if it satisfies the parity condition and is won by player env otherwise. A *finite run* is *won* by player sys if it ends in a state of env and there is no applicable move for env and vice versa.

---

[9] Γ^+ denotes the set of nonempty sequences over Γ.
[10] The symbol $\cdot$ denotes string concatenation.

A strategy sets the next move for a player; to do so for the infinite state spaces of pushdown games we use a pushdown transducer.

Definition 10 (Strategy). A *strategy* for player sys is a pushdown transducer, which reads moves of env to produce the next move for sys. A *winning strategy* is a strategy such that a run $\sigma = \sigma_0 \sigma_1 \sigma_2...$ is won by sys, if for each σ_i where $part(\sigma_i) = $ sys the output function λ produces a move to the state σ_{i+1}.

Theorem 1 (Parity Pushdown Games are Decidable [16]). Finding a winning strategy for a parity pushdown game is decidable.

4 From HR-Grammar to Pushdown Process

In this section, we construct a pushdown process from an ordered hyperedge replacement grammar and a temporal graph condition.

4.1 Simulating a HR-Grammar by a Pushdown Process

To construct a parity pushdown game from a grammar, we first need to construct a pushdown process. Any run over the transition system of the grammar has a corresponding run using the same rules over the transition system of the pushdown process. Additionally, the states of the pushdown process are sets of the atomic conditions of the winning condition which must be satisfied by the corresponding graphs generated by the grammar.

Definition 11 (Simulation). Let $\mathfrak{G}$ be a HR-grammar, ψ be a temporal graph condition and $\mathcal{P}$ a pushdown process with sets of conditions over $At(\phi)$ as states. $\mathcal{P}$ *simulates* $\mathfrak{G}$ with respect to ϕ, if
  (iso) there exists an isomorphism $iso\colon \mathcal{T}_u(\mathfrak{G}) \to \mathcal{T}_u(\mathcal{P})$ between their unlabelled transition systems,
  (rules) for every transition e in $\mathcal{T}(\mathfrak{G})$, the transition $iso(e)$ in $\mathcal{T}(\mathcal{P})$ is labelled with the same rule as the edge e in addition to any stack changes, and
  (sat) for every state v in $\mathcal{T}(\mathfrak{G})$ labelled with a graph G and the state $iso(v) = (q, s)$ in $\mathcal{T}(\mathcal{P})$, if $G \models c$ with $c \in At(\phi)$ then $\exists c' \in q : c' \Rightarrow c$ and if $c \in q$ then $G \models c$.

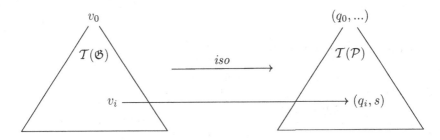

4.2 Partial Conditions

To be able to conclude which atomic conditions hold in a state of the pushdown process, we track which fragments of the condition are satisfied. We refer to these fragments as *subconditions*.

Definition 12 (Subcondition). For a condition $\exists(C)$, the condition $\exists(C')$ with $C' \subseteq C$ is called a *subcondition* of $\exists(C)$. The set of all subconditions of a condition c is denoted by $\mathsf{Sub}(c)$. We write $c_s \sqsubseteq c$ for $c_s \in \mathsf{Sub}(c)$.

If a condition is satisfied, its subconditions are also satisfied.

Lemma 2 (Subconditions preserve Satisfaction). For a graph G and a condition $c = \exists(C)$, $G \models c$ implies $G \models c_s$ for all $c_s \in \mathsf{Sub}(c)$.

Proof. If $G \models c$, then there exists an injective morphism $q : C \hookrightarrow G$. Since c_s is a subcondition of c, $C_s \subseteq C$ and then there exists a morphism $a_s^+ : C_s \to C$, such that $a_s^+ ; q$ is a morphism, implying $G \models c_s$. □

Subconditions with additional nonterminal hyperedges enable the application of rules to conditions, we call these *partial conditions*.

Definition 13 (Partial Condition). Let $c = \exists(C)$ be an atomic condition, and $c_s = \exists(C_s)$ a subcondition of c. A *partial condition* $c_p = \exists(C_p)$ *with respect to* c, is a condition with $C_s \subseteq C_p$, such that there exists a derivation $C_p \Rightarrow_{\mathcal{R}'} C^+$ to $C^+ \supseteq C$ by some set of rules $\mathcal{R}'$ where the number of hyperedges in $C_p \setminus C_s$ is at most the number of items in $C \setminus C_s$. For a condition c, $\mathsf{Part}(c)$ is the set of all partial conditions of c.

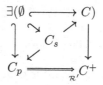

Lemma 3 (Finiteness of Partial Conditions). The set of partial conditions for a given condition c is finite.

Proof. Follows directly from the finiteness of c and the limit on the additional hyperedges. □

4.3 Construction of the Pushdown Process

To create a pushdown process we construct states as sets of partial conditions with respect to the atomic conditions of ϕ and use the rules of $\mathfrak{G}$ to construct transitions between such states.

Let $c = \exists(C)$ be a partial condition, $r : X :: = R$ a rule, and $C \Rightarrow_{r,e} C'$ a derivation. Then $c' = \exists(C')$ is the derived condition. We write $c \Rightarrow_{r,e} c'$ or $c \Rightarrow_r c'$.

$$\exists(\emptyset \xrightarrow{\ a\ } C)$$
$$a' \searrow \quad \Vert r$$
$$C'$$

If a condition is satisfied by a graph, deriving a new condition will also allow the derivation of a graph that satisfies this condition. For ordered hyperedge replacement, this is only true if we replace the first nonterminal in the respective orders.

Lemma 4 (Satisfaction of Derived Conditions). Let G be an ordered hypergraph and $c = \exists(C)$ a partial condition, such that $G \models c$ by a morphism q. If $q(e_1) = e_1'$ where $e_1 \in C$ and $e_1' \in G$, a derivation $c \Rightarrow_{r,e_1} c'$ implies a derivation $G \Rightarrow_{r,e_1'} G'$, such that $G' \models c'$.

Proof. Satisfaction of c implies the existence of a morphism $sat \colon C \hookrightarrow G$. Assuming r replaces an edge e in C, we derive G' by applying r to $sat(e)$. We can construct a morphism $sat' \colon C' \to G'$ by restricting sat to $C \setminus e$ and expanding it to include $R \subseteq C' \to R \subseteq G'$. The existence of sat' implies that $G' \models c'$.   □

In general derived conditions will not be partial conditions. We split derived conditions by collecting all of their subconditions that are partial conditions with respect to atomic conditions. Since there are only finitely many partial conditions, we can use split to ensure that the construction generates a finite state set. The pushdown process is constructed by repeated application of rules to partial conditions, such that each rule application mirrors a rule application to a corresponding graph in the grammars transition system. Therefore, we also need to ensure that the conditions produced by split have no "gaps" with respect to the corresponding graphs.

Definition 14 (Split). The condition $c = \exists(C)$ *split* according to the atomic condition $c_t = \exists(C_t)$, results in the set

$$Split(c, c_t) = \{\exists(C_u) \mid \exists(C_p) \in \text{Part}(c_t) \cap \text{Sub}(c) : C_p \sqsubseteq C_u \sqsubseteq C,$$
$$\text{the order } o_{C_u} \text{ is the smallest uninterrupted subsequence of } o_C\}$$

For an index i, $Split_i(c, c_t) = \{\exists(C_u) \in Split(c, c_t) \mid \text{edge } e_i \text{ in } o_C \text{ is } e_1 \text{ in } o_{C_u}\}$ and for sets S, S_t of conditions, $Split_i(S, S_t) = \bigcup_{c_t \in S_t} \bigcup_{c \in S} Split_i(c, c_t)$.

Example 3 (Split). Let $c' = \exists(\bullet\!-\!\boxed{Y}\!-\!\bullet\!-\!\boxed{X})$ be a partial condition of the atomic condition $c = \exists(\bullet\!\!-\!\!\!\to\!\bullet\!\to\!\bullet)$. A condition $c'' = \exists(\bullet\!-\!\boxed{Y}\!-\!\bullet\!-\!\boxed{Y}\!-\!\bullet\!-\!\boxed{X})$ can be derived by applying the rule extend from Example 1 to c'. c'' however, is *not* a partial condition, since there are more hyperedges than there are items missing from c. We collect subcondition $c_s \sqsubseteq c''$ which are also partial conditions with respect to c, such that $Split(c', c) = \{\exists(\bullet\!-\!\boxed{Y}\!-\!\bullet\!-\!\boxed{X}), \exists(\bullet\!-\!\boxed{Y}\!-\!\bullet\!-\!\boxed{Y}\!-\!\bullet), \exists(\bullet\!-\!\boxed{Y}\!-\!\bullet), \exists(\bullet\!-\!\boxed{X})\}$.

To determine which conditions correspond to modifiable parts of the graph, we need to differentiate between conditions that have a satisfying morphism that matches their first nonterminal to the first nonterminal of the graph and conditions that do not.

Definition 15 (Accessibly Satisfied). A partial condition c is *accessibly satisfied (a-satisfied) with respect to a morphism* $q: C \hookrightarrow G$, if $q(e_1) = e_1'$ where e_1 and e_1' are the first nonterminals in the order of C and G, respectively, and is *inaccessibly satisfied (i-satisfied) with respect to* q, if $q(e_1) \neq e_1'$. A partial condition is *a-satisfied (i-satisfied) with respect to a graph* G, if the condition is a-satisfied (i-satisfied) with respect to some morphism $C \hookrightarrow G$.

The pushdown process is constructed from states consisting of three sets, a-satisfied conditions A, i-satisfied conditions I, and conditions with multiple i-satisfying morphism M. Additional states A', I', M' are constructed by application of rules only to the a-satisfying conditions A. There are two cases:

Rule Creates New Nonterminal Hyperedges. In the first case, the rule creates new *nonterminal* hyperedges. The new a-satisfying conditions A' are the conditions derived from A which contain the first nonterminal of the right-hand side of the rule. Additionally, new i-satisfying conditions might be created which must be added to I', as well as potentially be added to M' in case they already exist in I. The new stack content w contains the newly created nonterminals. The i-th nonterminal is paired with conditions in I' that contain the nonterminal at $i - 1$ in the order as their first. Additionally, the nonterminals are paired with conditions in M' whenever a new condition was added to M'. These are the sets α and μ, respectively.

Rule Creates Terminal Items Only. In the second case, we only produce *terminal* items. This will lead to previously i-satisfying conditions becoming a-satisfying, thus they must be added to A' in addition to the conditions derived from A. These conditions were previously recorded in the set α on the stack. Conditions in α have to be removed from I' unless there are multiple i-satisfying morphisms, i.e. they also occur in M. Lastly, conditions may have to be removed from M if this has previously been recorded on the stack in the set μ.

Construction 1 (Transition). Let $q = (A, I, M)$ consisting of three sets of partial conditions be a state of a pushdown process, $(X, \alpha, \mu) \in \Gamma$ be a triple consisting of a nonterminal X and two sets of partial conditions α, μ and $r : X:: = R$ be a rule.

We construct a new state $q' = (A', I', M')$ and new stack content w from the set of derived conditions $D = \{c \mid a \in A : a \Rightarrow_r c\}$. There are two cases for filtering the conditions D:

(1) $\mathrm{str}(R) = Y_n Y_{n-1} ... Y_1$
$\quad A' = Split_1(D, At(\phi))$
$\quad I' = I \cup \bigcup_{i=2}^{n} Split_i(D, At(\phi))$
$\quad M' = M \cup \bigcup_{i=2}^{n} (I_i \cap Split_i(D, At(\phi)))$
$\quad w = (Y_n, \alpha, \mu)(Y_{n-1}, \alpha_{n-1}, \mu_{n-1}) ... (Y_2, \alpha_2, \mu_2)(Y_1, \alpha_1, \mu_1)$

where $\alpha_i = Split_{i+1}(D, At(\phi))$, $\mu_i = I_{i+1} \cap Split_{i+1}(D, At(\phi)) \setminus M_{i+1}$, $I_j = I \cup \bigcup_{i=j+1}^{n} Split_i(D, At(\phi))$ and $M_j = M \cup \bigcup_{i=j+1}^{n}(I_i \cap Split_i(D, At(\phi)))$

(2) $str(R) = \epsilon$

$\quad A' = \{C_p^1 | C_p \sqsubseteq C_p^1 \sqsubseteq C, \exists(C) \in D, \exists(C_p) \in Split(D, At(\phi))$

$\quad\quad\quad C_p^1$ contains the first nonterminal in the order o_C,

$\quad\quad\quad o_{C_p^1}$ is the smallest uninterrupted subsequence of $o_C\} \cup \alpha$

$\quad I' = I \setminus (\alpha \setminus M)$

$\quad M' = M \setminus \mu$

$\quad w = \epsilon$

The resulting transition is $(q, (X, \alpha, \mu), r, w, q') \in \delta$.

Construction 2 (Pushdown Process $\mathcal{P}(\mathfrak{G}, \phi)$). Given a hyperedge replacement grammar $\mathfrak{G} = (G_0, \mathcal{R})$ and a temporal graph condition ϕ, $\mathcal{P}(\mathfrak{G}, \phi) = (Q, \Gamma, q_0, w_{init}, \delta)$ is the pushdown process where the set of states Q, the stack alphabet Γ, initial state q_0, initial stack content $w_{init} \in \Gamma^+$ and the transition relation δ are constructed as follows:

States are triples of sets of partial conditions. Let $q_{aux} = (\emptyset, \emptyset, \emptyset)$ be a helper state that is not part of Q and a let $(X, \emptyset, \emptyset) \in \Gamma$. The start state q_0 and initial stack content w_{init} are constructed from q_{aux} according to Construction 1, except that we assume $D = \{\exists(G_0)\}$. The generated state is q_0 and $w_{init} = \perp \cdot w$.

All other states and transitions are constructed by application of Construction 1 for as long as new states or transitions are generated.

By Lemma 1, we can determine the pushdown store language for each state by treating that state as the final state of the pushdown process, including the triples (X, α, μ) that may occupy the top of the stack, which allows us to construct additional states and transitions.

Notation. States $q = (A, I, M)$ of pushdown processes are represented as shown on the left below. The upper part of the node contains the set A, while the lower part contains I and M. Conditions c in the lower part are marked c^+ when they are present in both I and M. We abbreviate the partial conditions and triples $(X, \alpha, \mu) \in \Gamma$ as shown on the tables below.

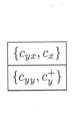

name	condition
c	$\exists(\bullet\!\!\longrightarrow\!\!\bullet\longrightarrow\!\!\bullet)$
c_x	$\exists(\bullet\!\!-\!\!\boxed{X}\!\!\;)$
c_y	$\exists(\bullet\!\!-\!\!\boxed{Y}\!\!-\!\!\bullet)$
c_{yx}	$\exists(\bullet\!\!-\!\!\boxed{Y}\!\!-\!\!\bullet\!\!-\!\!\boxed{X}\;)$
c_{yy}	$\exists(\bullet\!\!-\!\!\boxed{Y}\!\!-\!\!\bullet\!\!-\!\!\boxed{Y}\!\!-\!\!\bullet)$
$c_{y\rightarrow}$	$\exists(\bullet\!\!-\!\!\boxed{Y}\!\!-\!\!\bullet\longrightarrow\!\!\bullet)$

name	stack symbol
$X_{\emptyset,\emptyset}$	$(X, \emptyset, \emptyset)$
$X_{y,\emptyset}$	$(X, \{c_y\}, \emptyset)$
$X_{yy,\emptyset}$	$(X, \{c_{yy}, c_y\}, \emptyset)$
$X_{yy,y}$	$(X, \{c_{yy}, c_y\}, \{c_y\})$
$X_{yy,yy}$	$(X, \{c_{yy}, c_y\}, \{c_{yy}\})$

To make use of these pushdown processes for solving HR-games, we first need to show that they simulate the grammars they are constructed from.

Theorem 2 (Simulation). The pushdown process $\mathcal{P}(\mathfrak{G}, \phi)$ is finite and simulates $\mathfrak{G}$ with respect to ϕ.

Proof. By induction over a run γ over $\mathcal{T}(\mathfrak{G})$ and Lemmas 2 and 4. $\mathcal{P}(\mathfrak{G}, \phi)$ is finite: By Lemma 3 the number of partial conditions is finite and their uninterrupted versions are finite, since we have a finite set of rules. □

Example 4 (Pushdown Process with Partial Conditions). We take the grammar from Example 1 and the temporal graph condition from Example 2 to construct the pushdown process partially shown in Fig. 2.

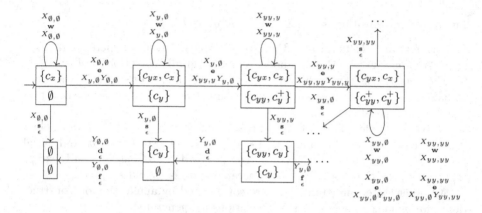

Fig. 2. Pushdown process with partial conditions

5 Construction of Hyperedge Replacement Games

The pushdown process from the previous section must be modified to generate a partition of its states and priority function to form a game. To generate a partition, we need to modify the pushdown process $\mathcal{P}(\mathfrak{G}, \phi)$ such that any state assigned to a player by the partition only has outgoing transitions that correspond to rules that belong to that player.

Example 5 (Player Order & Division of Rules). We specify the order in which players may make their moves with a transition system with states labelled over $\{\text{sys}, \text{env}\}$. In addition we set $\mathcal{R}(\text{sys}) = \{extend, delete\}$ and $\mathcal{R}(\text{env}) = \{wait, switch, fix\}$ for the rules introduced in Example 1.

The following transition system **ord** specifies alternating turns for the players sys and env:

$$\text{sys} \quad \text{env}$$

Construction 3 (Restriction). Let $\mathcal{P} = (Q, \Gamma, q_0, \bot, \delta)$ be a pushdown process over $\mathcal{R}$, $\mathbf{ord} = (T, s_0)$ a labelled transition system over $\{\mathbf{sys}, \mathbf{env}\}$.

The *restriction* of $\mathcal{P}$ by $\mathbf{ord}$ is constructed by synchronizing $\mathcal{P}$ and $\mathbf{ord}$ such that transitions $(q_i, (X, \alpha, \mu), r, w, q_j) \in \delta_{\mathcal{P}}$ are synchronized with edges in $\mathbf{ord}$ that start at a state labelled with $\mathbf{sys}$, if $r \in \mathcal{R}(\mathbf{sys})$ (analogously for $\mathbf{env}$). The labels $\mathbf{sys}, \mathbf{env}$ of states of $\mathbf{ord}$ induce a partition $part\colon Q \to \{\mathbf{sys}, \mathbf{env}\}$ over the states of of the modified pushdown process.

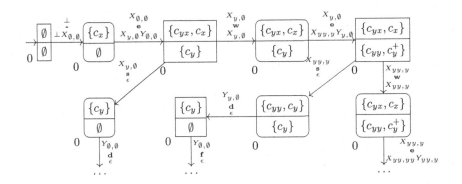

Fig. 3. Final pushdown process

We are left to integrate the temporal graph condition ϕ, which we translate into a priority function over the pushdown process.

Note. The result of Walukiewicz [16] assumes a pushdown process with an empty stack at the start. We can easily modify the pushdown process $\mathcal{P}(\mathfrak{G}, \phi)$ by reintroducing the auxiliary state q_{aux} used during construction as the new start state connected to q_0 by a transition that creates the initial stack. We set $part(q_{aux}) = \mathbf{env}$.

Lemma 5 (Temporal Graph Condition to Parity Condition). There is a transformation from a pushdown process $\mathcal{P}$ and a temporal graph condition ϕ to a priority function pri over $\mathcal{P}$, such that an infinite run σ over $\mathcal{T}(\mathcal{P})$ satisfies the parity condition $Par(pri)$ iff the run satisfies ϕ.

Construction 4 *(pri)*. Given a pushdown process $\mathcal{P}$ and a temporal graph condition ϕ, we modify $\mathcal{P}$ and construct a priority function pri over $\mathcal{P}$.

Convert ϕ to a Büchi-automaton $\mathcal{A}_\phi$ [15] and interpret $\mathcal{A}_\phi$ as a parity automaton where all accepting states have priority 0 and all other states have priority 1. To integrate the priorities into $\mathcal{P}$ we synchronize $\mathcal{P}$ with $\mathcal{A}_\phi$ by treating a transition $(q_i, (X, \alpha, \mu), r, w, q_j) \in \delta_{\mathcal{P}}$ with $q_j = (A, I, M)$ as if it is labelled c, if $\exists c' \in A \cup I : c \sqsubseteq c'$ and $\neg c$ otherwise for all $c \in At(\phi)$. We set $pri(q_{aux}) = 0$ and determine pri for other states by the component from $\mathcal{A}_\phi$.

Proof. [15] establishes this equality for ϕ and $\mathcal{A}_\phi$. The construction moves from a sequence of transitions in $\mathcal{A}_\phi$ to a sequences of states in $\mathcal{T}(\mathcal{P})$, the additional state q_{aux} has no influence on the satisfaction of $Par(pri)$.   □

Example 6 (Final Pushdown Process). The final pushdown process for the grammar from Example 1, the temporal graph condition from Example 2 and the player order from Example 5 is shown in Fig. 3. The partition function *part* is indicated by rectangles for env and rounded corners for sys. Additionally, the priority function *pri* is shown by a label at the bottom left corner of each state.

With these results, we define hyperedge replacement games.

Definition 16 (HR-Game). Let $\mathfrak{G}$ be an ordered hyperedge replacement grammar, ord a transition system with states labelled over $\{$sys, env$\}$ and ϕ a temporal graph condition. A *hyperedge replacement (HR) game* $\mathcal{G} = (\mathcal{P}, part, pri)$ consists of the pushdown process $\mathcal{P}(\mathfrak{G}, \phi)$ derived by Construction 2 and modified according to ord by Construction 3 and ϕ by Construction 4. *part* and *pri* are the partition function and the priority function induced by the latter two constructions.

Theorem 3 (HR-Games). Finding a winning strategy for HR-games is decidable.

Proof. Follows directly from the Theorems 1 and 2 and Lemma 5.   □

For the example game we have constructed throughout the paper, we cannot construct a winning strategy for sys. While there is no state in the restricted pushdown process that satisfies c, there is a strategy for the environment player env that forces the game to end in a state in which sys has no available moves.

Remark. (Rules with Application Conditions). The construction can be extended to rules with application conditions, by adding the application conditions to the set of atomic conditions. The applicability of these rules is then determined by checking for a-satisfaction of these conditions and transitions are omitted if application conditions are not satisfied.

6   Related Work

The combination of graph transformation and games has also been considered by Kaiser [10], referred to as *structure rewriting games*. In contrast to our approach rules are applied to all possible matches simultaneously. In addition, the approach uses a restricted class of graph transformation, called *separated handle rewriting*. The combination of restricted rewriting rules and simultaneous application to all matches also leads to decidable games.

Graph Transformation Games have independently been considered by Alabdullatif and Heckel [1], in the context of negotiation games. In contrast to our graph transformation games, players in the negotiation game play with the goal of minimizing costs rather than a binary win/loss. Consequently the solutions to these games are not winning strategies for either player, but an equilibrium for both players.

7   Conclusion and Future Work

In this paper we have proposed an approach to the verification of the correctness of graph grammars under adverse conditions, i.e. under the influence of an adverse environment. A hyperedge replacement game, consisting of an ordered hyperedge replacement grammar, a labelled transition system defining a player order and a temporal graph condition is introduced as a model for this purpose. We establish decidability of these games by showing that they can be reduced to parity pushdown games.

The main contributions of the paper are (1) a new notion of graph transformation games for modeling correctness under adverse conditions and (2) the identification of a decidable fragment of graph transformation games via a reduction to parity pushdown games.

It should be possible to extend the construction in such a way that winning conditions can be temporal conditions over any nested condition, since it should still suffice to consider a collection of finite subgraphs of a state. The main restriction of the translation to a pushdown process is the necessity for *ordered* hypergraph grammars. Dropping this restriction should still allow the construction of a Petri net, rather than a pushdown process, that similarly simulates a grammar. Unlike for pushdown games, however, we do not have a corresponding solution for finding winning strategies for transition systems generated by Petri nets.

Acknowledgements. We would like to thank Annegret Habel, Reiko Heckel, Berthold Hoffmann and Mark Minas for helpful feedback on earlier versions of this paper.

References

1. Alabdullatif, M., Heckel, R.: Graph transformation games for negotiating features. In: Graph Computation Models (GCM 2016) (2016)
2. Autebert, J.M., Berstel, J., Boasson, L.: Context-free languages and pushdown-automata. In: Handbook of Formal Languages, vol. 1: Word Language Grammar, pp. 111–172. Berlin (1997)
3. Baldan, P., Corradini, A., König, B., Lluch Lafuente, A.: A temporal graph logic for verification of graph transformation systems. In: Fiadeiro, J.L., Schobbens, P.-Y. (eds.) WADT 2006. LNCS, vol. 4409, pp. 1–20. Springer, Heidelberg (2007). https://doi.org/10.1007/978-3-540-71998-4_1
4. Drewes, F., Habel, A., Kreowski, H.J.: Hyperedge replacement graph grammars. In: Handbook of Graph Grammars and Computing by Graph Transformation, vol. 1, pp. 95–162. World Scientific (1997)
5. Ehrig, H., Ehrig, K., Prange, U., Taentzer, G.: Fundamental theory of typed attributed graph transformation based on adhesive HLR categories. Fundamenta Informaticae **74**(1), 31–61 (2006)
6. Grädel, E., Thomas, W., Wilke, T. (eds.): Automata Logics, and Infinite Games. LNCS, vol. 2500. Springer, Heidelberg (2002). https://doi.org/10.1007/3-540-36387-4

7. Habel, A.: Hyperedge Replacement: Grammars and Languages. LNCS, vol. 643. Springer, Heidelberg (1992). https://doi.org/10.1007/BFb0013875
8. Habel, A., Pennemann, K.H.: Correctness of high-level transformation systems relative to nested conditions. MSCS **19**, 245–296 (2009)
9. Hopcroft, J.E., Motwani, R., Ullman, J.D.: Introduction to Automata Theory, Languages, and Computation. Addison-Wesley Series in Computer Science, 2nd edn. Addison-Wesley-Longman, Boston (2001)
10. Kaiser, Ł.: Synthesis for structure rewriting systems. In: Královič, R., Niwiński, D. (eds.) MFCS 2009. LNCS, vol. 5734, pp. 415–426. Springer, Heidelberg (2009). https://doi.org/10.1007/978-3-642-03816-7_36
11. Keller, R.M.: Formal verification of parallel programs. Commun. ACM **19**(7), 371–384 (1976)
12. Peuser, C.: From hyperedge replacement grammars to decidable hyperedge replacement games. In: Graph Computation Models (GCM 2018) (2018, Preproceedings). https://www.gcm2018.uni-bremen.de/assets/gcm_2018_paper_10.pdf
13. Pnueli, A.: The temporal logic of programs. In: 18th Annual Symposium on Foundations of Computer Science, Providence, Rhode Island, USA, pp. 46–57. IEEE Computer Society (1977)
14. Poskitt, C.M., Plump, D.: Verifying total correctness of graph programs. Electron. Commun. EASST **61** (2013). https://journal.ub.tu-berlin.de/eceasst/article/view/827
15. Vardi, M.Y., Wolper, P.: An automata-theoretic approach to automatic program verification. In: Proceedings of the First Symposium on Logic in Computer Science, pp. 322–331. IEEE Computer Society (1986)
16. Walukiewicz, I.: Pushdown processes: Games and model-checking. Inf. Comput. **164**(2), 234–263 (2001)

Verifying a Copying Garbage Collector in GP 2

Gia S. Wulandari[1,2(✉)] and Detlef Plump[1]

[1] Department of Computer Science, University of York, York, UK
{gsw511,detlef.plump}@york.ac.uk
[2] School of Computing, Telkom University, Bandung, Indonesia

Abstract. Cheney's copying garbage collector is regarded as a challenging test case for formal approaches to the verification of imperative programs with pointers. The algorithm works for possibly cyclic data structures with unrestricted sharing which cannot be handled by standard separation logics. In addition, the algorithm relocates data and requires establishing an isomorphism between the initial and the final data structure of a program run.

We present an implementation of Cheney's garbage collector in the graph programming language GP 2 and a proof that it is totally correct. Our proof is shorter and less complicated than comparable proofs in the literature. This is partly due to the fact that the GP 2 program abstracts from details of memory management such as address arithmetic. We use sound proof rules previously employed in the verification of GP 2 programs but treat assertions semantically because current assertion languages for graph transformation cannot express the existence of an isomorphism between initial and final graphs.

1 Introduction

Poskitt and Plump developed Hoare-style proof systems for verifying the partial and total correctness of graph programs and showed that their proof calculi are sound with respect to the operational semantics of graph programs in the language GP 2 [12,13]. In these calculi, pre- and postconditions of programs are so-called E-conditions which extend nested graph conditions with support for expressions. E-conditions are limited to specify first-order graph properties and cannot express non-local properties such as connectedness or the existence of arbitrary-length paths. M-conditions [15] overcome this limitation in that they express monadic second-order properties of graphs.

In this paper, we present the verification of a graph program that cannot be proved correct by using E- or M-conditions because its correctness requires to establish a certain isomorphism between input and output graphs. We implement Cheney's copying garbage collector [3] in the graph programming language GP 2 and prove that it is totally correct. Cheney's algorithm is regarded as a challenge

G. S. Wulandari—Supported by Indonesia Endowment Fund for Education (LPDP).

© Springer Nature Switzerland AG 2018
M. Mazzara et al. (Eds.): STAF 2018 Workshops, LNCS 11176, pp. 479–494, 2018.
https://doi.org/10.1007/978-3-030-04771-9_34

for formal approaches to verifying pointer programs. This is because it works for possibly cyclic data structures with unrestricted sharing which cannot be handled by standard separation logics [5,16]. In addition, the algorithm relocates data which requires establishing an isomorphism between the initial and the final data structure of a program run.

While cycles and unrestricted sharing are not a problem for formal assertions based on nested graph conditions, the existence of an isomorphism between initial and final graphs of program runs cannot be expressed with such assertions. Therefore we treat assertions semantically, without a formal language, but use sound proof rules that were previously employed in GP 2 verification.

The remainder of this paper is structured is follows: Sect. 2 briefly describes the graph programming language GP 2, followed by Sect. 3, where we introduce the basic notions of graph program verification. In Sect. 4, we present an implementation of Cheney's copying garbage collector in GP 2. In Sect. 5, we precisely specify the garbage collector by pre- and postconditions. In Sect. 6, we prove that our implementation is partially correct, will terminate and cannot fail. In Sect. 7, we argue that our proof of partial correctness is shorter and less complicated than comparable proofs in the literature. Finally, we conclude and give some topics for future work in Sect. 8.

2   Graph Programs

We briefly describe a subset of the graph programming language GP 2 that is sufficient for our case study. A full definition of GP 2, including a formal operational semantics, can be found in [11]. The language is implemented by a compiler generating C code [1].

The principal programming constructs in GP 2 are graph-transformation rules labelled with expressions. For example, the program **cheney** in Fig. 4 contains the declarations of five rules. Rules operate on *host graphs* whose nodes and edges are labelled with heterogeneous lists of integers and character strings. Variables in rules are typed, where **list** is the most general type. In particular, integers and strings are considered as lists of length one. By abuse of terminology, we call items *unlabelled* if they are labelled with the empty list.

Besides a list label, nodes and edges may carry a *mark* which is one of the values **green**, **blue**, **grey** and **dashed** (where **grey** and **dashed** are reserved for nodes and edges, respectively). Marks are convenient to highlight items in input or output graphs, and to record which items have been visited during a graph traversal. For convenience, we sometimes refer to unmarked nodes as *white* nodes.

Moreover, nodes in rules and host graphs may be distinguished as *roots*. For example, in the rule **copy_root** of Fig. 4, nodes with a thick black border are roots. While roots are normally used to restrict the set of rule matches [1], we use them in this paper to specify reachable subgraphs.

The grammar in Fig. 1 gives the abstract syntax of graph programs in our subset (without the syntax of rule declarations). A program consists of a number of rule declarations and exactly one declaration of a main command sequence. The category RuleId refers to declarations of rules in RuleDecl. The call of a rule set $\{r_1, \ldots, r_n\}$ non-deterministically applies one of the rules whose left-hand graph matches a subgraph of the host graph. Rule matching is injective and involves instantiating the variables in rules with host graph labels. The call *fails* if none of the rules is applicable to the host graph. A loop command $\mathcal{R}!$ applies the rule set $\mathcal{R}$ repeatedly until it fails. When this is the case, $\mathcal{R}!$ terminates with the graph resulting from the last successful application of $\mathcal{R}$.

Prog	::= Decl {Decl}
Decl	::= RuleDecl | MainDecl
MainDecl	::= Main '=' ComSeq
ComSeq	::= Com {';' Com}
Com	::= RuleSetCall ['!']
RuleSetCall	::= RuleId | '{' RuleId {',' RuleId} '}'

Fig. 1. Abstract syntax of a subset of GP 2 programs

The semantics of graph programs is given in the style of structural operational semantics [9]. The meaning of a graph program P is the function $[\![P]\!]$ mapping an input graph G to the set $[\![P]\!]G$ of all possible outcomes of executing P on G. Possible outcomes include the value fail which indicates a failed program run, and the value $\perp$ which indicates divergence. We say that program P *can diverge from* graph G if there exists an infinite program run starting from G.

Writing $\mathcal{G}^\oplus$ for the set of all host graphs extended with the values fail and $\perp$, the semantic function $[\![\_]\!] : \text{ComSeq} \to (\mathcal{G} \to 2^{\mathcal{G}^\oplus})$ is defined by

$$[\![P]\!]G = \{X \in (\mathcal{G} \cup \{\text{fail}\}) \mid \langle P, G \rangle \xrightarrow{+} X\} \cup \{\perp \mid P \text{ can diverge from } G\}$$

where $\to$ is a small-step transition relation on *configurations* which is inductively defined by inference rules. In our setting, a configuration is either a command sequence together with a host graph, just a host graph or the special element fail: $\to \subseteq (\text{ComSeq} \times \mathcal{G}) \times ((\text{ComSeq} \times \mathcal{G}) \cup \mathcal{G} \cup \{\text{fail}\})$.

Configurations in $\text{ComSeq} \times \mathcal{G}$, given by a rest program and a host graph, represent states of unfinished computations while graphs in $\mathcal{G}$ are final states or *results* of computations.

Figure 2 shows the inference rules for the GP 2 commands used in this paper. The rules contain meta-variables for command sequences and graphs, where R stands for a call in category RuleSetCall (as defined by the grammar in Fig. 1), P and Q stand for command sequences in category ComSeq, and G, H stand for graphs in $\mathcal{G}$. The transitive closure of $\to$ is denoted by $\to^+$. We write $G \Rightarrow_R H$ if H results from host graph G by applying the rule set R, while $G \not\Rightarrow_R$ means that there is no graph H such that $G \Rightarrow_R H$ (application of R fails).

$$[\text{call}_1]\ \frac{G \Rightarrow_R H}{\langle R, G\rangle \to H} \qquad [\text{call}_2]\ \frac{G \not\Rightarrow_R}{\langle R, G\rangle \to \text{fail}} \qquad [\text{seq}_1]\ \frac{\langle P, G\rangle \to \langle P', H\rangle}{\langle P;Q, G\rangle \to \langle P';Q, H\rangle}$$

$$[\text{seq}_2]\ \frac{\langle P, G\rangle \to H}{\langle P;Q, G\rangle \to \langle Q, H\rangle} \qquad [\text{seq}_3]\ \frac{\langle P, G\rangle \to \text{fail}}{\langle P;Q, G\rangle \to \text{fail}} \qquad [\text{alap}_1]\ \frac{\langle P, G\rangle \to^+ H}{\langle P!, G\rangle \to \langle P!, H\rangle}$$

$$[\text{alap}_2]\ \frac{\langle P, G\rangle \to^+ \text{fail}}{\langle P!, G\rangle \to G}$$

Fig. 2. Semantic inference rules

$$[\text{ruleapp}]\ \frac{\models \{c\}\ r\ \{d\}}{\{c\}\ r\ \{d\}} \qquad\qquad [\text{ruleset}]\ \frac{\{c\}\ r\ \{d\}\ \text{for all } r \in \mathcal{R}}{\{c\}\ \mathcal{R}\ \{d\}}$$

$$[\text{alap}]\ \frac{\{inv\}\ \mathcal{R}\ \{inv\}}{\{inv\}\ \mathcal{R}!\ \{\neg\text{App}(\mathcal{R}) \wedge inv\}} \qquad [\text{comp}]\ \frac{\{c\}\ P\ \{d\} \qquad \{d\}\ Q\ \{e\}}{\{c\}\ P;Q\ \{e\}}$$

$$[\text{cons}]\ \frac{c \Rightarrow c' \qquad \{c'\}\ P\ \{d'\} \qquad d' \Rightarrow d}{\{c\}\ P\ \{d\}}$$

Fig. 3. Proof rules for graph program verification

3   Verification of Graph Programs

As mentioned in the Introduction, we treat assertions semantically and express pre- and postconditions in ordinary mathematical language (similar to [10]). As is usual in Hoare logic, we use triples $\{c\}\ P\ \{d\}$ to state that program P is partially correct with respect to precondition c and postcondition d. Intuitively, this means that for every graph G satisfying c, any graph H resulting from executing P on G will satisfy d.

Given a graph G and some assertion c, we write $G \models c$ if G satisfies c. If, in addition to partial correctness, P cannot diverge or fail from graphs satisfying c, the program is totally correct.

Definition 1 (Partial and total correctness [14]). *A graph program P is partially correct with respect to a precondition c and a postcondition d, if for every host graph G and every graph H in $\llbracket P \rrbracket G$, $G \models c$ implies $H \models d$.*

P is totally correct with respect c and d if it is partially correct and for every host graph G such that $G \models c$, $\llbracket P \rrbracket G \cap \{\bot, \text{fail}\} = \emptyset$.

We write $\models \{c\}\ P\ \{d\}$ if P is partially correct with respect to c and d. In Hoare logic, proof rules in the form of axioms and inference rules are used to construct proof trees decorated with Hoare triples. Proof trees are defined in Definition 2. The rules we use in this paper are shown in Fig. 3; they are taken from [12,13,15] except for [rule app], which replaces an axiom involving the weakest liberal precondition. As our semantic assertions do not come with an algorithm for calculating the weakest liberal precondition, determining and proving this condition would unnecessarily inflate our proofs.

Definition 2 (Proof tree [12]). *If $\{c\}$ P $\{d\}$ is an instance of an axiom X then* (a) *is a proof tree. If* $\{c\}$ P $\{d\}$ *can be instantiated from the conclusion of an inference rule X, and there are proof trees $T_1, \cdots, T_n$ with conclusions that are instances of the n premises of X, then* (b) *is a proof tree.*

$$(a) \quad X \; \frac{}{\{c\} \; P \; \{d\}} \qquad\qquad (b) \quad X \; \frac{T_1 \quad \cdots \quad T_n}{\{c\} \; P \; \{d\}}$$

Property App($\mathcal{R}$) in rule [alap] expresses that the rule set $\mathcal{R}$ is applicable. By the semantics of the as-long-as-possible command, $\mathcal{R}$ is not applicable to any graph resulting from the loop $\mathcal{R}!$

Definition 3 (App($\mathcal{R}$)). *Let $\mathcal{R}$ be a set of rules. A graph G satisfies App($\mathcal{R}$) if and only if there exists a graph H such that $G \Rightarrow_\mathcal{R} H$.*

The proof rules we use in this paper are known to be sound with respect to GP 2's operational semantics.

Theorem 1 (Soundness of proof rules [12]). *Given a program P and assertions c and d, $\vdash \{c\}$ P $\{d\}$ implies $\models \{c\}$ P $\{d\}$.*

Here $\vdash \{c\}$ P $\{d\}$ means that there exists a proof tree with root $\{c\}$ P $\{d\}$.

4   Cheney's Copying Garbage Collector in GP 2

Cheney's garbage collector assumes two disjoint, equally large regions of memory where the first region holds the data structure to be garbage collected and the second region consists of free cells. The structure that is reachable from the root cell in the first area is copied to the second region. Subsequently, the complete first region can be freed by the memory management system. Adopting this technique, we construct the graph program **cheney** in Fig. 4 to garbage collect an input graph. We model the free cells assumed by Cheney's method as unlabelled isolated nodes. This is similar to the store model used by [6] for pointer verification.

As input, our program assumes a graph that can be partitioned into two subgraphs: the graph to be garbage collected, and the graph that models a region of free memory cells. We differentiate the two regions by colours. White and grey nodes are used for the first region while green and blue nodes are used for the second region. The root cell in the first region is a unique root node. Hence, garbage collection involves identifying the subgraph reachable from the root node and copying it to the unlabelled subgraph. In Fig. 5, we give an example of the execution of **cheney**.

As in [5,16], we do not model the subsequent freeing of cells in the first region. This would be easy to achieve by a few rules which change all white and grey nodes into unlabelled green nodes and delete all edges between these nodes.

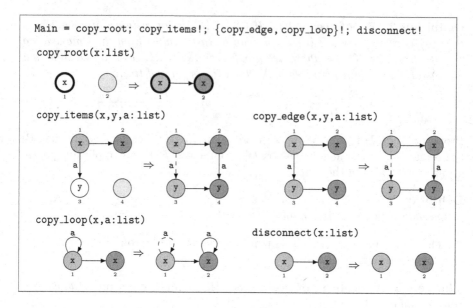

Fig. 4. Graph program cheney (Color figure online)

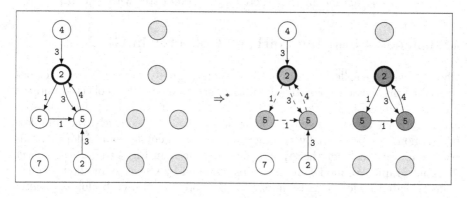

Fig. 5. A graph before and after the execution of cheney (Color figure online)

5   Case Study: Specification

We assume that the input graph of the program cheney can be partitioned into two subgraphs as described above. This partition will persist during program execution. Given an input graph G, we use Old_G and New_G to refer to these subgraphs, where Old_G is to be garbage collected.

Definition 4 (Old_G **and** New_G). *Given a graph G, we denote by Old_G the subgraph consisting of all unmarked and grey nodes and all edges between them. Also, New_G denotes the subgraph consisting of all green and blue nodes and all edges between them.*

The aim of program **cheney** is to copy to New_G the subgraph of Old_G consisting of all nodes and edges that are reachable from the root. We denote this subgraph by $\text{Reach}(\text{Old}_G)$.

Definition 5 ($\text{Reach}(G)$). *Given a graph G with a unique root node v, we denote by $\text{Reach}(G)$ the subgraph of G consisting all nodes and edges reachable from v by directed paths.*

As the garbage collector copies a subgraph of Old_G to New_G, its formal specification by pre- and postcondition needs to require an isomorphism between $\text{Reach}(\text{Old})$ in the input graph and $\text{Reach}(\text{New})$ in the result graph. However, program **cheney** uses marks to distinguish Old and New and reachable subgraphs. Therefore, we introduce graph morphisms that preserve labels, sources, targets, and roots, but ignore marks.

Definition 6 (Liberal graph morphism). *Given graphs G and H, a liberal graph morphism $f: G \to H$ is a pair of mappings $f = \langle f_V: V_G \to V_H, f_E: E_G \to E_H \rangle$ that preserve sources, targets, labels and roots.*

Then, an isomorphism is a bijective liberal morphism that reflects root nodes.

Definition 7 (Isomorphism). *A liberal graph morphism $f: G \to H$ is an isomorphism if f_V and f_E are bijective and if for each node v in G, v is a root if and only if $f_V(v)$ is a root.*

Given an input graph **Start**, program **cheney** has to produce a graph **Result** such that $\text{Reach}(\text{Old}_{\text{Start}})$ is isomorphic to $\text{Reach}(\text{New}_{\text{Result}})$. We specify the pre- and postcondition of **cheney** as follows.

Precondition. Each node in **Start** is either unmarked or green, and the number of unmarked and green nodes is the same. All edges are unmarked. All green nodes are isolated and unlabelled. There is a unique root node which is unmarked.

Postcondition. Each node in **Result** is either in $\text{Old}_{\text{Result}}$ or $\text{New}_{\text{Result}}$, and the number of nodes in $\text{Old}_{\text{Result}}$ and $\text{New}_{\text{Result}}$ is the same. There are no edges connecting $\text{New}_{\text{Result}}$ and $\text{Old}_{\text{Result}}$. There is a unique grey root node in $\text{Old}_{\text{Result}}$ and a unique blue root node in $\text{New}_{\text{Result}}$. In $\text{Reach}(\text{Old}_{\text{Result}})$, the nodes are grey and the edges are dashed, while other items in $\text{Old}_{\text{Result}}$ are unmarked. In $\text{Reach}(\text{New}_{\text{Result}})$, the nodes are blue and the edges are unmarked, while all other nodes in $\text{New}_{\text{Result}}$ are isolated green nodes which are unlabelled. Moreover, $\text{Reach}(\text{Old}_{\text{Start}})$ and $\text{Reach}(\text{New}_{\text{Result}})$ are isomorphic.

6   Case Study: Proof

6.1   Partial Correctness

To prove that program **cheney** is correct with respect to its pre- and postcondition, we consider an arbitrary execution of **cheney** that transforms an input graph Start satisfying the precondition into a result graph Result. Our proof rests on a property $\text{inv}_{\text{Start}}$, defined in Definition 8, which holds for Start and is an invariant for all five rules of cheney (shown in Lemma 2). Thus $\text{inv}_{\text{Start}}$ holds for each graph in the execution sequence Start $\Rightarrow^*$ Result.

In particular, for each graph G such that Start $\Rightarrow^* G \Rightarrow^*$ Result, $\text{inv}_{\text{Start}}$ asserts the existence of two isomorphisms: one between $\text{Old}_{\text{Start}}$ and Old_G and another one between Grey_G and Blue_G. Here Grey_G is the subgraph of G consisting all grey nodes and all dashed edges between them, and Blue_G is the subgraph of G consisting all blue nodes and all edges between them. We then establish that $\text{Grey}_{\text{Result}}$ equals $\text{Reach}(\text{Old}_{\text{Result}})$ while $\text{Blue}_{\text{Result}}$ equals $\text{Reach}(\text{New}_{\text{Result}})$.

Roughly, $\text{Old}_{\text{Start}}$ and Old_G are isomorphic because (1) no rule deletes or creates nodes, (2) no rule deletes, creates or relabels edges within Old (any edge created or deleted is incident to a blue node), (3) no rule can change the colour or label of a grey node, and (4) rules can change unmarked nodes only by turning them grey (while preserving the label).

Moreover, Grey_G and Blue_G are isomorphic because (1) $\text{Grey}_{\text{Start}} = \emptyset = \text{Blue}_{\text{Start}}$, (2) copy_root creates one-node in graphs Grey and Blue whose nodes are roots with the same label, and an unlabelled edge connecting Grey and Blue, called an *isomorphism edge*, which represents the node mapping of the isomorphism, (3) copy_items extends both Grey and Blue by one edge and its target node, where the edges have the same label and sources connected by an isomorphism edge, and creates an isomorphism edge between the target nodes, (4) copy_edge extends Grey and Blue by one edge each, where the edges have the same label and have their sources resp. targets connected by an isomorphism edge, (5) copy_loop works similar to copy_edge except that the new edges are loops, and (6) disconnect removes an isomorphism edge and hence does not alter Grey or Blue.

We use these isomorphisms to show that $\text{Reach}(\text{Old}_{\text{Start}})$, $\text{Reach}(\text{Old}_{\text{Result}})$ and $\text{Reach}(\text{New}_{\text{Result}})$ are all isomorphic, thus establishing the correctness of the garbage collector. We remark that verifying the existence of an isomorphism between (subgraphs of) the start graph and the result graph of a graph program execution is not possible with the approach of [12–15].

A proof tree for the partial correctness for cheney is provided in Fig. 6. The assertions in the tree are defined in Definition 8. One of these assertions is $\text{inv}_{\text{Start}}$ which acts as an invariant of cheney (see Lemma 2). We then give arguments about leaves in the proof tree in Lemma 3. The proof tree contains some applications of the proof rule [cons] whose validity is obvious by propositional logic, such as $c \wedge d \Rightarrow c$. We do not justify such applications, but we prove in Lemma 4 implications that are not obvious.

Definition 8. *Let G be a graph. We define the following assertions:*

reachOldGrey	:	in $\text{Reach}(\text{Old}_G)$, all nodes are grey
reachOldDashed	:	in $\text{Reach}(\text{Old}_G)$, all edges are dashed
reachNewBlue	:	in $\text{Reach}(\text{New}_G)$, all nodes are blue
nogreynode	:	there is no grey node
nobluenode	:	there is no blue node

nodashededge	:	there is no dashed edge
noconnect	:	there are no edges between Old_G and New_G

$\text{inv}_{\text{Start}}$:   :

(a) every node in G is either in Old_G or New_G, where Old_G and New_G have the same number of nodes

(b) there is a unique root node in Old_G and at most one root node in New_G

(c) each edge in G is either unmarked or dashed

(d) all grey nodes are in $\text{Reach}(\text{Old}_G)$

(e) all dashed edges are in $\text{Reach}(\text{Old}_G)$

(f) all blue nodes are in $\text{Reach}(\text{New}_G)$

(g) all green nodes are isolated unlabelled nodes

(h) there exists an isomorphism $f\colon \text{Grey}_G \to \text{Blue}_G$ where Grey_G is the subgraph of G consisting all grey nodes and all dashed edges between them while Blue_G is the subgraph of G consisting all blue nodes and all edges between them

(k) each edge e connecting Old_G and New_G is an isomorphism edge, that is, an unlabelled and unmarked edge satisfying $f_V(s_G(e)) = t_G(e)$

(l) Old_G is isomorphic to $\text{Old}_{\text{Start}}$

connect	:	if $f_V(v_1) = v_2$ then there exists an edge from v_1 to v_2
rootOldUnmark	:	there exists a unique unmarked root node in Old_G
rootOldGrey	:	there exists a unique grey root node in Old_G
norootNew	:	there is no root node in New_G
rootNewBlue	:	there exists a unique blue root node in New_G

From now on we denote the pre- and postcondition stated in Sect. 5 by precondition and postcondition, respectively.

Lemma 1 (Pre- and postcondition). *Using the assertions of Definition 8, the following holds:*

precondition $\Leftrightarrow$ $\text{inv}_{\text{Start}}(\text{a, b, c, g}) \wedge$ nogreynode $\wedge$ nobluenode $\wedge$ nodashededge
$\wedge$ rootOldUnmark $\wedge$ norootNew

postcondition $\Leftrightarrow$ $\text{inv}_{\text{Start}}(\text{a, b, d, e, f, g, h, l}) \wedge$ noconnect $\wedge$ reachOldGrey
$\wedge$ reachOldDashed $\wedge$ reachNewBlue

Proof. The first sentence of precondition is equivalent to $\text{inv}_{\text{Start}}(\text{a}) \wedge$ nogreynode $\wedge$ nobluenode, while the second sentence equivalent to $\text{inv}_{\text{Start}}(\text{c}) \wedge$ nodashededge. Then, the next sentence is equivalent to $\text{inv}_{\text{Start}}(\text{g})$, and the last sentence is equivalent to $\text{inv}_{\text{Start}}(\text{b}) \wedge$ rootOldUnmark $\wedge$ norootNew.

For postcondition, note that we write the result graph as Result. The first sentence in postcondition is equivalent to $\text{inv}_{\text{Start}}(\text{a})$, while the second sentence is equivalent to noconnect. Then, the next sentence is equivalent to $\text{inv}_{\text{Start}}(\text{b}) \wedge$ rootOldGrey $\wedge$ rootNewBlue. With the support of $\text{inv}_{\text{Start}}(\text{a})$, the fourth sentence is equivalent to reachOldGrey $\wedge$ reachOldDashed $\wedge$ $\text{inv}_{\text{Start}}(\text{d})$ $\wedge \text{inv}_{\text{Start}}(\text{e})$, and the fifth sentences is equivalent to reachNewBlue $\wedge$ $\text{inv}_{\text{Start}}(\text{f})$ $\wedge \text{inv}_{\text{Start}}(\text{g})$. The last sentence then equivalent to $\text{inv}_{\text{Start}}(\text{h}) \wedge \text{inv}_{\text{Start}}(\text{l}) \wedge$ ReachOldGrey $\wedge$ ReachOldDashed $\wedge$ ReachNewBlue.   □

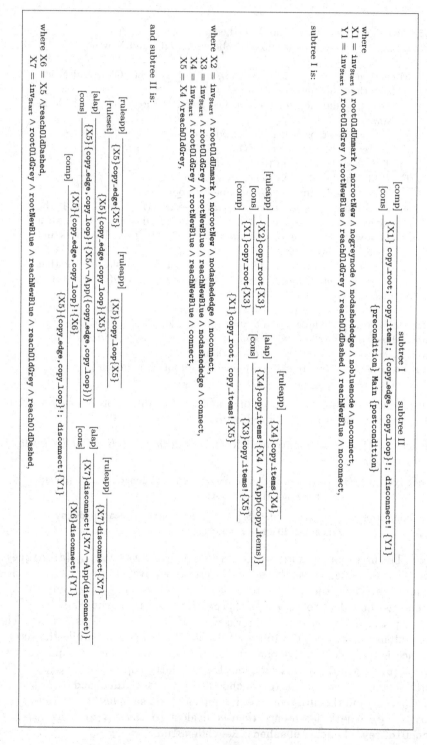

Fig. 6. Proof tree for partial correctness of **cheney**

Lemma 2 ($\text{inv}_{\text{Start}}$ **is invariant for all rules**). *The following holds:*

$$\models \{\text{inv}_{\text{Start}}\}\ \texttt{copy\_items}\ \{\text{inv}_{\text{Start}}\} \qquad \models \{\text{inv}_{\text{Start}}\}\ \texttt{copy\_loop}\ \{\text{inv}_{\text{Start}}\}$$
$$\models \{\text{inv}_{\text{Start}}\}\ \texttt{copy\_edge}\ \{\text{inv}_{\text{Start}}\} \qquad \models \{\text{inv}_{\text{Start}}\}\ \texttt{disconnect}\ \{\text{inv}_{\text{Start}}\}$$
$$\models \{\text{inv}_{\text{Start}} \wedge \texttt{norootNew}\}\ \texttt{copy\_root}\ \{\text{inv}_{\text{Start}}\}$$

Proof. We proof the lemma by checking each point of $\text{inv}_{\text{Start}}$.

(a) The application of any rule in cheney does not add or remove any node. It may change the colour of a node from unmarked to grey or from green to blue, which does not change the number of vertices in Old_G and New_G.

(b) Changes in root node only shown in copy_root, which change unmarked root node to grey root node and add a blue root node. This means the number of root nodes in Old_G never changes after any rule application, while the number of root nodes in New_G can increase from zero (because of norootNew) to one after the application of (copy_root), but never changes after the application of other rules.

(c) Every edge in each rule in the lemma is either unmarked or dashed. Therefore, for all rules in the lemma, since there is no other marks for edges exists before a rule application, they must not exist after the rule application.

(d) We only give the proof for copy_items and copy_root as the other rules do not change grey nodes and the triples must hold. For copy_root, the rule change an unmarked root node to a grey root node. From (b) we know that there is only one root node in Old_G, which implies there is no other root node than this new grey root node. The new grey root node is reachable from itself. Then for copy_items, the rule change an unmarked node, which is reachable from a grey node, to grey. Note that the existing grey node is reachable from the root node because $\text{inv}_{\text{Start}}$ holds before rule application. This means the new grey node is reachable from the root node as well.

(e) We can see that in every rule in the lemma, if there exists a dashed edge then its source and target must be grey. Since grey nodes are in $\text{Reach}(G)$, dashed edges must also be in $\text{Reach}(\text{Old}_G)$.

(f) Similar to the proof for (d).

(g) There is no rule in the lemma transform an isolated unlabelled green node into a green node that incident to an edge or not unlabelled.

(h) In every rule in the lemma, a production of a new grey node is always accompanied with a production of a new blue node of the same label. A new dashed edge also accompanied with a production of a new edge between blue nodes, and the label of their source node (or target node) is always the same. Then, the new grey node can map to the new blue node, and the new dashed edge can map to the new edge as an addition to the morphism f. The mappings are isomorphism as they preserve sources, targets, labels, and root.

(k) The edge between Old and New can be inserted only by rules copy_root and copy_items. This means that the edge must be an isomorphism edge.

(l) Every rule in the lemma does not add or delete any unmarked or grey nodes, or edges between them. Modification of these elements exists, where unmarked nodes can transform into grey nodes and unmarked edges can transform into dashed edges while labels are still preserved. However, the marks indicate no changes in area (New or Old) membership, and there are no changes in adjacency. Hence, sources, targets, and labels are preserved. □

Lemma 3. *For assertions* X2, X3, X4, X5, X7 *as defined in* Fig. 6, *the following holds:*

(1) $\models$ {X2} copy_root {X3}   (4) $\models$ {X5} copy_loop {X5}
(2) $\models$ {X4} copy_items {X4}   (5) $\models$ {X7} disconnect {X7}
(3) $\models$ {X5} copy_edge {X5}

Proof. Recall that by Lemma 2, each rule preserves $\text{inv}_{\text{Start}}$.

(1) We can see that the application of copy_root preserves the satisfiability of nodashededge. The assertion rootOldUnmark in the precondition guarantees rootOldGrey by the construction of copy_root. Then because the rule creates a new rooted node in the New subgraph, norootNew yields rootNewBlue after the rule application. connect must holds because the new edge must be the only one connecting the two areas as noconnect holds in the precondition. It also guarantees reachNewBlue because in New subgraph, the new blue root node is an isolated node, so it is the only node that is reachable from the root node.

(2) We can see that copy_items does not change any root, grey, or blue node, so it preserves rootOldGrey $\wedge$ rootNewBlue as well. Then, connect asserts there exists an edge between v_1 and v_2 for all v_1 and v_2 such that $f_v(v_1) = v_2$. From $\text{inv}_{\text{Start}}$, we know that v_1 is a grey node and v_2 is a blue node. copy_items yields a new grey and blue node with the same label and there is an edge between them. Hence, the new edge must be an isomorphism edge so that connect is preserved. The rule copy_items also changes the number of blue node, so we will need to see how it affects reachNewBlue. Follows from point (f) of $\text{inv}_{\text{Start}}$, the blue node in the left-hand side of copy_items must be in Reach(New$_G$). Therefore, the new blue node in the right-hand side is in Reach(New$_G$) because the new blue node is reachable from the existing blue node, so that reachNewBlue still holds.

(3) Because there are no changes in nodes, copy_edge preserves rootOldGrey $\wedge$ rootNewBlue. The adjacency between two grey nodes and between a grey and a blue node are not changed by copy_edge, so connect $\wedge$ reachOldGrey still holds. copy_edge adds new edge between two blue nodes. However, since the two are initially are in Reach(New$_G$) so that it does not change the condition of ReachNewBlue.

(4) The rule does not add or remove any node, also any edge between two nodes, so it preserves rootOldGrey $\wedge$ rootNewBlue $\wedge$ reachNewBlue $\wedge$ reachOldGrey $\wedge$ connect.

(5) Because disconnect does not change any node, also any edge between same-coloured nodes, it preserves rootOldGrey$\wedge$rootNewBlue$\wedge$reachNewBlue$\wedge$ reachOldGrey$\wedge$reachOldDashed.   □

Lemma 4 (Validity of implications). *For assertions* X1, X4, X5, X6, X7, Y1 *as defined in* Fig. 6, *the following holds:*

(1) precondition $\Rightarrow$ X1
(2) Y1 $\Rightarrow$ postcondition
(3) X5 $\wedge$ ¬App(copy_edge) $\Rightarrow$ X6
(4) X5 $\wedge$ ¬App(copy_loop) $\Rightarrow$ X6
(5) X4 $\wedge$ ¬App(copy_items) $\Rightarrow$ X5
(6) X7 $\wedge$ ¬App(disconnect) $\Rightarrow$ Y1

Proof. (1) We will show that precondition in Lemma 1 implies X1. In X1, we have additional conjunction point (d), (e), (f), (h), (k), and (l) of inv$_{\text{Start}}$. Point (l) is clearly satisfied as G is Start. Then the other points must hold because nogreynode $\wedge$ nobluenode $\wedge$ nodashedge implies the nodes or edges that must satisfies certain requirement do not exist so nothing negate those points. Then, noconnect holds because New area only consists of isolated nodes.

(2) By simplification, it is clear that Y1 implies postcondition.

(3, 4) Similar as above, the non-applicability of copy_edge and copy_loop implies that there is no unmarked edges (including loops) where its source and target is a grey node. Therefore, reachOldGrey implies all nodes in Reach(Old$_G$) are grey and the non-applicability implies that edges between these nodes are not unmarked, i.e. all edges between these nodes are dashed so that reachOldDashed holds. Hence, X6 holds.

(5) connect and isomorphism in inv$_{\text{Start}}$(h) assert that each grey node is a source for an edge where a blue node with the same label as the grey node is the target. rootOldGrey implies the existence of grey node. inv$_{\text{Start}}$ also implies that if there exists an unmarked node, then there must exist an isolated node, as the number of grey and unmarked nodes equal to the number of blue and isolated green nodes while there is a bijective function from grey nodes to blue nodes. Therefore non-applicability of copy_items implies that there is no edge from a grey node to an unmarked node, which means unmarked nodes are not reachable from grey nodes. Then because inv$_{\text{Start}}$ asserts grey nodes are reachable from the start node in Old area, the unmarked nodes must not reachable from the start node so that reachOldGrey holds. Hence, X5 holds.

(6) Non-applicability of disconnect implies there are no edges between any grey nodes and any blue nodes. inv$_{\text{Start}}$ implies that edges connecting Old$_G$ and New$_G$ are only edges incident to grey and blue nodes. Therefore, the non-applicability implies Old$_G$ and New$_G$ are not connected which means noconnect holds so that Y1 holds.   □

6.2 Total Correctness

A graph program P is totally correct with respect to a precondition c if the graph program is partially correct, also will not fail or diverge, with respect to c [14]. We have shown that the program cheney is partially correct, so we only need to show that cheney cannot fail or diverge.

Let us recall cheney at Fig. 4. The command sequence in the program consists of one rule set call and four loop commands. Precondition clearly stated the existence of an unmarked root node. Then, because precondition guarantees the same number of unmarked and green nodes, there must exists at least one green node as we have an unmarked root node. Therefore, the match of the left-hand side of copy_root is guaranteed by precondition so it will not fail. By the semantic of loop command, the other commands in the sequence will not fail either so that the absence of failure in the execution of cheney is guaranteed.

The rule copy_root is only applied once, so it will not diverge. For loop commands, elimination of an element is clearly can guarantee the absence of divergence. The rule copy_items, copy_edge, copy_loop, and disconnect eliminate unmarked nodes, unmarked edges between two grey nodes, unmarked loops on grey nodes, and edges between grey and blue nodes respectively.

7   Related Work

In this study, we implement Cheney's copying garbage collector [3] in GP 2 and reason about it. Several works in verification of Cheney's algorithm stated the difficulties in verifying the algorithm, such as in reasoning about reachability in graphs [8] and verifying programs involving cyclic data structures.

Torp-Smith et al. [16] is the extended version of [2]. In the study, they extend standard separation logic so that it can be used in cyclic data structures. Some remarks are stated to show the advantage in using local reasoning for the verification, such as ensuring an assignment is not affecting some assertions. The isomorphism between data structures from two different points in time; before and after a program execution; is also introduced in the study. Again, separating conjunction is used to reason about isomorphism as the update of bijective function can be seen in local reasoning. However, we think their proof is complicated as there are so many rules involved yet the validity of the rules is not provided. Moreover, there are 57 pages in the journal paper to discuss the verification of Cheney's garbage collector. They use about 48 triples in the proof, but reasoning about each step takes a lot of work as well.

In McCreight's PhD thesis [7], they use the definition of a morphism from [16] and study about mechanised verification of Cheney's algorithm. They also use separation logic for their verification. Their proof is detailed as they see all possible cases to mechanise the verification, but they use various lemmas, and it is not clear how the lemmas are proved. The proof is separated into five parts. The verification of each part requires between one and seven pages. However, to fully understand the verification, we need to understand the specification of each part which is not more concise than the verification itself. In total, there are about 50 pages of the thesis that deal with Cheney's algorithm.

This may result from the level difference in the language, as they use low-level programming and we use a programming language that abstracts from details of memory management such as address arithmetic. The other studies use separation logic for local reasoning in the verification. However, because sharing mostly exists in graph problems including garbage collector, they need to extend separation logic so that it can be used in the verification of Cheney's algorithm. The extension itself is not easy, and proofs following this extension is complex. In contrast, there is no need for us to extend the existing proof calculus for reasoning about our graph program. By using the existing proof calculus, which is sound in the sense of partial correctness, we are able to show verification of **cheney** in a simple way with clear justification for each step of verification.

Another extension of separation logic for the verification of Cheney's garbage collector can be found in [5]. The paper introduces the notion of sharing in separation logic, which is called ramification. This allows local reasoning while global effects are still accounted for when they are required, enabling reasoning about programs that manipulate data structures with unrestricted sharing. Different from [2,16], the paper uses inductive graph predicates and does the reasoning on the level of mathematical graphs. It is claimed that the verification is more concise than in other work. This is indeed the case as there are only about two pages to discuss Cheney's garbage collector and its verification. However, we find it difficult to see the reasoning about implications given in the proof. In addition, one needs to understand the intricate theory about ramification and its use in verification.

8   Conclusion and Future Work

We have implemented Cheney's copying garbage collector in GP 2 and verified the program using Hoare logic. To be compared to the previous work we described in the previous section, they use local reasoning and argue that this helps them so that their reasoning is less complicated [16]. To be compared with our work, the use of marks in our program implicitly helps us in separating properties that are not affected as we can focus on structures with specific marks. Similarly, the update of bijective function in our case can be seen with the use of marks.

We show a proof tree for the partial correctness of the program, and only from this, we argue that the proof is more straightforward than other proofs that have been done for the Cheney's algorithm. Moreover, in our work we use proof rules that are proven to be sound to connect one triple to another. But in other literature about verification of Cheney's algorithm, they do not have a clear reasoning about soundness of proof rules they use. Moreover, from the proof sketch, we only use 22 triples while the proof sketch in [16] has about 48 triples. This shows how concise our proof if we compare to theirs.

Our proof is more concise than others partly because we still use arbitrary mathematical language for the assertions, unlike others that have defined formal assertions for this. Although there are E-conditions [12] that can be used to express properties of graphs in graph programs, we still need to extend this. We need an assertion that can describe a condition between two graphs that exist at a different point in time, but E-condition we have now only expressed the graph that exists at one point in time. Moreover, E-condition that based on first-order logic is not enough to represent properties we need, e.g. the existence of two area Old and New. M-condition [15] can cover this, but the formal definition of this is yet to be defined. However, none of these can be used to express the isomorphism between two graphs that exist in different time. In the future, we plan to look the transduction in monadic second-order logic [4] and have assertion language that can express isomorphism between two structures.

References

1. Bak, C., Plump, D.: Compiling graph programs to C. In: Echahed, R., Minas, M. (eds.) ICGT 2016. LNCS, vol. 9761, pp. 102–117. Springer, Cham (2016). https://doi.org/10.1007/978-3-319-40530-8_7
2. Birkedal, L., Torp-Smith, N., Reynolds, J.C.: Local reasoning about a copying garbage collector. In Proceedings Symposium on Principles of Programming Languages (POPL 2004), pp. 220–231. ACM (2004). https://doi.org/10.1145/964001.964020
3. Cheney, C.J.: A nonrecursive list compacting algorithm. Commun. ACM **13**(11), 677–678 (1970). https://doi.org/10.1145/362790.362798
4. Courcelle, B., Engelfriet, J.: Graph Structure and Monadic Second-Order Logic: A Language-Theoretic Approach. Cambridge University Press, Cambridge (2012). https://doi.org/10.1017/CBO9780511977619
5. Hobor, A., Villard, J.: The ramifications of sharing in data structures. In Proceedings Symposium on Principles of Programming Languages (POPL 2013), pp. 523–536. ACM (2013). https://doi.org/10.1145/2480359.2429131
6. Klarlund, N., Schwartzbach, M.: Verification of pointers. DAIMI Report Series 23(470). Aarhus University (1994). https://doi.org/10.7146/dpb.v23i470.6943
7. Mccreight, A.E.: The Mechanized Verification of Garbage Collector Implementations. Ph.D thesis, Yale University (2008)
8. Myreen, M.O.: Reusable verification of a copying collector. In: Leavens, G.T., O'Hearn, P., Rajamani, S.K. (eds.) VSTTE 2010. LNCS, vol. 6217, pp. 142–156. Springer, Heidelberg (2010). https://doi.org/10.1007/978-3-642-15057-9_10
9. Plotkin, G.D.: A structural approach to operational semantics. J. Log. Algebraic Program. **60–61**, 17–139 (2004). https://doi.org/10.1016/j.jlap.2004.05.001
10. Plump, D.: Reasoning about graph programs. In: Proceedings Computing with Terms and Graphs (TERMGRAPH 2016), Electronic Proceedings in Theoretical Computer Science, vol. 225, pp. 35–44 (2016). https://doi.org/10.4204/EPTCS.225.6
11. Plump, D.: From imperative to rule-based graph programs. J. Log. Algebraic Methods Program. **88**, 154–173 (2017). https://doi.org/10.1016/j.jlamp.2016.12.001
12. Poskitt, C.M.: Verification of Graph Programs. Ph.D thesis, University of York (2013)
13. Poskitt, C.M., Plump, D.: Hoare-style verification of graph programs. Fundamenta Informaticae **118**(1), 135–175 (2012). https://doi.org/10.3233/FI-2012-708
14. Poskitt, C.M., Plump, D.: Verifying total correctness of graph programs. In: Proceedings International Workshop on Graph Computation Models (GCM 2012) 2012. Revised version, Electronic Communications of the EASST, vol. 61 (2013). https://doi.org/10.14279/tuj.eceasst.61.827
15. Poskitt, C.M., Plump, D.: Verifying monadic second-order properties of graph programs. In: Giese, H., König, B. (eds.) ICGT 2014. LNCS, vol. 8571, pp. 33–48. Springer, Cham (2014). https://doi.org/10.1007/978-3-319-09108-2_3
16. Torp-Smith, N., Birkedal, L., Reynolds, J.C.: Local reasoning about a copying garbage collector. ACM Trans. Program. Lang. Syst. **30**(4), 24:1–24:58 (2008). https://doi.org/10.1145/964001.964020

Model-Driven Engineering
for Design-Runtime Interaction
in Complex Systems (MDE@DeRun)

MDE@DeRun 2018 Organizers' Message

The first edition of the international workshop on Model-Driven Engineering for Design-Runtime Interaction in Complex Systems (MDE@DeRun 2018) was held on June 28, 2018 at the ENSEEIHT (National Higher School of Engineering in Electrical Engineering, Hydraulics and Digital Sciences) in Toulouse, France in conjunction with the Software Technologies: Applications and Foundations (STAF 2018) confederation of conferences on software technologies.

Prior to the day of the event, the workshop followed regular submission guidelines. Papers have been submitted in PDF format, strictly adhering to the LNCS proceedings format for later publication in this STAF'18 Workshop post-proceedings volume. All submissions have been peer-reviewed by at least three members of the program committee before making a final decision. Two types of papers were considered: (i) Research papers (maximum 10 pages) describing elaborated technical work, experiments or evaluations, and (ii) Short papers (maximum 6 pages) describing new ideas, practical experience reports or tool demonstrations.

At the end of the submission and selection process, 5 papers have been accepted out of 6 initial submissions. According to this number of accepted publications, the actual day of the workshop was composed of two main times. In a first time, two slots were dedicated to the standard presentation of the accepted papers, including time for questions and related discussions. In a second time, a more interactive session was planned to foster open exchanges between all the workshop participants. The main objective of this last session was to start building something in common within the community, on which we could work further in the coming years. This has notably resulted in a report paper, also included in this STAF'18 Workshop post-proceedings volume, proposing some scientific challenges and a related roadmap.

The MDE@DeRun 2018 workshop would not have been successful without the precious help and support of the program committee members, as well as of the paper authors and event participants (without forgetting the STAF 2018 organizers). Thus, we would like to thank again all of them. After the success of this first edition of our MDE@DeRun 2018 workshop, and the fruitful discussions we had during the event and also afterward, we hope to be able to organize more editions in the coming years.

September 2018

Hugo Bruneliere
Romina Eramo
Abel Gómez

Organization

MDE@DeRun 2018 - Organization Commmittee

Hugo Bruneliere	IMT Atlantique & LS2N (CNRS), France
Romina Eramo	University of L'Aquila, Italy
Abel Gómez	Internet Interdisciplinary Institute (IN3) - Universitat Oberta de Catalunya (UOC), Spain

MDE@DeRun 2018 - Program Committee

Orlando Ávila-García	Atos Spain SA, Spain
Alessandra Bagnato	Softeam, France
Simona Bernardi	Universidad de Zaragoza, Spain
Alessio Bucaioni	Arcticus Systems AB, Sweden
Jordi Cabot	ICREA - Universitat Oberta de Catalunya, Spain
Federico Ciccozzi	Mälardalen University, Sweden
Cristóbal Costa-Soria	ITI - Instituto Tecnológico de Informática, Spain
Juergen Dingel	Queen's School of Computing, Canada
Davide Di Ruscio	University of L'Aquila, Italy
Sébastien Gérard	CEA LIST, France
Jesús Gorroñogoitia Cruz	Atos Spain SA, Spain
José Merseguer	Universidad de Zaragoza, Spain
Saad Mubeen	Mälardalen University, Sweden
Gerson Sunyé	University of Nantes & LS2N (CNRS), France
Jagadish Suryadevara	Volvo CE, Sweden
Massimo Tisi	IMT Atlantique & LS2N (CNRS), France
Connie U. Smith	L&S Computer Technology, Inc., USA
Aitor Urbieta	IKERLAN, Spain

From Modeling to Test Case Generation in the Industrial Embedded System Domain

Aliya Hussain[1], Saurabh Tiwari[1(✉)], Jagadish Suryadevara[2],
and Eduard Enoiu[1]

[1] Mälardalen University, Västerås, Sweden
ahn16022@student.mdh.se, {saurabh.tiwari,eduard.paul.enoiu}@mdh.se
[2] Volvo Construction Equipment AB, Gothenburg, Sweden
jagadish.suryadevara@volvo.com

Abstract. Model-based testing (MBT) is the process of generating test cases from specification models representing system requirements and the desired functionality. The generated test cases are then executed on the system under test in an attempt to obtain a pass or fail verdict. While different MBT techniques have been developed, only a few target the real-world industrial embedded system domain and show evidence on its applicability. As a consequence, there is a serious need to investigate the use of MBT and the evidence on how modeling and test generation can improve the current way of manually creating test cases based on natural language requirements. In this paper, we describe an on-going investigation being carried out to improve the current testing processes by using the MBT approach within an industrial context. Our results suggest that activity and structure diagrams, developed under MBT, are useful for describing the test specification of an accelerator pedal control function. The use of MBT results in less number of test cases compared to manual testing performed by industrial engineers.

Keywords: MBT · Systems engineering · Test cases · Modeling

1 Introduction

Model-based testing (MBT) is an approach of automatically designing test cases based on behavioral models of system requirements [3]. These models represent the expected behaviour of the system under test (SUT). The testing process mainly consists of three high-level steps namely, *creation*, *execution* and *evaluation* of a test case. The test case *creation* is the most important part of this process as it involves the design of the preconditions, test steps and the expected output. The test case *creation* is a challenging activity and it has a direct impact on the ability to find faults and the quality of the resulting product. MBT automates the test creation by using abstract models developed at an earlier stage

© Springer Nature Switzerland AG 2018
M. Mazzara et al. (Eds.): STAF 2018 Workshops, LNCS 11176, pp. 499–505, 2018.
https://doi.org/10.1007/978-3-030-04771-9_35

of the development process and promises to be a more efficient and effective method than manual testing [1, 2].

In this study we present the results of an investigation at VCE (Volvo CE[1]), the stakeholder's requirements, needs, and concerns written in natural language. Manual test cases are manually created using these requirements based on the test engineer's domain knowledge and experience. In Fig. 1, we illustrate the overview of how MBT differs in its high-level process to manual testing.

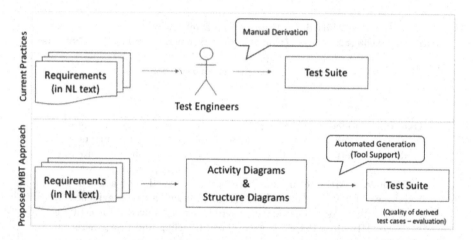

Fig. 1. Overview of MBT test case creation method and the current manual testing practice (NL stands for natural language).

We describe the modelling and test generation process using Conformiq Creator as well as an exploratory comparison between manual testing and MBT in terms of number of test cases and test goal categories. The goal is to facilitate the use of automated test case creation using models of the system specification and show its applicability. We demonstrate how the MBT process is used (as described in Fig. 1) for modeling a realistic function controlling the 'Accelerator Pedal' using activity diagrams (i.e, to specify the actions) and structure diagrams (i.e, to visualize the possible set of input and output parameters used). These diagrams are used by the MBT tool (Conformiq Creator[2]) to automatically generate test cases. Based on our initial investigations, we report our findings as well as point to future work.

2 Background

The study evaluates MBT use in an industrial scenario using a system provided by VCE. In this company, a management solution for systems engineering and

---

[1] Volvo Construction Equipment AB, Sweden.
[2] https://www.conformiq.com/.

software development (simply referred as the SE-Tool) is used as an adaption of the commercial tool *Systemweaver*[3]. This solution is a generic system modelling solution that supports the use of models (e.g., EAST-ADL[4] standard for automotive domain) and is a collaborative environment with support for system development. In this study we focus on the `Complete Analysis Function` (CAF) implemented in the SE-Tool framework and representing the functional architecture (i.e., the analysis level) of the Electrical and Electronic (E2E) control system w.r.to corresponding machine feature.

The CAF acts as a container for a collection of `Analysis Functions` (AF) and `Function Devices` (FD). An analysis function specifies a required function (within the E2E system) as a black-box mapping of inputs to outputs and a functional device (FD) that specifies the interface to other sub-systems, sensors or actuators. The HMI functional device is a special kind of functional device that is intended to be used for the operator interface; it defines components such as levers, switches and buttons for the operator interface. The SE-tool also provides the graphical overview of a CAF by showing all inputs and outputs as well as the interface with other subsystems.

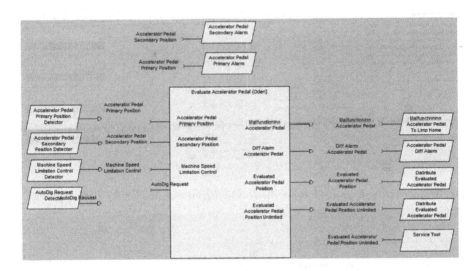

Fig. 2. View of Complete Analysis Function (CAF) for *Accelerator Pedal* function

The CAF function for the '*Accelerator Pedal*' is shown in Fig. 2. The purpose of this function is to evaluate pedal position requested from the *operator* (person who operates a machine through an appropriate interface). The inputs and outputs specified for the function are described, in terms of interface, as follows:

---

[3] http://systemweaver.se/.

[4] We refer the reader to the standard for further details: http://www.east-adl.info/.

- **Input Parameters:** *Accelerator Pedal Primary Position, Accelerator Pedal Secondary Position, Machine Speed Limitation Control,* and *AutoDig Request.* The values of both *Accelerator Pedal Positions, primary and secondary,* are obtained form the two sensors attached to the *"Acceleration Pedal".* On the other hand, the *Machine Speed Limitation* function provides *Machine Speed Limitation Control values* and the *AutoDig function* provides the *AutoDigRequest values.*

- **Output Parameters:** *Accelerator Pedal Primary Position, Evaluated Accelerator Pedal Position Unlimited, Evaluated Accelerator Pedal Position,* and *Malfunctioning Accelerator Pedal value.* In a nutshell, the *"Accelerator Pedal"* function translates the accelerator request from the operator into the corresponding "propulsion force request" which is passed on to and finally actuated by the Drive-Line System (DLS).

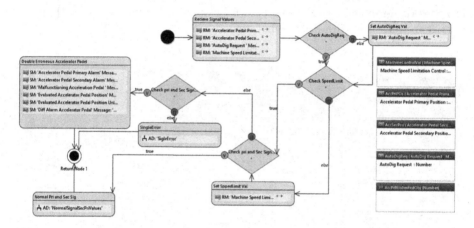

Fig. 3. An activity diagram showing the *Double Erroneous Accelerator Pedal* behavior.

3   The Modeling Approach

As shown in Fig. 1, in this paper, we describe a modeling approach to develop test models that enables automatic test case generation. The first step of the approach is to create, albeit manually (in future to be partly automated based on requirement models) a model from the CAF-based function specifications. Essentially, two types of models are created, namely, *activity* diagrams (i.e., representing behavioral models) and *structure* diagrams (i.e., representing a combinatorial model). We note here, that the structure diagram is limited to the input and output specifications. These diagrams created for the *Accelerator Pedal* function are described as follows:

– **Activity diagrams**: The activity diagram shown in Fig. 3 specifies the system behavior corresponding to the "Double Erroneous Accelerator Pedal" state of *Accelerator Pedal*. In the first activity node all input values are initialized and saved in the corresponding data objects. The value of *AutoDigRequest* is checked if its value falls out of range. In case this is true, the variable is reset in the next state. Similarly, *Machine Speed Limitation Control* value is adjusted. In addition, the Accelerator Pedal Primary Position and Accelerator Pedal Secondary Position are checked. If both values are out of range the output is set accordingly.

– **Structure Diagram:** The structure diagram as shown in Fig. 4, is created based on the *Accelerator Pedal* CAF for defining the interfaces available for testing. Firstly, the inputs and outputs of the function are identified. The Accelerator Pedal Input Signal interface contains several message objects and each message object corresponds to a specific input of a function. The message objects in the Accelerator Pedal Output Signal interface specifies the function outputs.

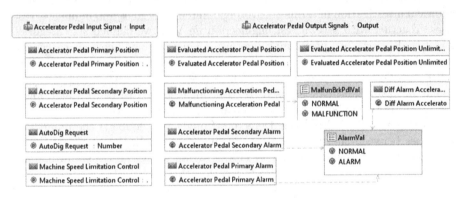

Fig. 4. Structure diagram for *Accelerator Pedal*

In the next section, we describe the main results obtained using the modelled diagrams in the context of generating test cases as well as a comparison between MBT and manual test cases.

4   Preliminary Results

The model of the Accelerator Pedal function is created manually and we validated the models by performing informal interviews with VCE test engineers responsible for testing the function under test to ensure model correctness and consistency. As a next step, the model is used as input to the Conformiq Creator tool to automatically generate test cases covering the created activity diagrams. Typically, the representation of a manually created test case in the SE-Tool is

performed in the test instruction language version 2 (TIL-2)[5] format to facilitate
the use of an automated test execution and evaluation environment. The test
cases derived from the proposed MBT approach are exported to a compatible
format (i.e., TIL-2). An example of a generated test case is shown in Table 1.

Table 1. Example of the test case derived in the TIL2 format compatible with the
VCE test environment

S.No.	Action	Expected result
1	Accelerator Pedal Primary Position = 101; Accelerator Pedal Secondary Position = −1; AutoDig Request = −1; Machine Speed; Limitation Control = -1	Accelerator Pedal Primary Alarm = ALARM; Accelerator Pedal Secondary Alarm = ALARM; Malfunctioning Acceleration Pedal = MALFUNCTION; Evaluated Accelerator Pedal Position = Do not Care; Evaluated Accelerator Pedal Position Unlimited = −1; Diff Alarm Accelerator Pedal = NORMAL

In order to contribute to the state-of-art, we compared MBT test cases with
manual test cases created by industrial engineers. We conducted a preliminary
empirical investigation in terms of covering different test goals and number of test
cases. Together with several test engineers from VCE we defined six categories
of test goals used when performing rigorous manual testing. These six categories
are shown in Table 2 and cover a set of realistic testing goals for the function
under test. Our results suggest that tests derived using the MBT approach are
similar in nature and can be used to cover all test goal categories at a lower
cost in terms of number of test cases created per each category; just for one of
these categories (i.e., Erroneous Detectors (Single and double)) the number of
test cases between the two techniques is similar. Overall, the total number of
test cases created using MBT (i.e., 8 TCs) is significantly lower than for manual
testing (i.e., 77 TCs). We have also found that these 8 TCs belong to multiple
categories. A more detailed efficiency and effectiveness measurement would be
needed to obtain more confidence in the results obtained in this study.

Table 2. Test goal category and number of test cases (TCs) comparison between
manually created test cases by industrial engineers and MBT-based test cases.

Test goal category	Manual TCs	MBT-based TCs
Normal operation	13	3
Differing detectors	6	1
Pedal position output	8	2
Erroneous detectors (single and double)	5	3
Erroneous autodig request and machine limitation control	22	3
All input erroneous combination	23	4
Total	77	8

[5] ISO/IEC/IEEE 29119-3:2013; Software and systems engineering – Software testing – Part 3: Test documentation.

5 Conclusions and Future Work

In this paper, we present an investigation into the use of model-based testing in the embedded system context. We use the Conformiq Creator tool to model the behavior and structure of a function controlling the accelerator pedal provided by Volvo CE. We automatically create test cases covering the model and compare these test cases in terms of test goal coverage and number of test cases to assess the applicability of MBT in this context. The approach has shown encouraging results. As future work, we plan to also investigate the efficiency and effectiveness of MBT test-case generation. We plan to semi-automatically generate diagrams out of CAF specifications to reduce the effort of creating test models. In addition, we need to investigate the use of complex data types and timing aspects into the test model, since Conformiq Creator does not support decimal numbers or how to directly represent timing requirements.

Acknowledgments. This work is partially funded from the Electronic Component Systems for European Leadership Joint Undertaking under grant agreement No. 737494 and The Swedish Innovation Agency, Vinnova (MegaM@Rt2). We would like to thank Kimmo Nupponen and the Conformiq team for their support.

References

1. Gudmundsson, V., Schulze, C., Ganesan, D., Lindvall, M., Wiegand, R.: An initial evaluation of model-based testing. In: 2013 IEEE International Symposium on Software Reliability Engineering Workshops (ISSREW), pp. 13–14 (2013)
2. Pretschner, A., et al.: One evaluation of model-based testing and its automation. In: Proceedings of the 27th International Conference on Software Engineering, ICSE 2005, pp. 392–401. ACM, New York (2005)
3. Schieferdecker, I.: Model-based testing. IEEE Softw. **29**(1), 14–18 (2012)

Automated Consistency Preservation in Electronics Development of Cyber-Physical Systems

Daniel Zimmermann[✉] and Ralf H. Reussner

Karlsruhe Institute of Technology (KIT), Karlsruhe, Germany
{d.zimmermann,reussner}@kit.edu

Abstract. Computer-aided development of complex cyber-physical systems usually takes place in engineering teams with several different expert roles using a range of various software tools. This results in numerous artifacts created during this process. However, these artifacts commonly contain plenty of overlapping information. Therefore, the editing of one model by a developer may lead to inconsistencies with other models. Keeping these artifacts manually consistent is time-consuming and error-prone. In this paper, we present an automated strategy to ensure consistency between two widely used categories of software tools in electrical engineering: an electronic design automation application for designing printed circuit boards (PCBs) and an electronic circuit simulator tool to predict system behavior at runtime.

Coupling these two types of tools provides the developers with the ability of efficiently testing and optimizing the behavior of the electric circuit during the PCB design process. For the proper preservation of consistency, assigning the model elements correctly between different tools is required. To avoid the disadvantages of ambiguous heuristic matching methods, we present a strategy based on annotated identifiers in order to ensure a reliable assignment of these model elements. We have implemented the described approach by using Eagle CAD as PCB software and Matlab/Simulink with the Simscape extension as the simulation tool.

Keywords: Cyber-Physical Systems (CPSs)
Consistency management · Electronics development

1 Introduction

Cyber-physical systems (CPSs) consist of a variety of mechanical, electronic and software components with increasing complexity. For example, more than 100 control units (ECUs) are installed in modern vehicles. The total number of lines of code in such systems can be up to 100 million, while now several thousand software-based functions are realized in premium cars [2]. This complexity, together with the cross-domain property of CPSs, poses a particular challenge for the development process.

© Springer Nature Switzerland AG 2018
M. Mazzara et al. (Eds.): STAF 2018 Workshops, LNCS 11176, pp. 506–511, 2018.
https://doi.org/10.1007/978-3-030-04771-9_36

Consequently, a whole range of different software tools are used for the development of such systems. A common programming environment for the design of mechatronic systems is, for example, Matlab/Simulink. For the creation of electronic circuit boards, tools such as Eagle, Altium or OrCad have proven themselves. Program packages for mechanical CAD designs are Catia, SolidWorks or AutoCAD. Furthermore, there are established tools for software development, multi-body simulations, thermal analysis, flow simulations and many more. It should be noted that a large part of the tools used for the development of CPSs are proprietary closed-source programs. The models created with such programs usually have overlapping information. For example, the description of a specific electrical circuit is used several times in different tools. It is crucial that the shared information of these models is consistent, otherwise, there may be delays during development or errors in later operation. Manual consistency management is very time-consuming and prone to error with an increasing number of complex models. Therefore, the use of automated methods is necessary, which reliably ensure the consistency and are easily applicable by the developer.

The contribution of this paper is an approach to couple existing modeling tools as black-boxes into the Vitruvius-Approach to couple metamodels for automated consistency support. More specifically, this paper deals with the problem, that practical consistency support should work in fine grained delta changes while black-box tools most often don't offer delta logging of changes. We bridge this with an approach presented in this paper by extracting these delta changes from two consecutive model states by using annotated identifiers.

The coupling of the model of a PCB program for the creation of electronic circuit boards with the model of a simulation tool offers the developer the opportunity to test the run-time-behavior of the circuit during the design phase. This means that errors can be detected at an early stage and optimizations can be made on the circuit. In comparison to similar solutions like [7], we are not presenting a new modeling language. Instead, we are coupling the models of existing software tools. Therefore, the developer can work with the usual tools without the effort of learning a new modeling environment.

2   The Vitruvius Approach

The Vitruvius framework is a model-driven approach for view-based development; it was originally designed for software development. Vitruvius is influenced by the *Orthographic Software Modeling (OSM)*, which uses a *Single Underlying Metamodel* (SUMM) [1]. The *Single Underlying Model* (SUM) contains all information without redundancies to inherently avoid inconsistencies. The user only gets access to the SUM via the views. The disadvantage of this approach is that the creation of a SUMM is complex and subsequent adjustments are difficult.

Vitruvius avoids this disadvantage by using a Virtual Single Underlying Metamodel (V-SUMM). In contrast to the SUMM, this V-SUMM consists of several metamodels, which are coupled with each other via consistency relationships. To simplify the definition of consistency relationships between metamodels, domain-specific languages have been developed [5]. Also with the Vitruvius approach, model changes can only be made via views. For the developer, the V-SUM behaves outwardly like the SUM proposed by Atkinson. The definition of consistency relationships is not made by the developer, but by the so-called methodologist.

Vitruvius follows a change-driven approach, meaning that the atomic model changes must be passed to the V-SUM. Each of these atomic changes is then gradually propagated through participating models based on the defined consistency rules [3]. However, this procedure requires the ability to track atomic changes during model editing by the developer.

3   Vitruvius for Closed-Source Tools

As already mentioned, the development of CPSs predominantly uses proprietary closed-source tools. Access to internal resources of such programs, e.g. via plug-ins, is usually not possible. However, it is possible to read and edit saved models. Some of the development tools use text-based file formats for persistence, some manufacturers rely on XML for example. From such files, models can be reconstructed and then edited. However, this approach only allows to view model states. There is no direct possibility to track the developer's atomic changes required by Vitruvius. These changes must first be extracted from two chronologically consecutive model states.

The basis for such a change extraction is the correct assignment of model elements, there are different matching algorithms (i.e. SiDiff, EMF Compare, Epsilon Comparison Language) [8,9]. However, an unambiguous mapping of model elements is only possible if universally unique identifiers (UUIDs) are present [4]. Heuristic methods can be used to resolve the ambiguities that are arising during the development process in the absence of UUIDs. These map the corresponding model elements based on structure and attributes [6]. However, since such procedures are faulty, they must be observed and controlled by the developer during execution, which in turn means more effort. In addition, incorrect element mappings cannot be ruled out by heuristic methods, even with the support of a developer.

When working with development tools, copying a model element is a common processing step. In the specific case of an electrical circuit, these may be components such as resistors, capacitors or transistors. During the copying process, the question is how to handle attributes of the copied element from other tools. For example, consider copying a resistor in a circuit simulation tool. We denote R_1 with the element to be copied and R_2 with the copy of R_1. After copying, both elements R_1 and R_2 have the same simulation attributes, including, for example, stray capacitances or inductances. Since the model of the simulation tool is coupled with that of the PCB program via the V-SUMM, R_1 implicitly also has attributes which occur exclusively in the PCB program, for example, information about packages of the components. Such information is not visible in the simulation tool. Now the question arises, which of the attributes, which are exclusively present in the PCB program, should have the element R_2 after the copying process. In our view, it is necessary for good usability that R_2 obtains all such attributes from R_1. The element R_2 should therefore also receive all the corresponding attributes from other tools after the copying process in the simulation tool. In this case, R_2 should have the same package as R_1.

In order for the consistency-keeping method to be able to fulfill this requirement when a model file is read, it must be recognized whether a newly added element originates from a copying process or not. This is indistinguishable without the presence of identifiers, and even when using UUIDs. To meet this requirement, we suggest annotating model elements with identifiers. During copying, this annotated identifier is adopted, meaning the original element and the copy have the same identifier. When reading a model file, copied elements can be recognized and attributes from other tools are correctly transferred to those elements. The identifiers are then dissolved into UUIDs, meaning that each element has a unique identifier once the consistency-keeping process has been completed. The annotated identifiers are manipulated only through the algorithm, whereas the developer should not make any changes to these identifiers.

4 Validation Case Study

A coupling between the PCB design program Eagle and the Simscape circuit simulation tool was implemented and tested on various circuits (Fig. 1). Simscape is an extension of Matlab/Simulink for the simulation of physical systems.

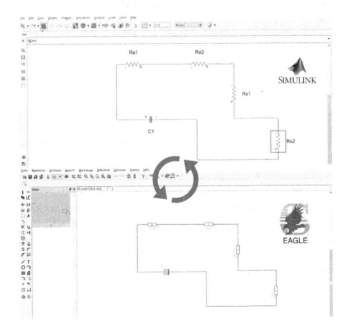

Fig. 1. Coupling between Eagle and Simscape

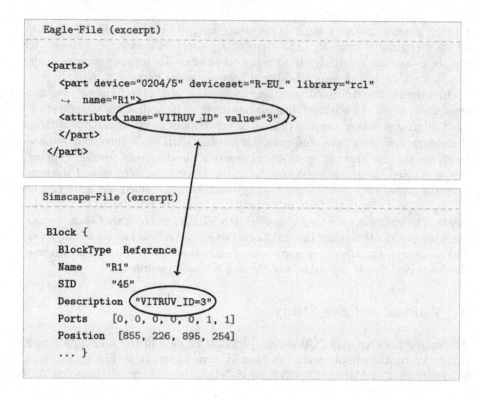

Fig. 2. Annotation of identifiers through adding attributes to the Eagle file and block comments to the Simscape file

The annotation is done in Simscape by entering identifiers in the block comments, in Eagle this is done by adding component attributes (Fig. 2). Even though in both tools the identifiers are visible to the developer during model editing, in our opinion these adjustments are hardly disturbing. The developer only may not change or remove the identifiers.

Eagle uses an XML format for persistence, so an ordinary XML parser is used to read out the Eagle file. In Matlab/Simulink, on the other hand, the .mdl-files use a text-based format, which is not XML-compliant. To parse these files, we use XText and have defined corresponding grammar rules.

The prototype allows to build circuits in Simscape and couple them with Eagle. Thus, it is possible for the designer to control and adjust the runtime behavior of the electrical circuit during the design process. In contrast to existing import/export functionalities, the presented approach enables seamless bidirectional work with both tools.

5   Conclusion and Future Work

The viability and applicability of coupling a simulation tool to a PCB program using annotated identifiers were tested on a prototype using Eagle and Simscape. In addition to electrical systems, metamodels of other domains, such as mechanical and other software systems will be integrated to the V-SUMM using annotated identifiers in the future and the advantages of the development process will be analyzed.

References

1. Atkinson, C., Stoll, D., Bostan, P.: Orthographic software modeling: a practical approach to view-based development. In: Maciaszek, L.A., González-Pérez, C., Jablonski, S. (eds.) ENASE 2008. CCIS, vol. 69, pp. 206–219. Springer, Heidelberg (2010). https://doi.org/10.1007/978-3-642-14819-4_15
2. Broy, M.: Challenges in automotive software engineering. In: Proceedings of the 28th International Conference on Software Engineering, ICSE 2006, pp. 33–42. ACM, New York (2006)
3. Burger, E.J.: Flexible views for view-based model-driven development. In: Proceedings of the 18th International Doctoral Symposium on Components and Architecture, WCOP 2013, pp. 25–30. ACM, New York (2013)
4. Diskin, Z., Xiong, Y., Czarnecki, K., Ehrig, H., Hermann, F., Orejas, F.: From state- to delta-based bidirectional model transformations: the symmetric case. In: Whittle, J., Clark, T., Kühne, T. (eds.) MODELS 2011. LNCS, vol. 6981, pp. 304–318. Springer, Heidelberg (2011). https://doi.org/10.1007/978-3-642-24485-8_22
5. Kramer, M.E.: Specification languages for preserving consistency between models of different languages. Ph.D. thesis, Karlsruhe Institute of Technology (KIT), Karlsruhe, Germany (2017)
6. Langer, P., et al.: A posteriori operation detection in evolving software models. J. Syst. Softw. 86(2), 551–566 (2013)
7. Neema, H., et al.: Design space exploration and manipulation for cyber physical systems. In: IFIP First International Workshop on Design Space Exploration of Cyber-Physical Systems (IDEAL 2014). Springer, Berlin (2014)
8. Schmidt, M., Gloetzner, T.: Constructing difference tools for models using the SiDiff framework. In: Companion of the 30th International Conference on Software Engineering, ICSE Companion 2008, pp. 947–948, ACM, New York (2008)
9. Stephan, M., Cordy, J.R.: A survey of model comparison approaches and applications. In: Modelsward, pp. 265–277 (2013)

A System Modeling Approach to Enhance Functional and Software Development

Saurabh Tiwari[1](✉), Emina Smajlovic[1], Amina Krekic[1],
and Jagadish Suryadevara[2]

[1] Mälardalen University, Västerås, Sweden
saurabh.tiwari@mdh.se, {esc17001,akc17003}@student.mdh.se
[2] Volvo Construction Equipment AB, Gothenburg, Sweden
jagadish.suryadevara@volvo.com

Abstract. This paper presents a SysML-based approach to enhance functional and software development process within an industrial context. The recent changes in technology such as electromobility and increased automation in heavy construction machinery lead to increased complexity for embedded software. Hence there emerges a need for new development methodologies to address flexible functional development, enhance communication among development teams, and maintain traceability from design concepts to software artifacts. The discussed approach has experimented in the context of developing a new transmission system (partially electrified) and its functionality. While the modeling approach is a *work-in-progress*, some initial success, as well as existing gaps pointing to future works are highlighted.

Keywords: Modeling · SysML · Systems engineering

1 Introduction

In recent times, there has been a significant paradigm shift within construction equipment industry in terms of introducing new technologies such as electromobility and increased automation. For instance, electrification (i.e. battery-powered parts) is being introduced into products, hydraulic motors are being replaced with electric versions, new versions of drive-line system (DLS) where electrified hub motors (instead of torque power from the engine) are introduced into wheels.

The advanced technological changes in large complex products causes enormous challenges for existing software development teams. While the functionality remains largely unchanged in comparison with legacy systems and software, the new *design concepts* lead to major changes in hardware and software. Hence the traditional function development techniques largely based on small incremental changes to existing software is no longer valid and may lead to quality issues as well as maintainability and traceability problems. Model-based methodologies such as *Model-based Systems Engineering* (MBSE) and *Model-based Design*

© Springer Nature Switzerland AG 2018
M. Mazzara et al. (Eds.): STAF 2018 Workshops, LNCS 11176, pp. 512–518, 2018.
https://doi.org/10.1007/978-3-030-04771-9_37

(MBD) are industry-wide considered as effective solutions in addressing, above described development challenges [1,2]. While traditionally MBD methodologies are associated with only Simulink-based development techniques, currently these techniques are being extended using SysML/UML-based modeling approaches. In this paper, we present the SysML-based modeling approach considered within the project for development of a new transmission system (partially electrified) and its software.

In this paper, we describe a modeling approach developed within VCE (Volvo CE[1]). The approach is presented using the *'Brake'* functionality to capture the transmission system behavior, in response to *brake requests* from the operator/machine. The modeling approach captures the functional behavior from both problem (as seen externally) and solution domain (albeit implementation independent) perspectives. Later, the SysML-based solution models can be further refined into *hardware* and *software views* explicitly reflecting the overall design concept(s), paving the way for traceable software architecture(s) which in turn implemented using traditional *Simulink-based* techniques.

2   Background

Software Engineering Framework at VCE referred to as SE-Tool, is a customization of the commercial tool *Systemweaver*. It is influenced by EAST-ADL[2] framework, to support complete software development processes at VCE. It is primarily used to develop the complete Electrical and Electronic (E2E) System in software as well as hardware i.e., ECUs, Sensors, and Actuators.

MathWorks Simulink[3] is a graphical development tool used to run simulations, generate code, and test and verify embedded systems. All functionalities in the Simulink represented by the blocks. The Simulink connects different blocks and signals to simulation models that can be executed. Also, the block in a Simulink work similarly to functions in a C/C++ program. Blocks are divided into pre-defined MATLAB libraries[4] based on their functionality. These libraries include Logic and Bit Operations (e.g., blocks like Relational Operator and Logical Operator) and Math Operations (e.g., blocks like Product, Divide, Add, Subtract are included).

While both SE-Tool and Simulink-based frameworks satisfactorily cover the development processes within Software domain, currently there are huge gaps related to systems engineering domain like maintainability, traceability, incorporating new design concepts etc. Hence, there is a need for the *"Model-based System"* approach compared to traditional function development approach.

---

[1] Volvo Construction Equipment AB, Sweden.
[2] We refer the reader to the standard for further details: http://www.east-adl.info/.
[3] https://se.mathworks.com/products/simulink.html.
[4] https://se.mathworks.com/help/simulink/block-libraries.html.

3   Braking Functionality: An Example

The drive-line system consists of a *clutch*, a *transmission*, a *drive shaft*, and an *axle* connecting the engine and the drive wheels. To describe the system modeling approach, we model the 'Brake' functionality, based on the logical distribution of the system behavior in terms of the system components described above. Please note, to simplify the presentation of this paper both scope and all the figures and illustrations are limited to the behavior of the 'Brake' functionality.

Corresponding to required "Brake behavior", the DLS system "implements" corresponding "Braking" behavior within its scope, e.g., to create a tractive force on the machine and gives the machine the capability to move. Additional subsystems and components (besides described below) may be required to increase the quality of the movement, but they are skipped in this paper, to keep the presentation simple. In order to perform braking, mainly following subsystems and external entities are involved:

- **Operator** represents a person who operates a machine by sending a "braking request" through appropriate interface.
- **Powertrain** is a subsystem that includes following subsystems: Engine, Drivetrain and Wheels (#4).
- **Requester** represents the braking pedal of the physical machine.

4   SysML-Based Modeling Approach

The overall modeling methodology, as shown in Fig. 1, is primarily based on a reverse-engineering approach, i.e., capturing functionality from legacy concepts and corresponding implementations in the hardware and software (e.g., simulink-based environment). The modeling has been done using IBM Rhapsody tool[5]. However, in this paper, for illustration purpose, the models have been re-drawn using other tool.

The overall system modeling approach is divided into three stages.

4.1   Functional Modeling (Structure)

The first phase of the modeling activity (refer to Fig. 1), is based on the product breakdown structure. Thus the modeling focuses on "structural aspects" using SysML BDD (Block Definition Diagram) and IBD (Internal Block Definition) Diagrams (as illustrated in Figs. 2 and 3 respectively). Besides modeling the physical architecture of the system-of-interest, the function behavior in logical terms (i.e. implementation independent manner) is captured too. The "braking behavior" is described below.

The *Operator* sends the signals to *Requester*, the *'braking request'* is created. *Requester* represents the braking pedal. It creates a "propulsion torque event", with return value of braking torque. The *'braking request'* is then forwarded to

---

[5] https://www.ibm.com/se-en/marketplace/rational-rhapsody.

Functional Modeling

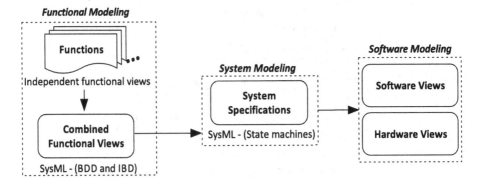

Fig. 1. Overview of the SysML-based modeling approach

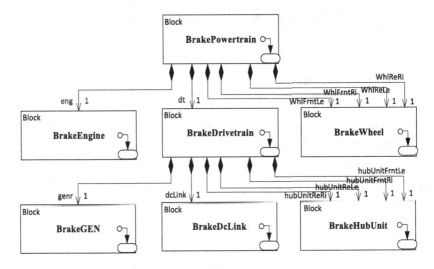

Fig. 2. BDD for Powertrain subsystem: description of the *Brake* function

Powertrain which communicates with *Wheels*, *Engine* and *Drivetrain*. *Powertrain* forwards the *'braking request'* to the *Drivetrain*, where *braking* happens in actual. It is consisted of three subsystems: *Generator*, *Dclink* and four *Hub Units*. The *Drivetrain* transform, transmit and modulate mechanical input torque to actualize requested mechanical torques at wheel interfaces. After receiving the *'braking request'*, engine requests how much power needs to be generated and sends that to *Generator* through the *Drivetrain*. *Generator* transfers mechanical energy to electrical and forwards it to *DcLink*, and then *DcLink* transmits that energy and forwards it to four *hub units* which modulate it and send to *Wheels*.

The operations and signals identified to realize (logically) the "braking behavior" is represented in a block diagram as shown in Fig. 3 (the color scheme to be explained later). It can be noted that the model elements (structure) illustrated are named with prefix "Brake" to indicate the modeling is focused only

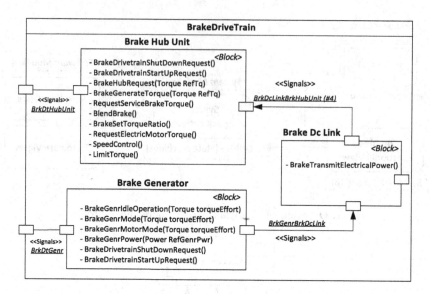

Fig. 3. BrakeDrivetrain IBD representing *Operations* and *Signals* (Color figure online)

on "analyzing" and capturing the "Braking" behavior in isolation. The structure indicates the logical decomposition or "allocation" of the function w.r.to the overall product breakdown structure. This is an important phase for both requirement and system engineers, and enhance communications within development teams. The results of this phase are also reviewed with the stakeholders.

4.2 System Modeling (Behavior)

It is the next level of modeling activity using SysML Statemachine diagrams to capture the functional behavior of the structural "parts" (w.r.to the system-of-interest). While in this paper, we restrict the behavior specification to that of "Braking", this specification is "incrementally" developed by considering each of the machine functions separately and eventually "combined" (manually). For instance, in Fig. 4, the behavior of the HubUnit part of BrakeDrivetrain is presented. It can be noted the granularity of the (behavior) modeling effort is not arbitrary, but carefully chosen to cover the "new" parts, in this case the HubUnit (electrically steering the wheels).

As result of the modeling activity described in previous subsection, it can be noted, there will be multiple state machines for the *HubUnit* (in other words, multiple *HubUnits* each pre-fixed with the individual function names). These state machines are "combined" to create a single state machine, at suitable granularity, that serves as the System Specification (for the DLS). Thus, this modeling phase also contributes to the overall system design decisions. For example, as shown in Fig. 4, the color scheme indicates the design decision to implement the corresponding operation in *Software* or *Hardware* (further explained in subsection below).

4.3 Modeling System Design (S/W and H/W Views)

This is the final phase of the SysML-modeling activity and concerns the detailed design modeling. As described in the previous subsection, the "software" and "hardware" parts are identified during behavior modeling phase, as part of the system specification. This phase further requires extensive domain expertise (both system and software level), for the technical trade-offs to be made regarding whether a certain SysML Operation is to be implemented in software or hardware (e.g. sensor). For instance, as shown in Fig. 4, the *blue* color represents the design decision that the corresponding operation has been allocated to the software modules and *red* color operations allocated to the hardware components for realization of the overall system. Based on these, allocation views are modeled in SysML (skipped in this paper due to lack of space).

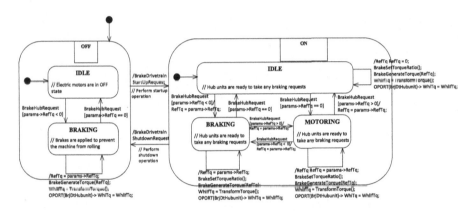

Fig. 4. State machine of *BrakeHubUnit* subsystem (Color figure online)

5 Conclusions

The SysML-based modeling approach presented in this paper is primarily a *reverse-engineering* effort in capturing functionality from legacy implementations in the hardware and software. However, the approach is generic enough to be extended into a useful modeling approach complimentary to existing software development approaches.

Acknowledgments. This work is partially funded from the Electronic Component Systems for European Leadership Joint Undertaking under grant agreement No. 737494 and The Swedish Innovation Agency, Vinnova (MegaM@Rt2).

References

1. Friedenthal, S., Griego, R., Sampson, M.: INCOSE model based systems engineering (MBSE) initiative. In: INCOSE 2007 Symposium (2007)
2. Friedenthal, S., Moore, A., Steiner, R.: A Practical Guide to SysML: The Systems Modeling Language. Morgan Kaufmann, Burlington (2014)

Embedded UML Model Execution to Bridge the Gap Between Design and Runtime

Valentin Besnard[1]([⊠]), Matthias Brun[1]([⊠]), Frédéric Jouault[1]([⊠]),
Ciprian Teodorov[2]([⊠]), and Philippe Dhaussy[2]([⊠])

[1] ERIS, ESEO-TECH, Angers, France
{valentin.besnard,matthias.brun,frederic.jouault}@eseo.fr
[2] Lab-STICC UMR CNRS 6285, ENSTA Bretagne, Brest, France
{ciprian.teodorov,philippe.dhaussy}@ensta-bretagne.fr

Abstract. The number and complexity of embedded systems is rising. Consequently, their development requires increased productivity as well as means to ensure quality. Model-based techniques can help achieve both. With classical model-driven development techniques, developers start by building design models before producing actual code. Although various approaches can be used to validate models and code separately, models and code are however separated by a semantic gap. This gap typically makes it hard to link runtime measures (e.g., execution traces) to design models. The approach presented in this paper avoids this semantic gap by making it possible to execute UML design models directly on embedded microcontrollers. Therefore, any runtime measure is directly expressed in terms of the design model. The paper introduces our UML bare-metal (i.e., not requiring an operating system) interpreter. Its use is illustrated on a motivating example, which can be simulated, or debugged, and for which message sequence charts can be generated.

Keywords: UML execution · Model interpretation
Embedded systems

1 Introduction

Embedded systems become more and more complex due to the emergence of new needs and applications (e.g., Internet of Things, autonomous cars, smart cities). This increasing complexity renders software programs more difficult to design, maintain, and evolve. One of the main consequence is that bugs and design faults are more difficult to detect and fix. To validate the system behavior, it becomes necessary to execute the system during early design phases, and to link design and runtime concepts together to ease the system analysis.

With model-driven engineering, a classical approach consists in simulating a model of the system under study on a desktop computer. Then, the application code is produced using code generation and executed on an embedded

© Springer Nature Switzerland AG 2018
M. Mazzara et al. (Eds.): STAF 2018 Workshops, LNCS 11176, pp. 519–528, 2018.
https://doi.org/10.1007/978-3-030-04771-9_38

target. However, code generation creates a semantic gap between design models and executable code that makes it more complicated to link design models to execution concepts. Therefore, diagnosis activities (e.g., simulation, debugging) and runtime measures analysis (e.g., execution traces) can become complex. It is even more challenging to visualize the execution of a system running on an embedded target and to interact with its design model at runtime.

To partially address these issues, we introduce a model interpreter that can be used to execute UML models. This tool has been presented in [2] but in this paper, we will focus on interactions between design and runtime, which have not been presented yet. In our approach, the design model is directly loaded in our model interpreter for being executed. This technique avoids the semantic gap created by code generation and ensures that the same concepts (here UML concepts) are used between design and runtime. Indeed, the model execution can be directly visualized in terms of UML concepts through two kinds of interactions. Online interactions used during simulation and debugging can be employed to interact with the model during its execution. Offline interactions are also available to visualize the model execution through the generation of message sequence charts (MSC) from execution traces. These MSC are directly expressed in terms of the design model elements. This approach is a first step towards the goal of executing design models for complex embedded systems. This work shows that it is possible to do it on bare-metal for small embedded devices (e.g., Internet of Things) but this approach can be generalized to use operating systems for more complex embedded systems applications.

Our UML model interpreter shows encouraging results towards feasibility. It can be used to execute UML models on desktop computers and embedded microcontrollers using model interpretation. This interpreter can be connected to a simulator for simulating and visualizing the system execution using a dedicated communication protocol. It is also possible to print execution traces into a formalism for generating MSC diagrams from these traces. Experiments have been made on a level crossing system to illustrate these features. These improvements contribute to reinforce the link between design and runtime as well as reducing time-to-market and increasing both productivity and quality.

The remainder of this paper is structured as follows. Section 2 introduces our model interpreter and the technique used to interpret a UML model on a bare-metal target. Then, we describe multiple interactions modes between design and runtime in Sect. 3. In Sect. 4, we discuss advantages of this approach before reviewing some related work in Sect. 5. Finally, we conclude this paper in Sect. 6.

2   Interpretation of Executable UML Design Models

To link design and runtime concepts, our approach is based on a model interpreter that can execute the model of the system produced during the design phase. In this section, we will present the process used to serialize a design model into source code before being loaded in and executed with our prototype.

The first step consists in designing a model of the system under study in UML. This activity can be performed with either graphical editors (e.g., Papyrus

[11]) or textual editors (e.g., tUML tool [9,10]). Using these tools, the design model can then be exported into the XML metadata interchange (XMI) format. To be executable, this model must specify explicitly the system behavior. In our case, the behavior of active classes is specified using state machines composed of states and transitions. Each transition can have a guard and an effect encoded respectively in an opaque expression and an opaque behavior. To write these guards and effects, we use an action language based on the C programming language but with specific syntactic extensions to simplify access to UML instances (i.e., instances of UML classes). These extensions can be used to send events, get and set values of attributes, and access content of event pools in a relatively simple way. With this syntactic sugar, users do not need to know the internal structure of the interpreter to use the action language.

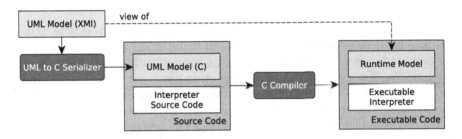

Fig. 1. Overview of the model generation process.

Once the executable model has been saved into XMI, it can be serialized into C source code using a transliteration, as shown in Fig. 1. This serialization can be seen as the way to load the model into our interpreter. In fact, it only adapts the syntax of the model to C programming language without performing any semantics change. The serializer is used to generate a C struct initializer for each UML element needed for model interpretation. With struct initializers the C compiler constructs the binary representation of the model in the initialized data section of the memory. This can be seen as compile-time model loading. Hence, this technique differs from classical code generation that generates both data and program required to execute the system. We only generate data that represents the static part of the model. The only exception concerns transition guards and effects that are serialized as C functions to which the C representation of transitions point (using function pointers). In fact, in UML with opaque expression guards and opaque behavior effects, the code of guards and effects is represented as strings stored into a body property. These C functions provide executable behaviors for these bodies without requiring to parse these strings or to perform expensive operations directly on the target. Apart from transition effects and guards, no code is generated from the UML model, only data. Moreover, this data is no more than an in-memory representation of a loaded UML model, similar to the result of EMF XMI loading.

Then, a C compiler is used to compile both the UML model in C language and the source code of the interpreter, which are then linked together into executable code. This executable code includes the runtime model composed of both the static and the dynamic part of the model. At this point, the reference model is the runtime model because this is the model really executed on the target. The design model is only a view of it. The resulting executable may be executed either on a desktop computer or on a microcontroller-based embedded system. The execution results in interpretation of the model using both the UML model of design (data) and the operational semantics implemented into the model interpreter (program). The implemented semantics tends towards the precise semantics for UML state machines (PSSM [13]) based on fUML [14].

3   Interactions with Design Tools

To reinforce the link between design and runtime, our approach is able to deal with two kinds of interactions between the runtime model and design tools. On the one hand, online interactions enable to interact with model execution for simulation or debugging purposes. On the other hand, our model interpreter is also able to generate traces at runtime that can be analyzed after execution. These interactions are supported by a choice of three possible interaction modes that are typical of embedded systems development process: simulation, debugging, and execution. The interpreter may be compiled with any of these features except the debugging loop which has not been implemented yet. In order to be deployed on the actual embedded system, the interpreter is compiled only with the execution loop. Therefore, interactions for simulation or debugging loops are not provided in the final product in order to avoid leaving a potential attack vector open.

3.1   Simulation

To interact with the model at design time, it is possible to use a simulator. The simulation mode enables making online interactions to explore the model and visualize its execution. Using our approach, model execution can be controlled through the interpreter running locally on a desktop computer or remotely on an embedded microcontroller. This second possibility can be employed to make hardware in the loop simulation directly on the board that will be used on the actual embedded system. To control model execution, our model interpreter provides the following application layer protocol:

Get configuration collects the current memory state of the interpreter.
Set configuration loads a configuration as the memory state of the interpreter.
Get fireable transitions collects transitions that can be fired on the next step.
Fire transition fires a transition of an active object's state machine.

Reset interpreter restarts the interpreter from the initial state of the model.

In this communication protocol, the memory state of the interpreter is called *configuration* and represents the dynamic part of the executed model. The configuration is composed of current states of state machines, contents of event pools (i.e., all events received by UML instances of active classes), and values of attributes. To get and set the configuration, we prefer the use of two global commands rather than multiple small and complex commands. This simplifies the protocol and gives the possibility to have an overview of the whole configuration at each simulation step. To improve performance, it is possible to use a *diff* mode that enables exchanging only bytes that are different between the current configuration and the previous one. For instance, if one wants to change the value of only one attribute, only the value of this attribute and its position into the configuration will be transmitted rather than the whole configuration. Virtual peripherals communicate with the model by directly reading or writing into event pools, which can also be performed in *diff* mode. With this simulation loop, execution flow is entirely controlled by the simulator. Therefore, it is possible to implement an execution loop in this tool to run model execution. Figure 2 presents the user interface of our simulator applied to a level-crossing model [2]. This interface shows the list of fireable transitions available in the selected configuration, the content of this configuration, and the part of the model state-space discovered since the beginning of the simulation.

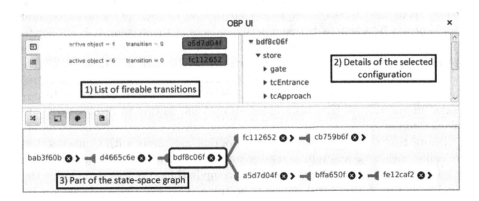

Fig. 2. User interface of the simulator.

3.2 Debugging

Debugging is another kind of online interactions. It can be used to control model execution in the same way than previously introduced simulation purpose, or to automatically execute the model with the actual embedded system. For this reason, it is a mix between both simulation and execution modes. The debugging loop can be used to control model execution using the communication protocol and to observe the configuration of the model. This protocol enables injecting an event, changing the value of an attribute, or changing the value of the current state of a state machine using the *Set configuration* request. The *diff mode* can be used to reduce the cost and optimize communication performance. This communication protocol can also be used to make omniscient debugging [3,5,8] to go back-in-time. Indeed, received configurations can be stored and reloaded at any time as the current memory state of the interpreter. In debugging mode, it is also possible to execute the system using the execution loop implemented in the interpreter. The only difference with the execution mode is that it will check if there is a command (sent by the debugger) to process, so the runtime cost is small. In our prototype of model interpreter, these debugging interactions have some limitations. The first one is that execution of opaque behaviors and evaluation of opaque expressions cannot be debugged because they are implemented as C functions. It would become possible if we used UML activities to specify their behaviors, which we might explore in the future. The second limitation is that we do not support breakpoints for the moment. Hence, it is not possible to stop the execution automatically when reaching a given state of a state machine. This is the main feature that lacks in our interpreter for supporting this mode.

3.3 Execution

The execution mode is the main loop actually used on the deployed system. For offline interactions, we add the possibility to generate execution traces and to display them using messages sequence charts (MSC). MSC are a kind of diagram that captures interactions between active objects of the system. It is similar to a sequence diagram but enhanced with states of state machines, such that it is possible to know the current state of each active object at any time. MSC give an overview of a scenario and enable to visualize interactions between active objects (i.e., exchange of events) and their state machine progression. In our model interpreter, we have also added an optional feature to display attribute values changes.

In practice, we instrumented the code of our interpreter with C macros that are called each time an event is sent, a state machine updates its current state, or an attribute has its value updated. At compile time, the user can choose the MSC formalism to use for displaying the trace. This will replace C macros by calls to appropriate functions in charge of displaying the trace. If no trace is required, (e.g., on the deployed embedded system), these macros are replaced by no instruction to have no impact on execution performance of the actual system. At runtime, the trace will be printed either on the standard output stream (e.g., a serial port of the embedded target) or directly in a text file when running on a desktop computer. Afterwards, the trace can be loaded into a tool in order to generate a graphical diagram that gives a better visualization of it. In the current version of our model interpreter, we have chosen to display traces using the PlantUML[1] formalism. Traces are then converted into diagrams using

---

[1] http://plantuml.com/.

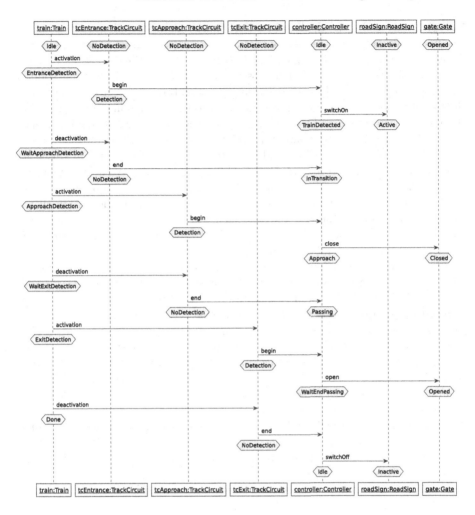

Fig. 3. Message sequence chart of a level crossing model.

the PlantUML tool. However, additional transformations towards different MSC formalisms can be easily added to our tool. Figure 3 shows an example of MSC diagrams obtained with our model interpreter. This example represents a trace of a level crossing model example introduced in [2].

4   Discussion

Our approach based on a model interpreter tackles issues to link design and run-time concepts. It thus should contribute to reduce time-to-market and increase both quality and productivity.

The first advantage of our approach is that our model interpreter can be deployed either on desktop computers or on embedded targets. Indeed, our prototype is adapted to be deployed on bare-metal microcontrollers without intermediate software layers like an operating system. This means that this model interpreter can run on embedded microcontrollers with relatively small memory size and relatively slow CPU. This possibility can be used to make simulation or debugging at the model level directly on embedded targets. For instance, this can be useful to detect some bugs linked to the hardware by making hardware in the loop simulation. In most of the classical approaches, the design model is specified and validated on desktop computers before being transformed into executable code through code generation, and executed on microcontrollers. In this case, the link between design and runtime is difficult to set up. With our approach, this link is easier to establish thanks to the possible interactions between design and runtime that it offers, and because we use the same model all along the development process. Indeed, our approach provides a continuum from design to runtime by applying simulation, debugging, and trace generation either on desktop computers or embedded microcontrollers.

The second point is that a single semantics implementation is used for execution and simulation. Indeed, the execution semantics used to interpret UML models is implemented in our model interpreter. In most of the classical approaches, the code generation step is a transformation that creates a semantic gap between design and runtime that may not ensure that simulation results are still valid at runtime. With our model interpreter, there is no problem of equivalence between the design model and the model used at runtime because all activities (execution, simulation, and debugging) are made through the interpreter. Hence, only one implementation of the semantics is used. This contributes to increase the development quality of the system.

The last key point deals with traces analysis as well as simulation and debugging results. In our approach, the design model is directly used for execution through a model serialization into C programming language. Therefore, the mapping between design and runtime concepts is straightforward. Simulation and debugging techniques can be used to simulate the model directly in terms of design concepts. This also facilitates execution traces analysis to inject feedbacks in the design model and fix design faults. As a result, we expect that this will increase productivity and reduce time-to-market.

5   Related Work

Other works have shown abilities to execute models and establish links between design tools and runtime measures through various kinds of interactions.

Multiple implementations of fUML [14] or PSSM [13] have been realized to execute models conforming to these executable UML standards. Moka [1] and Moliz [12] are two of these implementations that are able to support execution, simulation, and debugging of UML models. GEMOC Studio [4,7] is another tool that contains a modeling workbench to design models conforming to any domain-specific languages. This tool has four different execution engines and several add-ons can be used to perform simulation, debugging, and trace generation.

All these tools are well-integrated into modeling development environments. For instance, Moka has an Eclipse-based user interface and can be used with the Papyrus [11] editor to simulate UML models with graphical feedbacks over diagrams. The main drawback of all these tools is that they are not adapted to execute models on embedded targets. Indeed, these tools use too much memory for being executed on a small microcontroller. The generic approach used to build these tools also induces a lack of performance because they are not adapted for embedded systems execution.

In comparison to these works, some approaches aim at executing models on embedded targets with small memory footprints and good execution performance. UML virtual machine (UVM) [15] defines a runtime environment to execute bytecode in the binary UVM format generated from models and includes extensions for fine grained concurrency and precise timing. In the same way, a front-end, called GUML [6], has been defined for GCC to compile directly UML models into optimized binary code. Both tools have similarities to our model interpreter but they cannot be remotely controlled by diagnosis tools to analyze model execution in terms of design concepts.

6 Conclusion

To bridge the gap between design and runtime, this paper has presented our approach based on a UML model interpreter. This interpreter uses the same model for design and runtime to offer a direct link between design and runtime concepts. To take advantage of this link, we have put in place online and offline interactions between design and runtime. Simulation and debugging activities can be applied directly in terms of UML concepts. This eases the integration of simulation feedbacks and the correction of bugs into the design model. To facilitate the visualization of model execution, our approach also relies on execution traces generated at runtime to produce MSC diagrams with PlantUML. We expect that these improvements should help engineers to analyze model execution and fix design faults in the design model. In fact, this should reduce time-to-market and increase productivity because the model analysis will be easier.

Another significant key point of our approach is that this technique remains valid for embedded systems. Indeed, the same model interpreter can be used to execute models on bare-metal targets equipped with small embedded microcontrollers. For simulation, the interpreter can be remotely controlled through a communication protocol that is sufficient to get/set dynamic data of the runtime model, and control model execution by firing state machine transitions. Hence, the boundary between design and runtime virtually disappears and the transition from one to the other can be realized in a continuous way using multiple activities (e.g., simulation, debugging, execution).

To reinforce the link between design and runtime, we are currently investigating other possibilities offered by our approach. Indeed, the protocol used for simulation can also be reused to connect other diagnosis tools, such as a model-checker. This should offer a new kind of online interactions to make the verification of formal properties on models.

Acknowledgments. This work is partially funded by Davidson Consulting. The authors especially thank David Olivier for his advice and industrial feedback.

References

1. Papyrus: Moka overview. https://wiki.eclipse.org/Papyrus/UserGuide/ModelExe cution
2. Besnard, V., Brun, M., Dhaussy, P., Jouault, F., Olivier, D., Teodorov, C.: Towards one model interpreter for both design and deployment. In: Proceedings of EXE 2017, Austin, United States, September 2017
3. Bousse, E., Corley, J., Combemale, B., Gray, J., Baudry, B.: supporting efficient and advanced omniscient debugging for xDSMLs. In: Proceedings of SLE 2015, pp. 137–148. ACM, New York (2015)
4. Bousse, E., Degueule, T., Vojtisek, D., Mayerhofer, T., Deantoni, J., Combemale, B.: Execution framework of the GEMOC studio (tool demo). In: Proceedings of SLE 2016, pp. 84–89. ACM, New York (2016)
5. Bousse, E., Leroy, D., Combemale, B., Wimmer, M., Baudry, B.: Omniscient debugging for executable DSLs. J. Syst. Softw. **137**, 261–288 (2017)
6. Charfi Smaoui, A., Mraidha, C., Boulet, P.: An optimized compilation of UML state machines. In: Proceedings of ISORC 2012, Shenzhen, China, April 2012
7. Combemale, B., et al.: A solution to the TTC'15 model execution case using the GEMOC studio. In: 8th Transformation Tool Contest. CEUR, Italy (2015)
8. Corley, J., Eddy, B.P., Gray, J.: Towards efficient and scalabale omniscient debugging for model transformations. In: DSM 2014, pp. 13–18. ACM, New York (2014)
9. Jouault, F., Delatour, J.: Towards fixing sketchy UML models by leveraging textual notations: application to real-time embedded systems. In: Brucker, A.D., Dania, C., Georg, G., Gogolla, M. (eds.) OCL 2014. OCL and Textual Modeling: Applications and Case Studies, Valencia, Spain, vol. 1285, pp. 73–82 (2014)
10. Jouault, F., Teodorov, C., Delatour, J., Le Roux, L., Dhaussy, P.: Transformation de modèles UML vers Fiacre, via les langages intermédiaires tUML et ABCD. Génie logiciel **109** (2014)
11. Lanusse, A., et al.: Papyrus UML: an open source toolset for MDA. In: Proceedings of ECMDA-FA 2009, pp. 1–4 (2009)
12. Mayerhofer, T., Langer, P.: Moliz: a model execution framework for UML models. In: Proceedings of the 2nd International Master Class on Model-Driven Engineering: Modeling Wizards, MW 2012. ACM, New York (2012)
13. OMG: Precise Semantics of UML State Machines, February 2017. https://www.omg.org/spec/PSSM/1.0/Beta1/PDF
14. OMG: Semantics of a Foundational Subset for Executable UML Models, October 2017. https://www.omg.org/spec/FUML/1.3/PDF
15. Schattkowsky, T., Engels, G., Forster, A.: A model-based approach for platform-independent binary components with precise timing and fine-grained concurrency. In: Proceedings of HICSS 2007. IEEE Computer Society, USA (2007)

Sketching a Model-Based Technique
for Integrated Design and Run Time
Description
Short Paper - Tool Demonstration

Andreas Kästner[⊠], Martin Gogolla, Khanh-Hoang Doan, and Nisha Desai

Computer Science Department, University of Bremen, Bremen, Germany
{andreask,gogolla,doankh,nisha}@informatik.uni-bremen.de

Abstract. The paper sketches a UML- and OCL-based technique for the coherent description of design time and run time aspects of models. The basic idea is to connect a design model and a run time model with a correspondence model. We show two simple examples, one for structural modeling and one for behavioral modeling, that explain the underlying principles. As all three models are formulated in the same language, UML and OCL, one can reason about the single models and their relationships in a comprehensive way.

1 Introduction

In recent years, design time (DT) and run time (RT) models of software as well as their interplay have become a major topic in research and development. Often, it is said that the advantage of using a model instead of code lies in its power to abstract away unnecessary technical details. But up to now, a common agreement about the distinguishing characteristics of DT and RT models and their relationship is still open. This paper proposes to formulate an explicit DT and an explicit RT model and to formally link both.

For expressing these models, we use a mainstream language, the UML (Unified Modeling Language) [7], which includes the OCL (Object Constraint Language) [9]. Our approach is explained with examples that are worked out in our tool USE (Uml-based Specification Environment)[1].

As said, to catch DT and RT modeling aspects, we propose to introduce three connected models as sketched in Fig. 1: (i) a design time model, (ii) a run time model, and (iii) a correspondence model that connects and constrains the first two models. All three models can be full models containing, e.g., classes, associations, and constraints, but a model may also consist of associations (as first-class citizens) and constraints only. The correspondence model depends on and imports the other two models. All interactions and dependencies between design time and run time are modeled here. Figure 1 displays in the upper part

---

[1] https://sourceforge.net/projects/useocl/.

© Springer Nature Switzerland AG 2018
M. Mazzara et al. (Eds.): STAF 2018 Workshops, LNCS 11176, pp. 529–535, 2018.
https://doi.org/10.1007/978-3-030-04771-9_39

the three contributing models. In order to be more concrete, an example is given in the lower part with classes, associations and constraints for the structural modeling example to be discussed in detail further down.

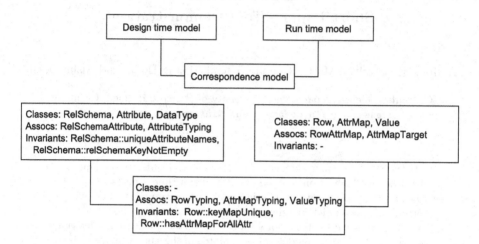

Fig. 1. Design time, run time and correspondence model.

The research contribution of this paper lies in the proposal for the distinction of the three different models and in the proof-of-concept that it is possible to realize this structure in a software design tool. We are not aware of another proposal for a correspondence model. The advantage that we see in such an explicit model lies in the option to analyze the relationship between DT and RT model, e.g., to check RT errors and to trace and to identify the 'guilty' parts either in the DT model or in the RT model or in both models.

The rest of this contribution is structured as follows. Section 2 introduces the structural example model. Section 3 focuses on the behavioral example model. Both examples show a RT error in form of an invariant violation, and both are implemented in USE [3,4]. Section 4 discusses some related approaches. Section 5 ends the paper with concluding remarks and future work.

2   Structural Modeling Example

The class model in Fig. 2a shows a tiny SQL subset: (i) in the DT model on the left, we see that a relational schema (class `RelSchema`) has attributes and that an attribute is typed through a data type; (ii) in the RT model on the right, a relational schema is populated with rows in which each attribute gets a value by means of attribute map objects; (iii) the correspondence model consists of three typing associations that allow to connect the RT objects with a unique type.

In Fig. 2b, further rules are shown in the form of invariants that restrict the possible object models. We informally explain the constraint purpose in the order

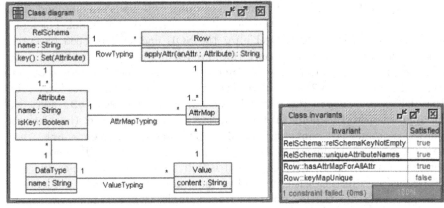

(a) DT, RT model.   (b) Restriction rules.

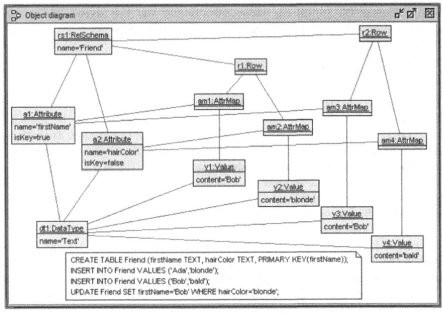

(c) Usage scenario.

Fig. 2. DT, RT and correspondence elements for a relational database.

in which the invariants appear: (i) the set of key attributes of each relational schema has to be non-empty, (ii) the attributes names have to be unique within the relational schema, (iii) each row must have an attribute value for each of its attributes, and (iv) each row must have unique key attribute values.

In Fig. 2c, we see a usage scenario in concrete SQL syntax. One table (relational schema) is added with a `create` command, populated by two SQL `insert` commands and finally modified with an additional SQL `update` command. This usage scenario is represented in the form of an evolving object model. The figure shows only the last object model after the SQL `update` has been executed: (i) after the `create` command only the four left-most objects (`rs1`, `a1`, `a2`, `dt1`) are present; (ii) after the first `insert` command the five middle objects (`r1`, `am1`, `v1`, `am2`, `v2`) appear, however we will have `v1.content='Ada'`; (iii) after the second `insert` the five right-most objects (`r2`, `am3`, `v3`, `am4`, `v4`) will appear; up to this point all four invariants evaluate to `true`; (iv) after the `update` command the `content` value of `v1` changes (`v1.content='Bob'`) and the evaluation of the invariant `keyMapUnique` turns to `false`. This constraint violation corresponds to a RT error that is indicated to the developer and that can be analyzed further with our tool so that the `Value` object `v1` is identified as being 'guilty' for the RT error. In this example, the correspondence model consists of associations and invariants only, but one could think of more complicated situations with RT objects introduced at different points in time and having different DT types (e.g., `ada:Student` and `ada:Employee`). This could be reflected by a correspondence class and appropriate objects.

3   Behavioral Modeling Example

Figure 3a shows a DT and RT model for simple protocol state machines. In the class model on the left side, we have the class `State` and the association class `Transition` making up the DT model. On the right side, `TraceNode` and `TraceEdge` constitute the RT model. The association between `State` and `TraceNode` establishes the correspondence model.

The class model is illustrated by an object model (Fig. 3c) that instantiates in particular the DT and RT classes. The object model pictures an automatically generated [4] fitness example. It shows in the middle a protocol state machine with states named `BOILING`, `FREEZING`, and `COLD` as well as transitions labeled `jog`, `run` and `stretch`. This instantiates the DT model. In the left and in the right of the class model, two examples traces, i.e., executions of the protocol state machine, instantiate the RT model: the actual event sequences are in the first execution on the left {`stretch`; `run`} and in the second execution on right the sequence {`jog`; `run`; `stretch`} and through links belonging to the correspondence model, the `TraceNode` objects are connected to `State` objects.

In Fig. 3b the names of needed OCL invariants are presented: (i) the OCL invariants for the DT part require deterministic transitions, each state to lie between the initial and the final state, unique state names, and the existence of a single initial and a single final state; (ii) the OCL invariants for the RT part require each trace to be a cycle-free string of pearls; (iii) the invariants for the correspondence part demand each trace to be connected to the initial state and the traces to show events corresponding to transition events.

The invariants in particular check that the sequence of events from the two traces is correct traces from the specified protocol state machine. In this case, the right event sequence {`jog`; `run`; `stretch`} is an acceptable sequence, however

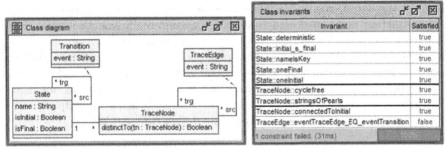

(a) DT, RT model.   (b) Restriction rules.

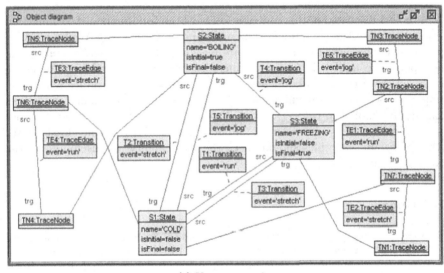

(c) Usage scenario.

Fig. 3. DT, RT and correspondence elements for a protocol state machine.

the left event sequence {`stretch`; `run`} is not a sequence allowed by the protocol state machine. This leads to the observation that the invariant `TraceEdge::`
`eventTraceEdge_EQ_eventTransition` evaluates to false: the link between TN6 and TN4 violates the determined protocol. Our tool USE offers options in terms of a so-called evaluation browser to analyze the object model and to identify the source for invariant violation: in the example the `TraceNode` objects TN6 and TN4 could be brought into the foreground.

4   Related Work

In [2], the authors propose an approach for improving user interaction modeling by adopting a design uncertainty model into an IFML model. Uncertainty is then solved by integrating the results of a run time log analysis. The approach in [1] discusses the Requirements Modeling Languages (RML) and proposes a conceptual distinction between design time and run time requirements models. Run time models extend design time models with additional information about execution of system tasks. In [6], the authors introduce an aspect-oriented modeling approach to enhance software adaptation by unifying design time and run time adaptation. [5] gives an overview on run time verification specification languages. [8] discusses through a controlled experiment whether it helps for comprehension of run time phenomena when corresponding design time models are provided.

5   Conclusion

The problem discussed in this contribution has been to formulate the connection between a design time and a run time model in a coherent way. We have shown by two examples how to use a software design tool to represent a connecting correspondence model. Future work includes finding a general way to set up the structure of the correspondence model. One may also introduce schematic, template-based correspondence models that establish unique typing connections from the RT model to the DT model. Tool support must be extended in order to formally distinguish between the different models. Last but not least, larger case studies and examples should check the applicability and usefulness of the proposed technique.

References

1. Borgida, A., Dalpiaz, F., Horkoff, J., Mylopoulos, J.: Requirements models for design- and runtime. In: Atlee, J.M., et al. (eds.) Proceedings of 5th International Workshop on Modeling in Software Engineering (MiSE 2013), pp. 62–68. IEEE Computer Society (2013)
2. Brambilla, M., Eramo, R., Pierantonio, A., Rosa, G., Umuhoza, E.: Enhancing flexibility in user interaction modeling by adding design uncertainty to IFML. In: Burgueño, L., et al. (eds.) Proceedings of MODELS 2017 Satellite Events, CEUR, vol. 2019, pp. 435–440 (2017)
3. Gogolla, M., Büttner, F., Richters, M.: USE: a UML-based specification environment for validating UML and OCL. J. Sci. Comput. Program. **69**, 27–34 (2007)
4. Gogolla, M., Hilken, F., Doan, K.H.: Achieving model quality through model validation, verification and exploration. J. Comput. Lang., Syst. Struct. (2017). Online. 02 Dec 2017
5. Havelund, K., Reger, G.: Runtime verification logics a language design perspective. In: Aceto, L., Bacci, G., Bacci, G., Ingólfsdóttir, A., Legay, A., Mardare, R. (eds.) Models, Algorithms, Logics and Tools. LNCS, vol. 10460, pp. 310–338. Springer, Cham (2017). https://doi.org/10.1007/978-3-319-63121-9_16
6. Parra, C.A., Blanc, X., Cleve, A., Duchien, L.: Unifying design and runtime software adaptation using aspect models. Sci. Comput. Program. **76**(12), 1247–1260 (2011)
7. Rumbaugh, J., Jacobson, I., Booch, G.: The Unified Modeling Language 2.0 Reference Manual. Addison-Wesley, Boston (2003)

8. Szvetits, M., Zdun, U.: Controlled experiment on the comprehension of runtime phenomena using models created at design time. In: Baudry, B., Combemale, B. (eds.) Proceedings of ACM/IEEE 19th International Conference on MODELS, pp. 151–161. ACM (2016)

9. Warmer, J., Kleppe, A.: The Object Constraint Language: Precise Modeling with UML, 2nd edn. Addison-Wesley, Boston (2003)

Model-Driven Engineering for Design-Runtime Interaction in Complex Systems: Scientific Challenges and Roadmap
Report on the MDE@DeRun 2018 Workshop

Hugo Bruneliere[1]([✉]), Romina Eramo[2]([✉]), Abel Gómez[3]([✉]), Valentin Besnard[4], Jean Michel Bruel[5], Martin Gogolla[6], Andreas Kästner[6], and Adrian Rutle[7]

[1] IMT Atlantique, LS2N (CNRS) and ARMINES, Nantes, France
hugo.bruneliere@imt-atlantique.fr
[2] University of L'Aquila, L'Aquila, Italy
romina.eramo@univaq.it
[3] Internet Interdisciplinary Institute (IN3), Universitat Oberta de Catalunya (UOC), Barcelona, Spain
agomezlla@uoc.edu
[4] ERIS, ESEO-TECH, Angers, France
valentin.besnard@eseo.fr
[5] IRIT (CNRS) and Université de Toulouse, Toulouse, France
bruel@irit.fr
[6] University of Bremen, Bremen, Germany
{gogolla,andreask}@informatik.uni-bremen.de
[7] Western Norway University of Applied Sciences, Bergen, Norway
adrian.rutle@hvl.no

Abstract. This paper reports on the first Workshop on Model-Driven Engineering for Design-Runtime Interaction in Complex Systems (also called MDE@DeRun 2018) that took place during the STAF 2018 week. It explains the main objectives, content and results of the event. Based on these, the paper also proposes initial directions to explore for further research in the workshop area.

Keywords: Design time modeling · Runtime modeling
Interactions · Correspondences · Traceability · Feedback

This workshop has been supported by the MegaM@Rt2 project. MegaM@Rt2 has received funding from the Electronic Component Systems for European Leadership Joint Undertaking under grant agreement No. 737494. This Joint Undertaking receives support from the European Union's Horizon 2020 research and innovation program and from Sweden, France, Spain, Italy, Finland & Czech Republic. Webpage - https://megamart2-ecsel.eu/mde-derun-2018/.

M. Mazzara et al. (Eds.): STAF 2018 Workshops, LNCS 11176, pp. 536–543, 2018.
https://doi.org/10.1007/978-3-030-04771-9_40

1   Introduction

Complex systems are now predominant in several domains such as automotive, health-care, aerospace, industrial control and automation [2]. Such systems call for modern practices, such as Model-Driven Engineering (MDE), to tackle advances in productivity and quality of these Cyber-Physical Systems (CPSs) [4]. However, the proposed solutions need to be further developed to scale up for real-life industrial projects and to provide significant benefits at execution time. To this intent, one of the major challenges is to work on achieving a more efficient integration between the design and runtime aspects of the concerned systems: the system behavior at runtime has to be better matched with the original system design in order to be able to understand critical situations that may occur, as well as corresponding potential failures in design. Methods and tools already exist for monitoring system execution and performing measurements of runtime properties. However, many of them do not rely on models and, usually, do not allow a relevant integration with (and/or a traceability back to) design models. Such a feedback loop from runtime is highly relevant at design time, the most suitable level for system engineers to analyze and take impactful decisions accordingly. It might also be useful to let the final users have some sort of control and manipulation possibilities over elements they would not be able to access otherwise. This last benefit implies that the models at runtime might be quite different from those at design time, especially in terms of programming/engineering background.

MDE@DeRun 2018[1] has been planned as a meeting point where both researchers and practitioners on model-driven and model-based techniques and architectures for complex systems can share their experiences and thoughts on this area of work. Its main goal was to disseminate and exchange related ideas or challenges, identify current and future key issues as well as explore possible solutions. The potentially relevant topics concern traceability between design time and runtime models, as well as related runtime information. They notably include (but not only):

- Model-based techniques, methods and tools allowing any interaction between design time and runtime, possibly resulting from heterogeneous engineering practices.
- Model-based techniques, methods and tools for inferring design deviations and identifying affected elements over a possibly large spectrum of runtime system configurations or conditions.
- Methods and techniques allowing to practically integrate, possibly in different ways, any feedback collected at runtime into design level models.
- Integrated model-based methods and techniques for runtime analysis and design artifacts input collection, e.g. based on probes injection to some runtime artifacts.

---

[1] https://megamart2-ecsel.eu/mde-derun-2018/.

- Validation and verification mechanisms for linking results of runtime analysis, e.g. from execution traces, with design models expressing systems' both functional and non-functional requirements.
- (Industrial) case studies, experience reports, literature reviews or visionary positions related to any of the previously mentioned topics.

The remainder of this paper is structured as follows. Section 2 briefly introduces the different papers accepted and presented during the workshop. Possible future challenges on design/runtime interactions in the MDE context are then discussed in Sect. 3, before we finally conclude this paper in Sect. 4.

2 Contribution Summary

In what follows, we list the 5 papers (4 short papers and 1 long paper) that have finally been accepted and presented during the workshop. A short summary is provided for each one of them.

Aliya Hussain, Saurabh Tiwari, Jagadish Suryadevara and Eduard Enoiu: *From Modeling to Test Case Generation in the Industrial Embedded System Domain* — This short paper presents an on-going investigation being carried out at Volvo CE[2] to improve testing processes by using a Model-based testing (MBT) approach. The goal has been to investigate the use of MBT and the evidence on how modeling and test generation can improve the current way of manually creating test cases based on natural language requirements. The authors used the Conformiq Creator tool to model the behavior and structure of a function controlling the accelerator pedal provided by Volvo CE. The authors automatically created test cases covering the model, and compare these test cases in terms of test goal coverage and number of test cases to assess the applicability of MBT in this context. The approach has shown encouraging results.

Saurabh Tiwari, Emina Smajlovic, Amina Krekic and Jagadish Suryadevara: *A System Modeling Approach to Enhance Functional and Software Development* — This short paper presents a SysML-based modeling approach to enhance functional and software development process within Volvo CE. The increased complexity of embedded software demands for new development methodologies to address flexible functional development, enhance communication among development teams, and maintain traceability from design concepts to software artifacts. The discussed approach has been experimented in the context of developing a new transmission system (partially electrified) and its features. While the underlying modeling approach is still work-in-progress, both initial success and existing gaps have been highlighted.

---

[2] Volvo Construction Equipment AB, Sweden.

Daniel Zimmermann: *Automated Consistency Preservation in Electronics Development of Cyber-Physical System* — This short paper presents an automated strategy to ensure consistency between two widely used categories of software tools in electrical engineering: an Electronic Design Automation application (EDA) for designing Printed Circuit Boards (PCBs) and an electronic circuit simulator tool to predict system behavior at runtime. Coupling these two types of tools provides the developers with the ability of efficiently testing and optimizing the behavior of the electric circuit during the PCB design process; to avoid the disadvantages of ambiguous heuristic matching methods, a strategy ensuring a reliable assignment of these model elements is needed. The approach has been implemented by using Eagle CAD as the PCB software and Matlab/Simulink with the Simscape extension as the simulation tool.

Valentin Besnard, Matthias Brun, Frédéric Jouault, Ciprian Teodorov and Philippe Dhaussy: *Embedded UML Model Execution to Bridge the Gap Between Design and Runtime* — This long paper proposes a solution to bridge the gap between design and runtime aspects in model-based software development. In fact, with classical model-driven development techniques, developers start by building design models before producing actual code. Although various approaches can be used to validate models and code separately, models and code are however separated by a semantic gap. This gap typically makes it hard to link runtime measures (e.g., execution traces) to design models. The approach presented in this paper avoids this semantic gap by making it possible to execute UML design models directly on embedded microcontrollers. Therefore, any runtime measure is directly expressed in terms of the design model.

Andreas Kästner, Martin Gogolla, Khanh-Hoang Doan and Nisha Desai: *Sketching a Model-Based Technique for Integrated Design and RunTime Description* — This short paper sketches a UML- and OCL-based technique for the coherent description of design time and runtime aspects of models. The basic idea is to connect a design model and a runtime model with a correspondence model. The authors show two simple examples, one for structural modeling and one for behavioral modeling, that introduce the underlying principles. As all three models are formulated in the same languages—UML and OCL—one can reason about the single models and their relationships in a comprehensive way.

3 Discussion: Challenges and Roadmap

After the paper presentation sessions (as summarized in previous Sect. 2), we then had a discussion panel in which we identified common challenges and a high-level research roadmap related to the topics of the workshop. The result of this collaborative work is described in what follows.

Although many contributions could be achieved in the last decade in the MDE community, there are still several open challenges towards a complete and relevant integration between runtime and design aspects in complex systems. Firstly, explicit correspondences and/or traceability links are needed between runtime and design molidels. Secondly, a better understanding of the nature of the available runtime information (and its possible impacts on the design information) is required. Thirdly, the objectives and benefits of leveraging such correspondences and information need to be defined. We foresee a set of challenges that can be used as a research roadmap.

Correspondences/traceability between runtime and design models —
The aim to match the system behavior at runtime with the original system design can be achieved in several ways. This is mainly related to the concept of traceability. As widely treated in the literature, traceability relationships may help designers to understand the associations and dependencies that exist among heterogeneous models and their correspondences [5,6].

In MDE, a *trace link* is a relationship between one or more source model elements and one or more target model elements, whereas a *trace model* is a structured set of trace links, e.g., between source and target models. Trace links may be defined between entire artifacts (e.g., a requirements document and a design model) or between parts of artifacts.

The correspondence between runtime and design models might also take advantage of the MDE capabilities. For instance, in the case of (automated) model transformations, the traceability links are not only obvious but also allow some syntactic adaptation (e.g., different levels of abstraction) as well as some semantic adaptation (e.g., different viewpoints) on the way.

In order to integrate runtime and design aspects of the system several aspects need to be considered.

1. *Types of correspondences*—Correspondences between models could be defined through the following means: *(a)* traceability link, *(b)* consistency specification, *(c)* (bidirectional) model transformation, *(d)* model viewpoints and views. *(e)* megamodeling.

2. *Approaches*—Correspondences between models can be defined by means of the following approaches: *(a)* by integrating correspondences inside models, that implies a modification of the original models, or *(b)* by defining external correspondences between models, in this case the consistency of the original models is preserved (no modifications).

3. *How correspondences are produced*—Correspondences can be defined both in a manual manner, requiring engineers and domain experts, or automatically, starting from executable correspondence specifications. There can also exist mixed approaches where correspondences are automatically initiated/proposed and refined manually.

4. *When correspondences are produced*—Correspondences can be produced *(a)* at design-time (e.g., when creating the design model), between design-time and runtime phases (e.g., by applying some processes/transformations on the design model), *(b)* at system initialization (e.g., by creating all traceability links), or *(c)* on the fly at runtime (e.g., by creating a new trace link for each new runtime object created/used).

Runtime information — Runtime information can be considered as any software, architectural information or model of the runtime system that can be obtained during the system execution. For instance, through observation and instrumentation, logs and metrics (that can be also considered as kinds of runtime traces), runtime information can be collected to enable comprehension of the inner workings of already deployed software system [3].

Such models containing runtime information should not be confused with models@run.time [1] that, in general, aims at applying model-driven techniques for adapting and evolving software behavior while it is executing. On the contrary, we are interested in exploiting information collected only at runtime. This information can then be used offline to improve the initial system design through trial and error, eventually with the help of verification and validation tools (for instance).

In the following, we describe several aspects we believe important to consider.

1. *Types of runtime information*—Runtime information can be of different types, such as simulation models, executable models, model representing logs/traces, model representing states or configurations of the system, models expressing dynamic information or runtime measures on design models, test models.

2. *How they are obtained*—Runtime information can be collected by means of various mechanisms, such as simulation, monitoring, execution, debugging, profiling, verification.

3. *How they are represented*—Runtime information can be represented by: *(a)* specific models representing runtime information (i.e., using a common and/or a general metamodel); or *(b)* measures that are directly expressed in terms of the design model.

4. *How are they visualized*— Runtime information can be visualized over sequence diagrams, graphical diagrams of the design model (e.g., with particular tools like Papyrus), state-space graphs, or various textual representations (using some DSLs). These models give either a snapshot of the system execution, a representation of the current execution trace, or a representation of the whole execution history (i.e., a part of the system state-space corresponding to all explored execution traces).

5. *Who uses runtime information*—Runtime information should take into account the users; e.g., end-users, architects, designers, developers of the system, and also "test engineers" in charge of verifying and validating the system. This will have a strong impact on the type of chosen runtime models.

6. *Viewpoints*—A same runtime information can take on different roles depending on the context/perspective from which it is analyzed (e.g., business, system, technology). In the same vein, some software artifacts (or parts of them) can be considered as design time or runtime ones depending on the specific viewpoint from which they are observed.

Objectives — The vision underlying the integration of design and runtime models is to create awareness of problems in design or critical situations that may occur. The understanding of this class of problems can be exploited for different purposes.

1. *Using/Analyzing correspondences*—Correspondences (i.e., traceability relationships) between elements in models can be exploited to perform operations on models. Some of the key operations are: *(a) match*, that takes two models and returns a mapping between them; *(b) compose*, that composes a pair of correspondences; *(c) merge*, that uses correspondences between two models to create a new model that is the merge of them; and *(d) set operations* on models, such as *union, intersection, difference*. Such correspondences can also be used to build views combining together several models that can possibly conform to different metamodels. This can be realized according to corresponding viewpoints specifying the nature/type of these correspondences at metamodel-level.

   Furthermore, correspondences can be used to feed both functional (e.g., consistency, requirement traceability) and non-functional analysis (e.g., performance, reliability, availability, security).

2. *Inference capabilities*—Correspondence between design and runtime information can be used to achieve inference capabilities, discovering the system properties deviations and affected design components based on trace analysis. For instance, inference methods offer a control loop across the whole design chain between runtime and design time of the system, including non-functional aspects. This way, additional information from runtime models can be used to enhance system/design models.

3. *Requirements*—Correspondences can be used to reconcile the requirements and the system's runtime behavior in case of system deviations from the initial requirement specification.

4. *Reverse engineering*—Going backwards through the development cycle, correspondences can be used in reverse engineering guiding the specification of the system design from the runtime behavior.

4   Conclusion

Achieving an efficient integration between the design and runtime aspects of complex systems proved to be an interesting challenge for MDE methods and tools. The industrial relevance of this research area has also been confirmed by the participation of some companies to the workshop, such as Volvo Construction Equipment that submitted and presented a couple of papers during the event.

The first International Workshop on Model-Driven Engineering for Design-Runtime Interaction in Complex Systems (MDE@DeRun 2018) aims at providing a place for the community to share ideas and results in this research area we believe important. This paper summarized the main objectives and contributions of this first edition. Furthermore, it discussed and proposed some first directions for further research in this area, which we plan to explore in the future in our respective works. We hope to be able to capitalize on the success of this initial edition of the MDE@DeRun workshop in order to organize a second edition of this event next year.

Acknowledgements. We would like to thank everyone who took part in the success of this first edition of the workshop, including the program committee members, the paper authors and everyone who attended the workshop or took part in the interesting discussions we had.

References

1. Blair, G., Bencomo, N., France, R.B.: Models@ run.time. Computer **42**(10), 22–27 (2009). https://doi.org/10.1109/MC.2009.326
2. Boccara, N.: Modeling Complex Systems. Graduate Texts in Comtemporary Physics. Springer, Heidelberg (2004). https://doi.org/10.1007/b97378
3. Cito, J., Leitner, P., Bosshard, C., Knecht, M., Mazlami, G., Gall, H.C.: PerformanceHat: augmenting source code with runtime performance traces in the IDE. In: Proceedings of the 40th International Conference on Software Engineering: Companion Proceeedings, ICSE 2018, pp. 41–44 (2018)
4. Derler, P., Lee, E.A., Vincentelli, A.S.: Modeling cyber-physical systems. Proc. IEEE **100**, 13–28 (2012)
5. Paige, R.F., et al.: Rigorous identification and encoding of trace-links in model-driven engineering. Softw. Syst. Model. **10**(4), 469–487 (2011)
6. Winkler, S., von Pilgrim, J.: A survey of traceability in requirements engineering and model-driven development. Softw. Syst. Model. **9**(4), 529–565 (2010)

Microservices: Science and Engineering (MSE)

Third Edition of "Microservices: Science and Engineering" Workshop - MSE 2018[1]

Antonio Bucchiarone[1], Sophie Ebersold[2], and Florian Galinier[2]

Fondazione Bruno Kessler, Trento, Italy
bucchiarone@fbk.eu
University of Toulouse, France
{sophie.ebersold,florian.galinier}@irit.fr

Abstract. The MSE ("Microservices: Science and Engineering") Workshop constitutes a forum for scientists and engineers in academia and industry to present and discuss their latest ongoing research as well as radical new research directions that represent challenging innovations, which can advance the status quo and the understanding in the microservices area and its applications, where the scaling in the small approach is of major importance. The goal of this paper is to report the outcomes of the one-day workshop held in Toulouse, France in June 25, 2018.

1 Motivation and Objectives

After the previous edition of the Workshop at SEFM 2017 in Trento[2], in 2018 the same workshop is held in Toulouse, France, under the STAF 2018 umbrella[3]. This workshop aims at bringing together contributions by scientists and practitioners to shed light on the development of scientific concepts, technologies, engineering techniques and tools for a service-based society. In particular, the focus is on Microservices, i.e., the use of services beyond the traditional cross-organizational B2B approach and the implementation of the model inside of applications, scaling in the small the concepts previously seen in the large. In Microservices, each component of a software is a service with the related issues of scalability and distribution of responsibility. Topics of interest include:

- Design and implementation of Service-oriented Architectures and Microservices
- Software engineering techniques for Microservices
- Requirements Engineering for Microservices
- Model-Driven Engineering for Microservices
- Security in Microservices
- Formal models and analyses of Microservice systems

---

[1] https://mse-staf18.fbk.eu/.

[2] https://mse-sefm17.fbk.eu/.

[3] http://www.staf2018.fr/.

- Validation and Verification techniques for Microservices
- Coordination models for Microservices
- Empirical studies on services and Microservices
- Programming languages for Microservices
- Static analysis of Microservices
- Testing of Microservice systems
- Migration to Microservices
- Adaptation and Evolution of Microservices

2 Accepted Papers

Five papers were accepted and presented in two sessions, each characterized by a theme. The first session was about *Model-Driven Engineering for Microservices* while the second was about *Resilience and Security in Microservices*. All the papers accepted to MSE 2018 explored key issues and uses of microservice-based engineering approaches, in both abstract and applied settings.

In the following, details on the papers presented are given.

2.1 Model-Driven Engineering for Microservices

- **Chair: Vaidas Giedrimas – Department of Computer Science, Siauliai University, Lithuania.**
- **Paper 1.** Jonas Sorgalla, Florian Rademacher, Sabine Sachweh and Albert Zündorf. *On Collaborative Model driven Development of Microservices.* **Presenter:** Jonas Sorgalla – University of Applied Sciences and Arts Dortmund.
- **Paper 2.** Maroun Koussaifi, Sylvie Trouilhet, Jean-Paul Arcangeli and Jean-Michel Bruel. *Ambient Intelligence Users in the Loop: Towards a Model-Driven Approach.* **Presenter:** Jean-Michel Bruel – University of Toulouse CNRS/IRIT Laboratory.
- **Paper 3.** Philip Wizenty, Florian Rademacher, Jonas Sorgalla and Sabine Sachweh. *Design and Implementation of a Remote Care Application Based on Microservice Architecture.* **Presenter:** Philip Wizenty – University of Applied Sciences and Arts Dortmund.

2.2 Resilience and Security in Microservices

- **Chair: Jean-Michel Bruel – University of Toulouse CNRS/IRIT Laboratory.**
- **Paper 4.** Vaidas Giedrimas, Samir Omanovic and Dino Alic. *The Aspect of Resilience in Microservices-based Software Design.* **Presenter:** Vaidas Giedrimas – Department of Computer Science, Siauliai University, Lithuania.
- **Paper 5.** Mohsen Ahmadvand, Alexander Pretschner, Keith Ball and Daniel Eyring. *Integrity Protection Against Insiders in Microservices: From Threats to a Security Framework.* **Presenter:** Mohsen Ahmadvand, Technical University of Munich.

3   Workshops Organizers

Antonio Bucchiarone: is a senior researcher at Fondazione Bruno Kessler (FBK), Trento, Italy. He received the PhD degree from IMT of Lucca, Italy in 2008. His research interests include self-adaptive (collective) systems, applied formal methods, run-time service composition and adaptation, specification and verification of component-based systems, and dynamic software architectures.

Sophie Ebersold: received the PhD degrees from the University of Toulouse 3, Toulouse, France. She is currently an associate professor at the University of Toulouse and is member of the SM@RT Research Team of IRIT Laboratory. Her main research interests include Model Driven Engineering, Languages Engineering, Requirements Engineering and more particularly Multi-Modeling in Software Engineering.

Florian Galinier: received the BS and MS degrees in computer science from the University of Montpellier, France, and he is currently a Ph.D student at University of Toulouse, France, in the SM@RT Research team of IRIT laboratory. His research interests include using model driven engineering to improve software quality through requirements engineering.

4   Acknowledgment

The workshop chairs would like to thank STAF 2018 organizers to have accepted the proposal and to have supported the organization and the management of the workshop. In particular, we would like to thank Manuel Mazzara, STAF 2018 Workshops Co-Chair, for his kind encouragement, and, for his support in dealing with workshop aspects. We thank the authors of the submitted papers, to have chosen the workshop as place where to propose their work. We thank also the reviewers, for their careful work in evaluating the papers.

Design and Implementation of a Remote Care Application Based on Microservice Architecture

Philip Nils Wizenty, Florian Rademacher[✉], Jonas Sorgalla[✉],
and Sabine Sachweh[✉]

University of Applied Sciences and Arts Dortmund,
Institute for the Digital Transformation of Application and Living Domains,
Otto-Hahn-Straße 23, 44227 Dortmund, Germany
{philipnils.wizenty,florian.rademacher,jonas.sorgalla,
sabine.sachweh}@fh-dortmund.de

Abstract. Microservice Architecture (MSA) is an architectural style for service-based software systems. MSA puts a strong emphasis on high cohesion and loose coupling of the services that provide systems' functionalities. As a result of this, MSA-based software architectures exhibit increased scalability and extensibility, and facilitate the application of continuous integration techniques. This paper presents a case study of an MSA-based Remote Care Application (RCA) that allows caregivers to remotely access smart home devices. The goal of the RCA is to assist persons being cared in Activities of Daily Living. Employing MSA for the realization of the RCA yielded several lessons learned, e.g., (i) direct transferability of domain models based on Domain-driven Design; (ii) more efficient integration of features; (iii) speedup of feature delivery due to MSA facilitating automated deployment.

Keywords: Microservice Architecture · Smart home · Remote Care

1 Introduction

In the upcoming years, the number of people aged 60 and older will steadily increase and is predicted to worldwide grow from 901 million in 2015 to approximately more than 1.4 billions in 2030 [13]. This will result in an increasing demand for caregivers which can not be covered by the labor market [10]. Hence, new solutions are needed to cope with the resulting *care gap*. The IT sector is one of the central domains from which such solutions are expected. That is, because it is perceived of being able to provide additional support for both persons being cared and caregivers by developing new supportive technologies [3,10]. Next to mainly hardware-based solutions like wearables, Internet of Things based distributed software systems could aid in coping with the broadening care gap [3].

This research is partially funded by the German Federal Ministry of Education and Research in the project "QuartiersNETZ" (grant number 02K12B061.).

© Springer Nature Switzerland AG 2018
M. Mazzara et al. (Eds.): STAF 2018 Workshops, LNCS 11176, pp. 549–557, 2018.
https://doi.org/10.1007/978-3-030-04771-9_41

In this paper we present a distributed software system that addresses the domain of ambulant care. More specifically, the system denotes a Remote Care Application (RCA) [8], which leverages Microservice Architecture (MSA) [5] as its underlying architectural style. Its main purpose is to provide a platform for professional caregivers and nursing relatives to remotely interact with *smart home devices* in households of persons being cared and hence support them in their Activities of Daily Living (ADL) [9], e.g., housekeeping, multimedia, taking medicine, or personal hygiene. We present the RCA in the form of a case study with the following objectives in mind: (i) provide MSA researchers with a practice-related, well-documented research object; (ii) present our experiences in MSA development; and (iii) elucidate our lessons learned in practical MSA development. Therefore, we describe the design, implementation and deployment of the RCA with a strong focus on architectural challenges and requirements.

The remainder of the paper is organized as follows. Section 2 identifies functional and non-functional requirements for the RCA. Section 3 describes the RCA's design and implementation based on the requirement elicitation. Section 4 discusses the realized MSA solution for the RCA and the lessons learned during its implementation. Section 5 concludes the paper.

2   Functional and and Non-functional Requirements of the Remote Care Application

This section describes the identified functional and non-functional requirements of the RCA. The requirements elicitation process was part of a holistic, iterative *participatory design methodology*, which we developed and proved within the research project of which the RCA was one result [12]. Among others, the methodology comprises application-specific phases for stakeholder identification, as well as selection and application of the requirements elicitation process model being most appropriate for the stakeholders and the application to develop participatory. Employing the methodology resulted in (i) persons being cared, professional caregivers and nursing relatives being the relevant RCA stakeholders; (ii) the *future workshop* method [11] in combination with *goal-oriented requirements elicitation* [4] being the most sensible process model for requirements elicitation. Tables 1 and 2 show the functional and non-functional requirement goals resulting from applying the process model. However, due to space constraints, we only list the tier1- and tier2-top-level goals and omit more fine-grained sub-goals.

The goals T1-FG-1 and T1-FG-2 in Table 1 describe the general purpose of the RCA. Accordingly, the RCA provides means to remotely assist household residents in human-technology interaction scenarios, e.g., programming the washing machine. Additionally, the RCA enables ambulant caregivers to dynamically prepare for their service remotely, e.g., heating up the bathroom in advance of their arrival. Based on tier 1, tier 2 Goal T2-FG-1 addresses the need to read data from smart home devices with the RCA to, e.g., display current and historical device states. Next to basic read access, selected stakeholders may have to control devices, as expressed in Goals T2-FG-2 and T2-FG-3.

Table 1. Tier 1 and tier 2 functional requirement goals of the Remote Care Application

ID	Goal	Description
T1-FG-1	Remote support	The RCA must enable caregivers to remotely assist persons being cared in human-technology interaction scenarios
T1-FG-2	Preparing household	The RCA must enable caregivers to remotely prepare a household in advance of an ambulant care visit
T2-FG-1	Smart home	The RCA must be connected with various smart homes and be able to read device states
T2-FG-2	Remote control	Devices in connected smart homes must be controllable
T2-FG-3	Access rights	Device control must be explicitly granted by admins

Table 2. Non-functional requirement goals of the Remote Care Application

ID	Goal	Description
NG-1	Scalability	The RCA must be able to handle thousands of households
NG-2	Security	Security must be high due to personal data being involved
NG-3	Availability	High availability on the basis of increased resilience, robustness and functional independence
NG-4	Extensibility	New functionalities need to be flexibly integrable and providable

Table 2 shows non-functional requirement goals related to the RCA. They were actually the main drivers for implementing the RCA on the basis of MSA (cf. Subsect. 3.1). Goal NG-1 expresses the need for high scalability of the RCA being particularly relevant for professional caregivers having a potential customer base of thousands of households. Additionally, because of the high sensitivity of data related to the persons being cared and in case of misuse the potential of burglary, data and communication security must follow a high state of practice (goal NG-2). The RCA must also exhibit a high degree of availability to enable quick reaction by professional caregivers and nursing relatives in cases of emergency (goal NG-3). Another relevant concern is extensibility (goal NG-4) to allow flexible integration of new smart home technologies and devices as well as new functionalities, e.g., means for data analysis, at runtime.

3 Design and Implementation of the Remote Care Application

This section describes the design and implementation of the RCA according to the identified requirements (cf. Sect. 2). First, Subsect. 3.1 elucidates our decision to apply MSA to the RCA w.r.t the requirements. Next, Subsect. 3.2 presents the application design. Finally, Subsect. 3.3 describes the RCA's implementation.

3.1 Motivation for Microservice Architecture

We chose MSA as the RCA's underlying architectural style mainly because of the high requirements for scalability, availability and extensibility, i.e., goals NG-1, NG-3 and NG-4 in Table 2. The scalability requirement is satisfied because microservices are scalable independently due to functional isolation and technical self-containment [5]. Availability can be achieved because MSA fosters the definition of well-defined, functional service boundaries. Eventually, compared to monolithic applications, this results in an increased resilience as the faulty service (i) fails instead of the whole application; (ii) can be identified more effectively than in tightly coupled monoliths [5]. Extensibility is an inherent characteristic of service-based architectural styles [1] and comes with well-partitioned service boundaries, which is one central characteristic of MSA [5].

3.2 Model-Based Design of the Application

The RCA's design process employed various types of models applicable to MSA for different design-specific concerns, i.e., capturing of domain concepts and microservice identification, interface modeling, and deployment modeling [7].

We applied the Domain-driven Design (DDD) methodology [2] to iteratively capture relevant domain concepts and their relationships. This resulted in the *domain model* shown in Fig. 1, which we created in collaboration with domain experts, i.e., representatives of the RCA stakeholders (cf. Sect. 1). Its notation and elements' semantics rely on a UML profile for DDD-based domain models [6], to prospectively enable semi-automatic model validation and code generation. Due to lack of space, however, we only present the result of the model creation process's final iteration. That is, a domain model with some technical information relevant to the RCA's implementation (cf. Subsect. 3.3).

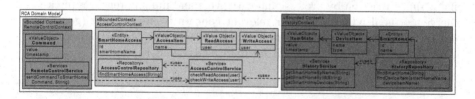

Fig. 1. Domain model of the Remote Care Application

The domain model is decomposed into three Bounded Contexts, of which each denotes a candidate for a functional microservice [5,7]. The `HistoryContext` bundles domain-specific concepts that model data of connected smart homes, devices' components (called *items*) and states. This corresponds to requirement goal T2-FG-1 (cf. Table 1), whereby the current state of a given `DeviceItem` is the `DeviceState` with the highest `timestamp`. A concrete `SmartHome` instance may then, for instance, contain a `DeviceItem` "ParlorLight_Color" with `DeviceState` value "(210,0.25,1)", which corresponds to light blue in the HSV color model. Furthermore, the context encapsulates a DDD Repository that models storage and retrieval of `SmartHome` instances and a Service to retrieve smart home and their device instances. The `RemoteControlContext` expresses characteristics for remote control of devices (cf. T2-FG-2). The stakeholders regarded smart home devices as objects that may receive descriptive `Commands` like "switch off palor light". Therefore, the context's technical Service realizes communication of commands to a concrete smart home. The `AccessControlContext` models regulation of access rights (cf. T2-FG-3). Within the collaborative domain modeling process we discussed several remote care control scenarios, that were identified in the future workshop with the stakeholders (see Sect. 2). Together with the representative domain experts, we came to the conclusion that simple read and write access rules are sufficient. Central to the context is the `AccessControlService`, which is used by the other contexts and deals with checking the access rights of a given `user`. Hence, they are organized in `AccessItems` to subsume concrete, regulated domain concepts like `Command` or `DeviceItem`.

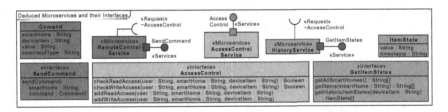

Fig. 2. Interface model of the Remote Care Application in MSA-adapted notation [7]

From the domain model, the *interface model* [7] depicted in Fig. 2 was deduced by mapping each Bounded Context in Fig. 1 to a microservice. As the interface model represents the technical implementation of the microservices, it needs to exhibit concrete technical information not present in the domain model, i.e., (i) interfaces with methods (deduced from the Bounded Contexts' Services of the domain model); (ii) types for exchanged data structures, e.g., `Command`, and their fields, e.g., `value`; (iii) service interaction relationships, e.g., the `HistoryService` consumes the `AccessControlService` (deduced from the `use` relationships in the domain model); (iv) additional elements necessary for the implementation, e.g., additional `add` methods in the `AccessControl` interface.

3.3   Implementation

Based on the interface model, we started to implement the RCA. Applied an MSA-specific, technically motivated Architectural Design (MSA-AD) [14]. Next to the functional microservices as business-related components, it comprises common infrastructure components of MSA.

Load Balancer and Circuit Breaker denote service-specific infrastructure components [14]. Load Balancers may cope with increased amounts of requests by measuring incoming network traffic and distributing requests to different service instances. Circuit Breakers on the other hand increase the resilience of microservices by blocking requests that continuously result in errors or communication faults. Satisfying requirement goals NG-1 and NG-3 (see Table 2), both infrastructure components contribute to the RCA's scalability and availability. Another key infrastructure component of the MSA-AD relevant to the RCA is the Discovery Service [14]. It allows functional and infrastructure microservices to expose their own interfaces, discover exposed interfaces of other services and establish a communication relationship with those services. The Discovery Services addresses requirement goal NG-4 (cf. Table 2) as it facilitates the flexible integration of new functionalities provided by microservices. The demand for security related to the RCA (goal NG-2 in Table 2) is satisfied by a dedicated Security Service [14]. It acts as an identity provider for client authorization and authentication. The services employ token-based security by populating each request's data with an access token. The necessary user data is managed by the User Management Service. Hence, the caller can be clearly identified, even when the request is transitively delegated from service to service. In combination with an additional API Gateway Service, the Security Service realizes a Single Sign-On Gateway, i.e., a central point for authentication. Besides that, the API Gateway Service denotes the entry point to the RCA for external callers.

The implementation of the RCA is based on Spring Cloud[1]. Consequently, each microservice is a standalone Java archive built with Spring Boot. The Discovery and API Gateway Service employ Eureka and Zuul, respectively. For architecture-internal communication synchronous RESTful HTTP is used. Furthermore, the API Gateway Service provides a REST endpoint for external requests. However, to increase the RCA's scalability (goal NG-1 in Table 2), asynchronous message-based communication via MQTT is applied with HiveMQ[2] as message broker for receiving data from connected smart homes. Eventually, the Security Service was based on OAuth2[3].

Figure 3 presents the deployment overview of the RCA and connected software components. The RCA communicates with various external clients. Administrators can configure access rights and control a connected smart home with the `ManagementPlatform` (cf. Subsect. 3.2). It is mainly used on the office computers of professional caregivers. The `RemoteAssistanceApp` is the counterpart of the platform for mobile devices. Both control applications, i.e., platform and app,

---

[1] http://projects.spring.io/spring-cloud.
[2] https://www.hivemq.com.
[3] https://oauth.net/2.

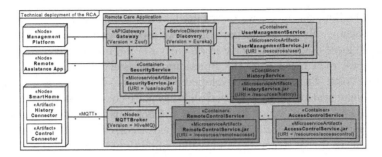

Fig. 3. Deployment model of the RCA in MSA-adapted notation [7]. It not otherwise stated, RESTful HTTP is used for communication purposes.

enable device control independent of a certain vendor. Additionally, the RCA acts as a mediator between smart homes and the control applications. Therefore, each SmartHome needs to execute an instance of Eclipse Smart Home[4], because both HistoryConnector and ControlConnector are based on this framework to abstract from vendor-specific protocols. While the HistoryConnector transmits status changes to the RCA, the ControlConnector receives and executes remote control commands (cf. Subsect. 3.2).

To provide MSA researchers with an operating case study, whose creation was mainly driven by practical requirements, we made the RCA's code available as open source on GitHub[5].

4   Discussion

This section discusses challenges we had to cope with in the RCA development.

First, we spent significantly more time with the engineering of infrastructure than functional microservices. The realization of the Security and API Gateway Service took the most time. The reasons for this are (i) a lack of documentation of the respective frameworks and (ii) the comparatively small business logic, i.e., while the RCA exhibits high degrees of scalability and extensibility its core functional capabilities are limited to a small number of microservices.

Second, the configuration of the development environment was partially cumbersome. By applying MSA, the application is decomposed into several small and autonomous services. This results in the physical development environment need to cope with a high amount of parallel processes, both functional and infrastructural. In our case this led to the regular development computers running out of resources when starting the RCA locally as a whole. Our solution was two-tiered. First we limited every microservices' available resources using JVM parameters. While thereby we were able to cope with the resource issue, this approach naturally reduced the application's performance and the opportunity

---

[4] https://www.eclipse.org/smarthome.
[5] https://github.com/SeelabFhdo/RemoteCareApplication.

to test scalability. Secondly, we distributed working services to a second development machine. Based on our experience we recommend to use a cloud server or multiple local machines directly in an early development stage.

Third, we recognized that the functional microservices contained a lot of boilerplate code. Therefore, we developed a *functional service template* [5], i.e., a stub implementation that comprised all boilerplate code and needed to be filled only with the business logic. To be able to adapt this template to subsequent MSA projects in other domains, we developed a corresponding reusable build management tool that generates and embeds functional service stubs as well as stubs for infrastructure components [14].

Fourth, the model-based design process (cf. Subsect. 3.2) eased the implementation of the RCA. However, it also introduced an additional amount of effort as we deduced the interface and deployment model manually from the domain model [7]. We expect that this extra work may be reduced by (semi-) automatically transforming the domain model into MSA-specific design models.

5   Conclusion

In this paper, we presented a case study on how to apply MSA in the remote care domain. We identified requirements for the RCA leveraging participatory design techniques and employed DDD to create an appropriate domain model. From this, we deduced further design models which enabled us to derive the RCA's implementation consisting of several functional and infrastructure microservices. Hence, the case study may not only shed light on MSA's applicability for remote care, but also on how model-based design may aid in microservice development.

References

1. Erl, T.: Service-Oriented Architecture (SOA) Concepts, Technology and Design. Prentice Hall, Upper Saddle River (2005)
2. Evans, E.: Domain-Driven Design. Addison-Wesley, Boston (2004)
3. Islam, S.M.R., Kwak, D., Kabir, M.H., Hossain, M., Kwak, K.S.: The internet of things for health care: a comprehensive survey. IEEE Access **3**, 678–708 (2015)
4. van Lamsweerde, A.: Goal-oriented requirements engineering: a guided tour. In: Proceedings of the Fifth International Symposium on Requirements Engineering, pp. 249–262 (2001)
5. Newmann, S.: Building Microservices. O'Reilly Media, Sebastopol (2016)
6. Rademacher, F., Sachweh, S., Zündorf, A.: Towards a UML profile for domain-driven design of microservice architectures. In: Cerone, A., Roveri, M. (eds.) SEFM 2017. LNCS, vol. 10729, pp. 230–245. Springer, Cham (2018). https://doi.org/10.1007/978-3-319-74781-1_17
7. Rademacher, F., Sorgalla, J., Sachweh, S.: Challenges of domain-driven microservice design: a model-driven perspective. IEEE Softw. (2018, in press)
8. Rashid Bashshur, G.S.: History of telemedicine: evolution, context, and transformation, New Rochelle (2009)
9. Rashidi, P., Mihailidis, A.: A survey on ambient-assisted living tools for older adults. IEEE J. Biomed. Health Inf. **17**(3), 579–590 (2013)

10. Redfoot, D., Feinberg, L., Houser, A.: The Aging of the Baby Boom and the Growing Care Gap: A Look at Future Declines in the Availability of Family Caregivers. AARP Public Policy Institute, Columbia (2013)
11. Robert Jungk, N.M.: Future Workshops: How to Create Desirable Futures. Institute for Social Inventions (1996)
12. Sorgalla, J., Schabsky, P., Sachweh, S., Grates, M., Heite, E.: Improving representativeness in participatory design processes with elderly. In: Proceedings of the 2017 CHI Conference Extended Abstracts on Human Factors in Computing Systems, pp. 2107–2114. ACM (2017)
13. United Nations: World Population Ageing 2015. No. ST/ESA/SER.A/390 (2015)
14. Wizenty, P., Sorgalla, J., Rademacher, F., Sachweh, S.: Magma: build management-based generation of microservice infrastructures. In: Proceedings of the 11th European Conference on Software Architecture (ECSA), pp. 61–65. ACM (2017)

Ambient Intelligence Users in the Loop: Towards a Model-Driven Approach

Maroun Koussaifi[✉], Sylvie Trouilhet, Jean-Paul Arcangeli,
and Jean-Michel Bruel

Institut de Recherche en Informatique de Toulouse, University of Toulouse,
Toulouse, France
maroun.koussaifi@irit.fr

Abstract. Ambient and mobile systems consist of networked devices and software components surrounding human users and providing services. From the services present in the environment, other services can be composed opportunistically and automatically by an intelligent system, then proposed to the user. The latter must not only to be aware of existing services but also be kept in the loop in order to both control actively the services and influence the automated decisions.

This paper first explores the requirements for placing the user in the ambient intelligence loop. Then it describes our approach aimed at answering the requirements, which originality sets in the use of the model-driven engineering paradigm. It reports on the prototype that has been developed, and analyzes the current status of our work towards the different research questions that we have identified.

Keywords: User in the loop · Ambient intelligence
Service composition · Software components · Emergence of services
Presentation of services · Model-driven engineering
Model transformation

1 Introduction

Ambient and mobile systems consist of fixed or mobile devices connected by one or several communication networks. These devices host services specified by interfaces and implemented by independently developed, installed, and activated software components. Components therefore provide services and, in turn, may require other services. They are blocks that can be assembled to build more complex services. For example, hardware or software interaction components (*e.g.*, buttons, sliders, screens) and functional components like a Polling Station and a Report Generator can be assembled if their interfaces match and provide a complete distributed "voting service".

Due to the high mobility of current devices and users, the environment is open and highly unstable: devices and software components, which are independently managed, may appear and disappear without this dynamics necessarily

© Springer Nature Switzerland AG 2018
M. Mazzara et al. (Eds.): STAF 2018 Workshops, LNCS 11176, pp. 558–572, 2018.
https://doi.org/10.1007/978-3-030-04771-9_42

being foreseen. Human users are plunged into these dynamic systems and can use the services at their disposal. Ambient intelligence aims at offering them a personalized environment, adapted to the current situation, anticipating their needs and providing them the right services at the right time, with as little effort as possible.

We are currently developing a solution in which services (in fact, microservices) are dynamically and automatically composed in order to build composite services and so customize the environment at runtime. Here, unlike the traditional "top-down mode" for building applications, services are built on the fly in "bottom-up mode" from the components that are present and available at runtime. This is supported by an *assembly engine* in line with the principles of autonomic computing and the MAPE-K model [11]: it senses the existing components, decides of the connections (it may connect a required service and a provided one if their interfaces are compatible) without using a pre-established plan (or not necessarily), and commands them. The heart of this engine is a distributed multi-agent system where agents, close to the software components, cooperate and decide on the connections between their services. Composite services (realized by assemblies of components) continuously emerge from the environment, taking advantage of opportunities as they arise. And to make the right decisions and offer the relevant services, the engine (*i.e.*, the agents) learns at runtime by reinforcement. The main advantages are proactivity and runtime adaptation in the context of openness, dynamics and unpredictability [15].

The user is at the core of ambient or cyber-physical systems. Here, unlike the traditional SOA paradigm, she/he does not necessarily demand or search for services (in "pull mode"); on the contrary, services adapted to the context and operational are supplied in "push mode". In this context of automation based on artificial intelligence, the sharing of decision-making responsibilities between the assembly engine and the user is in question. Anyway she/he must be kept "in the loop". On the one hand, it is essential to assist the user in the appropriation and control of the pushed services: she/he must be informed but also must keep some control over her/his ambient environment, or possibly be able to contribute herself/himself to the construction of personalized services. On the other hand, to make the right decisions, the assembly engine must rely on a model of the user in her/his environment. This model, which is unknown a priori, must be built at runtime and evolve dynamically.

Keeping the user in the loop therefore demands a number of requirements to be met. The objective of this work is to experiment and evaluate a solution based on model-driven engineering and model transformations in order to put the user in the control loop. The purpose of this paper is to explain and justify the interest of such an approach, to describe the main architectural principles, and to report on the development of a prototype solution (the design of the smart engine itself is out of the scope of this paper). The conducted experimentation allows us to conclude positively on the advantages of such an approach.

The paper is organized as follows. Section 2 describes in more details the problem through a use case. The concrete issues raised by the specifics of the domain, listed as requirements. Section 3 analyses the current state of the art and concludes that there is no current solution that fully addresses the requirements. Section 4 presents our initial ideas to address the research questions identified. Section 5 presents the prototype we have developed and experimented in order to validate our approach. Finally, a conclusion is given in Sect. 6 as well as the perspectives of this work.

2   Use Case and Requirements

2.1   Use Case

In order to illustrate the problem and motivate the requirements, we propose the following use case, divided into two phases: the first one describes an opportunistic adaptive service composition and the second one the emergence of an unanticipated service.

MissJane is a student at the university. This morning, she has a formative assessment: the teacher asks some questions and the students answer using a *Remote Control* device lent by the university for the year. The answers are collected by the teacher who makes comments in return. For that, the teacher activates a *Quiz* service implemented by three software components: a *Polling Station* available on the university network, a *Report Generator* and a *Remote Control* installed on his laptop. Then, the services provided by the students' remote controls connect with the required service of the *Polling Station* component. Unfortunately, MissJane has forgotten her remote control at home and is unable to answer. However, the ICE (Interactive Control Environment) interface which is at her disposal in order to control her smart environment suggests the use of a vertical slider currently available on her smartphone instead of the remote control. Even though it was not originally designed to be used with the *Quiz* service but as it matches the required service of the *Polling Station*, MissJane can use it, at least if she agrees, and therefore answer. In fact, the ICE interface could have suggested several other compatible interaction components (as an horizontal slider or a dimmer switch) also available in the environment. Then, MissJane would have chosen her favorite one.

Here, several available components have opportunistically been assembled by the smart engine. Then the resulting *Quiz* service that is adapted to the context has been presented to MissJane, who used it after acceptance. The corresponding assembly is depicted on the right side of Fig. 1 (we voluntarily use an informal notation of components and connections). Note that, in this example, we do not consider how the quiz questions are displayed to the students.

The course in now terminated. MissJane frequently goes to her favorite pub in the afternoon. To book a table and order drinks, she uses an *Order* service (see the left side of Fig. 1) implemented by three components (*Customer Input Interface, Menu Presentation, Order Generator*) provided by the pub and installed on her smartphone. As today it's her birthday, she would like to invite the other students to have a drink. But she doesn't want to enter all of the orders manually. Thus, she deactivates her *Customer Input Interface*. Then, in such a

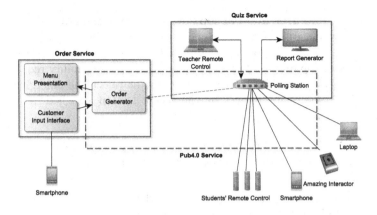

Fig. 1. Emerging composite services

context, the assembly engine proposes to bind the *Order Generator* component with the *Polling Station* still available in the environment, instead of the *Customer Input Interface*. Now, the new *Pub4.0* service allows each student to order her/his own drink with her/his remote control, and sends the global order to the pub. This service really emerges from the ambient environment as it was not designed beforehand and it is built from non-dedicated components provided by different authorities. The *Pub4.0* service is in the dotted frame of Fig. 1.

2.2 Requirements

Our goal in this project is to put the user in the loop. To achieve this goal, we have identified several requirements listed below. In a general way, the user must be aware of the emergence of new services that are pushed by the assembly engine, have the privilege to control this emergence, and be able to appropriate the services. On the other side, to improve its decisions, the intelligent assembly engine needs to learn from the user's actions and reactions to the situation and the proposals of services. We have organized the requirements in main concerns.

Presentation: An emerging service must be presented to the user. As unanticipated services may appear, the user must be informed of their availability. For example, in our use case, MissJane would receive a notification on her smartphone that she can use the vertical slider as a voting device. This implies that she has accepted to receive such a notification. This also raises some requirements related to acceptability and intelligibility. As a result, the research questions we are interested in are:

PRE 1. How to present an emerging service to a human user in an intelligible and personalized way?
PRE 2. When and how often must the emerging services be presented?

Acceptation: The user must accept or reject an emerging service. After it passes the presentation phase, user acceptation determines if the proposed service is relevant and has to be deployed or not. In our use case, MissJane would accept the use of the proposed vertical slider. This raises usability requirements: it demands an easy way for the user to accept or reject the emerging service (*e.g.*, MissJane would simply click on the accept button attached to the notification). Some related research questions are:

ACC 1. How the user must be notified that acceptation is required?
ACC 2. How the user could accept or reject an emerging service?

Modification: An emerging service should be modifiable by the user. The user should be able to remove or replace any component in the proposed service, more widely to modify the emerging service. For example, MissJane should be able to change from a vertical slider to an horizontal one. So, the user must have the necessary tools and services to modify the emerging service: alternative components and/or assemblies should be presented, editing should be easy and the user assisted in this task. This concerns the usability and ergonomics of the editing tools. In addition, the permission to use and bind a component, *i.e.*, security concerns, might be considered. Some related research questions are:

MOD 1. How the user can be assisted and tools be helpful?
MOD 2. How to insure, on the spot, that the modified service is still correct?
MOD 3. Which components of the ambient environment should be usable and presented to the user and how?

Creation: A composite service can be created by the user. Like the engine but without using its proposals, the user should be able to create her/his own composite service *i.e.*, an assembly from scratch, out of available components. For example, MissJane should be able to build by herself the *Pub4.0* service instead of the engine. To do this, the user must visualize the available components and be able to bind the ones she/he selects. Besides usability, user assistance, service correctness and relevance, another problem -partly related to scalability- concerns the identification of the available and useful components. This part of the requirements does not bring any new particular research question in addition to those related to the modification concern.

Feedback generation: The assembly engine must receive feedback from the user's actions. When a service is created, modified, accepted or rejected, positive or negative feedback must be generated for the engine, that could help to increase the quality of its decisions and fit to the user's behavior, practices and preferences (this means that a user profile is implicitly built). For instance, breaking a connection between services could trigger negative feedback for the engine in order to decrease the estimated value of the binding. In the same way, setting up a new connection could generate a positive feedback increasing consequently the estimated value of the binding. Thus, for example, after several times MissJane has modified an emerging service by choosing the horizontal slider, the engine would have finally learned her preference and proposed the service with the horizontal slider as a priority. In addition, when using a graphical editor, the user's actions such as swipe or pinch-spread may give information for the assembly engine. This way, the swipe of a service could mean that this one is interesting, and reinforce the interest of the component which implements this service. Concerning feedback and learning, some research questions are:

FBK 1. How to capture user's intentions from her/his manipulations?
FBK 2. How to translate the observed actions into useful information for the engine?

3   State of the Art

According to [9], as self-adaptive systems (*e.g.*, implementing the MAPE-K model) can behave in unexpected ways, humans must be involved in the adaptation process: they can help in conflict resolution and improve the adaptation strategy by giving feedback, even when they have limited attention or cognition. Transparency, intelligibility, trust to users, controlability, and management of user attention are major requirements. In [8], authors propose a solution to integrate the user in the self-adaptation loop, while usability and preference modeling are the main requirements. Adaptation relies on variability models built at design-time and user-level preferences. In addition, for acceptability and to avoid user trouble, "user focus" components (*i.e.*, components that are in the actual user focus, in opposition to "background" components) are kept out of dynamic adaptation. User contribution can be more or less explicit: she/he can select and adjust an application, accept or reject an application, change her/his preference, or even put off the adaptive behavior.

In order to succeed, putting the user in the loop must meet usability requirements. For that, End-User Development (EUD) aims to enable non-specialists in software development to create or modify applications. Common approaches consists in providing software elements to be customized and composed. According to [13], which reviews different projects in particular concerning mobile applications, a motivation is that "regular development cycles are too slow to meet the users' fast changing requirements". In [6], authors propose an EUD environment designed for home control as an alternative to artificial intelligence. Additionally, they report on their "lived-with" experiences with EUD at home. They conclude that if EUD and machine learning are competing approaches, "it should be possible to augment EUD with machine learning".

In [10], the emphasis is put on feedback and machine learning in adaptive smart homes. Authors argue that user preferences and profile can be learned (by semi-supervised reinforcement learning algorithms), associated to activity recognition that transforms raw data into sharp information about the user situation.

In the domain of human-computer interaction, several solutions for interface plasticity (*i.e.*, dynamic adaptation to changing environments) rely on component or service dynamic composition [7]: automation is demanded to overcome complexity (in number, dynamics, composability...), but keeping the user in the loop is imperative both to observe and to control the interactive ambient environment. The concept of Meta-UI (User Interface) [5] has been introduced as "the set of functions that are necessary and sufficient to control and evaluate the state of interactive ambient spaces". In [7], we have proposed the Meta-UI to present emerging user interfaces and allow for user's choice in the context of ambient systems.

Regarding the requirements analyzed in Sect. 2.2, the existing solutions are only partially satisfactory. They are *ad hoc* (EUD environments or Meta-UI), and none of them can support the description and edition of unanticipated emerging services. The next section introduces the principles of our approach, and Sect. 5 overviews our solution and details the prototype we have realized as a proof of concept.

4   Our Approach

From the previous section we can conclude that the problem we address requires to match and master links between concepts. It can be between a service and an assembly of components, between an intent and a set of model manipulations, etc. The key concerns here are: (i) the presentation/manipulation of services, which implies some form of editor, and (ii) the navigation/transformation between concepts. We have hence naturally explored the use of the recent Model-Driven Engineering (MDE) approaches to help in this concern.

Our team has a long experience in providing modeling and language engineering tools and approaches [4]. One of the most recent activity addresses the benefit of having, in the context of Cyber-Physical Systems (CPS) models directly manipulable by the final user in order to pilot and adapt their behavior [3]. Such manipulations are now possible thanks to the progress of language engineering environments such as GEMOC[1] that allow the definition of Domain-Specific Modeling Languages (DSML) and the automated generation of the language workbench that goes with it (graphical and textual editors, transformation languages, etc.).

In order for a human to manipulate concretely a model, a set of elements are required: (i) some tooling (viewers, editors, debuggers, interpreters, ...); (ii) some representations (concrete and abstract syntax, ...); (iii) some interpretations and rules (semantics, grammar, ...). This is the purpose of MDE approaches to provide such environments (see Fig. 2). In our context, we have to extract information from an ambient systems technical world (made of components, bindings, services, etc.) and present them from a user point of view (made of goals, expectations, required services, etc.). MDE will help to make the connections between the two domains by providing: (i) a detailed organization of

---

[1] http://gemoc.org/.

the concepts of each domain (called metamodels), (ii) a mapping between those concepts, (iii) the required environment to manipulate and navigate between those concepts. The detailed use of MDE to help solving the research questions we have listed in Sect. 2.2 will be given in Sect. 5.1.

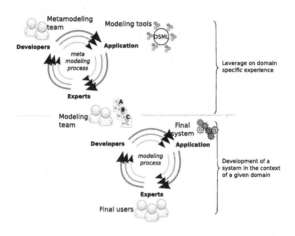

Fig. 2. Model-Driven Engineering in action (taken from [4])

Apart from our own efforts (*e.g.,* [1,3]) towards putting the final user in the loop of the monitoring and management of his/her own applications, we can cite several other approaches. In [14], the authors use MDE to control user interface adaptation according to explicit usability criteria. They focus on the generation of those interfaces and hence address more the variability concerns that the user interactions themselves. Let us also mention the work from [2], where the authors apply knowledge (inferred from large volumes of information, artificial intelligence or collective intelligence) to boost the performance and impact of a process. They nevertheless do not focus in user interaction. The following section provides details on the way we have implemented MDE techniques to answer the requirements identified in Sect. 2.

5   Proof of Concept

In order to experiment the base ideas of our approach, we have developed a solution that consists of a specialized model editor for user manipulations and tools to link the models with (an emulated version of) the ambient system. The full source code of our prototype can be found on Github[2]. The first tool generates the model of a service from the output of the assembly engine. The second tool allows the models that are created, modified, or accepted by the user to be deployed in the ambient environment.

---

[2] https://github.com/marounkoussaifi/MDE_Prototype_User_In_The_Loop.

Several technologies and frameworks support the implementation. They are used to define a metamodel from which models can be edited using a graphical editing framework, and to transform models by model-to-text transformation into codes that realize the deployment. In practice, we have used the Eclipse Modeling Framework (EMF[3]) which is a basic plugin for metamodeling on Eclipse, Ecore to define and create the metamodel, Sirius (See footnote 3) to define the editor's resources, and Acceleo (See footnote 3) which is a model-to-text transformation tool, to generate deployment code.

In the following, we present an overview of the implemented approach, and provide some more technical details.

5.1   Overview of the Prototype Solution

Figure 3 shows an overview of our prototype solution that is structured in three parts: an *editor*, a *service presenter*, and a *service deployer*.

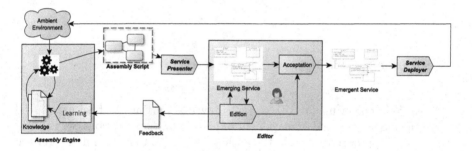

Fig. 3. Implementation of the complete loop

At first, the engine monitors the ambient environment to detect the available components and produces composite services in the form of scripts, *i.e.*, text files defining executable bindings of components. Figure 4 shows an example of such a script in Java, where the comments have been added by hand for a better understanding.

Then the *service presenter* transforms the script into an editable model of the emerging service to be presented to the user. This model conforms to the metamodel we have defined for this purpose (see Sect. 5.2). Via the *editor*, the service model can be manipulated either in the form of a text (for example for experimented users) or in a graphical form (possibly for non-specialists). Actually, this form can be adapted to the user thanks to the separation between the model and its representation, *i.e.*, the model can be represented in a domain-specific language (DSL). Figure 5 shows the graphical representation by the *editor* of the emerging *Pub4.0* service proposed by the engine (see Sect. 2.1). It consists of different components connected together. The students' remote controls are

---

[3] https://www.eclipse.org/[modeling/emf|sirius|acceleo].

```
// **** Emergence of the new Pub4.0 service ****
try {
    //Connecting the Order Generator to the Polling Station
    ambientEnv.bind(I2ofC8, I1ofC1, C8, C1);
    //Connecting the Vertical Slider to the Polling Station
    ambientEnv.bind(I2ofC1, I1ofC5, C1, C5);
    //Connecting 3 students remote controls to the Polling Station
    ambientEnv.bind(I3ofC1, I1ofC4, C1, C4);
    ambientEnv.bind(I3ofC1, I1ofC4bis, C1, C4bis);
    ambientEnv.bind(I3ofC1, I1ofC4beta, C1, C4beta);

} catch (BindingFailure e) {
    e.printStackTrace();
}
```

Fig. 4. Script for the assembly of Pub4.0 service

connected to the *Polling Station* by binding the *Vote* services together. Also, MissJane's *Vertical Slider* is used as the master remote control of *Pub4.0*: it's connected to the *Polling Station* by binding the *Master Control* service to the *Value* service. The *Value* service represents a generic type of service which is compatible with different other types, such as the *Master Control* service. In the same way, the *Polling Station* is connected to the *Order Generator* by binding the *Report* service to the *Order* service. Additionally, the *editor* may display several non-connected components which are available for connection if necessary. Once the emerging service is uploaded in the *editor*, the user can accept or reject it. She/he can also modify it, that is to say remove or change any binding between the components and use available components if one exists, or even define a new service by creating a new assembly.

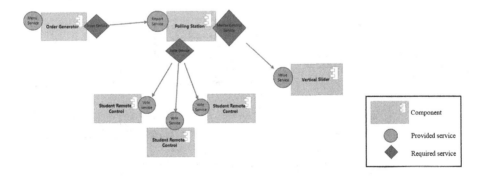

Fig. 5. Presentation of the Pub4.0 service

When editing, in order to generate feedback for the engine to enrich the agents' learning process, user's actions on bindings (in general on the interactive interface) are captured. The engine knowledge hence increases and therefore the engine future decisions will be more in line with the user expectations and profile.

At last, the emergent[4] service is transformed by the *service deployer* into a script to be executed in the ambient environment.

5.2 Service Edition

The graphical *editor* is the core element of the answer to the identified requirements listed in Sect. 2.2. It realizes the ICE interface introduced in Sect. 2.1: basically, it allows for visualization of emerging service models, service acceptation, and modification, deletion or creation of links between services. In addition, as a graphical editor, it enables to drag and drop any displayed component.

The *editor* relies on a metamodel that frames the definition of component assemblies as a service. The metamodel is classically defined by a class diagram relating together the metamodeling concepts (see Fig. 6). The figure was automatically generated by the Sirius Ecore Editor, a tool that allows the graphical representation and edition of an Ecore model (metamodel). It consists of three main classes. The *Service* abstract class is extended by two child classes, the *ProvidedService* and the *RequiredService* classes. The ambient environment (*ambientEnv* class) is composed of components (*Component* class). Components are composed themselves of at least one service (*Service* class). Bindings between component services are made to build the emerging service. Additionally, we have implemented Object Constraint Language (OCL) [16] rules to constrain the service models (*e.g.*, to control that a service does not exceed a maximal number of connections).

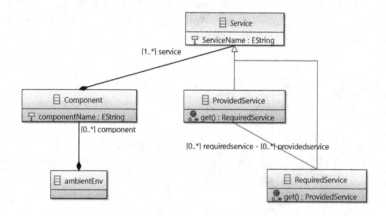

Fig. 6. Our service metamodel

To develop the *editor*, we have used the GEMOC Studio, and more precisely Sirius, a technology for designing customized graphic modeling tools. Sirius allows to define editors in a completely graphical way, without having to

---

[4] We deliberately use *emerging* to qualify services that are dynamically appearing. We reserve the use of *emergent* for emerging services that have been accepted by the user.

write any code. This is where the use of an MDE approach takes all its sense. Indeed, with such a strong coupling between the tool and the concepts, it is important that we take into account, in advance, the future evolutions of our metamodel. As the editor is completely automated from the metamodel itself, the metamodel evolutions have no impact on the editor from a workload point of view. At this point of our work, feedback generation has not yet been implemented. The GEMOC monitoring capabilities will be used in order to generate feedback for the learning process of the engine.

The *editor* should be integrated into the whole system and the ambient environment for example to present a short list of available components that are not connected but relevant for use (*e.g.*, an horizontal slider). At this stage, our *editor* is not fully integrated. Nevertheless, in order to test our prototype and simulate the arrival of new components, we have added to the editor a side panel that allows the user to design any component with its services.

5.3 Service Presentation

The *service presenter* is the element of our solution that transforms an emerging service into an editable model (which in turn will be presented to the user via the *editor*, as described in the previous section). Unlike the *editor*, the *service presenter* is not a user-manipulated tool.

The *service presenter* relies on the same metamodel as the *editor* to generate the model of the emerging service. Nevertheless, unlike for the editor but for fast prototyping concerns, we have not yet used an MDE approach to implement the *service presenter*. For the moment, we have developed a Java program that records all the bindings between different components, then generates the XML source of the graphical model while respecting the *editor* metamodel concepts. Whenever the metamodel changes, the *service presenter* must be rebuilt in order to become compatible with these changes. Using a MDE approach will be one of the major evolution of our future work.

However, in its current form, the *service presenter* is fully operational and is able to generate the model of an emerging service in the form of an assembly of components.

5.4 Service Deployment

The *service deployer* is the element of our solution that generates the bindings commands to be executed for the actual deployment of an emergent service in the ambient environment. It is also a non-user manipulated tool.

Likewise the *editor*, the *service deployer* must rely on the same metamodel while executing model-to-text transformation in order to properly generate the binding script. At this stage, this part suffers from the same limitation than the presenter described previously.

The *service deployer* consists of an Acceleo program that performs model-to-text transformation. Acceleo is an open source code generator from the Eclipse foundation. It allows the design of code generation modules that can generate outputs in a language chosen by the developer from one or more models as inputs. Currently, the *service deployer* performs model-to-Java code transformation.

At this stage of our work, the generated Java code implements the emergent service model to be injected in the ambient environment. This is enough for rapid prototyping and test.

6   Conclusion and Future Work

Infrastructure automation, commonly based on continuous integration, automated testing and deployment, helps in microservices management [12]. Our project aims to go a step further in this direction by automating the assembly of services that are available in the environment and operational. In such a context, the user must nevertheless be put into the loop to be informed of emerging services, to be able to edit, modify, validate them, and to give implicit feedback to the automatic system.

In this paper, we have proposed an MDE-based approach intended to answer the requirements to place the user in the ambient loop. The solution consists of an *editor* that enables the user to visualize an emerging service provided by a *service presenter*. Also, it enables her/him to accept or edit the service, before deployment by a *service deployer*. In such a way, the user is a full actor in the ambient system, especially as her/his actions may produce feedback for the intelligent system. At this stage of our work, tools for service presentation (*service presenter*) and deployment (*service deployer*) are working but should be consolidated *via* a full MDE-based development.

In the following, we discuss the current status of our solution towards the nine research questions we have identified. This discussion is summarized in Table 1 where the status regarding research questions are rated from none to three +.

Table 1. Current status of our solution towards the identified research questions

Research question	Current status
PRE 1 (How to present)	+
PRE 2 (When to present)	+
ACC 1 (How to notify user)	
ACC 2 (How the user accept)	++
MOD 1 (Help in manipulation)	++
MOD 2 (Correctness)	+++
MOD 3 (What to present)	+
FBK 1 (How to capture intentions)	+
FBK 2 (Feedback for the engine)	

The first group of research questions is directly related to the MDE-based approach we adopted in order to put the user in the loop: PRE 1, MOD 2, FBK 2. The experience presented in this paper shows that MDE meets the requirements of service presentation and editing, whereas the services are correct by construction since they conform to the metamodel. In addition, as the concrete service representation is separated from the service model itself, any dedicated language that is familiar to the user can be used (DSL). So, we do not expect any particular service manipulation abilities from the user; in the contrary we consider that it is up to ICE to adapt to the user. On the other hand, the view is currently only structural but does not present the function of the emerging service (neither of the components). Likewise, if a certain number of user actions can be observed, they still need to be interpreted in a way that is useful for learning. These points are fundamental, so we aim for a +++ level of response. To meet this objective, and fulfill intelligibility requirements both for the user and the engine, important work remains to be done concerning the enhancement of the metamodel and the transformation rules.

A second group of research questions concerns problems related to Human-Computer Interactions (HCI): PRE 2, ACC 1, ACC 2. They mainly concern acceptability, usability, and ergonomics. For the moment, the ambient environment and its changes are sensed periodically; at the same frequency, new emerging services are presented if there exist. We still have to deal with problems related to environment instability, awareness of user preferences, obtrusiveness or ergonomics in order to reach a solution rated between + and ++. Our proposal will rely on solutions elaborated in the HCI domain, and we do not really aim for a major contribution to the state of the art.

The last questions are strongly related to Artificial Intelligence issues: MOD 1, MOD 3, FBK 2. Currently, the *editor* supports the presentation of emergent services proposed by the intelligent system. We should go further in the choice of relevant services and components to present according to the context (user profile, situation. . .), and in the assistance to the user. Another challenge sets in the translation of user actions into learning knowledge useful to the engine. As these aspects are essential, we aim for a level response rated from ++ to +++. The further development of the engine's intelligence and its coupling with ICE will provide answers.

References

1. Bruel, J.M., Combemale, B., Ober, I.: Raynal, H.: MDE in practice for computational science. In: International Conference on Computational Science, Reykjavík, Iceland, June 2015. https://hal.inria.fr/hal-01141393
2. Cabot, J., Clarisó, R., Brambilla, M., Gérard, S.: Cognifying model-driven software engineering. In: Seidl, M., Zschaler, S. (eds.) STAF 2017. LNCS, vol. 10748, pp. 154–160. Springer, Cham (2018). https://doi.org/10.1007/978-3-319-74730-9_13
3. Combemale, B., Cheng, B.H., Moreira, A., Bruel, J.M., Gray, J.: Modeling for sustainability. In: Modeling in Software Engineering 2016 (MiSE 2016). ACM, Austin (2016). https://hal.inria.fr/hal-01185800

4. Combemale, B., France, R., Jézéquel, J.M., Rumpe, B., Steel, J.R., Vojtisek, D.: Engineering Modeling Languages. Chapman and Hall/CRC, Boca Raton (2016). https://hal.inria.fr/hal-01355374

5. Coutaz, J.: Meta-user interfaces for ambient spaces. In: Coninx, K., Luyten, K., Schneider, K.A. (eds.) TAMODIA 2006. LNCS, vol. 4385, pp. 1–15. Springer, Heidelberg (2007). https://doi.org/10.1007/978-3-540-70816-2_1

6. Coutaz, J., Crowley, J.L.: A first-person experience with end-user development for smart homes. IEEE Pervasive Comput. **15**, 26–39 (2016). https://doi.org/10.1109/MPRV.2016.24

7. Degas, A., et al.: Opportunistic composition of human-computer interactions in ambient spaces. In: Workshop on Smart and Sustainable City (Smart World Congress 2016 and International Conference IEEE UIC 2016), pp. 998–1005. IEEE Computer Society (2016). http://oatao.univ-toulouse.fr/18769/

8. Evers, C., Kniewel, R., Geihs, K., Schmidt, L.: The user in the loop: enabling user participation for self-adaptive applications. Futur. Gener. Comput. Syst. **34**, 110–123 (2014). https://doi.org/10.1016/j.future.2013.12.010

9. Gil, M., Pelechano, V., Fons, J., Albert, M.: Designing the human in the loop of self-adaptive systems. In: García, C.R., Caballero-Gil, P., Burmester, M., Quesada-Arencibia, A. (eds.) UCAmI 2016. LNCS, vol. 10069, pp. 437–449. Springer, Cham (2016). https://doi.org/10.1007/978-3-319-48746-5_45

10. Karami, A.B., Fleury, A., Boonaert, J., Lecoeuche, S.: User in the loop: adaptive smart homes exploiting user feedback-state of the art and future directions. Information **7**(2), 35 (2016). https://doi.org/10.3390/info7020035

11. Kephart, J.O., Chess, D.M.: The vision of autonomic computing. Computer **36**(1), 41–50 (2003). https://doi.org/10.1109/MC.2003.1160055

12. Lewis, J., Fowler, M.: Microservices (2014). https://martinfowler.com/articles/microservices.html

13. Paternó, F.: End user development: survey of an emerging field for empowering people. ISRN Softw. Eng. **2013** (2013). https://doi.org/10.1155/2013/532659

14. Sottet, J.-S., Calvary, G., Coutaz, J., Favre, J.-M.: A model-driven engineering approach for the usability of plastic user interfaces. In: Gulliksen, J., Harning, M.B., Palanque, P., van der Veer, G.C., Wesson, J. (eds.) DSV-IS/EHCI/HCSE -2007. LNCS, vol. 4940, pp. 140–157. Springer, Heidelberg (2008). https://doi.org/10.1007/978-3-540-92698-6_9

15. Triboulot, C., Trouilhet, S., Arcangeli, J.P., Robert, F.: Opportunistic software composition: benefits and requirements. In: Lorenz, P., Maciaszek, L.A. (eds.) International Conference on Software Engineering and Applications (ICSOFT-EA), pp. 426–431. INSTICC, July 2015. http://oatao.univ-toulouse.fr/15305/

16. Warmer, J., Kleppe, A.: The Object Constraint Language: Getting Your Models Ready for MDA, 2nd edn. Addison-Wesley Longman Publishing Co., Inc., Boston (2003). https://dl.acm.org/citation.cfm?id=861416

Integrity Protection Against Insiders in Microservice-Based Infrastructures: From Threats to a Security Framework

Mohsen Ahmadvand[1](✉), Alexander Pretschner[1], Keith Ball[2], and Daniel Eyring[2]

[1] Technical University of Munich, Munich, Germany
{ahmadvan,pretschn}@cs.tum.edu
[2] Brabbler AG., Munich, Germany
{kball,deyring}@brabbler.ag

Abstract. Building microservices involves continuous modifications at design, deployment, and run times. The DevOps notion together with the "you built it, you run it" paradigm often result in a much larger number of developers with direct access to the production pipeline than in the case of monolithic systems. Reproducible builds and continuous delivery entail practices that further worsen this situation as they grant insiders with indirect accesses (scripted processes) to production machines. Moreover, managing microservices is heavily aided by governance tools (such as Kubernetes) that are configured and controlled by insiders. In this setting, accounting for malicious insiders quickly becomes a major concern. In this paper, we identify representative integrity threats to microservice-based systems in the broader context of a development process by analyzing real-world microservice-based systems. We show that even end-to-end encryption may fall short without adequate integrity protections. From the identified threats, we then derive a set of security requirements for holistic protection. Finally, we propose a framework that serves as a blueprint for insider-resistant integrity protection in microservices.

1 Introduction

Microservice-based architectures are a relatively new paradigm for developing highly scalable distributed systems. In this paradigm, systems are decomposed into a set of independent subsystems (microservices) communicating over the network and collaborating with each other. In contrast to monolithic systems, microservices can be independently developed, deployed, executed and replicated, which yields shortened release cycles and vertically scalable systems [1].

This architecture paradigm, however, entails significant changes in the *organization processes* that were implemented for monolithic systems [16]. In microservice-based development, multiple disjointed teams are responsible for the entire lifecycle of their services. Each team has full knowledge about their

© Springer Nature Switzerland AG 2018
M. Mazzara et al. (Eds.): STAF 2018 Workshops, LNCS 11176, pp. 573–588, 2018.
https://doi.org/10.1007/978-3-030-04771-9_43

services and, often enough, limited knowledge about others (normally only API interfaces). As the system grows, bootstrapping services and handling their dependencies become a challenge.

To effectively address these issues, teams leverage container-based virtualization, e.g., Docker (https://docker.com), to bundle their services. Containers provide isolation and, more importantly, guarantee seamless portability of services from development to production. Developers are fully responsible for creating containers for their services utilizing Docker files and configurations.

Governing system containers, e.g., maintenance, orchestration, fault handling, load balancing, etc., is another complex procedure for which the state-of-practice suggests Kubernetes (https://kubernetes.io) or comparable tools [16]. Kubernetes honors developers' specified management policies in the form of configurations. Moreover, it provides a cockpit (*kubectl*) for system monitoring and management.

To resolve runtime problems, developers can, via *kubectl*, connect to running instances in the system to closely inspect or potentially even alter services. This effectively supports the "you built it, you run it" [12] paradigm, which aims at reducing the management complexity of such systems.

This new practice introduces a set of challenges with respect to protection of system integrity which we address:

1. *Reproducible builds:* To cope with the increased complexity, developers must ensure that their services run as expected in production. This entails a major change in the role of developers, known as *DevOps*, in setting up production services, be it preparing containers or scripting configurations. Consequently, production artifacts, including potentially sensitive data, are created and thus known by a larger number of insiders, which used to be restricted to only the operations team in monolithic systems. This extensive access by many parties increases the risk of user misbehaviors, which are very difficult to identify.

2. *Quis custodiet ipsos custodes:* The governance tools often allow for dynamic adaptation, e.g., spinning up new services in response to an increased load. They can potentially harm system assets if compromised. Insiders monitor the system and make necessary changes via their provided interface (*Kubectl*). However, if these insiders turn rogue, they can use the very same tool to harm the system or its users, known as Man-In-The-Cloud attacks [18]. In this setting, authenticating changes made through the tools is challenging.

3. *Continuous delivery:* Unlike monolithic systems in which the entire production system is updated at once, microservices and their settings change more frequently in a completely independent manner. This further complicates the authentication of changes in the system.

4. *Non-repudiation:* In contrast to monolithic systems, microservices split the internals of a system into disjoint subsystems. Each of them independently implements a specific part of a business goal upon request. In this setting, ensuring that sensitive operations are executed only by genuine requests is hard. That is, adversaries can potentially forge processes by issuing malicious

requests to services. Even signing requests fail to mitigate the risk because certificates/signing keys will usually reside inside the system nonetheless.

1.1   Problem Statement

These challenges are neither completely new nor exclusive to microservices. However, they impose a vastly increased risk to them. The induced complexity, the involvement of multiple parties in system configurations, the increased access to running services via governance tools and the expanded exposure of system artifacts altogether significantly increase the risk. In light of these emerging challenges, guaranteeing system and data integrity is problematic.

1.2   Gap

Section 7 will survey related work. In summary, to the best of our knowledge, we see the following gaps:

- Threats to integrity and their implications in microservice-based systems were not previously studied in a systematic and comprehensive way;
- Security requirements for a holistic integrity protection (expanding over build, deployment and execution processes) were not systematically analyzed;
- More importantly, there exists no solution for end-to-end integrity protection in microservice-based systems.

1.3   Contributions

We base our analysis on our experience with the security analysis of real-world microservice-based systems that were designed for security-sensitive contexts. For IP reasons, we cannot discuss these concrete systems themselves and will hence reflect on most parts of these systems in an abstract fictional state-of-the-art system (*SystemX*) as a case study. We consider our contributions to be the following:

- Carry out a comprehensive security analysis of *SystemX* to identify a set of integrity threats. We believe that this set of threats is representative for many microservice-based architectures;
- Derive a set of integrity protection requirements based on the threats; and
- Propose a security framework conforming to the requirements, which serves as a blueprint for holistic integrity protection in microservice-based systems.

2   Attacker Model: Rogue Insiders

In this paper, we assume that some of the organizational staff, developers, operations, etc. can go rogue. Such *insiders* may target arbitrary end users to steal their sensitive data, plant generic backdoors or (generally) perform any act of sabotage in the system. We, however, presume the organization itself is trust-worthy. That is, a majority of insiders aim for protecting both the system and its users.

As a consequence, we assume that system artifacts can be trusted when they are collectively approved by a subset of insiders upon commits to the source code control system (SCCS). This can be aimed at by reviews on the grounds of the four-eyes principle or other mechanisms. Our inside attacker of interest can, however, attempt to violate the integrity of system artifacts after creation (at various stages) or attack production machines.

3   Context

3.1   *SystemX*'s Architecture

SystemX is a structured four-tier architecture: (**a**) the *client tier* which delivers system functionalities to users, (**b**) the *API tier* which includes microservices that serve client requests, (**c**) the *internal* tier where system-level microser-vices reside, and (**d**) the *data* tier which contains the underlying distributed persistence services, e.g., an Apache Cassandra (cassandra.apache.org/) NoSQL database and a Ceph (ceph.com) distributed file system.

API services mediate requests to underlying internal services as necessitated by user requests. That is, internal services are not directly accessible from the outside world but through API services. Similarly, the persistence layer is reach-able strictly by internal services only. We refer to this access policy as *access zones* throughout the paper.

API services utilize two interaction models, *request-response* and *fire-and-forget*. The former enables direct communication between API and internal ser-vices while the latter queues requests in a message broker to be served by respec-tive services.

API services sign all requests with inter-service-authentication keys, which are stored as part of the Kubernetes secret storage. Similarly, the data layer APIs sign sensitive data before persisting them, so illegitimate data alterations, for instance by DB admins, can be detected. All signing keys are stored in a key management service (KMS).

SystemX uses end-to-end encryption for data exchange with users. Clients generate a key pair and subsequently register their public keys at the server. Consequently, all user data on the server will be encrypted.

The system utilizes various logs to track insiders' activities (e.g., inside kubectl). All these logs are signed and persisted in the data layer.

3.2   Organizational Processes

Development. There are three identical environments, viz. development, stag-ing, and production. To avoid surprises, both staging and production in terms of service configurations exactly mirror the development environment, which in turn yields effortless releases. Therefore, *system-wide configurations* (often including *initial secrets*) are checked into (internal) SCCS. Note that a management tool for sensitive data, e.g., Vault https://www.vaultproject.io/, could be used to move secrets away from configurations to protect their confidentiality. A vault can be configured to disclose secrets only after authenticating services' credentials. In this setting, microservices, however, need to be bootstrapped with valid credentials, which have to be hard-coded into services, fed into them at runtime, or reside in their configurations. All of the above are nonetheless susceptible to extraction attacks in the presence of malicious insiders.

Consequently, all secrets, whether they require credentials or not, including service and infrastructure credentials, signing certificates, KMS passphrases for key derivations, Kubernetes' secrets, inter-service authentication keys, and kubectls' admin certificates, are accessible to insiders. The same holds true for sensitive *configurations*, viz. Kubernetes' configuration, access control policies, continuous integration settings and build scripts.

Build. The continuous integration (CI) tool compiles and ships microservices in accordance with CI scripts (also checked into SCCS). Normally, each microservice is shipped in a separate Docker container. Build machines maintain a copy of the base docker images; if unavailable, they can fetch them from an image (e.g., DockerHub) repository. Both compiled binaries and prepared images are accessible to insiders and thus susceptible to manipulation attacks.

Deployment. The continuous delivery service (CD) automatically pushes newly compiled services to the development, staging and production environments. For manual updates, authorized developers (with access certificates) use kubectl. These certificates, however, are persisted in the same way as system secrets; and they are hence accessible to engineers.

Execution and Maintenance. For maintenance and monitoring purposes, developers can create a direct SSH tunnel to the production services (pods) via kubectl. Monitoring the data layer is a bit trickier, as access zones only allow API services to reach to this layer. However, this access policy is not a problem for insiders, as they can inject a container (via kubectl) to act as a proxy. It is noteworthy to mention that insiders' activity logs are recorded in the very same persistence layer.

To find other services running in the system, microservices consult Kubernetes' service discovery. That is, all services need to announce their addresses and identifiers to the service discovery.

3.3   Assets with Integrity Requirements

We identify two classes of integrity assets in *SystemX*.

Data. These assets include any sensitive information that is fed to, produced or processed by services or processes. In addition to user data, we specifically consider configuration files, system secrets (as listed before), and evidence (activity logs) in the database as data assets in *SystemX*.

Tampering with or accessing one or multiple of the above-mentioned data assets may violate system integrity. We will elaborate on this in Sect. 4.

Behavior. These assets include those functionalities of the services with which any tampering attacks put the system security at stake, e.g., access control mechanisms. We further classify such assets into two categories: *intra-service* and *inter-service*. Intra-service assets are concerned with the integrity of Docker images, microservices' logic (e.g., KMS), governance tools (e.g., Kubernetes' service registry/discovery and audit/logging system). We consider *process non-repudiation* (authenticating services on sensitive requests) and *access control mechanisms* (ensuring that only genuine services get access to system secrets) inter-service integrity assets.

4   Security Analysis

Utilizing microservices entails a new set of practices (see Sect. 3.2), which imposes some threats to the security of systems. In this section, we carry out a security analysis to identify such security threats targeting system integrity assets. We collected a comprehensive set of representative threats on data (Fig. 1) and behavior assets (Fig. 2). Each concrete attack (leaf) node is labeled with the organizational processes in which the threat can materialize - D for development, B for build, P for deployment and E for execution and maintenance. The labels are assigned by determining whether insiders have access to assets of interest in a particular stage or not (accesses were discussed in Sect. 3.2).

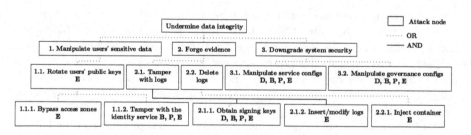

Fig. 1. Representative insider threats to data assets in microservice-based systems.

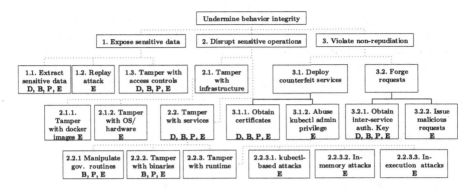

Fig. 2. Representative insider threats to behavior assets in microservice-based systems.

4.1 Threats to Data Integrity

Manipulate Users' Sensitive Data. End-to-end encryption schemes commonly boil down to the security of the *1.1. users' public key*. That is, if adversaries manage to forge them, e.g. temporarily exchange them with their own keys, they can mount an active MitM attack. Even if clients naively monitor key changes, e.g. by binding to users' first-seen key, they remain incapable of distinguishing a malicious key change from a legitimate one (e.g. due to a device change).

To maliciously rotate users' public keys, adversaries can *1.1.1. bypass access zones* at runtime and persist the forged key, or *1.1.2. tamper with the identity service* that supplies keys to requesters (clients).

Forge Evidence. *SystemX* fails to effectively protect the integrity of system logs. Therefore, adversaries can potentially *2.1. tamper with logs* given that they can *2.1.1. obtain signing keys* and subsequently *2.1.2. modify/insert arbitrary logs*. Worse yet, they can *2.2. delete* (all) *collected evidence* by bypassing data access zones, for instance, by *2.2.1. injecting a malicious container*.

Downgrade System Security. As the configuration files (*3.1. service configs* and *3.2. governance configs*) are accessible to users at all stages (D, B, P, E), malicious insiders can, for instance, add their certificate as one of the *kubectl* admins.

4.2 Threats to Behavior Integrity

Expose Sensitive Data. Sensitive data in the system suffers from deficient access control mechanisms. That is, attackers can *obtain sensitive data* at all stages.

Adversaries can *1.1. extract sensitive data* in the system by finding access credentials (e.g., in case of Vault usage), dumping the memory region containing sensitive data at runtime, or scanning configuration files. Similarly, attackers can trick services holding sensitive data to expose them, for instance, by *1.2. replaying authorized access calls*. Finally, they can *1.3. tamper with access control mechanisms* (e.g. their policy files) to circumvent protections.

Disrupt Sensitive Operations. There are two means for attackers to disrupt system operations - *2.1. tamper with the infrastructure*, and *2.2. tamper with services*.

To tamper with operations at the infrastructure level, adversaries can manipulate *2.1.1. docker images* or underlying *2.1.2. OS/drivers/libraries or the hardware level*.

At the service level (*2.2. tamper with services*) adversaries can tamper with governing tools or scripts, i.e. labeled as *2.2.1. Manipulate governance routines*, *2.2.2. tamper with service binaries* (e.g. by static patching attacks), or *2.2.3. tamper with the runtime*, i.e. dynamic attacks. For dynamic attacks, attackers from within can *2.2.3.1. abuse kubectl*, granting them admin access. Other means of runtime attacks are *2.2.3.2. in-memory patching* and *2.2.3.3. tampering with the execution*. Perpetrators can tamper with a service's process memory once it is loaded into memory, without modifying the underlying binary file, or disrupt its execution, for instance, bypass authentication mechanisms by flipping bits in CPU registers. Furthermore, malware can also be seen as another threat to the integrity of services. They may get loaded into the system by insiders or remote attackers (after a compromise).

Violate Non-repudiation. The setup of *SystemX* allows insiders to violate non-repudiation by two means - *3.1. deploy counterfeit services* and *3.2. forge requests*.

In order to deploy forged services, insiders need to first *3.1.1. obtain certificates*, which follows the same steps as extracting secrets. Then they can *3.1.2. abuse kubectl's admin privilege* to deploy any forged microservices to clusters.

Despite the signature-based authentication, perpetrators can forge requests and thus violate non-repudiation. The signing measure can be readily bypassed by *3.2.1. obtaining inter-service authentication key* and then using it to sign *3.2.2. arbitrary malicious requests*.

5   Requirements

Based on the security evaluation, we define six integrity requirements for an integrity-preserving system. Although these requirements are addressing SystemX's security problems, we believe they are a representative set of reoccurring problems in microservice-based systems as long as the organizational processes are similar to those that we discussed earlier (in Sect. 3.2).

5.1 Enable Authentication/Tracing of Sensitive Data Changes by End Users

As shown in Sect. 4.1, despite the utilization of end-to-end encryption, users' sensitive data is at risk of tampering attacks. Such tampering occurs in a covert manner, and thus users may never (or very late) become aware of them. A secure system must enable its users to track and authenticate any changes to their sensitive data.

5.2 Protect Confidentiality of System Secrets in All Processes

One of the root causes of the identified threats (Sects. 4.1 to 4.2) is insider-irresistible access control mechanisms and thus exposure of system secrets in various stages, even when a secure key management service (e.g., Vault) is employed.

Therefore, adequate secret management is crucial for microservices. All the production secrets shall be generated securely with no disclosure to insiders. However, the secret manager should enable developers to obtain secrets in the development environment for debugging purposes.

5.3 Collect Unforgeable Evidence of Insiders' Activities

Direct access to the production machines through kubectl enables rogue insiders to harm system assets without being held accountable, given that they can forge activity logs. Consequently, they can tamper with binaries at rest and runtime (Sect. 4.2), tamper with the infrastructure, or even submit counterfeit services to production (Sect. 4.2). Therefore, it is crucial to log all the insiders' actions in tamper-resistant storage securely.

5.4 Detect Tampering with Static Artifacts Such as Config, Script Files and Binaries

There exists no strong link between artifact origin (where system settings are defined as configurations) and destination (where they are being used). Consequently, attackers can modify sensitive settings (Sect. 4.1) without being noticed. Thus, it is necessary to authenticate configuration changes.

5.5 Raise the Bar Against Program Tampering Attack (Intra-Service Integrity Protection)

In the course of our security analysis, we identified several threats that target services' integrity both as binary and at runtime. Due to the high severity and likelihood of such attacks, it is of major importance to mitigate them, or at very least raise the bar against them.

5.6 Enable Services to Attest to the Integrity of Their Recipients and Senders (Inter-service Integrity Protection)

As seen above, the signature-based non-repudiation enforcement is ineffective. The risk primarily materializes when services need to serve other services' requests, without being able to verify whether requests are indeed originated from genuine services. The defeated access control on secrets is, in fact, a by-product of lacking integrity attestation.

6 A Framework for Integrity Protection

The extended access of insiders to system assets in the organizational processes, which microservice-based systems rely on, imposes numerous threats (see Sect. 4) to the system integrity. The combination of the extended access and the distributed nature of the systems introduce challenges in guaranteeing non-repudiation (see Sect. 4.2). Previously, we derived a set of requirements from those threats. In this section, we propose a framework depicted in Fig. 3 which satisfies our security requirements. As some of the identified threats are recurring problems (not exclusively specific to microservices), we suggest using existing solutions in the literature (see Sect. 7) that tackle similar problems as building blocks of our framework.

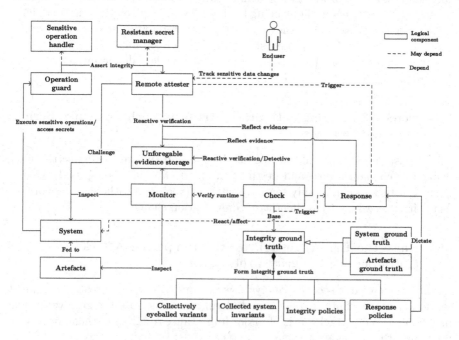

Fig. 3. Framework for microservice integrity protection

The proposed framework aims at holistic protection of a *system* (including governance tools) and its *artifacts*. It is comprised of *integrity ground truth, monitor, check, unforgeable evidence storage, response, remote attester*, and *operation guard* components. Some of these components could be implemented within one component in practice, however, for the sake of understandability, we keep them logically separated. In the following, we discuss these components, their interrelations and their contribution to the fulfillment of our security requirements.

6.1   Integrity Ground Truth

To evaluate integrity, the properties that distinguish a genuine system from a forged one shall be identified, which we refer to as the *integrity ground truth* component. It collects and maintains integrity properties of a system throughout its lifecycle, from development to execution. Depending on the nature of an artifact different properties may need to be extracted. Thus, this component is composed of four subcomponents, viz. *collective variant collector, invariant collector, integrity policies* and *response policies*.

Artifacts with frequent changes (e.g., configuration files and scripts) can be fed into the ground truth by utilizing a secure voting scheme, provided by the *collective variants collector* component. In this model, trusted people in the organization collectively accept or reject changes made to sensitive files. Invariant properties of services in development, e.g., their hashes, are automatically calculated and collected by the *invariant collector*.

A set of rules indicating which properties of the system at which point in time need to be evaluated are also fed into the integrity ground truth component via the *integrity policies* component. Similarly, a set of rule-based policies defining what shall be done after an inconsistency is detected in the system are fed into the *response policies* component. Based on the collected data, the *system ground truth* and *artifacts ground truth* are established.

It is crucial that the ground truth itself is protected from potential tampering attacks, possibly using tamper-resistant hardware. This component provides a baseline for the satisfaction of our integrity requirements.

6.2   Monitor, Check, Response and Unforgeable Evidence

The *monitor* component is tightly coupled with the system to inspect the integrity state of the artifacts as well as services. In practice, depending on which properties of the system are to be inspected, the monitor component is hooked on various representations of the assets in the system, throughout their entire lifecycle.

The *check* component later verifies the collected samples by the monitor. It bases its verification on the previously gathered system or artifacts ground truth. At verification time the check component treats any inconsistencies (mismatches) between the expected (available in the ground truth) and the inspected values (provided by the monitor) by triggering the *response* component, which effectively addresses requirements Sects. 5.4 and 5.5. What actions the response mechanism will take is dictated by the response policies (also in the ground truth). Consequently, the response reacts to a compromise according to the specified policies, e.g., a compromised service can be treated with an access blockage to the data layer.

All the three components (monitor, check, and response) unanimously reflect their actions into the *unforgeable evidence storage*. This is done to enable users to detect potential attacks on the integrity protection components themselves. This way, all the decisions made by the critical components are securely stored, so, for instance, a postmortem analysis could reveal from which point onward which integrity services were compromised.

Moreover, the unforgeable evidence storage enables the check component to function without direct interaction with the monitor component. In this model, the check component reads measurements (read by the monitor) from the storage and acts accordingly. The evidence storage plays a vital role in the fulfillment of requirement Sect. 5.3.

6.3   Remote Attester and Operation Guard

The *operation guard* mediates accesses to both the *sensitive operation handler* and the *resistant secret manager* components. To benefit from the guard, users need to move their system's sensitive operations (refactoring) into the sensitive operation handler. Consequently, such operations can only be reached through the operation guard.

In addition, all system secrets in production need to be handled entirely by the *resistant secret manager*. This component will attest to the integrity of services, in addition to their credentials, upon secret access requests. This, together with service integrity protection, prevents data exposure to insiders, which partially addresses requirement Sect. 5.2.

The secret manager comes in two variations: *development mode* and *production mode*. The former enables developers to obtain secrets for debugging purposes, while the latter only discloses secrets to authorized services. However, to avoid catastrophic events, e.g., a complete data loss due to hardware failures, we can securely back up production secrets, for instance, using secret sharing mechanisms [3].

To verify the authenticity of services requesting to either execute sensitive operations or access secrets, the operation guard consults the *remote attester*. The attester bases its judgment on the stored measurements in the unforgeable evidence storage. This component plays a crucial role in addressing requirements Sects. 5.2 and 5.6.

End users can also track their sensitive data changes via the remote attester (as per requirement Sect. 5.1). This will effectively detect attacks such as the malicious public key rotation presented in Sect. 5.6.

7   Related Work

7.1   Malicious Insider

The risk of insiders were analyzed in several papers. Callegati et al. [8] studied insider threats to federated mobility as a service provider. By means of a survey, Salem et al. [22] classified insiders into two groups of traitors and masquerades, and subsequently reviewed user behavior profiling and network sensors techniques for mitigation of risks of such. Kandias et al. [17] further mapped the problem of insiders to cloud-as-an-infrastructure model and thereby classified inside attackers to two subcategories, viz. malicious cloud provider and users in the organization who misuse their access to the cloud dashboard. The core assumption of the reviewed papers is the fact that insiders need access to system's sensitive assets to fulfill their duties. Therefore, their focus is on formulating the inside attacker problem as a behavioral intrusion detection problem at runtime. In contrast to these works, we identify a set of generic integrity assets in microservice-based systems throughout the entire development lifecycle (not only the runtime), which our insiders of interest need not access (e.g., system secrets). More importantly, we pin point a set of sensitive artifacts (e.g. service binaries and system configurations) whose authenticity shall be guaranteed throughout the development lifecycle, viz. build, deployment and execution. Finally, we propose a catalog of protection measures to secure those assets.

7.2   Technical Framework for Integrity Protection

To the best of our knowledge, in the literature there exists no solution that completely addresses our security requirements (see [2] for a survey of integrity protection techniques). In the following, we state some of the most relevant approaches to integrity protection that can serve as building blocks for implementing our integrity protection framework.

1. *Tracing sensitive data changes:*
   Neisse et al. in [21] proposed a hardware-aided scheme that captures sensitive configuration changes made by insiders and subsequently report them to a third-party verifier, which in turn enables a continuous authentication of changes.
2. *Protect system secrets from compromised services:*
   Dewan et al. [11] proposed a technique for authenticating programs' integrity on the sensitive data access according to an integrity manifest. That is, only processes whose invariants at runtime conforms with the requirements are granted access, and thus sensitive data are never exposed to compromised services.
3. *Collect unforgeable evidence:*
   To maintain unforgeable evidence/logs in adversarial environments, Schneier and Kelsey [24] proposed efficient schemes that preserve logs' integrity using hash chains. Zawoad et al. in [27] extended this by providing log confidentiality along with interfaces for cloud-based forensics.

4. *Protect (static) artifacts integrity:*

   Garfinkel et al. [13] and Santos et al. [23] proposed techniques based on the construction of a chain of trust. In their schemes, lower level programs hash and subsequently sign upper ones constituting a bottom-up verification mechanism. The starting point is a secure boot process that is aided by trusted hardware. Docker notary (docker.com/notary) is another tool that enables container integrity verification.

5. *Protect (dynamic) software integrity:*

   Software-based. Collberg et al. [9] defined tamper-proofing (integrity protection) as a technique, comprised of *check* and *respond* functions, that ensures a software system behaves as it should even in hostile environments. Banescu et al. [5] proposed a technique that authenticates control flows leading to sensitive operations. Sutter et al. [26] developed a protection toolchain to compose a wide range of protection techniques.

   Hardware-based. Intel SGX [10] is a trusted computing module that is capable of guaranteeing a tamper-free execution of desired (sensitive) regions in programs, which are referred to as *trusted regions*. SGX protects the trusted parts via CPU-level encryption and a signature-based mandatory access control so-called enclaves. Baumann et al. [6], Arnautov et al. [4] and Lind et al. [19] utilized SGX to protect integrity of services at different level of granularity of trusted regions. The very same tool was employed by Liang et al. [18] to protect cloud users' credentials from insiders. By the same token, Brenner et al. [7] proposed a secure Java-based middleware (powered by SGX) for protecting microservices' (sensitive) runtime data.

6. *Integrity attestation:*

   Some trusted hardware (e.g. SGX) natively support remote attestations [10]. For a software-based attestation, *timing-based* [14] and *challenge-based* [20,25] techniques were proposed in the literature. Furthermore, Jin and Lotspiech [15] developed a scheme in which a remote server detects integrity violations by analyzing collected (unforgeable) logs.

8   Conclusions

Adopting microservices entails new practices that are more susceptible to insider manipulations. In this work, we presented emerging integrity challenges and carried out a thorough security evaluation on a case study (based on real-world systems) to identify representative integrity threats. These threats capture the associated risk in such infrastructures, where practitioners may consciously accept, decline or seek measures to mitigate. In pursuit of protections, we then proposed a set of security requirements upon which we built a security framework for insider-resistant integrity protections. Our framework serves as a blueprint for integrity protection in microservice-based systems.

As for future work, we are planning to develop a prototype of our framework and carry out further evaluations, also concerning the expected trade-off between performance and security.

References

1. Ahmadvand, M., Ibrahim, A.: Requirements reconciliation for scalable and secure microservice (de)composition. In: 2016 IEEE 3rd Workshop on Evolving Security and Privacy Requirements Engineering (ESPRE). IEEE (2016)
2. Ahmadvand, M., Pretschner, A., Kelbert, F.: A taxonomy of software integrity protection techniques. In: Advances in Computers. Elsevier (2018)
3. Ahmadvand, M., Scemama, A., Ochoa, M., Pretschner, A.: Enhancing operation security using secret sharing. In: Proceedings of the 13th International Joint Conference on e-Business and Telecommunications - Volume 4: SECRYPT, (ICETE 2016), pp. 446–451. INSTICC/SciTePress (2016)
4. Arnautov, S., et al.: SCONE: secure linux containers with intel SGX. In: 12th USENIX Symposium on Operating Systems Design and Implementation (OSDI), vol. 16, pp. 689–703. USENIX Association, Savannah, GA (2016)
5. Banescu, S., Pretschner, A., Battré, D., Cazzulani, S., Shield, R., Thompson, G.: Software-based protection against changeware. In Proceedings of the 5th ACM Conference on Data and Application Security and Privacy, pp. 231–242. ACM (2015)
6. Baumann, A., Peinado, M., Hunt, G.: Shielding applications from an untrusted cloud with Haven. ACM Trans. Comput. Syst. (TOCS) **33**(3), 8 (2015)
7. Brenner, S., Hundt, T., Mazzeo, G., Kapitza, R.: Secure cloud micro services using Intel SGX. In: Chen, L.Y., Reiser, H.P. (eds.) DAIS 2017. LNCS, vol. 10320, pp. 177–191. Springer, Cham (2017). https://doi.org/10.1007/978-3-319-59665-5_13
8. Callegati, F., Giallorenzo, S., Melis, A., Prandini, M.: Cloud-of-things meets mobility-as-a-service: an insider threat perspective. Comput. Secur. **74**, 277–295 (2018)
9. Collberg, C.S., Thomborson, C.: Watermarking, tamper-proofing, and obfuscation-tools for software protection. IEEE Trans. Softw. Eng. **28**(8), 735–746 (2002)
10. Costan, V., Devadas, S.: Intel SGX explained. IACR Cryptology ePrint Archive 2016:86 (2016)
11. Dewan, P., Durham, D., Khosravi, H., Long, M., Nagabhushan, G.: A hypervisor-based system for protecting software runtime memory and persistent storage, pp. 828–835. Society for Computer Simulation International (2008)
12. Dragoni, N., et al.: Microservices: yesterday, today, and tomorrow. Present and Ulterior Software Engineering, pp. 195–216. Springer, Cham (2017). https://doi.org/10.1007/978-3-319-67425-4_12
13. Garfinkel, T., Pfaff, B., Chow, J., Rosenblum, M., Boneh, D.: Terra: a virtual machine-based platform for trusted computing. In: ACM SIGOPS Operating Systems Review, vol. 37, pp. 193–206. ACM (2003)
14. Jakobsson, M., Johansson, K.-A.: Practical and secure software-based attestation. In: 2011 Workshop on Lightweight Security & Privacy: Devices, Protocols and Applications (LightSec), pp. 1–9. IEEE (2011)
15. Jin, H., Lotspiech, J.: Forensic analysis for tamper resistant software. In: 14th International Symposium on Software Reliability Engineering, ISSRE 2003, pages 133–142. IEEE (2003)
16. Kalske, M., Mäkitalo, N., Mikkonen, T.: Challenges when moving from monolith to microservice architecture. In: Garrigós, I., Wimmer, M. (eds.) ICWE 2017. LNCS, vol. 10544, pp. 32–47. Springer, Cham (2018). https://doi.org/10.1007/978-3-319-74433-9_3

17. Kandias, M., Virvilis, N., Gritzalis, D.: The insider threat in cloud computing. In: Bologna, S., Hämmerli, B., Gritzalis, D., Wolthusen, S. (eds.) CRITIS 2011. LNCS, vol. 6983, pp. 93–103. Springer, Heidelberg (2013). https://doi.org/10.1007/978-3-642-41476-3_8

18. Liang, X., Shetty, S., Zhang, L., Kamhoua, C., Kwiat, K.: Man in the cloud (MITC) defender: SGX-based user credential protection for synchronization applications in cloud computing platform. In: 2017 IEEE 10th International Conference on Cloud Computing (CLOUD), pp. 302–309, June 2017

19. Lind, J., et al.: Glamdring: automatic application partitioning for Intel SGX. In: 2017 USENIX Annual Technical Conference (USENIX ATC 17), Santa Clara, CA, pp. 285–298. USENIX Association (2017)

20. Martignoni, L., Paleari, R., Bruschi, D.: Conqueror: tamper-proof code execution on legacy systems. In: Kreibich, C., Jahnke, M. (eds.) DIMVA 2010. LNCS, vol. 6201, pp. 21–40. Springer, Heidelberg (2010). https://doi.org/10.1007/978-3-642-14215-4_2

21. Neisse, R., Holling, D., Alexander, P.: Implementing trust in cloud infrastructures. In: Proceedings of the 2011 11th IEEE/ACM International Symposium on Cluster, Cloud and Grid Computing, pp. 524–533. IEEE Computer Society (2011)

22. Salem, M.B., Hershkop, S., Stolfo, S.J.: A survey of insider attack detection research. In: Stolfo, S.J., Bellovin, S.M., Keromytis, A.D., Hershkop, S., Smith, S.W., Sinclair, S. (eds.) Insider Attack and Cyber Security, vol. 39, pp. 69–90. Springer, US, Boston (2008). https://doi.org/10.1007/978-0-387-77322-3_5

23. Santos, N., Gummadi, K.P., Rodrigues, R.: Towards trusted cloud computing. In: Proceedings of the 2009 Conference on Hot Topics in Cloud Computing, Hot-Cloud 2009, Berkeley, CA, USA. USENIX Association (2009)

24. Schneier, B., Kelsey, J.: Secure audit logs to support computer forensics. ACM Trans. Inf. Syst. Secur. **2**(2), 159–176 (1999)

25. Seshadri, A., Luk, M., Shi, E., Perrig, A., van Doorn, L., Khosla, P.: Pioneer: verifying code integrity and enforcing untampered code execution on legacy systems. ACM SIGOPS Oper. Syst. Rev. **39**, 1–16 (2005)

26. De Sutter, B., et al.: A reference architecture for software protection, pp. 291–294, April 2016

27. Zawood, S., Dutta, A.K., Hasan, R.: SecLaaS: secure logging-as-a-service for cloud forensics. In: Proceedings of the 8th ACM SIGSAC Symposium on Information, Computer and Communications Security, ASIA CCS 2013, pp. 219–230. ACM, New York (2013)

The Aspect of Resilience in Microservices-Based Software Design

Vaidas Giedrimas[1]([⊠]), Samir Omanovic[2], and Dino Alic[2]

[1] Siauliai University, Šiauliai, Lithuania
vaigie@mi.su.lt
[2] University of Sarajevo, Sarajevo, Bosnia and Herzegovina
somanovic@etf.unsa.ba

Abstract. This paper discusses two approaches in microservices-based software design, from the perspective of failure possibility. The first approach accepts the fact that complex distributed software systems with many communicating components, such as microservices-based software, could fail (it is not important when), and is focused on the resilient software design. Resilient software design provides strategies and mechanisms for dealing with failures. While robust system just continues functioning in the presence of a failure, resilient system is prepared to adapt yourself while continuing functioning. Second approach is to try to build ideal software that will never fail. Lot of theory behind behavioral type systems is devoted to this – choreographic programming for example. Choreographic programming relies on choreographies as global descriptions of system implementations – behavior of all entities (e.g. microservices) in a system - are given in a single program. The first approach is in more tight relation with real software systems, while the second one has more theoretic background. In this paper authors discuss on the pros and cons of aforementioned methods and presents the ideas for its fusion (e.g. to use patterns for microservices).

Keywords: Microservices · Failure · Software resilience

1 Introduction

The concept of microservices is not extremely new, but nowadays the number of its applications is increasing rapidly. Thus, it is very important to have in mind as many as possible different aspects of microservices-based software systems design. Microservices as components are small and systems are composed of many components. That increases complexity and probability of failure. Software systems are influencing humanity more and more each day (from software in small embedded devices to social networks, intelligent agents, etc.), and software is a most frequently changed part of any system. That is the reason why a term software-intensive system is used to emphasize that software development and/or integration are dominant considerations. That means in general that we need reliable software. But in the context of microservices, having in mind complexity of such systems, this is yet more important.

© Springer Nature Switzerland AG 2018
M. Mazzara et al. (Eds.): STAF 2018 Workshops, LNCS 11176, pp. 589–595, 2018.
https://doi.org/10.1007/978-3-030-04771-9_44

Different approaches to microservices-based software design emerged as a response to aforementioned context. It is possible to classify them in different ways. One of most important perspectives is a failure possibility. From that point of view it is possible to talk about two approaches. The first approach accepts the fact that complex, distributed, communication-intensive software systems based on many components, such as microservices-based software is, could fail (it is not important when), and it is focused on the resilient software design. The second approach is to try to build ideal software that will never fail, which is harder to achieve.

The aim of this paper is to expose two major approaches for software quality assurance and to begin a discussion about the balance of aspects of the resilience and correctness by construction in microservice-based systems.

Next sections of the paper present these two approaches with their characteristics so that it is possible to capture main benefits from both approaches and synergistically apply them on microservices-based software design.

2   Resilient Design

Resilient software design provides strategies and mechanisms for dealing with failures on an adaptive way. Robustness [3], resilience [3, 4] and antifragility [5] are used in this context and it is necessary to explain the difference between them. Robust systems are resisting to failures and they continue functioning in the presence of a failure. So, robust systems are not affected by volatility. Resilient systems are prepared to adapt yourself while continuing functioning, i.e. they can recover from the failure. They have prepared mechanisms for reacting on volatilities and they can to recover from failures. Very precise definition of resilience is given in [4], where is stated that it encompasses avoidance of hostile acts or adverse conditions, robustness, reconstitution, and recovery, and that it is the ability to support the functions necessary for mission success in spite of hostile action or adverse conditions. Antifragility is beyond the resilience [5]. Antifragile design accepts volatility and system evolves to be able to respond in any situation, known or unknown in design-time.

At this moment, in the context of microservices-based software design from the failure possibility point of view, resilient design is more interesting than antifragile design, because it is trying to identify all possible failures and their characteristics so that adequate reactions can be prepared. If focus is on adapting to unknown failures, then system can evolve to something that we do not want. In other words, we need to try to stay, as much as possible, in known space, and only after that space is deeply investigated, from the resilience point of view, it is possible to go further and apply antifragility.

2.1   Aspects of Resilience

Microservices are small, highly independent components. From the resilience point of view this is good because it is aligned with one of the main principles of resilience – isolation, loose coupling, etc. However, this should be carefully observed when system includes a lot of microservices. Increased complexity and probability of failure must be taken in consideration also. So, let's list important aspects of resilience [1, 2, 4, 6–8] and observe the key point of that aspect in the context of microservices.

Isolation. This means that the system should be divided into smaller entities that are self-contained and not able to influence each other by propagating failures. To be able to prevent failure propagation it is important to identify failure units and use bulkheads to separate these units. For that, it is also important to have validation of all parameters to prevent malicious calls or bad responses. Good practice is to avoid general purpose data types and complicated validations. Properly designed microservices are well separated with validation of all parameters and failure is not propagated, which is one of the main advantages of microservices-based design. The separation also enables better scalability and redundancy – more than one service can perform some operation. By applying these principles we actually put some constraints on systems' behavior. It is very important to note this for connecting with a priori correct design approach that is elaborated later.

Loose Coupling. If isolation is achieved then one segment of loose coupling is also achieved. Second important thing is to avoid unnecessary waiting for responses. That can be done by using asynchronous communication so that sender sends request and does not wait for the response from the receiver. This also helps in preventing failure propagation. In this context is good to implement idempotency [23], i.e. that sender can send same request (identified by unique ID) multiple times and that receiver responds to the same request only once. This increases network traffic but makes nods more loosely coupled. To decrease dependency between sender and receiver, the sender does not need to know the exact location of the receiver (transparency). For this is possible to use dispatchers/mappers. This also isolates user from knowing that failure happened – when some service fails, another service can respond, if redundancy is applied. Event-driven design is aligned with loose coupling, but it is good practice to use some broker between sender and receiver to achieve transparency. Another good practice that supports loose coupling is to have stateless units to avoid recovery of the state if failure happens. Also, if possible, apply less strict rules related to consistency and use eventual consistency. In many situations is possible to relay on data that is not so "fresh" (cached responses or similar) which again supports loose coupling. All previously stated principles that support loose coupling can easily be applied on microservices-based software systems design. Again, all this adds some new rules and constraints related to systems' behavior.

Latency Control. It is very important to detect any latency and to prevent its propagation to other components involved. One mechanism that supports latency control is usage of timeouts for responds. Each respond should be given in the predefined timeout to avoid latency. In the case of breaking timeout, it is possible to apply alternative actions like: repeating request, sending request to replacement service, send alarms, etc. Beside timeouts, it is possible to use circuit breakers to switch off units that are failing repeatedly certain number of times. For latency control is important every aspect of time including time of failure. If failure happens it is important to fail fast is possible and recover fast is possible. Response time is important, but it is related to load. If system design allows, it is possible to apply quickest response. That means that one request is passed to several instances of a service and response from quickest one is returned while response from other instances were ignored. This spends resources and should be used only when necessary. Often it happens that service is cluttered with requests (normal or malicious). This should be prevented by limiting size of request queues and rejecting requests when queue is full. By doing this, senders that receive rejections can perform some alternative actions, and waiting in a queue doesn't influence total response time much. Not only size of request queues should be limited, but any resource overloading should be prevented by adding guards. All this can be applied on microservices-based software systems design and again, all this adds some new rules and constraints related to systems' behavior.

Supervision. Supervision aspect of microservices-based software systems should enable management of the failures on a higher level of abstraction – outside the failure unit. This mechanism ensures detection of failures of complete units in the system and alarming of problems. In that sense, each unit of the failure can be monitored by some monitor that will detect failure of that unit only. On the higher level of the abstraction (outside of the failure unit) is also possible to analyze causes of failure using information which is not available for failure handling within failure unit. So, the failure analysis can be on several levels of the abstraction and if one of levels is not capable to solve issue then problem is escalated to higher level.

3 A-Priori Correct Design

Another approach for ensuring software quality is the software development based on formal methods. Usually the specification of the software is made using some formalism (e.g. intuitionistic propositional logic [12], higher order logic [11, 16], process algebra, session types [10] or even some visual notation [12], etc.). Then the calculations are made using the same formalism, and the result (the derived formula, the prove of some theorem) is made. Because the elements of the formalism have one-to-one relation with software artefacts, the result shows how they should be connected or in what protocol they should communicate to achieve result software artefact (e.g. compound component or service). Because the derivation of result is proved formally, the result software is treated as a-priori correct and does not require (or do require much less) testing. For this reason, we refer this approach as a-priori correct design (or correctness by construction) approach.

During the decades different names of it has been used, such as *proofs-as-programs* structural synthesis etc. [12–14]. The black-box software artefacts which are used, also varies from functions to software services [12, 14, 16, 17]. However, as Wadler drew attention in [15], all similar approaches converge, because all they are based on universal theory. So, the Curry-Howard isomorphism is almost not depended on particular software developing paradigm. The achievements in this field could be adapted to new programing (or in more general case - software developing) paradigms, including microservice-based development. One of the "manuals" of such adoption is given by Poernomo et al. [13]. As the microservices could be considered as "black-boxes", the prerequisites of Curry-Howard protocol implementation are met. However, because the paradigm of microservices-based development differs from e.g. component-based development (e.g. by the scale), we need new forms of programming, e.g. choreographic programming.

3.1 Choreographic Programming

Choreographic programming relies on choreographies as global descriptions of system implementations – behavior of all entities (e.g. microservices) in a system - are given in a single program. In contrast to classical service-oriented architecture (SOA), compliant implementations are generated by compiler automatically [18]. This yields correctness-by-construction methodology, what helps to avoid deadlocks, communication errors etc.

One of disadvantages of this emerging paradigms could be small number of supported languages. However, the set of Jolie [19, 20], Chor [21] and AIOCJ [13] looks very promising. Existing applications of choreographic programming using microservices (e.g. [19, 20]) could be named as examples of good practice of adoption.

4 Use of Design Patterns and/or Choreographies?

A basic definition of software design patterns states that they are general, reusable solution for a common problem within a given context. In the microservices-based software design, the main focus is on the communication behavior between microservices as nodes and this paper is especially focused on failure possibility perspective. The main goal of any pattern is to specify preferred behavior which is further propagated in the real implementation. Similarly, choreography has a goal to specify preferred communication behavior as a global description that is further applied in choreography projections (real implementation). So, the choreography can be observed as one large specific pattern for communication behavior of the involved nodes. The main advantage of choreography is that produced software is guaranteed to be correct by construction, which means that failure should not happen. That is possible because choreography specifies the whole communication scenario (big picture of the system) while simple patterns target only one aspect (one part of the puzzle). On the other hand, creating choreographies for complex systems is not easy while using simple patterns is much easier.

The best practice should be somewhere in between, in the form of choreography patterns which are composed of hierarchy of smaller patterns. That way is possible to have several layers of abstractions (layered choreography) and achieve correctness by construction on each level of abstraction while lowest level contains simple patterns that are easy for implementation. Besides that, there is no need to be so strict about correctness by construction if resilience aspects are included. So, usage of design patterns that increase software resilience, decreases possibility of irresolvable failure and decreases need to formally prove correctness by construction. On the other hand, designing the software from high level of abstraction (through levels of choreographies) with resilience mechanisms included warranties (not necessary formally) that everything is covered.

There are design patterns dedicated for microservices-based software design like [9]: ambassador, anti-corruption layer, backends for frontends, bulkhead, gateway aggregation, gateway offloading, gateway routing, etc. These patterns and their application in a microservices-based software design support resilient design. For example, bulkhead isolates critical resources (CPU, memory, etc.) so that a single microservice can't consume all of the resources and starve the others. It also prevents cascading failures caused by some microservice. It is important to understand that the application of one pattern does not solve all the problems, but only one (or one group). Creating sets of complementary patterns organized in choreography layers so that they act as one whole should be a path to create truly resilient microservices-based software.

5   Conclusions and Future Work

Previous sections depict two approaches in microservices-based software design, from the perspective of failure possibility. Their main advantages and disadvantages where described. It is obvious that somehow these two approaches should meet. Thus, it is necessary to make some kind of compromise approach that this paper proposes. That compromise approach could be described in the following way:

- Choreography for the whole system should be defined in a layered manner starting with the highest level of abstraction. This ensures that all resilience aspects were covered and that they will act synergistically.
- Resilience aspects and patterns that support them should be included in the choreography levels so that choreography projections have resilience mechanisms. Use of listed resilience aspects and patterns that support them insures the quality of covering all resilience aspects.
- In one hand, there is no need to have formal correctness by construction since resilience mechanisms compensate lack of that. However, if the algorithm of resilience will be implemented not correctly, we still have potentially unsafe microservices-based software. Thus, it is reasonable to have hybrid approach with resilient design implemented using the elements of correctness by construction.

Our future work includes (but not limits to) following research actions:

- To propose the model for balance aspects of resilience and correctness by construction for choreographic microservices-based programming;
- To examine proposed model on all possible types of microservices according to well-known taxonomies (e.g. [22]).

References

1. Friedrichsen, U.: Patterns of resilience. https://www.slideshare.net/ufried/patterns-of-resilience. Accessed 23 Apr 2018
2. Friedrichsen, U.: The 7 quests of resilient software design. https://www.slideshare.net/ufried/the-7-quests-of-resilient-software-design. Accessed 23 Apr 2018

3. Monti, G.: Resilience Engineering #1: Robust Vs. Resilient (2011). http://www. activegarage.com/resilience-engineering-1-robust-resilient. Accessed 20 Apr 2018
4. Department of Defense: FACT SHEET: Resilience of Space Capabilities. National Security Space Strategy, Washington (2015)
5. Taleb, N.: Antifragile: Things That Gain from Disorder. Random House, New York City (2012)
6. Hanmer, R.: Patterns for Fault Tolerant Software. Wiley, Hoboken (2013)
7. Merkow, M.S., Raghavan, L.: Secure and Resilient Software Development, 1st edn. Auerbach Publications, Boca Raton (2010)
8. Mackey, A.: Building Resilient Systems. https://gooroo.io/GoorooTHINK/Article/16830/ Building-Resilient-Systems/23368#.Wt2zeBuFPZ4. Accessed 23 Apr 2018
9. Wasson, M.: Design patterns for microservices. https://azure.microsoft.com/en-us/blog/ design-patterns-for-microservices/. Accessed 23 Apr 2018
10. Hüttel, H., et al.: Foundations of session types and behavioural contracts. ACM Comput. Surv. **49**(1), 36 (2016). https://doi.org/10.1145/2873052. Article no. 3
11. Visser, E., Benaissa, Z., Tolmach, A.: Building program optimizers with rewriting strategies. In: Proceedings of the Third ACM SIGPLAN International Conference on Functional Programming (ICFP 1998), pp. 13–26. ACM, New York (1998). http://dx.doi.org/10.1145/ 289423.289425
12. Giedrimas, V., Omanovic, S., Grigorenko, P.: The evolution of automated component-based software development tools: from structural synthesis of programs to behavioral types. In: 2017 International Conference on Information Science and Communications Technologies (ICISCT), Tashkent, pp. 1–6 (2017)
13. Poernomo, J.H., Crossley, J.N., Wirsing, M.: Adapting Proofs-as-Programs: The Curry-Howard Protocol. Springer, Heidelberg (2005). https://doi.org/10.1007/0-387-28183-5
14. Gay, S., Ravara, A. (eds.): Behavioural Types: From Theory to Tools. River Publishers, San Francisco (2017). https://doi.org/10.13052/rp-9788793519817
15. Wadler, P.: Propositions as types. Commun. ACM **58**(12), 75–84 (2015)
16. Cazanescu, V.E.: Programming via rewriting. In: 13th International Symposium on Symbolic and Numeric Algorithms for Scientific Computing (2010)
17. Fiadeiro, J.L., Lopes, A.: A model for dynamic reconfiguration in service-oriented architectures. Softw. Syst. Model. **12**(12), 349–367 (2013)
18. Dragoni, N., et al.: Microservices: yesterday, today, and tomorrow (2017). https://arxiv.org/ abs/1606.04036. Accessed 28 Apr 2018
19. Cruz-Filipe, L., Montesi, F.: Choreographies in Practice. In: Albert, E., Lanese, I. (eds.) FORTE 2016. LNCS, vol. 9688, pp. 114–123. Springer, Cham (2016). https://doi.org/10. 1007/978-3-319-39570-8_8
20. Giaretta, A., Dragoni, N., Mazzara, M.: Joining Jolie to Docker - Orchestration of Microservices on a Containers-as-a-Service Layer. CoRR abs/1709.05635 (2017)
21. Chor - choreography programming language. http://www.chor-lang.org. Accessed 25 Apr 2018
22. Garriga, M.: Towards a taxonomy of microservices architectures. In: Cerone, A., Roveri, M. (eds.) SEFM 2017. LNCS, vol. 10729, pp. 203–218. Springer, Cham (2018). https://doi.org/ 10.1007/978-3-319-74781-1_15
23. Newman, S.: Building Microservices: Designing Fine-Grained Systems, 1st edn, pp. 215–216. O'Reilly Media, Newton (2015)

On Collaborative Model-Driven Development of Microservices

Jonas Sorgalla[1]([✉]) [iD], Florian Rademacher[1] [iD], Sabine Sachweh[1],
and Albert Zündorf[2]

[1] Institute for the Digital Transformation of Application and Living Domains,
University of Applied Sciences and Arts Dortmund,
Otto-Hahn-Straße 23, 44227 Dortmund, Germany
{jonas.sorgalla,florian.rademacher,sabine.sachweh}@fh-dortmund.de
[2] Department of Computer Science and Electrical Engineering Software Engineering
Research Group, University of Kassel, Wilhelmshöher Allee 73,
34121 Kassel, Germany
zuendorf@uni-kassel.de

Abstract. Microservice Architecture (MSA) denotes an emerging architectural style for distributed and service-based systems whereby each microservice is highly cohesive and implements a single business capability. A microservice system consists of multiple, loosely coupled microservices. It provides complex capabilities through services interacting in choreographies. A single dedicated team, typically practicing DevOps, is responsible for each microservice, i.e., it "owns" the service. However, while systems relying on MSA have several architectural advantages especially for cloud applications, their realization is characterized by an increased accidental complexity due to redundant handcrafting of implementation, e.g., to make each service standalone runnable. A promising way to cope with such complexity is the usage of Model-driven Development (MDD) whereby models are used as first-class entities in the software development process. Although there are already first steps taken on how MDD could be applied by a single team to implement its microservices, the question of how MDD can be adapted to MSA's development distribution across multiple teams remains an issue. In this paper we envision the application of Collaborative Model-driven Software Engineering (CMDSE) to MDD of MSA by surveying relevant characteristics of CMDSE and identifying challenges for its application to MSA. The present paper takes a first step towards enabling holistic MDD of MSA across microservice teams.

Keywords: Microservice architecture · Model-driven development
Collaborative model-driven software engineering
Model-driven microservice development

M. Mazzara et al. (Eds.): STAF 2018 Workshops, LNCS 11176, pp. 596–603, 2018.
https://doi.org/10.1007/978-3-030-04771-9_45

1 Introduction and Background

Microservice Architecture (MSA) denotes an emerging architectural style for distributed and service-based systems [9]. As such, MSA relies on the *service* concept as the fundamental architectural building block for a system's architecture. Each microservice is highly cohesive and represents a single business capability. Technically, a microservice is realized as an independent process that can be managed, i.e., designed, developed, deployed, and operated, autonomously. To realize complex business capabilities, multiple of these services can collaborate in service choreographies through interfaces [16]. Hereby, the service interaction is generally stateless and uses protocols like HTTP or AMQP[1] [15]. Furthermore, each microservice is organizationally aligned to exactly one service team which usually practices DevOps [11]. Resulting applications relying on MSA are, among other characteristics, vertical as well as horizontal scalable, flexibly extensible and have short release cycles which makes them especially suitable for cloud applications like Spotify or Netflix [15].

However, the advantages of MSA in terms of increased scalability, resilience and technology heterogeneity [15] come at the cost of an increased accidental complexity regarding the overall system development [16]. One reason for this increased complexity is that microservice architectures, compared to monolithic applications, are distributed by nature [8]. Resulting from this distribution, the realization of multiple services involves extensive and redundant handcrafting of implementation, e.g., to make each service independently runnable, or to provide and consume the necessary interfaces for complex operations [24].

An approach to cope with the *accidental complexity* of complex, distributed software systems such as MSA is Model-driven Development (MDD) [8]. MDD denotes the usage of models as first-class entities in the software development process. Applied to MSA, developers would use a modeling language to design services and use a Model-to-Code (M2C) transformation to (semi-)automatically derive service code [18]. In such a model-centric development scenario, modeling does not completely replace programming. Instead, the usage of models aims to ease accidental complexity by helping to avoid redundant programming, but does not replace the manual realization of *essential complexity*, e.g., programming service-specific, business-related behavior [20].

Although there are first approaches, e.g., [7] or [21], which address such an MDD for MSA (MSA-MDD), they currently only enable the generation of a microservice landscape from a centralized architectural perspective. Hence, we argue that a holistic approach to MSA-MDD needs to take MSAs organizational characteristics into account. That is, like the code-centric development process, a model-centric development process of MSA would need to consider Conway's Law in the context of MSA [15] and support a collaborative development spread across multiple teams [22].

In this paper, we present our vision of a collaborative modeling approach for MSA. For this purpose, we rely on methods and techniques from the research

---

[1] https://www.amqp.org.

area of Collaborative Model-driven Software Engineering (CMDSE) [6]. It defines approaches where multiple stakeholders use a set of shared models to collaborate.

The remainder of this paper is organized as follows. In Sect. 2 we elaborate on the collaborative aspects of microservice development and deduce challenges for a corresponding holistic MSA-MDD approach. Building on this, in Sect. 3 we describe our vision of a collaborative MSA-MDD approach by applying concepts from the area of CMDSE. Finally, Sect. 4 concludes the paper and Sect. 5 describes future work.

2   Challenges for Collaborative Model-Driven Microservice Development

In this section we identify and discuss major challenges for collaborative modeling in the context of MSA to enable holistic MSA-MDD. CMDSE is itself part of the broader research area of Collaborative Software Engineering (CoSE) [13], which investigates means for enhancing collaboration, communication and coordination (3C) among software engineers and project stakeholders. In the context of CoSE, the organizational structure of microservices can be separated into two hierarchical scopes of collaboration. In the *team-internal scope*, team members collaborate to manage one or more services. In the *team-external scope*, teams themselves collaborate with each other, e.g., by using an interface of another team's service for their service's realization. Furthermore, the act of assembling the overall system through autonomous services in its own right represents a form of team-external collaboration.

A holistic MSA-MDD may then be enabled by applying CMDSE to both team scopes. Based on 3C, full-fledged CMDSE approaches comprise the three main complementary dimensions *model management*, *collaboration means*, and *communication means* [10]. Each of the following subsections identifies and discusses challenges for collaborative MSA-MDD by analyzing the team-internal scope (cf. Subsect. 2.1) and the team-external scope (cf. Subsect. 2.2) with respect to these three dimensions of CMDSE.

2.1   Team-Internal Model-Driven Microservice Development

A team, which is responsible for one or more microservices, follows a *share-nothing* philosophy to foster agility and autonomy [9]. Therefore, each team is independent from other teams and services in their choices related to services' implementation regarding, e.g., programming languages, databases or employed tools. For example, this autonomy enables a single team to adopt an MDD approach for their services even if other teams do not use MDD [18].

However, in practice the team's technology stack and development process model is often influenced by an organization's culture [14], e.g., if the usage of GitLab[2] for managing the software lifecycle has proven successful in existing teams, a new team is highly likely to adopt GitLab, too. In certain cases,

---

[2] https://www.gitlab.com.

choices can be predetermined by the overall organization in order to maintain compatibility, e.g., with an existing deployment pipeline [1].

At this level, the possible application of MSA-MDD only differentiates itself from a traditional model-driven development process through the different roles within the team [2]. To utilize collaboration across team members, existing solutions, e.g., emfCollab[3] or the Eclipse Dawn Project[4] can be applied. Such solutions already realize means for the CMDSE dimensions model management and collaboration [10]. Depending on the tool, separate communication means like an instant messenger could be added to the collaboration tool stack. However, while these tools provide good means for collaboration, they still need an underlying modeling language for the microservice domain [17]. This motivates the first challenge for a collaborative MSA-MDD approach:

(C1) Support for Role-specific Team Tasks. For a model-centric development, this modeling language needs to support the different tasks and roles inside a DevOps-based MSA development team, i.e., the complete management process of a microservice.

2.2 Team-External Model-Driven Microservice Development

While the team-internal collaborative modeling scope can be covered leveraging existing CMDSE approaches (cf. Subsect. 2.1), especially for the application of collaborative MSA-MDD with regards to the team-external scope MSA-specific challenges arise which we discuss in the following.

With the distribution and loose coupling of functionality and service teams, MSA might not exhibit a central architecture viewpoint or entity, e.g., a team of dedicated software architects, for the overall microservice landscape. However, we expect that such a viewpoint or entity can be of great benefit in the context of MSA. First, it may be aware of the overall team structure and foster communication [17]. Second, it may document and comprehend the overall static structure and service interactions of a microservice architecture. Models are predestined to represent such structures and interaction relations [4]. Therefore, the second challenge for a collaborative MSA-MDD approach arise:

(C2) System Model Assembly Across Autonomous Microservices. How can such a holistic and model-based overview of an MSA be assembled from the involved services and interactions in a loosely coupled way, i.e., without contradicting MSA's paradigm of autonomous services.

Another aspect regarding the team-external scope results from Conway's Law. Due to the loose coupling of microservices, the responsible teams also collaborate more loosely preserving their autonomy [14]. Although there are mechanics to provide knowledge exchange across teams, e.g., Spotify joins persons with a similar skill set from different teams to horizontal organization

---

[3] http://qgears.com/products/emfcollab.
[4] https://wiki.eclipse.org/Dawn.

structures called *guilds* [12], knowledge exchanges generally happen on a non-technical and informal level [23]. However, next to provided interfaces of other teams' services, teams may also access the source code of microservices, e.g., through company-wide available code repositories or verbal requests [14]. This agile opportunities also need consideration in a collaborative MSA-MDD approach:

(C3) Collaboration Means for Teams. Like source-code, the models of a team need to be accessible and usable for other teams, e.g., to copy domain concepts [17] or retrieve interface descriptions, without contradicting the loose coupling characteristic of services and teams.

3   A Collaborative Modeling Approach for Model-Driven Microservice Development

Starting from the identified challenges and their discussion in Sect. 2, we derived a conceptual model for the prospective application of CMDSE to MSA. It is depicted in Fig. 1 as a UML class diagram enriched by indirect use relations.

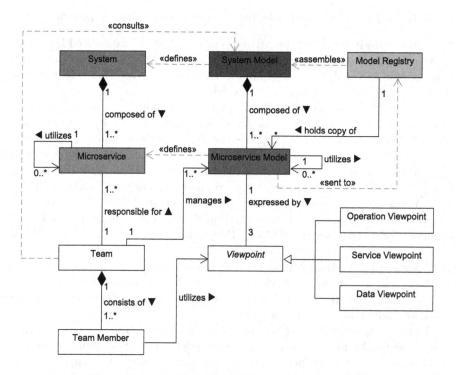

Fig. 1. Conceptual model of collaborative MSA-MDD

The overall microservice **System** is composed of many **Microservices**. For each of these services, a single **Team** which consists of multiple **Team Members** is considered responsible. For a model-centric development, our approach comprises a dedicated `Microservice Model`. Next to its services, each team is thus also responsible the defining models [17]. For the model-centric development inside a team, we suggest the usage of a separate model repository for each microservice model as means of management and a web- or eclipse-based workbench which works with a local model version repository.

With regard to the role-specific development tasks (cf. C1 in Subsect. 2.1), we propose the usage of such a model repository in combination with a set of integrable domain-specific modeling languages (DSMLs), which each addresses a specialized viewpoint for microservice development [19]. The common metamodel of the DSMLs defines three viewpoints. First, the `Data Viewpoint` holds concepts to specify a microservice?s information model. Second, the `Service Viewpoint` provides means to model interfaces and dependencies to other teams' services. Third, the `Operation Viewpoint` enables team members to model the information for deployment and operation of a service.

To compose an overall `System Model` (C2), our conceptual model involves a central `Model Registry` and an additional step in the continuous delivery pipeline, when a team releases a microservice. In this step, a copy of the corresponding service model is sent to the central model registry every time a microservice gets released. Thus, the registry is able to assemble the system model by weaving the microservice models according to their interface dependencies with other services. To ensure a successful composition of the system model, each microservice model is tested at each release for its integrability. A model which integration test fails, e.g., because an external service refers to a data object that is no longer published through the service's interface, is therefore marked as a conflict and has to be revised by the respective team.

As a result, our presented approach is able to provide teams with the ability to consult other teams' models through the assembled system model (C3). For realization, we envision the extension of the team-internal modeling workbench with the ability to access the system model and import other microservice models as dependencies inside the teams own model. While dependency information gets pushed to the model repository in the next release, the system model can also be consulted regarding change impact and conflict analysis [3], and perform appropriate measures, e.g., automatically protection of deprecated microservice releases because of other services' dependencies.

4 Conclusion

The usage of MDD for designing MSA is a promising way to cope with MSA's inherent accidental complexity. While there already exist approaches for MSA-MDD which support the development from a central architectural point of view, MSA's organizational characteristic of aligning services to teams is currently underrepresented.

Hence, we identified three major challenges for the realization of a holistic MSA-MDD across microservice teams by examining team-internal and team-external collaboration processes in microservice development (cf. Sect. 2).

As a result, we presented our vision of a collaborative MSA-MDD approach which foresees individual microservice models as model fragments of the overall system (cf. Sect. 3). Leveraging a model registry, such models get automatically woven to a system model which in the following can be used to provide team collaboration means, e.g., partial imports or dependencies of other microservice models across teams.

5   Future Work

For future work we are going to evaluate existing CDMSE approaches like Mondo[5] or Eclipse Dawn[6] for their applicability towards team-internal collaboration and extendability concerning our envisioned approach. In the following we plan to adapt our central modeling approach described in [19] to support a distributed modeling and implement a prototype for the model registry mechanism.

Beyond the realization of a model-centric development process at design time, we would like to further investigate the possibilities of runtime models [8] in the MSA software life cycle. Another interesting research direction we would like to further investigate comprises the usage of microservices as containers for language components in the context of globalizing modeling languages [5].

References

1. Balalaie, A., Heydarnoori, A., Jamshidi, P.: Microservices architecture enables devops: migration to a cloud-native architecture. IEEE Softw. **33**(3), 42–52 (2016)
2. Brambilla, M., Cabot, J., Wimmer, M.: Model-driven software engineering in practice. Synth. Lect. Softw. Eng. **1**(1), 1–182 (2012)
3. Briand, L.C., Labiche, Y., O'Sullivan, L.: Impact analysis and change management of UML models. In: Proceedings 2003 International Conference on Software Maintenance, 2003 ICSM, pp. 256–265. September 2003
4. Combemale, B., France, R., Jézéquel, J., Rumpe, B., Steel, J., Vojtisek, D.: Engineering Modeling Languages. Chapman & Hall/CRC innovations in software engineering and software development, Taylor & Francis, CRC Press (2016)
5. Combemale, B., Deantoni, J., Baudry, B., France, R.B., Jézéquel, J.M., Gray, J.: Globalizing Modeling Languages. Computer 10–13 (2014)
6. Di Ruscio, D., Franzago, M., Muccini, H., Malavolta, I.: Envisioning the future of collaborative model-driven software engineering. In: Proceedings of the 39th International Conference on Software Engineering Companion (2017)
7. Düllmann, T.F., van Hoorn, A.: Model-driven generation of microservice architectures for benchmarking performance and resilience engineering approaches. In: Proceedings of the 8th ACM/SPEC on International Conference on Performance Engineering Companion, ICPE 2017 Companion, pp. 171–172 (2017)
8. France, R., Rumpe, B.: Model-driven development of complex software: a research roadmap. In: 2007 Future of Software Engineering (2007)

---

[5] http://www.mondo-project.org.
[6] https://wiki.eclipse.org/Dawn.

9. Francesco, P., Lago, P., Malavolta, I.: Research on architecting microservices: trends, focus, and potential for industrial adoption. In: 2017 IEEE International Conference on Software Architecture (2017)
10. Franzago, M., Ruscio, D.D., Malavolta, I., Muccini, H.: Collaborative model-driven software engineering: a classification framework and a research map. IEEE Trans. Softw. Eng. (2017)
11. Kang, H., Le, M., Tao, S.: Container and microservice driven design for cloud infrastructure DevOps. In: 2016 IEEE International Conference on Cloud Engineering (IC2E), pp. 202–211, April 2016
12. Kniberg, H., Ivarsson, A.: Scaling Agile @ Spotify. Spotify, Inc. (2012)
13. Mistrík, I., Grundy, J., van der Hoek, A., Whitehead, J.: Collaborative Software Engineering: Challenges and Prospects, pp. 389–403. Springer, Heidelberg (2010). https://doi.org/10.1007/978-3-642-10294-3_19
14. Nadareishvili, I., Mitra, R., McLarty, M., Amundsen, M.: Microservice Architecture: Aligning Principles, Practices, and Culture, 1st edn. O'Reilly Media Inc., Sebastopol (2016)
15. Newman, S.: Building Microservices, 1st edn. O'Reilly Media Inc., Sebastopol (2015)
16. Rademacher, F., Sachweh, S., Zündorf, A.: Differences between model-driven development of service-oriented and microservice architecture. In: 2017 IEEE International Conference on Software Architecture Workshops (ICSAW), pp. 38–45 (2017)
17. Rademacher, F., Sorgalla, J., Sachweh, S.: Challenges of domain-driven microservice design: a model-driven perspective. IEEE Softw. **35**(3), 39–43 (2018)
18. Rademacher, F., Sorgalla, J., Sachweh, S., Zündorf, A.: Microservice architecture- and model-driven development: yet singles, soon married (?) In: Proceedings of the Second International Workshop on Microservices: Agile and DevOps Experience (MADE) (2018, in press)
19. Rademacher, F., Sorgalla, J., Sachweh, S., Zündorf, A.: Towardsaviewpoint-specific metamodel for model-driven development of microservice architecture (2018). arXiv:1804.09948
20. Schmidt, D.: Guest editor's introduction: model-driven engineering. Computer **39**(2), 25–31 (2006)
21. Sorgalla, J.: Ajil: a graphical modeling language for the development of microservice architectures. In: Extended Abstracts of the Microservices 2017 Conference (2017). www.conf-micro.services/papers/Sorgalla.pdf
22. Sorgalla, J., Rademacher, F., Sachweh, S., Zündorf, A.: Collaborative model-driven software engineering and microservice architecture: a perfect match? In: XP 2018 Workshops (2018). accepted
23. Wiedemann, A.: A new form of collaboration in it teams - exploring the DevOps phenomenon. In: PACIS 2017 Proceedings (2017)
24. Wizenty, P., Sorgalla, J., Rademacher, F., Sachweh, S.: Magma: build management-based generation of microservice infrastructures. In: Proceedings of ECSA 2017 (2017)

Security for and by Model-Driven Engineering (MDE)

SecureMDE 2018 Organizers' Message

There are at least two ways in which MDE and Security might be beneficially combined: using MDE to support the development of secure systems and, integrating security techniques in MDE to give support to new development scenarios such as collaborative and distributed modeling. Indeed, MDE has succeeded to play a key role in many critical tasks related to Information and Communications Technology (ICT) security. However, new domains such as Internet of Things, Cyber-physical systems, and Blockchain-based technologies stress the limitations of previous work and pose new challenges to current model-driven security techniques. Moreover, the increased adoption of MDE in collaborative scenarios highlights the need for security for MDE itself in order to deal with requirements such as confidentiality and integrity.

The goal of SecureMDE 2018 was to provide a forum for presenting and discussing new challenges and results related to this interplay between MDE and Security.

SecureMDE 2018 received four paper submissions, all selected for presentation at the workshop. Each paper was reviewed by at least three PC members. The workshop had two sessions, each section including two article presentations followed by a discussion time. In the first session, papers related to the specification of security aspects on system models (privacy and information flows) were presented. The two articles in the second session explored the security of communication between complex system components. Long and interesting discussions followed up each of the paper presentations, confirming the interest of these topics for the STAF attendees.

The organizers would like to thank the authors and presenters of submitted papers, the PC members, and the audience for the contribution to the success of the workshop.

September 2018

Salvador Martínez
Domenico Bianculli
Jordi Cabot

Organization

SecureMDE 2018 - Program Committee

Olivier Barais	Université de Rennes, France
Ameni Ben Fadhel	Université du Luxembourg, Luxembourg
Achim Brucher	University of Sheffield, UK
Marina Egea	Minsait - INDRA, Spain
Yehia ElRakaiby	University of Limerick, Ireland
Jan Jurgens	University of Koblenz-Landau, Germany
Alexander Knapp	Universität Augsburg, Germany
Nora Koch	University of Seville, Spain
Régine Laleau	Université Paris-Est Créteil, France
Yves Ledru	Université Grenoble-Alpes, France
Gabriel Pedroza	CEA-List, France
Alexander Pretschner	Technische Universität München, Germany
Daniel Varro	McGill University, Canada
Manuel Wimmer	Technische Universität Wien, Austria

A UML Profile for Privacy Enforcement

Javier Luis Cánovas Izquierdo[(✉)] and Julián Salas

Internet Interdisciplinary Institute (IN3), Universitat Oberta de Catalunya (UOC),
Barcelona, Spain
{jcanovasi,jsalaspi}@uoc.edu

Abstract. Nowadays most software applications have to deal with personal data, specially with the emergence of Web-based applications, where user profile information has become one of their main assets. Due to regulation laws and to protect the privacy of users, customers and companies; most of this information is considered private, and therefore convenient ways to gather, process and store them have to be proposed. A common problem when modeling software systems is the lack of support to specify how to enforce privacy concerns in data models. Current approaches for modeling privacy cover high-level privacy aspects to describe what should be done with the data (e.g., elements to be private) instead of how to do it (e.g., which privacy enhancing technology to use); or propose access control policies, which may cover privacy only partially. In this paper we propose a profile to define and enforce privacy concerns in UML class diagrams. Models annotated with our profile can be used in model-driven methodologies to generate privacy-aware applications.

Keywords: UML · UML-profile · Privacy

1 Introduction

In the last years, specially with the emergence of the Web, personal information has become one of the main assets of software applications. This kind of data usually includes information about users (e.g., email addresses or passport identifiers), personal information (e.g., geolocations, pictures or videos) or even composite information that can be discovered by mining the previous information (e.g., route to go to work or places to pass the night). Most of this information may be considered private, and therefore convenient ways to gather, process and store it have to be proposed to comply with existing regulations and to promote participation by providing accountability and transparency to data subjects.

Model-Driven Engineering (MDE) is a methodology focusing on using models to raise the level of abstraction and automation in software development. MDE relies on models and model transformations for the specification and generation of software applications, thus hiding the complexity of the target technology.

A common problem when modeling software systems is the lack of support to specify how to enforce privacy concerns in data models, that is, the mechanisms

© Springer Nature Switzerland AG 2018
M. Mazzara et al. (Eds.): STAF 2018 Workshops, LNCS 11176, pp. 609–616, 2018.
https://doi.org/10.1007/978-3-030-04771-9_46

(e.g., hashing or ciphering) that have to be applied to meet privacy requirements. Current approaches cover high-level privacy aspects [3,6,10] which address privacy concerns regarding to what elements are private but neglecting how to enforce privacy. The work by Basso et al. [5] proposes a UML profile for privacy-aware applications, however, it is mainly focused on defining privacy and user preferences. Other works (e.g., [1,2,4]) propose methodological approaches to address privacy but they do not focus on enforcement mechanisms. There are also approaches like XACML [12], PRBAC [11], UMLsec [9] or Ponder [7] proposing languages adapted to the definition of access control policies, which can be used to partially manage privacy concerns but they do not target enforcement.

In this paper we propose a profile to model privacy concerns in UML class diagrams with the aim of enabling privacy enforcement. Models are annotated by privacy experts, thus enabling developers (and model-driven tools) to understand how privacy has to be applied to the artifacts involved in model-based methodologies. We believe that our proposal promotes a better documentation of the models and could be easily adapted to existing methodologies to enable the generation of privacy-aware software applications.

The rest of the paper is organized as follows. Section 2 motivates the work and presents a running example. Section 3 describes the profile and Sect. 4 concludes the paper and presents the further work.

2   Motivation

Sharing and processing data has many benefits, but it also has risks to individual privacy: it can reveal information about individuals that would otherwise not be public knowledge. Privacy is a fundamental human right and it is commonly agreed it should be enforced by law. Moreover, developing privacy-aware software systems will also bring the benefits of increasing public engagement by promoting the participation and dissemination, and providing transparency and accountability on the data processing methodologies.

As suggested by the *privacy by design* concept [8], privacy should be protected throughout the whole process of any technological development, from the conception of a technology to its realization. Dealing with privacy at each stage of the data lifecycle (i.e., collection, maintenance, release, and deletion) will be enhanced by specific support when modeling software artifacts, thus enabling developers to easily define how data privacy has to be treated.

Along this paper we will use a running example to illustrate our approach. Let's imagine a public organization willing to publish some data regarding its employees (e.g., for statistical purposes). Figure 1 shows a UML class diagram model to represent companies, employees and positions. A company, which has a name and a tax number, is composed of employees, which have names, ages and passport numbers; and offers a set of positions, with a name and a salary.

Even with this small model, several concerns can be identified when publishing data conforming to this model. For instance, name and passport information uniquely identifies an employee and should be removed, encrypted or replaced;

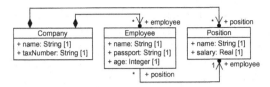

Fig. 1. Running example.

age information can be leveraged to uniquely re-identify an employee and should be treated (e.g., removing outliers to decrease its uniqueness); and salary information is generally considered sensitive information and could be masked by applying generalization (i.e., released using ranges of salaries).

It should be noted that there is no one-fits-all solution for providing privacy. Along with the possible benefits of releasing data there are some risks to individual privacy, this trade-off between the utility vs. privacy should be considered (i.e., performing the minimal number of privacy enforcement modifications to the data to preserve privacy). There are several methods for data protection, each one with its own strengths and weaknesses, and different trade-offs. An extensive analysis should be done to choose a method over others, however, by knowing the characteristics of each of them, a developer may provide certain guarantees of privacy by design to end-users.

In this paper we propose a UML profile to annotate class models with information regarding privacy concerns in order to enable their enforcement.

3   A Profile for Privacy Enforcement

Privacy enforcement covers the set of mechanisms deployed to protect private data [14]. To enforce privacy in UML we defined a profile following the standard recommendations [13]. The profile annotates UML classes and their properties. Class associations require special treatment, as we will show. Next we describe the main elements of the profile[1].

UML Property Privacy Type. UML properties can be classified according to a specific privacy type. This information is required for every property in the class model and classifies its sensitiveness, which is later used by the privacy type applied to the owning class, as we describe below. We identify four privacy types: *non-sensitive*, for non-confidential properties; *sensitive*, for confidential properties; *identifier*, for those properties that can unambiguously identify the owner of the property; and *quasi-identifier*, for properties that uniquely combined can be used to re-identify the owner of the property.

In the profile, the privacy type of a property is specified by the `PrivacyType` stereotype, which extends the `Property` metaclass. The actual values of privacy types are defined in the `PropertyPrivacyType`.

---

[1] The profile implementation and example are available at http://hdl.handle.net/20.500.12004/1/A/UMLPP/001.

UML Property Anonymization. UML properties can optionally be anonymized following a specific method. The anonymization of a property protects its values and can be used to configure how to store them. These methods are based on reducing the amount or precision of the data and follow two main principles: (1) masking the data and (2) using synthetic values instead of real ones. Masking the data can be divided in two categories: *non-perturbative* and *perturbative*.

Non-perturbative masking reduces the level of details without distorting it. Some well-known non-perturbative masking methods are: (1) *generalization*, which coarses a property by combining several (or a range) of values to a more general one; (2) *top/bottom coding*, which sets values above/below a given threshold into a single category; and (3) *suppression*, which removes outliers values of individual property values in order to decrease the uniqueness of the elements.

Perturbative masking includes (1) *noise addition*, which is applied to numerical properties and consists of adding a noise vector (most commonly) drawn from a $N(0, \alpha \Sigma)$, where Σ is the covariance matrix of the original data values; (2) *data/rank swapping*, which exchanges categorical property values in such a way that marginals are maintained; (3) *post-randomization*, where property values are changed according to a Markov matrix; and (4) *microaggregation*, which partitions the property values into groups containing each at least a specific amount of records and publishing the average record of each group.

In the profile, the anonymization method of a property is specified by the `PrivateMethod` stereotype, which extends the `Property` metaclass. The actual methods are defined in the `AnonymizationMethod`.

UML Class Privacy Type. UML classes can be annotated to indicate the privacy protection mechanism that has to be enforced. Annotating a class with this kind of information protects the way class instances are queried. Thus any instance of a class including this annotation will not provide information regarding its *identifier* properties and will protect *nonsensitive*, *sensitive* and *quasi-identifier* properties. The two main models for privacy protection, from which many others have been developed, are k-anonymity and ϵ-differential privacy (see `KAnonymity` and `DifferentialPrivacy` stereotypes in our profile).

The concept of k-anonymity was defined to release personal data while safeguarding the identities of the individuals to whom the data refer [15]. A dataset is k-anonymous if each record is indistinguishable from at least other $k-1$ records within the dataset, when considering the values of its quasi-identifiers. This model therefore aims to protect from attacks to obtain sensitive property values relying on quasi-identifiers. Applied to a UML class, this mechanism guarantees that individual instances of a UML class are indistinguishable from at least other $k-1$ instances.

To protect from inferences due to the low variability of sensitive properties in a k-group, ℓ-diversity and t-closeness models were proposed. A k-anonymous set of instances is said to be ℓ-diverse if, for each group of instances sharing quasi-identifier values, there are at least ℓ well-represented values for the sensitive property. A k-anonymous set of instances is said to have t-closeness if, for each group of instances sharing quasi-identifier values, the distance between the distribution of each sensitive property within the group and the distribution of the property in the whole set is no more than a threshold t.

The ϵ-differential privacy applied to UML classes establishes that the removal or addition of a single element to the set of class instances does not (considerably) change the results on an analysis. Therefore, the presence or absence of any individual element is not revealed by the computation (up to $exp(\epsilon)$) (Fig. 2).

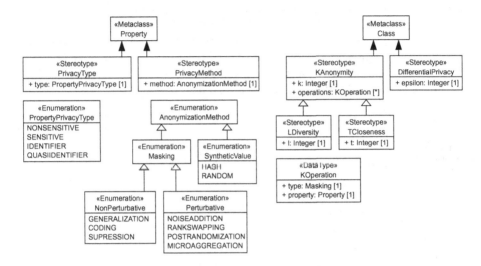

Fig. 2. Proposed UML profile to model privacy enforcement.

Privacy for UML Associations. In our approach, class associations obtain the privacy enforcement declared for the association endpoint. Although this solution could cover the privacy enforcement at UML class model level, it may become a challenging task when these models are transformed to low-level ones used to generate a software system. For instance, UML class models annotated with our profile can be used to generate a database schema, where resolving associations could involve the composition of different database tables. This composition is not trivial, specially if source/target tables corresponds to UML classes annotated with different privacy types. While it would be feasible to compose information of tables coming from UML classes annotated with ϵ-differential privacy, such composition would be challenging for k-anonymity (composability has been mentioned as open research question for Big Data privacy [16,17]).

Example. Figure 3 shows the running example described before annotated with our profile. As can be seen, the **name** properties of the **Company** and **Position** classes have been annotated as **NONSENSITIVE** as they not involve any privacy risk. The **taxNumber** property of the **Company** class, and the **name** and **passport** properties of the **Employee** class have been annotated as **IDENTIFIER**, as they can be used to uniquely identify the company and the employee, respectively (i.e., they will be removed in any query to the instances of such classes). The age and salary properties of the Employee and Position classes have been annotated as QUASIIDENTIFIER and SENSITIVE, as they store data that has to be protected. Additionally, for illustration purposes we use different anonymization methods for these properties, for instance, employees' names and passport information are protected using HASH and RANDOM mechanisms, respectively.

In the example we also indicate privacy protection mechanisms for Employee and Position classes, which apply k-anonymity. The k-anonymity for Employee class indicates a k value of 4 and applies the SUPRESSION method when retrieving the age property, thus decreasing the uniqueness of the class instances. On the other hand, the k-anonymity for Position class also indicates a k value of 4 and applies the GENERALIZATION method when retrieving the Salary property, thus the values of such property are expressed as ranges of values.

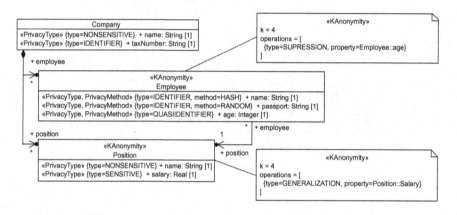

Fig. 3. Privacy enforcement profile applied to the running example.

This UML Class model annotated with our profile provides detailed information to enforce privacy when dealing with its instances. This information can later be used in model-driven methodologies to generate the needed artifacts in a privacy-aware software application. For instance, profile information can be used to customize the generation and configuration of the database schema, and to tune the behavior of queries in the data.

4   Conclusion and Further Work

In this paper we have presented a UML profile to model and enforce privacy concerns in UML class diagrams. We believe our approach paves the way to use models annotated with privacy enforcement information in model-based approaches to enable the validation and generation of privacy-aware applications.

As further work, we are interested in applying our approach to specific fields, such as Big Data and Web Engineering, where it is common to deal with sensitive information. We also plan to explore how privacy information could promote the Open Data movement, currently mainly lead by public organizations. We believe that offering better mechanisms to enforce privacy in Open Data datasets could encourage more organizations (even private companies) to join the movement.

References

1. Ahmadian, A.S., Peldszus, S., Ramadan, Q., Jürjens, J.: Model-based privacy and security analysis with carisma. In: Foundations of Software Engineering, pp. 989–993 (2017)
2. Ahmadian, A.S., Strüber, D., Riediger, V., Jürjens, J.: Model-based privacy analysis in industrial ecosystems. In: European Conference on Modelling Foundations and Applications, pp. 215–231 (2017)
3. Allison, D.S., Yamany, H.F.E., Capretz, M.A.M.: Metamodel for privacy policies within SOA. In: Workshop on Software Engineering for Secure Systems, pp. 40–46 (2009)
4. Alshammari, M., Simpson, A.: A UML profile for privacy-aware data lifecycle models. In: International Workshop on Computer Security, pp. 189–209 (2017)
5. Basso, T., Montecchi, L., Moraes, R., Jino, M., Bondavalli, A.: Towards a UML profile for privacy-aware applications. In: International Conference on Computer and Information Technology, pp. 371–378 (2015)
6. Busch, M.: Evaluating & engineering: an approach for the development of secure web applications (2016)
7. Damianou, N., Dulay, N., Lupu, E., Sloman, M.: The ponder policy specification language. In: International Workshop on Policies for Distributed Systems and Networks, pp. 18–38 (2001)
8. Hoepman, J.: Privacy design strategies - (extended abstract). In: International Conference on Systems Security and Privacy Protection, pp. 446–459 (2014)
9. Jürjens, J.: UMLsec: extending UML for secure systems development. In: 5th International Conference on the Unified Modeling Language, pp. 412–425 (2002)
10. Mont, M.C., Pearson, S., Creese, S., Goldsmith, M., Papanikolaou, N.: A conceptual model for privacy policies with consent and revocation requirements. In: International Summer School on Privacy and Identity Management for Life, pp. 258–270 (2010)
11. Ni, Q., et al.: Privacy-aware role-based access control. ACM Trans. Inf. Syst. Secur. **13(3)**, 24:1–**24**, 31 (2010)
12. OASIS: Extensible Access Control Markup Language (XACML). http://www.oasis-open.org/committees/tc_home.php?wg_abbrev=xacml. Accessed April 2018
13. OMG: Unified Modeling Language. https://www.omg.org/spec/UML/2.5/. Accessed April 2018
14. Salas, J., Domingo-Ferrer, J.: Some basics on privacy techniques, anonymization and their big data challenges. Mathematics in Computer Science (2018, in press)
15. Samarati, P., Sweeney, L.: Protecting privacy when disclosing information: k-anonymity and its enforcement through generalization and suppression. Technical report (1998)

16. Soria-Comas, J., Domingo-Ferrer, J.: Big data privacy: challenges to privacy principles and models. Data Sci. Eng. **1**(1), 21–28 (2016)
17. Torra, V., Navarro-Arribas, G.: Big data privacy and anonymization. In: Lehmann, A., Whitehouse, D., Fischer-Hübner, S., Fritsch, L., Raab, C. (eds.) Privacy and Identity 2016. IAICT, vol. 498, pp. 15–26. Springer, Cham (2016). https://doi.org/10.1007/978-3-319-55783-0_2

Specification of Information Flow Security Policies in Model-Based Systems Engineering

Christopher Gerking[(✉)]

Paderborn University, Heinz Nixdorf Institute, Paderborn, Germany
christopher.gerking@upb.de

Abstract. Model-based systems engineering provides a multi-discipli-nary approach to developing cyber-physical systems. Due to their high degree of interconnection, security is a key factor for cyber-physical systems and needs to be front-loaded to the beginning of the development. However, there is a lack of model-based systems engineering approaches that enable the early specification of security policies. As a consequence, security requirements frequently remain unspecified and therefore are hard to satisfy in the downstream development phases. In this paper, we propose to integrate model-based systems engineering with the theory of information flow security. We extend systems engineering models to information flow policies, enabling systems engineers to specify the information flow security requirements of a system under development. On refinement of the resulting models, our approach allows to derive security requirements for individual software components. We illustrate our approach using a model-based design of an autonomous car.

Keywords: Information flow · Security policies · Systems engineering

1 Introduction

Cyber-physical systems emerge from an interdisciplinary engineering that requires software engineers to work in close collaboration with control engineers, mechanical engineers, or electrical engineers. Model-driven engineering is widely accepted to bridge these different disciplines, using abstract models to integrate the heterogeneous landscape of discipline-specific artifacts. This discipline-spanning approach is known as *model-based systems engineering* [32].

Nowadays, a key quality factor for cyber-physical systems is *security* [6,14]. Thus, security properties such as confidentiality and integrity need to be *front-loaded* to the beginning of the engineering to make systems *secure by design*.

The theory of *information flow security* [25] allows to identify leaks in the information processing of software systems, and therefore enables reasoning about security at early development stages. Information flow security character-izes information leaks as non-authorized flows of information, thereby providing a *security policy* that the downstream stages of development must satisfy.

© Springer Nature Switzerland AG 2018
M. Mazzara et al. (Eds.): STAF 2018 Workshops, LNCS 11176, pp. 617–632, 2018.
https://doi.org/10.1007/978-3-030-04771-9_47

The problem we address in this paper is the missing support for the specification of security policies in model-based systems engineering. Thereby, the security requirements of a system under development are likely to remain unspecified at the early, discipline-spanning development stages. Instead, the need for security is implicitly deferred to the downstream, discipline-specific development phases, turning security into an *afterthought* [36]. This late handling of security requirements often forces engineers to revoke earlier design decisions. In the worst case, crucial security requirements might even go unrecognized. For cyber-physical systems, such *zero-day* vulnerabilities might escalate into serious safety hazards that need to be prevented by design.

Existing model-based systems engineering approaches like SysML [30] allow to design information flow as a crucial form of interaction between systems or subsystems. However, these approaches do not enable the specification of non-authorized flows and, therefore, fail to define full-fledged security policies. In contrast, the theory of information flow security provides so-called *flow policies* that enable engineers to specify confidentiality or integrity requirements of systems [23]. Nevertheless, this theoretical approach lacks an integration with model-based techniques used in systems engineering practice.

In this paper, we build upon our previous results [10–12] and propose a novel integration of model-based systems engineering and information flow security. To that end, we enrich structural systems engineering models with a specification technique to express non-authorized information flow that needs to be prevented. Thereby, we turn systems engineering models into full-fledged flow policies. As a benefit, the specified policies can be refined during the structural decomposition of models, allowing engineers to identify more fine-grained security requirements at the subsystem level. Finally, we describe how a refined security policy can be translated from the discipline-spanning systems engineering into discipline-specific software engineering models. Thereby, we obtain security requirements for individual software components that are amenable to formal verification. In summary, we enable systems engineers to front-load security requirements to the discipline-spanning development stage, and provide verifiable security policies for the downstream software engineering.

We illustrate our approach using an autonomous car that interacts with its environment both physically and digitally. Thus, the car must meet high security requirements to avoid leakage or manipulation of information.

In summary, this paper makes the following contributions:

- We enrich model-based systems engineering with a specification technique for information flow security policies of a system under development.
- We enable the refinement of the specified policies to derive fine-grained security requirements at the subsystem level.
- We describe a translation of refined policies into verifiable security requirements for individual software components.

Paper Organization: We give background information in Sect. 2, and integrate model-based systems engineering with information flow security in Sect. 3. In Sect. 4, we discuss related work, before concluding in Sect. 5.

2   Background

In this part, we describe our underlying model-based systems engineering approach in Sect. 2.1, and introduce information flow security in Sect. 2.2.

2.1   Model-Based Systems Engineering

Model-based systems engineering [32] promotes the usage of abstract, discipline-
spanning models for the initial design of a system. Our proposed approach is
based on CONSENS [7], a specification technique for the model-based systems
engineering of intelligent technical systems. CONSENS provides systems engineers with various types of abstract, semi-formal models, each one representing
a specific view on a system under development. One of these views is given by an
environment model that describes dependencies between the system and environmental elements. Dependencies are categorized as *energy flow, information
flow*, or *material flow*. As an example, Fig. 1 depicts an environment model of an
Autonomous Car. Information flow dependencies represent the data communication between the car and environmental elements, including a Passenger, a service
for Predictive Maintenance, a Cloud Storage, and a Traffic Service. Furthermore, the
propulsion is represented by an energy flow from the car to the Passenger.

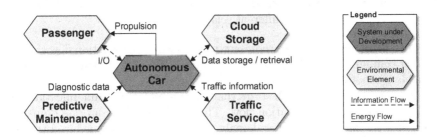

Fig. 1. Environment model of an autonomous car

In the remainder of this paper, we restrict ourselves to information flow
dependencies which are the most relevant type of flow with respect to security
requirements. In the scope of our example, the following two security requirements must be met by the Autonomous Car. First, no personal information about
the Passenger must be stored by the Cloud Storage, representing a confidentiality requirement. Second, it must not be possible for the Predictive Maintenance
to manipulate the information that the car gives to a Passenger, expressing an
integrity requirement. By considering only information flows, hidden information
leaks through energy or material flows are beyond the current scope of our work.
Nevertheless, since such flows might make cyber-physical systems vulnerable to
side-channel attacks, they need to be considered in future work as well.

In the scope of CONSENS, an environment model is further decomposed into internal system elements and their interdependencies at the subsystem level. The model resulting from this decomposition is referred to as *active structure* [7] and provides a structural view on the system under development. The decomposition is an iterative procedure, i.e., any internal system element might be decomposed into subsystems itself until a desired level of granularity has been reached.

Finally, the active structure also enables the transition from systems engineering to model-driven software engineering by deriving a software component model [9]. In contrast to the semi-formal models of CONSENS, this component model is equipped with formal semantics that are used to implement the information processing of each component.

2.2   Information Flow Security

The theory of information flow security [25] allows to detect information leaks in the information processing of a software system. To characterize an information leak, the information processed by a system is categorized according to different *security domains* [23]. Information flow security restricts the information processing such that no critical information from a certain domain must flow to particular other domains.

To specify concrete requirements for the information flow between domains, so-called *flow policies* have been introduced [23]. A flow policy interrelates the security domains using three different relations:

→ is an *interference relation* representing authorized information flow through direct communication. It states that the information in one domain is directly visible to another domain.

↝ is a neutral relation which states that there is no direct communication, but allows for indirect information flow. Thus, information from one domain is not directly visible to another domain, but is allowed to be deduced through indirect communication of other visible information.

⇸ is a *noninterference relation* that represents non-authorized information flow. It not only excludes direct communication between domains, but also forbids one domain to deduce any information from another domain through indirect communication.

To represent the security requirements of systems, a flow policy corresponds to a complete graph that interrelates any two security domains by exactly one of the above relations. In particular, information flow within a single domain is always authorized. Therefore, every domain interferes with itself, i.e., → is a reflexive relation. Formally, flow policies are defined as follows:

Definition 1 (Flow policy). *A flow policy [23] is a tuple $(D, \rightarrow, \rightsquigarrow, \nrightarrow)$ with a set D of security domains and relations $\rightarrow, \rightsquigarrow, \nrightarrow \subseteq D \times D$ forming a partition of $D \times D$. The relation $\rightarrow$ is reflexive, i.e., $d \rightarrow d$ holds for all $d \in D$.*

3   Specification and Refinement of Security Policies

In this section, we integrate CONSENS with information flow security concepts to enable the specification and refinement of security requirements in model-based systems engineering. In Sect. 3.1, we introduce our underlying engineering process. Next, in Sect. 3.2, we describe our extension of environment models to flow policies, before addressing the refinement of such policies at the level of active structures in Sect. 3.3. Finally, in Sect. 3.4, we describe the transition of security policies to the level of software components.

3.1   Engineering Process

Figure 2 illustrates our proposed engineering process that spans both systems engineering and the transition to software engineering. For a more general perspective on the integration of security measures into the engineering process, we refer the reader to our previous work [10]. In the initial activity named Analyze Environment, systems engineers produce an environment model as described in Sect. 2.1. The purpose of the next activity is to Specify Information Flow Requirements such as confidentiality or integrity. To that end, we propose to extend the environment model to a flow policy as defined in Sect. 2.2.

Next, in the activity Decompose System, the active structure (cf. Sect. 2.1) arises from the decomposition of the environment model. Alongside, we propose to refine the flow policy in the activity Refine Information Flow Requirements. During the activity Validate Refinement, we propose to automatically check the validity of the refined flow policy. In case of an invalid refinement, systems engineers need to revise the information flow requirements. Otherwise, an iterative decomposition of the active structure leads to recursive refinements of the flow policy.

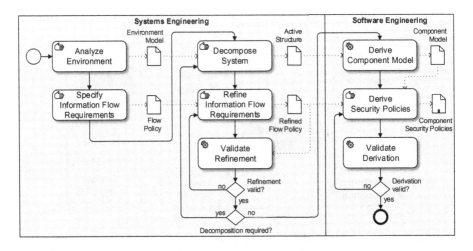

Fig. 2. Engineering process for the specification and refinement of security policies

Once no further decomposition is required, a software component model is automatically derived from the active structure in the activity Derive Component Model. Alongside, in the activity Derive Security Policies, software engineers derive corresponding component security policies that specify information flow requirements for individual software components. Finally, the validity of the derivation is automatically checked in the activity Validate Refinement. Beyond the scope of this paper, the resulting component security policies give rise to further refinements along with the decomposition of components into subcomponents.

3.2   Specification of Information Flow Security Requirements

Our approach is based on the observation that model-based systems engineering practices (e.g., CONSENS or SysML) and the theory of information flow security share a common notion of information flow between elements or domains, respectively. Thus, we integrate environment models with flow policies to specify information flow security requirements. In particular, we interpret each element of an environment model as an individual security domain, and regard the information flows between elements as interferences between the corresponding domains. Furthermore, we expand the models with additional flow relations known from flow policies. In particular, we add a noninterference relation that represents non-authorized information flow.

For example, in Fig. 3, we illustrate the extension of an environment model to a flow policy. The interference relation corresponds to the set of information flows known from Fig. 1. In addition, two noninterferences represent non-authorized information flow, thereby expressing the security requirements of the Autonomous Car described in Sect. 2.1. First, a noninterference between the Passenger and the Cloud Storage specifies the confidentiality requirement that no personal data should be stored in the cloud. Second, another noninterference is used to specify the integrity requirement that the information given to a Passenger must not be manipulated by the Predictive Maintenance.

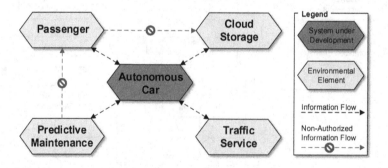

Fig. 3. Environment model of an autonomous car extended to a flow policy

Since a noninterference forbids information to be indirectly deducible through authorized communication, it represents a security requirement for the system under development. Thus, engineers need to ensure that the system's internal information processing does not leak information indirectly, and thereby violates one of the specified noninterference relations. For example, although the Autonomous Car communicates directly with both Passenger and Cloud Storage, the internal information processing of the car needs to ensure that no information is leaked indirectly from the passenger to the cloud.

To reduce the visual complexity of the resulting security policies, we leave the neutral relation between elements implicit. Thus, we assume neutral relations between any two elements that are related neither by an interference nor by a noninterference. For example, Fig. 1 includes implicit neutral relations from the Traffic Service to each of the other three environmental elements. Furthermore, we also leave the reflexivity of the interference relation implicit, i.e., we omit all self-loops from the visual representation.

3.3 Refining Security Policies at the Level of Active Structures

In the scope of CONSENS, the active structure results from the structural decomposition of an environment model, and describes internal interdependencies between nested elements of the system under development. In our approach, we adopt this refinement step and apply it to security policies as well. Thereby, we obtain refined security requirements that are specified at the level of the nested elements. In Fig. 4, we show an active structure that decomposes the Autonomous Car into a User Interface, a Storage Gateway, an Engine Control, and a Navigation System. Information flows between these nested elements represent the internal communication of the car. To refine the security policy that has been specified along with the environment model, we enrich the active structure with fine-grained noninterferences at the level of nested system elements. For example, Fig. 4 introduces two noninterference relations between Predictive Maintenance and User Interface, as well as between User Interface and Storage Gateway.

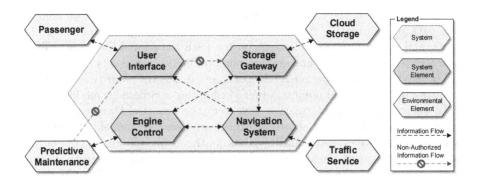

Fig. 4. Security policy refined during the decomposition into an active structure

The objective of our approach is to ensure validity of these refinements. To formalize validity, we relate the two flow policies by means of a *graph homomorphism*. In particular, we require a homomorphism (with respect to the interference relation) that maps every element of the active structure to the corresponding element inside the environment model. For example, in Fig. 4, all the nested elements are mapped to the Autonomous Car as the system under development, whereas the external elements are mapped to their corresponding identical elements inside the environment model. Furthermore, the homomorphism requires the active structure to include only such information flows that correspond to legitimate flows inside the environment model. Thus, if there is an interference between two elements of the active structure, the two corresponding elements inside the environment model must interfere as well. For example, in Fig. 4, all the internal information flows between the nested elements correspond to the interference of the Autonomous Car with itself.

Finally, in addition to the homomorphism, we also require every noninterference inside the environment model to be refined by appropriate fine-grained noninterferences at the level of the active structure. These fine-grained noninterferences ensure that every possible communication path between two noninterfering environmental elements is properly *illegalized* at the level of the active structure. We formalize these conditions as follows:

Definition 2 (Refinement). *A flow policy $Pol_a = (D_a, \to_a, \leadsto_a, \not\leadsto_a)$ is refined by a flow policy $Pol_b = (D_b, \to_b, \leadsto_b, \not\leadsto_b)$, if and only if*

- *there is a graph homomorphism f from the graph $(D_b, \to_b)$ to the graph $(D_a, \to_a)$, i.e., there is a function $f : D_b \to D_a$ where $d_1 \to_b d_2$ implies that $f(d_1) \to_a f(d_2)$, and*
- *for every noninterference $d_s \not\leadsto_a d_t$, a flow from each $d'_s \in f^{-1}(d_s)$ to each $d'_t \in f^{-1}(d_t)$ is illegalized by Pol_b.*

Definition 3 (Illegalization). *A flow policy $(D, \to, \leadsto, \not\leadsto)$ illegalizes a flow from $d_1 \in D$ to $d_n \in D$, if and only if for every path $(d_1 \to \ldots \to d_n) \in \to^*$ there is a noninterference $d_i \not\leadsto d_j$ where $1 \leq i < j \leq n$.*

Thus, to validate the refinement of an individual noninterference, we analyze each path of information flows between the corresponding environmental elements, and check if any two elements on the path are related by a fine-grained noninterference. If so, this fine-grained noninterference represents an illegalization of the information flow across the path, and fulfills the security requirement expressed by the original noninterference inside the environment model.

In our example, an information flow from the Predictive Maintenance to the Passenger is non-authorized according to the environment model. A communication path between these elements exists by traversing the Engine Control, the Navigation System, and the User Interface. However, the path is correctly illegalized by a noninterference between Predictive Maintenance and User Interface. Since an illegalization exists for all possible paths between Predictive Maintenance and Passenger, the initial noninterference has been correctly refined.

By checking each noninterference for appropriate illegalizations, the validity of a refinement is analyzable at the level of the active structure. Since the system elements inside the active structure may be recursively decomposed into more fine-grained system elements, the proposed approach can be iteratively applied to check the validity of lower-level refinements. Thus, during the decomposition of a system model, our approach enables systems engineers to iteratively check the validity of their refined security policies at each step of the refinement.

3.4   Transition from Systems Engineering to Software Engineering

In the scope of the CONSENS approach, the active structure of a system under development is systematically translated into a component-based software architecture [9]. In Fig. 5, we illustrate a component architecture that results from the active structure of the autonomous car. Each element of the active structure corresponds to a software component, whereas authorized information flows have been translated into connectors between ports of the corresponding components. Components communicate over these connectors by message passing. The information processing of a component drives its communication with other components, and is implemented by means of a stateful real-time behavior with formal semantics rooted in the theory of timed automata [2].

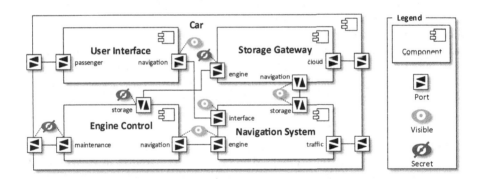

Fig. 5. Software component model including component security policies

We propose to refine security policies along with the translation from the active structure into a component model, thereby deriving verifiable security policies for individual components. Such a component security policy is specified by labelling the ports of the respective component according to their security-sensitivity, whereas possible sensitivity labels are *secret* and *visible*. A component security policy is fulfilled if the information processing of the component avoids an information flow from secret to visible ports. Figure 5 shows a set of component security policies that have been specified to refine the noninterference between Predictive Maintenance and User Interface. For the refinement of an individual noninterference, we propose the following validity conditions:

1. Ports that correspond to the source of the noninterference need to be labelled as secret. By treating the information processed by such a port as secret, we state that no such information must flow to other ports labelled as visible. Accordingly, in Fig. 5, the outer maintenance port is secret because it corresponds to the source of the refined noninterference.
2. Ports that correspond to the target of the noninterference need to be labelled as visible. By regarding the information processed by such a port as visible, we state that no flow of secret information to this port must be possible. For example, in Fig. 5, this applies to the navigation port of the User Interface as the target of the noninterference to be refined.
3. Every two ports that are connected by means of a connector must share identical sensitivities, i.e., must be either both secret or both visible. Thereby, we ensure that components agree on the sensitivity of information, preventing ports from upgrading or downgrading labels. Accordingly, in Fig. 5, the inner maintenance port of the Engine Control is also secret, whereas the interface port of the Navigation System needs to be visible.

The labels of other ports may be freely chosen, as long as they meet the above conditions. This degree of freedom enables software engineers to align the specified security requirements with the functional requirements of each component. Figure 5 illustrates a labelling that reduces the noninterference between Predictive Maintenance and User Interface to two effective component security policies. First, the information processing of the Engine Control needs to ensure that no information is flowing from its maintenance or storage ports to the navigation port. Second, an information flow from the engine port to the navigation port needs to be avoided by the information processing of the Storage Gateway. Since both User Interface and Navigation System comprise visible ports only, their component security policies are trivially fulfilled by definition. In combination, the set of local component security policies enforces the desired noninterference between Predictive Maintenance and User Interface.

Please note that, in general, refining multiple noninterferences at once might lead to conflicting sensitivity labels. Therefore, in our approach, each individual noninterference is refined separately, and may result in an individual set of component security policies. However, in order to refine a flow policy in its entirety, the information processing behavior of the components must fulfill all the resulting sets of component security policies at the same time.

The formal semantics of the information processing enables automated verification of the component security policies using our previous work [13]. However, a remaining problem to be addressed is that information flow security of individual components is not necessarily preserved on composition [24]. For example, in Fig. 5, even if both Engine Control and Storage Gateway fulfill their component security policies, an information flow between Predictive Maintenance and User Interface might nevertheless be present. Therefore, the goal of our current research [12] is to ensure that a composition of components fully preserves their security, and thereby satisfies the information flow requirements specified at the systems engineering level.

4   Related Work

Model-driven techniques are frequently applied to the engineering of secure software [29,31,40]. However, security also demands specific requirements engineering approaches surveyed in [8,26,34,37]. As shown by a recent study [27], such requirements-oriented approaches are still underrepresented among those works that emphasize security within the software development lifecycle. In this section, we focus on the intersection of model-driven and security requirements engineering. In particular, we are concerned with approaches addressing information flow security or systems engineering, as we do in this paper.

Model-Driven Engineering of Information Flow Security. FlowUML [1] validates UML sequence diagrams against logic-based security policies. Thereby, the approach enables reasoning about flow requirements at an early stage of the engineering process, similar to our work. Hoisl et al. [18] enable the specification of secure object flows in UML-based business process models. However, unlike our work, both aforementioned approaches do not address the refinement of security policies along with the engineering process.

RIFL [4] is a tool-independent specification language that explicitly targets information flow requirements. Thus, it naturally supports the specification of flow policies in terms of relations between security domains, similar to this paper. Due to its generality, RIFL is not restricted to a particular application domain. However, the approach has not yet been applied to the domain of model-based systems engineering, which is the goal of our work in this paper.

The STAIRS approach [35] enables reasoning about information flow properties of system specifications given in terms of UML sequence diagrams. The authors address the preservation of information flow properties under refinement of system specifications. This form of refinement is different from our work, which refines a security policy itself along with the engineering process. Furthermore, by using sequence diagrams as a notation for policy specification, the approach differs substantially from our work based on flow policies.

The most prominent approach towards model-driven design of secure systems is UMLsec [20]. Similar to our work, the approach integrates concepts from the field of information flow security to ensure confidentiality properties. Furthermore, the approach has been successfully integrated with security requirements engineering techniques [17,19]. Thereby, similar to our paper, UMLsec addresses a systematic transition from security requirements to a secure software design. IFlow [21] also supports the specification of information flow requirements in the scope of UML. To that end, the authors enable the specification of security policies that are conceptually similar to the flow policies used in this paper.

However, in summary, none of the above approaches is applicable to interdisciplinary models that are tailored to systems engineering. Instead, the approaches mainly focus on software engineering using UML. Thus, whereas information flow security has been frequently integrated into model-driven engineering, the transition from systems to software engineering is beyond the scope of the existing works.

Security in Model-Based Systems Engineering. Tropos is a model-based development methodology that has been extended to consider security requirements across the entire systems engineering process [28]. Due to its generality, the approach also enables engineers to specify and refine information flow restrictions. However, in contrast to our work, specific formal methods from the area of information flow security are no integral part of the methodology. ISSEP [33] is another systems engineering process that seamlessly integrates security practices. The authors use models as an interface to incorporate security solutions into the engineering process. However, compared to our work, information flow security is not among the incorporated solutions.

Another process that bridges security expertise and systems engineering is SEED [41]. Based on a separation between system and attack models, the authors enable risk analysis with respect to the confidentiality and integrity of data assets. Grunske and Joyce [15] propose another method for security risk analysis in SysML models. Similar to this paper, they take into account component-based architectures. However, whereas the authors of both these risk-centric works focus on quantitative security analysis, we take a more constructive approach by refining security policies along with the system specification.

SysML-Sec [3] is another approach that integrates security with model-based systems engineering based on SysML. The authors cover all phases of the engineering process. Thus, like our paper, they cover the transition from security requirements to the software design. To that end, SysML-Sec addresses a systematic refinement of software components along with the process. However, unlike our approach, information flow security and the refinement of corresponding information flow requirements are not considered.

Belloir et al. [5] support the elicitation of security requirements in model-based engineering of highly distributed systems of systems. The authors propose a process to translate such requirements into design models based on SysML. Thus, similar to our paper, they focus on the transition between requirements and design. SoSSec [16] is another method towards secure systems of systems. The authors provide a model-based description language for system architectures, and use simulative analysis to identify circumstances under which vulnerabilities might be exploited. In contrast to our work, none of the two approaches takes information flow requirements into account.

Lemaire et al. [22] analyze data flows in cyber-physical systems based on SysML. Thereby, similar to our paper, they seek to prevent violations of predefined security policies. However, unlike our work, the authors focus on hardware components as building blocks of systems. Thus, they do not provide a transition to the discipline of software engineering.

In summary, security has gained increased attention from the area of model-based systems engineering, especially in the context of SysML. However, existing approaches either provide security analyses based on full-fledged design models, or focus on the construction of specific security solutions. In contrast, none of the reviewed approaches takes the constructive refinement of information flow security policies into account, as we proposed in this paper.

5   Conclusions and Future Work

In this paper, we proposed a novel integration of model-based systems engineering and information flow security. We extended structural systems engineering models to flow policies. Thereby, we enabled the specification of security requirements in terms of non-authorized information flows that need to be prevented. On structural decomposition of these models, we described how the specified flow policies can be refined into more fine-grained security requirements. Finally, on the transition from systems engineering to software engineering, we demonstrated how to translate refined flow policies into security requirements for individual software components.

Our approach provides systems engineers with a specification technique for information flow security policies, allowing them to front-load the security of a system under development to an early development stage. Thereby, security requirements are made explicit, and are less likely to be deferred to an afterthought or even escalate into unrecognized zero-day vulnerabilities. In the downstream software engineering, our derivation of component security policies allows engineers to effectively derive verifiable security requirements that are amenable to verification using our previous work.

This work is part of our ongoing research on tracing information flow security in cyber-physical systems engineering [11]. In future work, we intend to extend our scope from information flows towards energy and material flows, enabling the detection of side-channel attacks. Furthermore, we are working on a compositional verification approach for security requirements at the level of component-based software architectures [12]. Thereby, we focus on the compositionality problem of information flow security [24]. Finally, whereas our work currently addresses the transition from security goals to a secure design, a seamless approach would need to take security threats into account as well [39]. Thus, in future work, we would like to enhance our approach with a *threat analysis* [38]. Thereby, we seek to enable engineers not only to specify security requirements, but also to identify these requirements systematically and thoroughly.

References

1. Alghathbar, K., Farkas, C., Wijesekera, D.: Securing UML information flow using FlowUML. J. Res. Pract. Inf. Technol. **38**(1), 111 (2006)
2. Alur, R., Dill, D.L.: A theory of timed automata. Theor. Comput. Sci. **126**(2), 183–235 (1994)
3. Apvrille, L., Roudier, Y.: Designing safe and secure embedded and cyber-physical systems with SysML-Sec. In: Desfray, P., Filipe, J., Hammoudi, S., Pires, L.F. (eds.) MODELSWARD 2015. CCIS, vol. 580, pp. 293–308. Springer, Cham (2015). https://doi.org/10.1007/978-3-319-27869-8_17
4. Bauereiß, et al.: RIFL 1.1: a common specification language for information-flow requirements. Technical report TUD-CS-2017-0225, TU Darmstadt (2017)
5. Belloir, N., Chiprianov, V., Ahmad, M., Munier, M., Gallon, L., Bruel, J.: Using relax operators into an MDE security requirement elicitation process for systems of systems. In: ECSA Workshops, pp. 32:1–32:4. ACM (2014)

6. Chattopadhyay, A., Prakash, A., Shafique, M.: Secure cyber-physical systems: Current trends, tools and open research problems. In: DATE 2017. pp. 1104–1109. IEEE (2017)
7. Dorociak, R., Dumitrescu, R., Gausemeier, J., Iwanek, P.: Specification technique CONSENS for the description of self-optimizing systems. In: Gausemeier, J., Rammig, F., Schäfer, W. (eds.) Design Methodology for Intelligent Technical Systems, chap. 4.1, pp. 119–127. LNME. Springer, Heidelberg (2014). https://doi.org/10.1007/978-3-642-45435-6_4
8. Fabian, B., Gürses, S.F., Heisel, M., Santen, T., Schmidt, H.: A comparison of security requirements engineering methods. Requir. Eng. 15(1), 7–40 (2010)
9. Gausemeier, J., Schäfer, W., Greenyer, J., Kahl, S., Pook, S., Rieke, J.: Management of cross-domain model consistency during the development of advanced mechatronic systems. In: ICED 2009, pp. 6:1–6:12. Design Society (2009)
10. Geismann, J., Gerking, C., Bodden, E.: Towards ensuring security by design in cyber-physical systems engineering processes. In: ICSSP 2018 (2018)
11. Gerking, C.: Traceability of information flow requirements in cyber-physical systems engineering. In: DS@MoDELS. CEUR Workshop Proceedings, vol. 1735 (2016)
12. Gerking, C., Schubert, D.: Towards preserving information flow security on architectural composition of cyber-physical systems. In: Cuesta, C.E., Garlan, D., Pérez, J. (eds.) ECSA 2018. LNCS, vol. 11048, pp. 147–155. Springer, Cham (2018). https://doi.org/10.1007/978-3-030-00761-4_10
13. Gerking, C., Schubert, D., Bodden, E.: Model checking the information flow security of real-time systems. In: Payer, M., Rashid, A., Such, J.M. (eds.) ESSoS 2018. LNCS, vol. 10953, pp. 27–43. Springer, Cham (2018). https://doi.org/10.1007/978-3-319-94496-8_3
14. Giraldo, J., Sarkar, E., Cárdenas, A., Maniatakos, M., Kantarcioglu, M.: Security and privacy in cyber-physical systems: a survey of surveys. IEEE Des. Test 34(4), 7–17 (2017)
15. Grunske, L., Joyce, D.: Quantitative risk-based security prediction for component-based systems with explicitly modeled attack profiles. J. Syst. Softw. 81(8), 1327–1345 (2008)
16. Hachem, J.E., Khalil, T.A., Chiprianov, V., Babar, A., Aniorté, P.: A model driven method to design and analyze secure architectures of systems-of-systems. In: ICECCS 2017, pp. 166–169. IEEE Computer Society (2017)
17. Hatebur, D., Heisel, M., Jürjens, J., Schmidt, H.: Systematic development of UMLsec design models based on security requirements. In: Giannakopoulou, D., Orejas, F. (eds.) FASE 2011. LNCS, vol. 6603, pp. 232–246. Springer, Heidelberg (2011). https://doi.org/10.1007/978-3-642-19811-3_17
18. Hoisl, B., Sobernig, S., Strembeck, M.: Modeling and enforcing secure object flows in process-driven SOAs: an integrated model-driven approach. Softw. Syst. Model. 13(2), 513–548 (2014)
19. Houmb, S.H., Islam, S., Knauss, E., Jürjens, J., Schneider, K.: Eliciting security requirements and tracing them to design: an integration of common criteria, heuristics, and UMLsec. Requir. Eng. 15(1), 63–93 (2010)
20. Jürjens, J.: Secure Systems Development with UML. Springer, Heidelberg (2005). https://doi.org/10.1007/b137706
21. Katkalov, K., Stenzel, K., Borek, M., Reif, W.: Modeling information flow properties with UML. In: NTMS 2015. IEEE (2015)

22. Lemaire, L., Vossaert, J., De Decker, B., Naessens, V.: Extending FAST-CPS for the analysis of data flows in cyber-physical systems. In: Rak, J., Bay, J., Kotenko, I., Popyack, L., Skormin, V., Szczypiorski, K. (eds.) MMM-ACNS 2017. LNCS, vol. 10446, pp. 37–49. Springer, Cham (2017). https://doi.org/10.1007/978-3-319-65127-9_4

23. Mantel, H.: Information flow control and applications — bridging a gap. In: Oliveira, J.N., Zave, P. (eds.) FME 2001. LNCS, vol. 2021, pp. 153–172. Springer, Heidelberg (2001). https://doi.org/10.1007/3-540-45251-6_9

24. Mantel, H.: On the composition of secure systems. In: S&P 2002, pp. 88–101. IEEE (2002)

25. Mantel, H.: Information flow and noninterference. In: van Tilborg, H.C.A., Jajodia, S. (eds.) Encyclopedia of Cryptography and Security, pp. 605–607. Springer, Heidelberg (2011)

26. Mellado, D., Blanco, C., Sanchez, L.E., Fernández-Medina, E.: A systematic review of security requirements engineering. Comput. Stand. Interfaces 32(4), 153–165 (2010)

27. Mohammed, N.M., Niazi, M., Alshayeb, M., Mahmood, S.: Exploring software security approaches in software development lifecycle: a systematic mapping study. Comput. Stand. Interfaces 50, 107–115 (2017)

28. Mouratidis, H., Giorgini, P., Manson, G.: Integrating security and systems engineering: towards the modelling of secure information systems. In: Eder, J., Missikoff, M. (eds.) CAiSE 2003. LNCS, vol. 2681, pp. 63–78. Springer, Heidelberg (2003). https://doi.org/10.1007/3-540-45017-3_7

29. Nguyen, P.H., Kramer, M.E., Klein, J., Traon, Y.L.: An extensive systematic review on the model-driven development of secure systems. Inf. Softw. Technol. 68, 62–81 (2015)

30. Object Management Group: OMG System Modeling Language, May 2017. https://www.omg.org/spec/SysML

31. Ouchani, S., Debbabi, M.: Specification, verification, and quantification of security in model-based systems. Computing 97(7), 691–711 (2015)

32. Ramos, A.L., Ferreira, J.V., Barceló, J.: Model-based systems engineering: an emerging approach for modern systems. IEEE Trans. Syst. Man Cybern. 42(1), 101–111 (2012)

33. Ruiz, J.F., Maña, A., Rudolph, C.: An integrated security and systems engineering process and modelling framework. Comput. J. 58(10), 2328–2350 (2015)

34. Salini, P., Kanmani, S.: Survey and analysis on security requirements engineering. Comput. Electr. Eng. 38(6), 1785–1797 (2012)

35. Seehusen, F., Solhaug, B., Stølen, K.: Adherence preserving refinement of traceset properties in STAIRS: exemplified for information flow properties and policies. Softw. Syst. Model. 8(1), 45–65 (2009)

36. Steward, C., et al.: Software security: The dangerous afterthought. In: ITNG 2012, pp. 815–818. IEEE Computer Society (2012)

37. Tøndel, I.A., Jaatun, M.G., Meland, P.H.: Security requirements for the rest of us: a survey. IEEE Softw. 25(1), 20–27 (2008)

38. Tuma, K., Calikli, G., Scandariato, R.: Threat analysis of software systems: a systematic literature review. J. Syst. Softw. 144, 275–294 (2018)

39. Türpe, S.: The trouble with security requirements. In: RE 2017, pp. 122–133. IEEE Computer Society (2017)

40. Uzunov, A.V., Fernández, E.B., Falkner, K.: Engineering security into distributed systems: a survey of methodologies. J. Univers. Comput. Sci. **18**(20), 2920–3006 (2012)
41. Vasilevskaya, M., Nadjm-Tehrani, S.: Quantifying risks to data assets using formal metrics in embedded system design. In: Koornneef, F., van Gulijk, C. (eds.) SAFE-COMP 2015. LNCS, vol. 9337, pp. 347–361. Springer, Cham (2015). https://doi.org/10.1007/978-3-319-24255-2_25

Towards Scenario-Based Security Requirements Engineering for Cyber-Physical Systems

Thorsten Koch[(✉)]

Software Engineering and IT Security, Fraunhofer IEM, Paderborn, Germany
thorsten.koch@iem.fraunhofer.de

Abstract. Cyber-physical systems are characterized among others by strong interconnection with each other, but also with their environment. This interconnection enables on the one hand new functionality with a high complexity and leads on the other hand to a high demand on the security of the systems. Both aspects require tailored development processes with a rigorous requirements engineering. However, current requirements engineering approaches focus either on the functional or on the security aspects but lack an integrated view on modeling and analysing both aspects. Therefore, we present in this paper ongoing research for a formal, model- and scenario-based requirements engineering approach for cyber-physical systems. Our approach enables the requirements engineer in an early stage of the development whether the modeled security requirements are sufficient to mitigate attacks and whether the security requirements influence the functional behavior. We illustrate the approach by means of an advanced driver assistance system from the automotive domain.

1 Introduction

Cyber-physical systems (CPS) [5] are characterized by complex functionality and a strong interconnection between each other and their environment. They exchange digital information to coordinate themselves and to perform complex tasks in a collaborative manner. Since most cyber-physical systems also interact with people in their environment, cyber-physical systems are highly safety-critical and require a rigorous requirements engineering (RE). Scenario-based RE formalisms like Modal Sequence Diagrams [12] enable an intuitive specification and the simulative validation of functional requirements on the behaviour of cyber-physical systems.

However, the interconnected nature of cyber-physical systems raises the possibility of cyber-attacks significantly and security has become a major quality attribute in the development. Thus, development processes and especially the requirements engineering need to address security requirements from the beginning in order to prevent vulnerabilities in the final system by design (e.g. by means of threat modeling) [2].

M. Mazzara et al. (Eds.): STAF 2018 Workshops, LNCS 11176, pp. 633–643, 2018.
https://doi.org/10.1007/978-3-030-04771-9_48

In secure software engineering, many approaches for the security requirements engineering exist. However, these approaches either lack in their modeling and analysis capabilities for functional and security requirements or they are not tailored to the characteristics of cyber-physical systems such as the discipline-spanning development [22] or the limited computing power of dedicated computing platforms [1].

Therefore, in this paper, we present ongoing research on the extension of our formal, model- and scenario-based requirements engineering approach based on Modal Sequence Diagrams (MSDs) with approaches from security engineering. Thereby, we conceive an RE approach for secure cyber-physical systems that covers the modeling of functional and security requirements in an integrated and intuitive manner. Furthermore, our RE approach enables the analysis of functional requirements, security requirements and their interplay. Thereby, the requirements engineer is able to determine in an early phase of the development, whether the modeled security requirements are sufficient to avoid the threats found in a threat analysis and whether the security requirements influence the functional behavior of the system in a negative way. In addition, we discuss the integration of our RE approach in the model-driven development process for secure cyber-physical systems proposed by Geismann et al [6]. The integration enables the automatic refinement of existing high-level information, e.g. from a threat model, and, thereby, reduces the manual effort of the requirements engineers for remodeling the information.

We illustrate our approach by means of an advanced driver assistance system taken from the automotive domain as depicted in Fig. 1. The purpose of the ADAS is to reduce the risk of rear-end collisions in case of appearing obstacles in front of a vehicle. Therefore, each vehicle is equipped with radar sensors to detect obstacles in front and a car-to-car communication systems to coordinate the reaction to dangerous situations with other vehicles. Besides the functional requirements on ADAS, there are further requirements concerning the security. For example, it should not be possible that an attacker is able to spoof a vehicle and cause the dangerous situations for the road users.

The remainder of the paper is as follows: The following section introduces related work. Section 3 presents the requirements engineering methodology for secure cyber-physical. Finally, Sect. 4 summarizes this paper and provides an outlook on future work.

2   Related Work

In secure software engineering, different stakeholder identify potential threats of the system and analyze their potential risk. If the stakeholders decide to mitigate a certain threat, they have to specify security requirements and mechanism. As in functional requirements engineering, use-case and scenarios help to elicit, document and analyze requirements. Hence, for secure software engineering, many approaches exist that specify misuse cases [19] or abuse cases [17] as negative scenarios to specify what is not allowed to happen during the execution of the

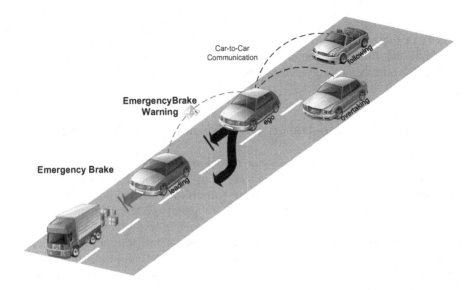

Fig. 1. Purpose of the advanced driver assistance system

system. Furthermore, there are several other approaches that worked on the elicitation and specification of security requirements, for example security use cases [3,4]; UMLsec [13,14], a framework for security requirements engineering [9]; SQUARE [16]; security requirements methods based on i* framework [15]; Secure Tropos [7].

However, all mentioned approaches mainly work on the elicitation and documentation of threats and security requirements only for software systems and do not cover characteristics of cyber-physical systems, for example security threats induced by the interplay of different engineering disciplines. Furthermore, they do not provide any integration into existing functional requirements engineering methodologies or development processes. In addition, they do not provide sufficient analysis techniques to validate & verify whether the specified security requirements are fulfilled and that a potential attacker is not able to execute the specified attack.

To overcome the issues with informal and non-analyzable misuse-cases, Whittle et al. [21] develop an approach to formalize by means of extended interaction overview diagrams (EIODs) and execute misuse-cases against scenario-specification. However, in contrast to our scenario-based RE approach, EIODs require a lot of meaningful pre- and post-conditions to be specified. Since these conditions are not fully available during the early design of a cyber-physical system, the approach of EIODs is not well suited for the development of a cyber-physical system.

To summarize this section, the scenario-based requirements engineering is well suited to support the textual requirements engineering of cyber-physical systems. However, the current challenges in the requirements engineering of interconnected cyber-physical system and the resulting requirements on the security of those systems is not covered by state of the art approaches. Hence, it is necessary to extend the existing approaches to conceive a systematic formal, model- and scenario-based requirements engineering methodology for secure cyber-physical system.

3   Secure Scenario-Based Requirements Engineering

In this section, we introduce our formal, model- and scenario-based requirements engineering methodology for cyber-physical systems. The RE methodology is based on previous work [12], in which we conceived a RE methodology for the functional behavior of cyber-physical systems based on Modal Sequence Diagrams. The main purpose of our new RE approach is to requirements engineer is able to determine in an early phase of the development, whether the modeled security requirements are sufficient to avoid the threats found in a threat analysis and whether the security requirements influence the functional behavior of the system in a negative way.

Therefore, we extend the functional RE methodology in three parts: First, we extend the modeling capabilities to enable the modeling of security properties within MSDs (cf. C1 in Fig. 2). Furthermore, we introduce attack-scenario as a formalization of misuse-case to model the behavior of a potential attacker. Second, we extend the analysis capabilities to validate whether security properties in MSDs influence the functional requirements in a negative way (cf. C2 in Fig. 2). In addition, we introduce an analysis to validate whether is able to finish an attack-scenario successfully on the designed system. If this is the case, the requirements engineer founds a vulnerability and has to add further security properties. Third, we provide the integration of our RE approach in the model-driven development process for secure cyber-physical systems proposed by Geismann et al [6] (cf. C3 in Fig. 2).

In the following sections, we introduce our methodology in further details. In Sect. 3.1 we introduce the integration of our approach in the model-driven development process for secure cyber-physical systems proposed by Geismann et al [6]. In Sect. 3.2, we introduce the modeling capabilities of our methodology. Finally, Sect. 3.3 describes the simulative validation of our specification.

3.1   Development Process for Secure CPS

The development of cyber-physical systems requires the symbiotic interaction of different engineering disciplines like mechanical engineering, electrical engineering, control and software engineering. This symbiotic interaction is called systems engineering and requires discipline spanning development processes. In [6], Geismann et al. stated that existing development processes for CPS (e.g. [18,20]) only focus on the functional but lack the security characteristics of the system under development. Hence, they presented ongoing research on the integration of secure software engineering practices into discipline-spanning engineering processes.

Figure 2 depicts an excerpt of the discipline-spanning engineering process. The development usually starts with the two-discipline spanning system-level phases *systems requirements analysis* and *systems architectural design*. Afterwards, the development continues in discipline-specific sub-processes for the involved engineering disciplines. For example, in the software engineering phases, the artifacts from the discipline-spanning phases are first refined to derive software requirements and then the software design and implementation are executed based on the derived software requirements. To keep the project time and costs under control, it is very important that artifacts of previous process phases are reused in a certain way to reduce manual and error-prone work for the specification of already known information.

Therefore, Holtmann et al. [11] developed a systematic transition from systems engineering models to model-based software requirements engineering. By automating several steps of this transition, they could avoid error-prone and time-consuming tasks.

In [6], Geismann et al. introduced concepts from secure software engineering for the specification of security characteristics throughout the development for cyber-physical systems. In the discipline-spanning development phases (*systems requirements analysis* and *systems architectural design*), they propose the integration of a threat analysis "'to support the identification of valuable assets and potential attack vectors of the system under development.'" We plan to extend the systematic transition of Holtmann et al. [11] to include the security relevant information. Thereby, we enable the automatic refinement of threats to attack-scenarios (cf. C3 in Fig. 2).

3.2   Functional Requirements

In this section, we introduce basic concepts for the modeling of functional requirements by means of Modal Sequence Diagrams as described in [12]. An MSD requirements specification consists of a UML class diagram and a set of MSDs. The UML class diagram is used to define the structure of the system under development and its environment. Furthermore, it specifies the possible messages each system can receive by operations of the defined classes.

Our running example consists of the two classes Vehicle and Environment depicted in Fig. 3. The Vehicle is the system under development and realizes the advanced driver assistance system as described in the following. The ADAS is supposed to reduce the risk of rear-end collisions in case of appearing obstacles in front of the vehicle.

The purpose of our running example is as depicted in Fig. 1. The vehicles are driving in a platoon with a constant velocity on a two-lane motorway. As mentioned in Sect. 1, each vehicle is equipped with radar sensors to detect obstacles in front and a car-to-car communication system. If an obstacle is detected in front of the vehicle, the advanced driver assistance system takes over control and communicates with the rear-end cars to negotiate a reaction of the situation.

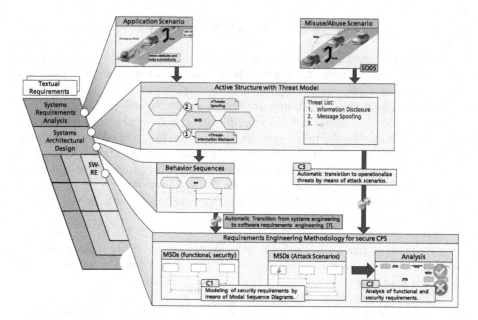

Fig. 2. Overview of our formal, model- and scenario based requirements engineering methodology for secure cyber-physical systems.

Therefore, the leading vehicle sends a warning message to the ego vehicle. After receiving the message, ego has to decide how to react. This situation is, on the one hand, based on its own distance to leading vehicle and whether it is possible to brake safely. On the other hand, the decision is based on the situation in the back.

The scenario of the advanced driver assistance system is specified in the MSDs in Fig. 4. An MSD basically consists of lifelines and messages. Lifelines refer to structural entities defined in a UML class diagram. The MSD depicted in Fig. 4 encompasses the three lifelines env:Environemnt and leading:Vehicle. Messages, depicted by arrows between lifelines, define requirements on the communication between objects. A concrete message exchange between two objects (send and receive) is called message event.

Messages have a temperature and an execution kind. The temperature of a message can be cold (c) or hot (h) visualized by blue and red arrows in Fig. 4. A cold message may be sent/received after any preceding and before any subsequent message of the same MSD, but it is not required to occur (e.g., obstaccle depicted in Fig. 4). If any other message of the same MSD occurs when a cold message is expected, the MSD is terminated/discarded (but the requirement is not violated). A hot message, on the contrary, has to strictly occur in the order as specified in the MSD (e.g., emcyBrakeWarning depicted in Fig. 4). If any other message of the same MSD occurs when the hot message is expected, the MSD is violated (i.e., the requirement is not fulfilled). The execution kind of a message

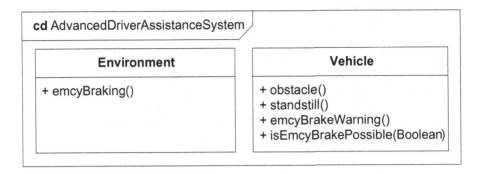

Fig. 3. System context of the advanced driver assistance system.

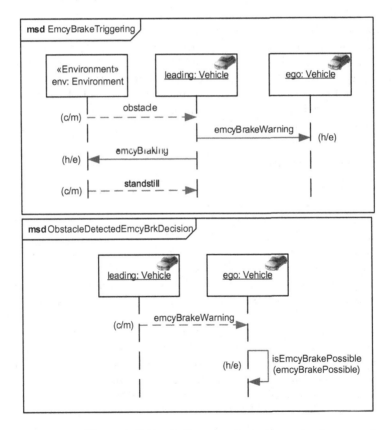

Fig. 4. Exemplary MSDs specifying the functional requirements of our running example. (Color figure online)

can either be executed (e) or monitored (m) depicted by solid and dashed arrows in Fig. 4, respectively. A monitored message can be observed during the execution of the MSD but its occurrence is not required. An executed message, on the contrary, is required to occur during the execution of an MSD. If it is not sent/received, the MSD is violated.

Furthermore, MSDs can contain assignments and conditions. Graphically, assignments are represented by rectangular boxes that cover one or multiple lifelines and contain a textual expression in the form <var> = <expr> where <var> is a variable name and <expr> is an OCL expression. The variable <var> can be any variable of an object bound to one of the lifelines covered by the assignment. Conditions enable requirements engineers to specify that an MSD may only advance under certain conditions specified by a Boolean formula. Graphically, conditions are depicted by convex hexagons with parallel opposing edges. The MSD may only advance past the condition if it is fulfilled. If the Boolean formula of a cold condition evaluates to false, the MSD is terminated/discarded. On the contrary, if the Boolean formula of a hot condition evaluates to false, the MSD only advances if the formula evaluates to true. However, if the Boolean formula can never be fulfilled the MSD is violated.

The consistency and correctness of the MSD specification is validated by means of the play-out algorithm [10]. The play-out algorithms is able to simulate selected paths of the overall state space to validate the requirements. Furthermore, it is possible to check for the consistency of the overall MSD specification by synthesizing a global controller implementing the requirements. If it is possible to synthesize such a controller, the MSD specification is consistent [8].

3.3   Security Requirements

In this section, we introduce our ongoing research on modeling and analysis security requirements by means of MSDs- In the current stage of our work, the modeling of security requirements encompasses two extensions. First, we enable the requirements engineer to express security properties of messages as depicted in Fig. 5. Therefore, we introduce new stereotypes in the Modal profile to specify that a message is signed (e.g. emcyBrakeWarning in Fig. 5), encrypted or both. Furthermore, we use conditions to model the validation of the security properties. For example, the condition "isSignatureValid?" checks whether the previous received message is correctly signed. If it is not correctly signed, the condition evaluates to false and a cold violation occurs.

Second, we introduce a new kind of scenarios so-called attack scenario for the specification of actions an attacker can perform. We assume that the attacker is part of the environment of the system under development and that the system has to operate correctly under the assumed behavior of the attacker. Therefore, an attack-scenario is a special kind of environment assumptions. In general, the attack scenario formalizes the idea of misuse-cases as proposed by Sindre and Opdahl [19] to enable the automatic validation of the specification.

In the future, we plan to extend the modeling capabilities to enable the specification of different attack models describing the capabilities and knowledge

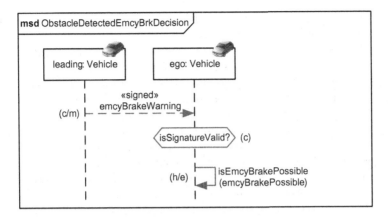

Fig. 5. Exemplary MSDs specifying the security requirements of our running example.

of the attack. Furthermore, we have to investigate on the modeling of different cryptographic keys and their management.

As described in Sect. 2, most approaches for secure requirements engineering lack in supporting analysis techniques to validate & verify whether the specified security requirements are fulfilled and that a potential attacker is not able to execute the specified misuse cases. Hence, we enhance the play-out algorithm to support the extensions to the Modal profile, especially the "attack scenario". Thereby, the software requirements engineer is able to analyze in an iterative process whether the software requirements are vulnerable to the "attack scenarios" and whether the "attack scenario" are able to prevent the potential attacks. The integrated analysis of functional and security requirements enables the software requirements engineer to detect conflicts between functional and security requirements.

4   Conclusion and Future Work

The development of highly interconnected cyber-physical systems, like advanced driver assistance systems from the automotive domain, requires development processes that cover the interdisciplinary nature of these systems and the emergent need of safety and security. Especially, in the requirements engineering phase, it is important to consider functional and security requirements as well as their mutual influence. For example, it is not sufficient to use always the strongest cryptographic algorithms since cyber-physical systems are built upon embedded devices with limited computing power. Hence, it might be possible that the embedded device is not able to handle the encryption of all messages; instead, the engineers have to decide which messages must be encrypted. While existing requirements engineering approaches either focus on functional or on security requirements, we presented in this paper ongoing research for conceiving a formal, model- and scenario-based requirements engineering methodology for secure cyber-physical systems integrated in the model-driven development process proposed by Geismann et al. [6].

In our approach, we extend previous work to enable the modeling and analysis of security requirements by means of Modal Sequence Diagrams. Therefore, we enable the specification of security properties for messages (e.g. signature and encryption) and the specification of attack-scenarios describing potential actions an attacker is able to perform. However, in the current stage of our work, there is no possibility to specify which keys are used in the system and its environment to sign and encrypt message or to further describe the capabilities of an attacker (e.g. knowledge of keys). In addition, we showed how the new modeling capabilities could be simulative validated by means of the Play-Out algorithm. Thereby, the requirements engineer is able to determine in an early stage of the development whether the functional behavior of the system successfully mitigates the specified attacks and whether the security properties influence in a negative way. Finally, we described the integration of our approach in a model-driven development process. The integration enables the refinement of development artefacts on a higher abstraction-level by means of (semi-) automatic model-transformations. This reduces manual effort of the requirements engineer.

In future work, we plan to develop the open parts of our requirements engineering methodology as well as extending the existing tool-suite SCENARIOTOOLS to fully support the new concepts. After completing the implementation of our tool-suite, we plan to empirically evaluate our work and its benefits in terms security.

References

1. Basin, D., Doser, J., Lodderstedt, T.: Model driven security: from UML models to access control infrastructures. ACM Trans. Softw. Eng. Methodol. **15**, 39–91 (2006)
2. Chattopadhyay, A., Prakash, A., Shafique, M.: Secure cyber-physical systems: current trends, tools and open research problems. In: Design, Automation Test in Europe Conference Exhibition (DATE), pp. 1104–1109, March 2017
3. Firesmith, D.: Security use cases. J. Object Technol. **2**(3), 53 (2003). http://www.jot.fm/issues/issue_2003_05/column6.pdf
4. Firesmith, D.G.: Engineering safety and security related requirements for software intensive systems. In: 29th International Conference on Software Engineering, p. 169. IEEE Computer Society, Los Alamitos (2007)
5. Fitzgerald, J., Larsen, P.G., Verhoef, M.: From embedded to cyber-physical systems: challenges and future directions. In: Fitzgerald, J., Larsen, P.G., Verhoef, M. (eds.) Collaborative Design for Embedded Systems, pp. 293–303. Springer, Heidelberg (2014). https://doi.org/10.1007/978-3-642-54118-6_14
6. Geismann, J., Gerking, C., Bodden, E.: Towards ensuring security by design in cyber-physical systems engineering processes. In: International Conference on Software and System Processes (ICSSP), 26–27 May 2018
7. Giorgini, P., Mouratidis, H., Zannone, N.: Modelling security and trust with secure tropos. In: Integrating Security and Software Engineering: Advances and Future Vision, pp. 160–189 (2006)

8. Greenyer, J.: Scenario-based Design of Mechatronic Systems. Ph.D. thesis, University of Paderborn (2011). http://dups.ub.uni-paderborn.de/hs/urn/urn:nbn:de:hbz:466:2--7690

9. Haley, C.B., Laney, R., Moffett, J.D., Nuseibeh, B.: Security requirements engineering: a framework for representation and analysis. IEEE Trans. Softw. Eng. **34**(1), 133–153 (2008)

10. Harel, D., Marelly, R.: Come, Let's Play: Scenario-Based Programming Using LSC's and the Play-Engine. Springer, New York (2003). https://doi.org/10.1007/978-3-642-19029-2

11. Holtmann, J., Bernijazov, R., Meyer, M., Schmelter, D., Tschirner, C.: Integrated and iterative systems engineering and software requirements engineering for technical systems. J. Softw. Evol. Process. **28**(9), 722–743 (2016)

12. Holtmann, J., Fockel, M., Koch, T., Schmelter, D., Brenner, C., Bernijazov, R., Sander, M.: The MechatronicUML requirements engineering method: process and language (2016)

13. Jürjens, J.: UMLsec: extending UML for secure systems development. In: Jézéquel, J.-M., Hussmann, H., Cook, S. (eds.) UML 2002. LNCS, vol. 2460, pp. 412–425. Springer, Heidelberg (2002). https://doi.org/10.1007/3-540-45800-X_32

14. Jürjens, J.: Secure Systems Development with UML. Springer, Heidelberg (2005). https://doi.org/10.1007/b137706

15. Liu, L., Yu, E., Mylopoulos, J.: Security and privacy requirements analysis within a social setting. In: Proceedings of the 11th IEEE International Requirements Engineering Conference, 2003, pp. 151–161 (2003). https://doi.org/10.1109/ICRE.2003.1232746

16. Mead, N.R., Stehney, T.: Security quality requirements engineering (SQUARE) methodology (2005)

17. Pauli, J.J., Xu, D.: Misuse case-based design and analysis of secure software architecture. In: ITCC 2005, vol. 2, pp. 398–403. IEEE Computer Society, Los Alamitos (2003)

18. Ramos, A.L., Ferreira, J.V., Barceló, J.: Model-based systems engineering: an emerging approach for modern systems. IEEE Trans. Syst. Man Cybern. Part C (Appl. Rev.) **42**(1), 101–111 (2012)

19. Sindre, G., Opdahl, A.L.: Eliciting security requirements with misuse cases. Requir. Eng. **10**(1), 34–44 (2005)

20. VDI: Design methodology for mechatronic systems (VDI 2206)

21. Whittle, J., Wijesekera, D., Hartong, M.: Executable misuse cases for modeling security concerns. In: Schäfer, W. (ed.) Proceedings of the 30th International Conference on Software Engineering, p. 121. ACM Press, New York (2008)

22. Win, B.D., Scandariato, R., Buyens, K., Grégoire, J., Joosen, W.: On the secure software development process: CLASP, SDL and touchpoints compared. Inf. Softw. Technol. **51**(7), 1152–1171 (2009). http://www.sciencedirect.com/science/article/pii/S0950584908000281. Special Section: Software Engineering for Secure Systems

Towards Model-Based Communication Control for the Internet of Things

Imad Berrouyne[1(✉)], Mehdi Adda[2], Jean-Marie Mottu[1], Jean-Claude Royer[1], and Massimo Tisi[1]

[1] Naomod Team, IMT Atlantique, LS2N, Nantes, France
{imad.berrouyne,jean-marie.mottu,jean-claude.royer,massimo.tisi}@ls2n.fr
[2] Mathematics, Computer Science and Engineering Department,
University of Quebec At Rimouski, Rimouski, QC G5L 3A1, Canada
mehdi.adda@uqar.ca

Abstract. Most of existing Model-Driven Engineering (MDE) approaches for the Internet of Things (IoT) focus on means of modeling the behavior of end devices. Little attention has been paid to network-related abstractions and communication control. The paper introduces an approach towards enabling model-based communication control in a network of things. First, we suggest a Domain Specific Language (DSL) to abstract basic network features. Second, we propose a policy language to control the communications within the network. Finally, as a proof-of-concept, we present a code generation process to enforce the expressed policy at runtime.

Keywords: Internet of Things · Model-Driven Engineering
Networking · Publish/subscribe · Communication control

1 Introduction

The IoT is reshaping our society's relationship with information and technology. Gartner reports that more than 8 billion connected devices are in use, and forecasts that this number will grow to 20.4 billion by 2020 [9]. Communication is the backbone of the IoT, which consists of connecting various computational platforms ranging from tiny and resource-constrained sensors and actuators to smartphones and computers.

In the light of recent large-scale network attacks such as Mirai and Persirai [13,25,27] targeting numerous devices, the need of new security approaches with respect to communication has resurfaced. As a matter of fact, existing engineering models for the IoT have shown their limits w.r.t security [23]. Indeed, according to the SANS Institute, almost 90% of security professionals affirm that changes to security controls are required when it comes to the IoT [20].

Most of these approaches are rather time-consuming and require learning platform specificity in detail as well as expertise in order to build efficient and

© Springer Nature Switzerland AG 2018
M. Mazzara et al. (Eds.): STAF 2018 Workshops, LNCS 11176, pp. 644–655, 2018.
https://doi.org/10.1007/978-3-030-04771-9_49

secure IoT applications. Because of these difficulties, buggy and insecure IoT applications may easily be delivered [23].

MDE is an emerging and promising paradigm having the potential to overcome such issues (e.g., platforms heterogeneity, inconsistent security specification). All the more so that recently MDE has successfully been applied to adaptive and distributed systems, by the model@runtime approach [3] as well as in model-driven security [2,16]. MDE can help in designing correct communications and secure systems by abstracting network and security features. Then, by means of code generation tools, guarantee that properties are enforced at runtime. Furthermore, it also allows for reasoning formally on models for various purposes such as security analysis and threat assessment [17], to name just a few. However, although the ongoing work on abstracting device heterogeneity is rather significant [8,11], modeling then enforcing security policies in the IoT is understudied.

This paper represents a first step towards a MDE approach focusing on communication control in a network of distributed things. Our approach relies on the abstract description of the network configuration and its access control policy as well as a code generation process for enforcement at runtime.

The paper is structured as follows. Section 2 presents a running example of IoT system. Section 3 gives an overview of the existing works. Section 4 provides our concrete solution based on a DSL and a code generation procedure. Finally, Sect. 5 presents the conclusion and future work.

2   Running Case

Figure 1 depicts an overall view of a small running case, including the used material as well as the possible interactions. We consider two rooms, each one containing the following things: a Temperature Sensor (TS) and a Smart Air Conditioner (SAC). A user monitors the temperature in both rooms, using a mobile interface. From a technical perspective, we use Arduino boards for the sensors and actuators in the network.

As customary in IoT, communication between things is ensured by a Publish and Subscribe (PubSub) channel. A thing publishes its data to a topic, then another thing can consume this data by subscribing to this topic. On the one hand, the TSs collect the current temperature in the room and publish it to a given topic in the broker. On the other hand, each SAC subscribes to the temperature measurements of the room it is located in, in order to decide how to behave. The monitor receives data from all devices and shows it on its screen and commands remotely the SACs. Concretely, Message Queuing Telemetry Transport (MQTT) is used as a PubSub communication channel and Mosquitto [14] as a PubSub broker. MQTT is a popular communication protocol [15] to build applications where things need to collaborate towards a common goal.

Figure 2 depicts the internal behavior of the Ts and SAC using statecharts. In particular, the TS statechart's state SendTemperature executes the action

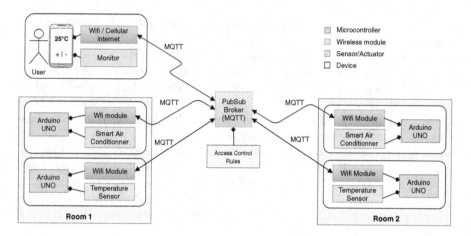

Fig. 1. Overview of the running case

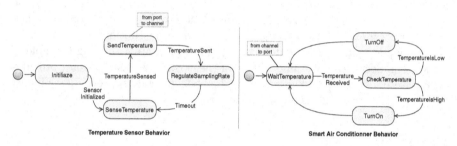

Fig. 2. Behavior of things in the running case

of sending measurements through a channel. On the other side, the SAC state-chart's state WaitTemperature waits for the temperature measurements from the channel to adjust its behavior.

State-of-art MDE tools for IoT allow developers to define such statecharts and generate code from them. In particular, ThingML [11] is a DSL used to model the things behavior as communicating event-based statecharts, typically encapsulating platform-specific code (e.g., C code on Arduino).

To ensure secure interactions among things we need to control the communications using a network policy. A policy is a flexible means to secure a network, through various control points. Controls can be enforced in the channel or directly in the devices. In particular, things cannot communicate between each other unless they are authorized to do so. For example, we have to ensure that the SAC from room 1 can only access the temperature data of room 1, and is denied access to data of room 2. Moreover, to avoid an unexpected behavior in the SAC, we use the policy to allow for communication between the SAC and the sensors only when the temperature is within a given range. For example the SAC can receive temperature measurements only when it is between −20 °C and 50 °C.

Existing MDE approaches like ThingML do not include a model of the network, thus hampering global reasoning on the network behavior, and lack mechanisms to model and enforce security measures.

3   Related Work

ThingML [11] proposes a methodology for the IoT using established MDE techniques [19]. The language has shown its efficiency at abstracting hardware and programming languages [18,26]. The approach provides a DSL to design the things' internal behavior using statecharts and an extensible multi-platform code generation framework. The latter also provides a plug-in system to add a network client to things. However, abstractions w.r.t communication are rather minimal in the DSL, simply consisting in declaring the used protocol and its attributes. In other words, the proposed language does not offer abstractions capturing network aspects such the communication channel that can be used between things. Our approach aims at studying these communication abstractions.

Eclipse Vorto [8] provides a solution to abstract the device capabilities into functions. A function consists of a set of attributes and a set of operations using the attributes. The functions are grouped inside a model to describe the behavior of the device. Code generators for various platforms permit to produce code from this model. The solution also offers a repository to share and reuse models and code generators. Compared to ThingML, modeling the device behavior is limited, only few operations are achievable. Communication is not modeled.

SensIDL [22] provides a MDE approach to tackle the data format heterogeneity among IoT devices. Indeed, a developer describes a platform-agnostic representation of the data generated by devices. Then, a multi-platform code generator produces the communication interfaces as well as the mechanisms to encode and decode this data on every device. Abstraction w.r.t to the network as well as security are not covered. In addition, contrary to ThingML, modeling of the device behavior is not included in the process.

Most of the existing MDE approaches that address network-related modeling, target Wireless Sensor and Actuators Networks (WSAN). For instance in [7], the authors map the Specification and Description Language (SDL) with TinyOS component models to enable a formal description of communication protocols. Then, a general scheme for creating code from these models is proposed.

From a model-driven security perspective, Basin et al. [2] present a comprehensive overview of model-driven security approaches. The considered works allow for modeling security requirements along with the system design, and generate security mechanisms at runtime. The authors show, using a concrete example, how a security policy is transformed by a code generation tool to control the behavior of a Graphical User Interface (GUI) at runtime. However, distributed systems such as the IoT and platform heterogeneity are not considered.

In [17], Mavropoulos et al. suggest a metamodel to describe IoT systems along with their security aspects. In this respect, a DSL is used to abstract hardware, software, social and security concepts. The approach is not meant for code generation, but rather for security analysis and visualization.

The OASIS consortium provides a framework to express and enforce communication policies. It defines a language called eXtensible Access Control Markup Language (XACML) to express an Access Control (AC) policy in Extensible Markup Language (XML) format [4]. It relies on a request-response model, AC decisions are taken dynamically. It also defines the mechanisms to process this policy. The security framework needs systematically a centralized Policy Decision Point (PDP) to evaluate access requests vis-a-vis the policy, while we are interested in distributing the enforcement of the security policy.

Martínez et al. [16] propose an approach to obtain a Platform-Independent Model (PIM) of the global AC policy in a network. The approach uses the firewalls configuration files in the system to extract all AC rules. Those rules are transformed into PIMs for each firewall then merged into a global AC model. A XACML policy can be easily generated from this model. We plan to provide an integrated modeling language for the IoT, including device behavior and network structure, and a policy language on top of those.

Alshehri et al. [1] introduce an approach to control communication between things using their virtual representation in the cloud. The approach separates the operational part from the administrative one. Existing AC models (e.g, Attribute-Based Access Control (ABAC), Role-Based Access Control (RBAC), Access Control List (ACL)) are used, when possible, in both parts to express the policy. The approach covers only controls on topics and does not allow modeling a network of things along with its policy.

Fadhel et al. [10] presents a comprehensive taxonomy of the RBAC concepts existing in the literature. The authors also provide a generalized RBAC framework encompassing all these concepts. In our approach, we cover few of them such as role assignment. Other concepts introduced in their paper will be subject to future work.

4   Approach

Our objective is providing a model-based methodology to control communications in a network of heterogeneous, distributed and connected devices. In this paper we design the main components of this methodology: a DSL to model IoT networks (Sect. 4.1), a policy language to control the network communications (Sect. 4.2), and a code generation process to enforce the expressed policy at various points of the architecture (Sect. 4.3). Our proposal is built on top of ThingML, from which we reuse the models of the thing behavior and the multi-platform code generator. The language development is open, and source code can be accessed online[1].

Throughout the paper, we use the running case to illustrate different facets of the methodology. For the sake of simplicity, we use a basic authentication mechanism, identifying things by a username and a password. Moreover, considerations on trust are beyond the scope of the paper.

---

[1] https://github.com/atlanmod/CyprIoT.

4.1   DSL for Network Modeling

To express the features of the network we define a textual language whose meta-model is depicted in Fig. 3. The latter shows the concepts introduced in this paper (Dark gray classes) and brings to light the reused concepts of ThingML (White classes). We use Xtext[2] to define the grammar of the concrete textual syntax.

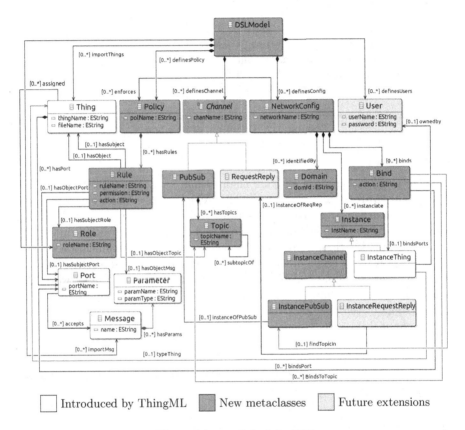

Introduced by ThingML   New metaclasses   Future extensions

Fig. 3. Metamodel of the DSL

A thing's internal behavior is described by importing a ThingML model. Listing 1.1 depicts the declaration of the things in the example. For instance, **import** Temperature ''temperature.thingml'' imports the model (i.e., statechart) of the TS.

Network communication is abstracted by a concept of **channel**. The current language supports only one type of channels, **channel : pubsub**. We plan to include other types of channel, such as request-reply (e.g., HTTP, CoAP). As it

___
[2] https://www.eclipse.org/Xtext/.

```
1  import Temperature "temperature.thingml" assigned sensor // assigned role
      sensor
2  import AirConditionner "airconditionner.thingml" assigned actuator
3  import Monitor "monitor.thingml" assigned actuator
```

Listing 1.1. Import of ThingML files

```
1  channel:pubsub MQTTChannel {
2      topic room1 // One topic per room
3      topic room2
4      topic temperatureData1 subtopicOf room1
5      topic commands1 subtopicOf room1
6      topic temperatureData2 subtopicOf room2
7      topic commands2 subtopicOf room2
8  }
```

Listing 1.2. Definition of channels

can be seen in Listing 1.2, a PubSub channel may contain multiple topics. The keyword **subtopicOf** provides a basic hierarchical structure for the topics.

The **networkConfig** section describes the global network topology. For instance, it defines which instances of things and channels are available in the network, then it binds a things' ports to channels to create a communication scheme. Listing 1.3 provides a configuration of the running case. A **networkConfig** has a **domain**, that is unique and serves as a global identifier for the network [21]. For instance, in our running case we use the domain in the topic structure as the root topic of the channel. A **bind** declaration connects a thing's port to a PubSub channel, by subscribing or publishing to its topics.

A **networkConfig** can also enforce a policy in the network. Multiple policies can be enforced. For instance, in Listing 1.3, both **roleBasedPolicy** as well as **attributeBasedPolicy** are enforced. Control strategies are discussed further in the next section.

4.2 Policy Language

A policy contains a set of rules. We define a rule as the composition of a subject (Thing, InstanceThing, Port or Role), a permission (allow or deny), an action (send or receive) and an object (Thing, InstanceThing, Port, Message or Topic). At this stage we only cover few mechanisms of the RBAC [5] and ABAC [12] models. You can find examples of the policy language in Listings 1.4 and 1.5.

As an illustration we apply these control strategies in our running case. The main goal is to avoid any unexpected behavior from the network.

RBAC. This is a coarse-grained strategy consisting of defining roles then assigning them to things. All the permissions given to a role will be applied to all things

```
 1  networkConfig smarthomeConfiguration {
 2      domain "fr.naomod.smarthome"
 3      enforce roleBasedPolicy, attributeBasedPolicy
 4      ....// Instances declaration
 5      bind instanceTS1.temperaturePort => MQTTChannel{temperatureData1}
 6      bind instanceTS2.temperaturePort => MQTTChannel{temperatureData2}
 7      bind instanceSAC1.temperaturePort <= MQTTChannel{temperatureData1}
 8      bind instanceSAC2.temperaturePort <= MQTTChannel{temperatureData2}
 9      bind instanceSAC1.commandsPort <= MQTTChannel{commands1}
10      bind instanceSAC2.commandsPort2 <= MQTTChannel{commands2}
11      bind instanceMonitor.temperaturePort <= MQTTChannel{temperatureData1,
            temperatureData2}
12      bind instanceMonitor.commandsPort => MQTTChannel{commands1}
13      bind instanceMonitor.commandsPort2 => MQTTChannel{commands2}
14  }
```

Listing 1.3. Network configuration (=> publish, <= subscribe)

with that role. This allows to decouple permissions from the concrete development of things.

In our running case we define two roles: one for sensors and one for actuators. The first role gives only send permission to all topics while the second one gives only receive permission from all topics. We assign the sensor role to the TS, the actuator role to the SAC, and both roles to the monitor as it needs to receive the temperature and to send commands. Listing 1.4 shows how this is defined.

ABAC. A more fine-grained strategy consists on dynamically deciding to allow the communication, based on contextual attributes. As a proof-of-concept we provide basic ABAC mechanisms.

For instance, in Listing 1.5, the rule in line 2 allows communication based on the source and destination ports (Temperature.temperaturePort and Monitor.temperaturePort). Lines 4–5 specify that only temperature messages whose value is in a certain range, can be communicated. Being able to decide based on the content of the communication, provides a fine granularity for access control.

```
 1  policy roleBasedPolicy {
 2      rule role:sensor allow:send topic:room1,room2
 3      rule role:actuator allow:receive topic:room1,room2
 4  }
```

Listing 1.4. Role-Based policy

```
1   policy attributeBasedPolicy {
2       rule Temperature.temperaturePort allow:send port:Monitor.temperaturePort
3       rule Temperature.temperaturePort allow:send thing:AirConditionner
4       rule Monitor allow:receive message:temperatureMessage.currentTemperature
            < 50 and temperatureMessage.currentTemperature > −20
5       rule Temperature allow:send message:temperatureMessage.
            currentTemperature < 100
6   }
```

Listing 1.5. Attribute-Based policy

4.3   Code Generation Process

Our code generation process is depicted in Fig. 4. The code generator takes as input a file containing the **networkConfig**. It performs two main functions: first it transforms ThingML models to bind them with specific network channels, second it enforces the policy at various enforcement points.

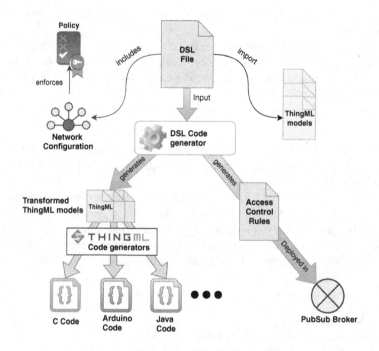

Fig. 4. Code generation procedure

As depicted in Fig. 5, controls are enforced at various points of the network architecture: (1) in the broker, by controlling the access to topics, or (2) in the thing by changing its internal behavior in the model.

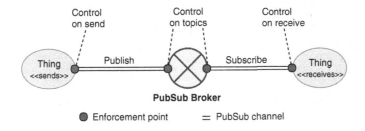

Fig. 5. Enforcement points

```
1  if (currentTemperature<100) { // Added control
2      temperaturePort!temperatureMessage(currentTemperature)
3  }
```

Listing 1.6. Control on send in ThingML

For our previous RBAC example, controls are applied only in the broker. In particular, our current generator is able to produce Access Control Rules (ACR) for the Mosquitto, specifying which MQTT topics can be accessed by each thing.

Content-based policies, like in Lines 4–5 of Listing 1.5, cannot usually be implemented in the broker because, for performance reasons, only few brokers provide content-based PubSub [24]. In this case, the control will be performed in the things rather than the broker, during the operations of send and receive. Distributed content-based PubSub has also the advantage to be more scalable and flexible. It avoids the "single point of failure" risk associated with control on the broker. This also contributes to a better security by design [6] as well as to reduce the attack surface of the thing.

In our language we can decide to control communication on the send or receive. As shown in Fig. 2, the TS sends its data in the SendTemperature state. To implement the rule in Line 5 of Listing 1.5 the generator adds an **if** condition before performing the send in the SendTemperature state, as shown in Listing 1.6. Temperature measurement is sent only when it is lower than 100. Likewise, Fig. 2 also shows that the SAC can receive this data at the WaitTemperature state. To control the temperature received by the SAC according to the rule in Line 4 of Listing 1.5, the generator adds a guard to the incoming event, as shown in Listing 1.7. Temperature is accepted only when it is between −20 and 50.

Controlling communication on receive requires checking whether the message satisfies the control conditions before reception. The message can still be intercepted, and demands superfluous processing for a message, that probably will not be used. When communication is controlled on send, the message remains until it satisfies the control conditions, this is more secure as the thing keep control over the message. However a malicious developer could easily remove a control on send, with the objective of controlling another connected device.

```
1  internal event receivedTemperature : temperaturePort?temperatureMessage
2  guard receivedTemperature.currentTemperature < 50
3      and receivedTemperature.currentTemperature > −20 // Added control
4  action do
5  ... // Actions
6  end
```

Listing 1.7. Control on receive in ThingML

5   Conclusion

We extended the current work on MDE for the IoT with a model-based communication control approach. In this respect, we proposed a DSL to tackle the lack of network modeling.

Network-related abstractions are proposed. The study focuses on PubSub communication channels and permit to model a network of things. Communication control is achieved using rule-based policies. The policy language permits to describe basic concepts of established security models such RBAC and ABAC.

A code generation process enforces the policy at various points of the network architecture. In this respect, AC rules are generated to be deployed in the broker and things' internal behavior may be modified.

In future work, we will enrich this first approach with more network-related abstractions. Then, we will formalize the model transformations of ThingML models using the AtlanMod Transformation Language (ATL). Finally, we plan to improve the security mechanisms already in place with smarter controls distribution throughout the enforcement points.

References

1. Alshehri, A., Sandhu, R.: Access control models for virtual object communication in cloud-enabled IoT. In: 2017 IEEE International Conference on Information Reuse and Integration (IRI), pp. 16–25. IEEE (2017)
2. Basin, D., Clavel, M., Egea, M.: A decade of model-driven security, pp. 1–10(2011)
3. Blair, G., Bencomo, N., France, R.B.: Models@ run. time. Computer, **42**(10) (2009)
4. OASIS XACML Technical Committee, et al.: Extensible access control markup language (XACML) version 3.0. Oasis standard, OASIS (2013)
5. Cugini, J., Kuhn, R., Ferraiolo, D.: Role-based access control: features and motivations (1995)
6. Davis, N., Humphrey, W., Redwine, S.T., Zibulski, G., McGraw, G.: Processes for producing secure software. IEEE Security & Privacy (2004)
7. Dietterle, D., Ryman, J., Dombrowski, K., Kraemer, R.: Mapping of high-level SDL models to efficient implementations for TinyOS. In: Euromicro Symposium on Digital System Design 2004, DSD 2004, pp. 402–406. IEEE (2004)
8. Eclipse: Eclipse Vorto - IoT Toolset for standardized device descriptions

9. UK Egham: Gartner says 8.4 billion connected "things" will be in use in 2017, up 31 percent from 2016. Gartner Inc. 7 (2017)

10. Fadhel, A.B., Bianculli, D., Briand, L.: A comprehensive modeling framework for role-based access control policies. J. Syst. Softw. **107**, 110–126 (2015)

11. Harrand, N., Fleurey, F., Morin, B., Husa, K.E.: Thingml: a language and code generation framework for heterogeneous targets. In: Proceedings of the ACM/IEEE 19th International Conference on Model Driven Engineering Languages and Systems, pp. 125–135 (2016)

12. Hu, V.C., Richard Kuhn, D., Ferraiolo, D.F.: Attribute-based access control. Computer **48**(2), 85–88 (2015)

13. Kolias, C., Kambourakis, G., Stavrou, A., Voas, J.: DDoS in the IoT: Mirai and other botnets. Computer **50**(7), 80–84 (2017)

14. Light, R.A.: Mosquitto: server and client implementation of the MQTT protocol. J. Open Source Softw. **2**(13) (2017)

15. Luzuriaga, J.E., Cano, J.C., Calafate, C., Manzoni, P., Perez, M., Boronat, P.: Handling mobility in IoT applications using the MQTT protocol. In: Internet Technologies and Applications (ITA), 2015. IEEE (2015)

16. Martínez, S., Garcia-Alfaro, J., Cuppens, F., Cuppens-Boulahia, N., Cabot, J.: Model-driven extraction and analysis of network security policies. In: Moreira, A., Schätz, B., Gray, J., Vallecillo, A., Clarke, P. (eds.) MODELS 2013. LNCS, vol. 8107, pp. 52–68. Springer, Heidelberg (2013). https://doi.org/10.1007/978-3-642-41533-3_4

17. Mavropoulos, O., Mouratidis, H., Fish, A., Panaousis, E.: Asto: a tool for security analysis of IoT systems. In: 2017 IEEE 15th International Conference on Software Engineering Research, Management and Applications (SERA), pp. 395–400. IEEE (2017)

18. Morin, B., Harrand, N., Fleurey, F.: Model-based software engineering to tame the IoT jungle. IEEE Softw. **34**(1), 30–36 (2017)

19. Mukerji, J., Miller, J.: MDA Guide. Object Management Group (2003)

20. Pescatore, J., Shpantzer, G.: Securing the internet of things survey. SANS Institute, pp. 1–22 (2014)

21. Pesonen, L.I.W., Eyers, D.M., Bacon, J.: Access control in decentralised publish/-subscribe systems. JNW **2**(2), 57–67 (2007)

22. Rathfelder, C., Taspolatoglu, E.: SensIDL: towards a generic framework for implementing sensor communication interfaces (2015)

23. Seralathan, Y., et al.: Iot security vulnerability: a case study of a web camera. In: 2018 20th International Conference on Advanced Communication Technology (ICACT), pp. 172–177. IEEE (2018)

24. Shen, H.: Content-based publish/subscribe systems. In: Shen, X., Yu, H., Buford, J., Akon, M. (eds.) Handbook of Peer-to-Peer Networking, pp. 1333–1366. Springer, Boston (2010). https://doi.org/10.1007/978-0-387-09751-0_49

25. Trend Micro: TrendLabs Security Intelligence BlogPersirai: New Internet of Things (IoT) Botnet Targets IP Cameras - TrendLabs Security Intelligence Blog (2017)

26. Vasilevskiy, A., Morin, B., Haugen, Ø., Evensen, P.: Agile development of home automation system with thingml. In: 2016 IEEE 14th International Conference on Industrial Informatics (INDIN). IEEE (2016)

27. Woolf, N.: DDoS attack that disrupted internet was largest of its kind in history, experts say. The Guardian, 26 (2016)

Author Index

Printed in the United States
By Bookmasters